Unless Recalled Earlier

Learning, Motivation, and Cognition

Learning, Motivation, and Cognition

THE FUNCTIONAL BEHAVIORISM OF ROBERT C. BOLLES

EDITED BY

Mark E. Bouton
Michael S. Fanselow

AMERICAN PSYCHOLOGICAL ASSOCIATION

WASHINGTON DC

Published by
American Psychological Association
750 First Street, NE
Washington, DC 20002

Copies may be ordered from
APA Order Department
P.O. Box 92984
Washington, DC 20090-2984

In the UK and Europe, copies may be ordered from
American Psychological Association
3 Henrietta Street
Covent Garden, London
WC2E 8LU England

Typeset in Century Schoolbook by EPS Group Inc., Easton, MD

Printer: Data Reproductions Corporation, Auburn Hills, MI
Jacket Designer: Berg Design, Albany, NY
Technical/Production Editor: Edward B. Meidenbauer

Library of Congress Cataloging-in-Publication Data
Learning, motivation, and cognition : the functional behaviorism of Robert C.
   Bolles / edited by Mark E. Bouton and Michael S. Fanselow.
      p.   cm.
   Includes bibliographical references and index.
   ISBN 1-55798-436-0 (hardcover : acid-free paper)
   1. Learning, Psychology of.   2. Motivation (Psychology).
3. Cognition.   4. Bolles, Robert C.   I. Bouton, Mark E.
II. Fanselow, Michael S.
BF318.L394   1997
153.1'534—dc21   97-25299
                                                                                        CIP

British Library Cataloguing-in-Publication Data
A CIP record is available from the British Library

Printed in the United States of America
First edition

Contents

Contributors

D. Caroline Blanchard, *Department of Anatomy and Reproductive Biology, John A. Burns School of Medicine, University of Hawaii, Honolulu*

Robert Boakes, *Department of Psychology, University of Sydney, Australia*

Elizabeth A. Brownson, *DepoTech, San Diego, CA*

Larry Cahill, *Center for Neurobiology of Learning and Memory, University of California, Irvine*

Byron Campbell, *Department of Psychology, Princeton University, Princeton, NJ*

Kathleen C. Chambers, *Department of Psychology, University of Southern California, Los Angeles*

Alexis C. Collier, *Department of Psychology, Ohio State University, Columbus*

George Collier, *Department of Psychology, Rutgers University, New Brunswick, NJ*

Anthony Dickinson, *Department of Experimental Psychology, University of Cambridge, England*

Michael Domjan, *Department of Psychology, University of Texas, Austin*

Paul M. Fedorchak, *Department of Psychology, Plymouth State College, Plymouth, NH*

John Garcia, Professor Emeritus, *University of California, Los Angeles; Mt. Vernon, WA*

Pamela S. Hunt, *Department of Psychology, The College of William and Mary, Williamsburg, VA*

Deanne Johnson, *Department of Psychology, Rutgers University, New Brunswick, NJ*

James L. McGaugh, *Center for Neurobiology of Learning and Memory, University of California, Irvine*

Ronald Mehiel, *Department of Psychology, Shippensburg University, Shippensburg, PA*

Robert D. Ogilvie, *Department of Psychology, Brock University, St. Catherines, Ontario, Canada*

Lewis Petrinovich, *Berkeley, CA*

Douglas S. Ramsay, *Departments of Orthodontics and Pediatric Dentistry, University of Washington, Seattle, WA*

Anthony L. Riley, *Department of Psychology, The American University, Washington, DC*

Benno Roozendaal, *Center for the Neurobiology of Learning and Memory, University of California, Irvine*

Randy J. Seeley, *Department of Psychology, University of Washington, Seattle*

Ronald A. Sigmundi, *Department of Psychology, St. Lawrence University, Canton, NY*

John Staddon, *Department of Psychology, Duke University, Durham, NC*
Yuan Wang, *Department of Psychology, University of Southern California, Los Angeles*
Stephen C. Woods, *Departments of Psychology and Medicine, University of Washington, Seattle*
David Yuan, *Asian American Network, El Monte, CA*
B. Silvano Zanutto, *Facultad de Ingeniería, Universidad de Buenos Aires, Argentina; Department of Experimental Psychology, Duke University, Durham, NC*

Foreword

Robert C. Bolles:
From Mathematics to Motivation

I met Bob Bolles circa 1952, when we were both employed by the U.S. Naval Radiological Defense Laboratory (NRDL) on the shores of San Francisco Bay. The mission of the "Rad Lab" was to devise protection against nuclear bombs and radioactive fallout. I was on leave from graduate school, studying the psychobiological responses to a new stimulus—ionizing rays and particles—in the biomedical branch of the Rad Lab. Bolles studied the purely physical energetics of radioactive material as a mathematician in the chemical–technical branch, and he left an enduring mark on that field. Some 30 years later, I met a physicist who had been at the Rad Lab, and as often happens at such meetings, we were commenting on what happened to former NRDLers, as we called ourselves. I said, "Remember Bob Bolles? He is now a prominent psychologist." He looked puzzled. "Bolles? Surely you don't mean Bolles, the coauthor of that handbook on radioactive decay functions? I still use the book."

Let's go back to 1954. Bolles was a new graduate student at the University of California, Berkeley. In that era, under the tolerant umbrella of Edward Chace Tolman, students were free to develop their own ideas. When I entered graduate school in 1949, students such as Dick Christie, Henry Gleitman, and Julie Hochberg were thriving in that democractic atmosphere and moved on to faculty jobs.

Three young turks, Bob Bolles, Jim McGaugh, and Lew Petrinovich, willfully pushed the department toward an emphasis on biology and neuroscience with their ingenious experiments. I was a witness to this passing parade of raw talent for over 16 years. (I finally received a PhD in 1965 at age 48. I am what is known, post hoc, as a "late bloomer.") Although it may be said that these three graduate students were inspired by Professors David Krech and Edward Tolman, it was also the other way around. All three were independent thinkers who influenced their elders. Their seminal papers do not have a professor as coauthor.

McGaugh and Petrinovich postulated that, after the trial, right or wrong, the rat still has an active memory of the trial on its mind and in its brain, so they injected a neural stimulant at that point in time and improved its learning performance. Jim McGaugh stayed with the study of neural memory activation throughout his career, as the reader knows (see chapter 18, this volume). Lew Petrinovich developed a strong interest in evolutionary theory (see chapter 1, this volume). Ultimately he took to the field, recording songs and describing nests of white-crowned sparrows over successive generations.

Petrinovich and Bolles ran an experiment with rats on a T maze foreshadowing Bolles's future career. They showed that hungry rats preferred to alternate between the two ends of the T maze, whereas thirsty rats preferred to go consistently to one end. Bolles did not plot the decay of motivation over time and repeated reinforcement. The conclusions and speculations of the article dealt with the differences in the geographic distributions of food as opposed to water in the natural history and evolution of the foraging rat. Bolles, the mathematician, had vanished forever. Bolles, the psychologist, took up Tolman's task, developing, refining, and advancing traditional learning theory.

At that time, learning theorists treated motivation like the gasoline in an automobile. Motivation made the rat go, but it had little effect on which way the rat turned at the choice point. Bolles and Petrinovich's experiment was crucial; one motive facilitated response variation, and the other motive inhibited such variation. The data should have negated the gas-tank hypothesis, but alas, learning theory is resistant to negative evidence. Perhaps no one else got the message, but I received it loud and clear.

Since then, various fixed-action patterns, each with its own little gas tank, have invaded learning theory. Putting static compartments into motivation does not help much; nobody will ever know where to look for neurological correlates of wellsprings of motivation, independent of behavioral mechanisms.

Bolles was much more thoughtful. He studied the interactions of specific propensities of the driven animal with the explicit demands of the test situation, articulating a new functional analysis of learning capacity, wherein motive variation is as important as task variation. Bolles's detailed, pragmatic approach to patterns of spurred activity will bear empirical fruit for decades to come, and the data will mesh well with findings in behavioral neuroscience.

Since my mind was going along the same path, or perhaps stuck in the same rut, one might think that Bolles and I always agreed. Not so! In about 1980, I sent an article to *Psychological Review*. The article got three negative reviews, and the editor sent it out to three more reviewers. I got two more negative reviews and one affirmative one that I knew came from Bolles. He ended his comments with, "I would not say all those things myself, but, I think that Garcia should be allowed to say them." That is the classic freedom of speech declaration attributed to Voltaire; Bolles modified it to fit the journals of psychology. It is the strongest support anyone requires or deserves in our business.

Our disagreements were minor. Bolles thought that novelty was important in aversion learning. I argued that people and wild animals easily acquire aversions for familiar flavors in one trial. Novelty is perhaps more important for the laboratory rat with its notoriously diminished cortex.

Bolles and I agreed on a substantial matter, namely, the spatiotemporal context: Tolman's cognitive map is more basic than the association, be it S-R, S-S, or R-R. To repeat this point in the practical terms of an experimental report, the information gained by the animal in the preliminary habituation phase, usually glossed over in the methods section, is often more important for the science of learning than the data so punctiliously detailed in the results section. During habituation, a cognitive substrate is laid down to receive the sense impressions, be they singular or in association.

This may be a general phenomenon. Petrinovich reported that white-crown nestlings habituated to a live zebra finch, rather than a white-crown tape recording, subsequently learn to sing like zebra finches. Similarly, a human infant habituated to parental talking picks up a functional language background before it can talk, and receptive fields of visual cells are organized by early habituation to environmental features.

Bolles went one step beyond Tolman. The contextual map and the subsequent sense impressions must be congruent with the evolution of the particular species under observation. In practice, the signals and tactics developed in training rabbits should not be applied, willy-nilly, to grizzly bears.

It was an honor and a pleasure to lock horns with a mind as brilliant as Bolles's. He knew how to expand people's vision by adding facts and projecting implications. Laboratory experimentation and learning theory have lost an important advocate, a constructive critic, and a great contributor in Robert C. Bolles, and I lost a very good friend.

JOHN GARCIA

About This Book: The Life and Influence of Robert C. Bolles

Michael S. Fanselow and Mark E. Bouton

Robert C. Bolles helped shape an era in the study of the biobehavioral aspects of learning and motivation. When he entered the field in the 1950s, it was dominated by mechanistic ideas about drive, reinforcement, and temporal contiguity. When he left it at his death in 1994, it had been radically changed. Ethological and cognitive themes had emerged and become part of the language used to describe learning and motivation. Bolles had a significant part in that change. The purpose of this book is to celebrate the man and his many scientific contributions.

As detailed in the foreword by John Garcia, Bolles began his scientific career, not as a psychologist, but as a mathematician working at the U.S. Naval Radiological Defense Laboratory in San Francisco. Born in Sacramento, California, in 1928, he was schooled at home until the age of 12; he earned a BA in 1948 and an MA in 1949 in mathematics from Stanford University. His work on behavior did not begin until he arrived at the University of California at Berkeley in the early 1950s to study psychology with Edward Tolman and David Krech. Bolles, along with several other graduate students, including Garcia, Lewis Petrinovich, and James McGaugh (all of whom have contributed to this volume), helped shape an interest in biopsychology in the department at Berkeley. The results of experiments from an early collaboration with Petrinovich (e.g., Bolles & Petrinovich, 1954) showed that food-deprived rats tended to choose alternate arms of a T maze on successive trials but that thirsty rats tended to stick with a single arm. This research anticipated several of the later themes in Bolles's work, and these themes are still major influences on the field. For example, the idea that a win–shift strategy characterizes foraging has had strong influences on the field of spatial memory (e.g., Olton, 1978). The idea that motivation and learning have selective effects on behavior led to the behavior systems approach (e.g., Timberlake & Fanselow, 1994). Bolles received his PhD from Berkeley in 1956 for a dissertation entitled "Deprivation and Behavior Variability in the Rat."

Bolles moved East and held brief academic appointments at the University of Pennsylvania and at Princeton University. Two of his colleagues during this period were Byron Campbell (Princeton) and George Collier (Rutgers), who shared Bob's interest in motivation and also contributed chapters to this book. In 1959, Bob took a position at Hollins College. There he examined the motivating effects of food deprivation, anticipation of feeding times, general activity, and biological clocks and rhythms. Sometime during this period, he conducted a legendary but unpublished experiment. After reading that the National Aeronautics and Space Administration (NASA) was about to spend $22 million (or so) on an experiment to determine whether gravity influences diurnal cycles, Bolles set about conducting a study for a cost of less than $20. NASA put a monkey in space; Bob bolted an electric motor to a 6-foot plank. He set the apparatus up so that the plank could rotate like a propeller in the horizontal plane. He then attached a bean plant in a flower pot to each end. On a table nearby were two more bean plants: a control group that showed natural diurnal cycling after a single cycle of light exposure. The rotating plants, the experimental group, were subjected to both the pull of Earth's gravity and the centrifugal force of rotation. Weeks later, Bolles concluded that gravity has no effect on the diurnal cycle. As legend has it, months later NASA arrived at the same conclusion.

Bolles liked to argue that simple observations often lead to the greatest insights. During the Hollins period, he watched and recorded all the behaviors of rats from birth to weaning. When the article that reported the results (Bolles & Woods, 1964) was declared a "Citation Classic" in *Current Contents*, Bolles wrote, "I have always believed in the idea that experimenters should look at their animals . . . the human eyeball is the instrument of choice if you want to observe a new phenomenon, and par-

Robert C. Bolles, June 1966

ticularly if you want to gain a new understanding of it" (Bolles, 1981, p. 115). Bolles, an active teacher as well as researcher, impressed this message on his students. An emphasis on detailed observation of behavior is at the core of contributions to this book by D. Caroline Blanchard and Robert Ogilvie, who were Hollins undergraduate and master's degree students working under Bolles, respectively.

One of Bolles's finest contributions was undoubtedly his classic book, *Theory of Motivation* (1967). This scholarly work took historical perspective and synthesized a broad range of data that marked the downfall of Hullian drive theory and the beginning of a new era. The book served as a review and introduction to the field for several generations of undergraduate and graduate students. It advocated a new interest in radical empiricism, a strong infusion of biological issues, and a focus on the purposiveness of goal-oriented behavior. Behavior was most often motivated by the anticipation of goals, rather than the drive or need for them.

Bolles returned to the West Coast in 1966, when he joined the faculty at the University of Washington. He remained there for the rest of his career. A faculty colleague (Stephen Woods) and a large number of PhD students from this extended period (Mark Bouton, Kathleen Chambers, Alexis Collier, Michael Fanselow, Paul Fedorchak, Ron Mehiel, Anthony Riley, and Ronald Sigmundi) have contributed chapters to this volume. At Washington, Bolles's research program included the analysis of aversively motivated behavior and avoidance, for which he is perhaps best known. His classic article on species-specific defense reactions (Bolles, 1970) had a large impact on the field and is another Citation Classic. This article, among others of his, fostered a new blend of psychology and ethology that grew into an important trend within learning theory to recognize biological constraints and adaptive function.

Bolles's appreciation of the naturalness of fear-motivated behavior led him to the view that animals often need to learn more about stimuli in their environment than about their own actions. This emphasis on "stimulus learning" appeared in several articles published in the 1970s and also flavored his second textbook, *Learning Theory* (1975, 1979). As is true of the biological trend in animal learning, Bolles is often credited with being an initiator of the "movement" in animal cognition (e.g., Bolles, 1972). However, for Bolles, biological constraints and the cognitive abilities of animals reflected the same thing: that learning and behavior are organized according to functional systems that provide natural and necessary problem-solving capabilities. The integration of cognition and biology into the psychology of learning and motivation can be appreciated by examining the second edition of his book *Theory of Motivation*, published in 1975.

In the early 1980s, Bolles's interests returned to problems of feeding, regulation, and appetitive motivation. At this point he focused on how tastes can be associated with calories and how this learning affects the rat's flavor preferences and food selection. His early work anticipated the discovery that rats have a unique taste receptor that detects complex carbohydrates (e.g., Bolles, Hayward, & Crandall, 1981; Sclafani, 1991). Unlike humans, rats can taste starch directly, and they like it. Bolles and his involved in ingestion can influence the expression of associatively mediated taste preferences (e.g., Fedorchak & Bolles, 1988).

Bolles was editor of *Animal Learning & Behavior*, the learning journal published by the Psychonomic Society, between 1981 and 1984. In those years, he also became increasingly involved in his hobby of astronomy. We remember a late-1970s seminar at Washington in which, freshly returned with stubble on his face from a drive he had taken in the mountains to photograph a total eclipse of the sun, Bob presented a detailed mathematical analysis of the eclipse phenomenon. (We had expected a discussion of configural conditioning.) In the 1980s, he took several trips to Australia to study the southern sky, and he had a book in manuscript on the subject when he died. During the same period, his passion for the history of psychology reemerged. He became the first historian of the Psychonomic Society. His third textbook, *The Story of Psychology: A Thematic History* (1993), appeared in print after several years in the writing. Through that book, Bob spoke to the student much the way he did in his own history course. He was an engaging and inspiring teacher.

Robert C. Bolles, July 1979, at home in Seattle.

This book really began in August 1993, when Bob and the two of us were together at the American Psychological Association meeting in Toronto. Over a glass of wine in a hotel room, Bob told us of his plan to retire from the University of Washington in the spring. We were surprised but quickly hatched the idea to hold a conference in Seattle that June to honor him. The conference was to be a unique gathering of Bolles's colleagues and students from all the periods of his long and distinguished career. A conference did take place on June 24, 1994, but circumstances intervened to make it very different from the one we had planned. On April 8, 1994, Bob suddenly died of a heart attack. Through a difficult and deliberate transformation, what had been planned as a retirement celebration became a memorial symposium instead. John Garcia read the piece that now appears as the foreword to the volume, and 13 of Bob's students (from the early 1960s through the 1980s) gave presentations. By September 1994, we had invited a mixture of Bolles's students and colleagues, as well as a number of respected researchers in the fields in which he had been active, to contribute to a book that would further honor him. The response was enthusiastic. Thus we arrived at the present volume, whose goal is to describe the current state of the art in Bob's field, present and evaluate his multiple impacts, and provide some personal reflections on one of the field's most colorful thinkers.

We have used the subtitle "The Functional Behaviorism of Robert C. Bolles" for the following reason. Although Bob's contributions to the field were varied and broad, we believe there were two themes that always shaped his thinking: behavior and function. He was a behaviorist in the sense that his ultimate goal was to explain and understand behavior; his level of analysis was how the environment determined behavior. The first chapter in *Theory of Motivation* provides one of the clearest analyses we know of what it takes to be scientific in the study of behavior. In Bolles's more recent text on the history of psychology (Bolles, 1993), he made the observation that there are several forms of behaviorism. He did not use this book as a forum to advance his own scientific views, but he made it clear that his flavor of behaviorism was closer in form to that of his mentor Tolman than it was to that of Watson. His approach was molar rather than atomistic or reductionistic. Bolles expanded on Tolman's purposive approach by considering behavior in terms of both its immediate or proximal purpose and its ultimate or evolutionary one. He always put behavior in the context of its function. Of paramount importance to him were the environmental problems that a particular behavior had evolved to solve (in both the ontogenetic and phylogenetic sense). Functional behaviorism, then, seeks an understanding of behavior that is guided by a consideration of function. The understanding is not complete until behavior can be placed in its functional context.

It makes sense to begin the book with a section entitled "Evolution, Phylogeny, and Ontogeny" to emphasize the functional aspects of behavior. In this section, Lewis Petrinovich, one of Bolles's earliest collaborators, describes his early research with Bolles, the general atmosphere in the department at Berkeley, and his own subsequent work on bird song development and human morality. Michael Domjan describes his work on learning and sexual behavior in Japanese quail, with an emphasis on the demise of the equipotentiality principle, the idea that animals can learn equally well about all potential combinations of stimuli and responses. Pamela Hunt and Byron Campbell then move to the subject of ontogeny and describe how a particular functional system (in this case, one of Bolles's favorites, defensive behavior) develops into a coherent coordination of individual responses to stimuli. Alexis Collier continues the ontogeny theme by analyzing how different environments can influence learning, memory, and elicited behavior in the developing rat.

Bolles's first research topic was how motivation for commodities such as food and water affects behavior (Bolles, 1963; Bolles & de Lorge, 1962; Bolles & Petrinovich, 1954). The second section, "The Motivation of Behavior," reflects Bolles's broad interests in this theme. One of the points of his work was that learning and drive are not independent agents that passively combine to produce behavior. Learning is often the source of the motivation for behavior. Randy Seeley, Douglas Ramsay, and Stephen Woods expand on this theme by describing the intimate interactions of learning with regulatory physiology. George Collier and Deanne Johnson review some of their work showing that the motivational principles derived from experiments with deprived animals working for food in short sessions can be very different from those derived from more "natural" studies in which the animal controls the pattern and amount of its daily intake. John Staddon (another master's student at Hollins) and Silvano Zanutto show how far an astonishingly simple model of feeding dynamics can go in explaining fundamental data concerning food intake. Robert Boakes then connects Bolles's early research interest in drive and food-anticipatory activity with his subsequent focus on constraints on learning, and he relates them to current work on chronobiology and activity-based anorexia in the rat. Finally, if a portion of the diurnal cycle is made up of activity, an even greater portion is taken up by the profound state of inactivity called sleep. Robert Ogilvie's chapter treats sleep as a behavior and embarks on a behavioral analysis of the subject.

Later in his career, Bolles turned to the question of how past behavioral experience guides an animal's selection among various foods. Our third section deals with these learned food preferences and aversions. In the early 1970s, Bolles's interest in the relation of behavior to both learning and function, as well as his friendship with John Garcia, sparked his work on conditioned taste aversions (e.g., Bolles, Riley, & Laskowski, 1973). Two of Bolles's students during this period, Anthony Riley and Kathleen Chambers, describe their current research using conditioned taste aversions. Chambers, David Yuan, Elizabeth Brownson, and Yuan Wang use the taste-aversion procedure as a method to investigate sexual dimorphisms in learned behavior. Riley uses the taste-aversion procedure as a tool to elucidate the stimulus properties of drugs. In the 1980s, Bolles turned to the acquisition of food preferences rather than aversions (e.g., Bolles et al., 1981). Paul Fedorchak describes some work of this type and tells how Bolles's research group first came to focus on calorie-based preference learning. Ronald Mehiel puts research on taste preferences into the context of Bolles's belief that behavior is fundamentally organized around hedonics and affect.

In the years between Bolles investigation of food aversions and his study of flavor preferences, his major focus was on aversive motivation. By taking a functional behavioristic approach to fear, he changed the analysis of fear and aversive motivation processes from an analysis of reinforcement (e.g., Miller, 1948; Mowrer, 1939) to a study of defensive behavior (Bolles, 1970; Bolles & Fanselow, 1980). Bolles's impact on the study of fear was enormous, and the fourth section of the book, "Defensive Behavior," pays tribute to his work on the problems of aversively motivated behavior. Caroline Blanchard demonstrates that by taking a naturalistic setting into the laboratory and making careful observations, one can reveal the complexities of the defensive behavioral repertoire. Ronald Sigmundi's chapter derives the rules by which animals choose between various defensive behaviors in their repertoire. Michael Fanselow charts the development of species-specific defense reaction theory (Bolles, 1970) from its beginning as an alternative paradigm to reinforcement approaches to the current behavioral and neurophysiological understanding of this functional behavior system.

As Bolles studied defense, he began to understand the important role that the animal's knowledge about the environment plays in the selection of behavior. Classical conditioning became an important explanatory principle, and its methods became one of the tools he used to study defensive behavior. A major theoretical issue in classical conditioning (as in any kind of learning) has always been the content of the learning—the question of what is learned. Bolles's answer to the question was again derived from the work of Tolman. He believed that exposure to Pavlovian relationships resulted in an animal's approaching a situation with acquired expectancies (e.g., Bolles, 1972). His view was frankly cognitive, and the final section of the book addresses cognitive processes in animal learning. Anthony Dickinson's chapter describes the progress that has been made in understanding the contents of instrumental learning and how those contents get translated into action. Larry Cahill, Benno Roozendaal, and James McGaugh demonstrate that emotional experience can enhance memory consolidation and describe the physiological mechanisms that cause this memorial modulation. Mark Bouton describes a distinction Bolles drew between how animals learn about signals for *whether* events will occur and how they learn about signals for *when* events will occur. Bouton explains how this distinction anticipated several important themes that later developed in learning theory.

Throughout his career, Bolles's writings, lectures, and presentations were characterized by a deep perspective and a wry sense of humor. One of our favorite examples is his discussion (Bolles, 1985) of the claim that there is only a quantitative difference in the temporal gaps that taste aversion learning and other types of learning can bridge. Bolles observed that the ratio between the gaps was about 1000:1, roughly the same as the ratio between the length of the legs of a racehorse and the size of the leg bumps that can be found on the vertebrae of certain snakes. Only a matter of degree.

Bolles was an outstanding thinker, scientist, and writer. He was also a humorous, irreverent presence at scientific meetings and an unpredictable pedagogical force. This book celebrates his many contributions and interests. We also hope it captures something of the man, as well as the affection and respect so many of us had for him.

Acknowledgments

Preparation of the book's final manuscript was supported by National Institute of Mental Health Grant MH 39786 to Michael S. Fanselow, National Science Foundation Grant IBN 92-09454 to Mark E. Bouton, and the Department of Psychology at the University of Vermont.

The order of editorship (and the order of this chapter's authorship) were decided using an unbiased method Bob Bolles taught us. In the equivalent of a verifiable coin toss conducted during a long-distance telephone call, one of us guessed whether a randomly chosen article from *Animal Learning and Behavior* (edited by Bolles) ended on an odd or an even page number.

Much of the information in this chapter was gathered during the preparation of an obituary we wrote for the *American Psychologist* (1996, Vol. 51, p. 733). There is overlap, therefore, between this chapter and that article. We wish to thank Steve Woods for his help at all stages of this project, especially those related to the 1994 conference at the University of Washington. We are also indebted to Bob's widow, Yasuko, for graciously providing the photographs that are printed here. Ralph Miller contributed the NASA anecdote, which was corroborated by several Hollins students.

References

Bolles, R. C. (1963). Effect of food deprivation upon the rat's behavior in its homecage. *Journal of Comparative and Physiological Psychology, 56,* 456–460.

Bolles, R. C. (1967). *Theory of motivation.* New York: Harper & Row.

Bolles, R. C. (1970). Species-specific defense reactions and avoidance learning. *Psychological Review, 71,* 32–48.

Bolles, R. C. (1972). Reinforcement, expectancy, and learning. *Psychological Review, 79,* 394–409.

Bolles, R. C. (1975). *Learning theory.* New York: Holt, Rinehart & Winston.

Bolles, R. C. (1975). *Theory of motivation* (2nd ed.). New York: Harper & Row.

Bolles, R. C. (1979). *Learning theory* (2nd ed.). New York: Holt, Rinehart & Winston.

Bolles, R. C. (1981, August 3). This week's citation classic. *Current Contents,* p. 115.

Bolles, R. C. (1985). The slaying of Goliath: What happened to reinforcement theory. In T. D. Johnston & A. R. Peitrewictz (Eds.), *The ethological study of learning.* Hillsdale, NJ: Erlbaum.

Bolles, R. C. (1993). *The story of psychology: A thematic history.* Pacific Grove, CA: Brooks/ Cole.

Bolles, R. C., & de Lorge, J. (1962). Exploration in a Dashiell maze as a function of food deprivation, current deprivation, and sex. *Canadian Journal of Psychology, 16,* 221–227.

Bolles, R. C., & Fanselow, M. S. (1980). A perceptual-defensive-recuperative model of fear and pain. *Behavioral and Brain Sciences, 3,* 291–301.

Bolles, R. C., Hayward, L., & Crandall, C. (1981). Conditioned taste preferences based on caloric density. *Journal of Experimental Psychology: Animal Behavior Processes, 7,* 59–69.

Bolles, R. C., & Petrinovich, L. (1954). A technique for obtaining rapid drive discrimination in the rat. *Journal of Comparative and Physiological Psychology, 47,* 378–380.

Bolles, R. C., Riley, A. L., & Laskowski, B. (1973). A further demonstration of the learned safety effect in food-aversion learning. *Bulletin of the Psychonomic Society, 1,* 190–192.

Bolles, R. C., & Woods, P. J. (1964). The ontogeny of behaviour in the albino rat. *Animal Behaviour, 12,* 427–441.

Fedorchak, P. M., & Bolles, R. C. (1988). Nutritive expectancies mediate cholecystokinin's suppression-of-intake effect. *Behavioral Neuroscience, 102,* 451–455.

Miller, N. E. (1948). Studies in fear as an acquirable drive: I. Fear as motivation and fear-reduction as reinforcement in the learning of new responses. *Journal of Experimental Psychology, 38,* 89–101.

Mowrer, O. H. (1939). A stimulus-response analysis of anxiety and its role as a reinforcing agent. *Psychological Review, 46,* 553–564.

Olton, D. S. (1978). Characteristics of spatial memory. In S. H. Hulse, H. F. Fowler, & W. K. Honig (Eds.), *Cognitive processes in animal behavior.* Hillsdale, NJ: Erlbaum.

Sclafani, A. (1991). Starch and sugar tastes in rodents: An update. *Brain Research Bulletin, 27,* 383–386.

Timberlake, W., & Fanselow, M. S. (1994). Symposium on behavior systems: Learning, neurophysiology, and development. *Psychonomic Bulletin & Review, 1,* 403–404.

Part I

Evolution, Phylogeny, and Ontogeny

1

Evolved Behavioral Mechanisms

Lewis Petrinovich

I begin with a discussion that places in a historical context some of the early collaborative research findings Robert Bolles and I published. This discussion highlights the origins of our views regarding animal learning and motivation, how those early views influenced all subsequent work we did throughout our separate careers, and how we both (in completely different ways) always paid proper attention to the evolved tendencies of organisms behaving in their natural environment, be they rats, birds, or humans.

The initial research with rats led to the realization that it is necessary to consider natural evolved response tendencies to understand behavior, even in the laboratory. This realization led me to the research program involving birds that is described here. The aim was to identify the prepared learning system, to inquire why the system had been selected, and to understand its functional significance in the birds' behavioral economy.

Having realized some success in that research program, as well as an understanding of evolutionary biology, I turned my attention to the problem of understanding the role of evolved mechanisms in one of the most complex aspects of humanity—human morality. This program began with empirical studies of the structure of human moral intuitions and has moved to the development of a biologically based ethical system that can be applied to issues regarding the permissible use of animals and humans by humans who have full moral standing and responsibilities. I describe here the highlights of that system, aspects of which are still being developed.

The general principles regarding morality are expanded to provide an understanding of an evolved human nature, which lays the foundation for an evolutionary psychology. Exemplars of the power of this evolutionary psychology are provided by studies of human language, problem solving, and the evolved human social condition. This essay is offered as testimony to the power of naturalism, both in observation and in theory building, as an essential tool for behavioral science.

In the Beginning

In our first year of graduate school in psychology at the University of California, Berkeley, Bolles and I spent a considerable amount of time socially talking about the philosophy of science. (The Conference for the Unified Sciences was in Berkeley during our first summer there.) During that first spring quarter, we talked with David Krech about a study in drive discrimination he was trying to do with no success. After some discussion, we decided what was wrong and figured out how a rat could be taught rapidly to go one way when hungry and the other when thirsty. Krech agreed it was a good idea, gave us his extensive apparatus and his best wishes, and we ran the rats; the results constituted our first joint publication (Bolles & Petrinovich, 1954).

With such signal success, we decided we could separate the cue and context aspects of a drive and use the cue aspects as discriminative stimuli in a T-maze task. Freed from the general contextual aspects of the drive, the cue components would have the same efficiency as typically found for external cues. We began a study in which rats were either hungry or thirsty and were trained on three trials a day; there were a number of different groups and many conditions with either light or drive stimuli presented in comparable manners; and each stimulus type was manipulated to have a sudden or gradual onset. All summer we took turns running rats most of the day, 7 days a week. On completion of the study, we met to analyze the results. After a couple of long nights looking at the data, considering every hypothesis we could think of, we found that it all made no sense—except for the simple fact that all the hungry rats did worse than the thirsty rats (no matter what the stimulus manipulations). The hungry rats were as good as the thirsty ones on the first and third trials, but they were significantly worse on the second trial, which meant the hungry rats were spontaneously alternating more than were the thirsty ones. That fact interested us, and in the fall we drew more rats from the colony and started the alternation studies that resulted in our next two published articles (Bolles & Petrinovich, 1956; Petrinovich & Bolles, 1954).

We then realized that there was a 15-minute intertrial interval between each of the three trials in the alternation studies. Because the only cue the rat could use to respond correctly was the turn made on the preceding trial (the first one being correct no matter which side was chosen), these animals were remembering the cue for the 15 minutes, even though they were placed in holding cages between trials while the other rats in the squad were being run. But everyone familiar with the literature knew that the rat's symbolic memory lasted only a few seconds. So we kept the best performers from the Bolles and Petrinovich (1956) study and trained them until they regained their high performance levels; the result was the Petrinovich and Bolles (1957) study, which showed that rats could perform significantly above chance when the delays between trials were increased to as long as several hours.

Subsequently, Bolles began digging more deeply into the motivational issues that our initial research involved. He brought his incredible analytic finesse to bear, and his massive output over the next few years attests to the success of that journey. We maintained contact and renewed our mutual intellectual interests on publication of his article on the species-specific defense response (SSDR; Bolles, 1970). By that time I had switched to the study of models for bird song learning and was doing both laboratory and field research with a bird species (the white-crowned sparrow) that learned dialects. As the years wore on, I did more and more field work and became increasingly interested in the evolutionary question of why the birds learned a dialect: What function did dialects serve in the overall regulation of the breeding system, and how did they develop? The results of that research program are summarized in a chapter I wrote (Petrinovich, 1990) and are discussed in the next section.

Although both Bolles and I were nurtured in the classical learning theory tradition, it was of the Tolmanian variety, which tended to be inclusive regarding admissible conceptualizations. We both were attracted to evolutionary ways of thinking, as was our friend and colleague John Garcia, who authored one of the first heresies to the classical learning theory tradition (Garcia & Koelling, 1966). When we submitted our alternation study for publication, we suggested (cautiously) that the results might be interpreted using an evolutionary hypothesis with an ecological slant. Our speculation was that the connection between hunger and variability (and thirst and stereotypy) had biological survival value. The omnivorous rat must continually explore its natural environment to hunt for food, whereas its water supply is presumably more fixed. Therefore, returning to the place where water was found previously would be adaptive, but returning to where food was last found might not be as adaptive because of the uncertainties of food sources. We suggested that this sort of "hunger exploration" would be more evident in carnivores, whose food supply is constantly on the move, and less evident in herbivores, who have a more stationary food supply. It could be that the difference in variability that was observed between hungry and thirsty animals was a manifestation of behavior patterns resulting from the evolutionary process of natural selection: an unusual interpretation from budding rat psychologists of those days. Tinbergen's *The Study of Instinct* (1951) was still thought by many of our psychological colleagues to have reintroduced that banished *I* word to the scientific vocabulary. The journal editor, Harry Harlow, was not comfortable with the paragraph about natural selection but was persuaded (by Krech and a reviewer) to let it remain.

Bolles's SSDR article (1970) applied ideas that came from the ethological tradition to a classical learning paradigm: avoidance learning. He argued that a rat brought a set of innate SSDRs into the avoidance learning situation. These SSDRs consisted of such behaviors as fleeing, freezing, and fighting. He started the article with a typical Bollesian fable regarding a bunny rabbit and an owl, and he refuted the basic reinforcement interpretation through an appeal to the actions of real predators and their prey, arguing that the explanations generated by classical learning theory are not adequate when one considers behaviors in the field. The SSDR is an innate response to a new or sudden stimulus and is evident whenever a response must be acquired quickly if the animal is to survive. The traditional approaches are okay if the animal can afford the luxury of slow learning, but the aversive stimulus probably is effective because its termination provides feedback rather than serving as a neutral aversive conditioned stimulus. In Bolles's view, the aversive stimulus converts a friendly and inquisitive domestic animal into a furtive and hostile wild one, who flees if possible. He then discussed several classic avoidance learning experiments to demonstrate the analytic power of his approach.

Garcia and others (Garcia & Brett, 1977; Rozin & Kalat, 1971) demonstrated that some responses cannot be learned at all, or only after extensive training, if they run counter to the natural behaviors evoked by the context, and Bolles noted that the task in training animals in such situations is to inhibit undesirable SSDRs and to allow the desirable one to come into play. The power of the research programs developed by Bolles and Garcia is that they were done within the settings used by those in the mainstream reinforcement tradition but with the focus on the animal as an organism adapting to the demands of its ecology rather than as a reinforcement-regulated automaton.

Bird Song Development

Meanwhile, I had developed a research program that was within the mainline ethological and evolutionary tradition: studying the development of the song of white-crowned sparrows (*Zonotrichia leucophrys nuttalli*) in the laboratory and gathering data regarding the distribution, transmission, and function of the song dialects in the field. Bolles brought the ethological tradition into psychological laboratory settings, and I brought the psychological tradition into traditional ethological settings. It was necessary for me to locate large numbers of nests to obtain enough young birds to use in tutoring studies. In these studies, nestlings were raised in acoustic isolation and allowed to hear only one or a selected set of songs presented either by tape recordings or live tutors. The results of these studies are described below. After nests were located, they were checked daily to establish the day eggs hatched so that the young could be removed at the proper early age. Because there is immense labor and time involved in locating nests, I decided to conduct some field experiments while waiting for the eggs to hatch and the nestlings to develop. These experiments examined the rates of habituation and sensitization to the presentation of meaningful stimuli (playback of territorial song) to birds in the field. The results of these studies are summarized in Petrinovich (1984). The careful observations necessary to locate nests forced an interest in the dynamics of the breeding system and led me to learn the intricacies of evolutionary theory as well as to understand the basics of ornithology.

Field Studies of Song

The birds of the sedentary Nuttall subspecies are located in the San Francisco Bay region. Most adult males have a single 2-second-long song, the elements of which are organized into a relatively few phrases. An interesting aspect of the song of this subspecies is that there are a number of noticeable dialects within a relatively restricted geographic region. The boundaries of the dialect areas that have been studied in the San Francisco Bay region have been quite stable for a number of years, and the size of each dialect area is small compared to those of any other subspecies. Given that these dialect regions are stable, it is of interest to determine the reasons that they form and persist. It was suggested (e.g., Nottebohm, 1969) that one function of these learned regional dialects is to maintain the integrity of local populations that have become well adapted to the requirements of the particular breeding habitat. The singers in the region have successfully reproduced; it was argued that if song is one of the adaptations that promote reproductive success (and if it is heritable), then young males who sing a particular song, and the females who breed with them, might continue along the successful singing and reproducing path.

To evaluate this argument, it is important to determine from whom young acquire their song. Birds that were hatched and fledged from a region and who subsequently acquired breeding territories in that natal dialect region were found to sing a song with many of the characteristics of the local dialect. However, there was considerable variability in song types within the dialect region. Some breeding males sang the same song as their fathers; some sang a song that was different from that of their fathers but that resembled the song of neighbors; and some sang a song with idiosyncratic elements not found anywhere in the region (Petrinovich, 1988). I concluded that males do not necessarily learn the song of their fathers.

Several other findings suggested that the song dialects are not produced by a process of assortative mating on the basis of song. After a male has obtained a territory, the characteristics of his song change very little (Petrinovich, 1988). However, a song learned in the natal region can be modified after a newly fledged bird leaves the region. DeWolfe, Baptista, and Petrinovich (1989) found that newly arrived first-year birds often sang a song with different dialect markers from those of the local region but changed their song to resemble that of the local dialect region. This finding suggests that social interaction with a neighbor might direct the course of the change in song. No tendency has been found for females to be mated with males who sing a song of the same dialect as their own (Baptista & Morton, 1982; Petrinovich, 1988; Petrinovich & Baptista, 1984).

The lack of a simple relationship between song type and mate choice, combined with the finding that song learned when birds are younger than 50 days can be modified after that age (Petrinovich & Baptista, 1987), suggests that song does not function as a reliable marker of the birds' natal area. It is unlikely, therefore, that song serves to promote patterns of positive assortative mating. I concluded that song learning in this subspecies is not related to selective mating but has a role in the interaction between males when they are establishing territories. Individual song types provide a marker for individual recognition and are generated by an imperfect song-learning mechanism. The females care only about being in a desirable territory and that the male who occupies that territory is of high quality; to attain these ends, they need to be able to recognize the male at a distance. Young birds from other regions modify their songs to resemble those of neighbors because songs resembling that of neighbors elicit fewer aggressive responses than do novel songs, as revealed by playback studies.

Laboratory Studies of Song

Marler (1970) concluded that the critical period for learning in the species is 10–50 days when young birds are hand-raised, individually isolated, and tutored with recorded song. If the birds were not exposed to song during that critical period, they developed abnormal song, as did birds exposed to recorded songs of alien species. I reported data from tape-tutored male birds (Petrinovich, 1985) that replicated Marler's findings, and I identified some of the factors involved in song learning. I found that the birds could learn quite readily the songs of either of two alien subspecies. When they were tutored by songs from two different dialects, their adult song was either one of these or a hybrid song. With a large number of presentations, a few birds could copy the tape-recorded song of an alien species. These findings contradicted the idea that birds are unable to learn alien song because it is rejected at the sensory level: If presented a sufficient number of times, the alien song can be an effective tutoring stimulus, even if tape-recorded songs are used for tutoring.

I performed a series of studies to investigate whether or not birds raised in the laboratory could learn a song after they were 50 days old, as had been observed in the field (Baptista & Petrinovich, 1984, 1986; Petrinovich & Baptista, 1987). Birds exposed to a social tutor rather than a tape-recorded one learned the song even though the exposure was not begun until after 50 days of age. If a song was learned between Days 10 and 50 (either in the laboratory or in the field) and the birds subsequently were exposed to a social tutor, they modified the initial song to resemble that of the new tutor. The song-learning mechanism remains accessible even after normal song learning has taken place in either the laboratory or the field.

The seemingly trivial effect of using a single method to present song stimuli in the laboratory resulted in an inaccurate view of the song-learning mechanism and led to the postulation of an unnecessary set of physiological entities, such as sensory gating mechanisms and central sensory templates. The choice of a single method to present stimuli led not only to a misunderstanding of the possible physiological mechanisms but also to erroneous ideas about the role of song dialects in the regulation of mate choice by females in the wild (see Petrinovich, 1990). Bouton (personal communication, 1996) noted that Bolles often stressed the point that if people had studied avoidance learning in Skinner boxes or shuttle boxes, the result would have produced some strange ideas about avoidance learning.

It was concluded that these difficulties in conceptual focus could have been avoided had more careful attention been paid to studies of the distribution patterns and stability of song types in the breeding population. Given the extensive training of psychologists in research design and statistics, I suggested (Petrinovich, 1990) that our pivotal role should be to direct careful attention to the details of measurement and quantification and to establish the construct validity of the different theoretical concepts being considered. To accomplish these goals, we should not lose sight of the variation in behaviors animals exhibit in different environmental contexts (including both laboratory and field) and should allow this natural range of behavior to express itself as much as possible—a point compatible with one advocated by Bolles in his 1970 paper.

Human Evolution

After I spent a few years learning the basics of evolutionary biology, two events led me to the areas of research and writing that I am involved in regarding human evolution. The first was a seminar I conducted when E. O. Wilson's *Sociobiology* (1975) appeared, a seminar that was enlivened by the arguments of strong supporters and avid detractors, especially concerning the issues of the last chapter regarding the application of sociobiological principles to humans. My interest in this subject was renewed on the publication of two books by two of the participants in that seminar, Martin Daly and Margo Wilson (1978, 1988), and of two books by R. D. Alexander (1979, 1987).

The other influence came from the large lecture course in comparative psychology that I taught every year. I had decided that I should treat the questions of animal rights and animal welfare seriously. Many students are interested in these issues, and I came to believe that it is necessary for animal researchers to present a reasoned and balanced presentation of the subject rather than simply stating, "I am a scientist and understand the paramount value of using animal research for the benefit of humans," as did many of my colleagues. I examined the issues and found them to be much more complicated than I had thought at the outset. Questions regarding the permissible uses of animals by humans become mired in all sorts of passions, ill-defined terms, confrontational politics, and muddy philosophical thinking.

At about this time there was a destructive attack by members of the animal rights movement on the animal psychology laboratories at the university. I knew that those of us who engaged in laboratory and field studies of animals had an extensive set of implicit assumptions that justified our research. However, these assumptions were seldom made explicit, whether to ourselves, our colleagues, our students, or the public. I began examining the underlying implicit presuppositions on which animal research is based and to read literature in moral philosophy to deepen my understanding.

To examine the moral and biological issues regarding the permissibility of animal research, I formed a seminar on the evolution of ethics. Two moral philosophers in the department of philosophy, John Fischer and

Mark Ravizza, met with the seminar on several occasions, giving the participants an introduction to the area. We decided that issues regarding human nature could be approached empirically, and we designed a series of moral dilemmas to investigate people's moral intuitions, studies that have resulted in three articles to date (O'Neill & Petrinovich, 1996; Petrinovich & O'Neill, 1996; Petrinovich, O'Neill, & Jorgensen, 1993). I wrote two books (1995, 1996) that deal with the permissible use of humans by humans, using an evolutionary model to ground the moral principles, and I am now completing a third book using the same theoretical models to deal with the topic of original interest, the permissible use of animals by humans.

The research program is based on the assumption that everything human, including mind and culture, originated during human evolution. Ruse and Wilson (1986) argued that there are three biological premises that can ground morality: reproductive success, inclusive fitness, and reciprocal altruism. *Reproductive success*, at the ultimate level, is the currency that is cashed in by counting the number of genes put back into the gene pool relative to the performance of others in the population, counting at least as far as the number of grandoffspring produced. *Inclusive fitness* is a concept that considers reproductive success beyond the boundaries of the individual reproducer and its offspring. Although it is a property that pertains to the individual organism, it includes the reproductive success of kin multiplied by the degree of relatedness of these kin. Daly and Wilson (1978) noted that the idea that organisms are designed by natural selection to contribute to the replication of their genes is more general and powerful than the idea that they are designed merely to reproduce.

Kin might contribute directly to the promulgation of an individual's genes, because they share a proportion of those genes. They also can assist the reproducer indirectly through activities that would enhance the likelihood that progeny will be raised successfully. Such assistance may also be provided by those who are not kin but who are members of the cooperating social community. The combination of these indirect components to fitness with the direct components is called inclusive fitness.

A question arises concerning why unrelated individuals might aid one another at all. The answer is that it depends on the third biological premise, *reciprocal altruism*. If someone provides critical assistance to an individual when that individual needs assistance, that individual is expected to assist the first one when he needs help. Reciprocal altruism enhances the success of reproducers in small communities, such as those that probably existed in the environment of evolutionary adaptation (EEA). This reciprocity depends on memory because everyone in the social group benefits by knowing the reputation and status of the different members of the group, with all members assessing and being assessed and reassessed by the individuals with whom they interact.

Empirical Study of Moral Intuitions

The assumption that there is an evolved human nature led my research group to investigate the attitudes people hold regarding basic issues concerning life and death. We identified and focused on the important dimensions that could be involved in morality and built these into a series of hypothetical moral dilemmas. The questionnaire we constructed included problems in which individuals were asked to imagine that an event with specified dire consequences was about to occur but they could cause an alternative event to occur through their action, even though this action would have its own dire consequences.

One dilemma is called the "trolley problem" (Thomson, 1976); a participant is told to imagine that a trolley is hurtling down a track out of control. If it continues on the track, it will kill the beings on the track straight ahead of it. However, there is a switch that can be thrown to shunt the trolley to a sidetrack, but the beings on that sidetrack will be killed. The composition of the beings on the main track and sidetrack can be varied, and the participant is asked to make the life-or-death choice by deciding to allow the train to continue or to throw the switch.

The second fantasy dilemma was the "lifeboat problem" (Regan, 1983). In this dilemma the problem is that a ship has sunk, there is a lifeboat with survivors, but one person has to be thrown over because of the limited capacity of the lifeboat. The composition of the lifeboat occupants can be varied, and the participants are asked to decide either to choose who is to drown or to choose that the occupants of the boat draw lots.

By varying the composition of the individuals involved in the different options, the researchers were able to determine the importance of several dimensions including the willingness to act versus not act (action-inaction) and the number of individuals involved in each option (numbers). Were individuals there because it was their job or were they innocent bystanders (social contract)? Were they members of an abhorrent political organization (Nazis)? Were they kin or friends who could assist in time of need (inclusive fitness)? Were they elite and productive members of society (elite)? Were they humans or members of some other species (species)? Were they nonhuman members of an endangered species (endangered)? The participants in the first study (Petrinovich et al., 1993) were 465 undergraduate students at the University of California at Riverside. Participants responded to a questionnaire that involved the two hypothetical dilemmas, answered a series of questions regarding their stated beliefs, and provided personal demographic data.

It was found that the personal beliefs stated by the participants were related to expressed religious preferences. Two religious clusters appeared. One included Catholics, Protestants, and Fundamentalists, and these students were less permissive in their views toward contraception, abortion, and capital punishment; the other included Jews and those expressing a preference for no religion, and they were more permissive in these areas.

The pattern of responses to the dilemmas was coherent for 90 percent of the individuals and did not relate to their religion, gender, or responses regarding stated beliefs. The species dimension was extremely strong: Individuals chose outcomes that benefited members of the human species regardless of the alternative, even when a 75-year-old man was pitted against the last remaining members of an endangered species of gorilla.

The inclusive fitness effect was also strong, as expected on the basis of evolutionary theory. A third sizable effect was the Nazi dimension. The social contract dimension was of moderate importance; if the individuals were present as employees, they were killed in preference to innocent individuals. The numbers dimension was weaker than the others, being important only if no other factors were involved, but overridden if the choice pitted any human against animals, Nazis, or when kin were involved.

The resolution of the fantasy moral dilemmas revealed a consistent pattern in the structure of people's moral intuitions. This study provided a "moral ethogram." My colleagues and I succeeded (just as the ethologists succeeded with nonhuman animals) in developing a strong descriptive base for the pattern of human moral intuitions, and this pattern was found for almost all individuals studied.

One criticism is that the results of the first study, using only university students in the United States, cannot be generalized because the sampling of people was too limited. Therefore, a study was conducted in Taiwan using 173 Taiwanese University students and a U.S. control sample of 120 (O'Neill & Petrinovich, 1996). The first language for all of the Taiwanese was Chinese; over half of the participants were affiliated with an Eastern religion; and few were affiliated with a Western Judeo-Christian religion. This sample was chosen to determine whether religious upbringing is an important factor influencing the resolution of the dilemmas; if so, those raised in households emphasizing the beliefs of an Eastern religion would be expected to resolve the dilemmas differently. Such results would limit the generality of the first study across people; the opposing results would support the generality argument, which would strengthen the idea that the moral dimensions found reflect underlying universals.

Once again, the analyses of the dilemmas indicated that the responses formed a coherent pattern for most of the individuals (82% compared with 87% for the new U.S. control sample). Species and inclusive fitness again were the two most important dimensions, and social contract, again, was moderate. The numbers effect was very small for the Taiwanese but not for the U.S. control sample. In short, there were few differences in the moral intuitions of the U.S. and Taiwan samples.

The dimensions that were identified and included in these studies were drawn from the literature in evolutionary biology and moral philosophy, and I believe they indicate how human moral intuitions are organized. These results provide an understanding of some of the biases that exist as a result of universal biological and cultural factors. This information could make it possible to advocate moral positions that capitalize on human moral biases and to recognize that there may be some undesirable predispositions that must be counteracted to promote a just society.

These empirical studies support the idea that patterns of moral intuitions are coherent and consistent with what would be expected on the basis of the Darwinian hypothesis of inclusive fitness. Although the Darwinian dimensions are important, other cultural influences have an effect as well. When alternatives were phrased in terms of killing, the action-inaction effect was larger than when they were phrased in terms of letting die. People agreed more strongly to act when the questions used the words "to save" than when they used the words "to kill," although the outcomes of the choices were identical. This effect could be primarily the result of social factors due to cultural influences (Petrinovich & O'Neill, 1996). Although personal beliefs differed for different religions, the resolution of the moral dilemmas did not. It is suggested that the structure of these moral intuitions is at a deeper moral level than socially influenced personal beliefs or cultural manifestations.

Evolutionary Psychology

I argue the merits of an evolutionary psychology that uses the basic principles of evolutionary theory to enhance the understanding of human behavior. Many social scientists still reject the idea that biological factors are important influences on the structure and functioning of human social systems. This rejection is based on at least three misconceptions: (a) that the introduction of biological factors entails an implicit or explicit acceptance of genetic determinism at some level; (b) that the variability in social structures across cultures makes it unlikely that there are strong biological universals; and (c) that the reference to biological factors represents a renascent version of social Darwinism. Because I have spoken to these rejections at length (Petrinovich, 1995), here, I address each only briefly. Regarding the first point, contemporary evolutionists and sociobiologists understand and agree that genes do not code for any behavior and that there are many steps between the proteins that genes do code and any behavior that is produced. It is essential to consider ecological and cultural influences on the development of behavior because it is within their context that genes are expressed. Alexander (1979) noted that evolutionary determinism includes all the events in the process of natural selection that fixed certain genes during the period when the initial members of the species were in the EEA. This view does not involve genetic determinism because evolutionarily determined traits can be altered if the environment within which individuals develop is modified. A broad interactionist view is at the heart of modern sociobiology and evolutionary psychology.

Concerning the second objection, the fact that cultures vary so much in their customs, rules, and laws is taken by some to mean there are few, if any, biological universals that influence human nature. Although there are a variety of structures that characterize different cultures, there are numerous general features that characterize all societies, and many of these are rules regarding reproduction and inheritance.

The third objection—the political and ideological concern—is based in part on the claim that evolutionary ideas lead to a hopeless pessimism when the inclusive fitness construct is used. However, the importance of inclusive fitness does not mean that people are destined to benefit kin and friends to the detriment of all outsiders, thus condemning humans to an environment consisting of "us" and "them." It only means that there are propensities to communicate and cooperate with familiars more than with strangers. The fact that biases exist does not mean that people are hopelessly bound to follow their lead into the depths of xenophobia.

It is a mistake to assume that behavioral plasticity demands an entirely open-ended, all-purpose mind. Cronin (1991) emphasized that humans have been selected to act adaptively using specially tailored information-processing machinery, with specific content rules that generate flexible behavior. The evolved rules for behavior need not be rules for behavioral rigidity. Humans have inherited a complex bundle of capabilities and propensities, along with preferences and taste, powers of discrimination, and preferred ways of doing things. These predispositions and capabilities enhance our dignity more than would coming into the world with a sparsely structured tabula rasa on which environmental factors work their wiles.

One reason to expect great uniformity in the development of many basic sensory and response categories is that the traits appearing early in the life of a developing organism have been selected so that, given the almost inevitable circumstances that surround conception and birth, the organism is provided with the necessary elements to sustain further physiological and behavioral development. It is critical that these early developmental processes run off in some appropriate sequence and that alternative avenues of stimulation or input can be used if the most commonly occurring events are not encountered. The necessary inputs can be provided through the activation of tuned sensory systems (experience-expectant in the terms proposed by Greenough, Black, & Wallace, 1987); these early inputs are received and activate a second system (experience-dependent). Lacking the expected stimulation, an organism is able to use other sensory modes to generate the stimuli necessary to continue the process of development.

There is a third, activity-dependent, system (Locke, 1993), which uses the activity of the organism to develop such processes as speech and language, thereby providing the organism with the ability to generate actively the stimulation necessary for development to proceed. The conception of these three systems is quite different from the traditional concept, which considers development in terms of innate versus learned influences. It is not the case that only one system is active for a time, to be followed by one of the others: There is a continuous interaction of the three systems from the outset. With this conceptualization of development, it is meaningless to invoke the specter of genetic or biological determinism. All organisms begin with genetically established experience-expectant systems. However, phenotypic development is a continuous function of the complex interplay between experience-expectant, experience-dependent, and activity-dependent systems.

Evolution and the Human Condition

For any species in which the young depend on parental care for early survival, there should be bonding mechanisms, certainly between the newborn and the primary caregiver (almost always the mother). Social bonds are cemented almost from the moment of birth, and in humans the bonding process between the mother and the fetus begins in utero, on the basis of chemosensory stimulation and the auditory input received from the mother's heartbeat and voice (Mehler & Dupoux, 1994). Such social bonds are important because they provide the basis on which moral standing is accorded to the neonate, who enters into the world as a human player interacting with members of the social community. At this point the neonate gains personhood, and the organism becomes a *human moral patient*—an individual who does not yet have the full moral standing of a moral agent (a standing that imposes duties and responsibilities on that agent)—and moral patients are due respect (see Petrinovich, 1995, 1996).

It is agreed that all humans have sensory receptors that react preferentially to selected types of stimulation that are also often difficult to habituate. Retinal cells are stimulated or inhibited by such things as edges and by lines with certain characteristics. Without prior experience, neonates group together figures of particular shapes, detect as basic units objects moving in common directions, and appreciate depth of field. The physiological mechanisms for many of these gestalt phenomena have been identified for many species.

Humans have mechanisms that "automatically" process certain kinds of visual stimuli preattentively. Such stimuli are said to "pop out" of displays, and the time required to detect these stimuli is independent of the number of elements. Detection of certain other stimuli requires the use of an attentional mechanism that checks each item in the display in a serial fashion; the more elements to be checked, the longer the search time (Treisman, 1988). Such simple sensory and perceptual mechanisms could have undergone strong selection and would have conferred a survival advantage in the EEA. At such simple levels of functioning, few would reject the argument that these processes represent evolved, content-specific information-processing adaptations. Many social scientists and humanists, however, have become increasingly resistant to attempts to extend the arguments much beyond such simple behavioral processes.

There is an enormous body of evidence (see Hauser, 1996) indicating that animals of many species have specialized detection systems and that these systems allow the animals to adapt to the demands of their environment. Emotional bonding takes place at the point of birth for many species. In humans, the neonate is able to respond to and to imitate certain adult facial expressions, an activity that would further strengthen the emotional bond with the mother and the social community (Meltzoff, 1996). Animals of many species have content-specific learning mechanisms that enhance the likelihood that certain kinds of events will be learned quickly.

There is evidence for content-specific learning mechanisms in a wide variety of situations that are critical to the survival of organisms. These mechanisms include SSDR's (Bolles, 1970), learned food aversions mediated by taste in rats and vision in birds (Garcia & Brett, 1977), and selective learning of certain sounds under certain conditions by birds

(Petrinovich, 1990). When learning mechanisms are studied within the context of the ecology within which organisms exist and cope, one is led to the conclusion that searching for content-general intellectual mechanisms is not of much use if the intent is to understand an animal's functioning in response to environmental contingencies.

Language Development

Pinker (1994) argued that human language, including the underlying rules that produce grammar and syntax, evolved through the process of natural selection. The use of "motherese," the language mothers use when addressing infants, directs the attention of the infant in ways that support emotional development, identifies linguistic units within the stream of speech, and enhances the acquisition of new words. These functions assist caregivers to be more efficient and make it more likely that offspring will survive to reproduce. These language precursors precede and prepare the way for the development of human language. Bickerton (1990), Locke (1993), and Pinker (1994) have all argued that the universality of critical elements in the development of human speech, grammar, and syntax supports the idea that language has evolved. When infants are born deaf, the development of signing exhibits the same essential characteristics as oral language does for those who hear, which means that what has evolved is not specific to speech but represents a communication mechanism that is active no matter what the sensory or response mode.

The human speech and language literature indicates that the development and use of language, among the most cherished of human abilities, has yielded many of its secrets to evolutionary analyses. The languagelike behaviors that have been laboriously taught to members of nonhuman species are faint shadows of the complex grammar that spontaneously develops in all young humans. Some aspects of adult language, such as categorical perception of speech sounds and a preference for the intonation patterns of the language heard in the uterus, are present at birth (Eimas, 1982; see Mehler & Dupoux, 1994).

In investigating the biologically primary abilities, Pinker (1994) noted that the brain organizes the world into discrete, bounded, and cohesive objects and arranges these objects into categories of the same kind. He argued that babies expect a language to contain words for kinds of objects and kinds of action, display basic elements of a universal grammar, and reflect the prosodic elements of their language community, all well before they have had any extensive exposure to a wide range of language exemplars.

Human Problem Solving

There is an immense literature bearing on the development of sensory and intellectual capacities of neonates and young infants that supports the conclusion that there is a universal theory of mind that develops in all normal humans with the regular patterns that characterize evolved mechanisms (see Gazzaniga, 1995; Hirschfeld & Gelman, 1994).

Geary (1995) used an evolution-based framework to gain understanding of the development of the cognitive processes involved in mathematics. He identified numerical abilities that appear to be universal primary abilities, many of which are shared with animals of other species and develop inevitably given normal experience. He analyzed the development of early mathematical abilities in infants and found that tendencies to group objects of the same kind involve an implicit understanding of the number of objects in small arrays and that these tendencies and understandings occur as early as the first week of life. This sensitivity is intermodal, and by 18 months of age, infants show a sensitivity to ordinal relationships and engage in primitive counting behavior. The strategies used to conceptualize linguistic and mathematical development (Wynn, 1992) provide insights into human nature, and these successes indicate it might be possible to develop an extensive base of cognitions and actions that people engage in consistently enough to be considered universals.

Premack and Premack (1995) developed the argument that the principles of morality could be formed from the simple properties of physical causation that all infants experience. One of the most important of these properties is the attribution of cause, which supports the attendant ideas of intentionality, value, reciprocation, possession, and group. Beliefs regarding relations between intentional objects arise from these basic, physically defined properties; they are coded in terms of right and wrong; and only relations among members count initially. Human moral beliefs develop from this innate set of properties, which are the frame into which the content of moral belief is poured, beliefs that reflect the power struggles of culture.

What about the complex human abilities involved in solving logical problems? There has been a biophobia and intellectual isolationism among social scientists that Tooby and Cosmides (1992, 1995) argued has become more extreme with time. These authors believe that the human brain is organized functionally to construct information, make decisions, and generate behaviors that would promote inclusive fitness in the ancestral environment of Pleistocene hunter-gatherers (the EEA).

Studies by Cosmides and Tooby (1992) and by Gigerenzer and Hug (1992) have indicated that the standard, domain-general model of problem solving fails when the cognitive behaviors studied are representative of those that would be adaptive within the natural social ecology of humans. One of the most important processes used to explain the evolution of social cooperation and competition is that of inclusive fitness. Cognitions involving social exchanges, having undergone selection pressure for many thousands of years, should incorporate design features that are particularly appropriate to deal with such problems. Individuals should be especially adapted to reason efficiently when social contracts are involved and should be attuned to detect cheating (a violation of a social contract), and they are. People reason more efficiently when solving problems that require the detection of rule violations involving social contracts than when the same formal rule violation does not involve such contracts. They also perform better on problems that are posed within a perspective in which a person needs to detect a cheater than one in which a person is only searching for information regarding the operative rule. There are a multitude of domain-specific mechanisms that were selected to enhance the adaptation of organisms coping with evolutionarily significant problems.

The Evolved Human Social Condition

A great deal of evidence supports adaptational explanations of complex human social behaviors. There are universal behavioral tendencies that influence patterns of homicide (Daly & Wilson, 1988), the different patterns of jealousy exhibited by men and women (Wilson & Daly, 1992), sex differences in the age and status preferred for mates (Kenrick & Keefe, 1992), and the different strategies used by males and females to assess a potential partner's reproductive potential (Buss, 1994).

Although different specific rules and structures are found in different societies, there are general features that characterize all societies, and a large number of these features relate to reproduction and inheritance— inheritance of goods as well as genes. The traits of cooperation and communication provide the cohesive elements for the sexual partnerships on which society depends. Such relatively permanent unions, based on economic and social cooperation, constitute the norm.

My research odyssey that began with the collaboration with Robert Bolles has taken many turns, but each was influenced by the belief that animals are trying their best to cope with the world out there and that they do the best they can with the abilities and resources available. In fact, if they did not do well in adapting to these demands, they would not be around. Bolles and I both were led to this enduring belief in the rational basis of nature by listening carefully to Tolman, who always had more positive queries about our research than we thought possible, to Brunswik, who instilled the romance by insisting that one use the broadest possible conceptual framework while suffering a minimal loss of rigor, and to Krech, who filled us with enthusiasm and curbed us with sharp criticism when necessary.

References

Alexander, R. D. (1979). *Darwinism and human affairs*. Seattle, WA: University of Washington Press.

Alexander, R. D. (1987). *The biology of moral systems*. New York: Aldine de Gruyter.

Baptista, L. F., & Morton, M. L. (1988). Song learning in montane white-crowned sparrows: From whom and when. *Auk, 99*, 537–547.

Baptista, L. F., & Petrinovich, L. (1984). Social interaction, sensitive phases and the song template hypothesis in the white-crowned sparrow. *Animal Behaviour, 32*, 172–181.

Baptista, L. F., & Petrinovich, L. (1986). Song development in the white-crowned sparrow: Social factors and sex differences. *Animal Behaviour, 34*, 1359–1371.

Bickerton, D. (1990). *Language and species*. Chicago: University of Chicago Press.

Bolles, R. (1970). Species-specific defense reactions and avoidance learning. *Psychological Review, 77*, 32–48.

Bolles, R., & Petrinovich, L. (1954). A technique for obtaining rapid drive discrimination in the rat. *Journal of Comparative and Physiological Psychology, 47*, 378–380.

Bolles, R., & Petrinovich, L. (1956). Body-weight changes and behavioral attributes. *Journal of Comparative and Physiological Psychology, 49*, 177–180.

Buss, D. M. (1994). *The evolution of desire*. New York: Basic Books.

Cosmides, L., & Tooby, J. (1992). Cognitive adaptations for social exchange. In J. H. Barkow, L. Cosmides, & J. Tooby (Eds.), *The adapted mind* (pp. 163–228). New York: Oxford University Press.

Cronin, H. (1991). *The ant and the peacock*. Cambridge, England: Cambridge University Press.

Daly, M., & Wilson, M. (1978). *Sex, evolution, and behavior*. North Scituate, MA: Duxbury Press.

Daly, J., & Wilson, M. (1988). *Homicide*. New York: Aldine de Gruyter.

DeWolfe, B. B., Baptista, L. F., & Petrinovich, L. (1989). Song development and territory establishment in Nuttall's white-crowned sparrows. *Condor, 91*, 397–407.

Eimas, P. D. (1982). Speech perception: A view of the initial state and perceptual mechanisms. In J. Mehler, E. C. T. Walker, & M. Grant (Eds.), *Perspectives on mental representation* (pp. 339–360). New York: Erlbaum.

Garcia, J., & Brett, L. P. (1977). Conditioned responses to food order and taste in rats and wild predators. In M. Kare (Ed.), *The chemical senses and nutrition* (pp. 277–289). New York: Academic Press.

Garcia, J., & Koelling, R. (1966). Relation of cue to consequence in avoidance learning. *Psychonomic Science, 4*, 123–124.

Gazzaniga, M. S. (1995). *The cognitive neurosciences*. Cambridge, MA: MIT Press.

Geary, D. (1995). Reflection of evolution and culture in children's cognition. *American Psychologist, 50*, 24–37.

Gigerenzer, G., & Hug, K. (1992). Domain-specific reasoning: Social contracts, cheating, and perspective change. *Cognition, 43*, 127–171.

Greenough, W. T., Black, J. E., & Wallace, C. S. (1987). Experience and brain development. *Child Development, 58*, 539–559.

Hauser, M. D. (1996). *The evolution of communication*. Cambridge, MA: MIT Press.

Herrnstein, R. J., & Hineline, P. N. (1966). Negative reinforcement as shock-frequency reduction. *Journal of the Experimental Analysis of Behavior, 9*, 421–430.

Hirschfeld, L. A., & Gelman, S. A. (1994). *Mapping the mind*. Cambridge, England: Cambridge University Press.

Kenrick, D. T., & Keefe, R. C. (1992). Age preferences in mates reflect sex differences in human reproductive strategies. *Behavioral and Brain Sciences, 15*, 75–91.

Locke, J. (1993). *The child's path to spoken language*. Cambridge, MA: Harvard University Press.

Marler, P. (1970). A comparative approach to vocal learning: Song development in white-crowned sparrows. *Journal of Comparative and Physiological Psychology, 71*, 1–25.

Mehler, J., & Dupoux, E. (1994). *What infants know*. Cambridge, MA: Basil Blackwell.

Meltzoff, A. N. (1988). The human infant as "homo imitans." In T. R. Zentall & B. G. Galef (Eds.), *Social learning* (pp. 319–341). Hillsdale, NJ: Erlbaum.

Meltzoff, A. N. (1996). The human infant as imitative generalist: A 20-year progress report on infant imitation with implications for comparative psychology. In C. M. Heyes & B. G. Galef, Jr. (Eds.), *Social learning in animals: The roots of culture* (pp. 347–370). New York: Academic Press.

Mowrer, O. H., & Lamoreaux, R. R. (1946). Fear as an intervening variable in avoidance conditioning. *Journal of Comparative Psychology, 53*, 72–78.

Nottebohm, F. (1969). The song of the chingolo, *Zonotrichia capensis* in Argentina: Description and evaluation of a system of dialects. *Condor, 71*, 299–315.

O'Neill, P., & Petrinovich, L. (1996). A cross-cultural study of moral intuitions. Manuscript submitted for publication.

Petrinovich, L. (1984). A two-factor, dual-process theory of habituation and sensitization. In H. V. S. Peeke & L. Petrinovich (Eds.), *Habituation, sensitization, and behavior* (pp. 17–55). New York: Academic Press.

Petrinovich, L. (1985). Factors influencing song development in the white-crowned sparrow (*Zonotrichia leucophrys*). *Journal of Comparative and Physiological Psychology, 99*, 15–29.

Petrinovich, L. (1988). Cultural transmission of song in white-crowned sparrows (*Zonotrichia leucophrys nuttalli*). *Behaviour, 107*, 208–240.

Petrinovich, L. (1990). Avian song development: Methodological and conceptual issues. In D. A. Dewsbury (Ed.), *Contemporary issues in comparative psychology* (pp. 340–359). Sunderland, MA: Sinauer Associates.

Petrinovich, L. (1995). *Human evolution, reproduction, and morality.* New York: Plenum Press.

Petrinovich, L. (1996). *Living and dying well.* New York: Plenum Press.

Petrinovich, L., & Baptista, L. F. (1984). Song dialects, mate selection, and breeding success in white-crowned sparrows. *Animal Behaviour, 32*, 1078–1088.

Petrinovich, L., & Baptista, L. F. (1987). Song development in the white-crowned sparrow: Modification of learned song. *Animal Behaviour, 35*, 961–974.

Petrinovich, L., & Bolles, R. (1954). Deprivation states and behavioral attributes. *Journal of Comparative and Physiological Psychology, 47*, 450–453.

Petrinovich, L., & Bolles, R. (1957). Delayed alternation: Evidence for symbolic processes in the rat. *Journal of Comparative and Physiological Psychology, 50*, 363–365.

Petrinovich, L., & O'Neill, P. (1996). The influence of wording and framing on moral intuitions. *Ethology and Sociobiology, 17*, 145–171.

Petrinovich, L., O'Neill, P., & Jorgensen, M. (1993). An empirical study of moral intuitions: Toward an evolutionary ethics. *Journal of Personality and Social Psychology, 64*, 467–478.

Pinker, S. (1994). *The language instinct.* New York: Morrow.

Premack, D., & Premack, J. (1995). Origins of human social competence. In M. S. Gazzaniga (Ed.), *The cognitive neurosciences* (pp. 205–218). Cambridge, MA: MIT Press.

Regan, T. (1983). *The case for animal rights.* Berkeley: University of California Press.

Rescorla, R. A., & LoLordo, V. M. (1965). Inhibition of avoidance behavior. *Journal of Comparative and Physiological Psychology, 59*, 406–412.

Rozin, P., & Kalat, J. W. (1971). Specific hungers and poison avoidance as adaptive specializations of learning. *Psychological Review, 78*, 459–486.

Ruse, M., & Wilson, E. O. (1986). Moral philosophy as applied science. *Philosophy, 61*, 71–92.

Thomson, J. J. (1976). Killing, letting die, and the trolley problem. *The Monist, 59*, 204–217.

Tinbergen, N. (1951). *The study of instinct.* Oxford, England: Oxford University Press.

Tooby, J., & Cosmides, L. (1992). The psychological foundations of culture. In J. H. Barkow, L. Cosmides, & J. Tooby (Eds.), *The adapted mind* (pp. 19–136). New York: Oxford University Press.

Tooby, J., & Cosmides, L. (1995). Introduction. In M. Gazzaniga (Ed.), *The cognitive neurosciences* (pp. 1181–1183). Cambridge, MA: MIT Press.

Treisman, A. (1988). Features and objects. *Quarterly Journal of Experimental Psychology, 40a*, 201–237.

Wilson, E. O. (1975). *Sociobiology: The new synthesis.* Cambridge, MA: Harvard.

Wilson, M., & Daly, M. (1992). The man who mistook his wife for a chattel. In J. Barkow, L. Cosmides, & J. Tooby (Eds.), *The adapted mind* (pp. 243–276). New York: Oxford University Press.

Wynn, K. (1992). Addition and subtraction by human infants. *Nature, 358*, 749–750.

2

Behavior Systems and the Demise of Equipotentiality: Historical Antecedents and Evidence From Sexual Conditioning

Michael Domjan

Robert Bolles lived through an exciting and turbulent time in the study of associative learning, and he relished contributing to and participating in the turbulence. One of the major changes in the field has been a shift away from the principle of equipotentiality. This chapter traces the demise of the principle of equipotentiality and its replacement by behavior systems approaches to the study of learning.

I begin the chapter with a description of the principle of equipotentiality. I then describe early challenges to equipotentiality in the 1960s, including challenges posed by Bolles's research on avoidance learning. In response to the new evidence, Bolles and others adopted broader conceptualizations in which learning was considered in the context of functional systems of behavior that are shaped by both phylogenetic and ontogenetic influences. As an illustration of a behavior systems approach, I describe research from my laboratory on learning in a sexual behavior system. I conclude with a discussion of the contributions of the behavior systems approach to the understanding of learning processes more generally.

The Principle of Equipotentiality

How organisms form associations has been the traditional subject of investigations of conditioning and learning. The elements of those associations were stimuli and responses. Theories and mechanisms of associative

The preparation of the chapter and much of the reported research on sexual conditioning were supported by National Institute of Mental Health Grant MH39940. A modified version of the chapter was given as a G. Stanley Hall Lecture at the annual convention of the American Psychological Association (1995) and at meetings of the Midwest Psychological Association (1996) and the Southwest Psychological Association (1996).

learning were assumed to apply equally to any type of stimulus and any type of response, an assumption known as the *principle of equipotentiality*.

The principle of equipotentiality had wide ramifications for the study of learning. It encouraged the formulation of theories in terms of generic stimuli (symbolized by "S") and generic responses (symbolized by "R"). The particular features of the stimuli and responses were assumed to be of little theoretical consequence. Such generic theories of learning dominated the field throughout much of the 20th century (Bower & Hilgard, 1981) and remain in evidence in contemporary research (e.g., Davis, Staddon, Machado, & Palmer, 1993; Pearce, 1994).

The principle of equipotentiality also encouraged the restriction of studies of learning to a few species (rats and pigeons, primarily) and a small number of experimental preparations (the Skinner box and the runway for the study of positive reinforcement, the shuttle box for the study of avoidance learning). Because the mechanisms of learning were assumed to be independent of the stimuli and responses involved in an association, only issues of convenience had to be considered in the selection of an experimental preparation (but see Timberlake, 1990).

With the focus on universal associative mechanisms encouraged by the principle of equipotentiality, investigators were satisfied to study a particular response isolated from the other activities of the organism. In fact, experimental preparations were specifically designed to limit the behavioral repertoire of the participants so that activities irrelevant to the response of interest would not intrude into the experiment. Because much of the data from studies of learning involved isolated responses, there was little interest in seeing how various responses were organized into functional systems of behavior.

Early Assaults on Equipotentiality: Biological Constraints on Learning

The principle of equipotentiality remained secure as long as investigators limited their attention to a few conventional experimental preparations. However, problems soon became evident when studies of learning were extended to nonconventional stimuli and responses. Breland and Breland (1961) pursued such extensions vigorously and soon found numerous problems with the principle of equipotentiality. They used reinforcement procedures to train chickens, pigs, raccoons, rabbits, ducks, and other species to perform various responses for entertainment displays and discovered that instrumental reinforcement did not invariably increase the rate of responding. With certain kinds of responses, continued reinforcement resulted in a deterioration rather than an improvement in performance. In one study, for example, Breland and Breland used raccoons that typically have a hearty appetite. The raccoons were reinforced with food for dropping a coin in a slot. As training progressed, the raccoons became increasingly reluctant to release the coin, showing a deterioration rather than an improvement in performance.

The nonequivalence of responses also became evident in studies of avoidance learning in the 1960s. Bolles (1969), for example, found that rats required to run in a running wheel to avoid shock learned the task much faster than rats required to rear on their hind legs. Others found that jumping out of a shock box occurred much more readily as an avoidance response in rats (Maatsch, 1959) than pressing a response lever (D'Amato & Schiff, 1964).

The principle of equipotentiality also ran into trouble when investigators turned their attention to new kinds of stimuli. For example, in what is now considered to be a classic experiment, Garcia and Koelling (1966) found that taste stimuli are much more easily associated with interoceptive malaise than are audiovisual cues, whereas audiovisual cues are more easily associated with cutaneous pain than are taste cues (for a review of subsequent research on this phenomenon, see Domjan, 1985).

Precursors of Behavior Systems

Efforts to understand examples of the nonequivalence of stimuli and responses quickly led to functional considerations. Bolles (1970), for example, pointed out that to avoid a predator, a rat has to make a successful avoidance response the first time. Failure to respond successfully during its first encounter with a predator may end the rat's life. Such considerations suggested to Bolles that much of defensive behavior must exist without learning as unconditioned responses to aversive stimuli. Bolles called unconditioned defensive responses *species-specific defense reactions*, or SSDRs.

Garcia also turned to functional considerations in his effort to explain why taste stimuli are associated with interoceptive malaise more easily than are audiovisual cues, whereas audiovisual cues are associated with cutaneous pain more easily than are taste cues (Garcia, Hankins, & Rusiniak, 1974). The propensity to associate taste cues with illness presumably evolved in omnivorous species such as the rat as a mechanism for avoiding poisonous food (Rozin & Kalat, 1971). A rat is more likely to experience food poisoning after eating a strange food than after encountering a distinctive auditory or visual cue. This correlation presumably led to the evolution of taste-aversion learning mechanisms. In contrast, cutaneous pain is presumably more likely in connection with distinctive auditory or visual cues than in connection with taste. That in turn presumably led to the evolution of learning mechanisms that favor the association of audiovisual cues with cutaneous pain.

Functional considerations of the sort entertained by Bolles and Garcia served to broaden the scope of studies of learning. Investigators started thinking about how learning may be involved in important tasks organisms perform that promote their reproductive fitness. In addition, instead of treating stimuli and responses merely as convenient tools to study the mechanisms of associative learning, investigators began to consider how learning may depend on the functional system of behavior in which the stimuli and responses participated.

Bolles (1971) pointed out that to understand what animals learn in aversive situations, one has to understand the organization of the defensive behavior system before learning occurs. He went on to speculate about the structure of the defensive behavior system and how the system might be altered by learning. Many of the details of Bolles's original theory turned out to be incorrect (e.g., Bolles & Riley, 1973). However, the basic idea that learning has to be studied within the context of functional systems of behavior rather than in isolated stimulus–response preparations has endured.

Garcia and his associates also relied on functional systems of behavior to explain their findings of selective associations with poison-induced internal malaise versus shock-induced cutaneous pain. They postulated that a specialized behavior system exists to regulate the organism's internal environment (*milieu interne*) and that a different system exists to regulate the organism's interactions with its external environment (*milieu externe*; Garcia et al., 1974). The two systems were assumed to be mediated by different neural structures, which in turn were assumed to mediate different forms of learning. For example, long-delay learning was presumed to occur in the interoceptive system but not in the exteroceptive system.

Bolles and Garcia were encouraged to consider systems of behavior in their efforts to deal with empirical results of learning experiments that violated the principle of equipotentiality. However, the idea that behavior is organized into complex functional systems did not originate with either of them. Rather, it originated with ethologists in their efforts to analyze the proximate mechanisms of naturally occurring behavior. On the basis of numerous observations, ethologists concluded that behavior was hierarchically and sequentially organized (see Baerends, 1988, for a recent review). When animals are in a particular motivational state (e.g., hunger), nondirected appetitive responses occur until a specific eliciting stimulus (a sign stimulus or releasing stimulus) is encountered. The sign stimulus elicits a consummatory response, which may or may not eliminate the drive state. If the original motivational state persists, appetitive responses reappear until a sign stimulus is again encountered.

The model of appetitive and consummatory behavior identified by ethologists is hierarchical because consummatory responses have precedence over appetitive behavior. Once the releasing stimulus for a consummatory response is encountered, appetitive behavior ends and the organism shifts to consummatory behavior. The model is sequential because appetitive responses typically precede consummatory responses.

The ethological model exemplifies a behavior system because it involves different types of responses (appetitive and consummatory behavior). Each response has its corresponding eliciting stimuli and control mechanisms, and activation of those control mechanisms is coordinated to produce sequentially organized and functionally effective behavior. A functionally effective organized set of responses constitutes a behavior system.

The Sexual Behavior System of Male Japanese Quail

Systems of behavior have been characterized for a variety of functions including homing, predatory defense, foraging, and territoriality. Some aspects of behavior systems are independent of learning; others are shaped or altered by experience. An issue of particular interest is whether all response and stimulus components of a behavior system are equally subject to modification by learning (equipotentiality) or are differentially sensitive to experience. I have been exploring this problem with a number of research collaborators in my study of the sexual behavior of male Japanese quail.

Early in our research on sexual learning in male quail, my colleagues and I distinguished between *species-typical cues*, which are unique to the animals we were studying, and *arbitrary cues*, which have no special relationship to the behavior at the outset of conditioning, events Pavlov (1927) defined as *conditioned stimuli*. At this point, we also followed the lead of classical ethology and distinguished between appetitive and consummatory sexual responses (e.g., Domjan, O'Vary, & Greene, 1988). However, these distinctions turned out to be inadequate to describe all of our findings. Our current working model of the sexual behavior system of male quail involves three types of stimuli (species-typical cues, local cues, and contextual cues) and three types of sexual responses (focal search, general search, and consummatory or copulatory behavior; see Domjan, 1994).

Species-typical cues are stimuli relevant to sexual behavior that are typical of a species, its habitat, or both. My group's studies have shown that species-typical cues relevant to the sexual behavior of male quail are provided by visual features of a female. These can be isolated from auditory, olfactory, and movement cues with the use of taxidermic models. Tests with taxidermic models containing various body parts of a female quail have shown that males are highly responsive to the plumage of a female's head and neck (Domjan & Nash, 1988), although other body parts of a female are also effective in stimulating sexual behavior (Crawford & Akins, 1993). Visual features of a female's head serve as social sign stimuli for the sexual behavior of male quail.

Local cues are spatially localized discrete stimuli (e.g., a spot of light or a three-dimensional object) that identify a particular location related to access to a potential sexual partner. In contrast, *contextual cues* refer to the spatial cues that distinguish a particular territory or area from other areas. Of course these various types of stimuli are not independent of each other. Species-typical cues and local cues exist in a particular area or territory. Therefore, species-typical cues and local cues occupy a subset of the spatial cues that make up the context in which sexual behavior may take place.

The most obvious type of sexual response in male quail is copulatory behavior, which involves consummatory aspects of sexual behavior, typically including physical contact between male and female and transfer of gametes. If a male quail cannot interact directly with a female, it will engage in one of two types of locomotor behavior, focal search or general search. *Focal search* involves approaching a particular place where a potential sexual partner might be found. *General search* refers to general locomotor behavior that is not directed toward a specific target location. Focal search and general search are different components of what ethologists previously considered to be appetitive behavior.

The sexual behavior sequence is presumed to start with general search for a potential sexual partner. Once a specific place where the sexual partner might be located has been identified, general search behavior is abandoned in favor of focal search of the target location. When the sexual partner has been located, focal search behavior is abandoned in favor of courtship and copulatory behavior. Each successive response in the behavior sequence is assumed to have priority over the previous one. If the conditions favorable to focal search behavior are encountered, general search behavior gives way to focal search, and if conditions favorable to consummatory behavior occur, focal search gives way to copulatory behavior.

The Sexual Behavior System Before Learning

Before one can describe how learning processes shape or alter a system of behavior, one has to characterize the preexisting state of the system. Figure 1 depicts my best guess as to the nature of the sexual behavior system before sexual conditioning. Different types of stimuli are represented on the vertical axis, and different types of sexual responses are represented on the horizontal axis. The density of the circles in each cell of the resultant matrix represents the presumed strength of control of a given response category by the various types of stimuli.

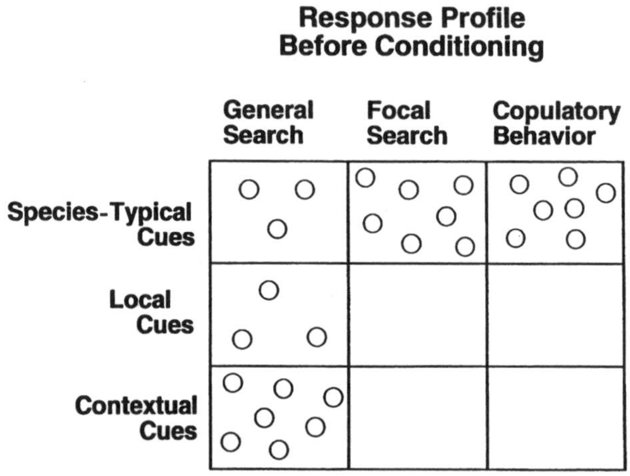

Figure 1.   The response profile of the sexual behavior system before conditioning. The density of the circles represents the degree of control of each type of stimulus over each type of response. From "Formulation of a Behavior System for Sexual Conditioning," by M. Domjan, 1994, *Psychonomic Bulletin & Review, 1,* 421–428. Reprinted with permission.

Although the efficiency of sexual behavior improves with experience (e.g., Lloyd, 1979), sexual responses can occur without practice. I assume that such unconditioned sexual behavior is primarily a result of species-typical cues provided by the potential sexual partner. Therefore, Figure 1 shows that species-typical cues can, to some extent, elicit general search, focal search, and copulatory behavior. Local cues and contextual cues may also elicit some behavior unconditionally. However, such unconditioned effects are likely to be limited to general search behavior. I assume that local cues and contextual cues do not elicit focal search and copulatory behavior unconditionally.

The Sexual Behavior System After Modification by Learning

Studies with male Japanese quail have shown that sexual conditioning can alter the stimulus control of sexual behavior in dramatic ways. Figure 2 depicts the conditioned response profile that I constructed on the basis

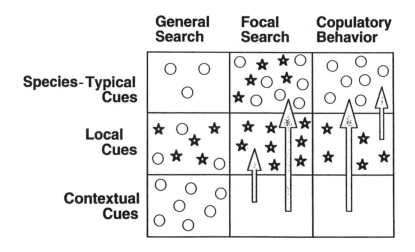

Response Profile After Conditioning

Figure 2. The response profile of the sexual behavior system after various types of conditioning procedures. Circles represent unconditioned effects (as in Figure 1), and stars represent conditioned effects. The density of either type of symbol reflects the degree of control of each type of stimulus over each type of response. Arrows represent modulatory influences between different types of stimuli created by conditioning. From "Formulation of a Behavior System for Sexual Conditioning," by M. Domjan, 1994, *Psychonomic Bulletin & Review, 1,* 421–428. Reprinted with permission.

of studies of sexual conditioning (see Domjan, 1994, for a summary of the specific experimental results). The unconditioned control mechanisms still operate after conditioning. This is shown by the circles in each of the cells of Figure 2, which are distributed the same way as in Figure 1. Conditioning effects are represented by the stars and arrows in the figure. The stars indicate that species-typical cues can become conditioned to elicit focal search behavior and local cues can become conditioned to elicit general search, focal search, and copulatory behavior. In addition to these direct response-eliciting effects of the stimuli after conditioning, I have identified modulatory, or interactive, effects among different types of stimuli. These conditioned modulatory influences are indicated by the arrows in Figure 2.

Modulatory influences refer to instances in which a stimulus alters the effectiveness of another cue in eliciting behavior. Conditioned modulatory influences among stimuli have become the focus of considerable attention among learning theorists because these influences sometimes involve special mechanisms of learning (e.g., Holland, 1992). My group's research, as summarized in Figure 2, shows how conditioned modulatory influences may contribute to a functional system of behavior. We have found that conditioned contextual cues can increase the effectiveness of species-typical cues in stimulating focal search behavior. Conditioned contextual cues can also increase the effectiveness of species-typical cues in eliciting copulatory behavior or of local cues in eliciting focal search behavior. Finally, conditioned local cues can increase the effectiveness of species-typical stimuli in eliciting copulatory behavior.

A comparison of Figures 1 and 2 provides an overview of how learning can modify the sexual behavior system. The most obvious consequence of learning is that sexual behavior is influenced by a much wider range of stimuli after learning (Figure 2) than before (Figure 1). Sexual conditioning increases the range of stimuli that control various aspects of sexual behavior, both directly and through interaction with other cues. This conclusion suggests that through experience, sexual behavior becomes more closely coordinated with environmental events.

In most of the experiments that contributed to the development of the model presented in Figure 2, the opportunity to copulate with a female served as the unconditioned stimulus (US). The results indicated that despite this uniformity in the unconditioned stimulus, a variety of sexual learning effects developed. As the following discussion illustrates, the results depended on the conditioned stimulus (CS) that was used, how the CS was presented in relation to species-typical cues, and how long the animals had to wait between presentation of the CS and access to a copulation partner (the CS–US interval). In the following sections, I explain why the available evidence has encouraged me to propose a behavior system with three response categories and three stimulus categories.

Functional distinction between general and focal search behavior: effects of the CS–US interval on sexual learning. Evidence that appetitive behavior in the sexual behavior system of male quail is not a homogeneous category came from studies of the CS–US interval. Temporal contiguity has been considered one of the fundamental factors determining the strength of association between conditioned and unconditioned stimuli. Konorski (1967), for example, wrote that CS–US contiguity is "the indispensable condition for the formation of every association (p. 292)." The general finding, consistent with this claim, has been that conditioned responding declines as the interval between the CS and the US is increased beyond about 0.5 second. The decline in conditioned responding is rapid in the conditioning of the nictitating membrane response of rabbits (Schneiderman & Gormezano, 1964). The CS–US interval function is not as steep in taste-aversion learning; however, a decline occurs even in that type of learning (Smith & Roll, 1967), and such effects have been interpreted as reflecting a decline in the strength of association between the CS and the US.

Akins, Domjan, and Gutiérrez (1994) conducted several experiments to evaluate how rapidly conditioned responding declines as the CS–US interval is increased in the sexual conditioning of male quail. The first experiment involved a localized CS, and we measured a form of focal search as the conditioned response: approach to the CS. Consistent with results reported with other conditioning preparations, conditioned approach behavior developed with a 1-minute CS–US interval but not with a 20-minute interval. One might conclude from this finding that learning did not occur with the 20-minute CS–US interval. However, Akins et al. noticed that birds that were conditioned with a 20-minute CS–US interval were more active than birds that did not receive a conditioning procedure.

Akins et al. pursued their incidental observation by making systematic measurements of the locomotor behavior of birds conditioned with different CS–US intervals. The results indicated that with a short CS–US interval, the predominant conditioned response is approach to the CS and increased locomotion in areas close to the CS. In contrast, with a 20-minute CS–US interval, the predominant conditioned behavior is increased locomotion throughout the experimental chamber. The CS used by Akins et al. was a foam block located at one end of an unusually large experimental arena (1.2 × 1.8 m). It is interesting that the conditioned response that developed with a 20-minute CS–US interval was not directed toward the CS but involved increased locomotion between one half of the apparatus and the other.

The results of the experiments by Akins et al. (1994) provided a new perspective on the effects of the CS–US interval on learning. They showed that one cannot automatically interpret CS–US interval effects as reflecting the strength of conditioning. Rather, the CS–US interval determines the nature of the conditioned response (CR). Others have also observed that Pavlovian conditioning can result in a variety of different types of conditioned responses. In a recent review of findings in aversive conditioning studies, for example, Lennartz and Weinberger (1992) distinguished between general CRs (e.g., heart rate changes) and US-specific CRs. However, they concluded that the nature of the conditioned response depends on the amount of training rather than the CS–US interval.

The findings of Akins et al. (1994) also suggested that appetitive aspects of sexual behavior include two functionally different response categories. Appetitive sexual behavior appears not to be a homogeneous category consisting primarily of approach to the location of a potential sexual partner. Rather, it also involves general locomotor behavior. Furthermore, CS-directed responses and general locomotor activity are functionally distinct. CS-directed activity develops with short but not long CS–US intervals, and general locomotion develops with long but not short CS–US intervals. Borrowing concepts from the literature on food foraging (e.g., Timberlake & Lucas, 1989), my colleagues and I refer to the general locomotor response as *general search behavior* and the CS-directed response as *focal search behavior* (see Figures 1 and 2).

Functional distinction between focal search and consummatory behavior. The sexual behavior system summarized in Figures 1 and 2 also involves a distinction between focal search and copulatory, or consummatory, behavior. Male copulatory behavior in quail involves a male grabbing the back of the female's neck (the grab response), mounting the female's back (the mount response), and bringing its cloacal protuberance in contact with that of the female (cloacal contact movement). Focal search involves approaching the CS. Both CS-approach and copulatory behavior can be observed as sexually conditioned responses if the conditioned stimulus is a terry cloth object that the male bird can grab, mount, and contact with its cloaca (Domjan, Huber-McDonald, & Holloway, 1992).

A number of investigators have looked for possible functional differences between appetitive and consummatory behavior. In much of this research, however, the appetitive response was a conditioned response whereas the consummatory behavior was an unconditioned response (e.g., Everitt & Stacey, 1987; Holland & Straub, 1979). Therefore, the differences obtained may have been related to the distinction between conditioned and unconditioned behavior rather than the distinction between appetitive and consummatory behavior.

Everitt and Stacey (1987), for example, first trained rats to press a response lever for sexual reinforcement provided on a second-order schedule. They then measured both lever pressing (the appetitive sexual response in this situation) and mount, intromission, and ejaculation responses when the males were given the opportunity to copulate with a receptive female (the consummatory response). The experimental manipulation was lesioning of the preoptic area. Preoptic area lesions severely disrupted copulatory behavior but had little effect on sexually conditioned lever pressing. This finding is consistent with a functional difference between appetitive and consummatory behavior. However, the result may also reflect differential sensitivity of conditioned and unconditioned sexual behavior to the lesions, because lever pressing is clearly a conditioned response, whereas mount, intromission, and ejaculation are unconditioned responses to a sexually receptive female.

In a recent study with male quail (Hilliard, Nguyen, Cusato, & Domjan, 1996), my associates and I avoided confounding the distinction between appetitive and consummatory behavior with differences in degree of conditioning by comparing the functional properties of conditioned appetitive and conditioned consummatory responses. Male quail first received sexual conditioning in which the CS was a three-dimensional object made of terry cloth the birds could both approach and copulate with. To encourage copulation (Domjan, Huber-McDonald, & Holloway, 1992), the CS object also contained some species-typical features: It was fitted with a taxidermically prepared female head and about 2.5 cm of neck feathers (see Figure 3). Such a stimulus object lacks sufficient species-typical features to elicit copulatory behavior unconditionally but readily elicits approach and copulation if it is paired with the opportunity to copulate with a live female bird (Köksal, Domjan, & Weisman, 1994).

Hilliard et al. (1996) presented the CS object paired with copulatory opportunity on seven occasions, which was sufficient to produce both conditioned approach to the CS (the appetitive response) and conditioned copulatory responses (the consummatory response). These investigators then measured the conditioned approach and copulatory behavior under different degrees of sexual satiation. The male quail received access to various numbers of female birds (0, 1, 4, or 8) before each test session to produce different degrees of sexual satiation.

The results of the experiment are summarized in Figure 4. Approach was measured in terms of how much time the participants spent in a small area (42 × 66 cm) surrounding the CS object. The copulatory responses shown are mounts and cloacal contact movements elicited by the CS object. Each response is expressed as a proportion of responding during the last acquisition trial. As expected, sexual satiation disrupted responding. Of particular interest, however, was the fact that conditioned copulatory behavior was disrupted much more than conditioned approach responding. The highest degree of sexual satiation virtually abolished mount and clo-

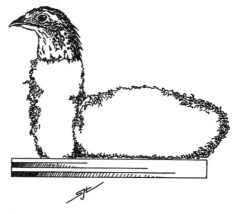

Figure 3. Sketch of the conditioned stimulus (CS) object used to study conditioned approach and copulatory behavior. The object is made of terry cloth filled with soft plastic fiber and has a taxidermically prepared female head and some neck feathers attached to the vertical section.

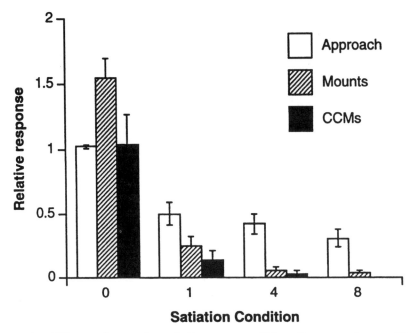

Figure 4. Effects of sexual satiation on conditioned approach, conditioned mount, and cloacal contact movements (CCM) in male quail. The birds were tested after exposure to 0, 1, 4, or 8 female quail to produce satiation. Each response is expressed as a proportion of responding during the last acquisition trial. Means and standard errors are shown.

acal contact responses. In contrast, approach behavior persisted at about 30 percent of the terminal acquisition level.

Hilliard et al. (1996) obtained similar results in a second experiment in which the effects of massed extinction trials were assessed. Again, conditioned copulatory behavior was disrupted to a greater degree than conditioned approach behavior. These results indicated that the controlling mechanisms of focal search behavior and copulatory behavior are different. Additional evidence in support of this claim is provided by research indicating that species-typical cues are much more important in the conditioning of copulatory behavior than in the conditioning of approach behavior (see "Conditioning of Copulatory Behavior," following).

Although it is clear that conditioned approach and copulatory behavior are differentially susceptible to sexual satiation, additional research is required to document the causes of that difference. One might suggest that the results represent only a quantitative difference between the two types of behavior. However, that begs the question of why such a quantitative difference exists. One possibility is that conditioned approach and copulatory responses reflect associations with different components of the sexual US. Conditioned approach may be mediated primarily by the visual features of a female quail that is presented as the US, whereas conditioned copulation may be mediated by tactile cues experienced during copulation with the female. Sexual satiation may serve to devalue the tactile US features more than the visual features, producing more of a disruption in conditioned copulatory behavior. Another possibility is that the two types of behavior are mediated to different degrees by stimulus–response and stimulus–stimulus associations. This possibility is consistent with Holland's (1979) observation that early components of a conditioned response are less specific to the US than are later components.

Distinction between species-typical cues and local cues. Another important feature of the sexual behavior system summarized in Figures 1 and 2 is that it involves three categories of stimuli: contextual cues, local stimuli, and species-typical cues. Furthermore, according to the system depicted, learning mechanisms can shape how an organism responds to each of these three types of stimuli. An important question from the standpoint of the principle of equipotentiality is whether it is necessary to postulate three different categories of stimuli for the behavior system.

TESTS OF BLOCKING. Recent studies using a blocking design have suggested that species-typical cues or social sign stimuli function in ways that are distinctively different from other types of stimuli. The blocking effect is one of the most important Pavlovian conditioning phenomena of the past quarter century (Kamin, 1969). Since its discovery, the blocking effect has been the focus of intense theoretical interest and has stimulated a family of information-processing models of Pavlovian conditioning such as the Rescorla–Wagner model (Rescorla & Wagner, 1972).

In the blocking effect, the presence of a previously conditioned stimulus (CS1) interferes with or blocks the conditioning of a newly introduced cue (CS2). In demonstrations of the blocking effect, animals receive two phases of training. During Phase 1, the blocking group receives CS1 paired with the US, whereas a control group receives exposures to CS1 and the US in an unpaired fashion. During Phase 2, both groups are exposed to a compound of CS1 together with the new conditioned stimulus, CS2, and the CS1–CS2 compound is paired with the US. Finally, the participants are tested for their response to CS2 presented alone. The blocking effect is manifested in less responding to CS2 in the blocking group than in the control group during the test phase.

My group recently completed experiments to see if an arbitrary local cue is more or less susceptible to blocking than a CS that contains some species-typical cues (Köksal et al., 1994). CS1 was an audiovisual cue presented above a door from which a female quail was released. Conditioning trials in Phase 1 consisted of presenting CS1 for 30 seconds, followed by release of the female bird for 5 minutes. For a control group, the female was presented about a half hour before each exposure to CS1. Conditioned approach to CS1 developed in the experimental group and reached an asymptote in 15 trials. At this point, both groups of birds were conditioned with a compound consisting of CS1 and a second stimulus, CS2. Presentations of the compound were paired with the release of a female quail.

In one experiment (Köksal et al., 1994, Experiment 2), CS2 consisted of a three-dimensional terry cloth object the birds could grab, mount, and contact with their cloaca. However, CS2 did not contain any species-typical female quail stimuli. Periodically during the course of compound conditioning, the animals were tested with CS2 alone. The researchers were interested in the extent to which the birds approached CS2. The test trials showed that CS2 came to elicit conditioned approach responding for participants in the control group but elicited much less conditioned responding in the experimental group. Thus, the presence of a previously conditioned stimulus (CS1) interfered with the conditioning of the added stimulus (CS2), an effect found in other studies of the blocking effect.

In another study (Köksal et al., 1994, Experiment 3b), the same procedure was used, but some species-typical cues were added to the terry cloth object that served as CS2. Namely, a taxidermically prepared head of a female quail was glued to the terry cloth object (see Figure 3). This time the blocking effect did not occur. The previously conditioned audiovisual CS did not block the conditioning of approach behavior to CS2. These results suggested that objects with species-typical features have special properties. Unlike objects lacking female cues, the conditioning of a terry cloth object with a female head cannot be blocked by a previously conditioned audiovisual cue. Thus, species-typical cues appear to be functionally different from more conventional localized conditioned stimuli.

CONDITIONING OF COPULATORY BEHAVIOR. Other evidence of the special status of species-typical cues has been obtained in studies of the conditioning of copulatory behavior. If a localized conditioned stimulus is paired with copulatory opportunity using a short CS–US interval, quail invariably come to approach the CS (Akins et al., 1994; Crawford & Domjan, 1993; Domjan, Lyons, North, & Bruell, 1986). Conditioned approach behavior requires minimal stimulus support: The CS only has to have a discrete location. In contrast, the occurrence of conditioned copulatory behavior requires that the CS have more elaborate features. A necessary condition is that the CS be a three-dimensional object that can support grab, mount, and cloacal contact movements. In addition, the CS has to include some species-typical features of a female quail, at least initially.

The first hint that species-typical cues have some unique properties in the control of copulatory behavior came from studies in which a small stuffed toy or an object made entirely of terry cloth was used as the conditioned stimulus (Domjan et al., 1988; Domjan, Huber-McDonald, & Holloway, 1992). These CS objects were repeatedly paired with the opportunity to copulate with a female quail. As a result of such pairings, males came to approach the CS objects; however, they rarely attempted to copulate with the CS objects, even though the objects could have been grabbed and mounted.

In contrast to the preceding findings, conditioned copulatory behavior readily develops when the CS object includes the head and neck feathers of a taxidermically prepared female quail (Domjan, Huber-McDonald, & Holloway, 1992; Köksal et al., 1994). A CS object containing the head and some of the neck plumage of a female does not elicit copulatory behavior unconditionally but becomes effective in eliciting copulatory responses if it is paired with access to a live female (Köksal et al., 1994).

My colleagues and I have been successful in inducing male quail to copulate with a terry cloth object entirely lacking in species-specific cues. However, we had to use a special fading procedure (Domjan, Huber-McDonald, & Holloway, 1992). Male quail were first conditioned to copulate with an object that included the head and neck plumage of a taxidermically prepared female quail. Once the males showed copulatory responses to such a CS object, the female plumage was gradually covered up with terry cloth. When the female plumage was covered up in sufficiently small steps, the males continued to copulate with the terry cloth object.

Our studies of blocking and conditioning of copulatory behavior indicate that an object that contains the species-typical cues of a female's head has privileged access to the sexual behavior system. An object with female head plumage is easily conditioned to elicit copulatory behavior and cannot be blocked from becoming conditioned to elicit focal search responding. The privileged status of visual cues provided by a female's head in sexual conditioning may represent a specialization of the sexual behavior system. Such a specialization may have evolved because quail live in grassy areas in which the female's head is likely to be the first part of a female's body males see as they approach a female (Schwartz & Schwartz, 1949; Taka-Tsukasa, 1967; Wetherbee, 1961). Stimuli of the head may also have a special role in the control of male sexual behavior because copulatory behavior begins with the male's grabbing the back of the female's head with its beak. However, these considerations do not rule out the possibility that the cues of a female's head are generally salient for male quail and are therefore especially effective as conditioned stimuli in a variety of contexts including feeding and defensive behavior. Additional research is required to evaluate that possibility.

Distinction between local cues and contextual cues. The behavior system depicted in Figures 1 and 2 also includes a distinction between local cues and contextual cues. What necessitates this departure from equipotentiality? The most compelling argument in support of the distinction between local and contextual cues is at the level of performance rather than learning process. Local cues are, by definition, isolated in space and therefore can support approach or focal search behavior. In contrast, contextual cues cannot elicit focal search directly. To date, my group has found no direct behavioral effects of the acquisition of an association between contextual cues and sexual reinforcement. Rather, sexually conditioned contextual cues influence behavior by increasing the effectiveness of local cues and species-typical cues in eliciting focal search (Domjan, Akins, & Vandergriff, 1992) and by increasing the effectiveness of species-typical cues in eliciting copulatory behavior (Domjan, Greene, & North, 1989). These modulatory or indirect effects of conditioned contextual cues are illustrated by the arrows in Figure 2.

A striking feature of the modulatory effects of contextual cues is that these conditioned properties can be acquired in just one trial. For example, in a recent study (Hilliard, Nguyen, & Domjan, 1997), male quail received a single conditioning trial in which they were first exposed to the contextual cues of a distinctive environment for 35 seconds and then given the opportunity to copulate with a female in that context for 5 minutes. A control group received the same context exposure, but for them copulatory opportunity was provided at some other time in their home cages. Each group was then tested in the distinctive environment with a terry cloth model that had a female head and about 2.5 cm of neck feathers attached. Response to the female cues was measured by observing how much time the males spent in a small area near the terry cloth model. The results of the test session, summarized in Figure 5, show that a single pairing of the context with sexual reinforcement was sufficient to enhance responding to the female cues. Birds in the paired group spent significantly more time near the female head than did those in the control group.

Contextual cues are probably not unique in the fact that they modulate the effectiveness of other types of stimuli. As is indicated in Figure 2, conditioned local cues can also increase the effectiveness of species-typical stimuli in eliciting copulatory behavior (Domjan et al., 1986). Furthermore, additional modulatory effects of conditioned local cues may be found

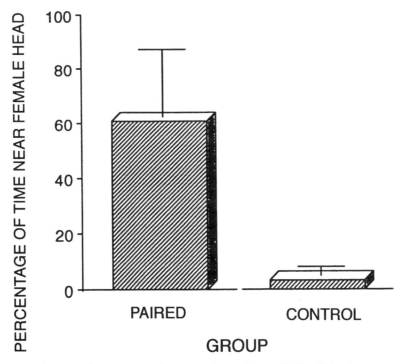

Figure 5. One-trial context conditioning in male quail. Conditioning was evident in increased time spent near a terry cloth model that included a taxidermically prepared female head and about 2.5 cm of neck plumage. During the conditioning trial, paired birds were given opportunity to copulate with a female quail in the CS context. Control birds received copulatory opportunity in their home cages unpaired with exposure to the contextual cues. Means and standard errors are shown.

once the proper experiments are performed. Thus, the distinction between local cues and contextual cues probably does not rest on the fact that contextual cues can modulate the effectiveness of species-typical stimuli whereas local cues cannot. However, conditioned contextual cues may be limited to modulatory influences on the effectiveness of other types of stimuli, whereas conditioned local cues can also elicit behavior directly.

The Sexual Behavior System and Equipotentiality

The sexual behavior system summarized in Figures 1 and 2 violates the principle of equipotentiality as that principle applies to both responses and stimuli. Instead of treating various sexual responses and stimuli as interchangeable, the sexual behavior system distinguishes among three types of responses (general search, focal search, and copulatory behavior) and three types of stimuli (contextual cues, local cues, and species-typical cues). As I have shown, general search, focal search, and copulatory behavior have functionally different controlling mechanisms. The evidence also suggests that learning proceeds differently if the conditioned stimulus contains species-typical features of a female quail than if the conditioned stimulus is an arbitrary local cue or a contextual stimulus. Furthermore, the various types of conditioned stimuli influence sexual behavior in different ways. Conditioned species-typical and local cues elicit sexual responses directly. In contrast, conditioned contextual cues influence sexual behavior primarily by modulating the effectiveness of species-typical and local cues.

Behavior Systems and Learning

Historically, violations of equipotentiality were considered to be "constraints on learning" (Hinde & Stevenson-Hinde, 1973) or "adaptive specializations of learning" (Rozin & Kalat, 1971). Such characterizations served to call attention to the phenomena but did not provide an integrated conceptual framework that could replace general process learning theory (Domjan & Galef, 1983). The behavior systems approach represents an effort to provide an integrated conceptual framework for adaptive specializations and constraints on learning. It is an effort to move from phenomena that challenge the principle of equipotentiality to a new general theory of learning and behavior (Timberlake & Lucas, 1989).

A behavior system is a set of behavioral mechanisms that is integrated and organized to enable the organism to achieve a particular biological function or goal. In the preceding sections, I described the outline of the system of behaviors that enable a male quail to find and copulate with a female conspecific. Bolles was particularly interested in the system of behaviors that is involved in predatory defense (Bolles, 1971; Bolles & Fanselow, 1980; see also Part D of this volume). Other systems of behavior are involved in foraging, temperature regulation, parental feeding, territoriality, and other important biological functions.

Each system of behavior involves various special features (e.g., specialized responses or stimuli) related to the unique function of that system. However, all systems of behavior are likely to have some common properties as well (Hogan, 1994; Shettleworth, 1994). One general characteristic is that behavior systems involve a set of different responses, each with its own controlling mechanism. In some cases it may be sufficient to categorize the responses as appetitive versus consummatory. However, additional response categories are likely to become necessary with more detailed analysis of the system. All behavior systems are also likely to involve sensitivity to several different types of stimuli, and each response is likely to have its own preferred activating stimulus. Finally, the stimulus–response modules are likely to be coordinated by a higher order regulatory or motivational process that determines performance.

Certain aspects of a behavior system are in place before a particular learning manipulation is introduced. Other aspects of the system are shaped by experience. Because of this, there are reciprocal influences between learning and behavior systems. The results of a particular learning manipulation are determined by the system of behavior that is under modification by the learning experience. The behavior system is in turn shaped by the learning manipulation. In some systems of behavior such as sexual behavior (see Figure 2) and foraging (Timberlake, 1994), the behavior system may be substantially modified by learning. In other cases (e.g., defensive behavior as conceived by Bolles), the learning influence may be much more restricted.

Although studies of learning from the perspective of systems of behavior are just in their infancy, the behavior systems approach promises several advantages. It forces researchers to think about learning not as an isolated process but as part of a more complex system with a specific biological function. Given its emphasis on function, the behavior systems approach encourages analysis of how learning is manifest in the organism's behavior; it encourages consideration of performance factors in learning. This emphasis on the functional behavioral consequences of learning is squarely in the tradition of Bolles's thinking about avoidance learning and species-specific defense reactions.

Also in the tradition of Bolles, the behavior systems approach integrates studies of learning with knowledge of the preexisting behavioral mechanisms of the organism. As such, it helps investigators to understand response constraints on learning not as isolated special cases but as manifestations of evolutionary processes that shape the mechanisms of both unconditioned and conditioned behavior.

Because behavior systems involve functionally distinct categories of stimuli, the behavior systems approach also helps integrate stimulus filtering and specialized perceptual processes into considerations of learning. Finally, given its functional emphasis, the behavior systems approach shows how motivation and learning are organized to achieve a biological goal. In this respect, the behavior systems approach represents many of Bolles's hopes and aspirations for a biological science of behavior.

References

Akins, C. K., Domjan, M., & Gutiérrez, G. (1994). Topography of sexually conditioned behavior in male Japanese quail (*Coturnix japonica*) depends on the CS-US interval. *Journal of Experimental Psychology: Animal Behavior Processes, 20*, 199–209.

Baerends, G. P. (1988). Ethology. In R. C. Atkinson, R. J. Herrnstein, G. Lindsey, & R. D. Luce (Eds.), *Stevens' handbook of experimental psychology* (Vol. 1, pp. 765–830). New York: Wiley.

Bolles, R. C. (1969). Avoidance and escape learning: Simultaneous acquisition of different responses. *Journal of Comparative and Physiological Psychology, 68*, 355–358.

Bolles, R. C. (1970). Species-specific defense reactions and avoidance learning. *Psychological Review, 77*, 32–48.

Bolles, R. C. (1971). Species-specific defense reaction. In F. R. Brush (Ed.), *Aversive conditioning and learning*. New York: Academic Press.

Bolles, R. C., & Fanselow, M. S. (1980). A perceptual-defensive-recuperative model of fear and pain. *Behavioral and Brain Sciences, 3*, 291–301.

Bolles, R. C., & Riley, A. L. (1973). Freezing as an avoidance response: Another look at the operant-respondent distinction. *Learning and Motivation, 4*, 268–275.

Bower, G. H., & Hilgard, E. R. (1981). *Theories of learning* (5th ed.). Englewood Cliffs, NJ: Prentice-Hall.

Breland, K., & Breland, M. (1961). The misbehavior of organisms. *American Psychologist, 16*, 681–684.

Crawford, L., & Akins, C. K. (1993). Stimulus control of copulatory behavior in male Japanese quail. *Poultry Science, 72*, 722–727.

Crawford, L., & Domjan, M. (1993). Sexual approach conditioning: Omission contingency tests. *Animal Learning & Behavior, 21*, 42–50.

D'Amato, M. R., & Schiff, D. (1964). Long-term discriminated avoidance performance in the rat. *Journal of Comparative and Physiological Psychology, 57*, 123–126.

Davis, D. G. S., Staddon, J. E. R., Machado, A., & Palmer, R. G. (1993). The process of recurrent choice. *Psychological Review, 100*, 320–341.

Domjan, M. (1985). Cue-consequence specificity and long-delay learning revisited. *Annals of the New York Academy of Sciences, 443*, 54–66.

Domjan, M. (1994). Formulation of a behavior system for sexual conditioning. *Psychonomic Bulletin & Review, 1*, 421–428.

Domjan, M., Akins, C., & Vandergriff, D. H. (1992). Increased responding to female stimuli as a result of sexual experience: Tests of mechanisms of learning. *Quarterly Journal of Experimental Psychology, 45B*, 139–157.

Domjan, M., & Galef, B. G., Jr. (1983). Biological constraints on instrumental and classical conditioning: Retrospect and prospect. *Animal Learning & Behavior, 11*, 151–161.

Domjan, M., Greene, P., & North, N. C. (1989). Contextual conditioning and the control of copulatory behavior by species-specific sign stimuli in male Japanese quail. *Journal of Experimental Psychology: Animal Behavior Processes, 15*, 147–153.

Domjan, M., Huber-McDonald, M., & Holloway, K. (1992). Conditioning copulatory behavior to an artificial object: Efficacy of stimulus fading. *Animal Learning & Behavior, 20*, 350–362.

Domjan, M., Lyons, R., North, N. C., & Bruell, J. (1986). Sexual Pavlovian conditioned approach behavior in male Japanese quail (*Coturnix coturnix japonica*). *Journal of Comparative Psychology, 100*, 413–421.

Domjan, M., & Nash, S. (1988). Stimulus control of social behavior in male Japanese quail, *Coturnix coturnix japonica*. *Animal Behaviour, 36*, 1006–1015.

Domjan, M., O'Vary, D., & Greene, P. (1988). Conditioning of appetitive and consummatory sexual behavior in male Japanese quail. *Journal of the Experimental Analysis of Behavior, 50*, 505–519.

Everitt, B. J., & Stacey, P. (1987). Studies of instrumental behavior with sexual reinforcement in male rats (*Rattus norvegicus*): II. Effects of preoptic area lesions, castration, and testosterone. *Journal of Comparative Psychology, 101*, 407–419.

Garcia, J., Hankins, W. G., & Rusiniak, K. W. (1974). Behavioral regulation of the milieu interne in man and rat. *Science, 185,* 824–831.

Garcia, J., & Koelling, R. A. (1966). Relation of cue to consequence in avoidance learning. *Psychonomic Science, 4,* 123–124.

Hilliard, S., Nguyen, M., Cusato, B., & Domjan, M. (1996). *Differential effects of sexual satiation and extinction on sexually conditioned appetitive and consummatory behavior.* Unpublished manuscript.

Hilliard, S., Nguyen, M., & Domjan, M. (1997). One-trial appetitive conditioning: Sexual learning about context. *Psychonomic Bulletin & Review, 4,.*

Hinde, R. A., & Stevenson-Hinde, J. (Eds.). (1973). *Constraints on learning.* New York: Academic Press.

Hogan, J. A. (1994). Structure and development of behavior systems. *Psychonomic Bulletin & Review, 1,* 439–450.

Holland, P. C. (1979). The effects of qualitative and quantitative variation in the US on individual components of Pavlovian appetitive conditioned behavior in rats. *Animal Learning & Behavior, 7,* 424–432.

Holland, P. C. (1992). Occasion setting in Pavlovian conditioning. In D. L. Medin (Ed.), *The psychology of learning and motivation* (Vol. 28, pp. 69–125). Orlando, FL: Academic Press.

Holland, P. C., & Straub, J. J. (1979). Differential effects of two ways of devaluing the unconditioned stimulus after Pavlovian appetitive conditioning. *Journal of Experimental Psychology: Animal Behavior Processes, 5,* 65–78.

Kamin, L. (1969). Predictability, surprise, and conditioning. In B.A. Campbell & R. M. Church (Eds.), *Punishment and aversive behavior.* New York: Appleton-Century-Crofts.

Köksal, F., Domjan, M., & Weisman, G. (1994). Blocking of the sexual conditioning of differentially effective conditioned stimulus objects. *Animal Learning & Behavior, 22,* 103–111.

Konorski, J. (1967). *Integrative activity of the brain.* Chicago: University of Chicago Press.

Lennartz, R. C., & Weinberger, N. M. (1992). Analysis of response systems in Pavlovian conditioning reveals rapidly versus slowly acquired conditioned responses: Support for two factors, implications for behavior and neurobiology. *Psychobiology, 20,* 93–119.

Lloyd, C. S. (1979). Factors affecting breeding of Razorbills *Alca torda* on Stokholm. *Ibis, 121,* 165–176.

Maatsch, J. L. (1959). Learning and fixation after a single shock trial. *Journal of Comparative and Physiological Psychology, 52,* 408–410.

Pavlov, I. (1927). *Conditioned reflexes* (G. V. Anrep, Trans.). London: Oxford University Press.

Pearce, J. M. (1994). Similarity and discrimination: A selective review and a connectionist model. *Psychological Review, 101,* 587–607.

Rescorla, R. A., & Wagner, A. R. (1972). A theory of Pavlovian conditioning: Variations in the effectiveness of reinforcement and nonreinforcement. In A. H. Black & W. F. Prokasy (Eds.), *Classical conditioning; II. Current research and theory* (pp. 64–99). New York: Appleton-Century-Crofts.

Rozin, P., & Kalat, J. W. (1971). Specific hungers and poison avoidance as adaptive specializations of learning. *Psychological Review, 78,* 459–486.

Schneiderman, N., & Gormezano, I. (1964). Conditioning of the nictitating membrane of the rabbit as a function of the CS–US interval. *Journal of Comparative and Physiological Psychology, 57,* 188–195.

Schwartz, C. W., & Schwartz, E. R. (1949). *A reconnaissance of the game birds in Hawaii* (pp. 90–99). Hilo, HI: Hawaii Board of Commissioners of Agriculture and Forestry.

Shettleworth, S. J. (1994). Commentary: What are behavior systems and what use are they? *Psychonomic Bulletin & Review, 1,* 451–456.

Smith, J. C., & Roll, D. L. (1967). Trace conditioning with X-rays as an aversive stimulus. *Psychonomic Science, 9,* 11–12.

Taka-Tsukasa, N. (1967). *The birds of Nippon.* Tokyo: Maruzen.

Timberlake, W. (1990). Natural learning in laboratory paradigms. In D. A. Dewsbury (Ed.), *Contemporary issues in comparative psychology* (pp. 31–54). Sunderland, MA: Sinauer.

Timberlake, W. (1994). Behavior systems, associationism, and Pavlovian conditioning. *Psychonomic Bulletin & Review, 1,* 405–420.

Timberlake, W., & Lucas, G. A. (1989). Behavior systems and learning: From misbehavior to general principles. In S. B. Klein & R. R. Mowrer (Eds.), *Contemporary learning theories: Instrumental conditioning theory and the impact of biological constraints on learning* (pp. 237–275). Hillsdale, NJ: Erlbaum.

Wetherbee, D. K. (1961). Investigations in the life history of the common coturnix. *American Midland Naturalist, 114,* 615–626.

3

Developmental Dissociation of the Components of Conditioned Fear

Pamela S. Hunt and Byron A. Campbell

Robert Bolles was a true functionalist. He, along with several other notable contemporaries, effectively merged the study of animal learning with the field of ethology (e.g., Bolles, 1970, 1985). Bolles was particularly struck by situations in which positive reinforcement seemed ineffective for modifying animal behavior. In one classic example, rats readily acquire a bar-press response to obtain food reward but appear to be unable to emit the same response to avoid shock. Although reinforcement theorists at the time were merely annoyed by such findings, Bolles found such situations of considerable interest and began to ask the pivotal question: Why?

A biologically oriented learning theorist, Bolles focused on understanding animal behavior with careful consideration for the organism's species-typical environment and ultimately formed theories for predicting the types of situational behavior an organism could acquire. Bolles not only focused on evolutionary pressures as a major determinant of this competence but also noted that during development, the young organism is faced with challenges that differ from those of its mature counterparts. Although he was not particularly well known as a developmental psychobiologist, Bolles made a number of important contributions to the study of behavioral development (Bolles & Woods, 1964; Collier & Bolles, 1980). In one article that related specifically to the ontogeny of learning capabilities, Collier and Bolles (1980) described what they termed "age-specific defense reactions" (ASDRs), an extension of Bolles's (1970) species-specific defense reaction (SSDR) hypothesis. Collier and Bolles found that the number of defensive reactions elicited by electric shock was relatively limited early in development but that the number and specificity of these reactions increased rapidly between 5 and 20 days of age. This sequential maturation of SSDRs along with Bolles's extensive use of one SSDR in particular (freezing) formed the groundwork of the research described in this chapter. In our group's investigation of Pavlovian conditioned

Preparation of this chapter and the research reported were supported by National Institutes of Mental Health Grants MH01562 and MH49496 to Byron A. Campbell and National Institutes of Child Health and Human Development postdoctoral Grant HD07694 to Pamela S. Hunt.

responses, we have similarly found that the behavioral response used to index aversive conditioning (e.g., fear) becomes extremely critical, because not all responses can be expressed at particular periods during development. There appears to be a highly invariant ontogenetic development of response systems.

The goal of this chapter is to examine critically the ontogenesis of conditioned fear in the young rat, using the results of ongoing research and previously published articles from our laboratory as the foundation. The chapter focuses on three simple but widely used measures of conditioned fear: behavioral suppression (i.e., freezing), changes in heart rate, and fear-potentiation of the acoustic startle response, each representing a species-specific component of defensive responding.

What Is Fear?

It is generally accepted that acquired fear is established through a process of Pavlovian conditioning (e.g., Bolles & Fanselow, 1980; McAllister & McAllister, 1971). In a Pavlovian paradigm, a "neutral" stimulus, the conditioned stimulus (CS), is paired with a stimulus of biological relevance (unconditioned stimulus, US) that elicits an observable or measurable response (unconditioned response, UR). As a result of this pairing, the CS comes to elicit a reaction known as the conditioned response (CR).

A widely held view is that most USs evoke a central emotional state as well as a number of specific autonomic and behavioral reactions and that both components become associated with the CS (Davis, Falls, Campeau, & Kim, 1993; Hollis, 1982; LeDoux, 1992; McAllister & McAllister, 1971). If the US is hedonically aversive, such as an electric shock or a loud noise, then the conditioned emotional response is assumed to be fear. Indeed, several contemporary theorists have explicitly included components reflecting the conditioning of affective states in their models of associative learning (e.g., Dickinson & Dearing, 1979; Konorski, 1967; Wagner & Brandon, 1989; cf. Pearce & Hall, 1980; Rescorla & Wagner, 1972; Wagner, 1981).

Because central emotional states such as fear are unobservable, the presence of acquired fear has to be inferred from changes in either overt behavior or physiological state. Behavioral indices include freezing, flight, suppression of ongoing behavior, and defensive burying (e.g., Blanchard & Blanchard, 1969; Bouton & Bolles, 1980; Fanselow, 1980, 1984; Pinel & Treit, 1978; Rudy, 1993). Hypoalgesia, typically opioid in nature, is also a predominant response (e.g., Fanselow & Bolles, 1979; Fanselow & Helmstetter, 1988). Variations in the activity of the autonomic nervous system are prevalent, and changes in heart rate and blood pressure are commonly measured (e.g., Campbell & Ampuero, 1985b; Kapp, Whalen, Supple, & Pascoe, 1992; Powell, 1992; Schneiderman, 1987). Another category of fear responses comprises the modulation of various reflexive behaviors. Modification of the eyeblink reflex to an orbital shock or loud noise in the presence of a fear cue has been used to index fear in rabbits (Weisz & LoTurco,

1988; Weisz & McInerney, 1990) and humans (Hamm, Greenwald, Bradley, Cuthbert, & Lang, 1991; Lang, Bradley, & Cuthbert, 1990). Rats show enhanced whole-body startle responses to an acoustic startle stimulus when the reflex is elicited in the presence of a stimulus previously paired with shock, a phenomenon known as *fear-potentiated startle* (Brown, Kalish, & Farber, 1951; Davis, 1992; Davis et al., 1993).

Psychologists and neuroscientists working in the animal-learning tradition have made a number of assumptions regarding conditioned fear. The first assumption is that fear is a central, phylogenetically constant state (Blanchard, Yudko, Rodgers, & Blanchard, 1993; LeDoux, 1993) that is inferred from the occurrence of a cluster of species-specific autonomic and behavioral responses to a CS that has been paired with an aversive US. However, the specific pattern of responses indicative of a central fear state is assumed to vary widely both within and between species, depending on the relevance of the stimulus to the species under investigation and the opportunities to escape or modify the consequences of the US. The second assumption, stemming from the first, is that all conditioned responses to a specific fear-eliciting stimulus are equally adequate for concluding that fear is present. Researchers studying the rat, for example, have inferred that widely used measures such as freezing, changes in heart rate, and fear-potentiated startle are equivalent reflections of the fear state. The choice of behaviors to index the central state of fear, therefore, is most often defined by other aspects of the experimental procedure or out of convenience to the experimenter. Hence, the use of a variety of measures is often viewed as unnecessary duplication (for discussions, see Archer, 1979; Lennartz & Weinberger, 1992).

This assumption of CR equivalence has gained wide acceptance from several sources of converging evidence. First, when multiple responses have been recorded at the same time, they tend to covary. The following response categories have been shown to co-occur: opioid analgesia, defecation, and freezing (Fanselow, 1984; Fanselow, Helmstetter, & Calcagnetti, 1991); freezing and fear-potentiated startle (Leaton & Borszcz, 1985; Leaton & Cranney, 1990); autonomic (heart rate and blood pressure) and motor (changes in general activity) responses (Campbell & Ampuero, 1985b; Hunt, Hess, & Campbell, 1997; LeDoux, 1993; Powell & Kazis, 1976); cardiac changes and potentiation of eyeblink reflexes (Bohlin & Graham, 1977; Whalen & Kapp, 1991), to name a few.

Second, the appearance of these responses is nonmonotonically related to the degree of conditioning. Conditioned response magnitude initially increases but thereafter declines with more training or with the use of relatively high shock intensities (Campbell & Ampuero, 1985a; Davis & Astrachan, 1978; Fanselow, 1984; Leaton & Borszcz, 1985; Millenson & Hendry, 1967; Powell, Schneiderman, Elster, & Jacobson, 1971). Third, these behaviors are all similarly affected (reduced) by administration of anxiolytic agents such as diazepam or midazolam, and most seem to be evoked by anxiogenic drugs such as dimethoxy-β-carboline (DMCM) or yohimbine (e.g., Davis, 1986; Davis et al., 1993; Fanselow & Helmstetter, 1988; Fanselow et al., 1991; Harris & Westbrook, 1995).

Finally, these behaviors have a common anatomical basis, such that the central nucleus of the amygdala seems to be critical for the expression of all of them. Electrical or chemical stimulation of the amygdala results in changes in blood pressure and heart rate, freezing, and startle response potentiation, whereas lesions of the amygdala block their elicitation as CRs (e.g., Davis, 1992; Davis et al., 1993; Kapp, Markgraf, Wilson, Pascoe, & Supple, 1992; LeDoux, 1992, 1993).

Emergence of Conditioned Fear During Development

Some time ago, Campbell and Ampuero (1985b) presented findings suggesting that classical Pavlovian fear conditioning produced conditioned behavioral responses considerably earlier during ontogeny than it produced conditioned autonomic responses such as a change in heart rate. In that study, an auditory or visual stimulus previously paired with shock suppressed appetitively motivated running several days earlier in development than it produced a conditioned change in heart rate. Unfortunately, drastically different procedures for training and testing the behavioral and cardiac CRs were used in that research, making it difficult to reach an unequivocal conclusion about the ontogenetic development of these two components of conditioned fear.

In the following sections, we describe the ontogeny of conditioned fear responses in the young rat, focusing on three specific measures: behavioral suppression (i.e., freezing; Blanchard & Blanchard, 1969; Fanselow, 1980; Rudy, 1993), changes in heart rate (Campbell & Ampuero, 1985b; Fitzgerald, Martin, & O'Brien, 1973; Kapp, Markgraf, et al., 1992; Kapp, Whalen, et al., 1992), and fear-potentiation of the acoustic startle response (Davis et al., 1993; Leaton & Cranney, 1990). These three measures were selected for several reasons. First, they can be consistently and rapidly established through classical conditioning procedures, and second, they have been widely used in the analysis of the neural circuits underlying the acquisition and expression of acquired fears in the adult laboratory rat. The chapter includes a brief description of our recent research findings followed by a discussion of the significance of these findings for contemporary analyses of the components of conditioned fear and some speculation about the neural mechanisms that might mediate the sequential emergence of the three expressions of conditioned fear.

The unconditioned stimulus used in all of these studies was a brief, intense noise burst, which we refer to as a *startle stimulus*. The startle US was selected because it can be used to study acquisition of fear-potentiated startle without having to wait 24 hours for the possible sensitizing effects of electric shock to dissipate. With electric shock, the prototypical aversive US for studying fear-potentiated startle, testing typically takes place 24 hours later to minimize the possibility of increased startle magnitude through shock sensitization of the startle response (Davis, 1989). The ability to measure fear-potentiated startle on-line with the use of the startle US was a particularly attractive feature because it eliminated the need for a retention interval between conditioning and testing. Retention intervals could make it difficult to draw conclusions about the relative age at which different conditioned fear responses emerge during development, given the possibility of age-related changes in rate of forgetting (e.g., Campbell & Campbell, 1962; Campbell, Misanin, White, & Lytle, 1974; Spear, 1979). By using a startle US, it was also possible to compare the development of conditioned freezing, fear-potentiated startle, and conditioned heart rate changes using the same CSs and US in all three experiments. In addition, when electric shock is used as the US, it briefly disrupts recording of ECG activity, whereas the acoustic startle stimulus permits continuous recording of heart rate during presentation of both the CS and US.

Ontogenesis of Conditioned Freezing to Auditory and Visual Stimuli

On the basis of the work of Campbell and Ampuero (1985b), it seemed likely that conditioned suppression of a behavioral response would appear early during development, before conditioned changes in heart rate and either before or simultaneously with the emergence of fear-potentiated startle. Since Campbell and Ampuero's (1985b) article was published, it has become clear that conditioned freezing (suppression of ongoing somatomotor activity) is probably the most sensitive and reliable technique for studying the emergence of conditioned behavioral responses during development. In an elegant series of studies, Moye and Rudy (1985, 1987) showed that conditioned freezing to an auditory CS followed by a shock US is first seen at approximately 15 days of age, and to a visual CS, at 17 days.

The purpose of the first of the following three experiments was to replicate Campbell's and Rudy's findings described previously (Campbell & Ampuero, 1985b; Moye & Rudy, 1985, 1987) using an acoustic startle stimulus as the US instead of electric shock. The specific goal was to determine the age at which the developing rat would show conditioned behavioral suppression to auditory and visual CSs paired with the startle stimulus. Some of these data have been published previously (Hunt, Richardson, & Campbell, 1994). The subjects were preweanling rats, ranging in age from 16 to 23 days, and were assigned to groups that were given either paired or explicitly unpaired presentations of a CS followed by the acoustic startle US (100-msec, 130-dB white noise with an instantaneous rise–fall time). The auditory CS was a 10-second pulsing 1600-Hz, 80-dB pure tone, and the visual CS was a flashing 25-watt white bulb. Conditioning consisted of 20 CS–US pairings during a single session. Following this training, animals were placed into a novel testing environment, where they were videotaped for 1 minute prior to CS onset and for 1 minute during which the CS was present. The total amount of time each subject remained immobile (absence of all visible movements) during each 1-minute epoch was subsequently scored from the videotapes.

As shown in the top panels of Figure 1, subjects previously given 20 pairings of the auditory CS with the startle stimulus US, even at the youngest age tested (16 days), showed conditioned suppression of activity. Little immobility was seen during the pre-CS period at any age. When the visual stimulus served as the CS, the 16-day-olds did not show conditioned freezing, whereas subjects 18 days of age and older responded to the CS with immobility (Figure 1, bottom panels). Once again, as Moye and Rudy (1985, 1987), Campbell and Ampuero (1985b), and others have reported,

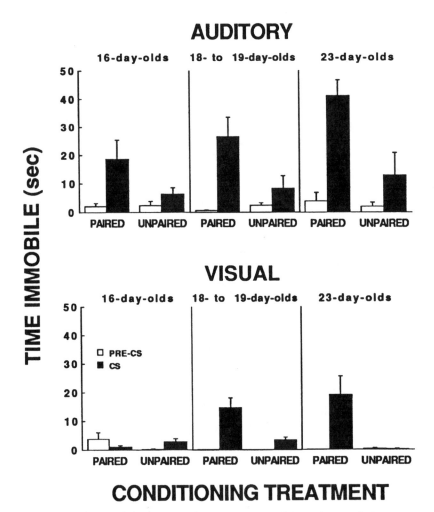

Figure 1. Conditioned fear to auditory (top panels) and visual (lower panels) stimuli as measured by the time (in seconds) spent immobile (freezing) during a 1-minute pre-CS (open bars) and a 1-minute CS (black bars) period by animals ranging in age from 16 to 23 days. Paired subjects were given 20 pairings of the CS with an acoustic startle US, and unpaired subjects were given these two events in an explicitly unpaired manner. The data shown represent mean ($+/-SEM$) time (in seconds) spent immobile.

conditioned responses to the auditory CS were observed earlier in development than conditioned responses to the visual CS.

Ontogenesis of Conditioned Heart Rate Responses to Auditory and Visual Stimuli

As noted earlier, Campbell and Ampuero (1985b) presented findings suggesting that conditioned changes in heart rate emerged later in development than conditioned suppression of appetitively motivated behavior. Although the differences between the ages at which conditioned suppression of behavior and conditioned heart rate responses appeared during development were substantial, procedural differences may have influenced the outcome, such as the use of food deprivation in one study but not in the other, differences in CS duration for training, and different routes of shock administration (subcutaneous versus footshock). In addition, it is also possible that conditioned heart rate would appear earlier in development with the use of the acoustic startle US than with electric shock. In a recent study by Hunt, Richardson, Hess, and Campbell (1997), it was shown that conditioned bradycardia to an olfactory CS using an acoustic startle US could be established in rats as young as 12 days of age (cf. 15 days with electric shock; Sananes, Gaddy, & Campbell, 1988).

The purpose of the following experiment was to compare the development of conditioned changes in heart rate (HR) with the development of conditioned freezing discussed previously. The results described in this section are taken from a recently published study: Richardson, Wang, and Campbell (1995) recorded heart rate during a training session in which a 10-second auditory CS (the same as that used in the previous experiments) was paired with the acoustic startle US. Heart rate was recorded for a brief period prior to CS presentation to establish a baseline and during the CS on each trial. The training procedures used were the same as in our prior behavioral experiment. We present some of the extensive data obtained in Figure 2 (top), which shows the change from baseline heart rate during the CS, averaged over blocks of two trials for selected age groups. It is readily apparent that a consistent conditioned change in heart rate to the auditory stimulus did not occur until the subjects were approximately 21 days of age. At 19 days there was a partial decrease in heart rate during the middle portion of the CS that did not persist, and at 17 days of age there was no evidence of a conditioned cardiac response to the auditory CS. This is in sharp contrast to conditioned freezing, which was shown to be fully established much earlier in development (16 days; see Figure 1). The delayed development of conditioned cardiac responses with respect to behavioral responses replicated the previously cited work using shock as the US (Campbell & Ampuero, 1985b).

The same developmental pattern occurred when the CS was a visual stimulus. In an unpublished study, Hunt, Hess, and Campbell (in preparation) repeated the Richardson et al. (1995) experiment using exactly the same procedures except that the visual CS described in Experiment 1 was

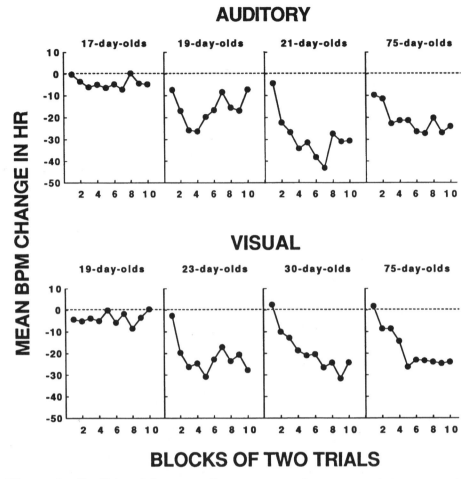

Figure 2. Conditioned fear to auditory (top panels) and visual (lower panels) stimuli as measured by mean beat-per-minute (BPM) changes in heart rate (HR) in subjects ranging in age from 17 to 75 days. The filled circles represent the cardiac change from baseline for subjects given 20 pairings of the CS with an acoustic startle US, averaged over blocks of two training trials.

substituted for the auditory CS. The results of this experiment are presented in the bottom panels of Figure 2. Here it is evident that the visual CS that produced conditioned suppression in 19-day-old rats did not produce a conditioned change in heart rate at that age. The youngest animals to show a consistent conditioned heart rate response in this experiment were the 23-day-old subjects.

The finding that pairing visual and auditory stimuli with an acoustic startle stimulus produces conditioned bradycardia conflicts with results of many other studies showing that another US, electric shock, often produces conditioned tachycardia in freely moving adult rats (Martin & Fitzgerald, 1980; Supple & Leaton, 1990). Shock, however, does not always produce conditioned tachycardia in freely moving animals (Campbell &

Ampuero, 1985b; Hunt, Hess, & Campbell, 1997; Teyler, 1971), and it nearly always produces conditioned bradycardia in restrained animals (Martin & Fitzgerald, 1980; Powell & Kazis, 1976). Our view is that brady-cardia and tachycardia can be equally indicative of intense fear states. In many feral animals, the approach of a predator can produce either a large increase *or* a large decrease in heart rate depending on the environmental circumstances. Smith and Woodruff (1980), for example, reported that the approach of a predator (human or dog) produced a pronounced increase in heart rate in woodchucks if the animal was in the open but an even greater decrease if it was in its burrow.

Many other dramatic examples of "fear bradycardia," the term used by behavioral ecologists to describe predator-elicited decreases in heart rate, have been reported. The approach of a predator produced heart rate decreases of approximately 90 percent in alligators (Smith, Allison, & Crowder, 1974), 60 percent in nesting ptarmigan hens (Gabrielsen, Blix, & Ursin, 1985), and 65 percent in concealed deer fawns (Jacobsen, 1979). In general, decreases in heart rate occur when concealment is used as the predator-avoidance strategy, and increases occur when flight or aggressive attack is the species- or situation-specific behavior. In the laboratory, stim-uli signaling imminent injury (pain) can elicit either conditioned brady-cardia or tachycardia depending on environmental circumstances (e.g., re-straint vs. freely moving) and possibly the nature of the injury-inducing stimulus. From this perspective, it is not at all surprising that the intense acoustic stimulus used in the present research produced conditioned bradycardia, because the unconditioned response to the startle stimulus is freezing and a substantial decrease in heart rate (Hunt, Richardson, et al., 1997).

Ontogenesis of Fear-Potentiated Startle to Auditory and Visual Stimuli

Two disparate lines of research make the study of the ontogeny of fear-potentiated startle particularly interesting. First, it has been shown that fear-potentiation of the acoustic startle response is related to conditioned behavioral suppression. Leaton and his colleagues (Borszcz, Cranney, & Leaton, 1989; Leaton & Borszcz, 1985; Leaton & Cranney, 1990) found that the whole-body startle reflex was significantly enhanced when sub-jects were immobile prior to response elicitation, relative to when they were active. We showed earlier in this chapter that when presented with a CS previously paired with an aversive stimulus, the typical response of laboratory rats is to freeze (see also Blanchard & Blanchard, 1969; Bolles & Fanselow, 1980; Fanselow, 1980). When the startle stimulus is pre-sented during this period of profound inactivity, the startle response itself is enhanced. These findings suggest that fear-potentiated startle should emerge concurrently with conditioned freezing.

In contrast, there is a substantial amount of research showing that motor reflex facilitation is accompanied by cardiac deceleration (e.g., Bohlin & Graham, 1977; Lang et al., 1990). The magnitude of the reflexive eyeblink responses to intense noise stimuli is increased in the presence of heart rate decreases (see also Whalen & Kapp, 1991). This suggests that fear-potentiated startle might emerge at the same time during development as conditioned changes in heart rate, assuming that the relation between cardiac deceleration and reflex potentiation is causal.

The purpose of the following two experiments was to determine when conditioned fear, as measured by fear-potentiated startle, appeared during the course of development relative to the two other measures: conditioned behavioral suppression and conditioned changes in heart rate. In the first experiment (Hunt et al., 1994), subjects ranged in age from 18 days (preweanlings) to 75 days (young adults). Training was exactly as in our previous studies. Subjects were given 20 pairings (or unpaired presentations) of the auditory CS with the startle stimulus US. Six randomly ordered test trials immediately followed the acquisition session, and the peak magnitude of the elicited whole-body startle reflex was recorded. On three of these trials, the startle stimulus was presented by itself to obtain a baseline measure of startle response magnitude. On the other three trials, the startle stimulus was preceded by the 10-second CS. Fear is inferred if the magnitude of the startle response is greater when the startle stimulus is preceded by the CS than when it is presented alone (e.g., Davis, 1992; Davis et al., 1993).

The data from the test trials are presented in Figure 3 (top). The magnitude of the whole-body startle reflex was enhanced when the startle stimulus was preceded by the auditory CS for animals 23 days of age and older, but not for 18-day-olds. Noteworthy is the failure to see potentiated startle in the 18-day-olds, even though animals at this age and even younger clearly display conditioned freezing to this auditory CS (Figure 1). Because of the ages of the rats studied, it is less clear whether the development of conditioned heart rate preceded or coemerged with fear-potentiated startle. Unfortunately, 21-day-olds, the youngest animals to show unambiguous conditioned changes in heart rate to an auditory CS, were not included in this experiment. The fact that 19-day-olds show a partial conditioned cardiac response to the auditory CS (see Figure 2) suggests that conditioned heart rate emerges earlier in development than fear-potentiated startle. The following experiment offers indirect support for this possibility in that it shows a substantial lag between the development of conditioned heart rate responses to a visual CS and fear-potentiated startle to the same CS.

The purpose of the final experiment to be described in this chapter was to determine when the visual CS could first support fear-potentiated startle during development. All of the experimental procedures were the same as those used previously except that the visual stimulus instead of the auditory stimulus was used as the CS. The data obtained from the test trials are shown in the bottom panels of Figure 3. The light CS potentiated the startle response in 30-day-old but not in 23-day-old subjects. This is much later in development than either conditioned behavioral sup-

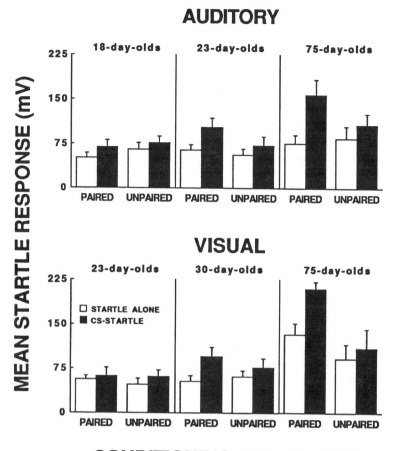

AUDITORY

VISUAL

CONDITIONING TREATMENT

Figure 3. Conditioned fear to auditory (top panels) and visual (lower panels) stimuli as measured by the fear-potentiated startle response technique in subjects ranging in age from 18 to 75 days. Paired subjects were given 20 pairings of an auditory CS (top panels) or visual CS (bottom panels) with the acoustic startle US, whereas unpaired subjects received the CS and US in an explicitly unpaired manner. The open bars represent the mean (+/−*SEM*) magnitude of the startle response (measured in millivolts, mV) when the startle stimulus was presented in isolation for some of the test trials, and the black bars represent the magnitude of the startle response when the startle stimulus was preceded by the 10-second CS on other test trials. From "Delayed Development of Fear-Potentiated Startle in Rats," by P. S. Hunt, R. Richardson, and B. A. Campbell, 1994, *Behavioral Neuroscience, 108,* pp. 71, 74, 77. Adapted with permission. Copyright 1994 by the American Psychological Association.

pression or even cardiac responses to the visual CS were observed. Further research confirmed this late emergence of fear-potentiated startle; even 28-day-old subjects failed to show potentiated startle to the visual CS. It is clear, particularly with the visual CS, that fear-potentiated startle does not emerge concurrently with either behavioral suppression or cardiac conditioned responses, the possibilities suggested in the introduction to this section.

Summary of Empirical Findings

The overall pattern of results from the preceding studies is summarized in Figure 4. This figure shows the approximate ages at which conditioned freezing, conditioned bradycardia, and fear-potentiated startle to auditory and visual stimuli paired with an acoustic startle stimulus first appeared during development. The ages shown were estimated from the previously described experiments. It is clearly evident from the figure that fear conditioning to auditory stimuli (open bars) occurs earlier in development than conditioning to visual stimuli (black bars). This developmental pattern of auditory function appearing before visual function has been documented repeatedly by many investigators using a variety of measures including learning, behavioral and cardiac orienting, and electrophysiological recordings (e.g., Aslin, Alberts, & Petersen, 1981; Campbell & Ampuero, 1985b; Gottlieb, 1971; Moye & Rudy, 1985, 1987).

More important, as emphasized repeatedly in the foregoing text, is the finding that the three manifestations of fear investigated in this research did not emerge at the same developmental age. Instead, there was a systematic pattern of development in which freezing to a conditioned fear-eliciting stimulus preceded the emergence of conditioned changes in heart rate to the same stimulus, which in turn preceded the appearance of fear-potentiated startle. The potential significance of these findings is discussed in the following sections.

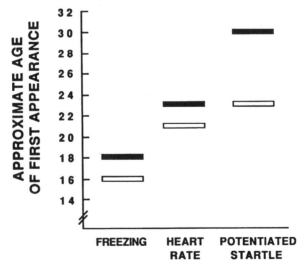

Figure 4. Summary graphic representing the approximate age at which conditioned freezing, conditioned bradycardia, and fear-potentiated startle to auditory (open bars) and visual (black bars) CSs paired with an acoustic startle stimulus first emerge during development.

This general pattern of sequential emergence of the different components of conditioned fear is further confirmed by similar findings in two other species. Both young rabbits (Sebastiani, Salamone, Silvestri, Simoni, & Ghelarducci, 1994) and pygmy goats (Fitzgerald, Francisco, Metcalfe, & Lawson, 1984), for example, showed conditioned behavioral responses (ear twitching and respiratory–motor activity, respectively) before they exhibited conditioned changes in heart rate to the same stimuli. The pygmy goat, for example, showed conditioned electromyographic (EMG) activity at 1 day of age, whereas conditioned changes in heart rate did not occur until the animals were 2 weeks of age. In both cases, the CS elicited an increase in skeletal–motor activity, rather than freezing, accompanied by a conditioned decrease in heart rate in one (Sebastiani et al., 1994) and a conditioned increase in the other (Fitzgerald et al., 1984). These results, coupled with our findings, suggest that conditioned changes in activity in general can be acquired earlier in development than conditioned changes in autonomic responding. This view is further supported by the finding that conditioned behavioral responses to olfactory stimuli can be established considerably earlier in development than autonomic responses (Kucharski & Spear, 1984; Sananes et al., 1988).

The finding that fear-potentiated startle emerges much later in development than behavioral immobility poses a serious challenge to the proposition that the behavioral response of freezing is the mechanism through which the CS comes to potentiate the acoustic startle response (Borszcz et al., 1989; Leaton & Borszcz, 1985; Leaton & Cranney, 1990). Although these two components of conditioned fear may co-occur in the adult rat, the results of the present experiments suggest that there is no causal relationship between freezing and fear-potentiated startle, because in the developing rat, the fear-induced behavioral response of freezing does not unequivocally lead to the potentiation of the acoustic startle response. It appears that the relationship between freezing and fear-potentiated startle is through the common central emotional state and not through peripherally mediated response summation.

Similarly, the developmental dissociation between the emergence of conditioned freezing and conditioned bradycardia shown in Figure 4 suggests that there is not a causal relationship between the decreased metabolic demands associated with behavioral immobility and the observed decrease in heart rate. Numerous investigators have noted that conditioned fear bradycardia typically occurs in animals that use behavioral immobility (freezing) to avoid detection by predators (e.g., Hollis, 1982), and some have assumed a causal relationship between behavioral immobility and bradycardia. Obrist, using data from both animal and human subjects (e.g., Obrist, 1968; Obrist, Webb, Sutterer, & Howard, 1970), was the first to advocate strongly that cardiac changes are intimately coupled to changes in somatomotor activity. Since that time, the role of cardiosomatic coupling in orienting and defense reactions has been the subject of considerable research (e.g., Black & de Toledo, 1972; Powell et al., 1971; Saiers, Richardson, & Campbell, 1989), with little evidence accruing to support a strong causal relationship between the two. In the present research, it is strikingly evident that CSs paired with an aversive US can produce decreases in behavioral activity that are not accompanied by decreases in heart rate. Again, cardiac decelerations and behavioral suppression often are observed concurrently, but their relation cannot be inferred as causal.

Maturation of the Neural Mechanisms Underlying the Development of Conditioned Fear: A Tentative Model

During the past decade, there has been an enormous increase in the understanding of the neural mechanisms mediating the acquisition and expression of conditioned fear (Davis, 1992; Davis et al., 1993; Fanselow, 1991, 1994; Kapp, Markgraf, et al., 1992; Kapp, Whalen, et al., 1992; LeDoux, 1992, 1993), but there has been little or no effort to study the maturation of those mechanisms and their relation to the development of conditioned fear. The intent of the following discussion is to (a) summarize what is currently known about the central structures and pathways associated with the acquisition of conditioned fear in the adult mammal and (b) propose a maturational model that might account for the sequential emergence of the components of conditioned fear described in the foregoing sections.

It is a given in developmental neurobiology that central pathways must undergo a sufficient level of development before they can support any change in behavior, including those involved in learning. In the rat, the hippocampus and cerebellum have been studied more intensely than other structures because they are both known to undergo considerable postnatal development (Altman, 1982; Altman & Bayer, 1975) and are required for various forms of learned behavior (Freeman, Barone, & Stanton, 1995; Rudy, 1991; Rudy & Morledge, 1994; Stanton, Freeman, & Skelton, 1992). In contrast, relatively little is known about the development of the amygdala, the structure that is central to most contemporary models of fear conditioning.

There is widespread agreement in the scientific community that the amygdala is a critical structure for both acquisition and expression of conditioned fear (see Aggleton, 1992, for review). Figure 5 presents a schematic summary of the major amygdalar inputs and outputs relevant to the forthcoming discussion. The convergence of CS and US information is hypothesized to occur in the lateral and basolateral nuclei of the amygdala (Davis, 1992; Davis et al., 1993; LeDoux, 1992, 1993), and it is presumably the site of associative links between the CS and US. The resulting associative information is then projected to the central nucleus of the amygdala (ACe), the major output center of the amygdalar complex. The ACe projects to a variety of brain stem and midbrain structures, each of which has been implicated in the generation of a specific fear response. Following is a summary description of the neural pathways mediating the three measures of conditioned fear discussed in this chapter. Extensive research using a broad range of experimental techniques has documented the follow-

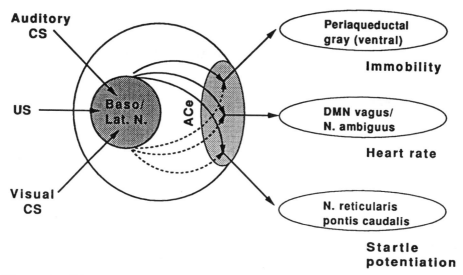

Figure 5. Hypothesized circuit for the neural basis of fear acquisition and expression (see text for details). CS = conditioned stimulus; US = unconditioned stimulus; Baso/Lat N. = basolateral and lateral nuclei of the amygdala; ACe = central nucleus of the amygdala; DMN vagus = dorsal motor nucleus of the vagus; N. ambiguus = nucleus ambiguus.

ing: (a) Conditioned freezing is mediated by a projection from the ACe to the ventral periaqueductal gray (Fanselow, 1991, 1994); (b) conditioned fear-induced autonomic responses (e.g., heart rate and blood pressure) involve projections from the ACe to the lateral hypothalamus (Francis, Hernandez, & Powell, 1981; LeDoux, 1992, 1993) and to the parasympathetic premotor neurons located in the dorsal motor nucleus of the vagus, nucleus ambiguus, or both (Kapp, Whalen, et al., 1992; McCabe et al., 1992; Schneiderman, 1987); and (c) potentiation of the startle response by fear stimuli is modulated at the level of the nucleus reticularis pontis caudalis (RPC; Davis, 1992; Davis et al., 1993) by a projection from the ACe.

This popular model has received wide conceptual support and empirical validation. However, as it stands, there is no place to incorporate the sensory-specific development of the three response systems we have described. As an example, take the conditioned response capabilities of the 23-day-old rat (see Figure 4). In this animal, visual stimuli that have been paired with a startle US produce conditioned freezing and conditioned bradycardia but do not produce a fear-potentiated startle response. This fact might lead to the conclusion that the pathways from the retina to the ACe are mature and suggests that the projections from the ACe to the RPC that mediate fear-potentiated startle are still incomplete. The latter inference is probably incorrect, however, because 23-day-old rats show fear-potentiated startle when the CS is an auditory stimulus. As shown in Figure 3, the auditory CS produces fear-potentiated startle at 23 days of age, whereas the visual CS does not. This finding suggests that the ACe → RPC projection is functional on Day 23 and that some other late-developing pathway must be responsible for the delayed emergence of fear-potentiated startle to the visual stimulus.

Similarly, an auditory CS previously paired with the startle stimulus US produces conditioned freezing but does not produce a conditioned decrease in heart rate at 16 days of age. As in the preceding case, one possible explanation of this developmental lag is that the pathways from the ACe to the vagal nuclei mediating conditioned bradycardia are not functional at this age. This appears not to be the case, however, because olfactory stimuli paired with the same US can produce parasympathetically mediated conditioned bradycardia in animals that are as young as 12 days (Hunt, Richardson, et al., 1997). Once again, the pathway or pathways between the ACe and the vagal effector nuclei appear functional in one context (olfactory conditioning) but not in another (auditory or visual conditioning). Following is a tentative model of the neural changes that might underlie the sequential emergence of conditioned freezing, conditioned changes in heart rate, and fear-potentiated startle during development.

From the summary schematic portrayed in Figure 5, it seems reasonable to assume that neither sensory afferents nor amygdalar efferents are likely to underlie the sequential emergence of the qualitatively different expressions of the conditioned fear response described in this review. Our assumption is that once the amygdalar afferent and efferent pathways are mature enough to carry one message to their target sites, it is likely that they can carry all messages to those sites. For example, if an olfactory CS can produce a conditioned change in heart rate through amygdalar efferents to the vagal nuclei, it seems reasonable to assume that those efferents should also be capable of transmitting conditioned changes in heart rate associated with auditory and visual stimuli.

If this is the case, the most likely locus of change underlying the sequential emergence of the various components of conditioned fear probably lies within the amygdala. Recent investigations have shown that there are extensive intra-amygdalar projections from the lateral and basolateral nuclei to the ACe (Krettek & Price, 1978; Pitkanen et al., 1995), and we hypothesize that they convey sensory-specific information (see Figure 5). The solid arrows represent associative information about the auditory CS being transmitted from the lateral–basolateral nuclei to specific areas of the central nucleus segregated according to efferent projection, whereas the dashed lines with arrows show corresponding projections relaying associative information about the visual CS. These intra-amygdalar connections, or their originating or target loci, could develop sequentially during ontogeny and be the basis for the observed sequential development of conditioned freezing, cardiac change, and fear-potentiated startle.

In summary, it seems apparent from the preceding analysis that (a) the three behavioral manifestations of fear described in this chapter emerge sequentially rather than simultaneously during development; (b) this sequential pattern of development is not the result of differential maturation of sensory inputs to the amygdala; and (c) sensory-specific connections, most likely within the amygdala, mature sequentially during development.

Conclusion

The study of the ontogenesis of learning capabilities can make an important contribution to knowledge of the neurobiological basis of acquired behavior and its maturation (e.g., Freeman et al., 1995; Rudy, 1991; Rudy & Morledge, 1994; Stanton et al., 1992). This knowledge has grown considerably over the past several decades owing to the work of many notable researchers. Researchers now take for granted knowledge of the sequential emergence of sensory system function (Aslin et al., 1981; Gottlieb, 1971); the development of sensory-specific information processing, learning, and memory capabilities (Moye & Rudy, 1985, 1987; Rudy, Vogt, & Hyson, 1984); and equally important to our own research, the concepts of species- and age-specific unconditioned defensive responses (Bolles, 1970; Collier & Bolles, 1980; Weihmuller & Collier, 1990) and their not infrequent interference with the acquisition of new response sequences.

The response system problem is certainly not new, but at the same time it has not been studied empirically to any great extent. Collier and Bolles (1980; Weihmuller & Collier, 1990) opened researchers' eyes almost 2 decades ago to the significance of response availability to the young animal's ability to solve and perform certain tasks. Bolles (1970) recognized that species-typical innate defensive reactions can affect the ability of a response to be instrumentally reinforced in avoidance learning situations; Collier and Bolles reasoned analogously that learning in the young animal may be affected similarly by whether or not a given response is available at the time learning is to occur. By paying careful attention to the behavioral abilities of the young animal, developmental psychobiologists have found tasks that specifically rely on age-appropriate response requirements. Still, one could never have foreseen that responses that do not involve complex motor patterns, such as changes in heart rate and fear-potentiated startle, would similarly show such a developmental pattern of emergence, not to mention their interaction with sensory competence. We hope that our description of the sequential emergence of these three defensive response systems during ontogeny will make developmental psychobiologists even more aware of the importance of the choice of response in the assessment of developmental changes in learning and memory. To this end we are indebted to Robert Bolles and his students, whose work continues to influence ours.

Byron Campbell's Recollections

Bolles's influence on my research and career began in 1956, when he and I were both appointed instructors in the Department of Psychology at Princeton University. For two young investigators concerned with animal learning, our views could not have been more different. Bolles came from the Tolmanian camp on the West Coast, and I came from the East Coast Hull–Miller bastion at Yale, albeit with a dissident as a mentor, Fred Sheffield. Our 2 years together were marked by lively discussion and some convergence of interests. After only a year or so, Bob found the conservative, formal traditions that then characterized Princeton too much to cope with and moved, with a brief stop at the University of Pennsylvania, to Hollins College, where Frank McGuigan had collected a spirited and enthusiastic group of young experimental psychologists. After 7 years at Hollins College, the University of Washington enticed him to return to the West Coast, where his research and career burgeoned with the help of many outstanding students, including the editors of this volume, Michael Fanselow and Mark Bouton. In the years after he moved to Washington, our interests converged a number of times. Collier and Bolles (1980) found, as we have, that the number of behavioral expressions of conditioned fear increase systematically with age. Another notable convergence is our heavy reliance on Michael Fanselow's behavioral findings and neural models in guiding and interpreting our research. For these and many other reasons, Pamela Hunt and I are both delighted to be a part of this tribute to Robert Bolles.

References

Aggleton, J. P. (1992). *The amygdala: Neurobiological aspects of emotion, memory, and mental dysfunction*. New York: Wiley-Liss.

Altman, J. (1982). Morphological development of the rat cerebellum and some of its mechanisms. In S. L. Palay & V. Chan-Palay (Eds.), *The cerebellum: New vistas* (pp. 8–49). Berlin: Springer-Verlag.

Altman, J., & Bayer, S. (1975). Postnatal development of the hippocampal dentate gyrus under normal and experimental conditions. In R. L. Isaacson & K. H. Pribram (Eds.), *The hippocampus: Structure and development* (Vol. 1, pp. 95–122). New York: Plenum Press.

Archer, J. (1979). Behavioural aspects of fear. In W. Sluckin (Ed.), *Fear in animals and man* (pp. 56–85). New York: Van Nostrand Reinhold.

Aslin, R. N., Alberts, J. R., & Petersen, M. R. (Eds.). (1981). *Development of perception: Psychobiological perspectives* (Vols. 1 and 2). New York: Academic Press.

Black, A. H., & de Toledo, L. (1972). The relationship among classically conditioned responses: Heart rate and skeletal behavior. In A. H. Black & W.F. Prokasy (Eds.), *Classical conditioning II: Current theory and research* (pp. 290–311). New York: Appleton-Century-Crofts.

Blanchard, D. C., & Blanchard, R. J. (1969). Crouching as an index of fear. *Journal of Comparative and Physiological Psychology, 67,* 370–375.

Blanchard, R. J., Yudko, E. B., Rodgers, R. J., & Blanchard, D. C. (1993). Defense system pharmacology: An ethological approach to the pharmacology of fear and anxiety. *Behavioural Brain Research, 58,* 155–165.

Bohlin, G., & Graham, F. K. (1977). Cardiac deceleration and reflex blink facilitation. *Psychophysiology, 14,* 423–430.

Bolles, R. C. (1970). Species-specific defense reactions and avoidance learning. *Psychological Review, 77,* 32–48.

Bolles, R. C. (1985). The slaying of Goliath: What happened to reinforcement theory? In T. D. Johnston & A. T. Pietrewicz (Eds.), *Issues in the ecological study of learning* (pp. 387–399). Hillsdale, NJ: Erlbaum.

Bolles, R. C., & Fanselow, M. S. (1980). A perceptual-defensive-recuperative model of fear and pain. *Behavioral and Brain Sciences, 3,* 291–323.

Bolles, R. C., & Woods, P. J. (1964). The ontogeny of behaviour in the albino rat. *Animal Behaviour, 12,* 427–441.

Borszcz, G. S., Cranney, J., & Leaton, R. N. (1989). Influence of long-term sensitization on long-term habituation of the acoustic startle response in rats: Central gray lesions, preexposure, and extinction. *Journal of Experimental Psychology: Animal Behavior Processes, 15,* 54–64.

Bouton, M. E., & Bolles, R. C. (1980). Conditioned fear as assessed by freezing and by the suppression of three different baselines. *Animal Learning and Behavior, 8,* 429–434.

Brown, J. S., Kalish, H. I., & Farber, I. E. (1951). Conditioned fear as revealed by magnitude of startle response to an auditory stimulus. *Journal of Experimental Psychology, 41,* 317–328.

Campbell, B. A., & Ampuero, M. X. (1985a). Conditioned orienting and defensive responses in the developing rat. *Infant Behavior and Development, 8,* 425–434.

Campbell, B. A., & Ampuero, M. X. (1985b). Dissociation of autonomic and behavioral components of conditioned fear during development in the rat. *Behavioral Neuroscience, 99,* 1089–1102.

Campbell, B. A., & Campbell, E. H. (1962). Retention and extinction of learned fear in infant and adult rats. *Journal of Comparative and Physiological Psychology, 55,* 1–8.

Campbell, B. A., Misanin, J. R., White, B. C., & Lytle, L. D. (1974). Species differences in ontogeny of memory: Indirect support for neural maturation as a determinant of forgetting. *Journal of Comparative and Physiological Psychology, 87,* 193–202.

Collier, A. C., & Bolles, R. C. (1980). The ontogenesis of defensive reactions to shock in preweanling rats. *Developmental Psychobiology, 13,* 141–150.

Davis, M. (1986). Pharmacological and anatomical analysis of fear conditioning using the fear-potentiated startle paradigm. *Behavioral Neuroscience, 100,* 814–824.

Davis, M. (1989). Sensitization of the acoustic startle reflex by footshock. *Behavioral Neuroscience, 103,* 495–503.

Davis, M. (1992). The role of the amygdala in conditioned fear. In J. P. Aggleton (Ed.), *The amygdala: Neurobiological aspects of emotion, memory, and mental dysfunction* (pp. 255–305). New York: Wiley-Liss.

Davis, M., & Astrachan, D. I. (1978). Conditioned fear and startle magnitude: Effects of different footshock or backshock intensities used in training. *Journal of Experimental Psychology: Animal Behavior Processes, 4,* 95–103.

Davis, M., Falls, W. A., Campeau, S., & Kim, M. (1993). Fear-potentiated startle: A neural and pharmacological analysis. *Behavioral Brain Research, 58,* 175–198.

Dickinson, A., & Dearing, M. F. (1979). Appetitive-aversive interactions and inhibitory processes. In A. Dickinson & R. A. Boakes (Eds.), *Mechanisms of learning and motivation: A memorial volume to Jerzy Konorski* (pp. 203–231). Hillsdale, NJ: Erlbaum.

Fanselow, M. S. (1980). Conditional and unconditional components of post-shock freezing. *Pavlovian Journal of Biological Sciences, 15,* 177–182.

Fanselow, M. S. (1984). Opiate modulation of the active and inactive components of the postshock reaction: Parallels between naloxone pretreatment and shock intensity. *Behavioral Neuroscience, 98,* 269–277.

Fanselow, M. S. (1991). The midbrain periaqueductal gray as a coordinator of action in response to fear and anxiety. In A. Depaulis & R. Bandler (Eds.), *The midbrain periaqueductal gray matter: Functional, anatomical, and neurochemical organization* (pp. 151–173). New York: Plenum Press.

Fanselow, M. S. (1994). Neural organization of the defensive behavior system responsible for fear. *Psychonomic Bulletin and Review, 1,* 429–438.

Fanselow, M. S., & Bolles, R. C. (1979). Triggering of the endorphin analgesic reaction by a cue previously associated with shock: Reversal by naloxone. *Bulletin of the Psychonomic Society, 14,* 88–90.

Fanselow, M. S., & Helmstetter, F. J. (1988). Conditional analgesia, defensive freezing, and benzodiazepines. *Behavioral Neuroscience, 102,* 233–243.

Fanselow, M. S., Helmstetter, F. J., & Calcagnetti, D. J. (1991). Parallels between the behavioral effects of dimethoxy-beta-carboline (DMCM) and conditioned fear stimuli. In L. Dachowski & C. F. Flaherty (Eds.), *Current topics in animal learning: Brain, emotion, and cognition* (pp. 187–206). Hillsdale, NJ: Erlbaum.

Fitzgerald, R. D., Francisco, D. L., Metcalfe, J., & Lawson, M. S. (1984). Classically conditioned heart rate and respiratory-motor activity in newborn and neonatal pygmy goats. *Animal Learning and Behavior, 12,* 217–222.

Fitzgerald, R. D., Martin, G. K., & O'Brien, J. H. (1973). Influence of vagal activity on classically conditioned heart rate in rats. *Journal of Comparative and Physiological Psychology, 83,* 485–491.

Francis, J., Hernandez, L. L., & Powell, D. A. (1981). Lateral hypothalamic lesions: Effects on Pavlovian cardiac and eyeblink conditioning in the rabbit. *Brain Research Bulletin, 6,* 155–163.

Freeman, J. H., Barone, S., Jr., & Stanton, M. E. (1995). Disruption of cerebellar maturation by an antimitotic agent impairs the ontogeny of eyeblink conditioning in rats. *Journal of Neuroscience, 15,* 7301–7314.

Gabrielsen, G. W., Blix, A. S., & Ursin, H. (1985). Orienting and freezing responses in incubating ptarmigan hens. *Physiology and Behavior, 34,* 925–934.

Gottlieb, G. (1971). Ontogenesis of sensory function in birds and mammals. In E. Tobach, L. R. Aronson, & E. Shaw (Eds.), *The biopsychology of development* (pp. 211–247). New York: Academic Press.

Hamm, A. O., Greenwald, M. K., Bradley, M. M., Cuthbert, B. N., & Lang, P. J. (1991). The fear-potentiated startle effect: Blink reflex modulation as a result of classical aversive conditioning. *Integrative Physiological and Behavioral Sciences, 26,* 119–126.

Harris, J. A., & Westbrook, R. F. (1995). Effects of benzodiazepine microinjection into the amygdala or periaqueductal gray on the expression of conditioned fear and hypoalgesia in rats. *Behavioral Neuroscience, 109,* 295–304.

Hollis, K. L. (1982). Pavlovian conditioning of signal-centered action patterns and autonomic behavior: A biological analysis of function. In J. S. Rosenblatt, R. A. Hinde, C. Beer, & M.-C. Busnel (Eds.), *Advances in the study of behavior* (Vol. 12, pp. 1–64). New York: Academic Press.

Hunt, P. S., Hess, M. F., & Campbell, B. A. (1997). Conditioned cardiac and behavioral response topography to an olfactory CS dissociates with age. *Animal Learning and Behavior, 25,* 53–61.

Hunt, P. S., Richardson, R., & Campbell, B. A. (1994). Delayed development of fear-potentiated startle in rats. *Behavioral Neuroscience, 108,* 69–80.

Hunt, P. S., Richardson, R., Hess, M. F., & Campbell, B. A. (1997). Emergence of conditioned cardiac responses to an olfactory CS paired with an acoustic startle US during development: Form and autonomic origins. *Developmental Psychobiology, 30,* 151–163.

Jacobsen, N. K. (1979). Alarm bradycardia in white-tailed deer fawns (*Odocoileus virginianus*). *Journal of Mammalogy, 60,* 343–349.

Kapp, B. S., Markgraf, C. G., Wilson, A., Pascoe, J. P., & Supple, W. F. (1992). Contribution of the amygdala and anatomically-related structures to the acquisition and expression of aversively conditioned responses. In L. Dachowski & C. F. Flaherty (Eds.), *Current topics in animal learning: Brain, emotion, and cognition* (pp. 311–346). Hillsdale, NJ: Erlbaum.

Kapp, B. S., Whalen, P. J., Supple, W. F., & Pascoe, J. P. (1992). Amygdaloid contributions to conditioned arousal and sensory information processing. In J. P. Aggleton (Ed.), *The amygdala: Neurobiological aspects of emotion, memory, and mental dysfunction* (pp. 229–254). New York: Wiley-Liss.

Konorski, J. (1967). *Integrative activity of the brain: An interdisciplinary approach.* Chicago: University of Chicago Press.

Krettek, J. E., & Price, J. L. (1978). A description of the amygdaloid complex in the rat and cat with observations on intra-amygdaloid axonal connections. *Journal of Comparative Neurology, 178,* 255–280.

Kucharski, D., & Spear, N. E. (1984). Conditioning of an aversion to an odor paired with peripheral shock in the developing rat. *Developmental Psychobiology, 17,* 465–479.

Lang, P. J., Bradley, M. M., & Cuthbert, B. N. (1990). Emotion, attention, and the startle reflex. *Psychological Review, 97,* 377–395.

Leaton, R. N., & Borszcz, G. S. (1985). Potentiated startle: Its relation to freezing and shock intensity in rats. *Journal of Experimental Psychology: Animal Behavior Processes, 11,* 421–428.

Leaton, R. N., & Cranney, J. (1990). Potentiation of the acoustic startle response by a conditioned stimulus paired with acoustic startle stimulus in rats. *Journal of Experimental Psychology: Animal Behavior Processes, 16,* 279–287.

LeDoux, J. E. (1992). Emotion and the amygdala. In J. P. Aggleton (Ed.), *The amygdala: Neurobiological aspects of emotion, memory, and mental dysfunction* (pp. 339–351). New York: Wiley-Liss.

LeDoux, J. E. (1993). Emotional memory systems in the brain. *Behavioural Brain Research, 58,* 69–79.

Lennartz, R. C., & Weinberger, N. M. (1992). Analysis of response systems in Pavlovian conditioning reveals rapidly versus slowly acquired conditioned responses: Support for two factors, implications for behavior and neurobiology. *Psychobiology, 20,* 93–119.

Martin, G. K., & Fitzgerald, R. D. (1980). Heart rate and somatomotor activity in rats during signalled escape and yoked classical conditioning. *Physiology and Behavior, 25,* 519–526.

McAllister, W. R., & McAllister, D. E. (1971). Behavioral measurement of conditioned fear. In F. R. Brush (Ed.), *Aversive conditioning and learning* (pp. 105–179). New York: Academic Press.

McCabe, P. M., Schneiderman, N., Jarrell, T. W., Gentile, C. G., Teich, A. H., Winters, R. W., & Liskowsky, D. R. (1992). Central pathways involved in classical differential conditioning of heart rate responses in rabbits. In I. Gormezano & E. A. Wasserman (Eds.), *Learning and memory: The behavioral and biological substrates* (pp. 321–346). Hillsdale, NJ: Erlbaum.

Millenson, J. R., & Hendry, D. P. (1967). Quantification of response suppression in conditioned anxiety training. *Canadian Journal of Psychology, 21,* 242–252.

Moye, T. B., & Rudy, J. W. (1985). Ontogenesis of learning: VI. Learned and unlearned responses to visual stimulation in the infant hooded rat. *Developmental Psychobiology, 18,* 395–409.

Moye, T. B., & Rudy, J. W. (1987). Ontogenesis of trace conditioning in young rats: Dissociation of associative and memory processes. *Developmental Psychobiology, 20,* 405–414.

Obrist, P. A. (1968). Heart rate and somatic-motor coupling during classical aversive conditioning in humans. *Journal of Experimental Psychology, 77,* 180–193.

Obrist, P. A., Webb, R. A., Sutterer, J. R., & Howard, J. L. (1970). The cardiac-somatic relationship: Some reformulations. *Psychophysiology, 6,* 569–587.

Pearce, J. M., & Hall, G. (1980). A model of Pavlovian learning: Variations in the effectiveness of conditioned but not of unconditioned stimuli. *Psychological Review, 87,* 532–552.

Pinel, J. P. J., & Treit, D. (1978). Burying as a defensive response in rats. *Journal of Comparative and Physiological Psychology, 92,* 708–712.

Pitkanen, A., Stefanacci, L., Farb, C. R., Go, G.-G., LeDoux, J. E., & Amaral, D. G. (1995). Intrinsic connections of the rat amygdaloid complex: Projections originating in the lateral nucleus. *Journal of Comparative Neurology, 356,* 288–310.

Powell, D. A. (1992). The prefrontal-thalamic axis and classical conditioning. *Integrative Physiological and Behavioral Sciences, 27,* 101–116.

Powell, D. A., & Kazis, E. (1976). Blood pressure and heart rate changes accompanying classical eyeblink conditioning in the rabbit (*Oryctolagus cuniculus*). *Psychophysiology, 13,* 441–447.

Powell, D. A., Schneiderman, N., Elster, A. J., & Jacobson, A. (1971). Differential classical conditioning in rabbits (*Oryctolagus cuniculus*) to tones and changes in illumination. *Journal of Comparative and Physiological Psychology, 76,* 267–274.

Rescorla, R. A., & Wagner, A. R. (1972). A theory of Pavlovian conditioning: Variations in the effectiveness of reinforcement and nonreinforcement. In A. H. Black & W. F. Prokasy (Eds.), *Classical conditioning: II. Current theory and research* (pp. 64–99). New York: Appleton-Century-Crofts.

Richardson, R., Wang, P., & Campbell, B. A. (1995). Delayed development of conditioned heart rate responses to auditory stimuli in the rat. *Developmental Psychobiology, 28,* 221–238.

Rudy, J. W. (1991). Elemental and configural associations, the hippocampus, and development. *Developmental Psychobiology, 24,* 221–236.

Rudy, J. W. (1993). Contextual conditioning and auditory cue conditioning dissociate during development. *Behavioral Neuroscience, 107,* 887–891.

Rudy, J. W., & Morledge, P. (1994). Ontogeny of contextual fear conditioning in rats: Implications for consolidation, infantile amnesia, and hippocampal system function. *Behavioral Neuroscience, 108,* 1–8.

Rudy, J. W., Vogt, M. B., & Hyson, R. L. (1984). A developmental analysis of the rat's learned reactions to gustatory and auditory stimulation. In R. Kail & N. E. Spear (Eds.), *Comparative perspectives on the development of memory* (pp. 181–208). Hillsdale, NJ: Erlbaum.

Saiers, J. A., Richardson, R., & Campbell, B. A. (1989). Pharmacological dissociation of heart rate and somatomotor components of the orienting response. *Psychobiology, 17,* 418–423.

Sananes, C. B., Gaddy, J. R., & Campbell, B. A. (1988). Ontogeny of conditioned heart rate to an olfactory stimulus. *Developmental Psychobiology, 21,* 117–133.

Schneiderman, N. (1987). Neurobiological bases of conditioned bradycardia in rabbits. In I. Gormezano, W. F. Prokasy, & R. F. Thompson (Eds.), *Classical conditioning* (3rd ed., pp. 37–63). Hillsdale, NJ: Erlbaum.

Sebastiani, L., Salamone, D., Silvestri, P., Simoni, A., & Ghelarducci, B. (1994). Development of fear-related heart rate responses in neonatal rabbits. *Journal of the Autonomic Nervous System, 50,* 231–238.

Smith, E. N., Allison, R. D., & Crowder, W. E. (1974). Bradycardia in a free ranging American alligator. *Copeia, 3,* 770–772.

Smith, E. N., & Woodruff, R. A. (1980). Fear bradycardia in free-ranging woodchucks, *Marmota monax. Journal of Mammalogy, 61,* 750–753.

Spear, N. E. (1979). Memory storage factors leading to infantile amnesia. In G. H. Bower (Ed.), *The psychology of learning and motivation* (Vol. 13, pp. 91–154). New York: Academic Press.

Stanton, M. E., Freeman, J. H., Jr., & Skelton, R. W. (1992). Eyeblink conditioning in the developing rat. *Behavioral Neuroscience, 106,* 657–665.

Supple, W. F., & Leaton, R. N. (1990). Lesions of the cerebellar vermis and cerebellar hemispheres: Effects on heart rate conditioning in rats. *Behavioral Neuroscience, 104,* 934–947.

Teyler, T. J. (1971). Effects of restraint on heart-rate conditioning in rats as a function of US location. *Journal of Comparative and Physiological Psychology, 77,* 31–37.

Wagner, A. R. (1981). SOP: A model of automatic memory processing in animal behavior. In N. E. Spear & R. R. Miller (Eds.), *Information processing in animals: Memory mechanisms* (pp. 5–47). Hillsdale, NJ: Erlbaum.

Wagner, A. R., & Brandon, S. E. (1989). Evolution of a structured connectionist model of Pavlovian conditioning (AESOP). In S. B. Klein & R. R. Mowrer (Eds.), *Contemporary learning theories: Pavlovian conditioning and the status of traditional learning theory* (pp. 149–189). Hillsdale, NJ: Erlbaum.

Weihmuller, F. B., & Collier, A. C. (1990). The role of age-dependent behaviors in the retention of an approach-avoidance response in preweanling rats. *Developmental Psychobiology, 23,* 265–283.

Weisz, D. J., & LoTurco, J. J. (1988). Reflex facilitation of the nictitating membrane response remains after cerebellar lesions. *Behavioral Neuroscience, 102,* 203–209.

Weisz, D. J., & McInerney, J. (1990). An associative process maintains reflex facilitation of the unconditioned nictitating membrane response during the early stages of training. *Behavioral Neuroscience, 104,* 21–27.

Whalen, P. J., & Kapp, B. S. (1991). Contributions of the amygdaloid central nucleus to the modulation of the nictitating membrane reflex in the rabbit. *Behavioral Neuroscience, 105,* 141–153.

4

How Typical and Atypical Contexts Influence Infant Behavior

Alexis C. Collier

Robert Bolles's influence in psychology has been pervasive and most notable in the field of learning and motivation. In his quest for parsimonious yet general principles of behavior, however, his thinking has also affected areas such as comparative, physiological, and developmental psychology, as well as writings about the history of psychology. The present chapter describes selected research in animal (rat) developmental psychobiology and illustrates how Bolles's views have influenced work on early learning and behavioral processes.

In addition to documenting the significance of his writings to the understanding of infant learning and behavior, I have organized the chapter with concepts that, in retrospect, can be credited to Bolles as well. As a graduate student under his tutelage, I was fortunate enough to have daily conversations with him. In one of those conversations, we were talking about what might at first appear to be a paradox: How does one study and understand general principles of behavior if behavior is so often constrained? One answer was that constraint itself can be a general principle and, procedurally, one needed to understand constraint by observing behavior in a variety of contexts (i.e., in different environments, using multiple tasks) and by observing many behaviors. Moreover, a clearer understanding of simple behavioral reactions under a variety of conditions could permit clearer distinctions among traditional learning and performance issues that might not necessarily be inferred from data collected in limited paradigms or tasks. In accordance with these ideas, two organizing concepts guided the research presented here.

The first organizing concept is that the physical and social context of an organism dramatically affects its psychological and physiological reactions (e.g., Levine, 1987). For an immature, altricial organism such as the rat pup, it may be obvious that manipulating primary motivators in

I thank Harvey G. Shulman for his reading of and helpful comments on this chapter and the many students and colleagues with whom I have collaborated on the research reported here.

the physical environment, such as pain, warmth, and nutrition, would affect responding, as it does in adults. The role of the social context might not be as obvious, however, other than the role of the dam as a provider of primary needs. Yet, as early as 1964, Bolles and Woods, in an observational study on the development of the albino rat, noted the following:

> The albino rat appears to be much more of a social animal, in the sense that it is subject to a great deal of social stimulation, than may be commonly realized. The social interactions among litter mates begins with competition during nursing, continues through the stage of social grooming, fighting, and playing, and includes the social facilitation (or imitation) in eating and jumping responses. These social influences no doubt have far-reaching effects upon the organism. The rat, then, offers interesting possibilities for research in this area. The apparently stunning effect of removing the mother is also an interesting social reaction which should receive further experimental investigation. (p. 440)

Indeed, mother–infant separation and pup isolation have become standard procedures for investigating maternal influences on the physiological and behavioral state of the infant (see Hofer, 1984, for a partial review) as well as an often used paradigm in infant learning to ensure approach motivation (e.g., Amsel, Letz, & Burdette, 1977). More recently, isolation effects have also been extended to the investigation of infant memory (Arnold & Spear, 1995).

The second conceptual framework guiding research in this chapter is that an understanding of an organism's typical reactions to the environment and events in it is important in assessing learning and memory. This idea is epitomized by Bolles's (1970) classic article on avoidance learning in which he argued that the rapidity of learning and extent to which an organism learns an avoidance response depends on its species-specific defense reaction (SSDR) to the controlling events of the avoidance problem. Ideas about species-specific reactions (SSRs) have been extended by others to incorporate age-specific reactions (ASRs) as well (e.g., Collier & Bolles, 1980; Smith & Bogomolny, 1983; Smith, Miller, Wigal, & Spear, 1989; Spear, 1984; Stehouwer & Campbell, 1980; Takahashi, 1992). By approaching the study of developmental processes with the recognition that very different reactions might be elicited to the same environmental event and modified accordingly in animals of different ages, one is posed to tap capabilities that might not otherwise be observed. If freezing were used to assess learning and memory ontogenetically, one might conclude that infants do not learn or remember. This could be erroneous, however, because very young rats do not freeze (Collier & Bolles, 1980). Thus assessing behaviors other than those commonly used as the adult standard might lead to different conclusions about early learning and memorial processes. Furthermore, to the extent that exposure to aversive events or stressors results in defensive patterns and activation of the hypothalamic-pituitary-adrenal (HPA) system in infants as in adults (e.g., Takahashi, Turner, & Kalin, 1991), ASRs may also be defensive (i.e., age-specific defense reactions, ASDRs) and further constrain infant behavior as in adults (Bolles,

1970). It may be expected, for example, that conditions in which infants are isolated from the mother or from cues associated with the nest would be aversive and that such contexts would represent another potential source for eliciting behavioral constraint on infant behavior (e.g., Spear, 1979, 1984).

With these concepts in mind, I review selective studies and report data from my laboratory that describe a variety of unlearned, elicited behaviors of infant rats in contexts defined as more (typical) or less (atypical) similar to their home environment. In this analysis, the dam, sensory stimuli associated with the dam, conspecific age-mates, and cues associated with the home nest, such as odor, constitute in varying degrees a more typical home environment. In many cases, a more typical context also is more familiar. The word *typical* is used as a more general term, however, to account for the frequently cited observation that few differences are found in rat pup reactions to surrogate mothers who are typical versus their own mothers who are more familiar (e.g., as in approach learning; Collier & Mast, 1979). Finally, I also review and report studies that take advantage of pups' unlearned responses in studying infant learning and memory. The goal of this chapter is not to provide a comprehensive review of the topic but to illustrate with representative studies that for infants, incorporating components of what would be a species-typical home environment influences both elicited and learned behavior in an age-dependent manner.

Age-Dependent Responding

Normative Developmental Findings

Normative rat developmental data were described as early as 1899 by Small. Bolles and Woods (1964) contributed to this knowledge base by using a noninvasive observational procedure and highlighting nest social behavior as well as sensory and motoric developmental changes in the rat. Altman and Sudarshan (1975) subsequently provided increased detail regarding locomotor and reflex changes during the preweaning period. Rat maternal behavior that characterizes changes in mother–infant interactions during development has also been described (e.g., Reisbick, Rosenblatt, & Mayer, 1975). These reports are consistent in describing newborn rats as immature in motor and sensory capabilities (blind, deaf, unable to walk, and without fur) and highly dependent on maternal care for survival, but also as organisms that develop rapidly into fully haired adultlike weanlings in about 3 weeks. Such a rapid developmental period offers the opportunity to study the rat through several adaptive periods and to track concomitant neural development with changes in broader behavioral processes such as learning and memory. The dramatic developmental changes also require the investigator to pay special attention to the particular needs of infants at different stages of development when attempting to assess learning and memory processes.

Most of the preceding studies were conducted to document typical pup responding with little emphasis on the context in which the investigations were done. With few exceptions (e.g., Bolles & Woods, 1964), however, the procedures used to gather information about infant rat developmental processes have resulted in some disruption within the infant's environment. Often pup behavior has been evaluated when the animal was completely separated from its mother and littermates. It is therefore likely that most studies on infant behavior incorporate to some extent an "atypical" and aversive context, which may need to be considered when inferences are drawn about developmental processes. At the extreme, failures of learning may need to be attributed to response constraints generated by an aversive context rather than lack of maturity. The recognition of this possibility encourages investigators to evaluate systematically the effects of atypical contexts on pup responding to improve understanding of normal developmental processes. An extreme variation of this strategy involves the study of pup developmental processes in planned maternal separation procedures or in isolation.

The Social Context and Elicited Responding

Maternal separation. Studies in which the separation or isolation procedure is used to learn about early developmental processes in the rat can illustrate the dramatic impact atypical contexts have on infant behavior at certain ages, even if the intention is not to evaluate context per se. Some of the varied effects of isolation in preweanling rats include increased general activity (e.g., Campbell, Lytle, & Fibiger, 1969; Randall & Campbell, 1976), increased ultrasonic vocalizations (e.g., Hofer, Shair, & Murowchick, 1989), increased motivation for play (Ikemoto & Panksepp, 1992), increased corticosterone but decreased growth hormone levels (e.g., Hennessy & Weinberg, 1990; Kuhn, Pauk, & Schanberg, 1990; Stanton & Levine, 1988; Takahashi et al., 1991), decreased heart rate and respiration (Hofer, 1987), decreased endogenous opioid peptides (Shoemaker & Kehoe, 1995), and decreased immune functioning (Kennedy & Collier, 1994). Isolation has been used as an effective unconditioned aversive stimulus for conditioning an odor aversion in preweanling rats (Smith, Kucharski, & Spear, 1985), and isolation during the retention interval before testing memory of an odor aversion has been shown to disrupt retention in preweanlings (Arnold & Spear, 1995).

Not all studies that have used the mother–infant separation procedure have also used the reunion procedure. Those that have, however, generally have shown reversal of the separation effects. For example, Stanton, Wallstrom, and Levine (1987) demonstrated that maternal contact inhibits pituitary–adrenal stress responses in preweanling rats. Richardson, Siegel, and Campbell (1988) demonstrated that the presence of the mother reduces the fear response, as measured by increases in heart rate, to an unfamiliar environment; they also demonstrated that the presence of the mother reduces typical reactions to shock (e.g., jumping and increased heart rate; Richardson, Siegel, & Campbell, 1989). Furthermore, the ameliorating effects of the dam are usually age-dependent, with the dam having greater impact in preweanlings. Although the mechanisms by which the separation procedure produces its varied effects are often unclear, these later studies nonetheless suggest that atypical contexts elicit a variety of stress-related defensive responses in young animals that the mother is particularly effective at reducing.

Stimuli associated with home. Besides the mother, the milieu of the infant rat includes other pups, the nest, and cues associated with the nest (e.g., odors), any of which might also be expected to influence infant behavior (e.g., Corby, Caza, & Spear, 1982; Rudy & Cheatle, 1979; Spear, 1979). If separation from the mother and nest creates a novel context that disrupts normal responding, as is the case in most experimental, controlled testing environments, then attempts to make the testing context more similar to the infants' home nest might allow for a more complete understanding of infant behavior. This idea has been supported most notably in the laboratories of Campbell (e.g., Randall & Campbell, 1976) and Spear (e.g., Smith & Spear, 1978). For example, the presence of home litter cues has been shown to enhance learning in aversive tasks, such as passive avoidance (Smith & Spear, 1978) and discrimination escape (Misanin & Hinderliter, 1989; Smith et al., 1989). Testing with conspecifics present can facilitate conditioned taste aversion (Smith & Spear, 1978, 1980) as well as decrease isolation-induced activity (Randall & Campbell, 1976) and vocalizations (Carden & Hofer, 1992). Other aspects of the home nest also influence infant behavior. Home litter cues can reduce isolation-induced activity (Campbell & Raskin, 1978) and dark preferences (Richardson & Campbell, 1988), whereas thermal and tactile cues associated with the dam reduce elevated heart rates (Siegel, Richardson, & Campbell, 1988).

Nest cues and huddling. In some of my work across several experiments, various students and I have investigated the impact of the dam and siblings on both elicited and learned behaviors. In one such study, Marie Peters and I were interested in the effects of home nest cues on pup–pup interactions. One kind of pup–pup interaction observed in most species that give birth to more than one altricial young is the huddling response (Rosenblatt, 1979). Huddling in rats has been shown to be an active response under multisensory control, regulated by thermotactile cues until about 15 days of age (15d), at which time olfactory cues become more important (e.g., Alberts, 1978a, 1978b; Alberts & Brunjes, 1978). Huddling might also be expected to be modulated by the familiarity of the context. Campbell and Raskin (1978) showed that unfamiliar surroundings evoke increased arousal related to fear and distress in young pups, and Randall and Campbell (1976) showed that conspecifics reduce such isolation-increased activity in 10d–20d pups. Although Randall and Campbell did not measure huddling per se, their findings suggest that an unfamiliar environment might motivate pups to make contact with conspecifics to reduce arousal and therefore huddle more.

Huddling has also been described as a form of "home nest settling" (Rosenblatt, 1979) that would be expected to increase only if cues associated with the home were present. With this analysis, on the other hand, huddling might be expected to be disrupted in atypical contexts. We measured huddling, defined as contact between at least three pups in groups of four, in 2d, 6d, 10d, and 14d male and female Sprague–Dawley rats, in familiar and unfamiliar contexts. A familiar context contained bedding (i.e., wood shavings) from the litter's own home nest; an unfamiliar context contained fresh, clean, cedar-scented wood shavings. Three hundred twenty rats from 40 litters were tested, with 10 litters represented in each age group (a group of four pups from a litter was considered the subject unit). Huddle groups were tested on a screen-covered wooden frame, scaled to size for the particular age condition and placed over the different beddings. The temperature was maintained at 26°C. Observations were made every 30 seconds for 30 minutes as to the quadrant location of the pup and the number of pups in contact. The average number of quadrant crossings may be seen in Figure 1, and the average number of minutes of contact time is shown in Figure 2 for the different aged pups in the familiar or unfamiliar context.

The activity data show a significant increase with age (10d and 14d more active than 2d and 6d, $ps < .05$), consistent with most reports on developing pups (e.g., Campbell & Raskin, 1978), but no effect of context familiarity. For huddling, however, both age and familiarity effects were observed. Less huddling was observed in younger pups (2d and 6d vs. 10d and 14d, $ps < .05$) and in the unfamiliar context ($p < .05$). Furthermore, proportionally more huddles over familiar bedding contained four instead

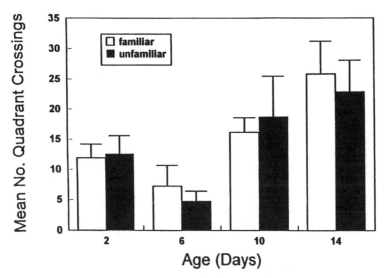

Figure 1. Activity levels, expressed as mean number of quadrants crossed, in different aged rats under familiar (home nest bedding) or unfamiliar (fresh bedding) context conditions. Vertical bars indicate standard errors of the means.

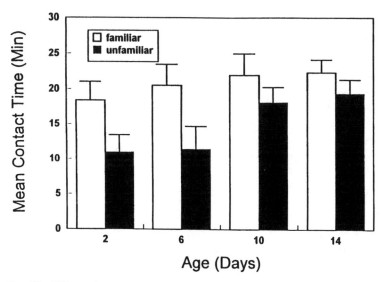

Figure 2. Huddling time, expressed as mean number of minutes that at least three of four pups were in contact, in different aged rats under familiar (home nest bedding) or unfamiliar (fresh bedding) context conditions. Vertical bars indicate standard errors of the means.

of three pups, and more huddles over unfamiliar bedding contained three instead of four pups (all $ps < .01$; see Table 1).

The findings of home familiarity effects on one measure (huddling) but not another (activity) indicate that conspecific interactions can serve multiple functions depending on the context and age of the organism. For activity, the lack of familiarity effects indicates that the presence of conspecifics, themselves part of a typical home context, mitigates against activity increases in older pups placed in unfamiliar surroundings (Randall & Campbell, 1976). The finding of more huddling in older pups is consistent with this interpretation. The contact data indicate that huddling is a typical behavior observed in the home nest that can be disrupted by unfamiliar surroundings, particularly for younger animals. Similar phenomena have been reported by Hofer (1972) with maternally separated rats; the young outside the home environment were observed to make contact but not remain together. Instead, pups were active until home was reached. Again, the context of the young dramatically affects their behavior, particularly in the drive to approach home.

Table 1. Proportion of Huddles Observed at 30-second Intervals Having Four Versus Three Pups in Contact for the Different Age and Context Conditions

Context condition	Age in Days			
	2	6	10	14
Unfamiliar	.21	.56	.09	.59
Familiar	.47	.79	.59	.72

Aversive cues and mother. Cairo Ali and I have also investigated pup behavior in a novel aversive context, but with the mother rather than conspecifics present, to assess any ASDR that could be directed toward her. We did so because accumulating evidence documented the importance of the mother in modulating infant learning (see the preceding discussion), including studies in which an anesthetized dam was used as the approach stimulus in appetitive learning (e.g., Amsel, Burdette, & Letz, 1976; Kenny & Blass, 1977). Furthermore, in earlier work with other collaborators (Collier, Mast, Meyer, & Jacobs, 1979), I had observed response differences in younger versus older pups in an approach-mother avoid-shock conflict learning task that led to the hypothesis that a very young infant's response to aversive stimulation was to approach mother, whereas an older pup would flee. This hypothesis was supported in part by observation of pups when shocked in the center of the runway without the mother present. Under these conditions, fleeing behavior improved with development. But direct tests of our ideas about shock-elicited responding with the mother present had not been done.

The present study was thus designed to assess pup responding under shock or no-shock conditions in a context that contained the dam, using the shock parameters employed in the Collier et al. (1979) study. We also were interested in opioid mediation of defensive responding and included morphine and naloxone pharmacological manipulations in this study. For the present discussion, however, only the nondrugged control conditions are presented. Different groups of 10d, 15d, and 20d pups (n = 6 per group) were either shocked or not shocked in a novel environment that contained an anesthetized dam. The environment was an enclosed area approximately 80 × 70 cm marked with 8-cm square grids and contained an 8-cm square shock grid in the center. The mother was located approximately 40 cm from the center in one of two extensions on either side of the apparatus; the approximate dimensions of the extensions were 20 × 30 cm. A pup was placed on the shock grid and given five 3-minute trials. These were a baseline no-shock trial; a 0.5-second, 0.75-mA shock trial; an observational no-shock trial; a 0.5-second, 1.4-mA shock trial; and a final observational trial. The intertrial interval (ITI) was 5 seconds. Latency to reach the dam, number of pups to reach the dam, number of grids crossed, number of ultrasonic vocalizations emitted, and general type of behavior occurring at 5-second intervals were recorded. Figures 3 through 6 show the results of these measures on the final observational trial for the different aged pups under shock or no-shock conditions.

APPROACH RESPONDING. For the approach-mother data, clear developmental trends emerged, but they were not in the direction we had anticipated. Younger (10d) pups took significantly longer to reach the dam (Figure 3), and significantly fewer of them did so ($ps < .05$; Figure 4). The activity data (Figure 5) were consistent with these findings in which only age effects were significant ($p < .05$). Ten-day pups crossed significantly fewer grids than 15d and 20d pups. Shock tended to decrease activity and approach responding but not significantly so on any of these measures. That shock had some effect, however, is revealed by the modal response

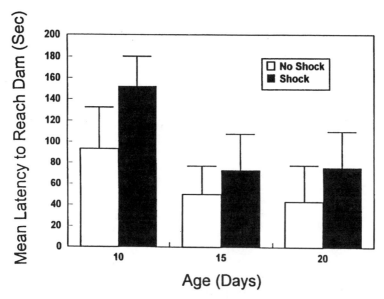

Figure 3. Mean latency in seconds for different aged pups to reach the dam under shock or no-shock conditions. Vertical bars indicate standard errors of the means.

of pups. The modal response was suckling for pups of all ages in the no-shock condition (46% for 10d and 15d pups, 36% for 20d pups). For shocked subjects, however, inactivity was the modal response for 10d (66%) and 20d (63%) pups, suggesting that shock interfered with the otherwise dom-

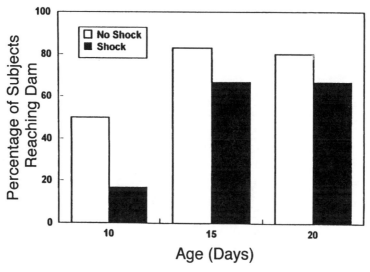

Figure 4. Percentage of pups of different ages that reached the dam under shock or no-shock conditions.

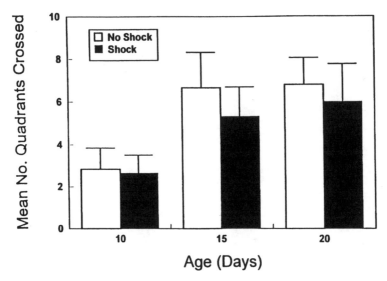

Figure 5. Mean number of quadrants crossed for different aged pups under shock or no-shock conditions. Vertical bars represent standard errors of the means.

inant suckling response. For 15d pups, suckling was the modal response (43%), followed by sniffing (39% even under the shock condition).

From the learning studies (Collier et al., 1979), we had expected that older pups would take longer to reach the dam because they have some freezing and fleeing defensive capabilities that younger pups do not have (Collier & Bolles, 1980), capabilities that could compete with approach tendencies. One explanation of why this did not happen is that the pres-

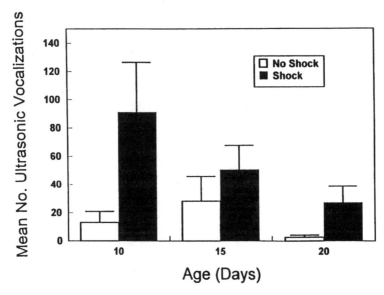

Figure 6. Mean number of ultrasonic vocalizations in different aged pups under shock or no-shock conditions. Vertical bars represent standard errors of the means.

ence of the dam blunted the alternative tendencies in older pups, thereby overriding the otherwise predicted shock effects. If so, this observation is reminiscent of the findings presented earlier in which testing with conspecifics seemed to mask expected novelty effects on activity. In these two instances, therefore, the social context appeared to moderate our aversive manipulations on some measures compared with the results of studies in which conspecifics or the mother was not present (e.g., Campbell & Raskin, 1978; Collier & Bolles, 1980; Collier et al., 1979). With conspecifics in the testing environment, novelty effects on activity were reduced; with a dam in the testing environment, shock effects on activity were mitigated.

DISTRESS CALLING. Measures of the ultrasonic vocalization, another defensive response in young pups (e.g., Takahashi et al., 1991), are shown in Figure 6. Vocalizations were in the range of 40–60 kHz for 10d pups, 25–40 kHz for 15d pups, and 15–25 kHz for 20d pups. For this measure, both age and shock effects were found (all $ps < .01$). Younger pups vocalized more than older ones, and all pups vocalized more in response to shock. The vocalization findings are consistent with reports of separation-induced distress calls reported by Hofer and Shair (1978) in 2-week-old pups and additionally show the cumulative effects of an added stressor (shock) on pup behavior.

Of note in these findings is the almost mirror image of the vocalization and approach data. Younger pups were less likely to reach the dam than older pups even though the approach data in the learning task showed they clearly had the locomotor abilities to do so (Collier et al., 1979). Instead, they were more likely to vocalize. Findings from other reports have suggested that pup vocalizations attract lactating mothers (e.g., Allin & Banks, 1972; Bell, Nitschke, Gorry, & Zachman, 1971); therefore, one explanation is that very young pups vocalize more to cue the mother to retrieve them. The findings of vocalizations in a context that contained the dam may also appear inconsistent with other reports that show that the dam reduces isolation-induced distress vocalizations (e.g., Hofer et al., 1989). However, in most of the work by Hofer and colleagues (Hofer & Shair, 1978; Hofer et al., 1989), only 14d pups were tested, and the testing context was much smaller than ours (22 × 15 cm vs. approximately 80 × 70 cm), permitting easier access to the dam. In our data, 15d and 20d pups also vocalized, but less often, and they were more likely to approach the dam themselves. Furthermore, informal observations revealed that for pups of all ages, vocalizations decreased or ceased if and when a pup reached the dam. Our findings, in conjunction with other reports, show not only that the social and experimental contexts affect infant behavior but also that the behavior likely to be expressed is age-dependent.

The Social Context and Learning

In addition to studying elicited responding, numerous students and I have also investigated the effect of the social and physical context on the expression of learning and memory in infant rats, with particular attention

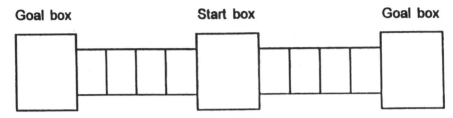

Figure 7. Schematic of apparatus for approach–avoidance conflict training.

to ASRs. The task we have used for these studies is the approach-dam avoid-shock conflict task referred to earlier. This task is informative in that it permits evaluation of both approach and avoidance learning and takes advantage of the finding that infant rats can learn quickly to approach an anesthetized dam for contact, dry suckling, or both, as a reward (e.g., Amsel et al., 1976; Kenny & Blass, 1977). The apparatus we have used for the approach–avoidance task is a version of one used by Maher, Elder, and Noblin (1962), scaled to size for the different aged pups. It consists of a startbox in the center with two alleys that run in opposite directions to goal boxes that can be discriminated on the basis of color (black or white) or texture (smooth or textured). A shock grid is located directly in front of the goal boxes. The apparatus is broken into 11 divisions to designate distinct locations (see Figure 7). This apparatus was originally designed to help evaluate the basis for deficiencies in passive avoidance stemming from lesions in adult rats (e.g., lack of inhibition, hyperactivity, persistence to the goal) by offering subjects alternative ways of solving the avoidance problem. For example, if shocked animals are unable to avoid passively by freezing because of lesions, or in this case because of immaturity, they may be able to flee down the alternative alley instead. Observing where subjects are in the apparatus thus permits better understanding of what their reaction is to the approach-dam avoid-shock conflict problem.

The typical training procedures we have employed are, first, to train a maternally deprived pup to approach the dam, usually with access to the alternative alley closed. Once a pup achieves a predetermined approach criterion, it is given 0.5-second shocks on the next two trials as it approaches. Following Maher et al. (1962), the first shock trial is designated as weak (0.75 mA), and the second is strong (1.4 mA). Access to the alternative alley is then opened, and the pup is given a final three-minute test trial. Latency to reach the dam is recorded. Pup location in the alley is also recorded at 5-second intervals, from which choices pups make and paths they take can be analyzed.

Reactions to the dam in approach–avoidance training. When preweanling rats were tested in this task, a clear developmental trend emerged. On the passive avoidance measure, 10d pups fail to avoid, 15d pups are somewhat better, and 20d pups are quite successful (e.g., Collier et al., 1979; Weihmuller & Collier, 1990; and observations following). The result of poorer passive avoidance in younger pups is consistent with other reports using step-down or step-through tasks (e.g., Campbell, Riccio, & Rohrbaugh, 1971) and is unlikely to be explained by differences based on appetitive approach (see Collier et al., 1979 for discussion; also, unpublished data from other studies in my laboratory show few differences in appetitive extinction in 10d–20d pups under most of the training conditions employed). However, if what the pups are doing on the test trial is assessed by analyzing their location in the apparatus at regular intervals, quite specific age-dependent reactions following shock are observed. The 10d pups approach the dam, hesitate in front of the shock grid demonstrating they have learned about the aversive contingency, but do not turn back. They eventually resolve any conflict by going to the dam and therefore fail to avoid. Fifteen-day pups do not often solve their conflict. They go back and forth, and some of the time they go on to reach the dam. Twenty-day pups appear to have little conflict in that they are good at avoiding, frequently running the other way. If these findings are conceptualized as ASRs in an aversive context or as ASDRs, and if Bolles's (1970) statement is accepted that avoidance will be observed to the extent a task is devised that captures an animal's typical responding, then successful avoidance might be expected even in a 10d pup if its ASR is required for avoidance.

Using pup-mother responding to express avoidance. To test the preceding idea regarding ASRs, Joelle Mast and I replicated the study described using 10d pups, but we gave them another dam to approach in the alternative alley near the goal box on the test trial. When we did this, the 10d pups were quite successful in avoiding the dam associated with shock by approaching the alternative dam nearby (Collier & Mast, 1979). Nonpunished pups continued in the original approach response even when the nearby alternative mother was available, suggesting that the successful avoidance was not solely mediated by offering an alternative source of reinforcement. Subsequently, Marie Peters and I (Collier & Peters, 1980) determined what aspects of the context were needed to permit successful avoidance in the 10d pups. Our findings revealed that it was necessary to make the alternative dam more attractive by having her closer than the original approach dam, although it did not matter whether the dam was the infant's own mother. Also, just providing pups with shavings from their home nest increased their vacillation, behavior not otherwise seen in this task in the 10d pups. Therefore, structuring the context to allow for age-appropriate response alternatives potentially motivated by either defensive (stress reducing) or appetitive (comfort gaining) characteristics permitted evidence of avoidance not otherwise observed.

The Physical Environment and Learning

The preceding work focused on how the social context might influence ASRs and infant learning (e.g., Collier & Mast, 1979), but other features of a learning context might be expected to influence behavior as well. One

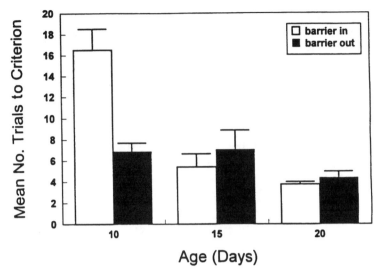

Figure 8. Mean number of trials to criterion for different aged pups to avoid shock passively under barrier-in or barrier-out conditions. Vertical bars indicate standard errors of the means.

simple contextual feature that seemed likely to affect avoidance or defensive behavior, or both, was the availability to the pups of other places to go if particular locations became unavailable or aversive. Using the same conflict task and apparatus, Fred Weihmuller, Cairo Ali, and I manipulated the physical characteristics of the apparatus by varying whether pups had access to the alternative alley once avoidance training began (barrier in or out). We first trained 10d, 15d, and 20d pups to the same approach-dam criteria and then initiated punishment. A 0.5-second, 1.4-mA footshock was delivered until pups did not return to the goal box containing the dam within 180 seconds on two consecutive trials or for a maximum of 30 trials. As can be seen in Figure 8, providing 10d pups access to the alternative alley eliminated avoidance differences otherwise seen (10d pups took significantly more trials to avoid but only if the barrier remained in; $ps < .01$). With adult rats, Bolles suggested that the geometry of a testing apparatus partly determines the expression of defensive responding and that a long alley, like the one we used, "invites" running (Bolles & Collier, 1976). Our data as well support the idea that defensive responses are partly controlled by the stimulus properties of the situation.

Age-Specific Responding and Memory

Different behaviors can evidence retention. If ASRs can constrain the expression of learning in young rats, they might also be expected to influence the assessment of memory. It is well established that memory in younger altricial rats is poorer than in older pups over the same retention interval, even though they learn equally well (Campbell & Spear, 1972). This finding is referred to as *infantile amnesia*. It is also known that reminder treatments, such as reinstatement (e.g., Campbell & Jaynes, 1966) and reactivation (Spear & Parsons, 1976), often alleviate some of these deficiencies. Reinstatement in these instances refers to reexposure of the original training procedures between original training and testing. Reactivation, as used by Spear and Parsons (1976), refers to a shock reminder cue given shortly before retention testing in aversive tasks. Weihmuller and I reasoned that if pups did remember, or could be reminded successfully, they might appear as if they had forgotten their original learning on a later test if their ASR had changed by that time (Weihmuller & Collier, 1990). Campbell and Coulter (1976) posed such a possibility, but the idea was not tested because few learning tasks elicit as distinct ASRs as the approach–avoidance task does. Ten-day pups in this task return to the dam following punishment and do not passively avoid, whereas 15d pups vacillate and do avoid.

We trained 10d and 15d pups in the approach–avoidance task and tested them 1 day later with or without a single shock reactivation before testing. Ten-day pups were also tested with or without reactivation 6 days later. Our findings showed forgetting, which could be alleviated with reactivation for the 1-day interval, with pups responding similarly on both the training and retention test (11d reactivated pups reapproached the dam as they had done at 10 days, whereas nonreactivated pups did not; 16d reactivated pups avoided as they had done at 15 days, whereas nonreactivated pups did not). A reactivation effect was also found for 10d pups tested after 6 days. At the longer retention interval, however, pups responded in the avoidance task as a trained 16d pup would rather than as they had at 10 days (i.e., 16d pups that received reactivation vacillated and avoided only if they had been trained at 10 days, whereas untrained or nonreactivated pups did not; Weihmuller & Collier, 1990). As had been shown regarding learning, therefore, we were able to confirm retention in pups that might not have been observed without consideration of their ASDRs.

Social and physical reactivation stimuli. In some of the work described previously, aspects of the infant's social or physical environment were shown to influence elicited as well as learned behaviors. It would therefore seem important to evaluate how features of the social or physical context might influence memorial processes as well. Weihmuller, working in my laboratory, has begun investigating how various aspects of an infant's social and physical context could influence the reactivation of memory using the approach-mother avoid-shock conflict task. Because the conflict task contains both appetitive (approach) and aversive (shock) components, any of several salient features of the task could be effective in alleviating ontogenetic forgetting. Weihmuller started this investigation with pups trained at 15 days and tested 6 days later. Before testing, he exposed pups to either a shock, the dam, or the location of the shock for a 2-second reactivation treatment. Untrained but reactivated controls were also tested. The findings to date indicate that only the shock reactivation treatment in trained subjects is effective in reinstating the avoidance response.

It may have been expected that using the dam as a reactivation treatment would permit the expression of memory. The findings that cues associated with the home environment result in passive avoidance learning not otherwise seen (e.g., Smith & Spear, 1978) and that isolation from the dam disrupts retention (Arnold & Spear, 1995) support this hypothesis. On the other hand, our preliminary findings are consistent with other reports showing that not all components of a learning episode are effective retrieval cues. In an appetitive task with human infants, for example, Rovee-Collier, Patterson, and Hayne (1985) showed reminder specificity effects and argued that they would be particularly adaptive to developing organisms by providing them with a buffer against memory retrieval in inappropriate contexts. Campbell and Randall (1976) suggested that different components of a learning contingency can be effective reinstatement treatments in infants depending on whether the task is appetitively or aversively motivated—another example of specificity. Furthermore, both internal and external contextual cues are known generally to control memory processes to the extent that they are present during training and testing (e.g., Richardson, Riccio, & Jonke, 1983; Richardson, Riccio, & McKenney, 1988; Spear, 1984). If the mother is not relevant to a target memory, therefore, in the sense of being a component of the learning contingency the pup is required to remember (shock punishment in my research), her effect on infant responding might be not influential. This is in contrast to the recently accumulating evidence demonstrating the mother to be a hidden regulator of a variety of pup responses, which theoretically could affect memorial processes or their expression (e.g., through separation- or stress-induced changes in internal endocrine states—one of many possibilities). It might also be true that any such general positive effects the dam could have on retention are age-dependent (we have evaluated maternal effects at only one age to date). Clearly, additional research on this question is required, because little information is available regarding maternal effects on memory across the early developmental period.

Stress Responding: Maternal Modulation and Learning

In the final set of studies reported here, Michael Hennessy and I continued to explore how the social context affects infant behavior within the approach–avoidance learning context. Of particular interest to us were reports from Levine and colleagues (Levine, Huchton, Wiener, & Rosenfeld, 1992; Stanton, Gutierrez, & Levine, 1988; Stanton & Levine, 1988) that maternal separation activates pups' HPA system, which has long been associated with arousal and stress (Mason, 1975; Selye, 1956). Furthermore, mother–infant reunion reduces separation-induced elevations of the HPA system (Stanton & Levine, 1990; Stanton et al., 1987). In most tests of infant learning, infants are typically removed from their nest and therefore from their mother and littermates. We (Hennessy, Collier, Griffin, & Schwaiger, 1988) thus hypothesized that standard training and handling procedures used in infant appetitive learning paradigms may also activate pups' HPA system. For instance, a common practice in approach-dam learning studies is to separate pups from their mother before training (e.g., Amsel et al., 1977). The procedure is likely patterned after appetitive tasks in adults, for which food is a common reward and hunger motivation is often necessary for the expression of learning (Bolles, 1975; Tolman & Honzik, 1930). However, pups of several ages will run for dry suckling or merely contact with the dam. This includes pups even younger than the age for which attracting maternal pheromones (Leon & Moltz, 1972) might explain their approach mother behavior. One possible basis for the approach behavior, therefore, is modulation of the HPA system.

My associates and I (Hennessy et al., 1988) began to investigate our ideas by measuring HPA activity in the context of the approach–avoidance task described earlier (Collier et al., 1979) in 10d and 15d pups. The approach–avoidance training methods were replicated, after which pups were returned either to an empty goal box or to one containing an anesthetized dam for either 15 or 60 minutes. The 60-minute isolation or contact periods following training allowed time for corticosterone changes to emerge, which lag behind the neural events that initiate HPA activity. Pups were then sacrificed and blood was collected for plasma corticosterone measures using standard radioimmunoassay procedures. Samples were also collected from deprived-only and nondisturbed pups. Our findings confirmed that the deprivation-plus-training combination elevated plasma corticosterone levels in both 10d and 15d pups, whereas deprivation alone was sufficient to do so in 15d pups. The presence of the dam reduced elevated levels, particularly for 15d pups after 60 minutes. On the basis of these findings, we hypothesized that some portion of the dam's reinforcing value may lie in her modulation of pups' HPA activity.

Although it is likely that the mother provides reward for an infant on the basis of multiple regulatory systems (Hofer, 1987), we have been interested in studying the HPA system as one of these for several reasons. First, our data indicate that the HPA system can be modulated in the infant learning task. Second, although the causal connection is not yet determined, there are striking relationships between approach learning to the dam and HPA activity across varied experiments. For instance, stimuli that support approach learning, such as contact with the dam but not with siblings, have been shown to correspond with stimuli that reduce the stress response in infants (i.e., contact with the dam but not siblings; Amsel et al., 1977; Stanton & Levine, 1990). Additionally, the ages in infancy at which the dam appears to be an effective reinforcer for instrumental approach learning parallel the ages for which contact with a dam inhibits the stress response (Smith & Bogomolny, 1983; Stanton & Levine, 1990). Finally, Blass and Kehoe (1987) identified at least four states that they argue appear to be reinforcing for infants. One of these is a calming by maternal (or sibling) stimulation that is not opioid-mediated. Reduction of stress could be interpreted as calming, implicating the HPA system as one candidate for this reinforcing system.

In ongoing collaboration with Michael Hennessy and students in my laboratory, Kimberly Caris and Tara Francis, I have continued to investigate how separation and reunion with the mother might influence HPA activity and pup performance within the approach-dam infant learning context. In one experiment, we manipulated maternal effects by varying the amount of maternal separation *before* approach training (0–12 hr). In general, we found a positive correspondence between increased separation periods and both HPA activity and performance. In a second experiment, we manipulated maternal contact *during* training by varying the number of rewarded (contact with the dam) or nonrewarded (extinction) trials pups were given after initial approach training was established (10–30 additional trials). At the end of training, all pups had elevated HPA activity except those given extended reward training (30 trials). Also, only pups given additional rewarded trials continued to approach. Although we have not demonstrated a causal relationship between HPA activity and performance in these studies, the results are nonetheless intriguing in that they demonstrate how differential contact with the mother affects both a physiological response indicative of stress and overt pup approach behavior. The results also remain consistent with the idea that part of what makes the dam so reinforcing to the infant lies in her ability to modulate changes in pup HPA activity.

Conclusion

Throughout this chapter, I have tried to illustrate, using representative examples from both my own work and others', the importance that various kinds of contextual stimuli can have in the study of early behavior. For a young altricial infant, the mother and cues associated with her are often critical determinants of this assessment. I have also attempted to show that it is equally important to recognize the rapidly changing characteristics of the infant and to consider how it might react, learn, and remember differently in various contexts as it matures.

These ideas are not novel; the study of any organism requires, at some level, an awareness of its evolutionary niche and both motor and sensory capabilities (e.g., Spear, 1979, 1984). For the infant rat, however, the effects of the social context, particularly the mother, on an array of processes are especially profound and striking. Furthermore, such social effects have not always been so obvious. This may have been because the rat mother historically was viewed primarily as a provider of basic needs (e.g., nutrition, warmth, and protection) and less as an important social stimulus that modulates a variety of psychological and physiological responses to the environment. The increasing evidence of dramatic effects of pup isolation on numerous processes forces consideration of the mother's role in these processes as well.

In closing, I note some caveats to the generalities I have stated. Whereas the mother is unquestionably critical to numerous developmental processes, her role may not always be enhancing from an investigator's perspective (e.g., the suckling context has been shown to interfere with taste-aversion learning; Martin & Alberts, 1979). The dam is not equally germane to all behavioral processes even at a single age (e.g., as in reactivation). Also in this chapter, I have focused my discussion on the relevance of contextual cues and age-specific responding, particularly defensive responding, to the study of infant development. However, there are other examples of age-specific characteristics, such as age dependencies in sensory responsiveness (Hyson & Rudy, 1987; Rudy, Vogt, & Hyson, 1984), that can provide insights into the ontogenesis of learning and memory. Finally, although I have characterized the dam as an important component of a broader social context for the infant rat, it is not certain that what is meant by social context is the same across species. For example, even if an infant rat is removed from a major social figure in its environment (its mother) and reacts with a stress response to the separation, it is premature to conclude that these are the same reactions being viewed when a young rhesus macaque, or even a human infant, is separated from its primary (usually mother) attachment figure (e.g., Levine, 1987). Nonetheless, recognizing the dam as part of a social environment that affects multiple aspects of an infant's behavior is likely to continue to have a critical role in the understanding of early developmental processes. Bolles's recognition of this fact (Bolles & Woods, 1964) well ahead of systematic research about it is but one of many demonstrations of his penetrating insight into the basics of behavior and the study of psychology.

References

Alberts, J. R. (1978a). Huddling by rat pups: Group behavioral mechanisms of temperature regulation and energy conservation. *Journal of Comparative and Physiological Psychology, 92,* 231–245.

Alberts, J. R. (1978b). Huddling by rat pups: Multisensory control of contact behavior. *Journal of Comparative and Physiological Psychology, 92,* 220–230.

Alberts, J. R., & Brunjes, P. C. (1978). Ontogeny of thermal and olfactory determinants of huddling in the rat. *Journal of Comparative and Physiological Psychology, 92,* 897–906.

Allin, J. T., & Banks, E. M. (1972). Functional aspects of ultrasound production by infant albino rats. *Animal Behaviour, 20,* 175–185.

Altman, J., & Sudarshan, K. (1975). Postnatal development of locomotion in the laboratory rat. *Animal Behaviour, 23,* 896–920.

Amsel, A., Burdette, D. R., & Letz, R. (1976). Appetitive learning, patterned alternation, and extinction in 10-day-old rats with nonlactating suckling as reward. *Nature, 262,* 816–818.

Amsel, A., Letz, R., & Burdette, D. R. (1977). Appetitive learning and extinction in 11-day-old rat pups: Effects of various reinforcement conditions. *Journal of Comparative and Physiological Psychology, 91,* 1156–1167.

Arnold, H. M., & Spear, N. E. (1995). Isolation disrupts retention in preweanling rat pups. *Behavioral Neuroscience, 109,* 744–758.

Bell, R. W., Nitschke, W., Gorry, T. H., & Zachman, T. A. (1971). Infantile stimulation and ultrasonic signaling: A possible mediator of early handling phenomena. *Developmental Psychobiology, 4,* 181–191.

Blass, E. M., & Kehoe, P. (1987). Emerging opioid systems in newborn rats. In N. A. Krasnegor, E. M. Blass, M. A. Hofer, & W. P. Smotherman (Eds.), *Perinatal development: A psychobiological perspective* (pp. 61–82). Orlando, FL: Academic Press.

Bolles, R. C. (1970). Species-specific defense reactions and avoidance learning. *Psychological Review, 77,* 32–48.

Bolles, R. C. (1975). *Theory of motivation* (2nd ed.). New York: Harper & Row.

Bolles, R. C., & Collier, A. C. (1976). The effect of predictive cues on freezing in rats. *Animal Learning and Behavior, 4,* 6–8.

Bolles, R. C., & Woods, P. J. (1964). The ontogeny of behaviour in the albino rat. *Animal Behaviour, 12,* 427–441.

Campbell, B. A., & Coulter, X. (1976). Ontogeny of learning and memory. In M. R. Rosenzweig & E. L. Bennett (Eds.), *Neural mechanisms of learning and memory* (pp. 209–235). Cambridge, MA: MIT Press.

Campbell, B. A., & Jaynes, J. (1966). Reinstatement. *Psychological Review, 73,* 478–480.

Campbell, B. A., Lytle, L. D., & Fibiger, H. C. (1969). Ontogeny of adrenergic arousal and cholinergic inhibitory mechanisms in the rat. *Science, 166,* 635–636.

Campbell, B. A., & Randall, P. K. (1976). The effect of reinstatement stimulus conditions on the maintenance of long-term memory. *Developmental Psychobiology, 9,* 325–333.

Campbell, B. A., & Raskin, L. A. (1978). Ontogeny of behavioral arousal: The role of environmental stimuli. *Journal of Comparative and Physiological Psychology, 92,* 176–184.

Campbell, B. A., Riccio, D. C., & Rohrbaugh, M. (1971). Ontogenesis of learning and memory: Research and theory. In M. E. Meyer (Ed.), *Second Western Symposium on Learning: Early learning* (pp. 76–109). Bellingham, WA: Western Washington State College Press.

Campbell, B. A., & Spear, N. E. (1972). Ontogeny of memory. *Psychological Review, 79,* 215–236.

Carden, S. E., & Hofer, M. A. (1992). Effect of a social companion on the ultrasonic vocalizations and contact responses of 3-day-old rat pups. *Behavioral Neuroscience, 106,* 421–426.

Collier, A. C. (1977). Preference for shock signals as a function of the temporal accuracy of the signals. *Learning and Motivation, 8,* 159–170.

Collier, A. C., & Bolles, R. C. (1980). The ontogenesis of defensive reactions to shock in preweanling rats. *Developmental Psychobiology, 13,* 141–150.

Collier, A. C., & Mast, J. (1979). Alleviation of avoidance deficits by approach alternatives in 10-day-old rats. *Physiology & Behavior, 23,* 615–618.

Collier, A. C., Mast, J., Meyer, D. R., & Jacobs, C.-E. (1979). Approach-avoidance conflict in preweanling rats: A developmental study. *Animal Learning & Behavior, 7,* 514–520.

Collier, A. C., & Peters, M. F. (1980). [Effects of alternative approach stimuli on approach–avoidance behavior in preweanling rats]. Unpublished raw data.

Corby, J. R., Caza, P. A., & Spear, N. E. (1982). Ontogenetic changes in the effectiveness of home nest odor as a conditioned stimulus. *Behavioral and Neural Biology, 35,* 354–367.

Hennessy, M. B., Collier, A. C., Griffin, A. C., & Schwaiger, S. (1988). Plasma corticosterone fluctuations in an infant-learning paradigm. *Behavioral Neuroscience, 102,* 701–705.

Hennessy, M. B., & Weinberg, J. (1990). Adrenocortical activity during conditions of brief social separation in preweaning rats. *Behavioral and Neural Biology, 54,* 42–55.

Hofer, M. A. (1972). Physiological and behavioural processes in early maternal deprivation. In *CIBA Foundation Symposium 8: Physiology, emotion and psychosomatic illness.* New York: Elsevier.

Hofer, M. A. (1984). Relationships as regulators: A psychobiologic perspective on bereavement. *Psychosomatic Medicine, 46,* 183–197.

Hofer, M. A. (1987). Shaping forces within early social relationships. In N. A. Krasnegor, E. M. Blass, M. A. Hofer, & W. P. Smotherman (Eds.), *Perinatal development: A psychobiological perspective* (pp. 251–274). Orlando, FL: Academic Press.

Hofer, M. A., & Shair, H. (1978). Ultrasonic vocalization during social interaction and isolation in 2-week-old rats. *Developmental Psychobiology, 11,* 495–504.

Hofer, M. A., Shair, H. N., & Murowchick, E. (1989). Isolation distress and maternal comfort responses of two-week-old rat pups reared in social isolation. *Developmental Psychobiology, 22,* 553–566.

Hyson, R. L., & Rudy, J. W. (1987). Ontogenetic change in the analysis of sound frequency in the infant rat. *Developmental Psychobiology, 20,* 189–207.

Ikemoto, S., & Panksepp, J. (1992). The effects of early social isolation on the motivation for social play in juvenile rats. *Developmental Psychobiology, 25,* 261–274.

Kennedy, S., & Collier, A. C. (1994). Stress-induced modulation of the immune response in the developing rat pup. *Physiology & Behavior, 56,* 825–828.

Kenny, J. T., & Blass, E. M. (1977). Suckling as incentive to instrumental learning in pre-weanling rats. *Science, 196,* 898–899.

Kuhn, C. M., Pauk, J., & Schanberg, S. M. (1990). Endocrine responses to mother-infant separation in developing rats. *Developmental Psychobiology, 23,* 395–410.

Leon, M., & Moltz, H. (1972). The development of the pheromonal bond in the albino rat. *Physiology & Behavior, 8,* 683–686.

Levine, S. (1987). Psychobiologic consequences of disruption in mother-infant relationships. In N. A. Krasnegor, E. M. Blass, M. A. Hofer, & W. P. Smotherman (Eds.), *Perinatal development: A psychobiological perspective* (pp. 359–376). Orlando, FL: Academic Press.

Levine, S., Huchton, D. M., Wiener, S. G., & Rosenfeld, P. (1992). Time course of the effect of maternal deprivation on the hypothalamic-pituitary-adrenal axis in the infant rat. *Developmental Psychobiology, 24,* 547–588.

Maher, B. A., Elder, S. T., & Noblin, C. D. (1962). A differential investigation of avoidance reduction versus hypermotility following frontal ablation. *Journal of Comparative and Physiological Psychology, 55,* 449–454.

Martin, L. T., & Alberts, J. R. (1979). Taste aversions to mother's milk: The age-related role of nursing in acquisition and expression of a learned association. *Journal of Comparative and Physiological Psychology, 93,* 430–455.

Mason, J. W. (1975). A historical view of the stress field, Part II. *Journal of Human Stress, 1,* 22–36.

Misanin, J. R., & Hinderliter, C. F. (1989). The role of homecage environmental stimuli in the facilitation of shock-motivated spatial discrimination learning in rat pups. *Developmental Psychobiology, 22,* 129–140.

Randall, P. K., & Campbell, B. A. (1976). Ontogeny of behavioral arousal in rats: Effect of maternal and sibling presence. *Journal of Comparative and Physiological Psychology, 90,* 453–459.

Reisbick, S., Rosenblatt, J. S., & Mayer, A. D. (1975). Decline of maternal behavior in the virgin and lactating rat. *Journal of Comparative and Physiological Psychology, 89,* 722–732.

Richardson, R., & Campbell, B. A. (1988). Effects of home nest odors on black-white preference in the developing rat: Implications for developmental learning research. *Behavioral and Neural Biology, 50,* 361–366.

Richardson, R., Riccio, D. C., & Jonke, T. (1983). Alleviation of infantile amnesia in rats by means of a pharmacological contextual state. *Developmental Psychobiology, 16,* 511–518.

Richardson, R., Riccio, D. C., & McKenney, M. (1988). Stimulus attributes of reactivated memory: Alleviation of ontogenetic forgetting in rats is context specific. *Developmental Psychobiology, 21,* 135–143.

Richardson, R., Siegel, M. A., & Campbell, B. A. (1988). Effect of maternal presence on the fear response to an unfamiliar environment as measured by heart rate in rats as a function of age. *Developmental Psychobiology, 21,* 613–633.

Richardson, R., Siegel, M. A., & Campbell, B. A. (1989). Effect of maternal presence on the cardiac and behavioral responses to shock in rats as a function of age. *Developmental Psychobiology, 22,* 567–583.

Rosenblatt, J. S. (1979). The sensorimotor and motivational bases of early behavioral development of selected altricial mammals. In N. E. Spear & B. A. Campbell (Eds.), *Ontogeny of learning and memory* (pp. 1–38). Hillsdale, NJ: Erlbaum.

Rovee-Collier, C., Patterson, J., & Hayne, H. (1985). Specificity in the reactivation of infant memory. *Developmental Psychobiology, 18,* 559–574.

Rudy, J. W., & Cheatle, M. D. (1979). Ontogeny of associative learning: Acquisition of odor aversions by neonatal rats. In N. E. Spear & B. A. Campbell (Eds.), *Ontogeny of learning and memory* (pp. 157–188). Hillsdale, NJ: Erlbaum.

Rudy, J. W., Vogt, M. B., & Hyson, R. L. (1984). A developmental analysis of the rat's learned reactions to gustatory and auditory stimulation. In R. Kail & N. E. Spear (Eds.), *Com-*

parative perspectives on the development of memory (pp. 181–208). Hillsdale, NJ: Erlbaum.

Selye, H. (1956). *The stress of life*. New York: McGraw-Hill.

Shoemaker, W. J., & Kehoe, P. (1995). Effect of isolation conditions on brain regional enkephalin and B-endorphin levels and vocalizations in 10-day-old rat pups. *Behavioral Neuroscience, 109*, 117–122.

Siegel, M. A., Richardson, R., & Campbell, B. A. (1988). Effects of home nest stimuli on the emotional response of preweanling rats to an unfamiliar environment. *Psychobiology, 16*, 236–242.

Small, W. S. (1899). Notes on the psychic development of the young white rat. *American Journal of Psychology, 11*, 80–100.

Smith, G. J., & Bogomolny, A. (1983). Appetitive instrumental training in preweanling rats: I. Motivational determinants. *Developmental Psychobiology, 16*, 119–128.

Smith, G. J., Kucharski, D., & Spear, N. E. (1985). Conditioning of an odor aversion in preweanlings with isolation from home nest as the unconditioned stimulus. *Developmental Psychobiology, 18*, 421–434.

Smith, G. J., Miller, J. S., Wigal, T., & Spear, N. E. (1989). Facilitation of acquisition and retention in preweanling but not postweanling rats by the presence of familiar home-nest material. *Behavioral and Neural Biology, 52*, 370–385.

Smith, G. J., & Spear, N. E. (1978). Effects of the home environment on withholding behaviors and conditioning in infant and neonatal rats. *Science, 202*, 327–329.

Smith, G. J., & Spear, N. E. (1980). Facilitation of conditioning in two-day-old rats by training in the presence of conspecifics. *Behavioral and Neural Biology, 28*, 491–495.

Spear, N. E. (1979). Memory storage factors leading to infantile amnesia. In G. Bower (Ed.), *The psychology of learning and motivation* (Vol. 13, pp. 91–154). New York: Academic Press.

Spear, N. E. (1984). Ecologically determined dispositions control the ontogeny of learning and memory. In R. Kail & N. E. Spear (Eds.), *Comparative perspectives on the development of memory* (pp. 325–358). Hillsdale, NJ: Erlbaum.

Spear, N. E., & Parsons, P. J. (1976). Analysis of a reactivation treatment: Ontogenetic determinants of alleviated forgetting. In D. L. Medin, W. A. Roberts, & R. T. Davis (Eds.), *Processes of animal memory* (pp. 135–165). Hillsdale, NJ: Erlbaum.

Stanton, M. E., Gutierrez, Y. R., & Levine, S. (1988). Maternal deprivation potentiates pituitary-adrenal stress responses in infant rats. *Behavioral Neuroscience, 102*, 692–700.

Stanton, M. E., & Levine, S. (1988). Maternal modulation of infant glucocorticoid stress response: Role of age and maternal deprivation. *Psychobiology, 16*, 223–228.

Stanton, M. E., & Levine, S. (1990). Inhibition of infant glucocorticoid stress response: Specific role of maternal cues. *Developmental Psychobiology, 23*, 411–426.

Stanton, M. E., Wallstrom, J., & Levine, S. (1987). Maternal contact inhibits pituitary-adrenal stress responses in preweanling rats. *Developmental Psychobiology, 20*, 131–145.

Stehouwer, D. J., & Campbell, B. A. (1980). Ontogeny of passive avoidance: Role of task demands and development of species-typical behaviors. *Developmental Psychobiology, 13*, 385–398.

Takahashi, L. K. (1992). Developmental expression of defensive responses during exposure to conspecific adults in preweanling rats *(Rattus norvegicus)*. *Journal of Comparative Psychology, 106*, 69–77.

Takahashi, L. K., Turner, J. G., & Kalin, N. H. (1991). Development of stress-induced responses in preweanling rats. *Developmental Psychobiology, 24*, 341–360.

Tolman, E. C., & Honzik, C. H. (1930). Degrees of hunger, reward and nonreward, and maze learning in rats. *University of California Publications in Psychology, 4*, 215–232.

Weihmuller, F. B., & Collier, A. C. (1990). The role of age-dependent behaviors in the retention of an approach-avoidance response in preweanling rats. *Developmental Psychobiology, 23*, 265–283.

Part II

The Motivation of Behavior

5

Regulation of Food Intake: Interactions Between Learning and Physiology

Randy J. Seeley, Douglas S. Ramsay, and Stephen C. Woods

The contributions of Robert Bolles to experimental psychology, especially to the theory of learning and motivation, are numerous and profound (see Bolles, 1975, 1979, 1993). Among them is the now widely accepted tenet that learning plays a fundamental role in all aspects of food intake, from assisting animals in finding food, to enabling the animal to adapt to different patterns of food availability, to preparing the body to deal with the food it is consuming and hence contributing to the physiology of regulation. Over the past 2 decades, the understanding of the physiological mechanisms involved in the regulation of food intake has grown at an unprecedented rate. For the most part, the study of the physiology of these systems has proceeded quite independently of a growing awareness of the pivotal role of learning in such behaviors. It is our intention in this chapter to provide a conceptual framework for integrating the physiological and associative components that are required for a thorough description and understanding of the regulation of food intake and body weight and thereby to provide an alternative explanation to the one afforded by current views of ingestive regulation.[1] Because body weight correlates so highly with body adiposity (i.e., total body fat content) in experimental animals, many experiments have monitored only one or the other; we use the two terms interchangeably in this review.

We do not discuss in this chapter the ability of animals to learn where to find food reliably or how to partition their time to integrate eating with other behaviors. The role of learning in these behaviors is self-evident and ubiquitous. Rather, we focus on the role of learning in food selection, determining meal size, and establishing the patterning of meals, as well as in the physiological changes that help prepare the body to process the food

The writing of this chapter was supported by several grants from the National Institutes of Health: DK-17844, AA-07455, DE-00379, and DA-07391.

[1]We had initiated a collaboration with Robert Bolles to amplify these points just before his untimely death (see Ramsay, Seeley, Bolles, & Woods, 1996).

that is consumed. The underlying tenet for this discussion is that the body runs most efficiently when disturbances in regulated systems can be anticipated and prevented. It is instructive to begin this discussion by considering the dominant theoretical approach to the understanding of the regulation of food intake: the concept of homeostasis.

Homeostasis

Mammals have elaborate control systems that under normal conditions are able to maintain appropriate levels of a multitude of critical internal parameters. Obvious examples are the maintenance of body temperature and of several parameters of the blood and other internal fluids (e.g., volume, pH, osmolality, oxygen and glucose concentration, electrolytes). Activities of most organ systems function best in a narrow range of each of these parameters, and it makes teleological sense that the level of each critical parameter can be monitored and controlled by complex response systems. The ability of the animal, in the face of changing environmental conditions, to detect and respond to perturbations of any of these parameters by making physiological or behavioral adjustments that return the value of the parameter toward preperturbation levels constitutes homeostasis (Cannon, 1932).

Most research on the physiology of the regulation of food intake and body weight has been predicated on the basic negative feedback model of homeostasis popularized by Claude Bernard (1878). In this schema, homeostatic regulation has three fundamental components: (a) a parameter that is critical to the animal and can be regulated, (b) a perturbation- or "error"-detecting mechanism, and (c) an effector mechanism that, when activated, corrects errors. For example (see Woods, Taborsky, & Porte, 1986), plasma glucose is normally maintained within a narrow range (75–100 mg/dl). Injecting the pancreatic hormone insulin into an organism enables tissues to remove glucose from the plasma at a higher rate than normal, resulting in a dose-dependent reduction of plasma glucose levels, or hypoglycemia. The reduced glucose is detected at several receptor sites, including the pancreas, liver, and brain, and this results in altered activity at several fronts. The B cells of the pancreas secrete less endogenous insulin, and the A cells secrete more glucagon, a hormone that causes increased secretion of glucose into the blood by the liver. The liver stops converting glucose to fats, secretes glucose that had been stored as glycogen into the blood, and begins converting certain amino acids into glucose. The brain, through direct autonomic nerves to the abdominal organs, enhances all of these activities at the pancreas and liver. The brain also stimulates the adrenal medulla to secrete epinephrine into the blood, and the epinephrine in turn also acts at the liver and pancreas to elevate plasma glucose. Finally, the brain motivates the animal to seek and eat food, thus providing a source of new glucose for the body. These physiological and behavioral responses are well coordinated and can be considered the collective effector mechanism in the negative feedback homeostatic control of plasma glucose.

As a second example, core body temperature is also normally maintained within very narrow limits in mammals. If an intervention imposed on an animal causes core temperature to decrease (i.e., causes hypothermia), an analogous cluster of physiological and behavioral responses is activated that enables the animal to regain normal temperature as rapidly as possible. Hence, any ongoing cooling mechanisms are inhibited (e.g., panting, sweating), warming mechanisms are stimulated (e.g., peripheral vasoconstriction, shivering), and the animal is likely to make consistent behavioral responses (e.g., increasing its general activity, moving into the sunlight; see Gordon, 1993).

We emphasize here two important aspects of these systems. The first concerns the parameter that is key to the regulatory process. It would be naive to assume that the same parameter conveniently assessed in an experiment (e.g., plasma glucose or body temperature at the tip of a sensor) is the one that is monitored and tied to response systems in the organism. For example, even though the administration of exogenous insulin lowers plasma glucose (the dependent variable) and the activated responses collectively restore plasma glucose to its preinsulin level, it is not necessarily true that plasma glucose per se is continuously monitored by the organism. The proof of this is that the same reflexes triggered when exogenous insulin lowers plasma glucose can also be triggered by drugs that block glucose utilization by tissues and in fact cause extreme hyperglycemia (e.g., 2-deoxyglucose). Hence, the administration of either insulin or 2-deoxyglucose activates a similar spectrum of physiological and behavioral sequelae (reduced lipogenesis, increased glucose secretion into the blood by the liver, and increased food intake), even though one drug is associated with hypoglycemia (insulin) and the other with hyperglycemia (2-deoxyglucose; Grossman, 1986). The point is that the commonality is not necessarily in the experimental dependent variable, but may be in some other implicit effect of the treatment. Both insulin and 2-deoxyglucose reduce the utilization of glucose for energy by tissues (insulin does it by reducing available substrate, and 2-deoxyglucose does it by blocking the process), and it is presumably this change in one or more receptor sites in the body that is key for activating the homeostatic responses.

In an analogous situation, body temperature can be lowered by placing a subject into a cold environment or by administering a drug that causes heat loss in most environments (e.g., ethanol; Kalant & Le, 1984). The responses activated are the same and are caused, presumably, by decreased temperature at some key receptor in the body. Some localized, altered cellular activity is therefore critical, and there may be any number of experimental methods that can accomplish the same change and thereby activate the same homeostatic response.

The second important aspect in a consideration of homeostasis is that everyday examples such as the ones we have used have most often been couched in terms of negative feedback systems. Effector control mechanisms exist that can move the value of a critical parameter in either direction (e.g., can raise or lower plasma glucose or body temperature). Under normal conditions, there is a balance between these opposing actions and little variation in the level of the critical parameter. As challenges or emergencies arise, the control system can be rapidly and effectively recruited to counter changes in the critical parameter, and the system responds and restores the variable to its homeostatically defended level. It is generally held to be a symmetrical process, with extreme increases or decreases in the critical parameter being undesirable, detectable, and rapidly neutralizable. In this model, if the value of a parameter moves outside an acceptable range, it is detected and corrected. However, many theorists suggest that such reliance on reactive measures is inefficient and can be avoided through learning. Hence, if an animal could, through experience, learn to recognize situations in which, with a high degree of reliability, plasma glucose is likely to change, it could make an a priori adjustment in the ongoing homeostatic control system over glucose and successfully minimize or possibly circumvent any change that would otherwise have occurred. Dworkin wrote a compelling review of this concept and applied it to homeostatically regulated systems (Dworkin, 1993).

There is in fact considerable evidence that this type of regulation normally occurs. As an example, when one consumes glucose-containing foods, glucose inevitably increases in the plasma. When the increase of glucose can be predicted, for example by the sweet taste of the food in the mouth or by some arbitrary stimulus reliably associated with elevations of plasma glucose in past experience, animals make homeostatic adjustments to lower levels of plasma glucose. Among other responses, they activate nerves from the brain to the pancreas and secrete insulin. It is important to note that this cephalic response is readily brought under stimulus control when the stimulus reliably predicts a carbohydrate meal (see reviews in Woods, 1991, 1995; Woods & Kulkosky, 1976). The contribution of this anticipatory insulin response to plasma glucose homeostasis becomes most evident when the response is blocked or prevented. In this instance, the same meal that otherwise would cause a modest increase of plasma glucose causes a much greater increase, one reminiscent of what occurs in diabetes (Berthoud, Bereiter, Trimble, Siegel, & Jeanrenaud, 1981; Louis-Sylvestre, 1978).

This kind of control is called *feedforward*, because the clever animal is able to predict when homeostatic perturbations will occur and can initiate anticipatory responses to deal with them. Hence, the magnitude of the disruption is reduced, and when the environment is especially predictable, there may be little observable disruption. Feedforward regulation occurs efficiently in the absence of significant errors, and the feedback arm of the system rarely needs to be activated (Ramsay, Seeley, Bolles, & Woods, 1996).

Drug Conditioning and Tolerance

A key factor in the development of the arguments we make in this chapter is based on a parallel between what happens when food is consumed and when drugs are taken. In both instances, the body is forced to cope with an influx of materials (ingested or otherwise) that interact with and disrupt many of the very systems that are controlled homeostatically. Drug-induced perturbations of any regulated variable can activate corrective responses through negative feedback loops (Dworkin, 1993; Eikelboom & Stewart, 1982; Poulos & Cappell, 1991; Ramsay & Woods, 1997). Furthermore, as these drug-induced disturbances become predictable, animals learn to activate the appropriate corrective responses in anticipation of the upcoming homeostatic challenge, and the result is that the disruption is considerably reduced if not circumvented altogether in a feedforward manner.

Animals to whom the same drug is repeatedly administered often develop tolerance to the drug's disruptive effects, meaning that the initial magnitude of the drug effect becomes substantially lessened over drug administration trials. There is considerable and quite compelling evidence that learning makes a substantial contribution to the tolerance that develops with chronic drug administration (Le, Poulos, & Cappell, 1979; Ramsey & Woods, 1997; Siegel, 1976; Siegel, Hinson, & Krank, 1981; Siegel, Hinson, Krank, & McCully, 1982; Wenger, Tiffany, Bombadier, Nicholls, & Woods, 1981). The concept is that individuals, faced with the imminent presence of a drug and its disruptive effects, make learned anticipatory responses that counter those effects before they develop. The combination of the drug effects and the effects of the learned compensatory responses results in little net perturbation of the variable that would have been affected. In a completely tolerant individual, a drug causes no observable effect, and there is therefore scant evidence that the individual is functioning in a drugged state. Homeostatic disturbances are not observed when the drug is administered because the animals successfully neutralize them with learned responses despite being in a drugged condition.

Drug-tolerant animals are often drug-dependent, that is, they need to receive their drug to avoid the onset of drug withdrawal. Withdrawal is the phenomenon in which drug-dependent (and drug-tolerant) individuals, in the absence of the drug, experience symptoms opposite in nature to the initial effects caused by the drug (Jaffe, 1985). With continued drug administration, dependence need not be evident. An animal's drug dependence may become apparent only when the drug is no longer available, the drug effect is consequently removed, and the symptoms of withdrawal emerge. The learned responses that are responsible for the development of tolerance are also thought to be responsible for the withdrawal associated with drug removal in a drug-dependent individual. This theoretical position, which was articulated by Siegel (1989), posits that the responses that compensate for the homeostatic disruption initially caused by a drug can be learned and thus result in the development of tolerance. Once learned, these compensatory responses prevent the homeostatic disturbances caused by the drug, and the animal functions in a drug-compensated, or drug-dependent, state. It also is possible to elicit the learned compensatory responses when the drug is not taken. If a learned compensatory response is made and no drug effect occurs, withdrawal-like effects are observed, and these can be as severe as the initial drug effect but in the opposite direction. Like other learned responses, these compensatory responses can be extinguished. Therefore, animals can return to homeostatic regulation in a drug-free state following a period of dysregulation associated with withdrawal.

The hypothermic effects of ethanol serve to illustrate these points (see Le et al., 1979; Mansfield & Cunningham, 1980; Ramsey & Woods, 1997; Woods, 1991, for specifics). Ethanol initially causes hypothermia, and with repeated administrations, its hypothermic effects become significantly attenuated (i.e., tolerance develops). The tolerance has been found to be situation-specific, and a withdrawal-like hyperthermic conditioned response can be elicited from these tolerant animals if the cue predicting ethanol administration is provided in the absence of the expected drug effect. Furthermore, this learned hyperthermic response extinguishes when the predictive relationship between the drug cue and the effect of ethanol no longer exists. Hence, both tolerance and dependence readily develop to the hypothermic effect of ethanol, and learning is a primary mechanism for both.

In summary, when initially administered, drugs disrupt important parameters that are normally defended by homeostatic control systems. If drug administration is repeated and predictable, animals learn to activate appropriate homeostatic responses in anticipation of taking the drug and hence neutralize the drug's effects. This is advantageous because the animal is able to function well (in a homeostatic sense) in spite of being in a drugged state. If the drug is not taken and the learned homeostatic response is elicited, there may be perturbations that are opposite in direction to the effects of the drug, resulting in the syndrome called withdrawal.

Animals can be considered to be dependent on food in a way that is analogous to their dependence on a drug; we have reviewed this position elsewhere (Ramsay et al., 1996; Woods, 1991; Woods & Strubbe, 1994). Like drug taking, the act of ingesting food confronts the regulatory mechanisms of the internal milieu with many homeostatically disruptive challenges. As an example, ingested carbohydrates threaten the carefully regulated level of plasma glucose. As we discussed previously, the animal easily copes with this because it is equipped with a sophisticated homeostatic control system to counter perturbations of plasma glucose. The animal anticipates meal-related perturbations of plasma glucose and makes learned anticipatory responses (e.g., increasing cephalic insulin) to minimize the perturbations. Indeed, animals can be considered to be operating in a food-dependent state that is analogous to a drug-dependent state. It would be easy to overlook the commonality of these situations because, unlike what occurs with chronic drug taking, it makes teleological sense that animals are evolutionarily prepared to cope with the everyday consequences of eating. A critical question concerns the nature of the mechanisms or strategies animals use to deal with these ingestive challenges to homeostasis. We believe that just as learning plays a crucial role in drug tolerance and dependence, it plays an essential role in the ingestion of food.

Homeostasis and Food Intake

Eating, especially by omnivores such as rats and humans, can be considered an effector response in the homeostatic control of plasma glucose (or of glucose utilization in the brain or elsewhere). However, application of a strict negative feedback model creates problems of interpretation. The seeking, consumption, digestion, and absorption of foods, even if pure glucose were to be consumed, are far too slow to be of practical help in alleviating reduced glucose metabolism when exogenous insulin or 2-deoxyglucose has been administered. It seems far more parsimonious to explain the increased eating as providing glucose for future needs that may arise. In this interpretation, the rapidly elicited autonomic and hormonal responses to insulin or 2-deoxyglucose administration might be considered to be working in a negative feedback manner, because they act within a reasonably short time frame to correct a detected "error" of glucose utilization. The behavioral response of eating, on the other hand, has a much longer time constant pertinent to plasma glucose and probably does not ameliorate the acute perturbation. In support of this view, plasma glucose eventually returns to normal whether food is eaten or not. In fact, if insulin is administered to an animal and no food is available for up to 6 hours, every measurable parameter of glucose and its utilization is corrected to normal. If food is then made available, the animal eats the same increment of food as it would have several hours previously (Ritter, Bellin, & Pelzer, 1981). It is almost as if the animal has a memory for the physiological perturbation and acts on it behaviorally when given the chance, even though acute needs are long since past. The point is that it is difficult to reconcile the temporal parameters of meals with the immediate needs for glucose. Hence, negative feedback models that posit the activation of a behavioral response that "corrects" a deviation of a parameter from normal cannot easily explain what has been called *glucostatic eating*. Note that this position acknowledges a strict negative feedback control of glucose parameters but that eating per se is not among the effector mechanisms.

To conceptualize eating as a behavior that serves a negative feedback role, it may be instructive to consider its other functions. Eating, after all, is a complex behavior, one that fulfills many needs in addition to supplying or replenishing glucose. It provides appropriate micronutrients (vitamins and minerals) and macronutrients (fats, carbohydrates, and proteins), and it provides osmoles and electrolytes as well. At a different level of analysis, eating provides all of the calories that enter the body. Eating might therefore be considered a negative feedback response to a perceived deficit of total body energy, which is mainly fat. In this schema, if an animal expends energy but does not eat for some period of time, it relies to an ever-increasing extent on the mobilization of stored energy from its fat stores.

If the amount of fat kept in storage is monitored, and if there is an "ideal" amount of stored fat in a homeostatic sense, it would be reasonable to consider eating the primary effector mechanism that is activated whenever fat stores fall below some threshold amount. Although it may not function to maintain ongoing plasma glucose levels, eating might serve to replenish depleted adipose stores. This might be an example of a homeostatic negative feedback system, one with a much longer time constant than required for the correction of disturbances of glucose metabolism.

There is compelling evidence to support this point of view. Evidence is reviewed in great detail elsewhere (Bray, 1976; Kaiyala, Woods, & Schwartz, 1995; Stallone & Stunkard, 1991), that animals behave as if adiposity were regulated homeostatically. Mammals tend to maintain relatively constant amounts of body fat as adults. When they are forced to lose fat (through forced food restriction, voluntary dieting, or even surgical lipectomy) and given the opportunity to eat freely, they tend to eat greater amounts than normal and to regain lost fat with a high degree of precision. Likewise, if animals are forced to consume excess food, they become fatter, and when given the opportunity, reduce their food intake and lose the fat they have gained. In both instances, the corrective responses, hyperphagia or hypophagia, may persist for days or weeks depending on the severity of the imposed change in the system. Such a time constant is considerably longer than that of the homeostatic systems generally considered by Bernard (1878) or Cannon (1932), but the overall outcome is consistent.

It is instructive to consider the physiology of the regulatory system that "controls" adiposity. If adiposity is indeed regulated homeostatically, the implication is that it is continuously monitored and the amount of food eaten is a major effector system in its regulation. Furthermore, the detection of adiposity must either occur within the brain or be relayed to the brain, and it must be interconnected with systems that influence feeding. One problem immediately arises. The fat mass is dispersed throughout the body. All mammals possess fat pads in the subcutaneous space as well as in the abdominal cavity, and most have additional pads elsewhere (e.g., the large epididymal fat pad in male rats). Hence, either (a) one fat pad serves as a bellwether for the rest and its size is continuously monitored by the brain; (b) all fat pads are simultaneously monitored, with the information being accumulated and integrated by the brain; or (c) there is a parameter highly correlated with total fat mass that is in turn accessible to and detectable by the brain. There is no compelling evidence that afferent nerves pass to the brain from each fat depot in the body, and no individual fat pad has been identified that has the requisite properties to serve as a bellwether (although Nicolaidis [1988] suggested that there is a fat "homunculus" in the brain whose size and activity reflect total body stores). On the other hand, there is compelling evidence that the level of one or more circulating factors is highly correlated with total body adiposity and influences food intake at the level of the brain.

The circulating factor that best meets all of these criteria is insulin. As we discussed previously, insulin is intimately involved in the regulation of plasma glucose, and insulin secretion from the pancreas and levels in the circulation are proportional to adiposity (Woods, Decke, & Vasselli, 1974). In humans and other mammals, higher levels of adipose tissue are associated with higher levels of insulin. Insulin crosses the blood–brain barrier from the circulation by way of a saturable, receptor-mediated process (Baura et al., 1993), and there are insulin receptors in many regions of the brain that are involved in the regulation of food intake (Baskin, Wilcox, Figlewicz, & Dorsa, 1988). These factors make insulin an obvious candidate to provide homeostatic feedback to the central nervous system about the state of peripheral fat stores.

Evidence that insulin acts within the brain as a negative feedback signal comes from numerous experiments indicating that when the level or action of insulin within the central nervous system is manipulated, there are predictable changes in food intake and body weight. When exogenous insulin is infused into the hypothalamus (MacGowan, Andrews, Kelly, & Grossman, 1990) or into the cerebral ventricular system of rats, baboons, or other mammals, there is a dose-dependent reduction of food intake and body weight (Brief & Davis, 1984; Riedy, Chavez, Figlewicz, & Woods, 1995; Woods, 1995; Woods, Stein, McKay, & Parte, 1979) that cannot be attributed to nonspecific effects such as illness or behavioral incapacitation (Chavez, Kaiyala, Madden, Schwartz, & Woods, 1995; Chavez, Seeley, & Woods, 1995). The infusion of insulin antibodies directly into the hypothalamus elicits increased food intake and body weight (MacGowan, Andrews, & Grossman, 1992), providing strong evidence that endogenous insulin normally reduces these parameters. It is consistent with this conclusion that when endogenous insulin is low (e.g., during starvation or untreated diabetes mellitus), there is a resultant robust increase of food intake that can be ameliorated by infusing insulin directly into the brain (Kaiyala et al., 1995; Woods, 1995). Collectively, these results strongly implicate endogenous insulin as a signal that reflects peripheral adipose stores and that modifies food intake and body weight–adiposity in a homeostatic manner.

Insulin is probably not unique in this regard. A second candidate for a circulating factor that homeostatically regulates adipose stores is the recently identified protein hormone that is synthesized in and secreted from adipose cells (Zhang et al., 1994). The protein, called "Ob" and recently dubbed "leptin," was identified in mice. Mice that make a mutant and evidently inactive form of leptin (ob/ob mice) have profound hyperphagia and morbid obesity compared to littermates that secrete the normal compound. The gene for Ob is expressed primarily in adipose tissue, and in normal animals and humans, leptin is secreted in proportion to the degree of stored fat. Several groups have found that the elevated food intake, adiposity, and body weight of ob/ob mice can be substantially reduced by the administration of Ob either systemically or directly into the brain (Campfield, Smith, Guisez, Deves, & Burn, 1995; Halaas et al., 1995; Pelleymounter et al., 1995). The presumption is that leptin provides a negative feedback signal to the central nervous system indicating the degree of energy stores in adipose tissue and influences food intake accordingly, a situation that is analogous to the effects of insulin.

The important point from this discussion is that adiposity appears to be regulated, circulating factors are implicated, and the overall system can be considered homeostatic. A critical question is whether this apparent homeostatic control over adiposity necessarily implies the existence of an ongoing negative feedback mechanism. If glucose is considered to be the pivotal parameter controlled by feeding, a strict negative feedback interpretation, especially one including altered food intake as the primary effector mechanism, is less consistent with the data than some sort of feedforward system in which eating provides the stores of glucose-yielding compounds that are then available as needed. In this schema, animals would eat the amounts of food (and perhaps types of foods as well) that previously were found to circumvent most effectively extreme reductions of available glucose. It is possible that, as occurs with glucose homeostasis, the amount of food that animals consume in a meal is not directly aimed at addressing ongoing energy expenditure, as a negative feedback model would dictate. Perhaps animals learn that eating a certain amount will lessen the probability that severe depletions of stored fat will occur, such that their intake is better described as a feedforward behavior. In such a schema, the amount of fat stored could be genetically determined, with decrements based on energy expenditure and increments based on a feedforward stocking of stores.

Learning and Ingestion

The position that we take in this chapter is that learning influences all aspects of food intake. As we discussed previously, the maintenance of a particular level of adiposity might be construed as the animal's having learned what amount of food best prevents depletions of a genetically determined basal amount of stored fat. Feedforward control systems, discussed in several excellent recent reviews, are based on experience and should be considered a form of learning (Dworkin, 1993; Houk, 1988; Weingarten, 1990). There are other, far more obvious, instances in which learning interacts with food intake. We only highlight them here and refer the reader to more thorough reviews.

Food Selection

Robert Bolles was a pioneer in the investigation of the associative factors that determine how animals come to prefer or avoid particular foods (e.g., Bolles, 1980); several other chapters in this volume, written by his students and collaborators, attest to this accomplishment. The crux of the argument is that successful omnivores are able to select adequate calories, adequate blends of macronutrients, adequate micronutrients, and adequate water from whatever choices are available. It is axiomatic that when animals have been deprived of food for a period of time and subsequently are allowed to feed freely, they demonstrate hyperphagia until lost calories and weight are compensated for. Curt Richter's work is legendary for demonstrating that when any of a number of physiological interventions is made, some omnivores (rats, in his experiments) alter their dietary choices to correct any consequent perturbations. For example, animals lacking the adrenal hormone aldosterone lose sodium in the urine; hence, adrenalectomized animals behaviorally compensate by increasing their consumption of sodium (Richter, 1936). Sodium-deficient animals seek sodium-rich foods, recognize them when they find them, and ingest them in quantities necessary to correct their deficit. Examples such as this conveniently fit the negative feedback model suggested by Bernard.

However, few corrective behaviors are as automatic as that for sodium. If an animal is rendered deficient in certain vitamins, there is not an automatic tendency to seek and consume foods that contain the vitamin. In an innovative series of experiments, Rogers and Rozin (1966) found that when animals consume foods that correct the symptoms of vitamin deficiency, they learn to eat those foods, and they associate the flavor of the food with recovery from the symptoms of vitamin deficiency. Hence, a learned association that develops between a flavor and recovery from illness is a major determinant of food choice in these animals.

Analogous to this discovery, and covered in far greater detail in other chapters in this volume, is the ease with which animals associate flavors with the onset of illness. The pioneering work of John Garcia and the rich literature that followed from it, combined with the work of Rozin and others, have allowed the strong conclusion that animals readily learn to consume flavors that are associated with reduced illness and to avoid flavors that are associated with increased illness.

Animals also readily learn to associate particular flavors with receiving calories. Fedorchak and Mehiel, who worked in Bolles's laboratory, found that rats learn to prefer flavors associated with receiving carbohydrates (Fedorchak & Bolles, 1987; Mehiel & Bolles, 1984). This finding has been replicated and expanded by Sclafani and his colleagues, who have found that fats can also serve as reinforcers for this kind of learning (Sclafani, 1991). Galef and his colleagues have found that learning which foods to avoid and which to eat occurs early in the life of rats and is a primary determinant of food choice (Galef, 1993). The point is that learning which foods to eat is based on the consequences of eating those foods, and the stimuli that guide the animals' behavior, rather than being calories or specific needed micronutrients, are flavors or other arbitrary sensory attributes.

Meal Patterning and Meal Size

Several examples can be cited to demonstrate that learning plays a fundamental role in the patterning of food intake. One of the earliest demonstrations came from Jacques Le Magnen (1959). He maintained rats on a schedule in which they had three 1-hour intervals when food was available each day. The rats easily adapted to this feeding schedule and ate sufficient food over the three meals to maintain body weight by consuming about the same amount of food at each meal. When the middle meal was eliminated and the animals had only two opportunities to feed per day, their strategy changed. For the first few days, the animals increased the size of the "dinner" meal. However, over the next few days, the first meal of the day (i.e., the "breakfast" meal) became larger and larger, and the dinner declined in size. Eventually, the animals compensated for the lost "lunch" by consuming very large breakfasts and normal dinners. Because weight was maintained throughout but the pattern changed, Le Magnen suggested that learning was responsible.

When animals are allowed to feed freely, they adopt species-specific patterns of eating. Nocturnal animals, such as rats, consume most of their daily food during the night (dark portion of the light–dark cycle), and diurnal animals eat mainly during the day. Although rats eat as many as 10 or more meals each day, the two largest meals occur in association with the twice-daily changing of the lights (i.e., at the time of lights-on and lights-off; Kersten, Strubbe, & Spiteri, 1980). Because rats readily learn the timing of lights on a 24-hour clock, Woods and Strubbe (1994) argued that the predictability of the light changes enables animals to make sufficient anticipatory responses to enable the consumption of particularly large meals at that time; that is, when the exact time of a meal is known, compensatory responses can be elicited to render the animal more tolerant at that time. One consequence is that it can consume more food without suffering severe perturbations of critical systems. Premeal changes of plasma glucose, metabolic rate, and body temperature can all be interpreted as serving this function (see Woods & Strubbe, 1994).

There is a subtle but important implication of the hypothesis that successfully anticipating when a meal will occur allows an animal to consume a larger meal. The implication is that the homeostatic perturbations caused by ingested food can be of sufficient magnitude or severity that they normally limit meal size. This argument has been developed in detail elsewhere (Woods, 1991; Woods & Strubbe, 1994); it is instructive to consider that, given a choice, animals eat only small meals except when the timing is most predictable and that when forced to eat their daily food in a small number of regularly scheduled large meals, several days are required before the large meals are consumed. It is as if the animals must learn responses to prepare the body to cope with the large amount of food entering the body at one time.

When diets are constant (such as a rat eating only pelleted chow) or at least predictable, animals presumably learn to gauge how much can be safely consumed at one time in a homeostatic sense. Because food supplies and content are often more variable in the real world than in the laboratory, omnivores have a sophisticated food-analyzing system, including the olfactory and gustatory organs and the chemosensory and other receptors lining the gastrointestinal tract. This system provides sensory information concerning what has been consumed and is important in controlling the progress of digestion. Because, as a rule, meals are completed long before most of the ingested components enter the blood, plasma levels of glucose or other nutrients are unlikely to be critical signals that cause satiety. Animals clearly use other, earlier events in the meal, and it is reasonable to assume that many of these are based on the same receptor system that influences digestion. For example, when the diet is constant and predictable, stomach volume during a meal is a reliable correlate of how many calories have been consumed. Hence, the clever animal could monitor its stomach volume and thereby estimate reasonably well how much digested food will enter the blood over the next hour or so. Likewise, the responses of chemosensors in the stomach and upper intestine could be monitored to provide an indication of the type and amount of specific macronutrients consumed, and so on.

There is evidence that at least some of these gastrointestinal signals are in fact monitored and contribute to the determination of meal size, and there is growing evidence that the information they provide is at least partly based on learning. Sham feeding occurs when the food animals consume is removed from the stomach during a meal. The first time animals sham feed, they consume more food than they would if they were eating normally, and over days, the amount consumed in one sham-feeding meal increases considerably. In an innovative series of experiments, Davis and Smith (1990) found that signals present in the real-feeding situation and absent in the sham-feeding situation are inhibitory in nature; that is, these signals, in the presence of the animal consumes smaller meals, and this response to these signals extinguishes over sham-feeding trials. The amount of food entering the stomach (or passing through the mouth) is clearly one possible cue animals use in the real-feeding situation, such that when a certain level of consumption is attained, eating stops. In the sham-feeding situation, when the previous association between amount eaten and subsequent absorption of a particular quantity of nutrients was broken, the control over amount eaten was lost. The animals ate more.

It has been repeatedly observed that animals respond to certain gastrointestinal peptides secreted during meals. In particular, animals eat less food when the levels of the duodenal peptide cholecystokinin (CCK) are increased (Gibbs, Young, & Smith, 1973; Smith & Gibbs, 1992; Woods & Gibbs, 1989). It is not difficult to imagine that over a lifetime of eating the same diet, a certain level of CCK becomes associated with a particular quantity of subsequently absorbed nutrients entering the blood. Hence, the clever animal could monitor the CCK levels at some receptor site and estimate reliably how much has been eaten. When exogenous CCK is given, animals respond by stopping a meal prematurely; likewise, when endogenous CCK is masked with the administration of antagonists, animals eat larger than normal meals (see Smith & Gibbs, 1992). That the response to CCK is not fixed was recently suggested by an experiment in which the predictive value of CCK was reliably changed over several days. In that experiment, the ability of CCK to control meal size disappeared over trials (Goodison & Siegel, 1995).

In short, many aspects of meals are governed by cues associated with past experience with specific foods, including the timing, size, and particular food selected. Animals behave in ways that ensure adequate intake while causing the least disruption to the body. This is a primary point we wish to make: The body runs most efficiently when disruptions or errors are minimized or prevented. Although there are protective systems always on the alert to detect and correct errors when they occur, it is maladaptive to rely on them for normal functioning. We believe that the most well-adapted individual anticipates perfectly through learning what and how much will be consumed, as well as when the food will be consumed, and then prepares the body to deal with that food so that minimal if any disruptions ever occur.[2]

References

Baskin, D. G., Wilcox, B. J., Figlewicz, D. P., & Dorsa, D. M. (1988). Insulin and insulin-like growth factors in the CNS. *Trends in Neuroscience, 11,* 107–111.

Baura, G., Foster, D., Porte, D., Jr., Kahn, S. E., Bergman, R. N., Cobelli, C., & Schwartz, M. W. (1993). Saturable transport of insulin from plasma into the central nervous system of dogs in vivo: A mechanism for regulated insulin delivery to the brain. *Journal of Clinical Investigation, 92,* 1824–1830.

Bernard, C. (1878). *Lecons sur les phenomenes de la vie communs aux animaux et aux vegetaux.* Paris: J. B. Bailliere.

Berthoud, H. R., Bereiter, D. A., Trimble, E. R., Siegel, E. G., & Jeanrenaud, B. (1981). Cephalic phase, reflex insulin secretion. *Diabetologia, 30,* 393–401.

Bolles, R. C. (1975). *Theory of motivation* (2nd ed.). New York: Harper & Row.

Bolles, R. C. (1979). *Learning theory* (2nd ed.). New York: Holt, Rinehart & Winston.

Bolles, R. C. (1980). Some functionalist thoughts about regulation. In S. M. Toates & T. R. Halliday (Eds.), *Analysis of motivational processes* (pp. 63–75). London: Academic Press.

Bolles, R. C. (1993). *The story of psychology: A thematic history.* Pacific Grove, CA: Brooks/Cole.

Bray, G. A. (1976). *The obese patient.* Philadelphia: Saunders.

Brief, D. J., & Davis, J. D. (1984). Reduction of food intake and body weight by chronic intraventricular insulin infusion. *Brain Research Bulletin, 12,* 571–575.

---

[2]When going through Bob's lab recently, I (S. Woods) uncovered a volleyball, a reminder of an endearing attribute of Bob Bolles that was well known to his many colleagues and friends, namely, a tremendous enthusiasm for all that he did. In the late 1970s and early 1980s, Bob had several graduate students and a very active lab, as I did. Our offices and labs were adjacent to one another in Guthrie Hall at the University of Washington, and one day, seemingly out of the blue, the Bolles lab challenged the Woods lab to a game of volleyball, the winners to have bragging rights for all time (as well as a certain volume of alcohol). Because I had several graduate students who prided themselves on their jocklike qualities, and because Bob's students seemed to be out of shape and to spend their lives in the lab, I gladly accepted. When the big day came and the participants were warming up, my students were planning strategies and generally looking very confident, whereas Bob's students appeared to be looking up the rules and figuring out how the game is played. Because I had cleverly gotten Bob to agree that as many students as showed up could take the court, and since six of my students were there as opposed to four of Bob's, I gladly agreed to sweeten the pot just before the start. At the instant the ball was to be put in play, Bob's students ripped off their (scruffy-looking) warmups to reveal sharp outfits including T-shirts saying "Bollesians." To make a long story short, Bob's team had in fact been practicing for weeks, were in excellent shape, and whipped our butts. Bob just stood there and smiled throughout. (The members of that team were Mark Bouton, Mike Fanselow, Steve Hirsch, and Ron Sigmundi.)

Campfield, L. A., Smith, F. J., Guisez, Y., Devos, R., & Burn, P. (1995). Recombinant mouse OB protein: Evidence for a peripheral signal linking adiposity and central neural networks. *Science, 269,* 546–549.

Cannon, W. B. (1932). *The wisdom of the body.* New York: Norton.

Chavez, M., Kaiyala, K., Madden, L. J., Schwartz, M. W., & Woods, S. C. (1995). Intraventricular insulin and the level of maintained body weight in rats. *Behavioral Neuroscience, 109,* 528–531.

Chavez, M., Seeley, R. J., & Woods, S. C. (1995). A comparison between the effects of intraventricular insulin and intraperitoneal LiCl on three measures sensitive to emetic agents. *Behavioral Neuroscience, 109,* 547–550.

Davis, J. D., & Smith, G. P. (1990). Learning to sham feed: Behavioral adjustments to loss of physiological postingestional stimuli. *American Journal of Physiology, 259,* R1228–R1235.

Dworkin, B. R. (1993). *Learning and physiological regulation.* Chicago: University of Chicago Press.

Eikelboom, R., & Stewart, J. (1982). The conditioning of drug-induced physiological responses. *Psychological Review, 89,* 507–528.

Fedorchak, P. M., & Bolles, R. C. (1987). Hunger enhances the expression of calorie- but not taste-mediated conditioned flavor preferences. *Journal of Experimental Psychology: Animal Behavior Processes, 13,* 73–79.

Galef, B. G. (1993). Functions of social learning about food: A causal analysis of effects of diet novelty on preference transmission. *Animal Behaviour, 46,* 257–265.

Gibbs, J., Young, R. C., & Smith, G. P. (1973). Cholecystokinin decreases food intake in rats. *Journal of Comparative and Physiological Psychology, 84,* 488–495.

Goodison, T., & Siegel, S. (1995). Learning and tolerance to the intake suppressive effect of cholecystokinin in rats. *Behavioral Neuroscience, 109,* 62–70.

Gordon, C. J. (1993). *Temperature regulation in laboratory rodents.* New York: Cambridge University Press.

Grossman, S. P. (1986). The role of glucose, insulin and glucagon in the regulation of food intake and body weight. *Neuroscience & Biobehavioral Reviews, 10,* 295–315.

Halaas, J. L., Gajiwala, K. S., Maffei, M., Cohen, S. L., Chait, B. T., Rabinwitz, D., Lallone, R. L., Burley, S. K., & Friedman, J. M. (1995). Weight reducing effects of the plasma protein encoded by the obese gene. *Science, 269,* 543–546.

Houk, J. C. (1988). Control strategies in physiological systems. *FASEB Journal, 2,* 97–107.

Jaffe, J. H. (1985). Drug addiction and drug abuse. In A. G. Gilman, L. S. Goodman, & A. Gilman (Eds.), *The pharmacological basis of therapeutics* (7th ed., pp. 532–581). New York: Macmillan.

Kaiyala, K. J., Woods, S. C., & Schwartz, M. W. (1995). New model for the regulation of energy balance and adiposity by the central nervous system. *American Journal of Clinical Nutrition, 62*(Suppl.), 11235–11345.

Kalant, H., & Le, A. D. (1984). Effects of ethanol on thermoregulation. *Pharmacology and Therapeutics, 23,* 313–364.

Kersten, A., Strubbe, J. H., & Spiteri, N. J. (1980). Meal patterning of rats with changes in day length and food availability. *Physiology & Behavior, 25,* 953–958.

Le, A. D., Poulos, C. X., & Cappell, H. (1979). Conditioned tolerance to the hypothermic effect of ethyl alcohol, *Science, 206,* 1109–1110.

Le Magnen, J. (1959). Etude d'un phenomene d'appetit provisionnel [Study of the phenomenon of provisional appetite]. *Comptes Rendus de l'Academie des Sciences (Paris), 249,* 2400–2402.

Louis-Sylvestre, J. (1978). Feeding and metabolic patterns in rats with truncular vagotomy or with transplanted B cells. *American Journal of Physiology, 235,* E119–E125.

MacGowan, M. K., Andrews, K. M., & Grossman, S. P. (1992). Chronic intrahypothalamic infusions of insulin or insulin antibodies alter body weight and food intake in the rat. *Physiology & Behavior, 51,* 753–766.

MacGowan, M. K., Andrews, K. M., Kelly, J., & Grossman, S. P. (1990). Effects of chronic intrahypothalamic infusion of insulin on food intake and diurnal meal patterning in the rat. *Behavioral Neuroscience, 104,* 373–385.

Mansfield, J. G., & Cunningham, C. L. (1980). Conditioning and extinction of tolerance to the hypothermic effect of ethanol in rats. *Journal of Comparative and Physiological Psychology, 94,* 962–969.

Mehiel, R., & Bolles, R. C. (1984). Learned flavor preferences based on caloric outcome. *Animal Learning and Behavior, 12,* 421–427.

Nicolaidis, S. (1988). Physiology of food intake and regulation of body weight. *Annals of Endocrinology (Paris), 49,* 89–97.

Pelleymounter, M. A., Cullen, M. J., Baker, M. B., Hecht, R., Winters, D., Boone, T., & Collins, F. (1995). Effects of the obese gene product on body weight regulation in ob/ob mice. *Science, 269,* 540–543.

Poulos, C. X., & Cappell, H. (1991). Homeostatic theory of drug tolerance: A general model of physiological adaptation. *Psychological Review, 98,* 390–408.

Ramsay, D. S., Seeley, R. J., Bolles, R. C., & Woods, S. C. (1996). Ingestive homeostasis: The primacy of learning. In E. Capaldi & T. Powley (Eds.), *Why we eat what we eat* (pp. 1–9). Washington, DC: American Psychological Association.

Ramsay, D. S., & Woods, S. C. (1997). Biological consequences of drug administration: Implications for acute and chronic tolerance. *Psychological Review, 104,* 170–193.

Richter, C. P. (1936). Increased salt appetite in adrenalectomized rats. *American Journal of Physiology, 115,* 155–161.

Riedy, C. A., Chavez, M., Figlewicz, D. P., & Woods, S. C. (1995). Central insulin enhances sensitivity to cholecystokinin. *Physiology & Behavior, 58,* 755–760.

Ritter, S., Bellin, S. I., & Pelzer, N. L. (1981). The role of gustatory and postingestive signals in the termination of delayed glucoprivic feeding and hypothalamic norepinephrine turnover. *Journal of Neuroscience, 1,* 1354–1360.

Rogers, W., & Rozin, P. (1966). Novel food preferences in thiamine-deficient rats. *Journal of Comparative and Physiological Psychology, 61,* 1–4.

Sclafani, A. (1991). Conditioned food preferences. *Bulletin of the Psychonomic Society, 29,* 256–260.

Siegel, S. (1976). Morphine analgesic tolerance: Its situation specificity supports a Pavlovian conditioning model. *Science, 193,* 323–325.

Siegel, S. (1989). Classical conditioning and opiate tolerance and withdrawal. In D. J. K. Balfour (ed.), *International encyclopedia of pharmacology and therapeutics: Section 130. Psychotropic drugs of abuse* (pp. 59–85). New York: Pergamon Press.

Siegel, S., Hinson, R. E., & Krank, M. D. (1981). Morphine-induced attenuation of morphine tolerance. *Science, 212,* 1533–1534.

Siegel, S., Hinson, R. E., Krank, M. D., & McCully, J. (1982). Heroin "overdose" death: The contribution of drug-associated environmental cues. *Science, 216,* 436–437.

Smith, G. P., & Gibbs, J. (1992). The development and proof of the CCK hypothesis of satiety. In C. T. Dourish, S. J. Cooper, S. D. Iversen, & L. L. Iversen (Eds.), *Multiple cholecystokinin receptors in the CNS* (pp. 166–182). Oxford, England: Oxford University Press.

Stallone, D. D., & Stunkard, A. J. (1991). The regulation of body weight: Evidence and clinical implications. *Annals of Behavioral Medicine, 13,* 220–230.

Weingarten, H. P. (1990). Learning, homeostasis, and the control of feeding behavior. In E. D. Capaldi & T. L. Powley (Eds.), *Taste, experience, and feeding* (pp. 14–27). Washington, DC: American Psychological Association.

Wenger, J. R., Tiffany, T. M., Bombadier, C., Nicholls, K., & Woods, S. C. (1981). Ethanol tolerance in the rat is learned. *Science, 213,* 575–577.

Woods, S. C. (1991). The eating paradox: How we tolerate food. *Psychological Review, 98,* 488–505.

Woods, S. C. (1995). Insulin and the brain: A mutual dependency. In S. Fluharty (Ed.), *Progress in psychobiology and physiological psychology* (Vol. 16, pp. 53–81). New York: Academic Press.

Woods, S. C., Decke, E., & Vasselli, J. R. (1974). Metabolic hormones and regulation of body weight. *Psychological Review, 81,* 26–43.

Woods, S. C., & Gibbs, J. (1989). The regulation of food intake by peptides. *Annals of the New York Academy of Sciences, 575,* 236–243.

Woods, S. C., & Kulkosky, P. J. (1976). Classically conditioned changes of blood glucose level. *Psychosomatic Medicine, 38,* 201–219.

Woods, S. C., Stein, L. J., McKay, L. D., & Porte, D., Jr. (1979). Chronic intracerebroventricular infusion of insulin reduces food intake and body weight of baboons. *Nature, 282,* 503–505.

Woods, S. C., & Strubbe, J. H. (1994). The psychobiology of meals. *Psychonomic Bulletin & Review, 2,* 141–155.

Woods, S. C., Taborsky, G. J., Jr., & Porte, D., Jr. (1986). CNS control of nutrient homeostasis. In F. Bloom (Ed.), *Handbook of physiology. Section 1. The nervous system: Vol. 4, Intrinsic regulatory systems of the brain* (pp. 365–411). Bethesda, MD: American Physiological Society.

6

Motivation as a Function of Animal Versus Experimenter Control

George Collier and Deanne Johnson

For many people, Robert Bolles represented an intellectual node. Each encounter produced a new idea or perspective. He was, in fact, the consummate intellectual: always interested, always critical, always stimulating, and always coming up with the unexpected. When first using Bolles's text to teach a motivation class, the first author was jarred loose from the classical learning and homeostatic models of behavior. Bolles was one of the first to consider species-specific behaviors in conventional laboratory paradigms, and he was willing to consider cognitive models of learning, because of the size of the window of time over which consequences acted, long before these became part of the zeitgeist.

It is presumptuous to write about motivation after Bolles's classic, encyclopedic, and critical books and defining articles on the subject. We wish to consider only one small aspect of this complex topic. In this chapter, we look at the role of the experimental paradigm in generating a model of motivation, that is, how one's concept of motivation may be affected by the paradigm in which one works. We compare the economics of open and closed economies with particular attention to the application of foraging theory to closed economies. In particular, we contrast the "session" and "foraging" paradigms.

The session paradigm has dominated experimentation in animal behavior for pragmatic as well as theoretical reasons (Collier, 1983). In an attempt to mimic the methods of physics, animal psychologists historically reduced their experimental variables to as few as possible and exerted as much control as possible (e.g., Skinner, 1938). This meant forgoing any attempt to mimic, or even consider, the problems presented by an animal's particular niche and thus essentially ignoring evolution. Also, because time, apparatus, and funds were limited, and great inherent variability necessitated using large numbers of subjects for statistical purposes, a paradigm was needed that allowed testing many animals in a "reasonable" period of time. The solution was to deprive animals of a commodity to ensure that they would be active and then have them work for it during

This research and the preparation of this chapter were supported by Grant DK 31016 from the National Institutes of Health to George Collier.

short, daily sessions. The economy in this paradigm is open in the sense that the supply of the commodity is unrelated to the consumer's demand: The animal consumes or uses less of the commodity during the session than it normally uses. Usually, in the case of food or water, supplements are supplied outside the session, although the total may still be less than the normal daily intake. No behavioral strategy of the animal can meet its physiological requirements. This experimental approach characterized both the Pavlovian and Thorndikian paradigms.

The foraging paradigm, on the other hand, is an attempt to simulate the animal's natural habitat. The animal is not deprived and lives in the experimental environment. The economy is closed because all of the animal's intake occurs in the experimental context, and supply is equal to or greater than demand. Additionally, because it is continuously in the experimental environment, the animal controls not only the amount but also the pattern of its intake, that is, the timing of feeding initiation, the size of subsequent bout of intake, bout frequency, bout distribution, and total resource use (Collier, Johnson, Hill, & Kaufman, 1986). Note that the animal in the session paradigm does not have this control because the experimenter determines these parameters. Giving control to the animal enables it to exhibit the full range of its phylogenetically and ontogenetically acquired solutions to the problems at hand. Making supply equal to or greater than demand allows the animal to regulate. We have found that the between-animal variability in this paradigm is relatively low; that is, the forms of the functions obtained are similar, and thus fewer subjects are required. We argue that the factors that motivate the behavior of foraging animals are different from those motivating deprived animals in sessions.

Session Paradigm

In his proto-operant procedure, Thorndike (1911) placed a hungry animal in a latched box and gave it a small bite of food when it escaped (we primarily discuss food, as an exemplar of many commodities or activities that may be used as reinforcers). Escape was first accomplished by "accidental encounters" with the latch. After each escape (trial), the animal was replaced in the box, and the increasing efficiency of and decreasing latency to escape over trials were observed. The animal was deprived of food to increase its activity level and thereby the likelihood of an encounter with the latch. The reinforcements were small and the number of trials was limited to prevent satiation. The nature of the problem (kind of latch); number of trials; length of the intertrial interval; quality, quantity, and timing of reinforcement; amount of food received; and time of occurrence and number of sessions all were controlled by the experimenter. What was left to the animal was random responding, the randomness of which might decrease over time. Such a decrease was regarded as evidence of learning (Thorndike, 1911). Analogous procedures were used in runway and T-maze studies.

Skinner adapted the session paradigm to his "repeating problem box" with two modifications: The behavior studied was reduced to a response that was already high in the animal's repertoire, and control of the inter-trial interval was taken from the experimenter and given to the animal (Skinner, 1932b). Control of the initiation and termination of the session, as well as the size of the contingent reinforcer, was still in the experimenter's hands. The intertrial interval and the increasing efficiency and decreasing latency over sessions were incorporated into one measure—response rate—and this became the currency of the operant and the measure of response strength. Because the problem was simple and the response rudimentary, rate was not an acquisition variable but a measure of performance, and problem solving was no longer a problem.

During the period of the development and refinement of the session paradigm, the Zeitgeist was homeostasis. Bernard (1865/1957) had exposed the conservative strategy of the internal milieu and explored the physiological mechanisms that preserved its constancy. Cannon (1932) added behavior, such as feeding and drinking, to the armamentarium of homeostatic mechanisms, and Richter (1942–1943) expanded the list of homeostatic behaviors, adding nest building, ambient temperature selection, diet selection, and others. The hypothesis that a state of depletion inspired consumption of the deficient commodity and that a state of repletion caused consumption to end—the depletion–repletion hypothesis—became the core concept in most behaviorally and physiologically based theories of motivation and was the basis for the concept of drive (Bolles, 1975; Booth, 1978; Cannon, 1932; Hull, 1943; Richter, 1942–1943; Skinner, 1932a, 1932b; Toates, 1986; Yamamoto & Brobeck, 1965). The induction of a state of depletion, or deprivation, is one of the defining characteristics of the session paradigm. Thorndike used deprivation to increase general activity rather than specifically to induce hunger, but for Hull and others, deprivation was the drive-producing operation and also specified the reinforcer (Hull, 1943), and for Skinner, deprivation was one source of the "dynamic laws of the reflex" (Skinner, 1938).

Time-Since Procedures

Three procedures have been used to induce deprivation. First is the "time-since" operation, in which the time between opportunities to engage in an activity is manipulated by the experimenter. The assumption is that, as the time since the last opportunity to perform an activity increases, the animal's tendency to perform that activity increases (e.g., Lorenz, 1950). Furthermore, the range of activities performed narrows, the intensity of the target activity increases, and the size or duration of bouts of that activity increases. In one example of the time-since procedure, feeding is the restricted activity. The experimenter presents food only for a restricted period each day, at some interval before the experimental session. In early studies of learning, this was the most common method of motivating animals. The increase in activity and the narrowing of the range of activities performed as a function of deprivation made it an attractive procedure.

One popular version of this procedure is to feed or water the animal once per day for an hour. This procedure disrupts the animal's normal patterns of feeding or drinking and has effects beyond increasing the tendency to eat or drink during the session. The initial restriction results in an abrupt decrease in intake and a precipitous fall in body weight (Collier, 1964, 1969; Ehrenfreund, 1959; Kanarek & Collier, 1983). There may be a slow recovery of intake and body weight over time, or the animal may continue to decrease intake, lose weight, and starve to death (Epling & Pierce, 1984; Kanarek & Collier, 1983; Navrick, 1969; Routtenberg & Kuznesof, 1967). This process is accelerated by access to a running wheel. To survive, the animal must reduce the latency to initiate feeding or drinking when an opportunity presents itself and must ingest rapidly and continuously, thereby ingesting more in the time available (Kanarek & Collier, 1983; Stellar & Hill, 1952).

The imperative for rapid consumption is paralleled by increasing rates of any instrumental behavior required for ingestion. However, as we show subsequently, even when there is no restriction on meal duration, rates of responding increase with weight loss. That is, there is a correlation between weight loss and activity that is independent of constraints on session time and intersession interval. Noninstrumental (spontaneous) activity, often measured with a running wheel, also increases with weight loss (Collier, 1969), and if this activity is made contingent on bar pressing, the rate of bar pressing also increases (Collier & Hirsch, 1971; Collier, Hirsch & Leshner, 1972; Marwine & Collier, 1971; Tang & Collier, 1971). This equivalence between feeding activity and spontaneous activity has always been a puzzle and fertile ground for short-lived hypotheses.

Large, rapidly consumed meals present a problem to the animal by taxing the homeostatic functions involved in processing ingested food (Woods, 1991; Woods & Strubbe, 1994); this may account, in part, for the failure of some animals to adapt and eat enough to survive. The likelihood and rate of recovery depend on age and metabolic rate (Rixon & Stevenson, 1957), the pattern of food availability, the quality of the food (e.g., caloric density, whether liquid or solid), and the availability of alternative activities. The availability of a running wheel or treadmill (Routtenberg & Kuznesof, 1967) or a sapid solution (Hamilton, 1971; Navrick, 1969; Sclafani, 1973) reduces the likelihood of the animal's eating enough to survive. If the occurrence of experimenter-determined meals is regular, the animal is more likely to come to "anticipate," both behaviorally and physiologically, the large meals required (Kanarek & Collier, 1983; Woods, 1991; Woods & Strubbe, 1994).

Experimenter-Controlled Weight Loss

Because of the individual differences in the rates of weight loss and recovery as a function of the variables discussed, the time-since procedure lost favor. A second deprivation operation, developed to eliminate this variability, entails experimenter-controlled weight loss. In this case, the daily amount of food is rationed to maintain each animal at a target body weight. The duration of the meal is no longer controlled: The animal eats the ration ad libitum, potentially bypassing the metabolic problems resulting from a large, rapidly consumed meal, and usually consumes all of what is offered. Weight loss is measured by comparison to either the weight of a nonrationed control group or the animal's own weight at the start of rationing (Marwine & Collier, 1971). For individual animals, the correlations between log percent body weight loss and the amount or intensity of activity, spontaneous or instrumental, are again high (> .90), stable, and path-independent (Collier, 1964, 1969; Collier et al., 1972; Collier & Levitsky, 1967; Marwine & Collier, 1971; Tang & Collier, 1971; Figure 1). For these reasons, experimenter-controlled weight loss has been adopted as the preferred method of depriving animals to manipulate their "motivation."

The interpretation of the relationship between body weight loss and activity is not straightforward. A period of adaptation is required before stable behavior is obtained (Collier & Levitsky, 1967; Marwine & Collier, 1971), and there is a threshold effect: Even in active animals, the correlation between activity and weight loss appears only when the animal's weight loss reaches a species- and age-specific criterion (7–10% for rats; Collier, 1964, 1969; Collier et al., 1972; Spence, 1956). Another intriguing finding is that when rationing ends and the animal is allowed unconstrained access to food and water, the correlation between weight loss and activity disappears during the period of weight recovery (Collier, 1964; Marwine & Collier, 1971; Tang & Collier, 1971). Also, there is no correlation between amount of weight loss and amount eaten during recovery (Levitsky, Faust, & Glassman, 1976). Although the function of the weight loss–activity relationship has never been clear, it has not been fertile ground for hypotheses.

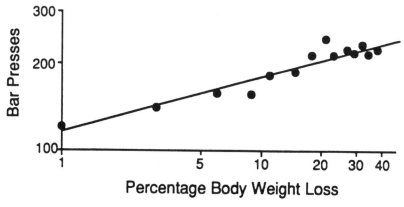

Figure 1.   Rate of bar pressing (bar presses per session) for food pellets by food-deprived rats as a function of percentage of body weight loss. Note log scales. From "Instrumental Performance as a Function of the Energy Content of the Diet," by G. Collier, D. Levitsky, and R. L. Squibb, 1967, *Journal of Comparative and Physiological Psychology, 64,* p. 70. Reprinted with permission.

Disrupting Homeostasis

The third deprivation procedure, pioneered by Richter (1942–1943), uses physiological or dietary interventions to produce perturbations of homeostasis, which again result in an increased tendency to engage in some activity that will mitigate the disturbance. For example, adrenalectomy leads to a failure to retain salt and a subsequent electrolyte imbalance. Adrenalectomized animals have an increased tendency to find, procure, and consume salt (Fitzsimons, 1972; Richter, 1942–1943). On the other hand, excessive salt intake leads to increased consumption of water (Collier, Johnson, & Stanziola, 1991; Fitzsimons, 1972). The success of these experiments led to the hypothesis that similar homeostatic perturbations underlay all three deprivation procedures.

The repletion side of the depletion–repletion hypothesis was supported by the form of the within-session rate-of-intake function, which is exponential with an initial high rate of intake decelerating to an asymptote. A great deal of experimental and intellectual effort has been expended attempting to account for this function (e.g., Collier & Myers, 1961; Davis, 1980; Davis, Collins, & Levine, 1976; Killeen, 1995; Skinner, 1932a; Smith & Gibbs, 1979; Staddon, 1983; Stellar & Hill, 1952). Most accounts include a depletion–repletion-based model in which the rate of intake is some function of the sum of an excitatory signal (which depends on the food's incentive value and the animal's state of depletion) and an inhibitory signal generated by the accumulation of the commodity or some surrogate.

The major effects of all three deprivation operations on behavior during an experimental session are (a) to increase the tendency to gain access to the needed commodity or activity, (b) to decrease the latency to respond when access is made available, (c) to increase rates of both instrumental and ingestive responding, (d) to increase the amount consumed within a bout, and (e) to increase noninstrumental, spontaneous activity. Our question is whether the relationships revealed in the session paradigm, that is, in studies of low-body-weight animals consuming an experimenter-determined amount of food in single, experimenter-instigated meals, are generalizable to animals that are controlling their bout patterns and regulating their intake in more naturalistic environments.

Foraging Paradigm

If the supply of a resource exceeds demand and the resource is continuously available, for example, oxygen and water for an aquatic animal or oxygen for a terrestrial animal, regulation is continuous and intake is proportional (although not always momentarily equal) to expenditure. On the other hand, if the resource is patchily distributed, behavior occurs in bouts. Intake is discontinuous and cumulative over bouts. The immediate relation between expenditure and consumption is broken. Long-term regulation is buffered by short-term storage mechanisms. Each resource must be discovered and identified, procured, and used (handled and ingested). The initial portion of this chain, gaining access to the resource, precedes actual contact with the resource and is conventionally called *foraging*. The terminal portion is called *consumption* or *exploitation*. The animal is faced with a number of decisions: what resource or activity to pursue at any given moment, how often to pursue it, and how much to take or how much time to spend in any patch.

The laboratory foraging paradigm simulates this situation and the problems facing such an animal. Certain procedures are borrowed from earlier research, such as making some activities contingent on operant responding; the operant responses simulate the time and effort an animal must expend foraging for and exploiting resources. The two most important features that distinguish the foraging from the session paradigm are that (a) the foraging paradigm is a closed economy (i.e., supply equals or exceeds demand and therefore the animal is never deprived by the experimenter) and (b) the foraging animal lives continuously, 24 hours per day, in the experimental environment, and therefore the animal (rather than the experimenter) controls the timing, size, frequency, and distribution of bouts of its activities as well as its total daily use of the resources. The "decisions" of the animal with regard to these parameters are the dependent variables in this paradigm.

In early studies of laboratory animals given continuous access to food and water, Richter (1927) observed that feeding by rats occurred in discrete bouts (meals) that varied in size (1–3 g) and occurred on the average nine times per 24 hours. Seventy percent occurred in the dark, but otherwise meals appeared to be randomly distributed. He stated that the discovery of the determinants of the initiation and termination of bouts was the central goal of psychological research (Richter, 1927), a view echoed by Skinner (Skinner, 1932a). The results of his subsequent research on physiological interventions led him to accept the depletion–repletion hypothesis. He argued, as did Le Magnen (1985) and others, that bouts of ingestion were instigated by depletion (perturbations in homeostasis) and were terminated by some surrogate of repletion. Skinner (1938) abandoned this goal when he adopted the session paradigm and focused on his operant analysis. Le Magnen (1969) expressed his model in terms of the prandial correlations between meal size and the length of the intermeal interval, which he came to believe reflected the difference between energy expenditure and energy assimilation (Le Magnen, 1985). Such correlations supported the depletion–repletion hypothesis. However, their generality is controversial (e.g., Campfield & Smith, 1986; Collier, 1982; de Castro, 1975; Panksepp, 1973; Woods, 1991), and evidence suggests that these correlations may depend on housing animals in small cages that restrict both stimulation and the behavioral repertoire (Woods & Kenney, 1979).

Bout Patterns

In the foraging paradigm, the depletion–repletion hypothesis does not explain bout patterns. For example, in a variety of situations and for a num-

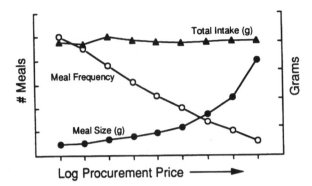

Figure 2. Meal frequency, meal size, and total daily intake as functions of the price of procuring access to food. These curves are generic; they are representative of the patterns seen in all species tested. From "The Time Window of Feeding," by G. Collier and D. F. Johnson, 1990, *Physiology & Behavior, 8,* p. 772. Reprinted with permission.

ber of resources, when the price of access to a resource increases, animals initiate access less often and consume more on each occasion, conserving daily intake while restricting the increase in daily cost (Collier & Johnson, 1990; Collier, Johnson, CyBulski, & McHale, 1990; Figure 2). For example, the completion of a number of bar presses may result in the presentation of a large cup of food from which the rat may eat any amount. The meal continues until the rat does not eat for 10 consecutive minutes and then the cup is withdrawn; the rat may initiate another meal by completing the bar-press requirement again. This *foraging cost* is operationally distinguished from *consumption cost* (e.g., a bar-press price on each 45-mg pellet of food) by the fact that it is paid only at the beginning of each meal (whereas consumption cost is paid throughout the meal) and is unaffected by the amount consumed in the meal (whereas the number of consumption bar presses per meal increases with meal size).

When the foraging cost is high, meal frequency is low and the intermeal interval is long, sometimes 20 hours or more in rats and even longer in other species (Collier & Johnson, 1990). One might consider the animal to be depleted at the end of such an intermeal interval. However, this does not appear to be the case. The increases in rate of responding and activity described previously for deprived animals in the session paradigm are not seen in foraging rats as a function of the length of the intermeal interval (Collier & Johnson, 1990; Mathis, Johnson, & Collier, 1995). That is, foraging rats' rates of responding (once procurement is initiated) and amounts and rates of daily running in an activity wheel are unaffected by the intermeal interval length (Collier et al., 1986; Mathis et al., 1995). Furthermore, there is no correlation between the length of an intermeal interval and the size of the preceding or subsequent meal (Collier & Johnson, 1990). Also, as cost increases, foraging rats actually wait longer after each meal to begin procuring access for the next meal. This delay is part of the strategy for economizing on the cost of feeding, that is, for reducing meal frequency (Collier & Johnson, 1990; Mathis et al., 1995).

The effects of depletion discussed previously for the session paradigm were on consumption within a meal rather than on foraging or gaining access to a resource. One may ask whether there are similar relations in the foraging paradigm between the length of the intermeal interval and within-meal behavior. The answer is *no*. For example, foraging rats do not eat at a faster rate when foraging costs are high and meals are infrequent and large; rather, they consume food at the same rate regardless of foraging cost (Collier et al., 1986). Furthermore, they do not show the typical "satiety function," in which intake slows as the resource is consumed; rather, the rate of intake is constant throughout the intake bout (Figure 3). Parenthetically, consumption rate is not inflexible in the foraging paradigm: Rats do respond faster as consumption cost (e.g., the price of each 45-mg pellet) increases (Collier et al., 1986) and for tastier or more calorically dense food (Johnson, Ackroff, Peters, & Collier, 1986). Taken together, the data for both foraging and consumption make it seem inappropriate to equate the length of the intermeal interval with the animal's state of depletion and difficult to accept the notion that depletion is the stimulus for meal initiation in the foraging paradigm.

Although *average* meal parameters under a given condition are relatively constant from day to day, meal size and intermeal interval are quite variable from meal to meal (Johnson & Collier, 1994). In fact, in agreement with Richter's original opinion (Richter, 1927), the best description seems to be that these variables vary randomly around their averages; there are no interval-to-size, size-to-size, or size-to-interval correlations. Meal size and intermeal interval do not appear to be functions of some momentary state of the animal. The averages vary as functions of the cost and quality of food, ambient temperature, physiological state (e.g., pregnancy, lacta-

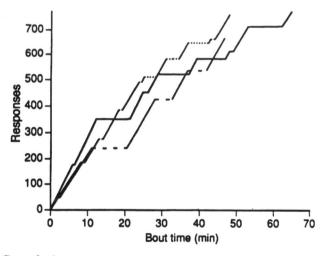

Figure 3. Cumulative responses made in three representative bouts of water consumption by a foraging rat earning sips (20 licks at a drinking spout) at a price of five bar presses per sip (generated from data gathered by Collier, Johnson, Borin, & Mathis, 1994).

tion), circadian rhythms, and so on (Collier & Johnson, 1990). In the foraging paradigm, meal parameters are tools in the service of the optimization of expenditures of time and effort to exploit resources. They do not reflect the cyclic processes of depletion and repletion and do not have the form of the classical discrepancy feedback models, suggesting that the controls of feeding must reside elsewhere. Although depletion is a sufficient condition to induce activity, it is not a necessary condition. The factors that motivate resource exploitation in the natural environment lie outside, rather than inside, the animal.

Regulation

Presumably, the state of the animal (e.g., growth, activity level, pregnancy) and the habitat (e.g., climate) determine the required nutrient intake. Regulation in a patchy environment can be framed in at least two ways. First, animals might cumulate the results of their meals, adjusting subsequent meals to meet their requirements. If this policy were followed, it should be possible to predict the size of the final meal or meals from the cumulative total of the prior ones. We have found no evidence for this strategy. Second, the habitat (resources available and their costs, climate, predation risk, and so on) could determine target values for meal size and intermeal interval that would minimize costs and combine to meet requirements. The actual size of each meal and intermeal interval would form distributions around the target values; total intake (e.g., grams per day) would be the quotient of their means. In this case, we would expect intermeal interval and meal size to be more variable than daily intake. The relations between the distributions of intermeal interval, meal size, and requirements would be phylogenetically determined characteristics of a species' niche. This nonfeedback model of meal parameters states that they are functions of overall requirements rather than momentary ones. The time window of feeding decisions would be long: hours or days depending on the constraints and the species. The unit of analysis in the foraging paradigm is the bout rather than rate.

How does the animal deal with the variations in total intake induced by the probabilistic nature of such a system? We have suggested that one mechanism is adjustments in physiological processes to compensate for any irregularities in intake (Collier, 1986; see also Woods, 1991; Woods & Strubbe, 1994). Similar physiological adjustments, such as in metabolic state or use of fat reserves, are made in response to variations in ambient temperature or activity level. With regard to feeding, this is a role reversal: Intake drives physiology rather than physiology driving intake. We have yet to test this model explicitly. This model of meal patterns clearly does not solve the problem of regulation. What it does suggest is that regulation does not occur at the level of the meal or at the level of meal patterns.

In its natural environment, the animal controls the allocation of its time and effort among activities. It anticipates its requirements and, in meeting them, attempts to maximize benefits relative to costs. It uses physiological processes to compensate for variable inputs. If successful, it is never depleted. We suggest that the processes motivating such an animal are different from those operating in deprived animals. A state of depletion threatens an animal's survival and has immediate behavioral consequences. Failure to optimize the use of time and energy may lead to a reduction in fitness (e.g., reproductive success) and affects longer term behavioral decisions. A nondepleted animal can afford to make behavioral decisions over a longer time window than can a depleted animal. It is inappropriate to generalize from one source of motivation to the other.

References

Bernard, C. (1957). *An introduction to the study of experimental medicine* (H. C. Greene, Trans.). New York: Dover. (Original work published 1865)

Bolles, R. C. (1975). *Theory of motivation* (2nd ed.). New York: Harper & Row.

Booth, D. A. (1978). *Hunger models: Computable theory of feeding control.* New York: Academic Press.

Campfield, L. A., & Smith, F. J. (1986). Functional coupling between transient declines in blood glucose and feeding behavior: Temporal relationships. *Brain Research Bulletin, 17,* 427–433.

Cannon, W. B. (1932). *The wisdom of the body.* New York: Academic Press.

Collier, G. H. (1964). Thirst as a determinant of reinforcement. In M. J. Wayner (Ed.), *Thirst, First International Symposium on Thirst in the Regulation of Body Water* (pp. 287–303). New York: Pergamon Press.

Collier, G. (1969). Body weight loss as a measure of motivation in hunger and thirst. *Annals of the New York Academy of Science, 157,* 594–609.

Collier, G. H. (1982). Determinants of choice. In D. J. Bernstein (Ed.), *1981 Nebraska Symposium on Motivation* (pp. 69–127). Lincoln: University of Nebraska Press.

Collier, G. H. (1983). Life in closed economy: The ecology of learning and motivation. In M. D. Zeiler & P. Harzem (Eds.), *Advances in the analysis of behavior* (Vol. 3, pp. 223–274). Chichester, England: Wiley.

Collier, G. (1986). The dialogue between the house economist and the resident physiologist. *Nutrition and Behavior, 3,* 9–26.

Collier, G., & Hirsch, E. (1971). Reinforcing properties of spontaneous activity in the rat. *Journal of Comparative and Physiological Psychology, 77,* 155–160.

Collier, G., Hirsch, E., & Leshner, A. I. (1972). The metabolic cost of activity in activity-naive rats. *Physiology & Behavior, 8,* 881–884.

Collier, G., & Johnson, D. F. (1990). The time window of feeding. *Physiology & Behavior, 48,* 771–777.

Collier, G., Johnson, D. F., Borin, G., & Mathis, C. E. (1994). Drinking in a patchy environment: The effect of the price of water. *Journal of the Experimental Analysis of Behavior, 63,* 169–184.

Collier, G., Johnson, D. F., CyBulski, K. A., & McHale, C. (1990). Activity patterns in rats as a function of the cost of access to four resources. *Journal of Comparative Psychology, 104,* 53–65.

Collier, G., Johnson, D. F., Hill, W. L., & Kaufman, L. W. (1986). The economics of the law of effect. *Journal of the Experimental Analysis of Behavior, 46,* 113–136.

Collier, G., Johnson, D. F., & Stanziola, C. (1991). The economics of water and salt balance. *Physiology and Behavior, 50,* 1221–1226.

Collier, G., & Levitsky, D. (1967). Defense of water balance in rats: Behavioral and physiological responses to depletion. *Journal of Comparative and Physiological Psychology, 64,* 59–67.

Collier, G., Levitsky, D., & Squibb, R. L. (1967). Instrumental performance as a function of the energy content of the diet. *Journal of Comparative and Physiological Psychology, 64*, 68–72.

Collier, G. H., & Myers, L. (1961). The loci of reinforcement. *Journal of Experimental Psychology, 61*, 57–66.

Davis, J. D. (1980). *Homeostasis, feedback and motivation.* London: Academic Press.

Davis, J. D., Collins, B. J., & Levine, M. W. (1976). *Peripheral control of meal size: Interaction of gustatory stimulation and postingestive feedback.* New York: Raven Press.

de Castro, J. M. (1975). Meal pattern correlations: Facts and artifacts. *Physiology & Behavior, 15*, 13–15.

Ehrenfreund, D. (1959). The relationship between weight loss during deprivation and food consumption. *Journal of Comparative and Physiological Psychology, 52*, 123–125.

Epling, W. F., & Pierce, W. D. (1984). Activity based anorexia in rats as a function of the opportunity to run on an activity wheel. *Nutrition and Behavior, 2*, 37–94.

Fitzsimons, J. T. (1972). Thirst. *Physiological Reviews, 52*, 463–561.

Hamilton, L. W. (1971). Starvation induced by sucrose ingestion in the rat: Partial protection by septal lesions. *Journal of Comparative and Physiological Psychology, 77*, 59–69.

Hull, C. L. (1943). *Principles of behavior.* New York: Appleton-Century-Crofts.

Johnson, D. F., Ackroff, K., Peters, J., & Collier, G. (1986). Changes in rats' meal patterns as a function of the caloric density of the diet. *Physiology & Behavior, 36*, 929–936.

Johnson, D. F., & Collier, G. (1994). Meal patterns of rats encountering variable procurement cost. *Animal Behavior, 47*, 1279–1287.

Kanarek, R. B., & Collier, G. H. (1983). Self-starvation: A problem of overriding the satiety signal. *Physiology & Behavior, 30*, 307–311.

Killeen, P. R. (1995). Economics, ecologics, and mechanics: The dynamics of responding under conditions of varying motivation. *Journal of the Experimental Analysis of Behavior, 64*, 405–431.

Le Magnen, J. (1969). Peripheral and systemic actions of food in caloric regulation of intake. *Annals of the New York Academy of Science, 268*, 3107–3110.

Le Magnen, J. (1985). *Hunger.* New York: Cambridge University Press.

Levitsky, D. A., Faust, I., & Glassman, M. (1976). The ingestion of food and the recovery of body weight following fasting in the naive rat. *Physiology & Behavior, 17*, 575–580.

Lorenz, K. (1950). The comparative method in studying innate behaviour patterns. *Symposium of the Society for Experimental Biology, 4*, 221–268.

Marwine, A. G., & Collier, G. (1971). Instrumental and consummatory behavior as a function of rate of weight loss and weight maintenance schedule. *Journal of Comparative and Physiological Psychology, 74*, 441–447.

Mathis, C. E., Johnson, D. F., & Collier, G. (1995). Procurement time as a determinant of meal frequency and meal duration. *Journal of the Experimental Analysis of Behavior, 63*, 295–309.

Navrick, D. J. (1969). *Effect of saccharin and sucrose consumption on the adjustment to a food deprivation schedule.* Unpublished master's thesis, Rutgers, The State University of New Jersey, New Brunswick.

Panksepp, J. (1973). Reanalysis of feeding patterns in rats. *Journal of Comparative and Physiological Psychology, 82*, 78–94.

Richter, C. P. (1927). Animal behavior and internal drives. *Quarterly Review of Biology, 2*, 307–343.

Richter, C. P. (1942–1943). Total self-regulatory functions in animals and human beings. *Harvey Lectures, 38*, 63–110.

Rixon, R. H., & Stevenson, J. A. F. (1957). Factors influencing survival of rats in fasting: Metabolic rate and body weight loss. *American Journal of Physiology, 188*, 332–336.

Routtenberg, A., & Kuznesof, A. Y. (1967). "Self-starvation" of rats living in activity wheels on a restricted feeding schedule. *Journal of Comparative and Physiological Psychology, 64*, 414–421.

Sclafani, A. (1973). Feeding inhibition and death produced by glucose ingestion in the rat. *Physiology & Behavior, 11*, 595–601.

Skinner, B. F. (1932a). Drive and reflex strength. *Journal of General Psychology, 6*, 22–37.

Skinner, B. F. (1932b). Drive and reflex strength: II. *Journal of General Psychology, 6*, 38–48.

Skinner, B. F. (1938). *The behavior of organisms*. New York: Appleton-Century-Crofts.

Smith, G. P., & Gibbs, J. (1979). Postprandial satiety. In J. M. Sprague & A. N. Epstein (Eds.), *Progress in psychology and physiological psychology* (Vol. 8, pp. 179–242). New York: Academic Press.

Spence, K. W. (1956). *Behavior theory and conditioning*. New Haven, CT: Yale University Press.

Staddon, J. E. R. (1983). *Adaptive behavior and learning*. Cambridge, England: Cambridge University Press.

Stellar, E., & Hill, J. H. (1952). The rat's rate of drinking as a function of deprivation. *Journal of Comparative and Physiological Psychology, 45*, 96–102.

Tang, M., & Collier, G. (1971). Effect of successive deprivations and recoveries on the level of instrumental performance in the rat. *Journal of Comparative and Physiological Psychology, 74*, 108–114.

Thorndike, E. L. (1911). *Animal intelligence*. New York: Macmillan.

Toates, F. (1986). *Motivational systems*. New York: Cambridge University Press.

Woods, S. C. (1991). The eating paradox. *Physiology & Behavior, 98*, 488–505.

Woods, S. C., & Kenney, N. J. (1979). Commentary: Alternatives to homeostasis. *The Behavioral and Brain Sciences, 2*(1), 123–124.

Woods, S. C., & Strubbe, J. H. (1994). The psychobiology of meals. *Psychonomic Bulletin & Review, 1*, 141–155.

Yamamoto, W. S., & Brobeck, J. R. (Eds.). (1965). *Physiological controls and regulations*. Philadelphia: Saunders.

7

Feeding Dynamics: Why Rats Eat in Meals and What This Means for Foraging and Feeding Regulation

John E. R. Staddon and B. Silvano Zanutto

Bob Bolles never separated learning from motivation, in his writing or in his laboratory research. He recognized that people, as well as rats, are driven much more by what they wish, want, and need than what they think and understand. Unfortunately, recent trends in psychology have downplayed the importance of motivation. The rat of the "cognitive revolution" is full of "representations" and "computations," but its "drives" and "needs" are kept hidden. Even in the study of topics that obviously involve motivational factors, like feeding and operant conditioning, recent emphasis has been away from motivation toward economics, with its implication of planful rationality as the basis of action. This chapter is a theoretical attempt to rerun the movie from the beginning—to look at feeding and foraging afresh, as biological, regulatory functions. To see—as Robert Bolles might have done—how much can be explained in purely motivational terms, *without* leaping at once to learning and cognition.

The argument is in three parts. First, we state the central question: Is there a simple dynamic process that might explain two key features of eating behavior in rats: eating in meals and the fact that feeding behavior is regulated? This question cannot be answered at the level of verbal description, which is rarely parsimonious or precise. Most important, verbal description does not allow us to see how the process should behave when subject to the constraints imposed by feeding schedules. A formal, real-time model can meet these objections. The second part of the argument is to describe such a model and show that it has the required properties. Fortunately, the necessary mechanism turns out to be astonishingly simple (see Figure 5 for a preview). The third part of the argument is to show that this same process can explain other experimental results concerning feeding and operant behavior, including some that are usually interpreted in much more complex ways.

Our research has been supported by grants from the National Science Foundation and the National Institute of Mental Health to Duke University. We thank Mark Bouton, Harvey Grill, and W. G. Hall for comments on earlier drafts.

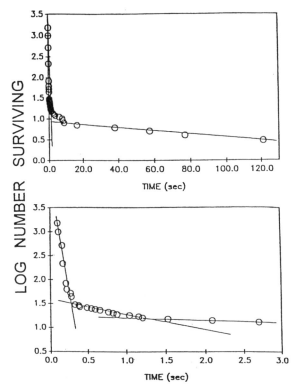

Figure 1. Eating in meals. Log-survivor distribution of interlick times for a rat licking at 0.4 M sucrose solution at two different time scales. From "The Microstructure of Ingestive Behavior," by J. D. Davis, 1989, *Annals of the New York Academy of Sciences, 575,* p. 106–121. Reprinted with permission.

The chapter is organized in three parts that correspond to the parts of this argument. First, we summarize the data on feeding regulation and eating in meals, then we derive a dynamic model to explain these data; and finally, we apply the model to experimental results on foraging.

The Data

The most obvious aspect of feeding is that it occurs in bouts, *meals*. The second most obvious property is that eating is *regulatory*. In this section, we first give an example of eating in meals and then describe experimental results that demonstrate feeding regulation at different time scales.

Figure 1 shows some quantitative data from Davis (1989) on rats licking sucrose solution. The plots show the distribution of time between eating episodes (licks of 0.4 M sucrose solution) at two different time scales. Data are from a single session in which an individual rat had ad-libitum access to sucrose solution. The lower graph shows the portion of the interlick-time distribution below 3 seconds. The licks occur in groups, which show up in this plot as subdistributions. The fitted lines show that

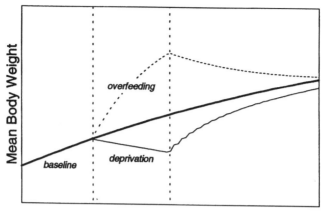

TIME (days)

Figure 2. Schematic of weight regulation in rats and many other animals. After perturbations that either increase (overfeeding) or reduce (deprivation) body weight, weight returns to the normal trajectory when a normal feeding regimen is restored.

the entire distribution is made up of three component exponential distributions, corresponding to random "lick generators," with short, intermediate, and long mean interlick times. The short and medium distributions are within "meals"; the long distribution corresponds to the time between meals. These data are typical of many sets of observations with both liquid and solid food: Under free conditions, rats eat in bouts, and the distribution of intereating times seems to be made up of at least two and probably three or more component distributions (Berdoy, 1993; Lucas & Timberlake, 1988; see also Machlis, 1977, for similar data on pecking in chicks). Any dynamic model for eating must first explain why eating occurs in meals, with this kind of temporal distribution in between-eating episodes.

Long-Term Regulation

The regulatory property of feeding is described in several ways, with more or less theoretical overtones. It is said, for example, that body weight is "defended" or "regulated" according to a "set point." All *we* mean by "regulated" *is that there are properties of the feeding system, such as body weight, that return more or less to their initial value after a perturbation.* The most neutral way to describe the regulatory property is as a stable fixed-point equilibrium.[1]

Note also the distinction between the variable (or variables) that is regula*ted* and the variable that does the regula*ting*. Body weight is reg-

---

[1]The fixed point (body weight) is increasing slowly, of course, as the rate matures. In most adult animals, however, the stable body weight changes very slowly or not at all. In all cases, the equilibrium properties are similar.

ulat*ed*, but eating rate is one of the variables that does the regulat*ing*. If body weight is reduced, eating rate increases (up to a point) until weight is restored to its normal level: Body weight is regulated; eating rate is the regulator. Over shorter time periods, however, eating rate is regulated and meal length is the regulator; over even shorter periods, meal length is itself regulated. This rather confusing terminology simply shows the limitations on purely verbal accounts of dynamic phenomena. As we move toward a mechanistic account, the picture will become clearer.

Figure 2 is a schematic illustration of body-weight regulation, a long-time-scale process. The figure shows the average body weight of a group of rats over time. Weight increases smoothly as the animals grow (heavy solid line). At the point where two light lines branch from the heavy solid curve, the group is split into three. A third are force-fed (light dotted line): Their weight increases to a level that is above the normal growth line. Another third are placed on a restricted diet (light solid line): Their weight decreases to a level below the growth line. At an intermediate point, both these groups are permitted to feed normally once again. The overfed rats eat less than normal, and the food-deprived rats eat more, until both groups return to the curve of normal growth (heavy solid line). The effects of almost anything that perturbs body weight—such as forced exercise, which usually reduces body weight, or diet-induced increased feeding (hyperphagia), which increases weight—are reversed when the treatment is terminated.

Body weight is regulated in two ways: through eating and in ways not directly related to ingestion. If an animal eats more (or less) than a base amount, its weight increases (or decreases), other things being equal. But weight is also controlled through noningestive processes, such as changes in general activity and in metabolic efficiency. In this chapter, we deal only with the rate, pattern, and regulation of eating and food-reinforced operant behavior.

Long-term energy intake is regulated through variations in eating rate. Most animals compensate well for changes in the caloric density of their diet. For example, casual observation shows that if large food pellets are replaced with smaller ones, rats eat proportionately more of the smaller pellets each day. When rats are fed a diet diluted with celluflour (a nonnutritive substance), they compensate by eating longer (but not more frequent) meals (Johnson, Ackroff, Peters, & Collier, 1986). Food deprivation also causes an increase in meal duration rather than meal frequency (Levitsky & Collier, 1968).

Weight is regulated over the long term—days or weeks. Feeding is also regulated over much shorter periods—minutes and hours. In the latter case, the regulated variable is not body weight but some property of ingestion: eating rate (grams per hour of rat chow consumed) or energy-intake rate (calories per hour of food ingested). The simplest way to show regulation over a short time scale is to interrupt the normal pattern of feeding for a while and watch what happens when the opportunity to eat is restored. The result is shown schematically in Figure 3. The figure shows eating episodes (e.g., pellets ingested, licks of sugar water) as ver-

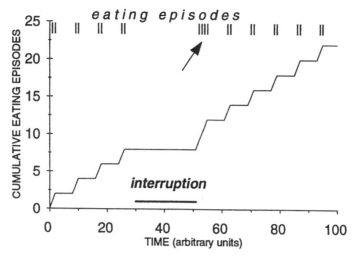

Figure 3. Schematic showing the effect on eating rate of perturbing eating. The curve is cumulative, showing pellets consumed as a function of time (the time of each pellet is indicated by the vertical hash marks at the top). Eating is prevented during the "interruption" period shown by the horizontal bar. The arrow shows the first postinterruption meal.

tical blips across the top and cumulative food intake underneath. Feeding is interrupted during the period marked by the heavy horizontal line. The figure shows three things: (a) Eating occurs in bouts (meals); (b) the effect of a moderate-duration interruption is restricted to the first postinterruption meal; and (c) the length of the first meal partially compensates for the effect of interruption. Now for the details of medium- and short-term regulation.

Medium-Term Regulation

Levitsky, Faust, and Glassman (1976) did an extensive study of the effects of longer periods of enforced fasting on the eating behavior of rats. They found that rats ate more postfast than under control conditions but ate no more after a 96-hour fast (the longest imposed) than after a 24-hour fast. In all cases, after a day or so postfast, eating rate was back to the normal prefast level. When the fast is longer than about 24 hours, the rat suffers a net intake deficit, which is greater the longer the period of fast. (It is interesting that even after 96 hours of food deprivation, body weight eventually returns to normal, despite the fact that cumulative food intake shows a persistent deficit. Clearly, the rat has means of regulating body weight in addition to its rate of ingestion: Bad news for [rat] dieters! We do not deal with noningestive regulation in this chapter.)

First-meal effect. If eating is interrupted for a period of hours, the effect is almost entirely on the first meal after eating resumes (the arrow in Figure 3). Le Magnen has written the following:

A food withdrawal from the beginning of the night for 2, 4, 6, . . . h, leads to a linear increase in the size of the first meal at the restoration of food access. Thus, the size of meal, unaffected by the duration of the pre-meal period of no eating in the ad libitum condition, becomes highly dependent on this pre-prandial interval of no eating when it is prolonged by the removal of food access. (Le Magnen, 1985, p. 22)

In Figure 3, meals are just two eating episodes, but after the interruption there is a single meal of length four; subsequent meals are again just two episodes long. We term this long postfast first meal the *first-meal effect* of interruption.[2]

Rats regulate eating rate when the natural eating pattern is perturbed in other ways. For example, Lucas and Timberlake (1988) looked at free feeding in rats when food pellets could be obtained only after different minimum interpellent times.[3] Under free conditions, each rat could eat from a trough containing a single pellet. Removal of the pellet immediately triggered (through a photocell arrangement) the delivery of another pellet, in a potentially endless supply. Under the delay conditions, however, a delay of 16, 32, 64, 128, 256, or 512 seconds was imposed between removal of one pellet and delivery of the next. The experimenters looked at mean meal size (in grams), meal duration, and intermeal interval, as well as total intake, at each delay value. They found that overall food intake declined slowly with increasing interpellet delay. Total intake declined significantly only at the longest delays. They also found that the shortest delay reduced meal size in comparison with free eating but longer delays caused no further reduction. Because meal size ceased to get any smaller as delay was increased from 16 to 512 seconds, the authors concluded that "meal size is determined . . . by a positive feedback component with a relatively short decay time probably based on gustatory stimulation from feeding." Because intermeal interval decreased to compensate partially for reduced meal size, the authors inferred the existence of "a negative feedback component capable of integrating total intake across delays of up to 1 hour" (Lucas & Timberlake, 1988, p. 259).

---

[2]Le Magnen also points out an interesting contrast between normal eating and eating following a perturbation. Under free conditions, even though both meal length and intermeal interval show some variability, there is no correlation between intermeal interval and the duration of the following meal; that is, the rat is no more likely to eat a long meal after a long intermeal interval than after a short interval. (There is a small and unreliable correlation between meal length and the length of the following intermeal interval, however [Le Magnen & Tallon, 1966; Panksepp, 1976; see also Clifton, 1987].) Rats are a bit more likely to wait a long time before eating again after they have just finished an extra-long meal.) Nevertheless, as Figure 3 shows, when the intermeal interval is *artificially* prolonged, a strong correlation emerges between the length of interruption and the length of the first meal after feeding is resumed. Thus, absence of a correlation between two variables (like meal length and intermeal interval) under free conditions does not rule out the possibility of a causal relation between them.

[3]These authors separated data from the day and night portion of the diurnal light cycle, but we will not consider this factor here. Given the uncertainties of defining a "meal," Lucas and Timberlake set a generous meal criterion: consumption of at least four pellets, followed by a pause of more than 10 minutes without eating after a pellet became available.

Short-Term Regulation

We have described feeding regulation across days (weight regulation), across hours (the effects of long interruptions), and across tens of minutes (the effect of interpellet delays). There is also regulation over seconds and minutes, that is, within a meal. Most of the work on short-term regulation has been done with liquid diets, such as sucrose solution, for which ingestion rate can be better controlled compared to solid food. There are several ways to do these experiments. Ingestion can be either free or controlled. In the first case, the rat laps at a spout connected to a graduated cylinder of liquid food. The animal therefore controls both the rate (how fast it laps) and timing (when it laps) of food delivery. In the second case, ingestion is through an intraoral infusion pump that fixes the rate, but not the timing, of food delivery. The interruptions can be in a single block or repeated. The best dependent measure is simply the experienced time pattern of eating episodes. But, such are the conventions of the field, a summary measure such as meal size or length is often used instead of the more comprehensive moment-by-moment record of ingestion. Here are two sets of typical experiments to show how "within-meal" eating is regulated in the face of interruptions.

Seeley, Kaplan, and Grill (1993) described two highly controlled experiments in which rats were infused intraorally with 12.5% glucose solution at a rate of 0.75 ml/min. The infusion system detected rejection by the rat and stopped the pump immediately. Each rat was tested once a day. No eating was permitted in the 5 hours before each test. During a test, after the first rejection, infusion was stopped for 30 seconds. If the rat rejected the glucose solution again within 60 seconds after infusion resumed, the intake test was terminated. If not, this procedure was repeated until the rat rejected twice within a 90-second period. The length and size of this single daily "meal" were defined between the time when infusion began and finally ceased.

In the two experiments, one or several interruptions were scheduled early during a meal, before the first rejection. Seeley et al. (1993) were interested in the effects on total session intake of interruption duration, time of onset (whether the interruption occurred early or late within the meal), and interruption pattern (whether the interruptions occurred in a block or were spaced). What were the effects of these different perturbations? In a word, *none*: The amount ingested was constant under all conditions. The rats in these two experiments defended their total intake per meal (where *meal* is defined in the rather complex way described previously) perfectly.

In a second set of experiments, Mook and Dreifuss (1986), maintained rats at 80 percent of their free-feeding weights and allowed them to lap freely at a spout connected to a cylinder of saccharin solution. Saccharin is nonnutritive and moderately attractive to rats, who treat it like food, not water: "The amount ingested increases with severity of food deprivation . . . whereas water intake declines" (Mook & Dreifuss, 1986, pp. 365–366). Under free conditions, the rate of lapping by rats at the sac-

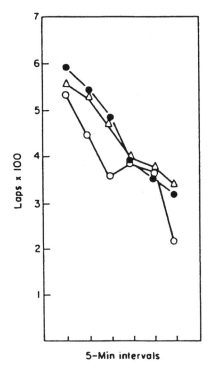

Figure 4. Mean number of laps by a group of rats at 0.2% saccharin solution when the spout was available continuously (triangles), during alternate 30-second intervals (filled circles), and during alternate 15-second intervals (open circles). From "Saccharin Drinking by Hungry Rats: Adjustment to Constraints," by D. G. Mook and S. Dreifuss, 1986, *Appetite, 7,* pp. 365–379, Figure 2. Reprinted with permission.

charin spout declined smoothly across a 30-minute test session (triangles in Figure 4). The striking result is that reducing lap opportunities by 50 percent, by interrupting lapping in alternating 15- or 30-second periods (open and closed circles in the figure), made almost no difference to the total number of laps. The rats simply lapped faster in the reduced time available to maintain overall lapping at an approximately constant rate. In this experiment, lap rate, ingestion rate, and meal duration were all simultaneously regulated. These experiments with saccharin show that there are short-term regulatory feeding processes that depend only on sensory feedback from the mouth. Because saccharin has no nutritive consequences, no negative feedback late in the digestive chain is involved.

These are the major experimental results on feeding regulation at different time scales. In the next section we consider what kind of dynamic process might underlie these effects.

What Kind of Dynamic Process Is This? The Model

Researchers do not know all the physiological processes—gustatory, gastric, metabolic, and neural—that underlie feeding behavior. Unfortunately, any attempt to assemble what is known about feeding physiology into a model that can successfully predict major features of feeding behavior will fail if the model lacks even one essential feature. Because knowledge of the relevant physiology is incomplete and likely to remain so for several years, trying to simulate the dynamics of feeding with a model limited to known physiology is unlikely to succeed. Perhaps this is why interest in physiologically based feeding models has faded in recent years. But we need not give up. Without knowing any of the physiological details, *the behavioral data alone* allow us to discern the broad outlines of the dynamic process that underlies feeding:

1. It must involve negative feedback. When the animal is food-deprived, its tendency to eat clearly increases. When it is allowed to eat, eating (eventually) ceases. Ergo, there must be some kind of negative feedback from the food. We term this hypothetical negative feedback a *satiation signal.*

2. The satiation signal is not simply linked to absorption. As we have seen, rats eventually cease to ingest saccharin solution, which is nonnutritive (although still a stimulus to the GI tract). And sham-fed animals also cease to feed, although they take longer to do so than normally fed rats (e.g., Davis & Smith, 1990). There seem to be several sources of negative feedback.

3. Because of regulation, there must be some fixed parameter, a set point of some sort, to act as reference, as a comparison.[4]

4. The fact that eating is episodic, occurring in meals, poses a special problem. Either different processes must turn eating on and off, or the feedback from food must be delayed in some way. The first possibility has been explored by Booth (1978; see also Guillot & Meyer, 1987) and Staddon (1988). It implies a process with two thresholds, a "start" threshold and a "stop" threshold. The idea is that eating begins when the tendency to eat rises above the start threshold; but once eating has begun, the eating tendency must fall below a second (lower), "stop" threshold before eating ceases. The two-threshold idea works surprisingly well, but there are at least three objections to it: (a) The definition of an eating bout is arbitrary. In simulations, a transition from not eating, in Time Step t, to eating, in Time Step $t + 1$, triggers a change in the effective threshold from θ_{start} to θ_{stop}, which is arbitrary because it depends on the size of the time step. If the time step is changed, a completely different pattern of real-time behavior may result. By the same token, (b) the two-threshold approach takes no account of the number of time steps in between eating bouts: Two

---

[4]Wirtshafter and Davis (1977) some years ago proposed "a simple feedback control model which contains no set point, and yet is able to account for . . . data which have been cited in support of the existence of a body weight set point" (p. 75). Their model does not invalidate our point, because it is in fact a controller that tracks the taste input, *S*, which acts as a reference. The general point is that there must be some fixed parameters in any system that has a fixed-point equilibrium.

eating episodes separated by 1 time step cause the same threshold change as two episodes separated by 2 or 100 time steps, which is not plausible. (c) The behavior is too perfect; every meal is uninterrupted, for example. The two-threshold assumption can never yield three-state intereating time distributions like those in Figure 1.

5. This analysis leads to the idea that the feedback signal that inhibits eating is *delayed*. Delay accounts for eating in meals in the following way. In the absence of food, the satiation signal decreases with time. When the signal falls below a threshold (the *set point*), eating begins (if food is available). Because of the lag between eating and its inhibitory feedback, however, the satiation signal continues to decline for a while during the meal. After a while, the delayed effects of the ingested food begin to catch up and the satiation signal begins to increase, eventually rising above the threshold, at which point eating ceases. Eating does not resume at once, because the lagged satiation signal continues to increase for a while even after eating has ceased. In this way, eating under ad-libitum conditions consists of temporally separated eating bouts.

6. The idea that the satiation signal is delayed is certainly plausible for inhibitory signals later in the chain of events initiated by ingestion: from the stomach and later in the digestive tract and from absorption. These effects are necessarily delayed with respect to ingestion. It is less plausible for the signals from food in the mouth. A clear implication is that these early signals, although they must exist (cf. the saccharin and sham feeding data), must be less important than the delayed signals.

The Model

Taken together, these properties have led us to a simple model that incorporates *delay*. Its dynamic properties are shown in Figure 5. The figure shows the hypothetical satiating effect of a single bit of food, at Time 0. The satiating effect of the food takes some time after ingestion to reach a maximum; it increases and then decreases. (The effect of a single brief stimulus is termed the *impulse response* of the system.[5] The impulse response needed to get eating in meals is biphasic, like the one in the figure.) The horizontal line shows the eating threshold: When the satiation signal is below the threshold (indicated by the heavy solid line), the system is ready to "eat" if food is available. When the satiation signal is above threshold (dashed line), the system will not eat. A system with a biphasic impulse response like this will produce eating in meals, for the reasons

---

[5]The satiation-signal model we describe is in fact linear, although the system as a whole is not, because of the threshold. The impulse response has a special significance for linear systems: It characterizes the system completely. Note that the impulse response is always biphasic, but it will only cross the satiation threshold if the initial bit of food is large enough.

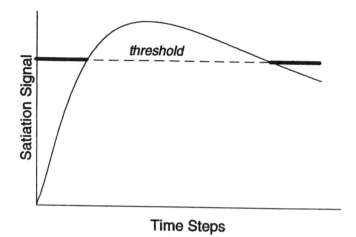

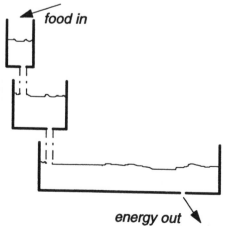

Figure 5. Biphasic impulse response of a system that will produce eating in meals. A single piece of food is delivered at Time 0. The satiating effects rise to a maximum only after a delay. The height of the peak depends on the size of the piece of food; if it is small, the satiation signal will follow the same biphasic pattern but may not reach the satiation threshold. This impulse response was obtained from a five-stage system of the type shown in Figure 7. The time constants for each integrator were determined as follows: $a_{i+1} = a_i + \lambda(1 - a_i)$ and $b_i = 1 - a_i$, where $i = 1$–5 and $\lambda = 0.5$.

described earlier in Point 5. What kind of process can produce a satiation signal with the properties shown in Figure 5? Will such a system show regulation? Will it regulate over different time scales?

Figure 6 shows a physical model with the necessary properties. It is a series of "leaky buckets," with the output of the first being the input to the second and so on down the chain. The chain can be of any length; three buckets are shown in the figure. The water level in successive buckets represents the effects (neural as well as metabolic) of food at different

Figure 6. A fluid-flow metaphor for feeding regulation.

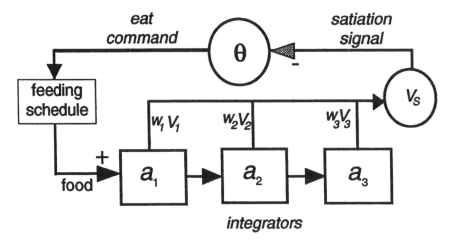

Figure 7. A three-stage cascaded-integrator (CINT) feeding model. The effects of food are the input to the first integrator (time constant: a_1), whose output is input to the second integrator, and so on. The values (V_i) of integrators later in the cascade are summed together as the satiation signal, V_S, which is compared with a threshold, θ, the set point of the system. In the models discussed in the text, the weights for early integrators in the chain are zero, and the weights for later stages are one. The eating command is the difference between satiation signal and a fixed threshold (set point): Eating command = $\theta - V_S$. If the eating command is positive and the feeding schedule makes food available, the system will eat; each quantum of food, $x(t)$, is input to the first integrator in the chain.

stages in the chain of events initiated by ingestion. The satiation signal from such a system is not shown in the figure. To get the required biphasic impulse response, all that is necessary is that the satiation signal be a weighted sum of all the water levels, *with later elements weighted more than earlier ones.*

This system is intrinsically regulatory. The fluid-flow metaphor shows pretty clearly that it tends toward a stable fixed-point equilibrium. Look again at Figure 6. Suppose we pour in fluid ("food in" = *eat*) only when some property of the fluid in the system (total fluid, level in the last compartment, and so on) exceeded a fixed threshold? It should be intuitively obvious that as long as inflow rate is not too large (so the top compartment overflows) or too small (lower than "energy out"), the average rate of inflow (i.e., total amount of fluid per unit time, averaged over a number of periods of inflow and no-inflow: *molar* ingestion rate) tends toward a constant. In the steady state, molar ingestion rate will equal energy outflow rate and be more or less independent of the local inflow rate.

It is not so obvious that a system like this will regulate at all the different time scales that feeding regulates: within a meal, following short interruptions, and after lengthy deprivation. To demonstrate this requires a formal model, to which we now turn.

Figure 7 shows a mathematical model with the same properties as the physical model in Figure 6. We term this the *cascaded-integrator* (CINT) model.[6] The leaky buckets shown in Figure 6 are replaced by *leaky integrators* linked in a cascade. Each leaky integrator is simply the familiar linear operator: in discrete-time notation, $V(t + 1) = aV(t) + x(t)$, where V corresponds to the water level in a given bucket in Figure 6, x is the inflow rate, and a is a constant between 0 and 1 representing the rate of outflow in relation to the size of the bucket (the larger a, the smaller the change in V during each time step). At each time step, therefore, each bucket (integrator) loses an amount proportional to its current level, $(1 - a)V(t)$, and gains an amount corresponding to the inflow rate, $x(t)$. In a cascade, the output, V_N, of integrator N is the input of integrator $N + 1$. There is a set point or threshold, represented by a fixed value, θ. The strength of the tendency to eat, or "eat command," is simply the difference between the sum of integrator states, V_i, and θ.

Formally, the cascaded-integrator model works as follows: The tendency to eat is simply the difference between a reference value, θ, and an aggregate *satiation signal*, V_S, which is the weighted sum of the states of all the integrators:

$$V_S = w_1V_1 + w_2V_2 + \cdots + w_NV_N = \sum_{i=1}^{N} w_iV_i, \qquad (1)$$

where w_i are the weights. Physiologically, Equation 1 reflects the well-established fact that the tendency to eat depends not only on the state of bodily deprivation (i.e., events late in the cascade) but also on taste factors and stomach fill (i.e., events at the beginning and in the middle of the cascade; cf. Mook, 1987).

To translate V_S into an eating command (response strength), we need a reference, θ: When V_S falls below θ, eating begins and the tendency to eat (which we term *reflex strength*) is proportional to the difference between V_S and θ. Thus, reflex strength = $\theta - V_S$. When eating actually occurs, *response strength*, the vigor of the measured response, is equal to reflex strength. For simplicity, we assume that eating is "all or none," occurring at a constant rate when reflex strength is above zero and not occurring when reflex strength is below zero. Our assumption resembles the controlled-infusion-rate-sucrose solution procedure of Seeley et al. (1993), but we are applying it to all eating. The model can only turn ingestion on and off; it has no control over the rate of ingestion in the "on" state. (This assumption must be relaxed when we use the model to drive operant responding.)

Theta is similar to the set point that figures prominently in most discussions of feeding regulation, but θ is different in three respects: (a) It

---

[6]This cascaded structure is similar to a class of models we have applied to data on simple habituation (Staddon, 1993; Staddon & Higa, in press). The probable importance of time delays in eating dynamics was noted by Schilstra (1978). The general idea that both long- and short-term food stores exert an inhibitory effect on eating was discussed briefly by Bolles (1980) and somewhat more extensively by Panksepp (1974) and Schilstra (1978).

corresponds to *no single physiological variable*, such as blood glucose level or the level of fat stores. Theta is a purely theoretical construct that may summarize the satiating effect of numerous physiological variables, (the V_i terms in Equation 1). (b) Theta does not necessarily correspond to a fixed *settling point* for body weight. We will show that different feeding regimens can lead to different steady-state eating rates, even though θ is constant. (c) Moreover, as we demonstrate, the system as a whole shows regulation of eating rate not just over the long term but also more or less locally.

To obtain eating in meals, we need a biphasic impulse response like the one shown in Figure 5. To get it, we order the weights so as to emphasize later integrators in the chain. For example, if the early weights are all zero, the early integrators serve only as delays and have no direct inhibitory effect on eating. As we will show, this delay is sufficient to produce eating in meals and does not interfere with useful regulatory properties of the cascaded system. In most of our simulations, the early w values are all equal to zero, and the last two or three are equal to one.

For the simple case, we assume that eating is all or none: The system eats at a fixed rate during a time step if the satiation signal is below threshold and not otherwise. The size of each eating input reflects the "satiating value" (SV) of each bit of food. Satiating value is presumably related to taste, texture, and bulk as well as nutrient value. These properties probably have separable effects on feeding, but it is simpler at this stage not to distinguish among them. The equations for this system are as follows:

$$x(t) = \phi(t) \text{ if } V_S < \theta; \quad 0 \text{ otherwise,} \tag{2}$$

$$V_1(t + 1) = a_1 V_1(t) + b_1 x(t), \tag{3}$$

$$V_i(t + 1) = a_i V_i(t) + b_i V_{i-1}(t), \quad 0 < i < N, \tag{4}$$

where $x(t)$ is the SV during each time step (i.e., the food actually eaten), $\phi(t)$ is the SV of each bit of food available (determined by the experimenter), V_i is the state of integrator i, a_i is the time constant of integrator i, and b_i is the input weight. In all our simulations $b_i = 1 - a_i$, and the a_i values are linked as described in the legend to Figures 5 and 14, limiting the number of free parameters to two, no matter how many integrators are in the model.

Equation 2 says that the system eats the food available (size: $\phi[t]$ in each time step) only if the satiation signal, V_S, is below threshold, θ. Equation 3 says that the state of the first integrator, $V_1(t + 1)$, is determined by its previous state, $V_1(t)$, and the SV during that time step, $x(t)$. Equation 4 says that the state of an integrator later in the cascade, $V_i(t + 1)$, is determined by its previous state, $V_i(t)$, and the state of the integrator earlier in the chain, $V_{i-1}(t)$.

Predictions

What kinds of things can this model predict? We emphasize at the outset that a purely regulatory model *should not explain everything* about feeding behavior, because rats do more than just regulate (e.g., Bolles, 1980). They come to the experiment with preexisting feeding patterns—the circadian pattern of eating, for example—and they *learn*. Indeed, they must learn at least some things to be able to eat at all in a new situation: what is food and what is not (not all foods are recognized instinctively by young rats) and where the food source is in the enclosure. Undoubtedly they learn other things as well, such as properties of the reinforcement contingencies. Because a minimal, regulatory model contains none of these things (circadian sensitivity must be added to get a fit to some data, as we show subsequently), we should not expect to explain every feature of the data. We should not expect, in other words, to fit a limited data set with high precision, in the fashion of traditional mathematical modeling. What we looked for is a pattern of results in a broad data set that is consistent with an underlying regulatory process. What is left over—the details that cannot be explained by a regulatory model—is then a proper domain for "higher" processes like learning and cognition. Our method is nothing more than a self-conscious application of Lloyd Morgan's (1894) canon: to refrain from attributing behavior to a complex process when a simpler one will do.

The steady-state pattern of eating shown by this system is illustrated in Figure 8 (top panel), which shows 50 time steps after a stabilization period of 900 steps. As one can see, the average meal duration is between three and four time steps, for a "bite" size, or SV, of 1. The bottom panel shows the effect of reducing the SV to 0.5: The meal duration increases to six or seven time steps, which means, of course, that the meal size in terms of amount eaten is approximately regulated. As in the actual behavior of rats, overall intake is also regulated, because meal frequency does not change (cf. Adolph, 1947; Johnson et al., 1986; Levitsky & Collier, 1968).[7] The doubling in meal duration caused by halving the satiation value, or bite size, of each eating episode shown by the model in Figure 8 is typical of real eating by rats. Meal duration is not regulated, but because of our all-or-none eating assumption, the model has no control over the amount ingested in each "bite" (i.e., no control over within-meal eating rate) so cannot simultaneously regulate both meal duration and meal size.

Effects of interruption. Figure 9 shows the effect on the model of deprivation and interruption. The system begins with all V values set equal to zero, maximal deprivation. When eating is allowed to begin, the satiation signal increases almost linearly and eating occurs in a long initial

---

[7]It is interesting that some herbivores, such as the guinea pig, do not adjust to dietary dilution by changing eating patterns (cf. Hirsch, 1973): If their diet is diluted, they simply get fewer calories and use other means to regulate body weight. The mechanisms that have evolved to regulate feeding are obviously adapted to different niches.

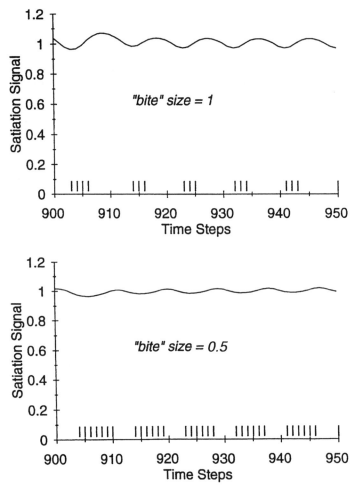

Figure 8. *Top panel*. Steady-state eating pattern for a five-integrator version of the system illustrated in Figure 7, with an eating threshold, $\theta = 1$, and a "bite" size, $\phi(t) = 1$. The wavy line is the satiation signal (i.e., ΣV_i, $i = M, N$, for $M = 3$, $N = 5$). The blips at the bottom show eating episodes. *Bottom panel*. Steady-state eating pattern for a "bite" size, $\phi(t) = 0.5$. Parameters are as in Figure 5.

meal (*A* in the figure), after which eating in the regular meal pattern resumes. A brief period (20 time steps) when eating is interrupted (horizontal line) is followed by a single long meal (*B*) and resumption of the regular pattern. The effect of a relatively brief interruption is precisely the first-meal effect that we described earlier.

Regulation: short and long term. If the initial long meal (14 time steps) represented in Figure 9 is briefly interrupted (e.g., for three time steps), the meal resumes after the interruption and its total size remains the same, exactly duplicating the results of Seeley et al. (1993) described earlier: Hungry rats "defend" the size of their first meal following a long (5-

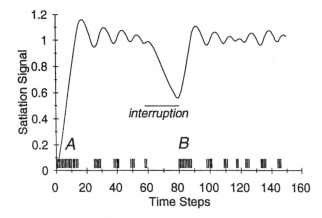

Figure 9. Effects of deprivation and interruption on the eating pattern of the CINT model. The system begins with all V values equal to zero (infinite deprivation). The horizontal line shows a brief period during which normal eating is interrupted. Blips at the bottom show eating episodes. Parameters are as in Figure 5.

hr) period of deprivation. The CINT model also duplicates the data of Mook and Dreifuss (1986) once a response assumption is introduced that relates eating rate (i.e., rate of ingestion of a sucrose or saccharin solution) to eating command (i.e., to the difference between threshold and the satiation signal).

In retrospect, neither of these experimental results is too surprising. Seeley et al. (1993) deprived their animals for 5 hours before the experiment; even a 38-minute interruption (their longest) during the initial meal adds relatively little, proportionately, to the state of deprivation with which the animals began the experiment. The Mook and Dreifuss animals were at 80 percent of their free-feeding weights, which implies an even longer deprivation period. In neither case was initial deprivation significantly increased by the local interruptions during the first meal. Given that in our model, as in the empirical data (Le Magnen, 1985), initial-meal length is determined by the initial state of deprivation of the animal, it is not surprising that the length of the initial meal was largely unaffected by the interruptions. But this was not obvious in the absence of a dynamic model.

The CINT model regulates pretty well over the long term. Recall that after an interruption of feeding, postfast intake increases with deprivation up to a maximum after fasts of 24 hours (Le Magnen, 1985; Levitsky et al., 1976); longer fasts produce no further effect. Moreover, eating rate after an initial extra-large postfast meal soon returns to normal. Figure 10 shows data from Levitsky et al. (1976), a study in which groups of rats were deprived of food for periods from 24 to 96 hours. The figure shows cumulative food intake (lines) for four groups of rats. The cumulative curves after the interruption show similar brief periods of acceleration and are thereafter approximately parallel both to each other and to the eating rate before the interruption. The symbols are predictions of the CINT

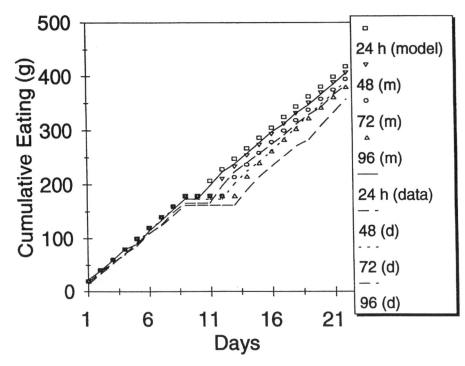

Figure 10. The effects of 24- to 96-hour food deprivation on cumulative eating. Lines show group-average data from Levitsky, Faust, and Glassman (1976). Symbols are predictions of a six-integrator CINT model with the parameter values shown in the legend to Figure 14; m = model; d = data.

model. The predictions are qualitatively the same as the data: brief acceleration (similar after all four deprivation periods) followed by a return to the same slope as before. Note that the cumulative eating deficit caused by deprivation of greater than 24 hours is never made up, either in the data or in the model. The model is not a perfect fit to the data. The reason is that we used parameter values based on a fit to extensive experimental foraging data from two studies by Collier, Hirsch, and Hamlin (1972). These data and simulation assumptions are described in detail subsequently.

Figure 11 shows how overall eating rate is affected by the satiation value of each bite. When each bite is less than about 0.4, the system "eats" during every time step, so that eating rate is proportional to bite size. Above that point, eating rate is regulated at about 34 per 100 time steps, with a slight tendency for the regulated level to increase with SV: Given a highly nutritious diet, the model will slowly "gain weight" unless non-ingestive mechanisms act to prevent it (in practice, they seem not to: cf. Sclafani & Springer, 1976).

The CINT model also regulates in the face of imposed delays between pellets (cf. Lucas & Timberlake, 1988). The heavy solid line in Figure 12 shows the effect of increasing the time between permitted bites (interpellet interval, IPI) from 1 to 128, using the same parameters as we used the

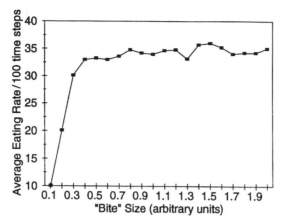

Figure 11. Effect of "bite" size (or infusion rate, in a controlled-infusion-rate procedure) on total ingestion rate in the CINT model. Parameters are as in Figure 5.

data from Levitsky et al. (1976) and the Collier foraging studies to be discussed shortly. Over a range of delays from 1 to 32, overall eating rate varies only by about 10 percent; thereafter, the decline is more substantial. The open squares are data from Lucas and Timberlake with one time step set equal to 8 seconds. The two curves show that data and model are

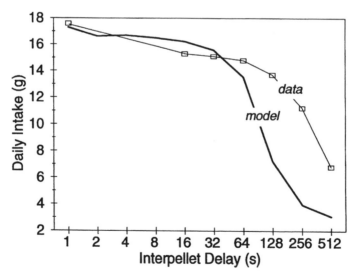

Figure 12. Effect of imposing a minimum interpellet interval (IPI) on overall eating rate. The data represented by the squares are from "Interpellet Delay and Meal Patterns in the Rat," by G. A. Lucas and W. Timberlake, 1988, *Physiology and Behavior, 43*. Reprinted with permission. Simulation of the CINT model (data from last 6 days of 22 days at each IPI). Note the drop in intake at the 2-second IPI with approximately constant intake thereafter, until IPI exceeded 32 seconds. Other details are as in Figure 14.

similar up to an IPI of about 64; thereafter, the model intake falls faster than the data.

Lucas and Timberlake suggested that their data on meal size imply some kind of positive feedback from each pellet (as well as regulatory negative feedback), because they found that meal size decreased at the shortest imposed interpellet interval (16 s) but further increases had no further effect. Our simulations show that the effect of IPI on overall eating rate at short IPIs can be reproduced by the CINT model, even though it lacks positive feedback.

Meal–intermeal correlations. There is a weak positive correlation between meal duration and subsequent intermeal interval in free-feeding laboratory rats but a negligible correlation between intermeal interval and duration of the next meal. Because the CINT model is deterministic, both meal duration and intermeal interval vary relatively little. Nevertheless, in our simulations there is a positive correlation between meal duration and duration of the subsequent intermeal interval and a smaller positive correlation between intermeal interval and duration of the subsequent meal—a pattern that matches the rat data.

Most of our predictions are not very sensitive to the time constants of the integrator series. With the exception of the effects of IPI on meal pattern, the properties of the CINT model are relatively independent of particular parameter values. Note also that although the model has five or six integrators, the 10 or 12 parameters are all linked, as described in the legends to Figures 5 and 14. In our simulations, there were only 2 free parameters. The qualitative predictions of the CINT model depend much more on its cascaded structure and the delay imposed by the initial non-satiating integrators than on details of parameter values.

The cascaded–integrator model seems to capture many of the salient features of feeding dynamics: eating in meals, the effects of long and short interruptions of feeding, and regulation at different time scales. These behavioral properties all flow from the idea that feeding is inhibited by the integrated, lagged effects of ingestion. Moreover, the model is consistent with known facts of psychobiology: that feeding is inhibited by both peripheral (taste, gastric content) and central (circulating metabolites, nutrient uptake) factors and that peripheral factors are less important than central ones.

We have become reasonably convinced that this model can account for the basic motivational dynamics of free and constrained feeding in the rat, but it may in fact do even more: It may account for at least some of the properties of food-reinforced operant behavior. In the final section of the chapter, we begin to explore the extent to which the CINT model can account for "optimal" behavior in experimental analogues to foraging, a data set usually assumed to require complex associative and even cognitive processes.

Extensions to Foraging

"Internal state" in the CINT model is defined by a handful of numbers, five or six in the models just discussed, corresponding to the V values of each integrator in the cascade. The input to the system, food, is defined by a single number: what we called bite size or satiation value.[8] The state of a real foraging animal cannot be defined so simply, however, and the essentials of a food source or a cuisine, even a cuisine for a rat, cannot be realistically represented by a single number. Foods' sources differ in palatability and accessibility, and organisms' sensitivity to both these factors is more or less dependent on associative learning. Palatability may depend partly on learning, but the *affordance* (e.g., Gibson 1979) of a particular food source—where the food is located, how it is to be obtained, how much effort is required and of what sort for each unit of food, and so on—is something that must be entirely learned. The attractiveness of a given food source depends not just on the animal's internal state but also on what might be termed its *incentive state*: the organism's "expectations" about affordance, taste, and other learned properties of a particular food source.[9] Incentive state must be represented by several numbers whose values depend on experience. In a comprehensive model, the food input itself must also be represented by several numbers, not only for food amount (the only variable we discuss in this chapter) but also for taste, texture, digestibility, specific nutrients and so on. Recognizing, therefore, the severe limitations on the simple regulatory approach, let's see how far it can go in explaining data from simulated foraging experiments.

Learning, particularly associative learning, involves processes more complex than feeding regulation. Moreover, it is often the first thing psychologists think of when they see an apparently complex behavior pattern well adapted to a particular set of reinforcement conditions. This tendency to attribute any apparently complex behavior to learning is not parsimonious and may not be the best way to understand what is really going on. In this section, we continue our strategy of self-conscious parsimony. We assume that foraging behavior is almost entirely *unlearned*[10]—until the failure of our regulatory model forces us to assume otherwise. When we find out how and where the regulatory model fails, we will see more clearly at what points something more complicated needs to be introduced. In this section, therefore, we look at a few of the definitive experiments showing

---

[8]The issues discussed in this paragraph are helpfully reviewed by Toates and Evans (1987). See also a good experimental example of the distinction between internal and incentive state in Weingarten (1985).

[9]Both incentive state and internal state are states of the animal; hence both are "internal" in a literal sense. Nevertheless, it is useful to have separate terms for aspects of internal state that reflect the nutritional state of the animal (*internal state*) and aspects that have to do with expectations about food sources (*incentive state*). We could have used terms like *drive state, hunger,* or *motivational level* for internal state, but these all carry historical baggage that we hoped to shed by using a more neutral term. Incentive value is termed *cue strength* by some authors (e.g., McFarland & Bösser, 1993).

[10]This assumption does not rule out the possibility that some of the parameters in our regulatory model may be tuned by experience, particularly during early development.

that foraging behavior by rats involves complex adaptive strategies, strategies that seem to require associative learning. We will find that their essential features can in fact be accounted for by feeding regulation alone.

Incentive Model and Response Rule

A model for feeding regulation needs to consider only the animal's internal state, but a model that hopes to encompass foraging must also deal with the attractiveness of each food source, that is, with *incentive*. We need to say something about incentive, even though, in our quest to push feeding regulation as far as it will go as an explanation, we will assume that incentive factors are constant. Foraging also involves different kinds of operant behavior: searching, lever pressing, and others. We must also, therefore, devise an appropriate *response rule*, an assumption about how internal state and incentive combine to produce operant responding.

In our model of feeding regulation, internal state was represented by several numbers (the V values of the cascaded integrators). However, the animal's tendency to eat is necessarily just a single number (threshold − satiation value: $\theta - V_S$), which we translated directly into an on−off eating command. In the feeding experiments discussed so far, the only behavior required of the animal was eating (assuming that going over to the feeder is an essentially costless activity so well learned that its associative aspects can be ignored for the moment). We will retain the on−off eating assumption. However, because in the experiments to be discussed now, an "arbitrary" operant response (sometimes many of them) like lever pressing is required for access to food, we need some way to use the model to drive operant behavior. The lever-press requirement has an effect on the attractiveness of a given food source (i.e., on its incentive value). If many responses are required for a small piece of food, the incentive value of the food source will be low; if few responses are required, or the food amount is large, the incentive value will be high. Presumably, the animal's net tendency to engage in lever pressing, the reflex strength of lever pressing (in our earlier terminology), depends in some way on both the animal's internal state *and* its incentive state with respect to lever pressing. How are these two states to be combined? This is a tricky question for at least two reasons. First, food-reinforced operant behavior can sometimes occur even when the animal's tendency to eat is below threshold. For example, we have observed that well-trained, hungry pigeons with free access to food nevertheless occasionally peck on a response key that produces the same food on an intermittent schedule, which implies that the threshold for eating may sometimes be lower than the threshold for food-reinforced operant behavior. Second, an incentive stimulus can sometimes induce eating in an apparently satiated animal (Weingarten, 1985), showing that incentive state can augment the tendency to eat even when the eating command is below threshold.

We cannot solve these problems here. In all our simulations, therefore, we assume that incentive state is constant, so that operant responding is determined entirely by internal state. Nevertheless, to make predictions, we need to make some assumption about how internal state translates into a real-time measure of operant responding, such as lever-response rate. The CINT models assume that feeding tendency is just the difference between a fixed threshold or set point, θ, and V_S, the satiation value. The quantity $p = (\theta - V_S)/\theta$ varies between 0 and 1, as long as θ equals or exceeds V_S, that is, as long as the model has some tendency to eat (reflex strength is greater than 0). Thus, we can treat p as a response probability, choosing our time step so that operant response rates fall in the typical range. For example, if p varies around a mean of 0.5, and the time step is equal to 1 second, response rates will be in the range of 30 per minute, which is typical of rats under many conditions. In practice, we modified the relation to ensure a nonzero "operant level" of responding, so that response probability is given by

$$p = k[(\theta - V_S)/\theta] + (1 - k), \qquad (5)$$

where $1 - k$ is the operant-level response probability.

With these preliminary assumptions—constant incentive value and a stochastic response rule[11]—we are ready to explore the extent to which free-operant "foraging" behavior can be explained by regulatory processes alone.

The Collier Experiments

George Collier and his associates have for several decades carried out ingenious and comprehensive behavioral experiments on feeding in rats. Collier acknowledges the importance of regulatory physiology (e.g., Collier, 1986), but he has argued consistently that *economic* factors are neglected in most treatments of feeding:

> The standard model is one in which deprivation results in depletion and hunger, and surfeit results in repletion and satiety. Feeding behaviors are presumed to begin and end *in response* to these deficits and surfeits. . . . This model is embedded in the concept of *homeostasis*. (Collier & Johnson, 1990, p. 771; italics in original)

Collier and his coworkers have done many experiments with results that appear to contradict the standard, homeostatic model:

---

[11]Note that this assumption is an oversimplification, because it ignores the effects of time discrimination. For example, when meals are spaced far apart, animals treat the situation like a long fixed-interval schedule. They wait a long time before making the first procurement response and then take some time to accelerate to their maximum response rate: "The primary effect of [variation in procurement cost] was on the inter-response times early in the ratio, which were longer in more expensive schedules" (Johnson & Collier, 1994, p. 1284). We do not deal with time discrimination because we are ignoring all associative factors.

When an animal can detect the structure of its habitat, its feeding behavior will tend to reduce the feeding cost/benefit ratio *in apparent anticipation* of both its nutritional requirements and the environmental conditions. This implies a system controlling when, where, and on what source the animal feeds, and how much and how fast it eats on any occasion, that is *quite different from the traditional homeostatic model.* . . . Hunger and satiety are not necessarily correlated with deficits and surfeits but rather with the patterns of intake required by different feeding strategies. (Collier & Johnson, 1990, pp. 775–776; italics added)

In chapter 6 of this volume, Collier and Johnson underline this message: "As cost increases [in the foraging paradigm], foraging rats actually wait longer after each meal to begin procuring access for the next meal. This delay is part of the strategy for economizing on the cost of feeding" (p. 124).

A strategy of anticipation is usually thought to depend on associative learning. We argue that the role of associative learning in feeding regulation may be much less than is often assumed. In this section, we take up the challenge of showing that a large part of the feeding data that Collier and Johnson have interpreted in economic and anticipatory terms can in fact be predicted by the perfectly homeostatic model discussed earlier.

Procedures

Collier has used procedures that differ in critical ways from "standard" operant conditioning studies: The animals are not food-deprived (other than through limitations on their ability to get food imposed by the reinforcement schedule), and "reinforcement" is not a fixed amount of food but a "meal" of indefinite duration. Collier's aim is to mimic natural foraging in which isolated "meals" (termed *consumption* by Collier) are separated by periods of searching (termed *procurement*) for the next meal. Experimental "sessions" are continuous throughout the 24-hour day, except for a brief daily maintenance period. This is sometimes called a *closed economy*, to be distinguished from the usual brief-session-followed-by-food-top-up *open economy* in standard conditioning experiments. Collier's basic procedure is diagrammed in Figure 13. Look at Figure 13 carefully, because the procedural details are quite complex and tend to conceal the simplicity of the underlying feeding dynamics. The basic idea behind the procedure is that the animal must make a large number of responses (usually lever pressing, for rat subjects) for the opportunity to eat (this is termed procurement or access cost: P_c); once food is available, however, it remains available (at small or no consumption cost: C_c) until the animal ceases to make the consumption response for a substantial period (usually 10 min), at which point it must again "pay" the access cost.

This procedure permits Collier to manipulate procurement cost either chronically (steady-state) or more frequently and look at the effect on eating. The experiments record eating patterns—meal size and frequency—

Collier Procedure

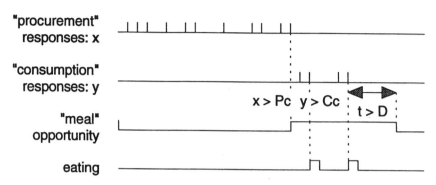

"procurement"
responses: x

"consumption"
responses: y

x > Pc   y > Cc   t > D

"meal"
opportunity

eating

Figure 13. Collier's experimental procedure. The figure shows the procedure used in most of the single-choice feeding experiments by Collier and his associates. Operant responses (usually, lever pressing) are of two types: "procurement" (or "access" responses and "consumption" responses. Procurement responses (x) are made for the opportunity to engage in consumption responses (y). Consumption responses are made for the opportunity to eat. (This is called a *chain* schedule, in operant terminology.) The procedure works like this: When the animal has ceased to make a consumption response (defined later) for experimenter-set Time D (D is usually 10 min), further consumption responses are ineffective, and the animal must make responses on the *procurement*, or *access*, lever to get more food. After it has made x procurement responses ($x = 11$ in the figure, but the usual requirement is much larger), a "meal opportunity" is offered. Now the animal must work on the *consumption* lever to get actual access to the food. After y consumption responses ($y = 2$ in the figure; usually y is much smaller than x; consumption cost is much less than procurement cost), a fixed amount of food is delivered. The animal can get additional food portions by paying the consumption cost again, and this possibility remains available indefinitely, until the animal again ceases to make consumption responses for Time D, at which point the procurement cost must be paid again and the cycle repeats. In some experiments, the only consumption response required is eating itself, detected by a photocell arrangement.

and correlations between meal size and the preceding or subsequent intermeal interval. What is the steady-state pattern of eating and operant responding after indefinite exposure to a given procurement cost? Dynamically, how does the pattern of eating and responding vary when procurement cost changes in various patterns? How well does the CINT model simulate these effects?

If procurement cost is increased (and consumption cost is low), both meal frequency and meal size change. As procurement cost increases, meal frequency decreases, so that the animal needs to pay the cost less often. At the same time, meal size increases, so that the animal does not reduce its total food intake. Typical steady-state results are shown in Figure 14 (squares and triangles) for an individual rat in a closed economy with food available according to the procedure diagrammed in Figure 13 (Collier, Hirsch, & Hamlin, 1972, Figures 5 and 7, Rat 1). Consumption cost was zero in this experiment; food was made unavailable 10 minutes after the

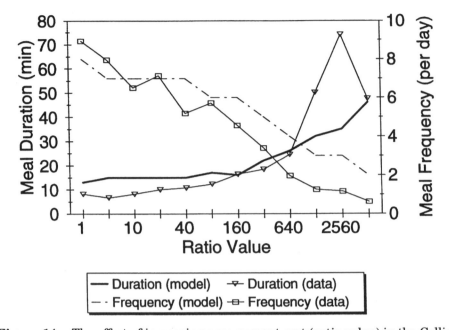

Figure 14. The effect of increasing procurement cost (ratio value) in the Collier, Hirsch, and Hamlin (1972) experiment. The open symbols represent mean meal duration (triangles) and meal frequency (squares). These are steady-state data from a single rat (the other two animals were similar) in a closed economy. In the *simulation*, the lines represent predictions of a six-stage CINT model. The parameter values (Equations 2–4) were determined as follows: $a_1 = \lambda_1$; $a_i = a_{i-1} + \lambda_2(1 - a_{i-1})$, $b_i = 1 - a_i$ (i.e., six stages, but only two free parameters). V_S was the sum of V values for the last three stages. For all the Collier simulations, plus the simulations shown in Figures 10 and 12, the parameters were $\lambda_1 = 0.87$, $\lambda_2 = 0.93$, $\Phi = 2$, and $\theta_{light} = 0.4$. To deal with the fact that rats eat more in the 12-hour light phase of these experiments than in the dark phase, we set θ_{dark} as follows: $\theta_{dark} = 0.3\theta_{light}$. Response probability was set by the equation $p = k[(\theta - V_S)/\theta] + (1 - k)$, with $k = 0.5$, which ensured a nonzero "operant level" of lever pressing of $p = k$. One time step = 1 second. To relate eating amount to Φ eating units/s (the output of the model), we assumed in all cases that 350 Φ units per time step = 1 g/s. To ensure appropriate initial conditions, the model was run for 10 days under free-food conditions before the first schedule constraint was imposed.

last eating episode, as measured by a photocell arrangement. The squares show per diem frequency of meals (defined according to the 10-min criterion) at different procurement costs, from 1 (continuous reinforcement, CRF) through 5,120 lever presses. The triangles show average meal duration, in minutes.

Figure 15 shows how well the animal in Figure 14 regulated its overall food intake. Overall ingestion rate (squares) was approximately constant up to ratio values of 200 or so and declined thereafter. The meal-frequency and meal-duration data in Figure 14 show that this defense of overall eating rate is accomplished primarily by large increases in meal size. As Collier pointed out, the animal behaves in a wonderfully adaptive fashion,

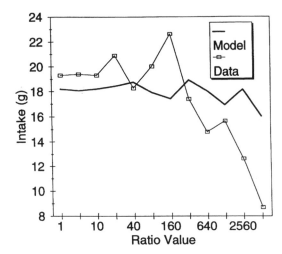

Figure 15.   Intake regulation in the Collier, Hirsch, and Hamlin (1972) experiment. Squares represent daily food intake in grams for the rat in Figure 14. The solid line represents predictions of the CINT model. Other details are as in Figure 14.

decreasing meal frequency as procurement cost increases (so the cost need be paid less and less often) but compensating for the resulting drop in eating rate by enormous, largely costless, increases in meal size. Similar effects have been found in cats and guinea pigs (Hirsch & Collier, 1974; Kanarek, 1975; see review in Collier, Hirsch, & Kanarek, 1977).

How might these results be explained homeostatically? The argument is as follows. As procurement cost (fixed-ratio size) is increased over the large range used in these experiments, the time between "meals" must also increase, because the rat does not increase its lever-press rate significantly at larger ratios. The question for the CINT models is whether this forced increase in intermeal interval is by itself sufficient to explain the effects of procurement cost. Recalling the effects of interruption discussed earlier, one is likely to answer "maybe," because following a forced interruption of feeding, the first meal is always extra-large (in fact and according to the CINT models). This is also what Collier's experiments show: When the procurement cost is high, so that intermeal interval is larger than it would be under unconstrained conditions, meal size is also large. Most recently, Mathis, Johnson, and Collier (1995) showed that procurement time and procurement cost are roughly equivalent: "The functions relating meal frequency and size to the procurement interval were of the same shape as those seen when cost is the completion of the bar-press requirement" (p. 295). The decline in meal frequency appears to be an adaptive response to increased procurement cost, but it may also be largely an incidental by-product of the time taken to complete large procurement-cost ratios.

Figures 14 and 15 show, along with the data from Collier et al. (1972), predictions of a six-stage CINT model, with the same parameters used earlier to fit the fasting data from Levitsky et al. (Figure 10). The CINT model predicts the meal-duration and meal-frequency data reasonably well; the model regulates total intake better than the rat does at high rat values. Apparently, the verbal argument is sound: The main effect of procurement cost on meal size can be explained by the same process that accounts for eating in meals and the first-meal effect of feeding interruption. The decrease in meal frequency with increasing procurement cost and the maintenance throughout of close to control levels of daily ingestion are also explained by the CINT model.

We have begun to extend our simulation to an extensive dynamic experiment by Morato, Johnson, and Collier (1995) in which procurement cost was changed daily or in blocks of days. The simulation duplicates the general pattern of results in this complex experiment, but space limitations preclude a detailed discussion here. We hope to present these results in an article devoted entirely to foraging and regulation.

Discussion

Johnson and Collier (1994) recently addressed the idea that meal duration increases as procurement cost increases, not because animals adapt to changed conditions but because "working harder to procure access to food stimulates a larger meal directly, and that consuming a large meal, in turn, delays the next meal" (p. 1279). This statement is close to our contention that the interruption of feeding by itself produces larger meals and that the effect on intermeal interval is a regulatory by-product. Johnson and Collier argued that this view implies that if "[procurement cost] varies across meals, an animal would eat larger meals after paying [larger costs]" (p. 1279). They tested the idea by varying procurement cost from meal to meal ("variable-price" conditions) as well as in blocks of days ("fixed-price" conditions) and comparing meal size versus cost functions under the two conditions, as well as looking at the correlation between meal size and preceding intermeal interval in the meal-to-meal condition. Their procedure is shown in Figure 13; the procurement cost varied from 1 to 512, and the consumption cost was 10. Johnson and Collier concluded that "within variable-price schedules there was no effect of the just-paid price on the size of the meal, *except in the highest-price schedules*, when meal frequency was low and somewhat larger meals followed higher prices" (1994, p. 1279; italics added). Another look at Figure 14 reveals that the meal-duration versus procurement cost (ratio value) function in the Collier et al. (1972) data and in our simulation is essentially flat until ratio values of 500 or so. In other words, even under steady-state conditions, ratio value has little effect on meal size until the ratio is quite large, which is just what Johnson and Collier reported and is perfectly consistent with the predictions of the CINT model. Johnson and Collier's data do indeed refute a simple meal-by-meal model, but they are completely consistent both with Collier's own early data and with a CINT-type homeostatic model.

Rats regulate both body weight and rate of eating at several time scales. We have proposed a very simple model for eating-rate regulation that is consistent with the major features of feeding experiments on long-, medium-, and short-term regulation and constraint. The model does not match every feature of the data perfectly. For example, with the parameters we used to account for the Collier et al. and Levitsky et al. results, the model regulates eating rate at the longest interpellet intervals (IPIs) less well than the rats in Lucas and Timberlake's constrained-IPI experiment (Figure 12) but better than the animals reported on by Collier et al. (Figure 15). The model predicts a meal frequency slightly higher than the data in the Collier et al. experiment (Figure 14). The model predicts slightly more compensation for long fasts than the data in the Levitsky et al. experiment (Figure 10). And eating in meals when IPI is constrained, as in the Lucas and Timberlake experiment, breaks down sooner in the model than in the data.

We expected some discrepancies of this sort, because a purely regulatory model necessarily ignores many factors that are known to affect eating behavior. We are not certain in every case which factor is responsible for which discrepancy. There are several possibilities: (a) *Noningestional regulatory processes.* As we pointed out earlier, the rats in the Levitsky et al. experiment all recovered their control body weights despite a persistent cumulative food deficit. Clearly there are important noningestional regulatory processes, which are not covered by the CINT model. At the longest fasts in the Levitsky et al. experiment, the animals lost substantial amounts of body weight, which might well affect the CINT model set point, θ. We assumed a constant θ value across all simulations. (b) *Associative factors.* The CINT model predicted a higher meal frequency than the Collier et al. data; however, the model takes no account of temporal discrimination, which is known to be a factor in the fixed-ratio "pause," the interruption in lever pressing that follows eating after long exposure to fixed-ratio schedules. Pausing should increase the intermeal interval and thus reduce meal frequency, by comparison with a pure regulatory model. Behavioral contrast (Reynolds, 1961), an associative phenomenon that depends on stimulus discrimination, may also affect bar-press rates in the procurement and consumption phases of Collier's experiment, elevating response rate in the consumption phase and depressing the rate in the procurement phase. (c) *Regulatory learning.* Davis and Smith (1990) showed in sham-feeding experiments that the satiating effect of taste diminishes with experience and is thus partly a learned effect. The CINT model takes no account of learning at all. (d) *Stochastic factors.* In many experiments, a "meal" is defined rather arbitrarily by a criterion intereating time. Such measures are very sensitive to stochastic factors: Adding "noise" to the eating threshold in a model can increase or decrease measured meal frequency under different conditions. We made no attempt to incorporate noise into the simple model.

The main point is that these deviations from the CINT-model predictions are all *second-order* effects. The major properties of all these experimental results—on feeding patterns, feeding regulation, and experimental analogues to foraging—seem to flow, not from learning, discrimination, or anticipation, but from a straightforward regulatory process in which the satiating effects of food are subject to multiple delays.

Epistemological Afterword

Some readers, particularly those whose interests are in physiology and anatomy, may find our account unsatisfying. They will ask in what sense the CINT model really *explains* feeding. What is really *true* about the model? (Or is it just a nerdy trick to baffle data gatherers?) We believe that the fundamental property we have discovered is the biphasic impulse response shown in Figure 5. Our primary conclusion is that the dynamics of eating behavior in rats derive almost entirely from the fact that the satiating effects of food are delayed. A secondary finding is that the satiation signal involves several time scales (this is implicit in the slow decline of the "tail" of the function in Figure 5). What about the specific architecture of the CINT model depicted in Figures 6 and 7? We are much less confident about this. We have made no serious attempt to link the different integrators to specifiable physiological processes in the chain of events that begins with ingestion. Indeed, we suspect that finding all such links will turn out to be extremely difficult. (Perhaps it was failure to construct viable models out of imperfectly known physiology that led to the desuetude of the whole feeding-model business.) In fact there are many ways to achieve the biphasic impulse response that seems to underlie feeding dynamics. Our suggestion is one of the simplest, but biology may well do the job in some other way.

The practical justification for modeling is that if psychobiologists know what job the physiology is doing, they will be better placed to figure out just how it does it. The economic justification is that it allows researchers to reduce a mass of unrelated empirical results to a few simple rules. The scientific justification is that it helps us to understand an apparently complex, purposive process in satisfyingly simple, causal terms.

References

Adolph, E. F. (1947). Urges to eat and drink in rats. *American Journal of Physiology, 151*, 110–125.

Berdoy, M. (1993). Defining bouts of behavior: A three-process model. *Animal Behaviour, 46*, 387–396.

Bolles, R. C. (1980). Some functionalistic thoughts about regulation. In F. M. Toates & T. R. Halliday (Eds.), *Analysis of motivational processes*. London: Academic Press.

Booth, D. A. (Ed.). (1978). *Hunger models*. London: Academic Press.

Clifton, P. G. (1987). Analysis of feeding and drinking patterns. In F. Toates & N. Rowland (Eds.), *Feeding and drinking*. Amsterdam: Elsevier.

Collier, G. (1986). The dialogue between the house economist and the resident physiologist. *Nutrition and Behavior, 3*, 9–16.

Collier, G., Hirsch, E., & Hamlin, P. (1972). The ecological determinants of reinforcement in the rat. *Physiology and Behavior, 9*, 705–716.

Collier, G., Hirsch, E., & Kanarek, R. (1977). The operant revisited. In W. K. Honig & J. E. R. Staddon (Eds.), *Handbook of operant behavior* (pp. 28–52). Englewood Cliffs, NJ: Prentice-Hall.

Collier, G., & Johnson, D. F. (1990). The time window of feeding. *Physiology and Behavior, 48,* 771–777.

Davis, J. D. (1989). The microstructure of ingestive behavior. In *Feeding disorders. Annals of the New York Academy of Sciences, 575,* 106–121.

Davis, J. D., & Smith, G. P. (1990). Learning to sham feed: Behavioral adjustments to loss of physiological postingestional stimuli. *American Journal of Physiology, 259,* R1228–R1235.

Gibson, J. J. (1979). *The ecological approach to visual perception.* Boston: Houghton Mifflin.

Guillot, A., & Meyer, J.-A. (1987). A test of the Booth energy flow model (Mark 3) on feeding patterns of mice. *Appetite, 8,* 67–78.

Hirsch, E. (1973). Some determinants of intake and patterns of feeding in the guinea pig. *Physiology and Behavior, 11,* 687–704.

Hirsch, E., &. Collier, G. (1974). The ecological determinants of reinforcement in the guinea pig. *Physiology and Behavior, 12,* 239–249.

Johnson, D. F., Ackroff, K., Peters, J., & Collier, G. H. (1986). Changes in rats' meal patterns as a function of the caloric density of the diet. *Physiology and Behavior, 36,* 929–936.

Johnson, D. F., & Collier, G. (1994). Meal patterns of rats encountering variable food procurement cost. *Animal Behavior, 47,* 1279–1287.

Kanarek, R. (1975). Availability and caloric density of the diet as determinants of meal patterns in cats. *Physiology and Behavior, 15,* 611–618.

Le Magnen, J. (1985). *Hunger.* London: Cambridge University Press.

Le Magnen, J., & Tallon, S. (1966). La periodicité spontanée de la prise d'aliments ad libitum du rat blanc [Spontaneous periodicity entrained by ad libitum feeding in the white rat]. *Journal de la Physiologie (Paris), 58,* 323–349.

Levitsky, D. A., & Collier, G. (1968). Effects of diet and deprivation on meal eating behavior in rats. *Physiology and Behavior, 3,* 137–140.

Levitsky, D. A., Faust, I., & Glassman, M. (1976). The ingestion of food and the recovery of body weight following fasting in the naive rat. *Physiology and Behavior, 17,* 575–580.

Lucas, G. A., & Timberlake, W. (1988). Interpellet delay and meal patterns in the rat. *Physiology and Behavior, 43,* 259–264.

Machlis, L. (1977). An analysis of the temporal pattern of pecking in chicks. *Behaviour, 63,* 1–70.

Mathis, C. E., Johnson, D. F., & Collier, G. H. (1995). Procurement time as a determinant of meal frequency and meal duration. *Journal of the Experimental Analysis of Behavior, 63,* 295–311.

McFarland, D., & Bösser, T. (1993). *Intelligent behavior in animals and robots.* Cambridge, MA: MIT/Bradford.

Mook, D. G. (1987). *Motivation: The organization of action.* New York: Norton.

Mook, D. G., & Dreifuss, S. (1986). Saccharin drinking by hungry rats: Adjustment to constraints. *Appetite, 7,* 365–379.

Morato, S., Johnson, D. F., & Collier, G. (1995). Feeding patterns of rats when food-access cost is alternately low and high. *Physiology and Behavior, 57,* 22–26.

Morgan, C. T. (1894). *An introduction to comparative psychology.* London: W. Scott.

Panksepp, J. (1974). Hypothalamic regulation of energy balance and feeding behavior. *Federation Proceedings, 33,* 1150–1165.

Panksepp, J. (1976). On the nature of feeding patterns—primarily in rats. In D. Novin, W. Wyrwicka, & G. Bray (Eds.), *Hunger: Basic mechanisms and clinical implications.* New York: Raven Press.

Reynolds, G. S. (1961). Behavioral contrast. *Journal of the Experimental Analysis of Behavior, 4,* 57–71.

Schilstra, A. J. (1978). Simulation of feeding behavior: Comparison of deterministic and stochastic models incorporating a minimum of presuppositions. In D. A. Booth (Ed.), *Hunger models: Computable theory of feeding control* (pp. 167–194). London: Academic Press.

Sclafani, A., & Springer, D. (1976). Dietary obesity in adult rats: Similarities to hypothalamic and human obesity syndromes. *Physiology and Behavior, 17,* 461–471.

Seeley, R. J., Kaplan, J. M., & Grill, H. J. (1993). Effects of interrupting an intraoral meal on meal size and meal duration in rats. *Appetite, 20,* 13–20.

Staddon, J. E. R. (1988). The functional properties of feeding, or why we still need the black box. *Appetite, 11,* 54–61.

Staddon, J. E. R. (1993). On rate-sensitive habituation. *Adaptive Behavior, 1,* 421–436.

Staddon, J. E. R., & Higa, J. J. (in press). Multiple time scales in simple habituation. *Psychological Review.*

Toates, F. M., & Evans, R. A. S. (1987). The application of theory, modelling and simulation to feeding and drinking. In F. M. Toates & N. Rowland (Eds.), *Feeding and drinking.* Amsterdam: Elsevier Science (Biomedical).

Weingarten, H. (1985). Stimulus control of eating: Implications for a two-factor theory of hunger. *Appetite, 6,* 387–401.

Wirtshafter, D., & Davis, J. D. (1977). Set points, settling points, and the control of body weight. *Physiology and Behavior, 19,* 75–78.

8

Wheels, Clocks, and Anorexia in the Rat

Robert A. Boakes

Two of the most important contributions Bolles made to the psychology of learning were his book *Theory of Motivation* (1967, 1975) and his research on constraints on learning. In its two editions, the book was a major influence for generations of psychology students in the 1960s and 1970s, for whom it served as the main introduction to the topic; it is still used in some undergraduate courses today. A dominant theme was an analysis of the many failings of Hull's (1943) theory of motivation. Later, Bolles's account of avoidance learning and his concept of species-specific defense reactions (SSDRs; Bolles, 1970, 1978) were major components, along with the attack by his former fellow graduate students, Garcia and Petrinovich (see Foreword and Chapter 1, this volume) on the equipotentiality principle, which had provided the bedrock of most theories of learning since Pavlov.

These two contributions may seem to have little in common, except that both attacked some of the most basic assumptions of neobehaviorism. The idea of the SSDR provided the basis for a number of new research developments (see Chapter 16, this volume, for example) that have continued to prove extremely fertile. In contrast, Bolles's earlier research of the 1960s, which was given prominence in his book, has had little continuing impact on the psychology of learning. Moreover, the central concern with motivational issues began to seem outdated even in the 1970s, when learning theorists put aside such questions, concentrating on associations and leaving performance for another day or another kind of researcher (e.g., Dickinson, 1980). Bolles's *Theory of Motivation* helped to close one era, and his research on avoidance learning was an influential factor in the start of a new one. At first sight, there appears to be no connection between the two.

In fact there was a connection, one provided by a piece of apparatus:

The research reported in this chapter was supported by a grant from the Australian Research Council. I am grateful for the hospitality of the Departament de Psicologia Basica, University of Barcelona, where this chapter was written using its resources. The comments of Mark Bouton, Dominic Dwyer, Ralph Mistlberger, and Stacey Young on an earlier version are greatly appreciated.

the running wheel. This apparatus produces two important phenomena that have been well documented since the pioneering work of Richter (1922). The first is that the speed with which a rat runs in such a wheel is highly sensitive to its degree of food deprivation: The hungrier the rat, the faster it runs. The second is that, if a rat is fed at a regular time each day, it develops what became known as *food anticipatory activity:* Its running accelerates during the few hours prior to the arrival of food, reaching a peak just before food becomes available. The first of these effects was crucial for Hull's theory. It provided a major empirical basis for his key assumption (Hull, 1943): As *general drive* increases (e.g., produced by food deprivation and adding in all other sources of drive), level of activity increases. More generally, how a rat behaves in a running wheel was for decades regarded as key for understanding motivation.

Bolles devoted a whole chapter of his book to the energizing effect of drives. His review of previous research led him to conclude that "the energizing of *certain classes of behavior* [my italics] . . [is] . . the *only* empirically defensible property of drive" (Bolles, 1975, p. 217). He went on to argue that "the drive concept is easily dispensed with entirely because there are other ways to explain the energizing effect" (p. 217). In the present context, the key section of this chapter is that devoted to the "energizing of general activity." This section examined the still prevalent belief that general activity can be seen as an unlearned and immediate reaction to an animal's need state. Following Sheffield and Campbell (1954), Bolles argued, partly on the basis of some of his own experiments (e.g., Bolles & Younger, 1967), that the effect of food deprivation is to enhance an animal's response to a stimulus; that is, it has no direct effect on general activity.

What then is the basis for the robust relationship between food deprivation and running in an activity wheel? Even at the time of publication of the book's second edition (1975), following a decade or more of research on this question in a number of laboratories including Bolles's own, he was unable to find a satisfactory account. There is clearly some kind of learned element, because when and to what degree an animal shows anticipatory running depend on the pattern of mealtimes and temporal relationships between access to the wheel and provision of food. For example, Bolles and Moot (1973) found that, when regularly fed two meals a day, rats showed increased running prior to both meals. On the other hand, familiar conditioning mechanisms cannot account for the long-documented finding that when an animal is placed for the first time in a running wheel, with no prior experience of comparable environment, its running speed shows a clear positive relationship to its degree of food deprivation (e.g., Duda & Bolles, 1963; Wald & Jackson, 1944).

What was clear by 1975 was that the result of giving a rat access to a running wheel and only limited access to food is a highly specific one. A rat given unlimited food but limited access to water shows a quite different pattern in that only a small increase in running occurs and this rapidly stabilizes (e.g., Bolles, 1968). Furthermore, if, instead of changing the deprivation state, some apparatus other than a running wheel is used for measuring activity, a hungry rat behaves in a different way. In a stabilimeter-type cage, the measured activity of a hungry rat given food once a day levels off after a day (Eayrs, 1954), in complete contrast to the steady increase of running often to dramatic levels seen when a running wheel is employed. As Bolles and Saunders (1969) confirmed using ultrasonic measuring devices, one can "obtain virtually any kind of functional relationship one might imagine between deprivation conditions and activation merely by varying the sensitivity (of activity recording devices)" (Bolles, 1975, p. 228). Finally, it appears that the different ways in which the rat responds to food and water in various kinds of equipment may be a poor predictor of how other species behave (Campbell, Smith, Misanin, & Jaynes, 1966). Bolles concluded: "So we see, perhaps to our surprise, that what was once considered to be a very general phenomenon, that is, that any kind of drive would stimulate general activity, now appears to be a very specific phenomenon . . . . we now see that this phenomenon is to a large extent specific to hunger, specific to the rat and specific to activity wheels" (Bolles, 1975, p. 228). Oddly, he did not label wheel running as a species-specific response of the rat to hunger; he kept the term to refer only to responses to fear.

Clocks

If the general effect of food deprivation, according to Bolles, is to enhance specific responses to specific stimuli, what kind of stimulus is functioning in the case of anticipatory wheel running? Until the 1960s, only two classes of stimuli were normally considered in attempts to answer this question: on the one hand, stimuli from the external environment, ones that might be correlated with the presentation of food, and on the other hand, internal stimuli generated by the physiological effects of food deprivation. In 1962 Bolles and de Lorge reported on a highly innovative experiment that suggested the role of another kind of internal stimulus, one generated by the animal's biological clock. This concept was only beginning to acquire general respectability at the time. Apparently the experiment was inspired by new results on circadian rhythms in bees (Renner, 1960). It compared three groups of rats, all having unlimited access to a running wheel except when fed for 1 hour. Whereas the control group was given food every 24 hours in the standard manner, the other two groups had adiurnal feeding cycles: every 19 hours in one group and every 29 hours in the other. The main result was that the controls showed the expected large increase in running prior to feeding, but little sign of this increase was found in the other groups (Bolles & de Lorge, 1962). The 29-hour group tended to display a continued 24-hour cycle of activity.

The experimental procedure was messy, the data variable with no statistics applied, and the conclusions far stronger than the reported results warranted. By today's standards, the article would be difficult to publish. Nevertheless, the results were replicated in a second experiment, which contained considerable procedural improvements over the first (Bolles & Stokes, 1965). This study also included a comparison with rats trained to lever-press for food. Although this behavior also showed an anticipatory pattern in the 24-hour controls, in the 19-hour and 29-hour groups, there was neither an anticipatory increase in lever pressing prior to feeding nor any sign that this response was sensitive to the normal 24-hour cycle. Thus, this experiment provided further grounds for wariness in generalizing from wheel running to other forms of activity. Overall, these results appeared to rule out the role of "drive stimuli" in controlling running. Rather, they indicated that "the rat cannot easily anticipate feedings given every 19 or 29 hours, because such cycles depart too far from its inborn circadian rhythm" (Bolles & Stokes, 1965, p. 294). To use the kind of phrasing that became current a few years later, there are strong biological constraints on the degree to which a rat can learn to adapt to an arbitrary feeding cycle.

It appears that at the University of Washington in the 1970s, Bolles's graduate students became less interested in such problems. This was at least partly due to his own increasing involvement in a number of other issues (Bouton, personal communication, 1996). The running wheel became an unfamiliar piece of apparatus in learning laboratories; however, it has retained its popularity in chronobiology laboratories, where the kind of research in which Bolles was a pioneer has turned out to be highly productive. As comprehensively summarized in recent reviews such as those of Mistlberger (1994) and Mistlberger and Rusak (1994), subsequent experiments have amply confirmed the main point made by Bolles and de Lorge (1962): Food anticipatory activity (FAA), and more generally a rat's running in a wheel, cannot be understood without reference to clocks inside the animal's brain, or neural oscillators. Research over the last 2 decades has increased understanding of some of the issues with which Bolles was concerned in the 1960s and early 1970s.

Most important, it has become clear that there are at least two clocks that affect running wheel activity and that can be distinguished both behaviorally and anatomically. By the end of the 1970s, the site of the oscillator primarily responsible for controlling rats'—and other mammals'—circadian activity had been clearly identified as the suprachiasmic nucleus (SCN) of the hypothalamus (e.g., Rusak & Zucker, 1979). In a rat with unrestricted access to food as well as to a running wheel, this clock plays the major role in determining the time at which feeding and bouts of running occur. It subsequently emerged, however, that the FAA effect could be obtained in animals in which this nucleus was ablated. Various experiments have converged in showing that there exists some other clock or clocks that can affect activity cycles related to food in addition to the "light clock" of the SCN. To date, the location in the rat's brain of the "food clock" remains unknown.

Bolles did not express his ideas in terms of the mathematical analysis of linked oscillators and the phenomenon of entrainment, which provide the framework for current research. Nonetheless, the general idea suggested by Bolles and de Lorge (1962) turned out to be correct. Both the light clock and the food clock have an innate periodicity, which can vary across individuals as well as across rat strains, that tends to be greater than 24 hours, and this can be entrained; that is, its period can change in the manner shown by any physical system with an inherent frequency of oscillation that is regularly stimulated by some outside source. Neural clocks can be entrained, their speed and setting changed and "tuned," by periodic environmental events (*zeitgebers*, or "timegivers"), but only by those regularly occurring with a restricted range of periods. With respect to wheel running, Stephan (1981) found that the entrainable range of the food clock was approximately 22–31 hours. These results may seem inconsistent with the claim by Bolles and de Lorge (1962) that FAA cannot be produced by providing food every 29 hours, but examination of their data suggests that in fact two of the animals did exhibit FAA under this condition. It seems that once the food clock is set to a particular time of day, it tends to remain at this value. Clarke and Coleman (1986) found that once FAA was generated by providing food every 24 hours and the animals were maintained in constant dim light, bouts of activity continued to occur during periods of food deprivation at about the time the animals had previously been fed. Also, if the periodicity of the food clock is reset, for example, to 22 hours, the setting survived a period of free feeding (Coleman, Harper, Clarke, & Armstrong, 1982).

As for the steady increase in FAA that occurs with prolonged exposure to regular, 24-hour feeding, Bolles (1975, pp. 223–226) remained convinced that it reflected some kind of conditioning process, even if he was far from clear on the form this might take. On the whole, following Finger (e.g., Finger, Reid, & Weasner, 1957), he tended toward an analysis in terms of superstitious instrumental reinforcement, although this was not the term he used, whereby a high rate of wheel running is "reinforced" adventitiously because it happens to be followed by the arrival of food (cf. Herrnstein, 1966; Skinner, 1948). He seemed curiously reluctant, as reflected in his classic article on species-specific defense reactions (Bolles, 1970), to explore the possibility that classical, or Pavlovian, conditioning might generate the effect, even though demonstrations that such conditioning can produce marked changes in skeletal responses had abounded following the discovery of autoshaping in the pigeon by Brown and Jenkins (1968). With hindsight, it seems obvious that internal signals from the food clock might serve as classical conditioned stimuli (CSs) that become associated with the arrival of food and thus, by some hardwired link, elicit increased running.

Recently, Mistlberger and Marchant (1995) argued that the phenomenon of FAA can be explained without reference to any kind of conditioning process. The concept of entrainment is all that is needed. In simple terms, one basic assumption is that there is an innate connection whereby during parts of its cycle, the food clock emits signals that trigger running in the rat. With increasing exposure of the animal to a regular feeding cycle with a period of about 24 hours, the clock becomes more precisely entrained and its phase shifts gradually so that the emission of signals that trigger running become more and more concentrated in the period immediately prior to the delivery of food. The discovery by Bolles and Moot (1973) that FAA can occur prior to both feeding periods if a rat is fed twice a day suggests that the emission of "activity signals" by the clock occurs at least twice during the normal 24-hour cycle. This is consistent with the observation that rats with free access to food tend to take their meals mainly during two parts of the dark periods. All that is needed to account for the increasingly high levels of running prior to receiving food that rats display when given access restricted to less than 2 hours is a motivational element: The running produced by such signals is enhanced by loss of body weight, an assumption quite consistent with Bolles's ideas on the subject.

Clearly associative processes play an important role in the development of other kinds of "anticipatory" activity. For example, both rats and pigeons can be easily trained to discriminate between two contexts, in which food is delivered in one but not in the other, as indexed by substantially more general movement in the food-associated context (e.g., Holland & Rescorla, 1975; Rescorla, Durlach, & Grau, 1985). However, the extent to which wheel running is sensitive to such associative factors and the possible role of Pavlovian processes in the FAA are currently important issues in light of the proposal by Mistlberger and Marchant (1995; see also Boulos & Logothetis, 1990).

Anorexia in the Rat

There is another major effect that can be obtained from hungry rats with access to a running wheel. If the daily period during which food is available is limited, their body weight can drop progressively until either they are removed from the apparatus or they die. Bolles knew about this phenomenon from firsthand experience. About half of the rats died in the 24-hour and 29-hour groups of Bolles and de Lorge (1962), so that they reported data only from the first six to survive in each group. However, Bolles appears to have seen this effect as unimportant, perhaps because its theoretical interest was not readily apparent. Routtenberg and Kuznesof (1967) provided a clear documentation of this dramatic effect, but otherwise Bolles's disinterest seems to have been shared by many contemporary researchers with laboratories containing running wheels. It was later discovered that rats under these conditions may develop a form of stomach ulceration quite unlike that produced by other forms of stress and more akin to human stomach ulcers. This finding revived interest in the procedure, termed the *activity-stress preparation* (Paré, 1975). More recently, the phenomenon has been seen as a model for some aspects of human anorexia (e.g., Epling & Pierce, 1988).

My initial interest in the phenomenon of *activity-based anorexia* (ABA)—which led to my reading the articles by Bolles's group on wheel running—was prompted by the realization that, after all these years and despite widespread use of the procedure in neurobiological research, there was no satisfactory explanation for such maladaptive behavior in rats. When a rat lives with access to a running wheel and food is made available once a day for 90 minutes, the most striking aspect of its behavior is how much it will run after a few days of exposure to these conditions. Distances equivalent to over 1 km per day are not uncommon. This fact suggests an obvious explanation for the rat's progressive loss of weight: Its calorie needs comes to outstrip its food intake. Even the name the phenomenon has recently acquired, activity-based anorexia, suggests this explanation. If it is correct, it implies that the more basic issue is to understand running rather than weight loss, which may be why Bolles and many other investigators concentrated on activity and paid little attention to the loss of body weight.

It turns out, however, that to assume that major weight loss is a direct consequence of a high level of activity is not correct. If rats are already fully adapted to a feeding schedule, allowing them subsequent access to a running wheel results in very high running rates. The important finding is that such running has only a small and transitory effect on their food intake and body weight, a result obtained by Dwyer and Boakes (1997, Experiment 1), whose data are shown in Figure 1. Group P, during a pre-adaptation period, was given 90-minute access to food starting at 1600 on a normal light–dark cycle (lights on: 0600–1800) for 14 days before the doors to the running wheels were opened. As shown in the top panel, running produced a further slight depression in the body weights of this group, but these weights soon recovered and were beginning to increase by the time the experiment was terminated. The same is true for food intake, as shown in the middle panel. In contrast, the body weights of Group N, which was given no prior exposure to the feeding schedule and instead had the 90-minute schedule imposed at the same time that the wheel access was introduced, continued to decrease precipitously, as seen in the top panel. Rats were removed if their weights reached the criterion of 70 percent or less of initial body weight on 2 successive days. All 8 rats in Group N reached this criterion (median: 16.5 days), whereas no rat in Group P did so. Indeed, all rats in the latter group instead reached a recovery criterion: body weight equal to or greater than its value 4 days earlier (median: 6.5 days).

That the substantial amount of running displayed by subjects in this experiment in fact was not responsible directly for the development of ABA in Group N is clearly indicated in the bottom panel. It can be seen that for the first 10 days or so, rats in Group P ran more than those in Group N, even though their body weight was beginning to recover during this period. Comparable results have been obtained from a study that examined stomach ulceration: A group of rats preadapted to a 1-hour feeding schedule ran faster than a group for which wheel access and food deprivation started at the same time, yet the rats in the former group showed no sign of the ulceration seen in the latter group (Morrow & Garrick, 1993). Therefore, both the progressive loss of weight of the full ABA effect and the ulceration that occurs when the weight drops below 70 percent of a rat's initial weight occur only when the running wheel is available at the time the rat is having to cope with a highly restricted feeding time. In summary, experiments that have adapted rats to the feeding schedule prior to giving access to a wheel suggest that excessive running is less a cause of weight loss than a consequence.

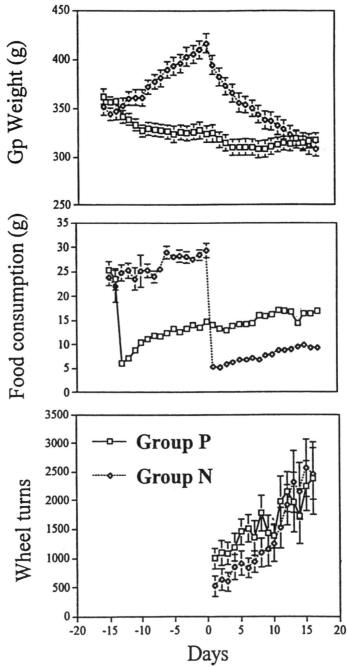

Figure 1. Body weight (top panel), food intake (center), and wheel turns (bottom) in rats preadapted to a 1.5-hour feeding schedule (Group P) for 14 days prior to wheel access and for a control group (Group N) who were given unrestricted food access until wheel access was provided. At this point, Day 1, Group C was also limited to 1.5-hours of food per day. Means ($N = 8$) and *SEM*s are shown, except when the latter were too small to print. From Experiment 1 in "Activity-Based Anorexia in Rats as a Failure to Adapt to a Feeding Schedule," by D. M. Dwyer and R. A. Boakes, 1997, *Behavioral Neuroscience, 111,* 197. Reprinted with permission.

Although the amount that a rat runs is not important for ABA, it turns out that *when* it runs is critical. My colleague and I compared two groups that were both placed on a 90-minute feeding schedule when first given access to a wheel but restricted the times when rats could enter the wheel (Dwyer & Boakes, 1997, Experiment 4). On a normal light–dark cycle (lights on: 0600–1800) and with feeding from 1300 to 1430, the early group was given 18.5 hours of access to the wheel, between 1430 and 0900, whereas the late group was given only 4 hours of access, from 0900 to 1300. The total amounts of running each day were comparable throughout the experiment. Nevertheless, the body weights of all but 1 of the 8 animals in the early group reached the recovery criterion (median: 14 days), whereas all 8 rats in the late group reached the removal criterion (median: 13 days). It therefore appears that for ABA to occur, it is critical that the rat be able to run for the few hours immediately preceding the arrival of food. In other words, a key factor is FAA, as Bolles might have guessed.

He might also have been pleased that the ABA phenomenon cannot be understood without reference to a rat's internal clock. Evidence for this statement comes from another experiment (Boakes & Dwyer, in press, Experiment 1). This resembled the first ABA experiment described, in that one group was given prior experience of feeding during the light period. However, in the present experiment, such preadaptation involved only a minor degree of deprivation, and this group was returned to unrestricted feeding for a period prior to the start of wheel access, a procedure that is important for understanding the possible role of a "reset" clock. The experiment also used a modification of the standard ABA procedure. In this case, instead of living in the activity wheel apparatus, rats were housed normally throughout the experiment and placed in the apparatus for only 3.5 hours each day. In the "training" phase, rats had access to the wheel from 1100 to 1300, and from 1300 to 1430, food was available.

The main question addressed by this experiment was whether prior experience of having to eat at this time of day would make subjects less vulnerable to the effects of wheel running, even though a period of free feeding had intervened to allow recovery of body weight. For the first 6 days of the experiment, one group, Group P (preadapted), was given food from 1300 to 1630 in the home cages, whereas their controls, Group N, remained on unrestricted food. This produced a transient decline in body weight in Group P to about 90 percent of its initial value before the weight started to climb once more. For the next 6 days, this group was returned to unrestricted feeding, and body weights recovered to just below those of Group N.

At this point training began, with the introduction for both groups of the wheel and a 1.5-hour food schedule, from 1300 to 1430. The amount of wheel running was comparable in the two groups: about 300 turns, about 330 m/hr after 14 sessions. However, the groups differed considerably in terms of how much they ate and the speed with which their body weights recovered from the initial impact of the 1.5-hour schedule. The recovery criterion was reached by Group P in a median of 9.6 days, whereas Group N took a median of 15.6 days. (The conditions of this ex-

periment were not sufficiently severe to produce the full ABA effect, i.e.,
complete failure to recover body weight.) This experiment suggests that
once the clock governing a rat's food intake has been reset to daytime
feeding, it retains this setting over a period of free feeding so that subsequently the animal can adjust more rapidly to the imposition of a more
limited daytime period of food access.

The key factor for ABA appears to be the process of adjusting to an
abnormally timed feeding schedule. Rats are normally nocturnal eaters,
consuming about 90 percent of their daily intake in the dark when access
to food is unrestricted. The imposition of a 1.5-hour feeding schedule during the dark period has a relatively minor impact on their body weights
compared to introduction of 1.5 hours of access during the day. Furthermore, if the standard ABA procedure is followed, but with feeding during
the dark period, the ABA effect disappears. As shown in Figure 2, Dwyer
and I found a dramatic difference between two groups given identical conditions, except that for the day group food was available from 1300 to 1430
(i.e., during the day, as has been standard in such research), whereas for
the night group access to food was from 1800 to 1930 (i.e., at the start of
the dark period). All 8 animals in the night group recovered, with a median
of 9 days to criterion, but all 8 animals in the day group had to be removed
from the experiment, their body weights reaching the criterion of 2 successive days at 70 percent or below in a median of 8.5 days (Dwyer &
Boakes, 1997, Experiment 3).

Findings from these and other experiments indicate strongly that the
ABA effect occurs as a result of the interaction of several factors. The first
two are those with which Bolles (1975) was so concerned: Wheel running
by the rat is an unlearned response to food deprivation and one that becomes pronounced in the period immediately prior to daily food delivery,
the FAA effect. The third factor is the process by which the rat adjusts to
eating at an unfamiliar time. Whether this is entirely based on the entrainment of a food clock, as suggested for wheel running by Mistlberger
and Marchant (1995), or also involves the synchronization of processes of
feeding and digestion by classical conditioning in the way that Pavlov originally suggested, is still unknown. Nevertheless, whatever the precise nature of this process, it is clear that the adjustment occurs more slowly if
the animal has been running a great deal before its daily food arrives. If
adjustment is sufficiently retarded, food intake will be insufficient to prevent a progressive decline in body weight.

There are other, minor factors that contribute toward the ABA effect.
Bolles would probably have found them of slight theoretical interest, but
they may bear on the puzzle of human anorexia. Social isolation accen-
tuates the effect in rats: When our subjects were communally housed between sessions in the wheel, they adjusted more rapidly to daytime feeding, whereas the standard ABA procedure is one that maintains rats in
complete isolation throughout an experiment. Also, the younger and
lighter the rat, the more likely it is that the simultaneous introduction of
a running wheel and a new feeding schedule will have a devastating effect
on its weight (Boakes & Dwyer, in press).

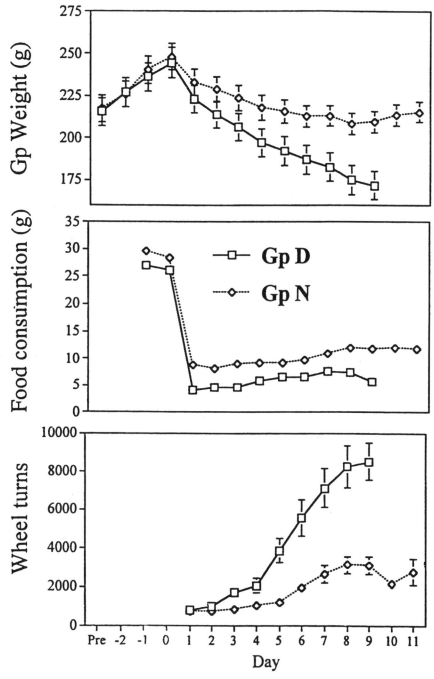

Figure 2. Body weight (top panel), food intake (center), and wheel turns (bottom) in rats given access to a wheel and a 1.5-hour food schedule from Days 1 to 11. Means ($N = 8$) and *SEM*s (except when too small to print) are shown for the two groups: Group D (Day) was fed in the middle of the light period and Group N (Night) at the start of the dark period. From Experiment 3 in "Activity-Based Anorexia in Rats as a Failure to Adapt to a Feeding Schedule," by D. M. Dwyer and R. A. Boakes, 1997, *Behavioral Neuroscience, 111,* 200. Reprinted with permission.

Conclusion

Experiments that involved placing rats in activity wheels were a major preoccupation for Bolles over a large part of his professional life. They were important for him as a way of studying the relationship between motivational factors and learning in order to understand behavior in general. The results from such experiments influenced his rejection of Hull's (1943) analysis of the same issues in terms of a general drive concept. The realization that wheel running by the rat is a species-specific unlearned response to food deprivation is likely to have shaped Bolles's ideas on avoidance learning. Just as one cannot understand a rat's response to food deprivation in terms of activity in general, one cannot understand a rat's reaction to fear-eliciting stimuli without understanding its repertoire of specific responses in such a motivational state.

It became clearly established during the 1970s not only that *performance rules*—the manner in which learning is expressed in behavior— are highly constrained by the inborn structure of an animal's brain but also that what it can learn is governed by such "biological constraints." Bolles's activity wheel experiments also provided an early example of such a constraint on learning, as demonstrated by the results suggesting that a rat can adapt only to a narrow range of adiurnal feeding cycles. This suggestion has been amply confirmed by more recent research that has concentrated on the properties of entrainable oscillators affecting wheel running—"light clocks," "food clocks," and perhaps others besides—and identifying their neural basis.

The ideas Bolles gained from the running wheel experiments helped in the analysis of a phenomenon they generated, activity-based anorexia, a phenomenon he chose to ignore. Understanding why a rat should run itself to death turns out to require the Bollesian concepts of a species-specific response that is augmented by food deprivation and of an internal clock, which he was among the first to show was necessary for the analysis of FAA. With his emphasis on the differences between species, Bolles would no doubt have wisely advocated great caution in looking for parallels between this startling phenomenon in the rat and the problem of human anorexia.

References

Boakes, R. A., & Dwyer, D. M. (in press). Weight loss in rats produced by running: Effects of prior experience and individual housing. *Quarterly Journal of Experimental Psychology*.

Bolles, R. C. (1967). *Theory of motivation*. New York: Harper & Row.

Bolles, R. C. (1968). Anticipatory general activity in thirsty rats. *Journal of Comparative and Physiological Psychology, 65,* 511–513.

Bolles, R. C. (1970). Species-specific defense reactions and avoidance behavior. *Psychological Review, 77,* 32–48.

Bolles, R. C. (1975). *Theory of motivation* (2nd ed.). New York: Harper & Row.

Bolles, R. C. (1978). The role of stimulus learning in defensive behavior. In S. H. Hulse, H. Fowler, & W. K. Honig (Eds.), *Cognitive processes in animal behavior* (pp. 89–108). Hillsdale, NJ: Erlbaum.

Bolles, R. C., & de Lorge, J. (1962). The rat's adjustment to a-diurnal feeding cycles. *Journal of Comparative and Physiological Psychology, 55,* 760–762.

Bolles, R. C., & Moot, S. R. (1973). The rat's anticipation of two meals a day. *Journal of Comparative and Physiological Psychology, 83,* 510–514.

Bolles, R. C., & Saunders, G. H. (1969). What does the ultrasonic recording device measure? *Behavioral Research Methods and Instrumentation, 1,* 180–182.

Bolles, R. C., & Stokes, L. W. (1965). Rat's anticipation of diurnal and a-diurnal feeding. *Journal of Comparative and Physiological Psychology, 60,* 290–294.

Bolles, R. C., & Younger, M. S. (1967). The effect of hunger on the threshold of behavioral arousal. *Psychonomic Science, 7,* 243–244.

Boulos, Z., & Logothetis, D. E. (1990). Rats anticipate and discriminate between two daily feeding times. *Physiology and Behavior, 48,* 523–529.

Brown, P. L., & Jenkins, H. M. (1968). Auto-shaping of the pigeon's key-peck. *Journal of the Experimental Analysis of Behavior, 11,* 1–8.

Campbell, B. A., Smith, N. F., Misanin, J. R., & Jaynes, J. (1966). Species differences in activity during hunger and thirst. *Journal of Comparative and Physiological Psychology, 61,* 123–127.

Clarke, J. D., & Coleman, G. J. (1986). Persistent meal-associated rhythms in SCN-lesioned rats. *Physiology and Behavior, 36,* 105–113.

Coleman, G. J., Harper, S., Clarke, J. D., & Armstrong, S. (1982). Evidence for a separate meal-associated oscillator in the rat. *Physiology and Behavior, 29,* 107–115.

Dickinson, A. (1980). *Contemporary animal learning theory.* Cambridge, England: Cambridge University Press.

Duda, J. J., & Bolles, R. C. (1963). Effects of prior deprivation, current deprivation, and weight loss on the activity of the hungry rat. *Journal of Comparative and Physiological Psychology, 56,* 569–571.

Dwyer, D. M., & Boakes, R. A. (1997). Activity-based anorexia in rats as a failure to adapt to a feeding schedule. *Behavioral Neuroscience, 111,* 195–205.

Eayrs, J. T. (1954). Spontaneous activity in the rat. *British Journal of Animal Behavior, 11,* 25–30.

Epling, W. F., & Pierce, W. D. (1988). Activity-based anorexia: A biobehavioral perspective. *International Journal of Eating Disorders, 7,* 475–485.

Finger, F. W., Reid, L. S., & Weasner, M. H. (1957). The effect of reinforcement upon activity during cyclic food deprivation. *Journal of Comparative and Physiological Psychology, 50,* 495–498.

Herrnstein, R. J. (1966). Superstition: A corollary of the principles of operant conditioning. In W. K. Honig (Ed.), *Operant behavior: Areas of research and application* (pp. 33–51). New York: Appleton-Century-Crofts.

Holland, P. C., & Rescorla, R. A. (1975). Second-order conditioning with food unconditioned stimulus. *Journal of Comparative and Physiological Psychology, 88,* 459–467.

Hull, C. L. (1943). *Principles of behavior.* New Haven, CT: Yale University Press.

Mistlberger, R. E. (1994). Circadian food-anticipatory activity: Formal models and physiological mechanisms. *Neuroscience and Biobehavioral Reviews, 18,* 171–195.

Mistlberger, R. E., & Marchant, E. G. (1995). Computational and entrainment models of circadian food-anticipatory activity: Evidence from non-24-hr feeding schedules. *Behavioral Neuroscience, 109,* 790–798.

Mistlberger, R. E., & Rusak, B. (1994). Circadian rhythms in mammals: Formal properties and environmental influences (pp. 277–300). In M. Kryger, A. Roth, & B. Dement (Eds.), *Principles and practice of sleep medicine.* New York: Saunders.

Morrow, N. S., & Garrick, T. (1993). Effects of preadaptation to restricted feeding and cimetidine treatment on gastric mucosal injury and wheel-running during exposure to activity stress. *Journal of Physiology (Paris), 87,* 245–252.

Paré, W. P. (1975). The influence of food consumption and running activity on the activity-stress ulcer in the rat. *American Journal of Digestive Diseases, 20,* 262–273.

Renner, M. (1960). The contribution of the honey bee to the study of time-sense and astronomical orientation. *Cold Springs Harbour Symposia on Quantitative Biology, 25.* Cold Springs Harbour, Biological Laboratory, NY, NY.

Rescorla, R. A., Durlach, P. J., & Grau, J. W. (1985). Contextual learning in Pavlovian conditioning. In P. D. Balsam, & A. Tomie (Eds.), *Context and learning* (pp. 23–56). Hillsdale, NJ: Erlbaum.

Richter, C. P. (1922). A behavioristic study of the activity of the rat. *Journal of Comparative Psychology Monographs, 1*(No. 2).

Routtenberg, A., & Kuznesof, A. Y. (1967). Self starvation of rats living in activity wheels on a restricted feeding schedule. *Journal of Comparative and Physiological Psychology, 64,* 414–421.

Rusak, B., & Zucker, J. (1979). Neural regulation of circadian rhythms. *Physiological Review, 59,* 449–526.

Sheffield, F. D., & Campbell, B. A. (1954). The role of experience in the "spontaneous" activity of hungry rats. *Journal of Comparative and Physiological Psychology, 47,* 97–100.

Skinner, B. F. (1948). "Superstition" in the pigeon. *Journal of Experimental Psychology, 38,* 168–172.

Stephan, F. K. (1981). Limits of entrainment to periodic feeding in rats with suprachiasmatic lesions. *Journal of Comparative Physiology, 143,* 401–410.

Wald, G., & Jackson, B. (1944). Activity and nutritional deprivation. *Proceedings of the National Academy of Science, 30,* 255–263.

9

The Behaviors of Sleep and Sleepiness: An Overview

Robert D. Ogilvie

This chapter will examine the role played by behavioral measures in enhancing scientific understanding of sleepiness, sleep onset, and sleep. Although electroencephalographic (EEG) assessment of sleep is common, definitions of sleep have always been behaviorally anchored. However, behavioral techniques have only recently been used to probe responsiveness during sleepiness, to study the sleep-onset period, and to establish depth of sleep. I show how this research led to the development of behaviorally based systems for assessing sleep and wakefulness and for devising alerting devices to awaken people reliably from sleep. Throughout the chapter, the usefulness of behavioral and physiological assessments of sleep and wakefulness are contrasted.

As Bob Bolles might have reminded us, the final test of the operation of an organismic system lies in its impact on the behavior of the organism. Bolles was *the* contemporary functional behaviorist. The first section of this book reviews his work and makes his contributions to psychology clear to those who did not know him. I was fortunate to study under his direction at Hollins College over 30 years ago, at the time when he was working on his influential book on motivation. His dedication to science and to the thoughtful measurement of behavior, always with a view to understanding function, profoundly influenced his students and his peers. Two brief anecdotes may help me describe the man: I remember sitting with a group of students on a porch on the main Hollins Quadrangle, when Bob, forever the Determinist, took on another Prof. in an impromptu "Free Will versus Determinism" debate. Bob's wonderful grasp of the roots of science, his brilliant mind and kind humour made the outcome very clear, very early! But perhaps most vivid were the examples of commitment to his science which we were exposed to daily. And nightly. The image of his old, two-tone green cadillac in front of his office at any hour told its own story.

So an important goal of this chapter is to demonstrate the applicability of Bolles's approach to areas of psychology he was never directly involved with, in this instance, the study of sleep and behavior.

Behavioral Measures and the Definition of Sleep

Historical Definitions

The following quote from Aristotle is a representative example of how sleep was viewed for the thousands of years that preceded the development of sophisticated physiological and behavioral measurements of wakefulness, sleepiness, and sleep:

> The criterion by which we know the waking person to be awake is identical with that by which we know the sleeper to be asleep; for we assume that one who is exercising sense-perception is awake, and that every one who is awake perceives either some external movement or else some movement in his own consciousness. (1908, p. 696)

Kleitman, in his influential book *Sleep and Wakefulness* (1939), was content to use Pieron's (1913) description of sleep as a state when complex sensorimotor activity was suspended, a time of increased sensory and reflex thresholds brought about by internal necessity but wherein an ability to arouse or be aroused is preserved.

EEG Definitions

Definitions of sleep changed dramatically with the advent of EEG recording. A consistent picture of the development of EEG definitions of sleep and its stages can be seen in the work of Loomis, Harvey, and Hobart (1935a, b), refined by Rechtschaffen and Kales (1968). On the basis of this work, the stages of wakefulness and sleep are characterized as follows: Alert wakefulness consists of low-amplitude, high-frequency, desynchronized EEG waves, characterized by mixed beta activity. In relaxed, eyes-closed wakefulness, alpha predominates in the tracings, although some people do not generate consistent alpha activity. Alpha gives way to theta frequencies as Stage 1 sleep is entered, and vertex sharp waves depict late Stage 1 activity, although this stage is viewed increasingly as a transition period between wakefulness and sleep (Hori, Hayashi, & Morikawa, 1994; Ogilvie & Wilkinson, 1988). Other sleep-specific waves (14-Hz sleep spindles and much slower, high-amplitude k complexes) are seen when Stage 2 sleep begins. Stages 3 and 4 are primarily identified by the presence of increasing amounts of slow, synchronized, high-amplitude (> 75 uV) delta waves. Stage 3 contains between 20 and 50 percent delta waves, whereas Stage 4 is composed of over 50 percent delta activity. Stage REM EEG resembles that of Stage 1, or wakefulness, in many ways, with its reversion to low-amplitude, desynchronized activity, marked this time by theta-frequency saw-toothed waves.

There has been a near-universal adoption of this EEG scoring system for describing normal and abnormal sleep, despite the absence of behavioral validation. Rechtschaffen (1994) discussed the issue, pointing out that to be useful, EEG criteria must correspond closely to behavioral standards. It is surprising that few such validating studies were performed. There were some unsystematic observations made by the Loomis team in the 1930s, but few direct comparisons existed until the Ogilvie and Wilkinson studies in the 1980s (1984, 1988; Ogilvie, Wilkinson, & Allison, 1989). That work indicated correspondences between behavioral and EEG (and other physiological) criteria for wakefulness and all sleep stages except Stage 1 (see discussion following). Rechtschaffen (1994) also pointed out that there are a number of compelling reasons to prefer the physiological measures: Physiological measures are often easier than observational ones to gather; they may provide information about the function of sleep; they can distinguish various sleep stages; they can be obtained continuously and without interrupting sleep; and they are useful in identifying sequences of activity within sleep. However, he also reminded the reader that physiological measures must be validated against fundamental sleep–wake behavior.

Behavioral and Phylogenetic Definitions

Although the advent of EEG measurement has largely pushed behavioral criteria for sleep identification into the background, this is not the case when one searches the phylogenetic scale for evidences of sleep in relatively primitive species. An article by Flanigan (1972) put the issue in an interesting perspective; he was looking for signs of sleep in a number of reptiles, including caiman, turtles, and tortoises. It soon became evident that the electrophysiological criteria used to identify sleep stages and wakefulness in mammals (muscle tension, eye movements, and EEG) were of limited use in reptiles. First, these animals show muscle atonia whenever muscles are not in active use, regardless of other evidence of sleep or wakefulness. Second, eye movement data are difficult to obtain. Third, EEG differences among states are unclear other than characteristic EEG spikes during quiescence in all three species. To resolve the issue, Flanigan refined earlier behavioral definitions of sleep:

> Sleep is a behavior and can therefore perhaps be best differentiated using at least four common criteria: 1) the assumption of a stereotypic or species-specific posture, 2) the maintenance of behavioral quiescence, 3) an elevation of arousal threshold which may be reflected in the intensity of an arousing stimulus and/or the frequency, latency, or duration of an arousal response, and 4) state reversibility with stimulation. (1972, p. 15)

In many situations, identifying sleep by behavioral criteria or describing active versus quiescent behaviors makes more sense than distorting mammalian EEG criteria in an attempt to learn about the phylogenetic beginnings of sleep.

Behavior and Sleep: Sensory Thresholds
During Waking and Sleep

This behavioral approach to plumbing the depth of sleep has a lengthy history. Kleitman (1963) referred to an 1862 article by Kohlschutter in which depth of sleep curves were determined by the hourly presentation of tones of increasing intensity. Kohlschutter noted that the deepest sleep occurred early in the night, followed by much lower auditory thresholds toward morning. Other studies that preceded the discovery of rapid eye movement (REM) sleep confirmed that auditory thresholds were highest within the first hour or two of sleep (i.e., Blake & Gerard, 1937). However, reevaluation of the threshold issue became important when the discovery of REM sleep led scientists to consider REM and non-REM sleep as separate states of existence. Rechtschaffen, Hauri, and Zeitlin (1966) conducted a careful experiment, using a rigorous definition of awakening, in which the sleeper, alerted by an ascending series of 5-second tones, had to identify the number of clicks presented subsequent to the arousal tone. These authors reported equal auditory arousal thresholds for Stage REM and Stage 2 sleep, higher thresholds for slow wave sleep, and a stage-independent decrease in arousal with increases in time asleep. Bonnet and Johnson (1978) found within-subject differences relating high arousal thresholds to subjectively better sleep and less time awake after initial sleep onset. Bonnet, Johnson, and Webb (1978), studying the reliability of auditory arousal thresholds, noted that thresholds from sleep were much more variable than those from waking. Bonnet and Moore (1982) wrote that the auditory threshold had increased to 64 percent of its highest level within 1 minute of the appearance of sleep spindles.

Okuma, Nakamura, Hayashi, and Fujimori (1966), using both photic and auditory stimuli, found that responses could be made in all but Stage 4 sleep and added that the perception of the correct number of stimuli was more accurate during REM than any other stage. The unresponsiveness of people in Stage 4 sleep was emphasized dramatically by Oswald (1962), who showed an EEG tracing of a subject deep in Stage 4 sleep who remained unresponsive in spite of having his eyelids pulled open in the presence of a strong light, being poked, and being spoken to loudly. Unresponsiveness to auditory stimuli is even more dramatic in children. Busby and Pivik (1985) found that 52 percent of both normal and hyperkinetic prepubertal children failed to awaken, even at sound levels of 123 dB.

The meaningfulness of arousal stimuli has been shown to have a marked effect on arousal thresholds from sleep. Oswald, Taylor, and Treisman (1960) used names as stimuli and found that a greater number of fist clenches and k complexes were made in response to the participant's own name than to the names of others. Langford, Meddis, and Pearson (1974) correctly predicted that personally significant stimuli would be processed more accurately during REM than in other stages. LeVere, Davis, Mills, and Berger (1976) found that people responded differentially to previously reinforced stimuli versus similar, nonreinforced tones presented in slow wave sleep.

The data on arousal threshold, therefore, reveal a great deal about sleep: Monitoring continues throughout all stages (at least in adults), but the rapid threshold increases at sleep onset suggest that information processing is dramatically attenuated throughout sleep. Responsivity, or the link to the outside world, is altered as a function of sleep stage and time of night.

Identifying Sleepiness

Objective Behavior

Although there are a number of objective measures of sleepiness, including performance tests, visually scored EEG indices, computer-generated EEG power spectra, measurement of slow rolling eye movements, the Maintenance of Wakefulness Test, pupillometry, and auditory evoked responses, by far the most popular index is the Multiple Sleep Latency Test (MSLT). This behavioral measure is reviewed here briefly, followed by a discussion of subjective sleepiness ratings. For reviews of sleep and performance, see books edited by Monk (1991) and by Broughton and Ogilvie (1992).

Carskadon and Dement (1979a, 1979b, 1981, 1982), interested in measuring physiological sleep tendency, reasoned that the most objective way to do so was to observe the behavior of falling asleep. They were particularly interested in looking at sleep onset latency at various times of day. They studied sleep latency in normal sleepers throughout the day and validated the new index by comparing latencies after sleep deprivation to those obtained after a normal night of sleep. They had conducted an earlier study looking at sleepiness during a sequence of consecutive 90-minute "days" in which volunteers were kept awake repeatedly for 60 minutes and then allowed up to 30 minutes of sleep (Carskadon & Dement, 1977). As one might expect, the authors detected circadian patterns in the sleep-latency data, with the shortest latencies corresponding to the times of normal nocturnal sleep. It was soon discovered that pathologically sleepy people could be separated from normal sleepers using sleep latencies (Zorick et al., 1982). This series of studies led to the development of the MSLT, which has become the standard tool for assessing pathological sleepiness. Typically, latencies are gathered during five 20-minute nap opportunities distributed at 2-hour intervals during the day. For example, it has been found that sleep latencies of less than 5 minutes, obtained during one or more of the five scheduled naps, can serve as an important index of narcolepsy (*International Classification of Sleep Disorders*, 1990). The MSLT has also been used successfully to identify other disorders involving excessive daytime sleepiness, such as sleep apnea (Zorick et al., 1982). Although the MSLT is widely employed, there are problems that limit its usefulness. Floor effects make it difficult to distinguish among subgroups of very sleepy individuals; similarly, ceiling effects reduce the sensitivity of the test as a measure in alert individuals. Also, "sleepability" is not considered; some people without sleep pathology are simply efficient sleepers who have learned to nap quickly in many situations. Finally, the test is cumbersome and expensive to administer: The testee must be kept in the sleep clinic all day because of the need for multiple testings at 2-hour intervals (Alloway, Ogilvie & Shapiro, (in press).

Subjective Behavior

The Stanford Sleepiness Scale (SSS) is the most widely used measure of subjective sleepiness. It was developed by Hoddes, Dement, and Zarcone (1972) from 52 items that subjects sorted into seven piles representing degrees of sleepiness. The investigators settled on a 7-point, single-item scale, in which 1 means *feeling active and vital, alert, wide awake* and 7 indicates *almost in reverie, sleep onset soon, lost struggle to remain awake*. Testing showed the scale to be useful in denoting changes when administered every 15 minutes. In a more detailed study, Hoddes, Zarcone, Smythe, Phillips, and Dement (1973) validated the scale against Wilkinson's (1968) Addition and Auditory Vigilance Tests. Six men were tested for 6 consecutive days; the SSS was given every 15 minutes during wakefulness, and the performance tests were given four times per day. The volunteers were sleep-deprived on Night 4. Following sleep deprivation, SSS scores were significantly "sleepier," and there was a significant drop in the performance measures. In another validation, Carskadon and Dement (1979a, b) compared MSLT and SSS ratings and reported significant negative correlations between MSLT latency and SSS scores. In 1981, the same authors noted that the SSS showed significant increases in sleepiness on the first day of reduced sleep.

SSS validation work continued. Glenville and Broughton (1979) assessed the SSS and found that following sleep deprivation, significant changes in simple reaction time, four-choice serial reaction time, and Wilkinson Auditory Vigilance Test scores were correlated with SSS scores. In the clinical arena, Pressman, Spielman, Pollak, and Weitzman (1982) found that SSS scores of people with narcolepsy and sleep deprivation were similar and indicated greater sleepiness than the scores of those who were not sleep-deprived when assessed in one morning and four evening sessions.

In short, the SSS was validated as an effective monitor of sleepiness in a number of settings and shown to be sensitive to changes in time of day and varying degrees of sleep loss. When these two variables were controlled, however, the SSS did not predict performance levels with sufficient accuracy to allow it to substitute for them (Glenville & Broughton, 1979).

Other useful subjective sleepiness scales have been developed. Akerstedt and Gillberg (1990) presented people with a 100-mm line, the ends of which were marked *very sleepy* and *alert*, and asked them to mark the line at a point that described their present state of sleepiness or alertness. The authors validated their Visual Analogue Scale (VAS) against alpha activity, related EEG spectral parameters, and other physiological signs of sleepiness such as the appearance of slow eye movements. High and low sleepiness estimates were clearly related to the physiological indicators, but the authors also noted that the VAS was sensitive to early signs of sleepiness, whereas the physiological indices primarily detected extreme sleepiness.

Additionally, Folkard, Spelten, Totterdell, Barton, and Smith (1995) found that even retrospective sleepiness assessments could be quite accurate. They used the VAS and a modified SSS administered at the end of a working shift to obtain nurses' estimates of their sleepiness every 2 hours across the shift they had just completed. Reliable and valid estimates were obtained when the two sleepiness scales were compared to reaction time and other performance measures.

Examining the Wake–Sleep Transition: The Sleep-Onset Period

There are two ways in which entry into sleep might begin. The process theoretically could commence almost instantly, as if with the flip of an electrophysiological switch or the precipitous activation of a brain stem nucleus. Alternatively, it might begin almost imperceptibly, marked by a series of gradual changes in a number of psychological and physiological processes. There seems to be evidence for both possibilities. Falling asleep can take only a moment for a sleepy child, or it can seem to take an eternity for a person with insomnia. But when does the process begin, and what does the actual transition look like? Does the individual with insomnia finally drop over a physiological cliff into another state? Does the child travel through a series of orderly changes swiftly and efficiently?

Ogilvie and Wilkinson (1984, 1988; Ogilvie et al., 1989) conducted three experiments aimed at answering those questions and characterizing the transition into sleep. They measured physiological (EEG, electrooculographic [EOG], electromyographic [EMG], respiration rate) and behavioral (response time, passive release of a switch, subjective sleepiness) activity simultaneously during daytime naps in sleep-deprived volunteers. Using the EEG to identify the standard Rechtschaffen and Kales (1968) Stage wake and Stages 1 and 2 of sleep, they noted that behavioral responsiveness did not cease uniformly at Stage 1 onset but deteriorated across that stage. They also saw wide individual differences such that some people ceased responding to the task (simply pushing a switch to terminate an intermittent faint tone) at or before the beginning of Stage 1 "sleep," whereas others responded to over 50 percent of all tones given during Stage 1 and occasionally responded within the first few moments of Stage 2 sleep. They also found that sleepiness degraded performance (lengthened response times) long before Stage 1 "sleep" was entered (Ogilvie & Wilkinson, 1984). It was also apparent that the physiological and behavioral changes were orchestrated differently from person to person; that is, the behavioral and physiological sequence of events leading to

Stage 2 sleep varied considerably across subjects. Even the behavioral measures did not match up uniformly; muscle relaxation (releasing a "deadman" switch) did not coincide precisely with behavioral response failure.

However, not all data clearly supported the notion of a gradual transition into sleep. Changes in respiratory parameters were often sudden; dramatic drops in abdominal amplitude frequently occurred from one breath to the next as sleep was entered (Ogilvie & Wilkinson, 1984). Overall, however, there were significant correlations among changes in EEG, abdominal respiratory volume, behavioral response latency, and subjective sleepiness throughout the wake–sleep transition period, suggesting that sleep onset is indeed an orderly, if not a highly regimented, process (Ogilvie et al., 1989).

Behavioral Sleep–Wake Monitoring

Passive Behavioral Measures

Actigraphs. Knowing more about sensory thresholds and sleep-related behaviors has allowed scientists to develop a number of behaviorally based alternatives to EEG-based polysomnography. It is highly unlikely that the methods described subsequently will entirely replace EEG recordings, but these methods have already begun to supplement the costly, cumbersome (but usefully detailed) polysomnography.

We discussed earlier the advantages of using activity and quiescence to look at sleep and its precursors in more primitive species; therefore, it seems reasonable to assume that relative changes in activity level might be a useful behavioral indication for studying sleep and wakefulness in people. Actigraphs have been particularly useful in allowing the monitoring of activity–inactivity (and presumably sleep) in the home relatively easily and inexpensively. The wrist actigraph has been used to study circadian rhythms (Brown, Smolensky, D'Alonzo, & Redman, 1990), insomnia (Brooks, Friedman, Bliwise, & Yesavage, 1993; Hauri & Wisbey, 1992), children with sleep disturbance (Sadeh, Lavie, Scher, Tirosh, & Epstein, 1991) and attention-deficit hyperactivity disorder (ADHD; Miller & Kraft, 1994). The devices have been validated against polysomnographic information (Sadeh et al., 1991); overall agreement was 85 percent for normal children but significantly reduced with children who had ADHD. The actigraphs also distinguished between the overall activity patterns of the two groups of children. Brooks et al. (1993) found that actigraphs could distinguish between control and sleep-restriction nights in elderly people with insomnia and concluded that the tool was a promising one for assessing insomnia. However, Hauri and Wisbey (1992) came to another conclusion. In an extensive study using actigraphs and EEG assessments of people with several subtypes of insomnia, they reported several shortcomings: Actigraphs overestimated sleep, typically disagreeing with EEG records approximately 10 percent of the time. On only 75 percent of cases did the two methods agree to within 1 hour on total sleep time.

It is self-evident that people can remain quiet yet not be asleep. This fact, coupled with evidence that some people move quite extensively while preparing for and even during sleep, probably accounts for the less than perfect correspondence between these measures. Nevertheless, actigraphs have been found to be useful adjuncts to other forms of sleep-related information, because they are easily worn day and night for considerable periods of time.

The Nightcap. Two complementary behaviors, body and eye movements, have been used as the basis of an ingenious new passive sleep–wake detecting system (Mamelak & Hobson, 1989). The sensors for this unit are integrated into cloth headgear that resembles an old-fashioned nightcap. The designers sought to build a passive sleep–wake monitor that could distinguish among wakefulness, REM sleep, and non-REM sleep. The system also needed to be portable and easy to use. They constructed their device on the basis of the idea that the three fundamental sleep–wake states could be distinguished by the different patterns of relative responsiveness characteristic of each: They reasoned that during wakefulness, both body and eye movements would be present. In non-REM sleep, there would be no movement from either detector, whereas in REM sleep, the eye movement detector would be active and the body movement sensor would be quiet. The investigators found that the algorithms they developed to identify the three primary sleep–wake states agreed with polysomnographic measures 85 percent of the time. Stickgold and Hobson (1994) went on to use the system to detect sleep onset. They also found that the Nightcap computer detected early evidence of sleep in a study of self-arousals during the hypnagogic period of Stage 1 sleep. The Nightcap appears to have great potential for in-home studies of dreams or hypnagogic imagery in which a device is needed to awaken the sleeper at a particular point during REM or non-REM sleep.

Active Behavioral Measures: Behavioral Response Monitors

Cued behavioral response systems have now been well validated as practical devices for describing fundamental sleep–wake parameters. The following paragraphs summarize that work.

Auditory systems. Work on behavioral responsiveness at sleep onset (Ogilvie & Wilkinson, 1984) showed that sleepiness and sleep onset could be traced quite accurately using a behavioral index. The Ogilvie and Wilkinson (1988) experiment showed that auditorily cued responses tracked nocturnal wakefulness, and response failures signified sleep. This simple system agreed overall with EEG sleep–wake assessments on 93.5 percent of all measurements taken on 11 sleep-lab-adapted participants. The simplicity and accuracy of behavioral sleep–wake measurement encouraged my group to try to validate further and make portable the behavioral response system. Bonato and Ogilvie (1989) found that the sleep of good and poor sleepers could be distinguished behaviorally. Kuderian, Ogilvie, McDonnell, and Simons (1991) extended that finding by comparing 8 people with insomnia with 8 good sleepers, using a portable behavioral response system in their houses for four consecutive nights. Those with insomnia had longer sleep latencies and less efficient sleep and tended to have a greater number of arousals from sleep than did normal sleepers.

Cote and Ogilvie (1994) returned to the issue of agreement between the EEG sleep–wake scoring and the behavioral cued-response paradigm. They found that agreement between the two systems was nearly identical to that reported by Ogilvie and Wilkinson in 1988: 94.2 percent. They used a special-purpose portable computer, the Sleepscope, which yielded 15 behavioral indices including total recording time, total sleep time, sleep efficiency, sleep-onset latency, and number of micro- and macroarousals. The computer also produced a sleep–wake histogram and many of the statistics usually computed from EEG sleep scoring to describe sleep patterns in clinically useful detail. Cote and Ogilvie reported another experiment in 1995 in which they successfully distinguished people with insomnia from normal sleepers, replicating and extending the work of Kuderian et al. (1991). Cote and Ogilvie (1995) found predicted differences in wakefulness, sleep-onset latency, total sleep percentage, and percentage of wakefulness prior to sleep onset.

Uses for auditory probes during sleep. It is important to consider that auditory stimulation during sleep was used for quite different purposes in the two preceding discussions. In the first, I considered evidence concerning auditory thresholds, whereas in the second, I reviewed studies using auditory cues to map sleep and wakefulness were reviewed. In the first case, systematic increases in the loudness of the tones were used to establish waking thresholds from various sleep stages and times of night. In an extreme example, Busby and Pivik (1985) reported that tones over 120 dB were often unsuccessful in awakening children. In contrast, the cued response technique uses tones that are less than 5 dB above background sound levels and requires people to respond when awake. All of the literature on auditory thresholds confirms that people ought not to be able to respond to these faint cues while in any true sleep state. Yet Ogilvie and Wilkinson (1988) and Cote and Ogilvie (1995) found that the cues are effective during brief and more lengthy arousals in reminding people to respond, thereby signaling wakefulness. From the detailed sequence of alternations between responding and quiescence, a clear picture of waking and sleeping emerges.

At some level, these cues *are* processed during sleep. This paradox was uncovered by Ogilvie, Simons, Kuderian, MacDonald, and Rustenburg (1991) when they showed that these faint 1000-Hz tones, which generated no overt behavioral responses, did produce stable event-related potentials (ERPs). That study showed that although latencies and amplitudes differed from those seen during wakefulness, a clear transformation of the

ERP signature took place as people fell asleep. Furthermore, Ogilvie, Battye, and Simons (1994) found that the ERP components to faint stimuli were preserved in some form in every sleep stage. Other work (Campbell, Bell, & Bastien, 1992) had shown that ERPs to much louder stimuli could be obtained from any phase of sleep. It appears from the information to date that sensory channels are much more easily accessed during sleep than is regulated motor activity.

In a related and ongoing debate, some researchers have claimed that behavioral responses (typically to auditory stimuli) are possible *during* sleep, whereas others are convinced that such responses occur during brief, stimulus-triggered *microarousals* from sleep. In part, the issue revolves around definitions of sleep. If one assumes that behavioral definitions of sleeping and waking provide the first and final criterion for sleep, as I do, then behavioral responses cannot occur within sleep. They must represent interruptions of sleep. However, others hold that EEG criteria are primary. Campbell and Webb (1981) asked participants to press a button whenever they were aware of being awake at night. These investigators reported that 52 percent of all responses came during wakefulness, 12 percent in EEG-defined sleep followed by wakefulness, and 36 percent in sleep not followed by wakefulness. However, of the latter 36 percent, 73 percent of the "sleep" responses were preceded by 4–6 seconds of alpha activity. Additionally, 31 percent of EEG-defined periods of wakefulness were not identified. Webb and Aber (1983) also found that a similar uncued response system failed to detect 60 percent of all EEG periods of more than 1 minute of wakefulness, testimony to the insensitivity of either the EEG-based definition of sleep–wakefulness, their response measure, or both.

Vibratory systems. MacLean and his students have been conducting parallel investigations to Brock's studies using vibratory stimuli. Mac-Lean, Arnedt, Biedermann, and Knowles (1992) used microswitch closures to a vibratory stimulus to examine sleep quality. They presented stimuli throughout the night and found no difference in sleep latency when EEG and behavioral methods were compared. They reported rank-ordered decreases in responsiveness after sleep onset from wakefulness to Stages 1, 2, REM, 3, and 4. Responsiveness varied from about 12 percent during wakefulness to zero for Stage 4. Alloway and MacLean (1994) examined vibrotactile thresholds during sleep. They found that thresholds in Stages 2, 4, and REM were significantly higher than those seen during wakefulness. Although different sensory modalities cannot be compared directly, the pattern of threshold variations as a function of sleep stage is similar when vibrotactile and auditory thresholds are examined.

Vibrotactile alerting devices. Auditory smoke detectors have saved countless lives, but these units are of limited use to those with severely impaired hearing. Although both strobe light and vibratory substitutes are on the market today, neither has received adequate independent testing until recently. Murphy et al. (1995) examined the usefulness of a vibrotactile device as a "smoke alarm" for the severely hearing impaired. They placed a commercially available vibrator–alarm system under the mattress and activated it during either REM or Stage 3–4 sleep. People without hearing problems awakened on 75.9 percent of all trials and awoke from REM sleep 92 percent of the time. Those with hearing loss awakened on 70.0 percent and 87.5 percent of experimental trials from those stages, respectively. These data represent superior awakening percentages to those reported by Bowman, Jamieson, and Ogilvie (1995), who used a visual alerting device that was brighter than those on the market for this purpose. They found awakening percentages for university students with normal hearing of just under 50 percent for Stage 4 stimulation and just over 50 percent for attempted arousals from Stage REM. The vibrotactile modality appears to be the most useful one for designing improved smoke detectors for the hearing impaired.

Conclusion

Sleep and behavior are integrally related. Sleep is most broadly defined in behavioral terms, and behavioral responses have been used to determine sensory thresholds and probe depth of sleep in all sleep stages. Self-rated sleepiness estimates have been shown to add an important dimension to earlier attempts to measure this construct solely in terms of performance or EEG changes. Both auditory and vibrotactile response systems have been constructed, providing cued active behavioral response devices that accurately describe sleep–wake patterns. Motoric behavior is the basis for actigraphs that provide yet another, although less sensitive, alternative to polygraphic sleep measurements, and the Nightcap system, which detects motor and eye movement, promises to distinguish REM and non-REM sleep from wakefulness. Knowledge of sensory thresholds has allowed scientists to devise auditory, visual, and vibrotactile alerting devices. Finally, by combining behavioral and physiological measures of sleep and sleepiness, the understanding of sleep and the transition from wakefulness to sleep has been advanced.

The theme of this chapter has been to demonstrate that behavioral measurements during sleep and wakefulness have played an important role in facilitating scientific understanding of sleep-related processes. From anchoring definitions of sleep to providing methods for probing sleepiness, falling asleep, and sleep thresholds, sleep-related behaviors remain central to the study of sleep.

References

Akerstedt, T., & Gillberg, M. (1990). Subjective and objective sleepiness in the active individual. *International Journal of Neuroscience, 52,* 29–37.

Alloway, C. E. D., & MacLean, A. W. (1994). Vibrotactile response thresholds during sleep. *Sleep Research, 23,* 175.

Alloway, C. E. D., Ogilvie, R. D., & Shapiro, C. M. (in press). The alpha attenuation test: Assessing physiological sleepiness in narcolepsy. *Sleep.*

Aristotle. (1908). *The works of Aristotle* (W. D. Ross, Ed.; J. I. Beare, Trans.). Oxford, England: Clarendon Press.

Blake, H., & Gerard, R. W. (1937). Brain potentials during sleep. *American Journal of Physiology, 119,* 692–713.

Bonato, R. A., & Ogilvie, R. D. (1989). A home evaluation of a behavioral response measure of sleep/wakefulness. *Perceptual and Motor Skills, 68,* 87–96.

Bonnet, M. H., & Johnson, L. C. (1978). Relationship of arousal threshold to sleep stage distribution and subjective estimates of depth and quality of sleep. *Sleep, 1,* 161–168.

Bonnet, M. H., Johnson, L. C., & Webb, W. B. (1978). The reliability of arousal threshold during sleep. *Psychophysiology, 15,* 412–416.

Bonnet, M. H., & Moore, S. E. (1982). The threshold of sleep: Perception of sleep as a function of time asleep and auditory threshold. *Sleep, 5,* 267–276.

Bowman, S. K., Jamieson, D.G., & Ogilvie, R.D. (1995). Waking effectiveness of visual alerting signals. *Journal of Rehabilitation Research and Development, 32,* 43–54.

Brooks, J. O., Friedman, L., Bliwise, D. L., & Yesavage, J. A. (1993). The use of the wrist actigraph to study insomnia in older adults. *Sleep, 16,* 151–155.

Broughton, R. J., & Ogilvie, R. D. (Eds.). (1992). *Sleep, arousal and performance: Problems and promises.* Cambridge, MA: Birkhauser Boston.

Brown, A. C., Smolensky, M. H., D'Alonzo, G. E., & Redman, D. P. (1990). Actigraphy: A means of assessing circadian patterns in human activity. *Chronobiology International, 7,* 125–133.

Busby, K., & Pivik, R. T. (1985). Auditory arousal thresholds during sleep in hyperkinetic children. *Sleep, 8,* 332–341.

Campbell, K., Bell, I., & Bastien, C. (1992). Evoked potentials as measures of information processing during sleep. In R. J. Broughton & R. D. Ogilvie (Eds.), *Sleep, arousal and performance.* Cambridge, MA: Birkhauser Boston.

Campbell, S. C., & Webb, W. B. (1981). The perception of wakefulness within sleep. *Sleep, 4,* 177–183.

Carskadon, M. A., & Dement, W. C. (1977). Sleepiness and sleep state on a 90-minute schedule. *Psychophysiology, 14,* 127–133.

Carskadon, M. A., & Dement, W. C. (1979a). Effects of total sleep loss on sleep tendency. *Perceptual and Motor Skills, 48,* 495–506.

Carskadon, M. A., & Dement, W. C. (1979b). Sleepiness during sleep restriction [abstract]. *Sleep Research, 8,* 254.

Carskadon, M. A., & Dement, W. C. (1981). Cumulative effects of sleep restriction on daytime sleepiness. *Psychophysiology, 18,* 107–113.

Carskadon, M. A., & Dement, W. C. (1982). The Multiple Sleep Latency Test: What does it measure? *Sleep, 5*(Suppl. 2), 67–72.

Cote, K. A., & Ogilvie, R. D. (1994). Identifying sleep and wakefulness: A comparison of behavioural and polysomnographic methods. *Journal of Psychophysiology, 8,* 305–313.

Cote, K. A., & Ogilvie, R. D. (1995). Behavioral home monitoring in insomniac and normal sleepers. *Canadian Journal of Behavioral Science, 27,* 438–449.

Flanigan, W. F. (1972). Behavioral states and electroencephalograms of reptiles. In M. H. Chase (Ed.), *The sleeping brain.* Los Angeles: UCLA Brain Information Service/Brain Research Institute.

Folkard, S., Spelten, E., Totterdell, P., Barton, J., & Smith, L. (1995). The use of survey measures to assess circadian variations in alertness. *Sleep, 18,* 355–361.

Glenville, M., & Broughton, R. (1979). Reliability of the Stanford Sleepiness Scale compared to short duration performance tests and the Wilkinson Auditory Vigilance Task. In P. Passouant & I. Oswald (Eds.), *Pharmacology of the states of alertness.* New York: Pergamon Press.

Hauri, P. J., & Wisbey, J. (1992). Wrist actigraphy in insomnia. *Sleep, 15,* 293–301.

Hoddes, E., Dement, W., & Zarcone, V. (1972). The development and use of the Stanford Sleepiness Scale (SSS). *Psychophysiology, 9,* 150.

Hoddes, E., Zarcone, V. P., Smythe, H., Phillips, R., & Dement, W. C. (1973). Quantification of sleepiness: A new approach. *Psychophysiology, 10,* 431–436.

Hori, T., Hayashi, M., & Morikawa, T. (1994). Topographical EEG changes and the hypnagogic experience. In R. J. Broughton & R. D. Ogilvie (Eds.), *Sleep, arousal and performance*. Cambridge, MA: Birkhauser Boston.

International classification of sleep disorders. (1990). Rochester, MN: American Sleep Disorders Association.

Kleitman, N. (1939). *Sleep and wakefulness*. Chicago: University of Chicago Press.

Kleitman, N. (1963). *Sleep and wakefulness* (2nd ed.). Chicago: University of Chicago Press.

Kuderian, R. H., Ogilvie, R. D., McDonnell, G., & Simons, I. A. (1991). Behavioral response home monitoring of good and insomniac sleepers. *Canadian Journal of Psychology, 45,* 169–178.

Langford, G. W., Meddis, R., & Pearson, A. J. D. (1974). Awakening latency from sleep for meaningful and non-meaningful stimuli. *Psychophysiology, 11,* 1–5.

LeVere, T. E., Davis, N., Mills, J., & Berger, E. H. (1976). Arousal from sleep: The cognitive value of auditory stimuli. *Physiological Psychology, 4,* 376–382.

Loomis, A. L., Harvey, E., & Hobart, G. A. (1935a). Further observations on the potential rhythms of the cerebral cortex during sleep. *Science, 82,* 198–199.

Loomis, A. L., Harvey, E., & Hobart, G. A. (1935b). Potential rhythms of the cerebral cortex during sleep. *Science, 81,* 597–598.

MacLean, A. W., Arnedt, T., Biedermann, H., & Knowles, J. B. (1992). Behavioural responding as a measure of sleep quality. *Sleep Research, 21,* 105.

Mamelak, A., & Hobson, J. A. (1989). Nightcap: A home-based sleep scoring system. *Sleep, 12,* 157–166.

Miller, L. G., & Kraft, I. A. (1994). Application of actigraphy in the clinical setting: Use in children with attention-deficit hyperactivity disorder. *Pharmacotherapy, 14,* 219–223.

Monk, T. H. (Ed.). (1991). *Sleep, sleepiness and performance*. Chichester, England: Wiley.

Murphy, T., Alloway, C. E. D., Lamarche, C. H., Bernstein, D. M., Ogilvie, R. D., MacLean, A. W., & Jamieson, D. G. (1995, September). How reliably does a vibro-tactile smoke alarm awaken individuals with hearing loss? Paper presented to the World Federation of Sleep Research Societies, Nassau.

Ogilvie, R. D., Battye, R. A., & Simons, I. A. (1994). Changing CNS priorities in sleepiness and sleep? EEG and ERP evidence. In R. D. Ogilvie & J. R. Harsh (Eds.), *Sleep onset: Normal and abnormal processes* (pp. 269–286). Washington DC: American Psychological Association.

Ogilvie, R. D., Simons, I. A., Kuderian, R. H., MacDonald, T., & Rustenburg, J. (1991). Behavioral, event-related potential (ERP), and EEG/FFT changes at sleep onset. *Psychophysiology, 28,* 54–64.

Ogilvie, R. D., & Wilkinson, R. T. (1984). The detection of sleep onset: Behavioral and physiological convergence. *Psychophysiology, 21,* 510–520.

Ogilvie, R. D., & Wilkinson, R. T. (1988). Behavioral versus EEG-based monitoring of all-night sleep/wake patterns. *Sleep, 11,* 139–155.

Ogilvie, R. D., Wilkinson, R. T., & Allison, S. (1989). The detection of sleep onset: Behavioural, physiological and subjective convergence. *Sleep, 12,* 458–474.

Okuma, T., Nakamura, K., Hayashi, A., & Fujimori, M. (1966). Psychophysiological study on the depth of sleep in normal human subjects. *Electroencephalography and Clinical Neurophysiology, 21,* 140–147.

Oswald, I. (1962). *Sleeping and waking: Physiology and psychology*. Amsterdam: Elsevier.

Oswald, I., Taylor, A. M., & Treisman, M. (1960). Discriminative responses to stimulation during human sleep. *Brain, 83,* 440–453.

Pieron, H. (1913). *Le problem physiologique du sommeil*. Paris: Masson et Cie.

Pressman, M. R., Spielman, A. J., Pollak, C. P., & Weitzman, E. D. (1982). Psychophysiological measures of daytime sleepiness in sleep deprivation and narcolepsy [Abstract]. *Sleep Research, 11,* 165.

Rechtschaffen, A. (1994). Sleep onset: Conceptual issues. In R. D. Ogilvie & J. R. Harsh (Eds.), *Sleep onset: Normal and abnormal processes* (pp. 3–17). Washington DC: American Psychological Association.

Rechtschaffen, A., Hauri, P., & Zeitlin, M. (1966). Auditory awakening thresholds in REM and NREM sleep stages. *Perceptual and Motor Skills, 22,* 927–942.

Rechtschaffen, A., & Kales, A. (Eds.). (1968). *A manual of standardized terminology, techniques and scoring system for sleep stages of human subjects*. Los Angeles: UCLA Brain Information Service/Brain Research Institute.

Sadeh, A., Lavie, P., Scher, A., Tirosh, E., & Epstein, R. (1991). Actigraphic home-monitoring in sleep-disturbed and control infants and young children: A new method for pediatric assessment of sleep-wake patterns. *Pediatrics, 87,* 494–499.

Stickgold, R., & Hobson, J. A. (1994). Home monitoring of sleep onset and sleep-onset mentation using the Nightcap. In R. D. Ogilvie & J. R. Harsh (Eds.), *Sleep onset: Normal and abnormal processes* (pp. 141–160). Washington, DC: American Psychological Association.

Webb, W. B., & Aber, W. R. (1983). Signalled arousals and EEG arousals within sleep [Abstract]. *Sleep Research, 12,* 166.

Wilkinson, R. T. (1968). Sleep deprivation and behaviour. In B. F. Reiss & L. A. Abt (Eds.), *Progress in clinical psychology*. New York: Grune & Stratton.

Zorick, F., Roehrs, T., Koshorek, G., Sicklesteel, J., Hartse, K., Wittig, R., & Roth, T. (1982). Patterns of sleepiness in various disorders of excessive daytime somnolence. *Sleep, 5,* S165–S174.

Part III

Learned Food Preferences and Aversions

10

Sexual Dimorphisms in Conditioned Taste Aversions: Mechanism and Function

Kathleen C. Chambers, David Yuan, Elizabeth A. Brownson, and Yuan Wang

In 1972, while pursuing a number of different problems in the hope that one would lead to a dissertation topic, I (the first author) inadvertently discovered a sexual dimorphism in the extinction of conditioned taste aversions (CTAs); males extinguished more slowly than females (Chambers & Sengstake, 1976). When I shared this result with Bob Bolles, he asked me what it meant. Having an acquired disposition to view things in biological ways, I began to expound on the role gonadal hormones play in sexual dimorphisms. He smiled and shrugged his shoulders, but it was clear my answer did not satisfy him. Several years later, after I had completed my dissertation on the role of testosterone (T) in the sexual dimorphism concerning extinction of CTAs and had begun to pursue this problem further in my own laboratory, Bolles again had occasion to ask me what it meant. At that time I was beginning to explore the particular aspects of behavior that T might be influencing during the taste aversion learning situation to cause a prolonged extinction. I told him that I thought females and males acquire taste aversions of equal strength but that during extinction females learn about the nonnegative consequences of consuming that food more readily than males and that T is responsible for slowing the relearning process. Although he remarked that he was happy I was bringing hedonics into my thinking, he still was not satisfied. Finally, in April 1984, when we were both participants at a New York Academy of Sciences conference on conditioned food aversions organized by Norman Braveman and Paul Bronstein (1985), I got it right. During my presentation, I suggested that there was a functional reason for the sexual dimorphism in extinction. Because adequate nutrition is essential for the survival of the fetuses the pregnant female is carrying or the pups she is nursing, it makes functional sense for the female to assess readily whether it was in fact the food she had eaten that caused malaise.

What I finally got right was the inclusion of a functionalistic view in my mostly mechanistic approach. Bolles began moving toward a functionalistic view long before the publication of his seminal paper on species-specific defense reactions (Bolles, 1970), and he was delighted when other investigators began to leave behind purely associationistic and mechanistic explanations of behavior and include functionalism. He suggested that any analysis of behavior should begin with function: that is, what the behavior was designed to do (Bolles, 1985).

Sexual dimorphisms have always been problematic to traditional associationistic learning theorists in the same way that species differences and CTAs have. They cannot be explained by the model. Indeed, sex differences in traditional learning experiments are either ignored by use of only male subjects or are regarded as error variance. Yet anyone who embraces functionalism must view sexual dimorphisms as a different kind of problem. It is a challenge to determine what role the sexual dimorphism in a particular behavior plays in the everyday survival of both the female and male, their progeny, or the species to which they belong. Indeed, sexual dimorphisms are a central part of a functionalistic approach. Ignoring them compromises the understanding of behavior.

There are differences between females and males in a number of behavior systems, and within each system there are a number of behavioral differences. For example, in the eating system there are sexual dimorphisms in energy expenditure or activity levels, food intake, innate taste aversions and preferences, and learned taste aversions (Beatty, 1979). For most behavior systems, the reason for the specific sexual dimorphism can be linked directly to differences in the reproductive and parental demands on females and males.

In this chapter, we first discuss the sexual dimorphisms that have been found in rats during CTA testing and the hormonal and neural mechanisms that control them. We attempt to relate these sexual dimorphisms to other dimorphisms within as well as outside the eating system on the basis of knowledge of hormonal and neural mechanisms. Finally, we attempt to explain these dimorphisms with respect to the function they play in the everyday life of the rat in a natural environment.

Sexual Dimorphisms in Conditioned Taste Aversions

Three separate sexual dimorphisms have been found in the taste aversion learning situation: (a) a dimorphism in sensitivity to the illness-inducing agent, (b) a dimorphism in the rate of extinction, and (c) a dimorphism in latent inhibition, or the effects of preexposure to a novel taste on its subsequent aversive conditioning. When a low dose of lithium chloride (LiCl) is paired repeatedly with a sucrose solution, a greater proportion of male than female rats acquire an aversion to the sucrose (Chambers, Sengstake, Yoder, & Thornton, 1981; Dacanay, Mastropaolo, Olin, & Riley, 1984). This dimorphism in acquisition appears to be due to differences in threshold sensitivity to LiCl rather than to differences in acquisition, because the rate of acquisition for females that acquired an aversion is similar to the rate for males. When a high dose of LiCl is paired once with a sucrose solution, males extinguish the aversion to the solution at a slower rate than females. This dimorphism has been found in different strains of rats, in mice, and in chicks (Brot, Bernstein, & Dorsa, 1992; Chambers & Sengstake, 1976; Clifton & Andrew, 1987; Ingram & Corfman, 1981; Weinburg, Gunnar, Brett, Gonzalez, & Levine, 1982) and has been shown to be due to factors associated with extinction, not acquisition (Chambers & Sengstake, 1979). Finally, when males and females are preexposed to a sucrose solution prior to pairing a high dose of LiCl with the solution, males exhibit stronger aversions and slower extinction rates than females (Chambers, 1985). This finding suggests that females learn the nonnegative consequences of consuming the novel sucrose solution more readily than males (Kalat & Rozin, 1973).

What Are the Functions of the Sexual Dimorphisms in CTAs?

Female rats are responsible for the primary care of the young. We have observed in seminatural environments that pregnant rats sequester the space around familiar food and water sites to build their nests. They also stock their nests with food. After the birth of their young, they defend this space against conspecific intruders, in particular, males. This forces males to seek other sources of food and water. It makes functional sense, therefore, for males to be more sensitive to the possibility that a food has illness-producing properties. We think that this is the principle expressed when males but not females acquire aversions to solutions with very low doses of LiCl. However, any food that causes illness after consumption is potentially life threatening, and it makes functional sense for both males and females to acquire equally strong aversions to this food. It is not surprising that there is no sexual dimorphism in the acquisition of aversions induced with high doses of LiCl.

Males pushed to the periphery are more likely to encounter all kinds of dangers, whereas females spending long periods of time in their nests nursing young and restricting their movement to a small known area are less likely to encounter the kinds of dangers to which males are exposed. In addition, the survival of her young is enhanced if the female is able to reassess quickly the illness-inducing value of the foods in her immediate environment. It makes functional sense, then, for males to be more cautious then females in assessing and reassessing danger value. This is expressed in the greater cautiousness of males when they become ill after consuming a relatively novel food previously associated with no illness and the slower extinction of males in a number of different aversive learning situations.

Hormonal and Neural Mechanisms

After I (the first author) outlined my vision of the function of the extinction sexual dimorphism, Bolles asked me whether I was now going to pursue more rigorously the *why* (or functional) approach to this problem and dispense with further investigations that use the *how* (or mechanistic) approach. I smiled and said *no*, but the question has never left my mind. In this section, we review the hormonal and neural mechanisms that control the sexual dimorphisms in CTAs and then show how an understanding of these mechanisms contributes to a further understanding of the functions of these dimorphisms.

Threshold Sensitivity to the Illness-Inducing Agent

Both ovarian and testicular hormones contribute to the sexual dimorphism in threshold sensitivity to LiCl (Chambers et al., 1981). Gonadectomy increases the proportion of females and decreases the proportion of males that acquire an aversion such that the proportion of both falls between those of intact females and males. T treatment increases the proportions of gonadectomized males and females that acquire an aversion to that of intact males. The ovarian hormone or hormones involved in this sexual dimorphism have yet to be determined. For this sexual dimorphism, then, it appears that T is necessary for the maximum number of animals to acquire an aversion, and some ovarian hormone is required for the minimum number of animals to acquire an aversion. Gonadectomy alone is not sufficient to minimize the number in males or maximize the number in females.

Extinction

The sexual dimorphism in extinction is dependent on the presence of T and estradiol (E; Chambers, 1976, 1980; Chambers & Yuan, 1990; Clifton & Andrew, 1987; Earley & Leonard, 1978, 1979).

Influence of testosterone. ACTIVATIONAL EFFECTS OF TESTOSTERONE. Gonadectomy increases the rate of extinction of males, and T replacement restores extinction to a slow rate. Females also have the behavioral capacity to respond to T; the extinction rates of gonadectomized females given T are prolonged. Thus, a critical difference between males and females that contributes to the sexual dimorphism in extinction is the higher level of circulating T in males. It is clear that the slowing of extinction is androgen-rather than estrogen-based because dihydrotestosterone, a metabolite of T that cannot be converted to E, also slows extinction rates in gonadectomized males and females (Chambers, 1976, 1980; Chambers & Yuan, 1990; Clifton & Andrew, 1987; Earley & Leonard, 1978, 1979).

Although females have the capacity to respond to T, the amount needed to induce a slow extinction rate is greater in females than males

(Sengstake & Chambers, 1991). We gave gonadectomized females and males T implants that yielded low, high, or supraphysiological levels of T (based on levels in intact males). In two separate studies, we (Sengstake & Chambers, 1991) found that implants resulting in low physiological levels of T slowed extinction in males but not females. In females, implants that resulted in supraphysiological T levels clearly slowed extinction. The size of implant that resulted in high physiological levels of T appears to be a threshold dose for females, because some females exhibited prolonged extinction with this dose and others did not. This sexual dimorphism in T sensitivity is not due to differences in circulating T levels, because there were no differences in the T levels of females and males given the different sizes of implants.

It is the presence of T during the perinatal period of development that influences T sensitivity. When females were exposed to T during late fetal and early neonatal life, they showed greater behavioral sensitivity to T. After gonadectomy in adulthood, they exhibited a slow extinction rate when given an implant that resulted in low physiological levels of T, whereas perinatally untreated females did not. Extinction rates also were not prolonged in adult gonadectomized females exposed to T during the fetal and neonatal period but not during adulthood. These results are similar to those of other investigators, who have found that only fetal females in a uterine position that exposed them to higher testosterone levels than other females showed prolonged extinction as adults when given low doses of T (Babine & Smotherman, 1984; Meisel & Ward, 1981; vom Saal & Bronson, 1980). The results of all these studies show that (a) the presence of T during the perinatal period alters subsequent sensitivity to T but that (b) it is the presence of sufficient T during adulthood and not the presence of T during the perinatal period that is critical for the expression of a slow extinction rate.

RELATIONSHIP BETWEEN LEVELS OF TESTOSTERONE AND RATE OF EXTINCTION. Although a slow extinction is dependent on sufficient circulating levels of T, we consistently have failed to find significant correlations between T level and extinction rate. This is not unusual; it is true of other androgen-dependent behaviors as well, such as male sexual behavior. There is one explanation that frequently has been offered to account for this finding (Chambers, Resko, & Phoenix, 1982). Mean T levels usually range from 2.2 to 3.5 ng/ml in adult male rats. Ejaculatory behavior in male rats can be stimulated when T levels are exogenously maintained at 0.2 ng/ml, and normal values for different components of sexual behavior, (e.g., intromission latency, intromission frequency, and postejaculatory interval) can be stimulated with doses of T that yield 0.5–0.7 ng/ml. During most of a normal day, therefore, there is more circulating T available than is needed to activate male sexual behavior when appropriate stimuli are present (Damassa, Smith, Tennent, & Davidson, 1977). Fluctuations in T levels due to pulsatile release and circadian rhythms do not affect the action of T on behavioral target tissues. Individual differences in behavior, then, are likely due to differences in sensitivity of target tissues to T.

Although individual differences in behavior cannot be accounted for by differences in T levels, there is a relationship between T dose and behavior. As the amount of circulating T increases from gonadectomized levels, there is an incremental slowing of extinction (Chambers & Sengstake, unpublished data; see Figure 1). T doses that yield circulating levels close to 1.0 ng/ml, however, are not sufficiently high to prolong extinction significantly. T doses that yield circulating levels within the range found in intact males significantly slow extinction, and extinction is significantly slowed even further as T levels begin to rise above the physiological range (Chambers, Sengstake, Brownson & Westfahl, 1993). The latter result differs from what has been found for male sexual behavior. The dose response curves for different components of male sexual behavior vary, but maximum levels of behavior are achieved with doses that yield physiological levels of T (Chambers & Phoenix, 1986; Damassa et al., 1977); that is, supraphysiological levels of T do not activate higher levels of sexual performance.

ALONE ON A DESERT ISLAND. Any behavior whose activation is dependent on the availability of circulating T levels potentially can be affected by factors that decrease T availability below the threshold amount needed to activate that particular behavior. There are three environmental factors that are known to cause reductions in circulating T levels: social isolation, food deprivation, and fluid deprivation (Chambers & Sengstake, 1978; Chambers, Sengstake, et al., 1993; Dessi-Fulgheri, Lupo Di Prisco, & Verdarelli, 1976; Howland & Skinner, 1973). Prolonged social isolation (3–6 months), imposed in either infancy or adulthood, disrupts male sexual behavior by decreasing the occurrence of mounts, intromissions, and ejaculations (Chambers, Sengstake, Walther, & Bullis, 1982; Gerall, Ward, & Gerall, 1967; Greundel & Arnold, 1969; Hard & Larsson, 1968). In adult male rats socially isolated for 6 weeks, mean T levels decrease to about 1 ng/ml and extinction is accelerated (Chambers & Sengstake, 1978). Food deprivation increases intromission latency and mount frequency prior to ejaculation in adult male rats, which is similar to the changes that occur following gonadectomy (Davidson, 1966; Sachs, 1965). Mean T levels decrease to about 1 ng/ml in adult male rats maintained on a 22-or 23-hour fluid-deprivation schedule, and extinction is accelerated even when the males are given a choice between water and the conditioned solution (Brownson, Sengstake, & Chambers, 1988; Chambers, 1982; Chambers, Sengstake, et al., 1993). These results suggest that there is a causal relationship between the environmentally induced decreases in T levels and the behavioral effects in males.

There are six other findings that support this hypothesis for fluid deprivation. First, adrenocorticotropic hormone (ACTH) increases T levels in fluid-deprived males and prolongs extinction only if the males are not gonadectomized (Chambers, 1982; Kendler, Hennessy, Smotherman, & Levine, 1976). Second, fluid deprivation does not accelerate extinction in a choice situation in females (Sengstake, Chambers, & Thrower, 1978). Third, the extinction rates of deprived and nondeprived males do not differ when the rats are gonadectomized, and the rates of intact and gonadectomized males do not differ when they are fluid-deprived (Chambers,

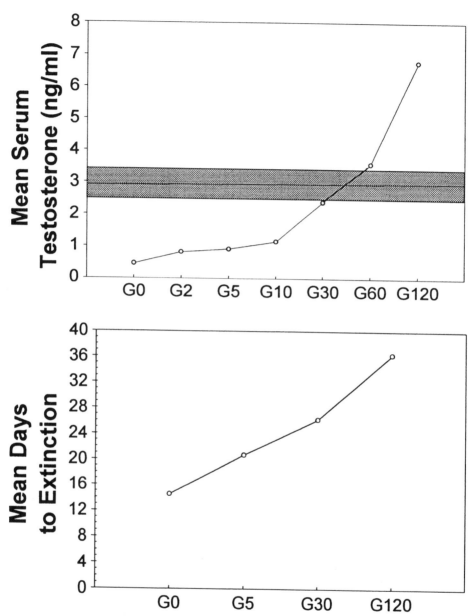

Figure 1. *Top*. Mean (± *SE*) serum testosterone (T) levels in intact Sprague–Dawley males (horizontal bar) and mean levels in gonadectomized males implanted subcutaneously with blank Silastic capsules (G0) or with various sizes of T-filled capsules (G2–G120). *Bottom*. Mean days to extinguish a conditioned taste aversion in gonadectomized Sprague–Dawley males implanted subcutaneously with blank Silastic capsules or with various sizes of T-filled capsules (G5–G120). The extinction rates for G30 and G120 were slower than those for G0, $F(1, 3) = 6.40$, $p = .003$, Newman–Keuls, $p < .05$).

Sengstake, et al., 1993). Fourth, T doses that produce physiological levels of serum T restore extinction rates of gonadectomized fluid-deprived males to the rates found in intact, nondeprived males (Chambers, Sengstake, et al., 1993). Fifth, both T and fluid deprivation affect extinction rate by acting during extinction but not during acquisition (Chambers & Sengstake, 1979; Sengstake & Chambers, 1979). Finally, fluid deprivation also produces a pseudocastration effect in intact males for another behavioral expression that depends on circulating T. It decreases the threshold sensitivity of intact males to LiCl (Chambers et al., 1981).

Although the acceleration of extinction in fluid-deprived males can be accounted for by the decreases in circulating T, fluid deprivation also has other effects on the androgen–target tissue system that can contribute to its behavioral effects. T treatment is less effective in prolonging extinction in fluid-deprived gonadectomized males than in nondeprived gonadectomized males (Chambers, Sengstake, et al., 1993). This suggests that fluid deprivation also reduces the sensitivity of target tissues to T.

The mechanisms by which fluid deprivation reduces circulating T and decreases target tissue sensitivity are yet to be delineated. There are two mechanisms by which circulating T levels could decrease. There could be decreases in the synthesis and release of T or increases in its degradation. It is unlikely that a degradation mechanism is involved, because the T levels of gonadectomized deprived and nondeprived males do not differ when subjects are given the same dose of T. We have suggested that either increases in systemic release or local testicular synthesis of arginine vasopressin causes decreases in circulating T levels (Chambers, Sengstake, et al., 1993). This hypothesis is based on the reports that circulating vasopressin levels are elevated and that this hormone is synthesized in the testes and inhibits the biosynthesis of T in the testicular Leydig cells (Adashi & Hsueh, 1981; Kasson & Hsueh, 1986; Kasson, Meidan, & Hsueh, 1985; Meidan & Hsueh, 1985). Reduced sensitivity of target tissues to T could be the result of a decrease in the number of androgen receptors or a decrease in androgen receptor affinity. The influence of fluid deprivation on these receptor characteristics is unknown.

WHAT IS TESTOSTERONE DOING? Because T is effective only when it is present during extinction, any hypothesis associated with acquisition can be eliminated. A number of extinction-associated hypotheses have been suggested (Chambers & Sengstake, 1979; Clifton & Andrew, 1987; Earley & Leonard, 1979). These include the following: (a) T delays the passive decay of the memory trace for the CTA; (b) T increases the focusing or narrowing of attention; (c) T reduces problem-solving ability or flexibility so that the animal is less able to relearn that the conditioned substance no longer causes illness; and (d) T improves performance in passive avoidance tasks so that the animal is better able to resist sampling the conditioned substance.

Our group tested the hypothesis that T delays the passive decay of the memory trace after acquisition (Chambers, 1985). Most females have extinguished their aversion after 2 weeks. We thus imposed a delay of 2 days, 2 weeks, or 4 weeks between acquisition and extinction tests. If passive decay contributes to the faster extinction rate of females, then one would expect females with delays of 2–4 weeks to have a faster extinction rate than those with a delay of 2 days. Because the extinction rates of the females given different time delays did not differ, it is unlikely that the effect of T is associated with memory decay.

Clifton and Andrew (1987) suggested that T-mediated effects on attentional processes provide an unlikely explanation because extinction of a CTA and attentional processes are modulated by different hormonal mechanisms. T prolongs extinction of a CTA in both rats and chicks, yet behaviors in tasks measuring attention in chicks are modulated by estrogen (Clifton & Andrew, 1986).

In examining the extinction in females and males, we found that once they begin to extinguish, the amount of time it takes them to reach preconditioning consumption levels (slope of the curve) is the same. The difference is in the amount of time it takes for females and males to begin to show the gradual increase in the amount of sucrose solution consumed. We are presently testing two hypotheses that could account for this difference. First, T may delay relearning by increasing the number of taste–no illness pairings needed by the animal to revise its learned assumptions about the consequences of consuming the substance. Second, T may delay risk taking by increasing the time interval between the taste–illness pairing and testing of whether the taste still predicts illness.

The action of T on extinction may not be specific to CTAs. Evidence suggests that T prolongs extinction of other avoidance tasks as well. Male rats gonadectomized neonatally exhibit accelerated extinction of a passive avoidance task, and adult gonadectomized male rats treated with T show delayed extinction of an active avoidance task (Negroni & Denti, 1977; Telegdy & Stark, 1973). The former effect is due to decreased levels of circulatory T at the time of testing rather than alterations in the development of neural tissues in the neonatally gonodectomized male because the extinction rates of neonatally androgenized females were not different from untreated females. It may be that T activates a particular neural site that then modulates extinction of aversive learning in general through its connections to neural areas controlling each type of aversive learning. If this is the case, it is unlikely that the action of T is simply to improve passive avoidance performance.

NEURAL MECHANISMS. In a preliminary study, we gonadectomized three groups of males and placed T directly into the dorsal medial preoptic area of one of the groups (Hung, Yuan, & Chambers, 1991; see Figure 2). The rates of extinction of these T-treated males were slower than those of the other two groups, the nonsurgical and surgical controls. In another study, we found that T had no effect when it was placed in the ventral medial preoptic area (Wang & Chambers, unpublished results; see Figure 2). Together these results suggest that the dorsal medial preoptic area is part of the neural pathway mediating T effects on extinction.

It was suggested recently that T influences extinction of CTAs by acting on the central vasopressin system (Brot, Bernstein, & Dorsa, 1990, 1992). Systemic injections of vasopressin or of a vasopressin agonist pro-

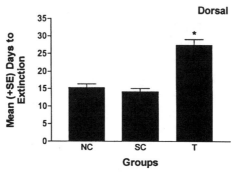

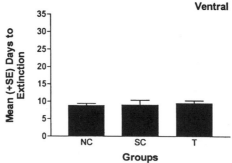

Figure 2. *Top*. Mean (+ *SE*) days to extinguish a conditioned taste aversion in gonadectomized Fischer 344 males with T-filled or empty cannulas (SC) implanted in the dorsal medial preoptic area or with no implantation surgery (NC). *Significantly different from both control groups, $p < .05$. *Bottom*. Mean (+ *SE*) days to extinguish a conditioned taste aversion in gonadectomized Fischer 344 males with T-filled or empty cannulas (SC) implanted in the ventral medial preoptic area or with no implantation surgery (NC).

long extinction, and intraventricular implants of a vasopressin antagonist produce fast extinction rates (Brot et al., 1989; Cooper, McNamara, & Thompson, 1980). In addition, Brattleboro rats, which do not have an intact vasopressin system but do have an intact testicular system, show rapid extinction of CTAs (Brot et al., 1990, 1992). Recently, we found a relationship between extinction rate and vasopressin levels in the hypothalamic paraventricular nucleus, a primary source of vasopressin (Brownson, 1992; Brownson, Chambers, & Brinton, 1997; Chambers, Brownson, & Brinton, 1993; see Figure 3). Vasopressin levels were measured in nondeprived and deprived male rats at three different time periods with respect to taste aversion conditioning: prior to conditioning, 23 hours after the first extinction trial, and 23 hours after the extinction trial in which each fluid-deprived rat drank 50–75 percent of its acquisition-day consumption. At each time period, a deprived rat was paired with a nondeprived rat and brains were removed from each member of a pair, for vasopressin measurements, within minutes of one another. None of the nondeprived rats had begun to extinguish at the last time period. Vaso-

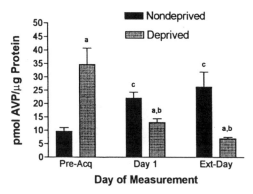

Figure 3.   Mean (+ *SE*) levels of arginine vasopressin (AVP) in the paraventricular nucleus of the hypothalamus in nondeprived and fluid-deprived Fischer 344 males before acquisition of a conditioned taste aversion (Pre-Acq), 23 hours after extinction day 1 (Day1), or 23 hours after the extinction trial in which each fluid-deprived male reached 50–75 percent of its acquisition-day consumption (Ext-Day; none of the nondeprived rats had begun to extinguish). [a] Significantly different from nondeprived males on the same day of measurement, *p* < .05. [b]Significantly different from Pre-Acq levels for deprived males, *p* < .05. [c]Significantly different from Pre-Acq levels for nondeprived males, *p* < .05.

pressin levels were higher in deprived than nondeprived males prior to conditioning; this is what one would expect as a result of the fluid deprivation. However, after acquisition of a CTA and during extinction, vasopressin levels of deprived males were lower than those of nondeprived males. The latter result is what one would expect if lower vasopressin levels in the paraventricular nucleus lead to faster extinction rates. Additional support for this suggestion comes from a reexamination of the histological data from our dorsal medial preoptic area study; the placements were just below the paraventricular nucleus. We suggest, therefore, that the implanted T stimulated neurons in the paraventricular nucleus, and as a result, vasopressin levels were increased and extinction was prolonged.

Influence of estradiol. ACTIVATIONAL EFFECTS OF ESTRADIOL. Although we have observed that the extinction rates of intact and gonadectomized females do not differ, the intact females were tested without taking the stage of their hormonal cycle into account (Chambers 1976). Therefore, any differences could have been obscured by having different females in different parts of their cycle and by testing each female during different stages of her cycle. There is evidence that suggests that E has an effect on extinction. T has a diminished effect in intact females compared to ovariectomized females, and E, but not progesterone, can block the effects of T on extinction in gonadectomized females (Chambers, 1976, 1980; Chambers & Yuan, 1990). In addition, E doses that result in high physiological blood levels accelerate extinction in ovariectomized females when they are administered without T (Yuan, 1992; Yuan & Chambers, 1989, 1997a; see Figure 4). Males also have the capacity to respond behaviorally to E,

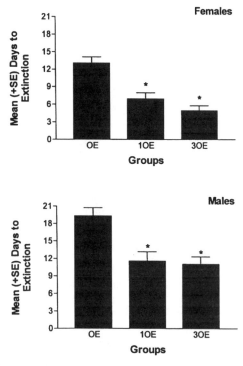

Figure 4. *Top.* Mean (+ *SE*) days to extinguish a conditioned taste aversion in gonadectomized females implanted subcutaneously with blank Silastic capsules (0E) or two different sizes of capsules filled with estrodiol (E; 10E or 30E). *Significantly different from 0E females, *p* < .05. *Bottom.* Mean (+ *SE*) days to extinguish a conditioned taste aversion in gonadectomized males implanted subcutaneously with bank Silastic capsules (0E) or two different sizes of E-filled capsules (10E or 30E). *Significantly different from 0E males, *p* < .05.

because in gonadectomized males, E blocks the effects of T and accelerates extinction when given without T (Chambers & Yuan, 1990; Earley & Leonard, 1979; Yuan, 1992; Yuan & Chambers, 1989, 1997a). It appears for this sexual dimorphism as well that gonadectomy alone is not sufficient to convert male behavior patterns into female patterns or female behavior patterns into male patterns.

WHAT IS ESTRADIOL DOING? There is an accumulation of evidence that suggests that the effects of E on extinction are due to the illness-inducing properties of E. A number of investigators have shown that E in different forms and administered through different routes can induce a CTA when paired with a novel flavor in rats, mice, and humans (De Beun et al., 1991; Gustavson & Gustavson, 1986, 1987; Gustavson, Gustavson, Young, Pumariega, & Nicolaus, 1989; Gustavson, Reinarz, Gustavson, & Pumariega, 1988; Miele, 1987; Miele, Rosellini, & Svare, 1988; Nicolaus, Farmer, Gustavson, & Gustavson, 1989; Nicolaus, Herrera, Nicolaus, & Gustavson, 1989; Peeters, Smets, & Broekkamp, 1992; Rice, Lopez, & Garcia, 1987). Recently, it has been established that the same route of administration of the same dose of E used to accelerate extinction can also induce a CTA (Wang, Yuan, & Chambers, 1992; Yuan, 1992; Yuan & Chambers, 1997b; see Figure 5). This suggests that the accelerated extinction induced by E is a result of its illness-inducing properties.

Further support for this hypothesis comes from studies examining the effects of preexposure to the illness-inducing agent before conditioning or extinction. Preexposure to an illness-inducing agent before acquisition of a CTA can attenuate the subsequent learning of an aversion, and preexposure to an illness-inducing agent after acquisition but before extinction of an aversion can accelerate the subsequent extinction of the aversion (Cannon, Baker, & Berman, 1977; Domjan, 1978; Mikulka, Leard, & Klein, 1977; Riley, Dacanay, & Mastropaolo, 1984; Switzman, Fishman, & Amit, 1981). The substance used in the pre- and postexposure phases can be the same as the illness-inducing agent used to induce the CTA, or it can be different. The former method has been termed *intraagent disruption*, and the latter has been called *interagent disruption* (Cannon et al., 1977). One of the explanations for this effect is as follows: Animals do not readily acquire aversions to familiar foods, especially foods eaten from puphood. Therefore, when an animal is exposed to an illness-inducing agent and only familiar foods are available, a dissociation between illness induced by the illness-inducing agent and food occurs. When a novel food is made available, this dissociation then interferes with the ability of an animal to associate the illness with the novel food. Two important predictions can be made on the basis of this explanation. When an illness-inducing agent is given before acquisition or before extinction of a CTA, the aversion will be attenuated, but when an illness-inducing agent is given during acquisition or extinction, the aversion will be strengthened.

We conducted several studies to test the hypothesis that the time of exposure to E determines extinction rate. In the first study, we gave E in combination with T before and during acquisition and before and during extinction (Chambers & Yuan, 1990; Yuan, 1992; Yuan & Chambers, 1989).

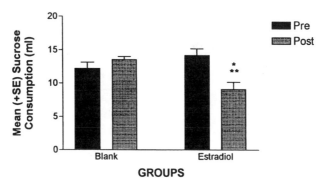

Figure 5. Mean (+ *SE*) amount of a sucrose solution consumed by gonadectomized females before (Pre) and after (Post) pairing consumption of the sucrose with implantation of blank Silastic capsules or E-filled capsules. *Significantly different from Pre consumption levels. **Significantly different from blank Post Consumption levels.

The prolonged extinction usually observed after T treatment was blocked in both cases; that is, extinction was accelerated. We then gave E without T during the same two time periods (Yuan, 1992; Yuan & Chambers, 1991b, 1997b; see Figure 6). Extinction was accelerated when E was given before and during acquisition. This result is similar to reports of other investigators that aversion learning is weaker or blocked and extinction is accelerated when E is given before acquisition of an E-induced aversion (De Beun, Peeters, & Broekkamp, 1993; Merwin & Doty, 1994). We found that E had a borderline effect, however, when it was given before and during extinction. This result was unexpected if one considers the strong effect E had during this time period when given in combination with T. However, it is not unusual if one focuses on a dissociation–association hypothesis. We decided to examine this borderline effect further by separating the time period of administration of E with respect to extinction (Yuan, 1992; Yuan & Chambers, 1991a, 1991b, 1997b; see Figure 7). In line with the predictions expressed previously, one would expect an accelerated extinction when E is given after acquisition but before extinction because of the learned dissociation between food and illness. Also, one would expect a prolonged extinction when E is given during extinction, because an illness-inducing agent is being administered coincident with consumption of a novel taste that already has been associated with illness. Both of these predictions were substantiated. The results of all of these studies support the hypothesis that E accelerates extinction and blocks the effects of T because of its illness-inducing properties.

NEURAL MECHANISMS. The preceding evidence strongly indicates that T and E affect extinction through different mechanisms. This hypothesis is supported by the evidence that androgens generally do not act as illness-inducing agents. Dihydrotestosterone prolongs extinction but does not induce CTAs (Chambers, 1980; Earley & Leonard, 1978; Gustavson et al.,

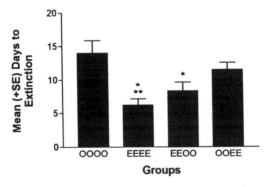

Figure 6. Mean (+ SE) days to extinguish a conditioned taste aversion in gonadectomized females implanted subcutaneously with blank or E-filled Silastic capsules before and during acquisition (0000) and extinction (EEEE), with blank capsules before and during acquisition and E-filled capsules before and during extinction (00EE), or with E-filled capsules before and during acquisition and blank capsules before and during extinction (EE00). *Significantly different from 0000, $p < .05$. **Significantly different from 00EE, $p < .05$.

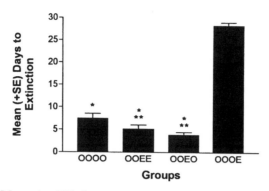

Figure 7. *Top.* Mean (+ *SE*) days to extinguish a conditioned taste aversion in gonadectomized females implanted subcutaneously with blank Silastic capsules before and during acquisition and extinction (0000), E-filled capsules before and during extinction and blank capsules before and during acquisition (00EE), E-filled capsules before extinction and blank capsules at all other times (00E0), or E-filled capsules during extinction and blank capsules at all other times (000E). *Significantly different from 000E, $p < .05$. **Significantly different from 0000 females, p < .05.

1989). The reports on the ability of T to induce CTAs have been inconsistent, but any conclusion that T can act as an illness-inducing agent is equivocal because T is aromatized to E endogenously (Gustavson et al., 1989; Miele et al., 1988; Peeters et al., 1992). The hypothesis also is supported by our findings that E does not accelerate extinction of other aversive learning situations, such as step-down passive shock avoidance, step-through active shock avoidance, and conditioned acoustical eyeblink response (Yuan, 1992; Yuan & Chambers, 1997a). Therefore, it is highly unlikely that these two hormones act on the same neural sites to produce their effects.

One of the problems with exploring further the neural pathways for E action is that when permanent lesions are used, it is difficult to assess whether the effect on CTAs is associated with gustatory processing, illness processing, integration, storage, retrieval, or motor response deficits. There is the additional problem that E causes decreases in food intake that are not associated with CTAs (Wade, 1972). Recently, we tested the feasibility of using a temporary lesioning technique, the cold probe (Wang, 1995; Wang, Lavond, & Chambers, 1997), which can reduce the temperature of discrete areas of the brain and thus inactivate the neurons in that area. The temperature can be controlled such that the neurons but not the axons of passage are affected (Brooks, 1983). When the cooling is turned off, the neurons are once more active. We can give an animal the novel substance with the brain area not cooled and therefore functional, which allows gustatory processing to occur; we can cool the brain area when illness processing is occurring; and we can test the animal with the brain area not cooled. This technique allows us to eliminate gustatory processing, retrieval, and motor response deficits as possible explanations for CTA deficits, but it does not allow us to eliminate integration or storage.

Because there were some technical problems that had to be worked out before E could be used in cooling experiments, we used LiCl as the illness-inducing agent in our first experiment. We chose this agent because studies indicated that the area postrema is essential for both an E-induced CTA (Bernstein, Courtney, & Braget, 1986) and a LiCl-induced aversion (Ritter, McGlone, & Kelley, 1980). Furthermore, preexposure to LiCl can weaken an E-induced aversion, and preexposure to E can weaken a LiCl-induced aversion, which suggests a common neural mechanism (De Beun, et al., 1993; Yuan, 1992; Yuan & Chambers, 1991b). It is likely that the neural pathway extending from the area postrema is the same for all agents for which the effectiveness as an illness-inducing agent in a CTA situation requires an intact area postrema. Future research, of course, is needed to verify this suggestion.

In two separate studies, we used LiCl or apomorphine as the illness-inducing agent (Wang, 1995; Wang, Lavond, & Chambers, 1994, 1997). We selected apomorphine as a control agent because it does not require a functioning area postrema to induce CTAs (Parker & Brosseau, 1990; Van Der Kooy, Swerdlow, & Koob, 1983). After the animals consumed a sucrose solution, cooling of the area postrema was initiated, and 5 minutes later, one of the illness-inducing agents was administered. Cooling was continued for 55 minutes. The male rats were tested for acquisition 2 days later while the neural function of the area postrema was preserved. Cooling attenuated a LiCl-induced CTA but not an apomorphine-induced aversion. These results replicated the findings of the permanent lesion studies and thus indicated the viability of cooling as a tool for investigating the illness circuitry of CTAs. They also extended previous findings. Although the area postrema is necessary for LiCl- and E-induced aversions, its precise role is unclear. It is the common assumption that the area postrema is part of the illness pathway, but some have suggested that it plays a role in taste processing (Chambers, 1990; Chambers & Bernstein, 1995; Kosten & Contreras, 1989). That the animals showed an attenuation of a LiCl-induced aversion when cooling was initiated after taste processing during acquisition and when testing for acquisition was done while the area postrema was functional makes it highly unlikely that this area is involved in taste processing. We now are applying this technique to the study of E action in the brain.

Function Revisited

There are three points that we can add to the discussion of the function of the sexual dimorphisms in CTAs. First, finding that the same hormone, testosterone, is involved in the establishment of sexual dimorphisms in the extinction of other kinds of avoidance learning lends support to the notion that the function of all of these sexual dimorphisms is related to the peripheralization of the male in loose-knit rat societies and the potential for increased exposure to danger. Second, environmental conditions such as scarcity of food or water place a male in a situation that is similar to that faced by a pregnant or nursing female. That is, his survival is enhanced if he is able to reassess quickly the illness-inducing value of the foods that do exist in his environment. It makes functional sense for a physiological system (i.e., the pituitary–testicular system) that ensures protection from poisoning when foods are plentiful to be deactivated to ensure protection from starvation when foods are scarce. Third, the social isolation data present a problem. Adult rats use social cues to increase their knowledge about acceptable food sources by following other rats to these sources (Galef, Mischinger, & Malenfant, 1987; Galef & Wigmore, 1983; Posadas-Andrews & Roper, 1983). Given this fact, one would expect that socially isolated males would be more cautious rather than less. Why this is not the case remains unresolved.

A Troublesome Strain

We conclude this chapter with data that have led us to expand our ideas about the function of the sexual dimorphism in the extinction of CTAs but also to revise our model of the way testosterone influences this sexual dimorphism. The data necessitating a revision of our ideas would have delighted Bolles, because the challenge to him was to find a model that best fit the data rather than finding data that best fit a model.

All the results gathered in our laboratory were based on the performance of Sprague–Dawley rats. Subsequently, Fischer 344 rats entered our laboratory. This happened at a time when the first author was involved primarily in studying the reproductive decline in aging rhesus males. Sexual performance declines in aging males of most species studied, and there is evidence of reduced T production in most of these species (Chambers, 1995). Fischer 344 males are not an exception (Chambers & Phoenix, 1984, 1986). However, attempts to associate the decreases in T with behavior have not been successful in any species. This has led several investigators to suggest that target tissues, central or peripheral, controlling sexual behavior are less responsive to T (Chambers & Phoenix, 1984; Jakubczak, 1964, 1967; Larsson, 1958). When the National Institute of Aging offered aging Fischer 344 rats at no cost to their grantees, we thought that using these animals would allow us to answer questions about T sensitivity that required invasive procedures and thus precluded use of our aged rhesus monkeys (Chambers, Thornton, & Roselli, 1991; Roselli, Thornton, & Chambers, 1993). Furthermore, we had hoped to study the mechanisms controlling T-dependent changes in sexual behavior and CTAs in the same aging animals. However, we encountered problems from the outset, problems associated with T effects and not E effects. E had similar effects in both Sprague–Dawley and Fischer 344 rats (Yuan, 1992; Yuan & Chambers, 1989, 1990).

Testosterone and Fischer 344 Males

For a given dose of LiCl, extinction is slower in Fischer 344 than in Sprague–Dawley males, yet T levels are lower in Fischer 344 males (Brownson, 1992; Brownson, Sengstake, & Chambers, 1990, 1991, 1994; see Figure 8). As is true in Sprague–Dawley rats, extinction is faster in gonadectomized Fischer 344 females than in intact males (Chambers, Brownson, & Yuan, 1991; see Figure 9). However, the extinction of gonadectomized Fischer 344 females also is faster than that of gonadectomized Fischer 344 males, and gonadectomy does not alter extinction rate in Fischer 344 males (Chambers, Brownson, & Yuan, 1991; Yuan, Hung, & Chambers, 1990b). Raising circulating T levels above mean levels for intact Fischer 344 males slows extinction further, but these are the same levels of T that restore the rate of extinction in gonadectomized Sprague–Dawley males to the rate observed in intact Sprague–Dawley males, and this rate is faster than that of intact Fischer 344 males (Chambers, Brownson, & Yuan, 1991; see Figure 10).

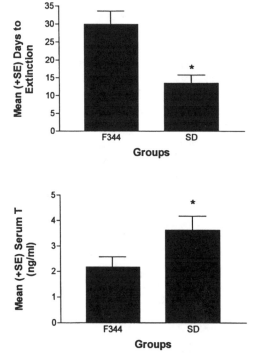

Figure 8. *Top.* Mean (+ *SE*) days to extinguish a conditioned taste aversion in intact Fischer 344 (F344) and Sprague–Dawley (SD) male rats given the same dose of LiCl to induce the aversion. *Significantly different from F344 males, *p* < .05. *Bottom.* Mean (+ *SE*) serum T levels in intact F344 and SD male rats. *Significantly different from F344 males, *p* < .05. From "The Role of Serum Tesosterone in the Accelerated Extinction of a Conditioned Taste Aversion in Fluid Deprived Male Rats," by E. A. Brownson, C. B Sengstake, and K. C. Chambers, 1994, *Physiology and Behavior, 55,* pp. 275–276. Adapted with permission.

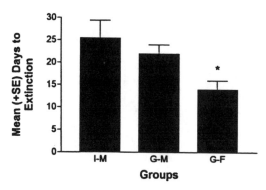

Figure 9. Mean (+ *SE*) days to extinguish a conditioned taste aversion in Fischer 344 intact males (I-M), gonadectomized males (G-M), and gonadectomized females (G-F). *Significantly different from the two male groups, *p* < .05.

Because gonadectomy has no effect on extinction, one would not expect a deprivation-induced decrease in T levels to cause an accelerated extinction. We found that deprived Fischer 344 males had a faster extinction rate than nondeprived males but that T levels did not differ (Brownson, 1992; Brownson et al., 1990, 1991, 1994; see Figure 11). The same supraphysiological doses of T that prolonged extinction in nondeprived, gonadectomized males had no effect in deprived, gonadectomized males (see Figure 12). Higher supraphysiological doses had a modest effect in deprived, intact males (Brownson, 1992).

What sense can be made of these data? It is more parsimonious to base any explanation on the assumption that the mechanisms controlling extinction of Fischer 344 males are similar to those of Sprague–Dawley males. Embracing this assumption, we suggest the following: The curve describing the relationship between extinction rate and T levels is set at a lower T threshold level for Fischer 344 males than for Sprague–Dawley males (see Figure 13). Fischer 344 males are more sensitive to the behavioral effects of T than are Sprague–Dawley males. This greater sensitivity

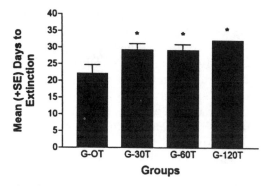

Figure 10. Mean (+ *SE*) days to extinguish a conditioned taste aversion in gonadectomized Fischer 344 male rats implanted with blank Silastic capsules (G-0T) or with various sizes of T-filled capsules (G-30T–G-120T). *Significantly different from G-0T, *p* < .05.

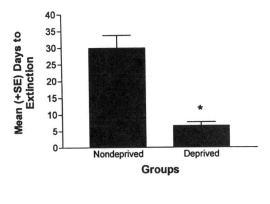

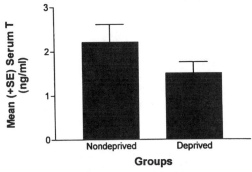

Figure 11. *Top*. Mean (+ *SE*) days to extinguish a conditioned taste aversion in nondeprived and fluid-deprived Fischer 344 male rats. *Significantly different from nondeprived males, $p < .05$. *Bottom*. Mean (+ *SE*) serum T levels in nonde-prived and fluid-deprived Fischer 344 male rats. From "The Role of Testosterone in the Accelerated Extinction of a Conditioned Taste Aversion in Fluid Deprived Male Rats," by E. A. Brownson, C. B. Sengstake, and K. C. Chambers, 1994, *Physiology and Behavior, 55*, pp. 275–276. Adapted with permission.

is such that the low levels of androgens circulating in gonadectomized Fischer 344 males are sufficient to prolong extinction. The strain differ-ence in responsiveness to T could be due to differences in the amount of T that is actually available at the target tissue site or in the effectiveness of the available T during prenatal–neonatal differentiation. The presence of T during this period of development has been found to influence sensi-tivity to T in adulthood for a number of behaviors that depend on the activational effects of T, such as intermale aggression and prolonged ex-tinction of a conditioned aversion (Babine & Smotherman, 1984; Bartley & Goldman, 1977a, 1977b; Sengstake & Chambers, 1991; Simon & Whalen, 1987). With respect to fluid deprivation, we provided evidence that indicates that deprivation affects the rate of extinction in Sprague–Dawley males both by reducing the serum T levels and by reducing sen-sitivity to T. The primary factor influencing extinction in this strain is the reduced level of T. We suggest that the primary factor in deprived Fischer 344 males is reduced sensitivity to T. The difference between these two strains, therefore, is in the relative contributions of reduced serum T levels

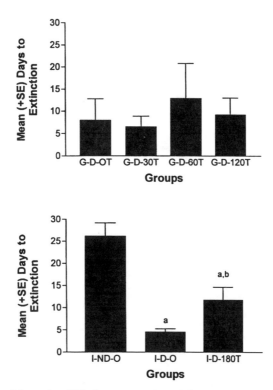

Figure 12. *Top.* Mean (+ *SE*) days to extinguish a conditioned taste aversion in gonadectomized (G-D) deprived Fischer 344 males implanted with blank Silastic capsules (0T) or with various sizes of T-filled capsules (30T–120T). *Bottom.* Mean (+ *SE*) days to extinguish a conditioned taste aversion in intact nondeprived (I-ND) and deprived (I-D) Fischer 344 males implanted with blank Silastic capsules or with T-filled capsules (180T). [a]Significantly different from I-ND-0, $p < .05$. [b]Significantly different from I-D-0, $p < .05$.

and reduced T sensitivity to accelerated extinction during fluid deprivation.

Aging and Fischer 344 Males

Data from several studies indicate that reductions in the T levels of Fischer 344 males begin to become evident at about 24 months of age (Chambers & Phoenix, 1984, 1986), whereas reductions in sexual performance are evident by 15 months of age. Therefore, as mentioned previously, decreased serum T levels cannot account for the reductions in sexual performance; rather, performance changes are probably due to reductions in sensitivity to T.

We pursued investigation of the effects of aging in Fischer 344 males on extinction of a CTA and on behavioral sensitivity to low doses of LiCl. We found no difference in the extinction rates of middle-aged (16–18

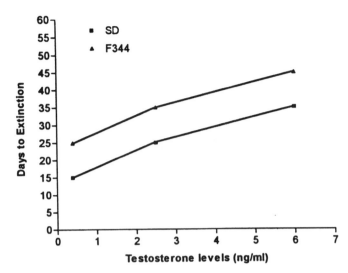

Figure 13. Hypothesized relationship between T levels and days to extinction in Sprague–Dawley (SD) and Fischer 344 (F344) male rats.

months) and young (3 months) males (Yuan, Hung, & Chambers, 1990a; see Figure 14, top). Behavioral sensitivity of middle-aged males to low doses of LiCl was significantly lower than that of young males, and increasing T levels in middle-aged males increased their sensitivity to LiCl (Yuan, Diego, & Chambers, 1991; Yuan, Hung, & Chambers, 1990a, 1990c; see Figure 15). Because extinction rate does not change in middle-aged males but sexual behavior and LiCl sensitivity do, reduced sensitivity to T appears to be either behavior-specific and not a general neural change or it occurs at different ages for different neural areas. However, it is important to note that there are inconsistencies in other reports on aging-related changes in extinction of CTAs. Some investigators have reported that extinction is slower in fluid-deprived middle-aged (12 months) and old (24 months) Fischer 344 males than in young males (Ingram & Peacock, 1980), whereas others have found a faster extinction rate in fluid-deprived middle-aged (19 months) and old (24 months) Sprague–Dawley males than in young males (Cooper et al., 1980). In addition, we have found slower extinction rates in nondeprived middle-aged Fischer 344 males than in young males when a month delay is imposed between acquisition and initiation of extinction trials (Yuan et al., 1990a; see Figure 14, bottom). At present, it is unclear what these contradictory findings mean, but they raise an interesting question. Are the inconsistencies due to an age-related strain difference or to differences in procedure (e.g., the fact that the Sprague–Dawley males were given a dose of LiCl that was considerably lower than that given to the Fischer 344 males)? Perhaps the results in Sprague–Dawley males are associated with age-related changes in a LiCl sensitivity mechanism, whereas the results in Fischer 344 males are associated with age-related changes in an extinction mechanism.

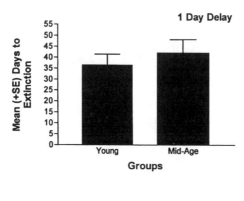

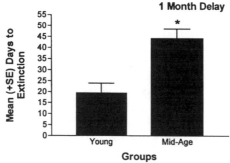

Figure 14. *Top.* Mean (+ *SE*) days to extinguish a conditioned taste aversion in young and middle-aged Fischer 344 males when the standard 1-day delay was imposed between acquisition and extinction trials. *Bottom*: Mean (+ *SE*) days to extinguish a conditioned taste aversion in young and middle-aged Fischer 344 males when a 1-month delay was imposed between acquisition and extinction trials. *Significantly different from young males, $p < .05$.

Function Revisited Once Again

We think that the divergence that is found in different strains tells something about the kinds of adaptations that take place in the face of environmental changes. We think that when food and water are plentiful, the hormonal milieu of the rat fetuses is such that an increase in sensitivity of the brain androgen receptors that modulate extinction of CTAs is produced and the adult male as a result is less affected by fluctuations in circulating T. On the other hand, when food and water are scarce, there is a decrease in brain androgen receptor sensitivity and the adult male is more affected by fluctuations in circulating T. The former circumstance is represented in the Fischer rats, and the latter in the Sprague–Dawley rats.

Conclusions

Being a rather recalcitrant student, it took me (the first author) years to realize the profound influence Bob Bolles had on my thinking and my

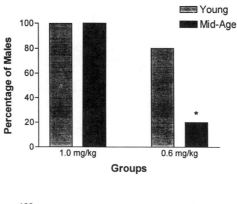

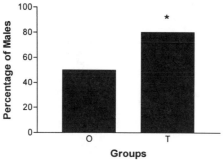

Figure 15. *Top.* Percentage of young and middle-aged Fischer 344 males acquiring an aversion when two different doses of LiCl were used to induce the aversion. *Significantly different from young males receiving 0.6 mg/kg, $p < .05$. *Bottom.* Percentage of intact middle-aged Fischer 344 males implanted with blank Silastic capsules (0) or T-filled capsules that acquired an aversion when a low dose of LiCl was used to induce the aversion. *Significantly different from 0 males, $p < .05$.

approach to scientific problems. This has been most evident in two areas. First, as we have indicated throughout this chapter, I have learned to take the animal out of the restricted environment in which it has been placed, at least mentally, and to ask how the behavior displayed in this environment fits into its natural environment and its daily existence. Second, I have learned to remain constantly open to the revision and possible abandonment of the models constructed to explain data. It is the latter attribute that set Bolles apart from most learning theorists. He truly was a Kuhnian revolutionary (Kuhn, 1970).

References

Adashi, E. Y., & Hsueh, A. J. W. (1981). Direct inhibition of testicular androgen biosynthesis by arginine-vasopressin: Mediation through pressor-selective testicular recognition sites. *Endocrinology, 109,* 1793–1795.

Babine, A. M., & Smotherman, W. P. (1984). Uterine position and conditioned taste aversion. *Behavioral Neuroscience, 98,* 461–466.

Bartley, M. S., & Goldman, B. D. (1977a). The effects of castration and Silastic implants of testosterone on intermale aggression in the mouse. *Hormones and Behavior, 9,* 32–48.

Bartley, M. S., & Goldman, B. D. (1977b). Testosterone-induced aggression in adult female mice. *Hormones and Behavior, 9,* 78–84.

Beatty, W. W. (1979). Gonadal hormones and sex differences in nonreproductive behaviors in rodents: Organizational and activational influences. *Hormones and Behavior, 12,* 112–163.

Bernstein, I. L., Courtney, L., & Braget, D. J. (1986). Estrogens and the Leydig LTW(m) tumor syndrome: Anorexia and diet aversions attenuated by area postrema lesions. *Physiology and Behavior, 38,* 159–163.

Bolles, R. C. (1970). Species-specific defense reactions and avoidance learning. *Psychological Review, 77,* 32–48.

Bolles, R. C. (1985). Introduction: Associative processes in the formation of conditioned food aversions: An emerging functionalism? *Annals of the New York Academy of Sciences, 443,* 1–7.

Braveman, N. S., & Bronstein, P. (Eds.). (1985). Experimental assessments and clinical applications of conditioned food aversions. *Annals of the New York Academy of Sciences, 443,* 1–441.

Brooks, V. B. (1983). Study of brain function by local, reversible cooling. *Reviews of Physiology, Biochemistry, and Pharmacology, 95,* 1–109.

Brot, M. D., Bernstein, I. L., & Dorsa, D. M. (1989). Chronic central administration of vasopressin antagonist hastens extinction of conditioned taste aversion in rats. *Society for Neuroscience Abstracts, 15,* 1069.

Brot, M. D., Bernstein, I. L., & Dorsa, D. M. (1990). Influence of the vasopressin-deficiency of Brattleboro (BB) rats on a sexually dimorphic behavior. *Society for Neuroscience Abstracts, 16,* 743.

Brot, M. D., Bernstein, I. L., & Dorsa, D. M. (1992). Vasopressin deficiency abolishes a sexually dimorphic behavior in Brattleboro rats. *Physiology and Behavior, 51,* 839–843.

Brownson, E. A. (1992). *Hormonal mechanisms for fast extinction of a conditioned taste aversion in fluid deprived rats.* Unpublished doctoral dissertation, University of Southern California, Los Angeles.

Brownson, E. A., Chambers, K. C., & Brinton, R. D. (1997). *Vasopressin content increases in select brain regions during maintenance of a conditioned taste aversion.* Manuscript submitted for publication.

Brownson, E. A., Sengstake, C. B., & Chambers, K. C. (1988). Effect of fluid deprivation on testosterone levels and the rate of extinction of a conditioned taste aversion in male rats. *Society for Neuroscience Abstracts, 14,* 100.

Brownson, E. A., Sengstake, C. B., & Chambers, K. C. (1990). Effects of fluid deprivation on testosterone sensitivity and extinction of a conditioned taste aversion. *Society for Neuroscience Abstracts, 16,* 766.

Brownson, E. A., Sengstake, C. B., & Chambers, K. C. (1991). Effectiveness of testosterone in prolonging extinction of conditioned taste aversions in fluid deprived male rats is dependent on LiCl dose. *Society for Neuroscience Abstracts, 17,* 1414.

Brownson, E. A., Sengstake, C. B., & Chambers, K. C. (1994). The role of serum testosterone in the accelerated extinction of a conditioned taste aversion in fluid deprived male rats. *Physiology and Behavior, 55,* 273–278.

Cannon, D. S., Baker, T. B., & Berman, R. F. (1977). Taste aversion disruption by drug pretreatment: Dissociative and drug-specific effects. *Pharmacology, Biochemistry and Behavior, 6,* 93–100.

Chambers, K. C. (1976). Hormonal influences on sexual dimorphism in rate of extinction of a conditioned taste aversion in rats. *Journal of Comparative and Physiological Psychology, 90,* 851–856.

Chambers, K. C. (1980). Progesterone, estradiol, testosterone and dihydrotestosterone: Effects on rate of extinction of a conditioned taste aversion in rats. *Physiology and Behavior, 24,* 1061–1065.

Chambers, K. C. (1982). Failure of ACTH to prolong extinction of a conditioned taste aversion in the absence of the testes. *Physiology and Behavior, 29,* 915–919.

Chambers, K. C. (1985). Sexual dimorphisms as an index of hormonal influences on conditioned food aversions. *Annals of the New York Academy of Sciences, 443,* 110–125.

Chambers, K. C. (1990). A neural model for conditioned taste aversions. *Annual Review of Neuroscience, 13,* 373–385.

Chambers, K. C. (1995). The roles of regulatory and modulatory processes in the decline of reproductive behavior of males. In D. K Sarkar & C. D. Barnes (Eds.), *Reproductive neuroendocrinology of aging and drug abuse* (pp. 119–150). Boca Raton, FL: CRC Press.

Chambers, K. C., & Bernstein, I. L. (1995). Conditioned flavor aversions. In R. L. Doty (Ed.), *Handbook of olfaction and gustation* (pp. 745–773). New York: Marcel Dekker.

Chambers, K. C., Brownson, E. A., & Brinton, R. D. (1993). Vasopressin content in the CNS changes during maintenance of conditioned taste aversion. *Society for Neuroscience Abstracts, 19,* 1007.

Chambers, K. C., Brownson, E. A., & Yuan, D. L. (1991). Effects of gonadectomy on extinction of conditioned taste aversions in Fischer 344 male rats. *Society for Neuroscience Abstracts, 17,* 1414.

Chambers, K. C., & Phoenix, C. H. (1984). Testosterone and the decline of sexual behavior in aging male rats. *Behavioral and Neural Biology, 40,* 87–97.

Chambers, K. C., & Phoenix, C. H. (1986). Testosterone is more effective than dihydrotestosterone plus estradiol in activating sexual behavior in old male rats. *Neurobiology of Aging, 7,* 127–132.

Chambers, K. C., Resko, J. A., & Phoenix, C. H. (1982). Correlation of diurnal changes in hormones with sexual behavior and age in male rhesus macaques. *Neurobiology of Aging, 3,* 37–42.

Chambers, K. C., & Sengstake, C. B. (1976). Sexually dimorphic extinction of a conditioned taste aversion in rats. *Animal Learning and Behavior, 4,* 181–185.

Chambers, K. C., & Sengstake, C. B. (1978). Pseudo-castration effects of social isolation on extinction of a taste aversion. *Physiology and Behavior, 21,* 29–32.

Chambers, K. C., & Sengstake, C. B. (1979). Temporal aspects of the dependency of a dimorphic rate of extinction on testosterone. *Physiology and Behavior, 22,* 53–56.

Chambers, K. C., Sengstake, C. B., Brownson, E. A., & Westfahl, P. K. (1993). Decreased testosterone levels and accelerated extinction of a conditioned taste aversion in fluid-deprived male rats. *Behavioral Neuroscience, 107,* 299–305.

Chambers, K. C., Sengstake, C. B., Walther, A. M., & Bullis, J. E. (1982). Disruption of sexual behavior in socially isolated adult male rats. *Behavioral and Neural Biology, 34,* 205–220.

Chambers, K. C., Sengstake, C. B., Yoder, R. L., & Thornton, J. E. (1981). Sexually dimorphic acquisition of a conditioned taste aversion in rats: Effects of gonadectomy, testosterone replacement and water deprivation. *Physiology and Behavior, 27,* 83–88.

Chambers, K. C., Thornton, J. E., & Roselli, C. E. (1991). Age-related deficits in brain androgen binding and metabolism, testosterone, and sexual behavior of male rats. *Neurobiology of Aging, 12,* 123–130.

Chambers, K. C., & Yuan, D. L. (1990). Blockage of the effects of testosterone on extinction of a conditioned taste aversion by estradiol: Time of action. *Physiology and Behavior, 48,* 277–281.

Clifton, P. G., & Andrew, R. J. (1986). Differing effects of gonadal steroids on attack and memory processing. *Physiology and Behavior, 37,* 701–708.

Clifton, P. G., & Andrew, R. J. (1987). Gonadal steroids and the extinction of conditioned taste aversions in young domestic fowl. *Physiology and Behavior, 39,* 27–31.

Cooper, R. L., McNamara, M. C., & Thompson, W. G. (1980). Vasopressin and conditioned flavor aversion in aged rats. *Neurobiology of Aging, 1,* 53–57.

Dacanay, R. J., Mastropaolo, J. P., Olin, D. A., & Riley, A. L. (1984). Sex differences in taste aversion learning: An analysis of the minimal effective dose. *Neurobehavior, Toxicology, and Teratology, 6,* 9–11.

Damassa, D. A., Smith, E. R., Tennent, B., & Davidson, J. M. (1977). The relationship between circulating testosterone levels and male sexual behavior in rats. *Hormones and Behavior, 8,* 275–286.

Davidson, J. M. (1966). Characteristics of sex behavior in male rats following castration. *Animal Behaviour, 14,* 266–272.

De Beun, R., Jansen, E., Smeets, M. A. M., Niesing, J., Slangen, J. L., & Van De Poll, N. E. (1991). Estradiol-induced conditioned taste aversion and place aversion in rats: Sex- and dose-dependent effects. *Physiology and Behavior, 50,* 995–1000.

De Beun, R., Peeters, B. W. M. M., & Broekkamp, C. L. E. (1993). Stimulus characterization of estradiol applying a crossfamiliarization taste aversion procedure in female mice. *Physiology and Behavior, 53,* 715–719.

Dessi-Fulgheri, F., Lupo Di Prisco, C., & Verdarelli, P. (1976). Effects of two kinds of social deprivation on testosterone and estradiol-17β plasma levels in the male rat. *Experentia, 32,* 114–115.

Domjan, M. (1978). Effects of proximal unconditioned stimulus preexposure on ingestational aversion learned as a result of taste presentation following drug treatment. *Animal Learning and Behavior, 6,* 133–142.

Earley, C. J., & Leonard, B. E. (1978). Androgenic involvement in conditioned taste aversion. *Hormones and Behavior, 11,* 1–11.

Earley, C. J., & Leonard, B. E. (1979). Effects of prior exposure on conditioned taste aversion in the rat: Androgen- and estrogen-dependent events. *Journal of Comparative and Physiological Psychology, 93,* 793–805.

Galef, B. G., Jr., Mischinger, A., & Malenfant, S. A. (1987). Hungry rats' following of conspecifics to food depends on the diets eaten by potential leaders. *Animal Behaviour, 35,* 1234–1239.

Galef, B. G., Jr., & Wigmore, S. W. (1983). Transfer of information concerning distant food in rats: A laboratory investigation of the "information centre" hypothesis. *Animal Behaviour, 31,* 748–758.

Gerall, H. D., Ward, I. L., & Gerall, A. A. (1967). Disruption of male rat's sexual behaviour induced by social isolation. *Animal Behaviour, 15,* 54–58.

Greundel, A. D., & Arnold, W. J. (1969). Effects of early social deprivation on reproductive behavior of male rats. *Journal of Comparative and Physiological Psychology, 67,* 123–128.

Gustavson, C. R., & Gustavson, J. C. (1986). Estrogen based conditioned taste aversion: A neuroethological model of anorexia nervosa. *Society for Neuroscience Abstracts, 12,* 1451.

Gustavson, C. R., & Gustavson, J. C. (1987). Estrogen induced anorexia in the rat: An LiCl comparison suggests it is estrogen induced nausea. *Society for Neuroscience Abstracts, 13,* 555.

Gustavson, C. R., Gustavson, J. C., Young, J. K., Pumariega, A. J., & Nicolaus, L. K. (1989). Estrogen induced malaise. In J. M. Lakoski, J. R. Perez-Polo, & D.K. Rassin (Eds.), *Neural control of reproductive function* (pp. 501–523). New York: Alan R. Liss.

Gustavson, C. R., Reinarz, D. E., Gustavson, C. R., & Pumariega, A. J. (1988). *Estrogen based conditioned taste aversion in a single human subject.* Paper presented at the meeting of the Western Psychological Association, San Francisco, CA.

Hard, E., & Larsson, K. (1968). Dependence of adult mating behavior in male rats on the presence of littermates in infancy. *Brain Behavior and Evolution, 1,* 405–419.

Howland, B. E., & Skinner, K. R. (1973). Effects of starvation on gonadotropin secretion in intact and castrated male rats. *Canadian Journal of Physiology and Pharmacology, 51,* 759–762.

Hung, C., Yuan, D. L., & Chambers, K. C. (1991). *Medial preoptic implant of testosterone can prolong the extinction of a conditioned food aversion in the male rat.* Poster session presented at the third Internation Brain Research Organization Congress of Neuroscience, Montreal, Canada.

Ingram, D. K., & Corfman, T. P. (1981). Strain-dependent sexual dimorphism in the extinction of conditioned taste aversion in mice. *Animal Learning and Behavior, 9,* 101–107.

Ingram, D. K., & Peacock, L. J. (1980). Conditioned taste aversion as a function of age in mature rats. *Experimental Aging Research, 6,* 113–123.

Jakubczak, L. F. (1964). Effects of testosterone propionate on age differences in mating behavior. *Journal of Gerontology, 19,* 458–461.

Jakubczak, L. F. (1967). Age, endocrines, and behavior. In L. Gitman (Ed.), *Endocrines and behavior* (pp. 231–245). Springfield, IL: Charles C Thomas.

Kalat, J. W., & Rozin, P. (1973). "Learned safety" as a mechanism in long-delay taste-aversion learning in rats. *Journal of Comparative and Physiological Psychology, 83*, 198–207.

Kasson, B. G., & Hsueh, A. J. W. (1986). Arginine vasopressin as an intragonadal hormone in Brattleboro rats: Presence of a testicular vasopressin-like peptide and functional vasopressin receptors. *Endocrinology, 118*, 23–31.

Kasson, B. G., Meidan, R., & Hsueh, A. J. W. (1985). Identification and characterization of arginine vasopressin-like substances in the rat testis. *Journal of Biological Chemistry, 260*, 5302–5307.

Kendler, K., Hennessy, J. W., Smotherman, W. P., & Levine, S. (1976). An ACTH effect on recovery from conditioned taste aversion. *Behavioural Biology, 17*, 225–229.

Kosten, T., & Contreras, R. J. (1989). Deficits in conditioned heart rate and taste aversion in area postrema–lesioned rats. *Behavioural Brain Research, 35*, 9–21.

Kuhn, T. S. (1970). *International encyclopedia of unified science: The structure of scientific revolutions* (Vol. II, no. 2). Chicago: University of Chicago Press.

Larsson, K. (1958). Sexual activity in senile male rats. *Journal of Gerontology, 13*, 136–139.

Meidan, R., & Hsueh, A. J. W. (1985). Identification and characterization of arginine vasopressin receptors in the rat testis. *Endocrinology, 116*, 416–423.

Meisel, R. L., & Ward, I. L. (1981). Fetal female rats are masculinized by male littermates located caudally in the uterus. *Science, 213*, 239–242.

Merwin, A., & Doty, R. L. (1994). Early exposure to low levels of estradiol (E_2) mitigates E_2-induced conditioned taste aversions in prepubertally ovariectomized female rats. *Physiology and Behavior, 55*, 185–187.

Miele, J. L. (1987). Conditioned taste aversion: Steroids as unconditioned stimuli. *Dissertation Abstracts International, 47*, 3574B.

Miele, J. L., Rosellini, R. A., & Svare, B. (1988). Estradiol benzoate can function as an unconditioned stimulus in a conditioned taste aversion paradigm. *Hormones and Behavior, 22*, 116–130.

Mikulka, P. J., Leard, B., & Klein, S. B. (1977). Illness-alone exposure as a source of interference with the acquisition and retention of a taste aversion. *Journal of Experimental Psychology: Animal Behavior Processes, 3*, 189–201.

Negroni, J. A., & Denti, A. (1977). One trial passive-avoidance learning in neonatally hormone treated rats: Its relation with activity. *Acta Physiologica Latinoamericana, 27*, 281–287.

Nicolaus, L. K., Farmer, P. V., Gustavson, C. R., & Gustavson, J. C. (1989). The potential of estrogen-based conditioned aversion in controlling depredation: A step closer toward the "magic bullet." *Applied Animal Behavior Sciences, 23*, 1–14.

Nicolaus, L. K., Herrera, J., Nicolaus, J. C., & Gustavson, C. R. (1989). Ethinyl estradiol and generalized aversions to eggs among free-ranging predators. *Applied Animal Behavior Sciences, 24*, 313–324.

Parker, L. A., & Brosseau, L. (1990). Apomorphine-induced flavor-drug associations: A dose-response analysis by the taste reactivity test and the conditioned taste avoidance test. *Pharmacology, Biochemistry and Behavior, 35*, 583–587.

Peeters, B. W. M. M., Smets, R. J. M., & Broekkamp, C. L. E. (1992). Sex steroids possess distinct stimulus properties in female and male mice. *Brain Research Bulletin, 28*, 319–321.

Posadas-Andrews, A., & Roper, T. J. (1983). Social transmission of food preferences in adult rats. *Animal Behaviour, 31*, 265–271.

Rice, A. G., Lopez, A., & Garcia, J. (1987). Estrogen produces conditioned taste aversions in rats which are blocked by antihistamine. *Society for Neuroscience Abstracts, 113*, 556.

Riley, A. L., Dacanay, R. J., & Mastropaolo, J. P. (1984). The effect of morphine preexposure on the acquisition of morphine-induced taste aversions: A nonassociative effect. *Animal Learning and Behavior, 12*, 157–162.

Ritter, S., McGlone, J. J., & Kelley, K. W. (1980). Absence of lithium-induced taste aversion after area postrema lesion. *Brain Research, 201*, 501–506.

Roselli, C. E., Thornton, J. E., & Chambers, K. C. (1993). Age-related deficits in brain estrogen receptors and sexual behavior of male rats. *Behavioral Neuroscience, 107,* 202–209.

Sachs, B. D. (1965). Sexual behavior of male rats after one or nine days without food. *Journal of Comparative and Physiological Psychology, 60,* 144–146.

Sengstake, C. B., & Chambers, K. C. (1979). Differential effects of fluid deprivation on the acquisition and extinction phases of a conditioned taste aversion. *Bulletin of the Psychonomic Society, 14,* 85–87.

Sengstake, C. B., & Chambers, K. C. (1991). Sensitivity of male, female, and androgenized female rats to testosterone during extinction of a conditioned taste aversion. *Behavioral Neuroscience, 105,* 120–125.

Sengstake, C. B., Chambers, K. C., & Thrower, J. H. (1978). Interactive effects of fluid deprivation and testosterone on the expression of a sexually dimorphic conditioned taste aversion. *Journal of Comparative and Physiological Psychology, 92,* 1150–1155.

Simon, N. G., and Whalen, R. E. (1987). Sexual differentiation of androgen-sensitive and estrogen-sensitive regulatory systems for aggressive behavior. *Hormones and Behavior, 21,* 493–500.

Switzman, L., Fishman, B., & Amit, Z. (1981). Pre-exposure effects of morphine, diazepam and 9-THC on the formation of conditioned taste aversions. *Psychopharmacology, 74,* 149–157.

Telegdy, G., & Stark, A. (1973). Effect of sexual steroids and androgen sterilization on avoidance and exploratory behaviour in the rat. *Acta Physiologica Academiae Scientiarum, Hungaricae, Tomus, 43*(1), 55–63.

Van Der Kooy, D., Swerdlow, N. R., & Koob, G. F. (1983). Paradoxical reinforcing properties of apomorphine: Effects of nucleus accumbens and area postrema lesions. *Brain Research, 259,* 111–118.

vom Saal, F. S., & Bronson, F. H. (1980). Sexual characteristics of adult female mice are correlated with their blood testosterone levels during prenatal development. *Science, 208,* 597–599.

Wade, G. N. (1972). Gonadal hormones and behavioral regulation of body weight. *Physiology and Behavior, 8,* 523–534.

Wang, Y. (1995). *The exploration of the neural mechanism of conditioned taste aversions with reversible blockade.* Unpublished doctoral dissertation, Los Angeles. University of Southern California, Los Angeles.

Wang, Y., Lavond, D. G., & Chambers, K. C. (1994). Investigation of neural areas controlling conditioned taste aversions in rats: Effects of cooling the area postrema. *Society for Neuroscience Abstracts, 20,* 1213.

Wang, Y., Lavond, D. G., & Chambers, K. C. (1997). The effects of cooling the area postrema of male rats on conditioned taste aversions induced by LiCl and apomorphine. *Behavioural Brain Research, 82,* 149–158.

Wang, Y., Yuan, D. L., & Chambers, K. C. (1992). Estradiol acts as an inter-agent to accelerate extinction of conditioned taste aversions. *Society for Neuroscience Abstracts, 18,* 522.

Weinburg, J., Gunnar, M. R., Brett, L. P., Gonzalez, C. A., & Levine, S. (1982). Sex difference in biobehavioral responses to conflict in a taste aversions paradigm. *Physiology and Behavior, 29,* 201–210.

Yuan, D. (1992). *The role of estradiol in extinction of a conditioned taste aversion and the mechanism of action.* Unpublished doctoral dissertation, University of Southern California, Los Angeles.

Yuan, D., & Chambers, K. C. (1989). *Temporal analysis of estradiol blockage of testosterone effect on conditioned taste aversion.* Poster session presented at the first annual meeting of the American Psychological Society, Alexandria, VA.

Yuan, D. L., & Chambers, K. C. (1990). *Age-related differences in the effect of estradiol on extinction of a conditioned food aversion.* Poster session presented at the second annual meeting of the American Psychological Society, Dallas, TX.

Yuan, D. L., & Chambers, K. C. (1991a). *Condition under which estradiol prolongs extinction of conditioned food aversions.* Poster session presented at the third annual meeting of the American Psychological Society, Washington, DC.

Yuan, D. L., & Chambers, K. C. (1991b). Effects of estradiol on extinction of conditioned taste aversions: Time of action. *Society for Neuroscience Abstracts, 17,* 1414.

Yuan, D. L., & Chambers, K. C. (1997a). *Differential effects of estradiol on extinction of avoidance behaviors.* Manuscript submitted for publication.

Yuan, D. L., & Chambers, K. C. (1997b). *Estradiol induces a conditioned taste aversion and alters rates of extinction of LiCl-induced aversions.* Manuscript submitted for publication.

Yuan, D. L., Diego, L. L., & Chambers, K. C. (1991). Testosterone increases the sensitivity to LiCl in old male rats. *Gerontologist, 31,* 31.

Yuan, D. L., Hung, C., & Chambers, K. C. (1990a). *Conditioned food aversion in young and old male rats.* Poster session at the annual meeting of the American Psycological Association, Boston.

Yuan, D. L., Hung, C., & Chambers, K. C. (1990b). *Effects of gonadectomy on extinction of a conditioned food aversion.* Poster session presented at the 70th annual meeting of the Western Psychological Association, Los Angeles.

Yuan, D. L., Hung, C., & Chambers, K. C. (1990c). Failure to observe age-related differences in extinction of a conditioned food aversion when low doses of LiCl are used. *Gerontologist, 30,* 115A.

11

Drug Discrimination Learning: Assessment of Opioid Receptor Pharmacology

Anthony L. Riley

When I entered Robert Bolles's laboratory in 1971, he had recently become fascinated with taste-aversion learning, the phenomenon in which animals come to avoid the consumption of previously poisoned foods and solutions. Like his own "species-specific defense reactions," taste aversions were not easily explained within traditional frameworks of learning; their explanation called for "knowing the animal." Because of his new-found interest in aversions, the lab was devoted to examining this unique behavior: its parameters, its mechanisms, and its implications. Bolles's genuine interest in and excitement over aversion learning was contagious, and I immediately took on this field as my major work. Some 25 years removed from this initial introduction, I find myself still intrigued by this phenomenon. My specific interests in aversion learning have changed over these years and now focus on the use of aversion learning as a tool in the classification and characterization of drugs and toxins (as opposed to its underlying mechanisms and implications for learning theory). My current interests are reflected in the present chapter, which describes the use of drugs as discriminative stimuli for behavior.

The chapter provides a general introduction to drug discrimination learning and to the general usefulness of this procedure in drug classification and characterization. The limitations of the basic drug discrimination procedure in the assessment of opioid antagonists are then presented, followed by a description and discussion of a modification of the drug discrimination design, specifically the taste-aversion baseline of drug discrimination learning, which offers a relatively sensitive assay of the discriminative properties of drugs. The chapter closes with an overview of work from my laboratory on the discriminative properties of mu, delta, and kappa opioid antagonists, which illustrates the specific advantages the aversion baseline may have over more traditional assessments of drug

The research on which this chapter is based was supported by a grant from the Mellon Foundation and a National Research Service Award from the National Institute on Drug Abuse (1 F31 DA04577-01).

discrimination learning. These advantages may reflect the unique nature of this form of learning—the very uniqueness that motivated Bolles's initial interest in this phenomenon.

Drug Discrimination Learning

Drug discrimination learning is a behavioral preparation in which drugs serve discriminative functions for behavior (for reviews, see Jarbe, 1987; Overton, 1984; for a bibliography, see Samele, Shine, & Stolerman, 1992; see also Colpaert & Balster, 1988; Colpaert & Rosecrans, 1978; Colpaert & Slangen, 1982; Glennon, Jarbe, & Frankenheim, 1992; Ho, Richards, & Chute, 1978; Lal, 1977; Lal & Fielding, 1989; Thompson & Pickens, 1971). Within such a preparation, an animal is reinforced for making a specific response, such as a press on the right lever following the administration of a specific drug. Responses on the other lever have no programmed consequences during this time. In other sessions, the animal is reinforced for making responses on the second lever, in this case the left lever, following administration of the drug vehicle. Again, responses on the other lever have no programmed consequences during these sessions. Under these conditions, the animal acquires the drug discrimination, and behavior comes under the control of the drug; that is, the animal performs drug- and vehicle-appropriate behavior following administration of the drug or its vehicle, respectively.

Following the initial demonstration of drug discrimination learning with alcohol (Conger, 1951; see Overton, 1991, 1992, for historical reviews), a wide range of compounds have been used with a number of different species within a variety of experimental designs and parameters (Barry, 1974; Jarbe, 1987; Overton, 1982). The interest in drug discrimination learning, however, goes considerably beyond the demonstration that drugs can serve as discriminative stimuli for specific behaviors. Specifically, the drug discrimination procedure is useful in both the classification and characterization of drugs (Riley, 1995). In relation to drug *classification*, once discriminative control has been established and animals are making drug-appropriate responses, other drugs can be administered and tested for their ability to substitute for the training drug, that is, to determine whether the stimulus control established to the training drug generalizes to the test drugs. Under such conditions, drugs from the same class as the training drug substitute and engender drug-appropriate responding (Barry, 1974; Overton, 1982). For example, in an analysis of the stimulus properties of the opioid agonist morphine, Lal, Gianutsos, and Miksic (1977) reported that animals trained to discriminate morphine from its vehicle generalized this control to a range of other narcotics, including methadone, fentanyl, codeine, heroin, and butorphanol (see also Holtzman, 1985; Holtzman & Locke, 1988), while displaying vehicle-appropriate responding when administered one of a number of nonopioid compounds (e.g., atropine, amphetamine, cocaine, lysergic acid diethylamide [LSD] and pentobarbital). Of course, compounds classified as belonging to one major group may in fact differ in terms of their activity at various receptor subtypes and in terms of their behavioral and physiological effects. The *characterization* of compounds in terms of such differences has also been investigated within the drug discrimination procedure. For example, animals trained to discriminate the mu opioid morphine from its vehicle fail to generalize this control to the kappa opioid U50,488H. Similarly, animals trained to discriminate U50,488H from its vehicle fail to generalize this control to morphine (Negus, Picker, & Dykstra, 1990; see also Holtzman, 1985; Ukai & Holtzman, 1988). Other mu and kappa agonists substitute appropriately for morphine and U50,488H, respectively. Such generalization functions give some insight into the mechanism or basis of drug action, in this case its receptor specificity.

The usefulness of drug discrimination learning in classifying drugs comes from the fact that with a relatively simple behavioral baseline, drugs can be appropriately catalogued into functional categories that provide the investigator with information about the drug. Its usefulness in characterizing drugs comes from a similar base in that a simple behavioral procedure provides a baseline to assess drug action and mechanism. The usefulness of drug discrimination learning, however, is not limited to behavioral classification and characterization. The design has also been used to identify and assess drug interactions. For example, once discriminative control has been established, other compounds can be coadministered with the training drug to determine if and to what degree these compounds either antagonize or potentiate the discriminative control of the training drug. In relation to the antagonism of the training drug, Locke and Holtzman (1985) reported that the administration of the opiate antagonist naltrexone blocked the stimulus control of morphine in animals trained to discriminate morphine from its vehicle. The antagonism was dose- and time-dependent and reversible, behaviorally indexing naltrexone as a competitive antagonist to morphine (see also Bartoletti, Gaiardi, Gubellini, Bacchi, & Babbini, 1989; Jarbe, 1978; Shannon & Holtzman, 1976).

Furthermore, if the training drug is known to act on a specific receptor system, one can administer antagonists with selective activity at the various subtypes of that receptor to identify exactly where the training drug is acting to produce its discriminative control. In such an analysis with the mu and kappa opioid agonists etorphine and ethylketocyclazocine, Dykstra, Bertalmio, and Woods (1988) reported that lower doses of the relatively selective mu antagonist quadazocine were required to antagonize the discriminative stimulus properties of etorphine than of ethylketocyclazocine. The differential ability of quadazocine to block the effects of these two compounds is consistent with the known and differential affinity of quadazocine at mu and kappa receptors. Similar analyses have been done with compounds that potentiate the stimulus properties of the training drug (see France & Woods, 1988; Goudie, 1992; Signs & Schechter, 1986; Snoddy & Tessel, 1985). Such assessments provide information not only regarding the general basis for the discriminative effects but also regarding the specific biochemical mediation of the drug stimulus.

Although the drug discrimination design has been effective in the behavioral classification and characterization of a range of drugs and in the identification and assessment of drug interactions, it should be noted that not all drugs can be assessed within this preparation (for an overview, see Overton, 1987), primarily because they are ineffective as such stimuli. One compound that has been extensively investigated in this regard is the opioid antagonist naloxone hydrochloride. Althought it is effective as an antagonist of opioid activity within a wide variety of physiological and behavioral preparations (see Braude, Harris, May, Smith, & Villarreal, 1973; van Ree & Terenius, 1978), it generally fails to support drug discrimination learning. For example, Lal, Miksic, and McCarten (1978) as well as Overton and Batta (1979) were unable to establish discriminative control with naloxone in rats (see also Overton, 1982; Weissman, 1978), prompting Overton (1987) to list naloxone as a compound "virtually undiscriminable" (see also France & Woods, 1988; Valentino, Herling, & Woods, 1983). Although these reports questioned the ability of naloxone to serve as a discriminative cue, Carter and Leander (1982) were able to train pigeons to discriminate naloxone from its vehicle. Even in that case, however, such control was evident only with extremely high doses of naloxone (30 mg/kg) and with extensive training. The inability of naloxone to serve as a discriminative stimulus has precluded the use of this design in its behavioral classification and characterization.

Conditioned Aversion Baseline of Drug Discrimination Learning

Recently, my laboratory and others have introduced a modification of the taste-aversion procedure that may be more sensitive in the assessment of the stimulus properties of drugs (Kautz, Geter, McBride, Mastropaolo, & Riley, 1989; Lucki, 1988; Martin, Gans, & van der Kooy, 1990; Mastropaolo, Moskowitz, Dacanay, & Riley, 1989; Riley, Jeffreys, Pournaghash, Titley, & Kufera, 1989; for reviews, see Mastropaolo & Riley, 1990; Riley, 1995; Riley et al., 1991). In this modification of the traditional taste aversion design (Garcia & Ervin, 1968; Revusky & Garcia, 1970; Rozin & Kalat, 1971; for a bibliography, see Riley & Tuck, 1985), every fourth day experimental subjects are given access to a novel solution to drink and are then immediately injected with a toxin. These pairings, however, are always preceded by administration of a training drug. On intervening recovery days, subjects are administered the drug vehicle prior to the same taste, but on these days the animals are not made sick. Under these conditions, the training drug serves as a stimulus signaling the subsequent taste−sickness pairing, whereas the vehicle serves as a stimulus signaling a safe exposure to the same taste (see Exhibit 1).

Discriminative control within this procedure is indexed by the differential consumption of the solution dependent on the administration of the training drug or the vehicle, that is, decreases in consumption following administration of the training drug and maintenance of consumption of the same solution following administration of the drug vehicle. Control

Exhibit 1. General Procedure for Group L (Experimental) and Group W (Control) During the Acquisition of Drug Discrimination Learning Within the Conditioned Taste Aversion Baseline

Day	Procedure	Group[a]	
		L	W·
—	Habituation	W-S	W-S
1	Conditioning	D-S-L	D-S-L
2–4	Recovery	W-S	W-S

[a]D, Drug; L, LiCl; W, water; and S, saccharin.
Note. The alternating cycle of conditioning–water recovery was repeated until discriminative control was established.

subjects that receive both the drug and its vehicle prior to receiving the solution alone maintain high levels of consumption following both injections, indicating that the differential consumption by the experimental group is a function of the discriminative control of the drug and not a generalized unconditioned suppression of fluid consumption.

In one of the first demonstrations of drug discrimination learning within this design from my laboratory (Mastropaolo et al., 1989), water-deprived rats were injected every fourth day with 1.8 mg/kg phencyclidine (PCP) 15 minutes prior to 20-minute access to a novel saccharin solution. Immediately following access to saccharin, subjects were injected with the emetic lithium chloride (LiCl; experimental subjects, Group PL) or the LiCl vehicle (control subjects, Group PW). On intervening recovery days, all subjects were injected with distilled water (the PCP vehicle) 15 minutes prior to getting saccharin alone. After only four such conditioning–recovery cycles, experimental subjects significantly decreased saccharin consumption following the injection of PCP, but consumed the same amount of saccharin at high levels following distilled water (see Figure 1). Control subjects drank saccharin following both PCP and the PCP vehicle. The relative rapidity with which the discrimination was acquired (relative to more traditional assessments of PCP discriminative control; see Jarbe, Johansson, & Henrikksson, 1975; White & Holtzman, 1983) suggested that this procedure may be sensitive in the general assessment of stimulus control.

Subsequent to my group's initial demonstration of discriminative control with PCP, a wide range of compounds were shown to be effective within the aversion baseline, for example, alcohol (Kautz, Logan, Romero, Schwartz, & Riley, 1989), alprazolam (Glowa, Jeffreys, & Riley, 1991), amphetamine (Revusky, Coombes, & Pohl, 1982), buprenorphine (Pournaghash & Riley, 1993; Riley & Pournaghash, 1995), chlordiazepoxide (van Hest, Hijzen, Slangen, & Oliver, 1992; Woudenberg & Hijzen, 1991), cholecystokinin (Melton, Kopman, & Riley, 1993; Melton & Riley, 1993, 1994), cocaine (Geter & Riley, 1993), diprenorphine (Smurthwaite & Riley, 1992), 8-OH-DPAT (Lucki, 1988; Lucki & Marcoccia, 1991; van Hest et al., 1992), estradiol (de Beun, Heinsbroek, Slangen, & van de Poll, 1991), fentanyl

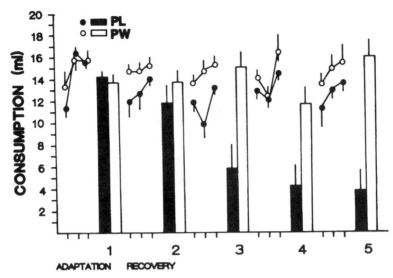

Figure 1. The mean amount of saccharin consumed (+/− *SEM*) for experimental subjects (Group PL) injected with phencyclidine (PCP) prior to a pairing of saccharin and lithium chloride (LiCl) and with the PCP vehicle prior to saccharin alone during adaptation and throughout the repeated conditioning and recovery cycles. Control subjects (Group PW) were injected with PCP and the PCP vehicle prior to saccharin alone. Consumption during adaptation and recovery is represented by filled and unfilled circles (Groups PL and PW, respectively). Consumption during conditioning is represented by filled and unfilled bars (Groups PL and PW, respectively). From "Conditioned Taste Aversions as a Behavioral Baseline for Drug Discrimination Learning: An Assessment with Phencycline," by J. P. Mastropaolo, K. H. Moskowitz, R. J. Dacanay, and A. L. Riley, 1989, *Pharmacology, Biochemistry, & Behavior, 32,* p. 3. Reprinted with permission of Elsevier Science Ltd.

(Jaeger & Mucha, 1990), morphine (Jaeger & van der Kooy, 1993; Martin, Bechara, & van der Kooy, 1991; Martin et al., 1990; Pournaghash & Riley, 1993; Skinner & Martin, 1992; Stevenson, Pournaghash, & Riley, 1992), nalorphine (Smurthwaite & Riley, 1994), naloxone (Kautz, Geter, et al., 1989; Smurthwaite, Kautz, Geter, & Riley, 1992), pentobarbital (Jaeger & Mucha, 1990; Riley et al., 1989), testosterone (de Beun, Jansen, Slangen, & van de Poll, 1992) and TFMPP (Lucki, 1988). In most of these cases, control is established rapidly, typically within four to eight conditioning trials, supporting the earlier suggestion that the aversion baseline may be a sensitive index of drug discrimination learning.

Discrimination Effects of Opioid Antagonists: Naloxone

Given the sensitivity of the aversion baseline in relation to the rapidity of establishing discriminative control, my colleagues and I suggested that the sensitivity of this design may also be reflected in its ability to establish control with compounds heretofore ineffective in more traditional operant procedures (see Kautz, Geter, et al., 1989). Accordingly, we attempted to establish discriminative control with the opioid antagonist naloxone hydrochloride. Specifically, water-deprived rats were injected every fourth day with naloxone (either 1 mg/kg, Group N1L, or 3 mg/kg, Group N3L) 10 minutes prior to a saccharin–LiCl pairing and, on intervening days, with the naloxone vehicle prior to saccharin alone. Control subjects (Groups N1W and N3W) received the same sequence of injections but were not injected with LiCl. After only two conditioning trials, the experimental subjects significantly decreased saccharin consumption following naloxone and consumed the same saccharin solution following the naloxone vehicle (see Figure 2). Control subjects consumed saccharin following both injections. Thus, under these training conditions, naloxone was effective as a discriminative stimulus at low doses and with only limited training. Following acquisition of the discrimination, other compounds were assessed for their similarity to naloxone. The procedure during testing was identical to that used during the acquisition of the discrimination except that on the second recovery day following each training trial, different compounds were injected (in place of naloxone) prior to saccharin access to determine whether these compounds substituted for the training drug. No injections were given following saccharin access on these probe sessions. Under such conditions, naloxone's stimulus control generalized to the opioid antagonist naltrexone (at doses lower than that needed to establish control with naloxone, an effect consistent with the relative potency of naloxone and naltrexone) but not to the opioid agonist morphine (see Figures 3 and 4), suggesting that naloxone's stimulus effects were based on its antagonist activity at the opioid receptor.

Receptor Mediation

In subsequent work, Smurthwaite et al. (1992) demonstrated that animals trained to discriminate naloxone from its vehicle within this baseline also generalized naloxone's control to diprenorphine, another opioid antagonist. Although the receptor activity of naloxone, naltrexone, and diprenorphine is not identical, all three have antagonist activity at the mu receptor subtype of the opioid receptor (Lord, Waterfield, Hughes, & Kosterlitz, 1977; Magnan, Paterson, Tavani, & Kosterlitz, 1982), leading my colleagues and I to conclude that naloxone's stimulus properties are based on its activity at this specific receptor subtype (see Smurthwaite et al., 1992), presumably owing to its blocking of endogenous opioid activity (see Riley & Pournaghash, 1995; Smurthwaite & Riley, 1992; see also Self & Stein, 1992; Shippensburg, 1993; Stolerman, 1985).

Although naloxone is an antagonist at the mu receptor subtype, its binding and antagonist characteristics are not limited to the mu receptor. Specifically, in addition to its high affinity for the mu receptor subtype, it binds to and blocks opioid activity at the delta and kappa receptor subtypes (Kosterlitz, Paterson, & Robson, 1981; Magnan et al., 1982; Wood,

1982). Accordingly, it is possible that naloxone's stimulus control is based
on its activity at each of these subtypes of the opioid receptor. Therefore,
although stimulus control with naloxone may be opioid-mediated, it is not
clear that its stimulus properties are mediated by a single receptor subtype. To test this possibility, my group recently trained animals to discriminate 1 mg/kg naloxone from its vehicle within the aversion baseline and
tested for the generalization of this stimulus control to a variety of opioid
antagonists with relatively selective binding at the three opioid receptor
subtypes (Klimczak & Riley, 1996). Specifically, we administered to nal-
oxone-trained rats various doses of the opioid antagonists naltrexone (*mu*:

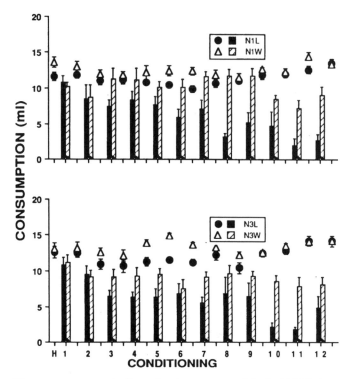

Figure 2.   The mean amount of saccharin consumed (+/− *SEM*) for experimental
subjects (Groups N1L and N3L) injected with naloxone prior to a saccharin–LiCl
pairing and with the naloxone vehicle prior to saccharin alone during adaptation
(H) and throughout the repeated conditioning–recovery cycles. Control subjects
(Groups N1W and N3W) were injected with naloxone and the naloxone vehicle
prior to saccharin alone. Consumption during adaptation and recovery is represented by filled circles and unfilled triangles (Groups N1L and N3L and Groups
N1W and N3W, respectively). Consumption during conditioning is represented by
filled and hatched bars (Groups N1L and N3L and Groups N1W and N3W, respectively). From "Naloxone as a Stimulus for Drug Discrimination Learning," by
M. A. Kautz, B. Geter, S. A. McBride, J. P. Mastropaolo, and A. L. Riley, 1989,
Drug Development Research, 16, p. 320. Reprinted with permission of John Wiley
and Sons, Inc.

Kosterlitz et al., 1981; Magnan et al., 1982; Wood, 1982), naltrindole (*delta*: Contreras, Tam, Drower, & Rafferty, 1993; Lever et al., 1992; Rogers, Hayes, Birch, Traynor, & Lawrence, 1990), and norBNI (*kappa*: Zimmerman & Leander, 1990) to assess their ability to substitute for the naloxone stimulus. As previously reported, naltrexone substituted for naloxone in a dose-dependent manner with subjects eventually avoiding saccharin consumption following increasing doses of naltrexone, an effect similar to that produced by the training dose of naloxone. It is interesting that neither the delta antagonist naltrindole nor the kappa antagonist norBNI substituted for the naloxone stimulus. In subsequent tests, the relatively selective kappa antagonist MR2266 (see Bansinath, Ramabadran, Turndof, & Puig, 1990; Calcagnetti, Calcagnetti, & Fanselow, 1990; Laorden, Carrillo, & Puig, 1991; Ohno, Yamamoto, & Ukei, 1991; Wollemann, Benyhe, &

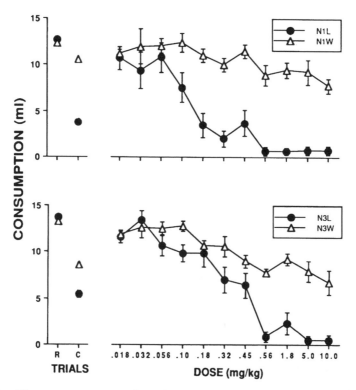

Figure 3. The mean amount of saccharin consumed (+/− *SEM*) for subjects in Groups N1L and N1W (upper panel) and Groups N3L and N3W (lower panel) following administration of naloxone and distilled water during conditioning (C) and recovery (R) and following naltrexone in naltrexone-substitution sessions. Consumption during recovery and conditioning sessions and over the increasing doses of naltrexone is represented by filled circles and open triangles (Groups N1L and N3L and Groups N1W and N3W, respectively). From "Naloxone as a Stimulus for Drug Discrimination Learning," by M. A. Kautz, B. Geter, S. A. McBride, J. P. Mastropaolo, and A. L. Riley, 1989, *Drug Development Research, 16,* 322, 323. Reprinted with permission of John Wiley and Sons, Inc.

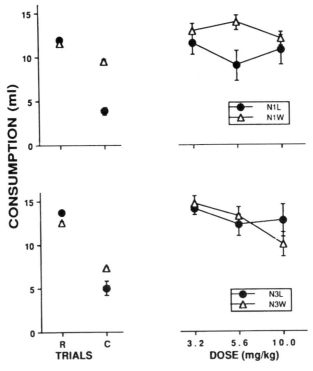

Figure 4. The mean amount of saccharin consumed (+/− *SEM*) for subjects in Groups N1L and N1W (upper panel) and Groups N3L and N3W (lower panel) following administration of naloxone and distilled water during conditioning (C) and recovery (R) and following morphine in morphine-substitution sessions. Consumption during recovery and conditioning sessions and over the increasing doses of morphine is represented by filled circles and open triangles (Groups N1L and N3L and Groups N1W and N3W, respectively). From "Naloxone as a Stimulus for Drug Discrimination Learning," by M. A. Kautz, B. Geter, S. A. McBride, J. P. Mastropaolo, and A. L. Riley, 1989, *Drug Development Research, 16,* 322, 323. Reprinted with permission of John Wiley and Sons, Inc.

Simon, 1993) also failed to substitute for naloxone. Naloxone's stimulus effects within the aversion design appear to be mediated by its antagonist activity solely at the mu receptor.

If antagonist activity at the opiate receptor mediates the acquisition of discriminative control to the opioid antagonists and various opioid antagonists differ in their activity at the receptor subtypes, it might be expected that animals could be trained to discriminate between opioid antagonists that differ in this respect. In a modification of the aversion baseline, a colleague and I (Kautz & Riley, 1990) reported that animals could be trained on such a discrimination. Specifically, we trained animals to discriminate between naloxone (a broad-based opioid antagonist with relative selectivity at the mu receptor subtype; Kosterlitz et al., 1981; Magnan et al., 1982; Wood, 1982) and diprenorphine (an opioid antagonist with equal affinity at mu, delta, and kappa subtypes of the opiate receptor; Chang, Hazum, & Cuatrecasas, 1981; Magnan et al., 1982; Sadee, Richards, Grevel, & Rosenbaum, 1983). In this study, experimental animals were administered naloxone prior to a saccharin–LiCl pairing and diprenorphine prior to saccharin alone. Although subjects initially generalized naloxone discriminative control to diprenorphine (see the preceding), they eventually acquired the two-drug discrimination, avoiding saccharin when it was preceded by naloxone and consuming the same saccharin solution when it was preceded by diprenorphine (see Figure 5). Clearly, the procedure can be modified to allow for a differentiation between compounds that may share sufficient properties to underlie generalization but that nevertheless differ in their activity (see also Kautz & Riley, 1993; Kautz, Smurthwaite, & Riley, 1992). Although this work with diprenorphine fur-

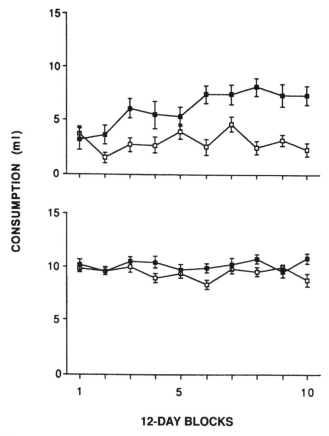

Figure 5. The mean amount of saccharin consumed for experimental subjects (Group L) injected with naloxone prior to saccharin–LiCl pairings and with diprenorphine prior to saccharin alone (top panel). Control subjects (Group W) were injected with naloxone and diprenorphine prior to saccharin alone (bottom panel). For both groups, consumption following naloxone and diprenorphine is represented by unfilled and filled circles, respectively.

ther suggests that antagonist activity at receptor subtypes other than mu may support drug discrimination learning (i.e., delta and kappa), conclusions regarding the ability of delta and kappa antagonists to serve a stimulus function necessitate selective training with these compounds (for a failure to see the acquisition of stimulus control with the relatively selective kappa antagonist MR2266, see Riley & Pournaghash, 1995).

Discriminative Effects of Partial Agonists: Nalorphine

Acquisition of Nalorphine Stimulus Control

My group's initial work within the taste-aversion design has focused on the opioid antagonist naloxone (both its ability to serve a discriminative function and the receptor basis for this control). More recently, we began assessing compounds generally classified as weak or partial opioid *agonists*. One such compound is nalorphine, which has been classified as an opioid with limited efficacy at the mu receptor subtype (Gilbert & Martin, 1986; Kosterlitz et al., 1981; Lord et al., 1977; Martin, 1967; Martin, Eades, Thompson, Huppler, & Gilbert, 1976). Although it is able to exert biological activity (as mediated by the mu subtype), the biological activity exerted by nalorphine is not as great as that produced by a strong or full opioid agonist such as morphine. This partial nature is supported by the fact that within a variety of procedures, animals trained to discriminate mu agonists from their vehicles do not consistently generalize this control to nalorphine, suggesting that as a partial agonist, nalorphine's mu stimulus effects are relatively weak (Colpaert & Janssen, 1984, 1986; Colpaert, Niemegeers, & Janssen, 1976; Hirschhorn & Rosecrans, 1976; Overton & Batta, 1979; Shannon & Holtzman, 1977). On the basis of our prior work with the opioid antagonists, my associates and I reasoned that the relatively weak mu agonist properties of nalorphine might also be detected within the more sensitive aversion design (Smurthwaite & Riley, 1995). To test this hypothesis, we injected rats with 5.6 mg/kg morphine 15 minutes prior to a saccharin–LiCl pairing and with the morphine vehicle prior to saccharin alone. Control subjects were administered both morphine and its vehicle prior to nonpoisoned exposures to saccharin. Following acquisition of the discrimination, all subjects were given various doses of nalorphine and naloxone prior to saccharin to assess the ability of these compounds to substitute for the morphine stimulus. In all experimental subjects, morphine generalized to nalorphine but not to naloxone, suggesting that nalorphine and morphine share stimulus properties, presumably on the basis of their agonist activity at the mu receptor. Within the aversion design, therefore, we were able to demonstrate the mu agonist properties of nalorphine.

Relative Efficacy of Nalorphine

Although nalorphine may share such properties with morphine, in earlier work from our lab, 5 of 12 rats trained to discriminate naloxone from its vehicle generalized naloxone's stimulus effects to nalorphine; that is, for a subset of subjects, naloxone and nalorphine appeared to share stimulus properties (see Smurthwaite et al., 1992). Therefore, depending on the training drug, nalorphine appears to share stimulus properties with both naloxone and morphine (at least for selective subjects). This ability of nalorphine to substitute for both an antagonist and an agonist is consistent with the position that nalorphine lies on a continuum of efficacy between pure opioid antagonists like naloxone (which have no ability to produce biological activity) and full agonists like morphine. (For discussions of relative efficacy of opioids, see Bertalmio, France, & Woods, 1993; Picker, 1994; Picker, Smith, & Morgan, 1994; Picker et al., 1993; Riley & Pournaghash, 1995.)

Although nalorphine may lie on a continuum between naloxone and morphine, it is not clear exactly where on this continuum it lies, that is, to which of these two compounds nalorphine is more similar. To examine this question, we recently trained subjects to discriminate morphine from naloxone and then assessed the degree to which nalorphine substituted for the training drugs to learn whether nalorphine would substitute for morphine, naloxone, both, or neither (Smurthwaite & Riley, 1995). Using a modification of the taste-aversion baseline of drug discrimination learning (i.e., a two-drug discrimination), we trained animals to discriminate between morphine (5.6 mg/kg) and naloxone (1 mg/kg). Under one training condition, subjects were injected with morphine prior to a saccharin–LiCl pairing and with naloxone prior to saccharin alone. Under the second condition, this procedure was reversed, such that naloxone signaled the saccharin–LiCl pairing and morphine signaled saccharin alone. Control subjects received both injections prior to saccharin access but were not injected with LiCl at any point during conditioning. Following acquisition of the discrimination, all subjects were injected with various doses of a number of mu agonists (e.g., morphine, methadone, buprenorphine) and antagonists (e.g., naloxone, naltrexone, diprenorphine) prior to saccharin access to assess their ability to substitute selectively for the training drugs. The substitution pattern with nalorphine was then assessed and compared with the patterns of the aforementioned mu agonists and antagonists.

Under these training conditions, all subjects acquired the two-drug discrimination, avoiding saccharin consumption when it was preceded by the LiCl-associated drug and consuming the same saccharin solution when it was preceded by the drug signaling the safe exposure to saccharin. This control was established independently of which drug (i.e., morphine or naloxone) signaled the saccharin–LiCl pairing. When tested with various mu agonists, all subjects displayed morphine-appropriate responding. Specifically, animals in the condition in which morphine signaled the saccharin–LiCl pairing avoided saccharin following both methadone and

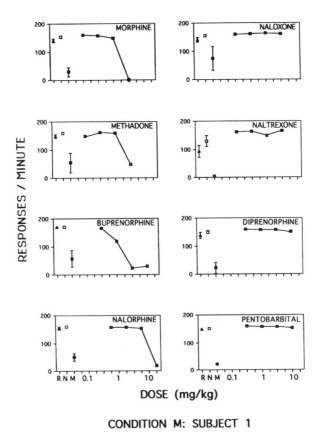

CONDITION M: SUBJECT 1

Figure 6. Response per minute following cumulative probe doses of test drugs for an individual subject that was trained on the morphine–saccharin–LiCl/naloxone–saccharin discrimination (Condition M). The mean numbers (+/− *SEM*) of response per minute during recovery (R) and following the training doses of naloxone (N) and morphine (M) are indicated by the triangle, open square, and closed square, respectively.

buprenorphine. Animals for which morphine signaled the unpoisoned exposure to saccharin readily consumed the saccharin solution (see Figure 6). When tested with mu antagonists, all subjects displayed naloxone-appropriate behavior. Specifically, animals in the condition in which naloxone signaled the saccharin–LiCl pairing avoided saccharin following both naltrexone and diprenorphine. On the other hand, animals for which naloxone signaled the unpoisoned exposure to saccharin readily consumed the saccharin solution (see Figure 7). When nalorphine was administered to experimental subjects, consumption was consistently *morphine*-appropriate, regardless of whether morphine signaled the saccharin–LiCl pairing or the nonpoisoned exposure to saccharin; the animals avoided and consumed the saccharin solution, respectively. Control subjects drank saccharin following all drugs, indicating that the specific patterns of consumption under the two experimental conditions were not unconditioned

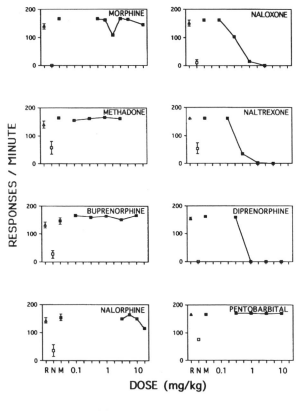

CONDITION N: SUBJECT 4

Figure 7.   Response per minute following cumulative probe doses of test drugs for an individual subject that was trained on the naloxone–saccharin–LiCl/ morphine–saccharin discrimination (Condition N). The mean numbers (+/− *SEM*) of response per minute during recovery (R) and following the training doses of naloxone (N) and morphine (M) are indicated by the triangle, open square, and closed square, respectively.

effects of the various drugs but were a function of the specific discrimination procedures (see Figure 8).

Taken together, these data clearly indicate that nalorphine shares stimulus properties with morphine more than with naloxone, even though when either morphine or naloxone is the training stimulus, nalorphine can substitute for both (see Smurthwaite et al., 1992; Smurthwaite & Riley, 1995). This conclusion regarding the efficacy of nalorphine relative to morphine and naloxone is supported by the fact that animals trained to discriminate nalorphine from its vehicle in a simple drug versus vehicle discrimination procedure within the aversion design generalize nalorphine control exclusively to morphine and not naloxone (see Smurthwaite & Riley, 1994). Therefore, the modified taste-aversion baseline in which compounds with different degrees of biological activity (in this case, antagonist

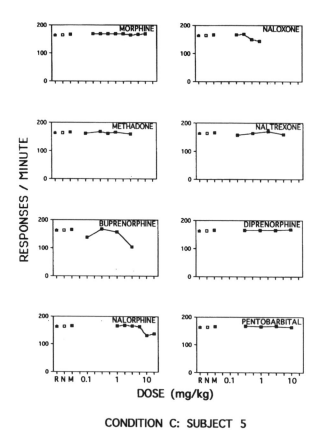

CONDITION C: SUBJECT 5

Figure 8. Response per minute following cumulative probe doses of test drugs for an individual control subject that was given morphine and naloxone prior to unpoisoned exposures to saccharin (Condition C). The mean numbers ($+/-$ *SEM*) of response per minute during recovery (R) and following the training doses of naloxone (N) and morphine (M) are indicated by the triangle, open square, and closed square, respectively.

and full agonist) serve as discriminative stimuli in a two-drug discrimination may be useful in identifying the *relative* efficacy of opioids with weak or partial agonist properties.

CCK–Opioid Interactions

Acquisition of CCK Stimulus Control

Although my group's initial focus on naloxone was on establishing it as a discriminative stimulus and assessing the similarity of this stimulus to other compounds as a manner of classifying opioid antagonists (and weak agonists), we recently extended our analysis of the opioid antagonists to assess their relationship to nonopioid compounds. One such compound we recently examined is the gut peptide cholecystokinin (CCK). Our interest in CCK stemmed from several reports documenting its ability to block the effects of morphine within a range of behavioral preparations (Dourish, Hawley, & Iversen, 1988; Faris, 1985; Itoh & Katsuura, 1982; O'Neill, Dourish, & Iversen, 1989; Wilson, Denson, Bedford, & Hunsinger, 1983). Because of the similarity of CCK to the opioid antagonists in terms of blocking the effects of morphine, CCK has been described as an endogenous opioid antagonist (Faris, 1985; Han, Ding, & Fan, 1985; O'Neill et al., 1989). Accordingly, a colleague and I decided to assess the similarity of CCK and naloxone within the drug discrimination procedure (see Melton & Riley, 1993).

Although CCK has been reported to support drug discrimination learning within traditional operant assessments (de Witte et al., 1985), the doses used in the establishment of discriminative control were quite large (e.g., 20 µg/kg). Given that at such doses CCK has been reported to have opioid agonist effects in analgesia assays (see Faris, 1985), it was important to establish control with substantially lower doses to test the similarity of CCK to opioid antagonists. To do so, we assessed CCK within the taste-aversion baseline of drug discrimination learning (Melton et al., 1993). Specifically, animals were administered 5.6 µg/kg CCK 5 minutes prior to 5-minute access to a novel saccharin solution. (These different temporal parameters were used because of the rapid onset and short duration of action of CCK; see Melton et al., 1993.) As in similar assessments with other drugs, subjects were injected with LiCl immediately following saccharin access. This procedure was repeated every fourth day. On intervening days, subjects received the CCK vehicle prior to a nonpoisoned exposure to the same saccharin solution. Control subjects were injected with both CCK and its vehicle prior to saccharin alone. Under these conditions, all subjects acquired the CCK–distilled water discrimination within approximately 10 conditioning trials, avoiding saccharin consumption when it was preceded by CCK and drinking the same solution when it was preceded by distilled water. When various doses of CCK were administered prior to saccharin access, discriminative control was dose-dependent. Specifically, subjects tended to consume saccharin following the lower doses of CCK and to avoid its consumption at and above the training dose. The discriminative control by CCK appeared to be receptor-mediated in that administration of the CCK_A receptor antagonist devazepide (but not the CCK_B receptor antagonist L-365,260) prior to CCK completely antagonized the CCK stimulus (see Melton & Riley, 1994).

Effects of Opioids on CCK's Stimulus Effects

Given that CCK clearly established discriminative control, Melton and I then assessed the interaction of CCK and the opioids within this preparation (see Melton & Riley, 1993). Animals were trained to discriminate CCK (13 µg/kg) from its vehicle and then administered opioid antagonists

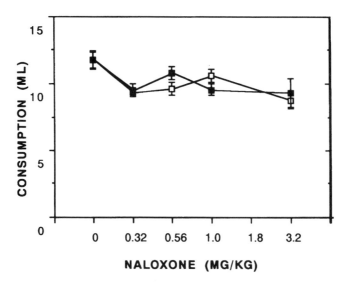

Figure 9. The mean amount of saccharin consumed (+/− *SEM*) for subjects trained to discriminate cholecystokinin (CCK) from its vehicle (Group L, filled squares) and subjects injected with CCK and its vehicle prior to unpoisoned exposures to saccharin (Group W, unfilled squares) during naloxone substitution sessions. From "An Assessment of the Interaction Between Cholecystokinin and the Opiates within a Drug Discrimination Procedure," by P. M. Melton and A. L. Riley, 1993, *Pharmacology, Biochemistry, & Behavior, 46,* pp. 239–240. Reprinted with permission of Elsevier Science Ltd.

alone and in combination with the training dose of CCK. When naloxone was administered prior to saccharin access in CCK-trained subjects, there was no evidence of substitution; that is, experimental subjects (Group L) drank at control levels (Group W) following all doses of naloxone (see Figure 9). Following this, dose-response functions for CCK were determined to establish the largest dose of CCK that could be given that did not produce saccharin avoidance, that is, the largest dose that did not substitute for the training dose. Various doses of naloxone that alone did not substitute for CCK were then administered in combination with the ineffective dose of CCK. For all experimental subjects, naloxone *potentiated* the stimulus effects of CCK: Ineffective doses of CCK resulted in complete suppression of saccharin consumption when combined with naloxone. As illustrated in Figure 10, control subjects also decreased consumption of saccharin with increasing doses of naloxone in combination with CCK, an effect likely due to a summation of the unconditioned effects these compounds have on consumption in general. This decrease, however, was not to the degree seen in the trained subjects, suggesting that the suppression in experimental subjects reflected the potentiating effects of naloxone on CCK's stimulus effects.

The fact that naloxone did not substitute for CCK is consistent with the position that CCK and naloxone do not act in an identical manner, for example, as antagonists at the same receptor (Hong & Takemori, 1989;

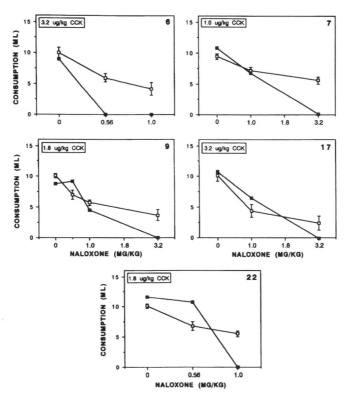

Figure 10. The absolute amount of saccharin consumed for individual experimental subjects trained to discriminate CCK from its vehicle (filled squares) following various doses of naloxone (0–3.2 mg/kg) administered in combination with a dose of CCK (noted in insert) that was ineffective in producing saccharin avoidance when administered alone. The mean amount (+/− *SEM*) of saccharin consumed for control subjects is represented by unfilled squares. From "An Assessment of the Interaction Between Cholecystokinin and the Opiates within a Drug Discrimination Procedure," by P. M. Melton and A. L. Riley, 1993, *Pharmacology, Biochemistry, & Behavior, 46,* pp. 239–240. Reprinted with permission of Elsevier Science Ltd.

Miller & Lupica, 1994; Ossipov, Kovelowski, Vanderah, & Porreca, 1994; Pournaghash & Riley, 1990; Wang & Han, 1990). The fact that naloxone potentiated the stimulus effects of CCK, however, indicates that the two drugs clearly interact, possibly by convergent activity at the same cell or through allosteric binding at a common receptor complex (see Bartolome, Lorber, & Bartolome, 1994; Dourish, 1992; Flood, Garland, & Morley, 1992; Hong & Takemori, 1989; Miller & Lupica, 1994). It is of interest that although naloxone appears able to influence the stimulus properties of CCK through its convergent or allosteric effects, its activity alone appears insufficient to produce a stimulus effect perceived as similar to that produced by CCK. (Similar examples of such dissociation of potentiation and stimulus effects have been reported with other drugs within more traditional assessments; see France & Woods, 1988; Snoddy & Tessel, 1985.) If

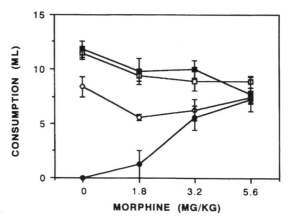

Figure 11. The mean amount (+/− *SEM*) of saccharin consumed for subjects in Group L (filled symbols) and W (unfilled symbols) following various doses of morphine (0–5.6 mg/kg) administered alone (squares) or in combination with 13 μg/kg CCK (circles). From "An Assessment of the Interaction Between Cholecystokinin and the Opiates within a Drug Discrimination Procedure," by P. M. Melton and A. L. Riley, 1993, *Pharmacology, Biochemistry, & Behavior, 46,* pp. 239–240. Reprinted with permission of Elsevier Science Ltd.

naloxone is able to potentiate CCK's stimulus effects (through its activity on a common system), it might be expected that opioid agonists would impact CCK's stimulus effects as well. Specifically, morphine might be expected to block CCK's stimulus properties.

In a test of this prediction, my colleague and I administered morphine sulfate (alone and in combination with CCK) to subjects trained to discriminate 13 μg/kg CCK from its distilled water baseline (Melton & Riley, 1994). Whereas morphine alone had no effect on saccharin consumption —experimental subjects (Group L) drank at control levels (Group W)— morphine (at doses of 7.5 mg/kg and higher) completely blocked the stimulus effects of CCK in CCK-trained animals (see Figure 11). CCK and morphine, therefore, interact in an antagonistic manner within the drug discrimination preparation (although the effects of CCK on morphine discriminative control have yet to be tested), an interaction consistent with the aforementioned possibility that opioids and CCK act by convergent and oppositional activity on some common system.

My group's work with the opioids and CCK has focused almost exclusively on naloxone and morphine, and our conclusions regarding the possible biochemical interactions have been limited to their convergent and oppositional activity at the mu receptor subtype (on the basis of the relative binding profiles for naloxone and morphine). Recently, however, Roques and his colleagues (see Dauge, Corringer, & Roques, 1995) noted that within other preparations (e.g., assays of locomotor activity), CCK may be acting through the delta opioid receptor subtype to antagonize opioid agonist effects. In this work, the antagonist effects of CCK on opioid-induced suppression of motoric behavior were potentiated by the highly specific delta antagonist naltrindole. To test whether other opioid antagonists with activity at other receptor subtypes may interact with CCK within the discrimination design, we recently assessed the ability of mu, delta, and kappa antagonists to substitute for or potentiate the stimulus properties of CCK (Riley & Melton, in press). The design used in this assessment was functionally identical to that described previously, except that a lower dose of CCK was employed as the training drug. Specifically, subjects were trained to discriminate 5.6 μg/kg CCK from its vehicle and were then administered either naloxone (mu), naltrindole (delta), or MR2266 (kappa), either alone or in combination with ineffective doses of CCK, prior to saccharin access. As previously reported, naloxone failed to substitute for the CCK stimulus yet clearly potentiated the stimulus effects of a dose of CCK that alone did not exert stimulus control. MR2266 also failed to substitute for CCK but potentiated its stimulus effects. Naltrindole, however, failed to substitute *and* failed to potentiate the effects of CCK, even at doses effective in other preparations (Dauge et al., 1995; Desmeules, Kayser, Gacel, Guilbaud, & Roques, 1993; Suzuki et al., 1994). Within the drug discrimination baseline, therefore CCK appears to act on systems that may be modulated by mu and kappa (but not delta) receptor subtypes to effect its stimulus properties. The specific basis for the interaction remains unknown.

Although full opioid agonists (e.g., morphine) and pure opioid antagonists (e.g., naloxone) act differentially on the stimulus properties of CCK (antagonize and potentiate, respectively), it is unclear how compounds with limited agonist efficacy might affect such control. In earlier work, my group found that partial agonists such as nalorphine substituted for both morphine and naloxone when these compounds were used individually as the training drugs (see Smurthwaite et al., 1992; Smurthwaite & Riley, 1995). When the two-drug naloxone versus morphine discrimination was established, nalorphine appeared to share stimulus properties with morphine more than with naloxone. To assess whether the agonist properties of nalorphine are generally more salient in drug discrimination learning, we recently assessed the effects of nalorphine on the stimulus properties of CCK (Ziervogel & Riley, 1996). Two different groups of subjects were used within this study, one trained on a morphine–distilled water discrimination (5.6 mg/kg morphine) and a second trained on a CCK–distilled water discrimination (5.6 μg/kg CCK). After subjects acquired their respective discriminations, various doses of nalorphine were given either alone or in combination with each of the two training drugs. As expected, nalorphine substituted for morphine in animals trained to discriminate morphine from its vehicle (Smurthwaite & Riley, 1995). The effects of nalorphine on the stimulus properties of CCK were varied and animal-dependent. For one subset of subjects, nalorphine blocked CCK's stimulus effects, an antagonism similar to that produced by morphine. For another subset, nalorphine dramatically potentiated CCK's stimulus control, an effect like that produced by naloxone. Thus, nalorphine appeared to produce effects within this design like those of an opioid agonist and antagonist, dependent on the specific subject tested. These data are consistent with the aforementioned work in which nalorphine substituted for both naloxone and morphine when each of these compounds alone served as the training drug. They further suggest that nalorphine lies between naloxone and morphine on an efficacy continuum, close to a point below which it is perceived as an antagonist and above which it is perceived as an agonist. Why some subjects treat nalorphine as an agonist and others treat it as an antagonist is not clear, although it is possible that animals differ in their sensitivities to nalorphine (in terms of where on the continuum it lies). Regardless of the basis, the differential effects of a partial agonist on CCK discriminative control might reveal (like the two-drug discrimination) its relative efficacy.

Conclusions

The present review has focused on the use of the taste-aversion baseline of drug discrimination learning to assess opioid receptor pharmacology, primarily in relation to opioid antagonists (and to some degree, weak and partial agonists). Heretofore, the analysis of such compounds generally was limited to investigations of their effects on the stimulus properties of opioid agonists in naive animals or the ability of such antagonists to serve a discriminative function in opioid-dependent subjects. For example, following the establishment of discriminative control with an opioid agonist, the concurrent administration of the training drug and an opioid antagonist provides insight into the opioid nature of the stimulus effects as well as the specific receptor system mediating these effects (e.g., see France & Woods, 1985; Holtzman, 1985; Picker, Doty, Negus, Mattox, & Dykstra, 1990; Picker & Dykstra, 1987; Schaefer & Holtzman, 1977; Teal & Holtzman, 1980). Furthermore, the administration of antagonists to opioid-dependent animals has revealed that withdrawal precipitated by the antagonist can serve as a discriminative stimulus itself. The effects of other opioid agonists and antagonists on the stimulus control produced by withdrawal can then be assessed to determine their ability to reverse or potentiate the withdrawal-associated state (France, de Costa, Jacobson, Rice, & Woods, 1990; France & Woods, 1989, 1993; Holtzman, 1985; Miksic, Sherman, & Lal, 1981; Valentino et al., 1983; see Emmett-Oglesby, Mathis, Moon, & Lal 1990, for a general discussion of withdrawal states as discriminative stimuli).

Although they are extremely useful for these purposes, such analyses provide little insight into the perceived similarities of opioid antagonists in opioid-naive subjects or the relationship of these stimulus properties to other opioid and nonopioid compounds. The ability within the taste-aversion baseline to assess these properties and their relationships to other compounds in opioid-naive subjects may provide a basis for identifying and characterizing antagonists selective for specific opioid receptor subtypes. The ability to identify and characterize drug interactions within the discrimination procedure may also provide insight into the mechanism of action of the opioids in their interaction with other compounds. Although use of the taste-aversion baseline is relatively new in the field of drug discrimination learning, and the extent to which data from such investigations parallel those of more traditional assessments is not known (see Sobel, Wetherington, & Riley, 1995), the assessments of the opioid antagonists within this baseline suggest that the method may be a useful tool in the classification and characterization of the stimulus properties of drugs.

References

Bansinath, K., Ramabadran, K., Turndof, H., & Puig, M. M. (1990). Effects of the benzomorphan κ-opiate, MR 2266 and its (+) enantiomer MR2267, on thermonociceptive reactions in different strains of mice. *Neuroscience Letters, 117,* 212–217.

Barry, H. (1974). Classification of drugs according to their discriminable effects in rats. *Federation Proceedings, 33,* 1814–1824.

Bartoletti, M., Gaiardi, M., Gubellini, C., Bacchi, A., & Babbini, M. (1989). Time-dependent generalization of morphine stimulus properties to meperidine: Antagonism by naloxone. *Pharmacology, Biochemistry, & Behavior, 34,* 429–431.

Bartolome, J. V., Lorber, B. A., & Bartolome, M. B. (1994). Brain cholecystokinin and β-endorphin systems may antagonistically interact to regulate tissue DNA synthesis in rat pups. *Brain Research, 661,* 19–24.

Bertalmio, A. J., France, C. P., & Woods, J. H. (1993). Establishing correlations between the pharmacodynamic characteristics of opioid agonists and their behavioral effects. In A. Herz (Ed.), *Handbook of experimental pharmacology: Opioids II* (Vol. 104/II, pp. 449–469). Berlin: Springer-Verlag.

Braude, M. C., Harris, L. S., May, E. L., Smith, J. P., & Villarreal, J. E. (Eds.). (1973). *Narcotic antagonists: Advances in biochemical psychopharmacology* (Vol. 8). New York: Raven Press.

Calcagnetti, D. J., Calcagnetti, R. L., & Fanselow, M. S. (1990). Centrally administered opioid antagonists, nor binaltorphimine, 16-methyl cyprenorphine and MR2266, suppress intake of sweet solution. *Pharmacology, Biochemistry, & Behavior, 35,* 69–73.

Carter, R. B., & Leander, J. D. (1982). Discriminative stimulus properties of naloxone. *Psychopharmacology, 77,* 305–308.

Chang, K.-J., Hazum, E., & Cuatrecasas, P. (1981). Novel opiate binding sites selective for benzomorphan drugs. *Proceedings of the National Academy of Sciences, 78,* 4141–4145.

Colpaert, F. C., & Balster, R. L. (Eds.). (1988). *Transduction mechanisms of drug stimuli.* Berlin: Springer-Verlag.

Colpaert, F. C., & Janssen, P. A. J. (1984). Agonist and antagonist effects of prototype opiate drugs in rats discriminating fentanyl from saline: Characteristics of partial generalization. *Journal of Pharmacology and Experimental Therapeutics, 230,* 193–199.

Colpaert, F. C., & Janssen, P. A. J. (1986). Agonists and antagonist effects of prototype opiate drugs in fentanyl dose-dose discrimination. *Psychopharmacology, 90,* 222–228.

Colpaert, F. C., Niemegeers, C. J., & Janssen, P. A. J. (1976). On the ability of narcotic antagonists to produce the narcotic cue. *Journal of Pharmacology and Experimental Therapeutics, 197,* 180–187.

Colpaert, F. C., & Rosecrans, J. A. (Eds.). (1978). *Stimulus properties of drugs: Ten years of progress.* Amsterdam: Elsevier.

Colpaert, F. C., & Slangen, J. L. (Eds.). (1982). *Drug discrimination: Applications in CNS pharmacology.* Amsterdam: Elsevier.

Conger, J. J. (1951). The effects of alcohol on conflict behavior in the albino rat. *Quarterly Journal of the Studies on Alcohol, 12,* 1–29.

Contreras, P. C., Tam, L., Drower, E., & Rafferty, M. F. (1993). [³H]Naltrindole: A potent and selective ligand for labeling d-opioid receptors. *Brain Research, 604,* 160–164.

Dauge, V., Corringer, P.-J., & Roques, B. P. (1995). CCK$_A$, but not CCK$_B$, agonists suppress the hyperlocomotion induced by endogenous enkephalin, protected from enzymatic degradation by systemic RB 101. *Pharmacology, Biochemistry, and Behavior, 50,* 133–139.

de Beun, R., Heinsbroek, R. P. W., Slangen, J. L., & van de Poll, N. E. (1991). Discriminative stimulus properties of estradiol in male and female rats revealed by a taste-aversion procedure. *Behavioural Pharmacology, 2,* 439–445.

de Beun, R., Jansen, E., Slangen, J. L., & van de Poll, N. E. (1992). Testosterone as appetitive and discriminative stimulus in rats: Sex- and dose-dependent effects. *Physiology & Behavior, 52,* 629–634.

Desmeules, J. A., Kayser, V., Gacel, G., Guilbaud, G., & Roques, B. P. (1993). The highly selective d agonist BUBU induces an analgesic effect in normal and arthritic rat and this action is not affected by repeated administration of low doses of morphine. *Brain Research, 611,* 243–248.

de Witte, P., Swanet, E., Gewiss, M., Goldman, S., Roques, B., & Vanderhaeghen, J.-J. (1985). Psychopharmacological profile of cholecystokinin using the self-stimulation and the drug discrimination paradigms. *Annals of the New York Academy of Sciences, 448,* 4470–4487.

Dourish, C. T. (1992). The role of CCKA and CCKB receptors in mediating the inhibitory effect of CCK on opiate analgesia. In C. T. Dourish, S. J. Cooper, S. D. Iversen, & L. L. Iversen (Eds.), *Multiple cholecystokinin receptors in the CNS* (pp. 455–472). Oxford, England: Oxford University Press.

Dourish, C. T., Hawley, D., & Iversen, S. D. (1988). Enhancement of morphine analgesia and prevention of morphine tolerance in the rat by the cholecystokinin antagonist L-364,718. *European Journal of Pharmacology, 147,* 469–472.

Dykstra, L. A., Bertalmio, A. J., & Woods, J. H. (1988). Discriminative and analgesic effects of mu and kappa opioids: In vivo pA2 analysis. In F. C. Colpaert & R. L. Balster (Eds.), *Transduction mechanisms of drug stimuli* (pp. 107–121). Berlin: Springer-Verlag.

Emmett-Oglesby, M. W., Mathis, D. A., Moon, R. T. Y., & Lal, H. (1990). Animal models of drug withdrawal symptoms. *Psychopharmacology, 101,* 292–309.

Faris, P. L. (1985). Opiate antagonistic function of cholecystokinin in analgesia and energy balance systems. *Annals of the New York Academy of Sciences, 448,* 437–447.

Flood, J. F., Garland, J. S., & Morley, J. E. (1992). Evidence that cholecystokinin-enhanced retention is mediated by changes in opioid activity in the amygdala. *Brain Research, 585,* 94–104.

France, C. P., de Costa, B., Jacobson, A. E., Rice, K. C., & Woods, J. H. (1990). Apparent affinity of opioid antagonists in morphine-treated rhesus monkeys discriminating between saline and naltrexone. *Journal of Pharmacology and Experimental Therapeutics, 252,* 600–604.

France, C. P., & Woods, J. H. (1985). Opiate agonist-antagonist interactions: Applications of a three-key drug discrimination procedure. *Journal of Pharmacology and Experimental Therapeutics, 234,* 81–89.

France, C. P., & Woods, J. H. (1988). Acute supersensitivity to the discriminative stimulus effects of naltrexone in pigeons. *Journal of Pharmacology and Experimental Therapeutics, 244,* 599–605.

France, C. P., & Woods, J. H. (1989). Discriminative stimulus effects of naltrexone in morphine-treated rhesus monkeys. *Journal of Pharmacology and Experimental Therapeutics, 250,* 937–943.

France, C. P., & Woods, J. H. (1993). U-50,488, saline and naltrexone discrimination in U-50,488-treated pigeons. *Behavioural Pharmacology, 4,* 509–516.

Garcia, J., & Ervin, F. R. (1968). Gustatory-visceral and telereceptor-cutaneous conditioning: Adaptations in internal and external milieus. *Communications in Behavioral Biology, 1,* 389–415.

Geter, B., & Riley, A. L. (1993). The ability of a D1 and D2 antagonist combination to antagonize the discriminative stimulus properties of cocaine. In L. Harris (Ed.), *Problems of drug dependence, 1992: Proceedings of the 54th annual scientific meeting* (p. 95). Washington, DC: U.S. Government Printing Office.

Gilbert, P. E., & Martin, W. R. (1986). The effects of morphine- and nalorphine-like drugs in the nondependent, morphine-dependent and cyclazocine-dependent chronic spinal dog. *Journal of Pharmacology and Experimental Therapeutics, 198,* 66–82.

Glennon, R. A., Jarbe, T. U. C., & Frankenheim, J. (Eds.). (1992). *Drug discrimination: Applications to drug abuse research. NIDA Monograph 116.* Washington, DC: U.S. Government Printing Office.

Glowa, J. R., Jeffreys, R. D., & Riley, A. L. (1991). Drug discrimination using a conditioned taste-aversion paradigm in rhesus monkeys. *Journal of the Experimental Analysis of Behavior, 56,* 303–312.

Goudie, A. J. (1992). Discriminative stimulus properties of amphetamine, cathione, and related compounds. In R. A. Glennon, T. U. C. Jarbe, & J. Frankenheim (Eds.), *Drug discrimination: Applications to drug abuse research. NIDA Monograph 116* (pp. 45–60). Washington, DC: U.S. Government Printing Office.

Han, J.-S., Ding, X.-Z., & Fan, S.-G. (1985). Is cholecystokinin octapeptide (CCK-8) a candidate for endogenous anti-opioid substrates? *Neuropeptides, 5,* 399–402.

Hirschhorn, I. D., & Rosecrans, J. A. (1976). Generalization of morphine and lysergic acid diethylamide (LSD) stimulus properties to narcotic analgesics. *Psychopharmacology, 47,* 65–69.

Ho, B. T., Richards, W. III., & Chute, D. L. (Eds.). (1978). *Drug discrimination and state dependent learning.* New York: Academic Press.

Holtzman, S. G. (1985). Discriminative stimulus properties of opioids that interact with mu, kappa and PCP/sigma receptors. In L. S. Seiden & R. L. Balster (Eds.), *Behavioral pharmacology: The current status* (pp. 131–147). New York: Alan R. Liss.

Holtzman, S. G., & Locke, K. W. (1988). Neural mechanisms of drug stimuli: Experimental approaches. In F. C. Colpaert & R. L. Balster (Eds.), *Transduction mechanisms of drug stimuli* (pp. 139–153). Berlin: Springer-Verlag.

Hong, E. K., & Takemori, A. E. (1989). Indirect involvement of delta opioid receptors in cholecystokinin octapeptide-induced analgesia in mice. *Journal of Pharmacology and Experimental Therapeutics, 251,* 594–598.

Itoh, S., & Katsuura, G. (1982). Effects of β-endorphin, thyrotropin-releasing hormone and cholecystokinin on body shaking behavior in rats. *Japanese Journal of Physiology, 32,* 667–675.

Jaeger, T. V., & Mucha, R. F. (1990). A taste aversion model of drug discrimination learning: Training drug and condition influence rate of learning, sensitivity and drug specificity. *Psychopharmacology, 100,* 145–150.

Jaeger, T. V., & van der Kooy, D. (1993). Morphine acts in the parabrachial nucleus, a pontine viscerosensory relay, to produce discriminative stimulus effects. *Psychopharmacology, 110,* 76–84.

Jarbe, T. U. C. (1978). Discriminative effects of morphine in the pigeon. *Pharmacology, Biochemistry, & Behavior, 9,* 411–416.

Jarbe, T. U. C. (1987). Drug discrimination learning: Cue properties of drugs. In A. J. Greenshaw & C. T. Dourish (Eds.), *Experimental psychopharmacology* (pp. 433–479). Clifton, NJ: Humana Press.

Jarbe, T. U. C. (1989). Discrimination learning with drug stimuli: Methods and applications. In A. A. Boulton, G. B. Baker, & A. J. Greenshaw (Eds.), *Neuromethods: volume 13. Psychopharmacology* (pp. 513–563). Clifton, NJ: Humana Press.

Jarbe, T. U. C., Johansson, J. O., & Henrikksson, B. G. (1975). Drug discrimination in rats: The effects of phencyclidine and Ditran. *Psychopharmacologia, 42,* 33–39.

Kautz, M. A., Geter, B., McBride, S. A., Mastropaolo, J. P., & Riley, A. L. (1989). Naloxone as a stimulus for drug discrimination learning. *Drug Development Research, 16,* 317–326.

Kautz, M. A., Logan, J. P., Romero, A. E., Schwartz, M. D., & Riley, A. L. (1989). The effects of Ro 15-4513 on ethanol drug discrimination learning. *Society for Neuroscience Abstracts, 15,* 633.

Kautz, M. A., & Riley, A. L. (1990). Drug-drug discrimination with the opiate antagonists naloxone and diprenorphine. *Society for Neuroscience Abstracts, 16,* 1192.

Kautz, M. A., & Riley, A. L. (1993). Morphine/nalorphine discrimination learning within a conditional two-drug discrimination procedure. In L. Harris (Ed.), *Problems of drug dependence, 1992: Proceedings of the 54th annual scientific meeting* (p. 247). Washington, DC: U.S. Government Printing Office.

Kautz, M. A., Smurthwaite, S. T., & Riley, A. L. (1992). Drug/drug discrimination learning within the conditioned taste aversion procedure. In L. Harris (Ed.), *Problems of drug dependence, 1991: Proceedings of the 53rd annual scientific meeting* (p. 382). Washington, DC: U.S. Government Printing Office.

Klimczak, A., & Riley, A. L. (1996). [Naloxone as a discriminative stimulus: An assessment of mu, kappa, and delta apioid mediation.] Unpublished raw data.

Kosterlitz, H. W., Paterson, S. J., & Robson, L. E. (1981). Characterization of the k-subtype of the opiate receptor in the guinea-pig brain. *British Journal of Pharmacology, 73,* 939–949.

Lal, H. (Ed.). (1977). *Discriminative stimulus properties of drugs.* New York: Plenum Press.

Lal, H., & Fielding, S. (Eds.). (1989). *Drugs as interoceptive stimuli.* New York: Alan R. Liss.

Lal, H., Gianutsos, G., & Miksic, S. (1977). Discriminative stimuli produced by narcotic analgesics. In H. Lal (Ed.), *Discriminative stimulus properties of drugs* (pp. 23–45). New York: Plenum Press.

Lal, H., Miksic, S., & McCarten, M. (1978). A comparison of discriminative stimuli produced by naloxone, cyclazocine and morphine in the rat. In F. C. Colpaert & J. A. Rosecrans (Eds.), *Stimulus properties of drugs: Ten years of progress* (pp. 177–180). Amsterdam: Elsevier/North-Holland.

Laorden, M. L., Carrillo, E., & Puig, M. M. (1991). Prevention of hyperthermia-induced convulsions in immature rat by MR-2266, a kappa antagonist. *Methods and Findings in Clinical Pharmacology, 13,* 605–608.

Lever, J. R., Scheffel, U., Kinter, C. M., Ravert, H. T., Dannals, R. F., Wagner, H. N., & Frost, J. J. (1992). In vivo binding of N1'-([^{11}C]methyl) naltrindole to d-opioid receptors in mouse brain. *European Journal of Pharmacology, 216,* 459–460.

Locke, K. W., & Holtzman, S. G. (1985). Characterization of the discriminative stimulus effects of centrally administered morphine in the rat. *Psychopharmacology, 87,* 1–6.

Lord, J. A. H., Waterfield, A. A., Hughes, J., & Kosterlitz, H. W. (1977). Endogenous opioid peptides: Multiple agonists and receptors. *Nature, 267,* 495–499.

Lucki, I. (1988). Rapid discrimination of the stimulus properties of 5-hydroxytryptamine agonists using conditioned taste aversion. *Journal of Pharmacology and Experimental Therapeutics, 247,* 1120–1127.

Lucki, I., & Marcoccia, J. M. (1991). Discriminated taste aversion with a 5-HT1A agonist measured using saccharin preference. *Behavioural Pharmacology, 2,* 335–344.

Magnan, J., Paterson, S. J., Tavani, A., & Kosterlitz, H. W. (1982). The binding spectrum of narcotic analgesic drugs with different agonist and antagonist properties. *Naunyn-Schmiedeberg's Archives of Pharmacology, 319,* 197–205.

Martin, G. M., Bechara, A., & van der Kooy, D. (1991). The perception of emotion: Parallel neural processing of the affective and discriminative properties of the opiates. *Psychobiology, 19,* 147–152.

Martin, G. M., Gans, M., & van der Kooy, D. (1990). Discriminative properties of morphine that modulate associations between taste and lithium chloride. *Journal of Experimental Psychology: Animal Behavior Processes, 16,* 56–68.

Martin, W. R. (1967). Opioid antagonists. *Pharmacological Reviews, 19,* 463–521.

Martin, W. R., Eades, C. G., Thompson, J. A., Huppler, R. E., & Gilbert, P. E. (1976). The effects of morphine- and nalorphine-like drugs in the nondependent and morphine-dependent chronic spinal dog. *Journal of Pharmacology and Experimental Therapeutics, 197,* 517–532.

Mastropaolo, J. P., Moskowitz, K. H., Dacanay, R. J., & Riley, A. L. (1989). Conditioned taste aversions as a behavioral baseline for drug discrimination learning: An assessment with phencyclidine. *Pharmacology, Biochemistry, & Behavior, 32,* 1–8.

Mastropaolo, J. P., & Riley, A. L. (1990). Drug discrimination studies in animals: A behavioral approach to understanding the role of neurotransmitter receptor complexes in mediating drug effects. In S. Deutsch, A. Weizman, & R. Weizman (Eds.), *Application of basic neuroscience to child psychiatry* (pp. 125–140). New York: Plenum Press.

Melton, P. M., Kopman, J. A., & Riley, A. L. (1993). Cholecystokinin as a stimulus in drug discrimination learning. *Pharmacology Biochemistry, and Behavior, 44,* 249–252.

Melton, P. M., & Riley, A. L. (1993). An assessment of the interaction between cholecysto-kinin and the opiates within a drug discrimination procedure. *Pharmacology, Biochemistry, and Behavior, 46,* 237–242.

Melton, P. M., & Riley, A. L. (1994). Receptor mediation of the stimulus properties of cho-lecystokinin. *Pharmacology, Biochemistry, and Behavior, 48,* 275–279.

Miksic, S., Sherman, G., & Lal, H. (1981). Discriminative response control by naloxone in morphine-pretreated rats. *Psychopharmacology, 72,* 179–184.

Miller, K. K., & Lupica, C. R. (1994). Morphine-induced excitation of pyramidal neurons is inhibited by cholecystokinin in the CA1 region of the rat hippocampal slice. *Journal of Pharmacology and Experimental Therapeutics, 268,* 753–761.

Negus, S. S., Picker, M. J., & Dykstra, L. A. (1990). Interactions between mu and kappa opioid agonists in the rat drug discrimination procedure. *Psychopharmacology, 102,* 465–473.

Ohno, M., Yamamoto, T., & Ueki, S. (1991). Effect of the k-receptor agonist, U50,488H, on cerebral ischemia-induced impairment of working memory assessed in rats by a three-panel runway task. *European Journal of Pharmacology, 193,* 357–361.

O'Neill, M. F., Dourish, C. T., & Iversen, S. D. (1989). Morphine-induced analgesia in the rat paw pressure test is blocked by CCK and enhanced by the CCK antagonist MK-329. *Neuropharmacology, 28,* 243–247.

Ossipov, M. H., Kovelowski, C. J., Vanderah, T., & Porreca, F. (1994). Naltrindole, an opioid d antagonist, blocks the enhancement of morphine-antinociception induced by a CCK_B antagonist in the rat. *Neuroscience Letters, 181,* 9–12.

Overton, D. A. (1982). Comparison of the degree of discriminability of various drugs using the T-maze drug discrimination paradigm. *Psychopharmacology, 76,* 385–395.

Overton, D. A. (1984). State dependent learning and drug discriminations. In L. L. Iversen, S. D. Iversen, & S. H. Snyder (Eds.), *Handbook of psychopharmacology* (pp. 59–127). New York: Plenum Press.

Overton, D. A. (1987). Applications and limitations of the drug discrimination method for the study of drug abuse. In M. A. Bozarth (Ed.), *Methods of assessing the reinforcing properties of drugs* (pp. 291–340). New York: Springer-Verlag.

Overton, D. A. (1991). Historical context of state dependent learning and discriminative drug effects. *Behavioral Pharmacology, 2,* 253–264.

Overton, D. A. (1992). A historical perspective on drug discrimination learning. In R. A. Glennon, T. U. C. Jarbe, & J. Frankenheim (Eds.), *Drug discrimination: Applications to drug abuse research. NIDA Monograph 116* (pp. 5–24). Washington, DC: U.S. Government Printing Office.

Overton, D. A., & Batta, S. K. (1979). Investigation of narcotics and antitussives using drug discrimination techniques. *Journal of Pharmacology and Experimental Therapeutics, 211,* 401–408.

Picker, M. J. (1994). Kappa agonist and antagonist properties of mixed action opioids in a pigeon drug discrimination procedure. *Journal of Pharmacology and Experimental Therapeutics, 268,* 1190–1198.

Picker, M. J., Doty, P., Negus, S. S., Mattox, S. R., & Dykstra, L. A. (1990). Discriminative stimulus properties of U50,488 and morphine: Effects of training dose on stimulus sub-stitution patterns produced by mu and kappa opioid agonists. *Journal of Pharmacology and Experimental Therapeutics, 254,* 13–22.

Picker, M., & Dykstra, L. A. (1987). Comparison of the discriminative stimulus properties of U50,488 and morphine in pigeons. *Journal of Pharmacology and Experimental Therapeutics, 243,* 938–945.

Picker, M. J., Smith, M. A., & Morgan, D. (1994). Assessment of the relative intrinsic efficacy of profadol and meperidine in a pigeon drug discrimination procedure: Relevance to partial substitution. *Behavioral Pharmacology, 5,* 61–70.

Picker, M. J., Yarbrough, J., Hughes, C. E., Smith, M. A., Morgan, D., & Dykstra, L. A. (1993). Agonist and antagonist effects of mixed action opioids in the pigeon drug dis-crimination procedure: Influence of training, dose, intrinsic efficacy and interanimal differences. *Journal of Pharmacology and Experimental Therapeutics, 266,* 756–767.

Pournaghash, S., & Riley, A. L. (1990). Failure of cholecystokinin to precipitate withdrawal in morphine-treated rats. *Pharmacology, Biochemistry, & Behavior, 38,* 479–484.

Pournaghash, S., & Riley, A. L. (1993). Buprenorphine as a stimulus in drug discrimination learning: An assessment of mu and kappa receptor activity. *Pharmacology, Biochemistry, and Behavior, 46,* 593–604.

Revusky, S., Coombes, S., & Pohl, R. W. (1982). Drug states as discriminative stimuli in a flavor-aversion learning experiment. *Journal of Comparative and Physiological Psychology, 96,* 200–211.

Revusky, S., & Garcia, J. (1970). Learned associations over long delays. In G. Bower & J. Spence (Eds.), *Psychology of learning and motivational advances in research and theory* (Vol. 4, pp. 1–83). New York: Academic Press.

Riley, A. L. (1995). Use of drug discrimination learning in behavioral toxicology: Classification and characterization of toxins. In L. Chang & W. Slikker (Eds.), *Neurotoxicology: Approaches and methods* (pp. 309–321). New York: Academic Press.

Riley, A. L., Jeffreys, R. D., Pournaghash, S., Titley, T. L., & Kufera, A. M. (1989). Conditioned taste aversions as a behavioral baseline for drug discrimination learning: Assessment with the dipsogenic compound pentobarbital. *Drug Development Research, 16,* 229–236.

Riley, A. L., Kautz, M. A., Geter, B., Smurthwaite, S. T., Pournaghash, S., Melton, P. M., & Ferrari, C. M. (1991). A demonstration of the graded nature of the generalization function of drug discrimination learning within the conditioned taste aversion procedure. *Behavioral Pharmacology, 2,* 323–334.

Riley, A. L., & Melton, P. M. (in press). The effects of mu and delta opioid receptor antagonists on the stimulus properties of cholecystokinin. *Pharmacology, Biochemistry, & Behavior.*

Riley, A. L., & Pournaghash, S. (1995). The effects of chronic morphine on the generalization of buprenorphine stimulus control: An assessment of kappa antagonist activity. *Pharmacology, Biochemistry, & Behavior, 52,* 779–787.

Riley, A. L., & Tuck, D. L. (1985). Conditioned food aversions: A bibliography. *Annals of the New York Academy of Sciences, 443,* 381–437.

Rogers, H., Hayes, A. G., Birch, P. J., Traynor, J. R., & Lawrence, A. J. (1990). The selectivity of the opioid antagonist, naltrindole, for d-opioid receptors. *Journal of Pharmacy and Pharmacology, 42,* 358–359.

Rozin, P., & Kalat, J. W. (1971). Specific hungers and poison avoidance as adaptive specializations of learning. *Psychological Review, 78,* 459–486.

Sadee, W., Richards, M. L., Grevel, J., & Rosenbaum, J. S. (1983). In vivo characterization of four types of opioid binding sites in rat brain. *Life Sciences, 33,* 187–189.

Samele, C., Shine, P. J., & Stolerman, I. P. (1992). *Forty years of drug discrimination research: A bibliography for 1951–1991.* NIDA Administrative Document, National Clearinghouse for Alcohol and Drug Information. Washington, DC: Department of Health and Human Services.

Schaefer, G. J., & Holtzman, S. G. (1977). Discriminative effects of morphine in the squirrel monkey. *Journal of Pharmacology and Experimental Therapeutics, 201,* 67–75.

Self, D. W., & Stein, L. (1992). Receptor subtypes in opioid and stimulant reward. *Pharmacology and Toxicology, 70,* 87–94.

Shannon, H. E., & Holtzman, S. G. (1976). Blockade of the discriminative effects of morphine in the rat by naltrexone and naloxone. *Psychopharmacology, 50,* 119–124.

Shannon, H. E., & Holtzman, S. G. (1977). Further evaluation of the discriminative effects of morphine in the rat. *Journal of Pharmacology and Experimental Therapeutics, 201,* 55–66.

Shippensburg, T. S. (1993). Motivational effects of opioids. In A. Hertz (Ed.), *Handbook of experimental pharmacology: Opioids II* (Vol. 104/II, pp. 633–650). Berlin: Springer-Verlag.

Signs, S. A., & Schechter, M. D. (1986). Nicotine-induced potentiation of ethanol discrimination. *Pharmacology, Biochemistry, & Behavior, 24,* 769–771.

Skinner, D. M., & Martin, G. M. (1992). Conditioned taste aversions support drug discrimination learning at low dosages of morphine. *Behavioral and Neural Biology, 58,* 236–241.

Smurthwaite, S. T., Kautz, M. A., Geter, B., & Riley, A. L. (1992). Naloxone as a stimulus in drug discrimination learning: Generalization to other opiate antagonists. *Pharmacology, Biochemistry, and Behavior, 41,* 43–47.

Smurthwaite, S. T., & Riley, A. L. (1992). Diprenorphine as a stimulus in drug discrimination learning. *Pharmacology, Biochemistry, and Behavior, 43,* 839–846.

Smurthwaite, S. T., & Riley, A. L. (1994). Nalorphine as a stimulus in drug discrimination learning. *Pharmacology, Biochemistry, and Behavior, 48,* 635–642.

Smurthwaite, S. T., & Riley, A. L. (1995). Animals trained to discriminate morphine from naloxone generalize morphine (but not naloxone) to nalorphine. In L. Harris (Ed.), *Problems of drug dependence, 1994: Proceedings of the 56th annual scientific meeting* (p. 94). Washington, DC: U.S. Government Printing Office.

Snoddy, A. M., & Tessel, R. E. (1985). Prazosin: Effect of psychomotor-stimulant cues and locomotor behavior in mice. *European Journal of Pharmacology, 116,* 221–228.

Sobel, B.-F. X., Wetherington, C. L., & Riley, A. L. (1995). The contribution of within-session averaging of drug- and vehicle-appropriate responding to the graded dose-response function in drug discrimination learning. *Behavioural Pharmacology, 6,* 348–358.

Stevenson, G. W., Pournaghash, S., & Riley, A. L. (1992). Antagonism of drug discrimination learning within the conditioned taste aversion procedure. *Pharmacology, Biochemistry, and Behavior, 41,* 245–249.

Stolerman, I. P. (1985). Motivational effects of opioids: Evidence of the role of endorphins in mediating reward and aversion. *Pharmacology, Biochemistry, & Behavior, 23,* 877–881.

Suzuki, T., Yoshiike, M., Mizoguchi, H., Kamei, J., Misawa, M., & Nagase, H. (1994). Blockade of d-opioid receptors prevents morphine-induced place preferences in mice. *Japanese Journal of Pharmacology, 66,* 131–137.

Teal, J. J., & Holtzman, S. G. (1980). Stereospecificity of the stimulus effects of morphine and cyclazocine in the squirrel monkey. *Journal of Pharmacology and Experimental Therapeutics, 215,* 369–376.

Thompson, T., & Pickens, R. (Eds.). (1971). *Stimulus properties of drugs.* New York: Appleton-Century-Crofts.

Ukai, M., & Holtzman, S. G. (1988). Morphine like discriminative stimulus effects of opioid peptides: Possible modulatory role of d-ala2-d-leu5-enkephalin (DADL) and dynorphin A(1-13). *Psychopharmacology, 94,* 32–37.

Valentino, R. J., Herling, S., & Woods, J. H. (1983). Discriminative stimulus effects of naltrexone in narcotic-naive and morphine-treated pigeons. *Journal of Pharmacology and Experimental Therapeutics, 224,* 307–313.

van Hest, A., Hijzen, T. H., Slangen, J. L., & Oliver, B. (1992). Assessment of the stimulus properties of anxiolytic drugs by means of the conditioned taste aversion procedure. *Pharmacology, Biochemistry, and Behavior, 42,* 487–495.

van Ree, J. M., & Terenius, L. T. (Eds.). (1978). *Characteristics and function of opioids.* Amsterdam: Elsevier/North-Holland Biomedical Press.

Wang, X.-J., & Han, J.-S. (1990). Modification by cholecystokinin octapeptide of the binding of m-, d- and k-opioid receptors. *Journal of Neurochemistry, 55,* 1379–1382.

Weissman, A. (1978). The discriminability of naloxone in rats depends on concomitant morphine treatment. In F. C. Colpaert & J. A. Rosecrans (Eds.), *Stimulus properties of drugs: Ten years of progress* (pp. 209–214). Amsterdam: Elsevier/North-Holland Biomedical Press.

White, J. M., & Holtzman, S. G. (1983). Three-choice drug discrimination: Phencyclidine-like stimulus effects of opioids. *Psychopharmacology, 80,* 1–19.

Wilson, M. C., Denson, D., Bedford, J. A., & Hunsinger, R. N. (1983). Pharmacological manipulation of sincalide (CCK8)-induced suppression of feeding. *Peptides, 4,* 351–357.

Wollemann, M., Benyhe, S., & Simon, J. (1993). The kappa-opioid receptor: Evidence for the different subtypes. *Life Sciences, 52,* 599–611.

Wood, P. L. (1982). Multiple opiate receptors: Support for unique mu, delta and kappa sites. *Neuropharmacology, 21,* 487–497.

Woudenberg, F., & Hijzen, T. H. (1991). Discriminated taste aversion with chlordiazepoxide. *Pharmacology, Biochemistry, & Behavior, 39,* 859–863.

Ziervogel, S. D., & Riley, A. L. (1996). [Nalorphine's opioid agonist and antagonist properties within the taste aversion baseline of drug discrimination learning.] Unpublished raw data.

Zimmerman, D. M., & Leander, J. D. (1990). Selective opioid receptor agonists and antagonists: Research tools and potential therapeutic agents. *Journal of Medicinal Chemistry, 33,* 895–902.

12

The Nature and Strength of Caloric Conditioning

Paul M. Fedorchak

During the 1980s, Robert Bolles's research interests moved away from fear conditioning and into the relatively new area of flavor preference learning. This chapter begins with a discussion of how the research group moved into this new area of research. The seminal studies by Bolles and his students are presented to chronicle the development of theory in flavor conditioning. The remainder of the chapter outlines a number of ways that caloric substances have been employed as unconditioned stimuli (USs) to generate flavor preferences and contrasts caloric conditioned flavor preferences (CFPs) with the relatively weaker preferences that have been generated by two noncaloric, though foodlike, US substances: saccharin and mineral oil. Following this, I discuss whether, in the CFP paradigm, the differential potency of caloric versus noncaloric reinforcers might represent a qualitative rather than quantitative difference. Evidence for a qualitative difference arises from the observation that although conditioned preferences reinforced by sucrose and other caloric substances are highly sensitive to postconditioning hunger level manipulations (the US revaluation effect), the same hunger changes have no effect on saccharin-mediated preferences. I also consider whether a similar insensitivity to US revaluation might show up in other conditioning paradigms using USs that, like saccharin, constitute only a logical subset (e.g., sweetness alone) of the components of an otherwise "complete" US event (e.g., sweetness plus caloric aftereffects). This section ends with the argument that saccharin-mediated flavor conditioning might best be viewed not as a case of first-order conditioning, with saccharin representing a US, but rather as a case of second-order conditioning, with saccharin playing the role of an "innate" first-order CS.

The chapter ends with a discussion of recent evidence that calorie-mediated CFPs may be unusually resistant to extinction, some observations suggesting that two different types of associations may contribute to their underlying framework (one that extinguishes quickly and another that lingers indefinitely), and the description of a method capable of distinguishing between these different associative links.

Because the bulk of this chapter focuses on Robert Bolles's research, I start with a short vignette about Bolles as a teacher, an image unfamiliar to most readers. Fittingly, this classroom story—the "poi lecture"—is one that also invokes the topic of the chapter.

Like a comic working a room, Bolles could really get rolling at times, and the poi lecture was one of those times. During his class on learning, while talking about taste preferences—how they might come about, their similarities from culture to culture—he began waxing disgustedly about poi, the official food of Hawaii. He feigned chewing, broke into a look of horror, then let loose with a loud "Yuk!" How can they eat this stuff?! It tastes just like wet newspapers! Wet newspaper *paste!*" The students convulsed with laughter. "But amazingly, they [Hawaiians] can't seem to get enough of it. Just as we eat potatoes with most meals, in Hawaii it's not a meal unless you have your poi." As the commotion subsided, Bolles made it clear how interesting it would be if we could understand how people come to like, and sometimes even crave, tastes that initially seem so aversive. The poi story captures the essential features of Bolles's lecture style: plenty of humor and speculation, with a constant emphasis on just how little is really known.

From Fears to Flavors

The movement of Bolles and his students toward the study of flavor preference learning began with a skeptical statement about whether such learning could occur. Near the end of the second edition of his book *Learning Theory*, Bolles wrote the following:

> We might expect to see an increased preference for a food that provides caloric value to a hungry rat. Such a mechanism, a "post-ingestive Garcia effect," would lead to animals having a convenient preference for foods of high caloric density. But so far such an effect has not been reported. (Bolles, 1978, p. 172)

He followed this statement with a discussion of the reasons such an effect might be difficult to find. Approximately 2 years after the preceding words were written, the fear conditioning era of the Bolles Lab came to an end with the departure of Mark Bouton, Michael Fanselow, and Ron Sigmundi and Bolles's recruitment of Linda Hayward (a visitor from Australia) and Christian Crandall (an undergraduate). Hayward and Crandall helped Bolles carry out what would eventually become the first published Bolles Lab flavor preference study.

The Initial Study

In their study, Bolles, Hayward, and Crandall (1981) mixed rat chow into wet mash, added a distinctive flavor (almond or vanilla), and then fed the mix to their rats every other day for several days. On the intervening days, the rats received an alternate mixture with the other flavor added. The second mixture was the same chow, but it was adulterated with nonnutritive chalk to reduce the caloric density from 4 calories/g to 2 calories/g. After the animals had an equal number of experiences with each substance, the authors created a single chow–chalk mixture that was calorically equidistant from the two original mixtures, flavored one portion with vanilla and the other with almond, and presented them simultaneously to the animals. The rats preferred the flavor that had been paired with the higher calorie mixture. Bolles and his students were not convinced this preference was due to the caloric difference between the training substances, however, and suggested that the rats may have avoided the flavor associated with the potentially aversive chalk dilutant. This was a reasonable possibility given what was known about taste-aversion learning (Garcia & Koelling, 1966). In that first article, Bolles et al. (1981) also identified a factor that seemed surprisingly ineffective at promoting a preference for one flavor over another: a differential *amount* of food. Whereas rats easily learn to prefer the arm of a T maze containing the greater amount of food, in the study reported by Bolles et al. (1981) no preference developed for a target flavor associated with the larger of two meals (12 calories versus 6 calories) when both were of equal caloric density (but see Hayward, 1983 for a different result using neonatal rats). By leaving open the possibility that caloric density could reinforce a flavor preference but simple amount could not, the Bolles et al. (1981) article set the direction for the next era of the Bolles lab.

A Switch to Flavored Solutions

In 1982 Ron Mehiel began working with Bolles on flavor preference research. After a few experiments using Bolles's methods with solid foods, he and Bolles started experimenting, instead, with flavored solutions. One of their first positive outcomes was obtained in an experiment in which they mixed up one flavored solution with saccharin (which, according to Bolles, rats "loved") and a differently flavored solution with alcohol (which he said they "hated"). The flavors were grape and orange Kool-Aid mixed up according to the standard package directions but without the cup of sugar. During the first few days of an 8-day series of day-long, single-bottle conditioning exposures, the rats behaved as anticipated: They drank a lot of flavored saccharin and very little flavored alcohol. Over time, however, they switched their affinities, and by the last day (i.e., after 4 days with each solution) they were drinking more flavored alcohol than flavored saccharin. After conditioning, the rats were given a choice of the two flavored solutions without the saccharin and alcohol reinforcers; they clearly consumed more of the flavor associated with alcohol. With the title of his talk implying that rats were *preferring* the alcohol flavor because of alcohol's caloric content, Bolles presented these data at the next Psychonomic Society Meeting (Bolles & Mehiel, 1982).

Isolating Alcohol as the Reinforcer

In 1983 I moved away from a line of research I had initially pursued with Bolles (endorphins and frustration behavior) to begin conducting flavor preference experiments. My motivation for becoming involved in this area was fueled by a desire to evaluate a counterintuitive alternative explanation for why Bolles and Mehiel's (1982) rats drank more alcohol-associated than saccharin-associated flavor: they were *rejecting* the saccharin flavor. Reasoning that the same pattern of results might emerge even with the alcohol omitted from the "alcohol flavor," I designed my first flavor conditioning experiment. Every other day during an 8-day conditioning period, rats in the first of three groups were given, as their only available liquid, a solution of 5% alcohol mixed with a distinctive flavor (either grape or orange). On alternate days, they received a saccharin solution mixed with the alternate flavor. In all important respects, this group provided a straight replication of Bolles and Mehiel's 1982 study. The two other groups were treated identically to the first, except that for one group, saccharin was omitted from the alternate flavor, and for the other group, ethanol was omitted. In all groups, flavors were counterbalanced across reinforcers to control for any unlearned affinities for grape or orange. Following conditioning, all rats were given a two-bottle preference test between the orange and grape solutions, with no reinforcers in either. If the apparent preference for the ethanol flavor reported by Bolles and Mehiel (1982) was really a rejection of the saccharin flavor, during the choice test the "saccharin only" group should have behaved just like the "saccharin–ethanol" group and avoided the saccharin flavor, and the "ethanol only" group should not have shown any preference. That would have been the counterintuitive outcome. When the rats were given the two-bottle test, however, the results were clear: The alcohol deserved all the credit. Rather than rejecting the saccharin flavor, the saccharin-only rats preferred the saccharin-associated flavor about 3:1 over the water-associated flavor, and the rats in both of the other groups preferred the ethanol-associated flavor. In fact, the ethanol-flavor preferences in the two ethanol-exposed groups were so similar that I was forced to conclude that when saccharin was contrasted with ethanol, as in the first group and in Bolles and Mehiel's study, it was the saccharin, rather than the ethanol, that had little if any effect.

Evaluating the Flavor–Flavor Account of Caloric Conditioning

In 1983 Bolles argued that flavor–calorie learning probably took place indirectly, through flavor–flavor associations. For example, for grape to increase in value by being paired with alcohol, alcohol's bad taste would first have to improve through association with its aftereffects (either pharmacological or caloric), and the new, positive value would have to shift over to the grape. This account of calorie learning held that if the flavor associated with alcohol were found to increase in value, the taste of alcohol would also have to have improved in a corresponding manner. A rat who preferred grape because it had been paired with alcohol should prefer the alcohol, and rats who preferred an alcohol-associated flavor over a saccharin-associated flavor should also prefer unflavored alcohol over unflavored saccharin. Shortly after the article containing that prediction went to press (Bolles, 1983), the group knew that this account of post-ingestively reinforced preference conditioning was not correct.

When rats who had already demonstrated a clear preference for an ethanol-associated flavor over a saccharin-associated flavor were given a postconditioning choice between plain ethanol and plain saccharin, they preferred the saccharin to the alcohol. In fact, their postconditioning behavior toward these US solutions was not all that different from their reactions prior to conditioning. What appeared to have happened during conditioning was something like *overshadowing*, with the natural taste of alcohol being edged out of the associative competition (or performance arena) by the artificial Kool-Aid flavors. In contrast to Bolles's (1983) conjecture that flavor cues might acquire value through indirect flavor–flavor conduits, the grape and orange target flavors seemed to have become directly associated with the aftereffects, or lack thereof, of their paired US substances.

Confronted with this almost complete lack of change in reinforcer solution preference, I decided to test an implication of the overshadowing explanation. If the grape and orange had indeed overshadowed the natural tastes, the absence of these flavors during conditioning should permit the alcohol and saccharin tastes to switch affective value. That is exactly what happened. When I gave new rats 8 days of alternating exposure to plain alcohol and plain saccharin, they progressively increased their alcohol intake and decreased their saccharin consumption, just like their predecessors had with flavored solutions. In a subsequent two-bottle test, they preferred the plain alcohol over the plain saccharin by a 4:1 ratio. This outcome indicated that the taste of alcohol, when not masked by grape or orange, was quite capable of acquiring the positive associative value that had previously accrued to those flavors, and the raw taste of saccharin was quite capable of losing its positive value, at least when compared to the taste of alcohol.

The US-Preexposure Effect With an Alcohol US

Shortly after finding that rats could learn to prefer alcohol's taste, just as they learned to prefer a flavor cue mixed with it, Bolles and I found that if we pretrained the animals to prefer the plain alcohol before pairing it with the grape, the preference for grape was weakened (Bolles & Fedorchak, 1984). This was the well-known US preexposure effect,[1] which is commonly explained with reference to the phenomenon of *blocking* (Kamin, 1969). The blocking account of our outcome holds that the exposure

---

[1]In light of evidence that a preferred taste *can* transmit positive value to an added cue (e.g., Fanselow & Birk, 1982; Holman, 1975), it would not have been surprising to find that the alcohol preexposure had produced the opposite effect on subsequent "grape" conditioning; the lessened aversiveness of alcohol's taste during preexposure—owing to reduced neophobia as well as rising associative value—might have further enhanced the grape preference.

to plain alcohol allowed the rats to associate alcohol's taste with its after-effects and that this association blocked learning about the novel grape or orange flavors that were later mixed with the alcohol. Because we did not have a ready way to separate the taste of alcohol from its aftereffects, we never completely evaluated the blocking account of this ethanol preexposure effect. However, using a similar, calorie-based flavor preference paradigm, Holder (1991) showed blocking of the taste component by the odor component, and vice versa, of a flavor conditioned stimulus (CS). Therefore, blocking does occur in flavor preference conditioning, and it remains a possible explanation of our ethanol-based US preexposure outcome.

In 1984 Bolles and I presented the "blocking" paper at a meeting of the Psychonomics Society in San Antonio, Texas (Bolles & Fedorchak, 1984); Ron Mehiel and Bolles published their initial data on caloric conditioning (Mehiel & Bolles, 1984); and with the exception of a brief period of time devoted to studying the *differential outcome effect* (see Fedorchak & Bolles, 1986), the transformation from a fear conditioning lab to a flavor conditioning lab was complete.

The Current Status of Research on Flavor Preference Conditioning

Since Bolles penned his skeptical words regarding flavor preference conditioning back in 1978, the need to account for the elusiveness of this phenomenon has been replaced by a stream of positive results. It is now clear not only that flavor preferences are conditionable but also that the very reinforcer Bolles (1983) had speculatively invoked—caloric density—is an unusually potent US for this type of learning.

Caloric Conditioning

Caloric substances, whether mixed directly with flavor CSs (e.g., Fedorchak & Bolles, 1987, 1988; Holder, 1991; Mehiel & Bolles, 1984, 1988; Simbayi, Boakes, & Burton, 1986), intubated into the stomach (e.g., Elizalde & Sclafani, 1990b; Puerto, Deutsch, Molina, & Rolls, 1976; Sherman, Hickis, Rice, Rusiniak, & Garcia, 1983; Tordoff & Friedman, 1986), or delayed a short time after CS exposure (e.g., Capaldi, Campbell, Sheffer, & Bradford, 1987; Elizalde & Sclafani, 1988; Holman, 1975), have been shown to be highly effective at increasing a rat's preference for a previously neutral flavor. Although there are some differences among these pairing methods (e.g., delayed conditioning is usually weaker than the "immediate" mixed or intubated methods), the *caloric* effect is quite reliable.

Taste and Texture Conditioning

Less impressive have been attempts to condition a preference using reinforcers with foodlike qualities, like sweet taste (saccharin) or oily texture (mineral oil), but no caloric aftereffects. Rats developed preferences for flavors paired with a concentrated (0.32%) saccharin solution (over a dilute saccharin-paired flavor) but only when the saccharin was mixed with the flavor or followed immediately after flavor ingestion (Holman, 1975). In the same study, when saccharin and a caloric dextrose solution were *delayed* by 30 minutes after CS ingestion, only the dextrose produced a flavor preference. Fedorchak and Bolles (1987) found, in both between-group and within-group comparisons, that 5% ethanol produced stronger flavor preferences than 0.028% saccharin (16 ml of ethanol flavor vs. 5 ml of water flavor and 18 ml of ethanol flavor vs. 7 ml of saccharin flavor, respectively). Raising the saccharin concentration to 0.25% had no effect; this concentration produced the same size preference for a saccharin-paired flavor as had the weaker concentration, about 7 ml of saccharin flavor versus 5 ml of water flavor, averaged across all tests. Capaldi, Owens, and Palmer (1994) obtained similar results using sucrose as a caloric reinforcer (test intakes: 14 ml of an 8% sucrose-associated flavor vs. 2 ml of a 1% sucrose-associated flavor) and 0.15% versus 0.03% saccharin as a taste reinforcer. In the latter case, intakes for the strongest preference observed were 7 ml of the 0.15% saccharin-associated flavor versus 3 ml of the 0.03% saccharin-associated flavor. Finally, Mehiel and Bolles (1988) paired one flavor with saccharin and an alternative flavor with one of a number of caloric solutions that rats had initially "rated" as being higher or lower in taste value than the saccharin. In all cases, the calorie-associated flavor was much more highly preferred than the saccharin-associated flavor, and the unconditioned taste value of each caloric reinforcer played little role in the degree to which it was preferred.

Concerning another type of tastable but noncaloric US, oiliness, Elizalde and Sclafani (1990a) found that flavor preferences reinforced by nonnutritive mineral oil were inferior to those reinforced by caloric corn oil emulsions, both when the oils were mixed with the flavors and when they were delayed by 10 minutes. In the delayed case, mineral oil's taste or oily texture alone was completely unable to generate a preference. Thus, the effectiveness of oiliness as a US parallels that of sweetness: Both are modestly effective as tastes or textures alone but not nearly as potent as their caloric counterparts. Calories promote stronger preferences and can do so across a temporal delay. To date, no one has successfully conditioned a flavor preference by presenting a noncaloric reinforcer after a temporal delay.

Are Caloric Associations Qualitatively Different From Others?

The preceding evidence suggests that caloric substances are a more potent reinforcer in the flavor preference paradigm than noncaloric tastes or textures. All of the studies in the preceding section have directly compared these two classes of reinforcers and have found that, across a variety of situations, caloric USs generate stronger preferences than noncaloric tastes, such as sweetness, or noncaloric texture–taste combinations, such as oiliness. In addition to this quantitative difference, there is some evidence that the type of preference generated by caloric substances might also be *qualitatively* different from the taste-mediated preference, at least when the taste quality is sweetness.

A number of researchers have found that caloric substances in a variety of forms produce a *hunger-sensitive* preference (Capaldi et al., 1994; Fedorchak & Bolles, 1987; Holder, 1991). In contrast, even though the noncaloric sweetness of saccharin effectively reinforces a flavor preference (e.g., Fanselow & Birk, 1982), such preferences have been shown by the same researchers (Capaldi et al., 1994; Fedorchak & Bolles, 1987; Holder, 1991) to be completely *insensitive* to hunger changes during preference testing. In my experiment with Bolles (Fedorchak & Bolles, 1987), rats in different groups had one flavor paired in solution with either 5% ethanol, 8% sucrose, 0.025% saccharin, or 0.25% saccharin and the other flavor paired with plain water. As in earlier experiments, each rat was exposed to the two conditioning solutions, the CS+ and CS−, on alternate days over an 8-day period. In subsequent "CS only" choice tests conducted after 24 hours of free feeding, rats showed similar-sized preferences for flavors associated with each of these reinforcers. However, when the choice tests were carried out after a night of food deprivation, the preference for flavors associated with both of the caloric solutions (ethanol and sucrose) dramatically increased, and the preference for flavors associated with both concentrations of saccharin were completely unaffected. It should be stressed that the effects of hunger being described here are *performance* effects that occur during the choice tests that follow conditioning. In the same study (Fedorchak & Bolles, 1987, Experiment 2), manipulations of hunger level during *conditioning* had no effect on the development of the flavor−ethanol association. Whether this lack of effect of hunger on learning is specific to an ethanol US is not clear at present, but there is some evidence that preferences mediated by sweet USs, whether caloric (sucrose) or not (saccharin), are enhanced by hunger during conditioning (Capaldi et al., 1994).

The Hunger Effect and Other US Revaluation Paradigms

One question prompted by the calorie versus taste hunger effect difference seen in the flavor preference paradigm is whether similar differences might also show up in more traditional conditioning situations. The ability of hunger to influence performance toward a calorie-associated flavor CS is an example of the well-known "US revaluation effect" documented in a number of learning situations. For example, when rats in an operant chamber expect an upcoming food reward, they show anticipatory nose-poking into the food hopper. In one recent study, Balleine (1992) found that reductions in hunger level led to immediate decreases in the number of such conditioned hopper entries. Perhaps if saccharin or the chance to see and smell (but not consume) food were used as a US, the revaluation effect might also fail to occur in this situation.

In a different type of US revaluation study, male Japanese quail were conditioned to respond to a styrofoam and feather CS that predicted an upcoming opportunity to copulate with a female quail (Holloway & Domjan, 1993a; see chapter 3, this volume). When, following conditioning, these researchers reduced the testosterone levels of their quail, and thus devalued the US, conditioned approach responding to the CS dropped off accordingly. In another experiment, Holloway and Domjan (1993b) found that exposure alone (without copulation) to the female quail served as a weaker, yet still effective, US. Similar to the results with saccharin-reinforced conditioned flavor preferences (CFPs), conditioned responding supported by Holloway and Domjan's "exposure only" US might be insensitive to the testosterone changes that altered the behavior of birds conditioned with a complete version of the US (i.e., copulation). Although the "nosepoking for saccharin" and "exposure to quail" revaluation experiments have not been conducted, any observed invulnerability to revaluation with these USs, in these very different paradigms, would expand the generality of this lack of effect and help define what US components are necessary to obtain the US revaluation effect.

Are Saccharin-Mediated CFPs a Form of Second-Order Conditioning?

Fedorchak and Bolles (1987) discussed a conceptualization of saccharin-mediated flavor conditioning that deserves restating here. This was the possibility of regarding saccharin not as a US but as an "innate" CS that elicits an expectancy of caloric aftereffects. Saccharin is consumed almost as avidly as sucrose (Smith & Duffy, 1957), and it also causes hypoglycemia (Deutsch, 1974). Just like the hypoglycemic CR to a glucose-associated flavor extinguishes when the glucose is removed, saccharin presented repeatedly (and, of course, without caloric aftereffects) also "extinguishes" its ability to cause hypoglycemia (Deutsch, 1974). For these reasons, if saccharin is recast as a CS (the CS1, in second-order conditioning parlance), then an arbitrary flavor attached to it could be considered a second-order CS (the CS2). Enhancing this argument are reports that conditioned responses to second-order CSs can be insensitive to the same US revaluation manipulations that effectively alter first-order conditioned responses (Holland, 1981; Holland & Rescorla, 1975). These findings strengthen the second-order flavor conditioning analogy because intake of saccharin-associated flavors (CS2) is not enhanced by hunger (Fedorchak & Bolles, 1987; Holder, 1991), even though consumption of saccharin itself (CS1) clearly is (Smith & Duffy, 1957).

Another way to test the second-order conceptualization of saccharin-mediated CFPs is suggested by a recent study by Yin, Barnet, and Miller (1994). These researchers found that second-order excitatory conditioned responses that appeared early in conditioning were eliminated (and eventually transformed into inhibitory responses) by extended CS2 → CS1 pairings (in the absence of the US). If the same pattern of results were to occur across extended flavor → saccharin pairings, it would suggest that the factor reinforcing the saccharin-associated flavor preference in the early stages of conditioning was the sweet-elicited expectation of caloric aftereffects and that the progressive weakening of that expectation through repeated noncaloric episodes eventually led to a corresponding loss of preference for the saccharin-associated flavor. The noted outcome, combined with the already documented invulnerability to US revaluation, would provide further support that saccharin behaves like a CS, rather than a US, in the way it transmits its positive affective value to a novel target flavor. If the conditioned responses generated by the US events described earlier—exposure to quail and seeing or smelling food in an anticipatory nosepoking situation—were found to be both invulnerable to US revaluation and eliminated by extended conditioning, these events also might be construed as CSs that derive their second-order reinforcing power from soon-to-be-violated, possibly innate, expectancies.

Resistance to Extinction of Conditioned Flavor Preferences

In addition to the greater asymptotic strength of calorie-mediated CFPs, there is also a growing body of evidence that such flavor preferences are extremely resistant to extinction. In the most recent report of this effect, Drucker, Ackroff, and Sclafani (1994, Experiment 2) conditioned a strong preference for a flavored solution CS+ through intragastric polycose infusion (the caloric reinforcer) and then observed how behavior toward this CS+ and a CS− flavor (that had been paired with water infusions) changed during a 20-day, two-bottle extinction period. Early in extinction, they observed a quick drop-off in absolute intake of the CS+ flavor combined with no change in CS− consumption, which was low throughout. After the seventh of these daily extinction sessions, the CS+ intake leveled off, but it remained at a point significantly higher than CS− intake. This relative difference, the basic "preference," remained stable throughout the remaining 14 days of extinction. Mehiel (1991) and Elizalde and Sclafani (1990b) earlier had noticed a similar persistence of preference during repeated choice tests.

In one of my last experiments in Bolles's lab (Fedorchak, 1988), I also attempted to extinguish the calorie-mediated preference of a group of rats. After 5% ethanol had served as the caloric US, I gave the rats 2 days each of nonreinforced, single-bottle exposure to the CS+ and the CS− (grape and orange Kool-Aid flavors). Prior to extinction, all rats had demonstrated a solid preference for the CS+ flavor over the CS− flavor while hungry (18 ml vs. 4 ml), as well as the typically smaller satiation-size preference when not hungry (approximately 6 ml vs. 3 ml). In a two-bottle choice test conducted after the single-bottle extinction exposures, all rats showed the smaller satiation-sized preference under both hunger and satiation conditions. What seemed to have extinguished was the associative quality that supported the hunger effect. The basic preference was still there, but now it was one that remained stable in the face of changing hunger levels. It is interesting that Ramirez (1994) found, after 4 days of extinction, that a still reliable dextrose-reinforced flavor preference was also unaffected by increases in hunger level. He did not evaluate the effect of hunger prior to extinction, so it is not clear whether his data show a loss of the effect or the hunger effect was not there to begin with. However, his rats lost some of their preference at the point in extinction when the hunger test was carried out, and they did fail to react to the hunger change; thus his finding may confirm mine.

In attempting to understand the particular changes in preference they observed during extinction (quick drop in CS+ intake, followed by a persistent and unchanging lower magnitude preference for CS+ over CS−), Drucker et al. (1994) suggested that nutrient-based flavor preferences "may involve 'expectancy learning' (the flavor comes to signal nutrition) as well as 'hedonic conditioning' (the flavor comes to 'taste better')" (p. 706) and that the former type of learning may be more vulnerable to extinction than the latter. To the extent that one could equate expectancy learning with vulnerability to US revaluation, the possibility that extinction might selectively eliminate the hunger effect (a form of US revaluation), but not the basic preference, could be seen as support for a dual "expectancy–hedonic" associative framework for calorie-mediated CFPs.

The Nature of Conditioned Flavor Preferences

One issue yet to be addressed regarding conditioned flavor preferences concerns whether flavor conditioning generates a new incentive value that independently drives up intake of the US-paired flavor or whether conditioning merely redistributes the rat's attention toward the paired flavor and away from the unpaired flavor, without creating new incentive for consumption per se. Most CFP studies have employed the differential (CS+/CS−) conditioning arrangement, in which one of two flavor alternatives is paired with a US. This two-bottle method is probably the most sensitive means of detecting learned associations (e.g., Elizalde & Sclafani, 1990b), but it does not reveal anything about the underlying dynamics of the preference generated by these associations.

One possibility regarding the nature of these conditioned preferences is that they reflect absolute increases in intake of the US-paired flavor, with no change in consumption of the alternate flavor. Alternatively, such CFPs might represent only a redistribution of the relative preference between the two flavor alternatives, with no real change in overall consumption (i.e., with no real added incentive to consume). One might envision the redistribution hypothesis as a case in which rats enter the flavor conditioning situation predisposed to treat any *taste* as food and all that flavor conditioning does is make one food relatively *better* than the other. Here, conditioned rats eat the same total amount as nonconditioned rats but satisfy most of this intake from the newly preferred source. Alternatively, perhaps the rat begins with no such "taste = food" preconception and conditioning creates the only food it will ever encounter in the choice test situation. In this case, "eating" is not even possible until after conditioning, and when hungry, conditioned rats naturally consume more than nonconditioned rats.

Regardless of how this issue might be conceptualized, the information needed to determine whether a preference for a CS+ flavor over a CS− flavor represents an absolute increase or a redistribution is relatively straightforward: One needs to know how much of both flavor cues rats would ingest if neither cue had ever been explicitly paired with the US throughout conditioning.

The value of this comparison condition is that it controls for changes in flavor value that might occur during the conditioning process that are independent of the developing CS-US association but may nevertheless be caused by experience with the US. Such nonspecific US effects could raise, lower, or have no effect on a rat's general motivation to eat or drink at test time, and having a baseline of such *nonassociative* changes is absolutely essential for understanding the precise nature of the types of intake changes specifically attributable to the CS-US *association*. In short, to know whether, for example, a 10-ml CS+ versus 2-ml CS− preference is the product of enhanced CS+ intake, decreased CS− intake, or some combination of these influences, one must know whether a "both flavors unpaired" control group would consume 4, 20, or 12 ml, respectively, of both flavor cues combined during the choice test. By clearly separating intake driven by the CS-US association from intake guided by nonassociative influences, this particular control arrangement has the potential to reveal fundamental differences in the underlying nature of seemingly similar flavor preferences.

In a recent experiment (Fedorchak, 1993), I employed the "both flavors unpaired" group to evaluate the underlying nature of an ethanol-reinforced flavor preference. Specifically, I compared the preference patterns of rats that had received explicit CS-US pairings, in which one of two flavor cues was always paired with a 5% ethanol reinforcer, with the preference patterns of control rats who always experienced both flavors unpaired with the ethanol US. All rats were presented with one flavored solution (e.g., grape) on Day 1, an alternate flavor (e.g., orange) on Day 2, and plain water on Day 3 of a series of 3-day conditioning cycles. For half the rats, 5% ethanol always accompanied one of the flavors but not the other. For the others, the ethanol was not paired with either flavor, but it appeared in the plain water on the 3rd day.

After conditioning, I gave all rats a two-bottle, "CS-only" choice test. During this test, the normally conditioned rats drank 12 ml of ethanol flavor versus 2.1 ml of neutral flavor (a typical preference), whereas the group in which both flavors were unpaired drank very little of either flavor (6.1 ml total, about equally distributed between both flavors). Because this 14.1 ml of total consumption by the normally conditioned rats represented an absolute increase over control levels (6.1 ml), I concluded that the ethanol US added new, intake-driving value to its associated flavor—that it created new incentive value, as opposed to merely redistributing existing incentive value without adding anything new to the system.

Ethanol is a caloric US, and it also supports a hunger-sensitive flavor preference. Thus an early prediction regarding other flavor preferences would be that all calorie-based preferences reflect new incentive value, with caloric USs perhaps generating a food quality that induces hungry rats to "eat" rather than drink the flavors (Mook & Cseh, 1981). Indeed, the factors that promote the hunger effect may be the same as those that create new incentive value. In contrast, preferences reinforced by noncaloric USs (e.g., tastable or pharmacological) may turn out to represent redistributions; that is, these USs might alter relative preference without changing the net incentive for consumption.

In addition to helping reveal the infrastructure of different types of CFPs, the "both flavors unpaired" condition might shed some light on the types of changes that occur during extinction. Perhaps, for example, the high intake of the CS+ early in extinction, as observed by Drucker et al. (1994), reflects the existence of new incentive (as evidenced by greater overall consumption compared to control animals). Later, however, when intake of the CS+ levels off yet remains above CS− levels, that lingering preference may represent only a redistribution of the same amount of total incentive available to the control animals. In other words, the normally conditioned rats at this point in extinction could be retaining their preference while consuming no more, overall, than unpaired animals. Finally, the point in extinction when preferences are no longer affected by hunger changes may also be the point when only redistribution forces remain, and that, in turn, may be when the preference stabilizes at a lower level that persists, with no reconditioning, perhaps indefinitely.

At this point it may be apparent that the "absolute incentive−relative redistribution" distinction that my "both flavors unpaired" comparison condition was designed to sort out sounds quite similar to the "expectancy−hedonic" distinction offered by Drucker et al. (1994). However, until the various interrelationships described in the last segment of this chapter are more fully evaluated, the possibility that they are the same will remain speculative. For now, what is clear is that different researchers have independently observed patterns in their data that have stimulated thinking about dual associative mechanisms in the underlying nature of conditioned flavor preferences. This suggests that there is something there worth pursuing. Funny, that is what Bolles would have said.

References

Balleine, B. (1992). Instrumental performance following a shift in primary motivation depends on incentive learning. *Journal of Experimental Psychology: Animal Behavior Processes, 18,* 236−250.

Bolles, R. C. (1978). *Learning theory* (2nd ed.). San Francisco: Holt, Rinehart & Winston.

Bolles, R. C. (1983). A "mixed model" of taste preference. In R. Mellgren (Ed.), *Animal cognition and behavior* (pp. 65−82). Amsterdam: North-Holland.

Bolles, R. C., & Fedorchak, P. M. (1984, November). *Blocking of an ethanol-mediated taste preference.* Paper presented at the 25th annual meeting of the Psychonomic Society, San Antonio, TX.

Bolles, R. C., Hayward, L., & Crandall, C. (1981). Conditioned taste preferences based on caloric density. *Journal of Experimental Psychology: Animal Behavior Processes, 7,* 59–69.

Bolles, R. C., & Mehiel, R. (1982). *Conditioned taste preferences based on the calories in ethanol.* Paper presented at the 23rd annual meeting of the Psychonomic Society, Minneapolis, MN.

Capaldi, E. D., Campbell, D. H., Sheffer, J. D., & Bradford, J. P. (1987). Conditioned flavor preferences based on delayed caloric consequences. *Journal of Experimental Psychology: Animal Behavior Processes, 13,* 150–155.

Capaldi, E. D., Owens, J., & Palmer, K. A. (1994). Effects of food deprivation on learning and expression of flavor preferences conditioned by saccharin or sucrose. *Animal Learning and Behavior, 22,* 173–180.

Deutsch, R. (1974). Conditioned hypoglycemia: A mechanism for saccharin-induced sensitivity to insulin in the rat. *Journal of Comparative and Physiological Psychology, 86,* 350–358.

Drucker, D. B., Ackroff, K., & Sclafani, A. (1994). Nutrient-conditioned flavor preference and acceptance in rats: Effects of deprivation state and nonreinforcement. *Physiology and Behavior, 56,* 701–707.

Elizalde, G., & Sclafani, A. (1988). Starch-based conditioned flavor preferences in rats: Influence of taste, calories, and CS-US delay. *Appetite, 11,* 179–200.

Elizalde, G., & Sclafani, A. (1990a). Fat appetite in rats: Flavor preferences conditioned by nutritive and non-nutritive oil emulsions. *Appetite, 15,* 189–197.

Elizalde, G., & Sclafani, A. (1990b). Flavor preferences conditioned by intragastric Polycose: A detailed analysis using an electronic esophagus preparation. *Physiology and Behavior, 47,* 63–77.

Fanselow, M. S., & Birk, J. (1982). Flavor-flavor associations induce hedonic shifts in taste preference. *Animal Learning and Behavior, 10,* 223–228.

Fedorchak, P. M. (1988). [Extinction eliminates the hunger effect.] Unpublished raw data.

Fedorchak, P. M. (1993, April). *Conditioned flavor preference: Absolute incentive or relative hedonic shift?* Paper presented at the 64th annual meeting of the Eastern Psychological Association, Washington, DC.

Fedorchak, P. M., & Bolles, R. C. (1986). Differential outcome effect using a biologically neutral outcome difference. *Journal of Experimental Psychology: Animal Behavior Processes, 12,* 125–130.

Fedorchak, P. M., & Bolles, R. C. (1987). Hunger enhances the expression of calorie- but not taste-mediated conditioned flavor preferences. *Journal of Experimental Psychology: Animal Behavior Processes, 13,* 73–79.

Fedorchak, P. M., & Bolles, R. C. (1988). Nutritive expectancies mediate cholecystokinin's suppression-of-intake effect. *Behavioral Neuroscience, 102,* 451–455.

Garcia, J., & Koelling, R. (1966). Relation of cue to consequence in avoidance learning. *Psychonomic Science, 4,* 123–124.

Hayward, L. (1983). The role of oral and postingestive cues in the conditioning of taste preferences based on differing caloric density and caloric outcome in weanling and mature rats. *Animal Learning and Behavior, 11,* 325–331.

Holder, M. D. (1991). Conditioned preferences for the taste and odor components of flavors: Blocking but not overshadowing. *Appetite, 17,* 29–45.

Holland, P. C. (1981). The effects of satiation after first- and second-order appetitive conditioning in rats. *Pavlovian Journal of Biological Science, 16,* 18–24.

Holland, P. C., & Rescorla, R. A. (1975). The effects of two ways of devaluing the unconditioned stimulus after first- and second-order appetitive conditioning. *Journal of Experimental Psychology: Animal Behavior Processes, 1,* 355–363.

Holloway, K. S., & Domjan, M. (1993a). Sexual approach conditioning: Tests of unconditioned stimulus devaluation using hormone manipulations. *Journal of Experimental Psychology: Animal Behavior Processes, 19,* 47–55.

Holloway, K. S., & Domjan, M. (1993b). Sexual approach conditioning: Unconditioned stimulus factors. *Journal of Experimental Psychology: Animal Behavior Processes, 19,* 38–46.

Holman, E. W (1975). Immediate and delayed reinforcers for flavor preferences in rats. *Learning and Motivation, 6,* 91–100.

Kamin, L. J. (1969). Predictability, surprise, attention, and conditioning. In B. A. Campbell & R. M. Church (Eds.), *Punishment and aversive behavior.* New York: Appleton-Century-Crofts.

Mehiel, R. (1991). Hedonic-shift conditioning with calories. In R. C. Bolles (Ed.), *The hedonics of taste.* Hillsdale, NJ: Erlbaum.

Mehiel, R., & Bolles, R. C. (1984). Learned flavor preferences based on caloric outcome. *Animal Learning and Behavior, 12,* 421–427.

Mehiel, R., & Bolles, R. C. (1988). Learned flavor preferences based on calories are independent of initial hedonic value. *Animal Learning and Behavior, 16,* 383–387.

Mook, D. G., & Cseh, C. L. (1981). Release of feeding by the sweet taste in rats: The influence of body weight. *Appetite, 2,* 15–34.

Puerto, A., Deutsch, J. A., Molina, F., & Roll, P. L. (1976). Rapid rewarding effects of intragastric injection. *Behavioral Biology, 18,* 123–134.

Ramirez, I. (1994). Flavor preferences conditioned with starch in rats. *Animal Learning and Behavior, 22,* 181–187.

Sherman, J. E., Hickis, C. F., Rice, A. G., Rusiniak, K. W., & Garcia, J. (1983). Preferences and aversions for stimuli paired with ethanol. *Animal Learning and Behavior, 11,* 101–106.

Simbayi, L., Boakes, R. A., & Burton, M. J. (1986). Can rats learn to associate a flavour with the delayed delivery of food? *Appetite, 7,* 41–53.

Smith, M., & Duffy, M. (1957). Consumption of sucrose and saccharin by hungry and satiated rats. *Journal of Comparative and Physiological Psychology, 50,* 65–69.

Tordoff, M. G., & Friedman, M. I. (1986). Hepatic portal glucose infusions decrease food intake and increase food preference. *American Journal of Physiology, 251,* R192–R196.

Yin, H., Barnet, R. C., & Miller, R. R. (1994). Second-order conditioning and Pavlovian conditioned inhibition: Operational similarities and differences. *Journal of Experimental Psychology: Animal Behavior Processes, 20,* 419–428.

13

The Consummatory Rat: The Psychological Hedonism of Robert C. Bolles

Ronald Mehiel

Robert Bolles was a psychological hedonist in the tradition of Epicurus, Bain, Bentham, and Young, among others. The purpose of this chapter is to show how my work investigating conditioned flavor preferences has been guided by his notion that behavior is ultimately organized by psychological hedonism. The animal's behavior is most simply explained by the organizing calculus of the greatest pleasure principle (Bentham, in Reese, 1980). I lead off with a discussion of psychological hedonism: how behavior is organized hedonistically and how food liking is a good example of this phenomenon. Next, I explore physiological mechanisms, specifically cholecystokinin (CCK) and the opioid antagonist naloxone. Finally, I examine the problem of the two-bottle test.

Psychological Hedonism Defined

There is an old but persistent idea that reason and intellect are somehow above emotion and that feelings, or affective responses, tend to cloud decision making. People are apt to make mistakes when they are angry. We "see red" and so behave in ways that later, under the cool light of nonemotional intellect, we wish we had not. We can all understand this kind of logic, because to one degree or another, we have all looked back on our own behavior and wished we had not been "swayed by emotion."

For as long as that idea has persisted, however, there has been another idea, developed in opposition, that the emotions are part of the intellect, that what feels good is the right thing to do, and that what hurts is wrong. This argument has been made on the molecular level, known as reinforcement theory (cf. Bain, 1859; Morgan, 1890; Spencer, 1855; Thorndike, 1898), and on the molar level (cf. Gassendi, 1649/1993; Mill, 1843), concerning what is moral for society in general. One can account for individual differences by postulating different frames of temporal or latitudinal reference (Locke, 1690).

Behavior Is Organized Hedonistically

When I first met Robert Bolles, he was talking about affective, or hedonic, responses and the way in which they organize behavior. If one thinks of the rat as an animal that can easily associate stimuli with its own hedonic responses to those stimuli and one that has a built-in set of behaviors that express the psychological (or hedonic) state, then we have an extremely efficient animal, capable of responding adaptively in almost any context. Bolles (1970) developed species-specific defense reaction (SSDR) theory as an example of this kind of organized behavior system. The wonderful thing about the system—the reason it was so successful for him—was that it was an elegant old idea. Once the animal learns that a particular context is dangerous (e.g., produces shock), its behavior is perfectly suited to avoid that context. It is suddenly extremely cautious, slow moving, and attentive. It will leave the area if at all possible. It need not, indeed it cannot, *learn* to perform these behaviors. The behaviors are all in place on the first trial. It is the organization of the behavior that is made possible by the negative hedonic psychological state of the animal.

Bolles talked about Garcia's work with conditioned taste aversions (e.g., Garcia & Koelling, 1966) and interpreted the phenomenon as another example of hedonic learning. The animal had to hate tastes that were paired with illness. It was the most parsimonious way of thinking about it. Eating behavior had to be subject to the same kinds of organization by hedonic state as defensive behavior was. It was no huge step to think that there must be some positive affective side to eating.

Food Liking as an Example of Hedonistic Behavior

When I was Bolles's student, he and I gathered as much evidence as we could to support the notion that animals learn to like flavors that are paired with the intake of energy. We used discrimination learning as a paradigm, pairing one flavor with any kind of calorie source we could find, another flavor with either sweet water or plain water, and looking at the change in intake of the flavors in two-bottle tests.

What does it mean to say that a hedonic response organizes behavior? One can take a reductionistic tack and think about the complex constellation of metabolic processes that prepare the animal for, and result from, ingestion. Few of these processes have been looked at through the lens of conditioned flavor preference learning, although some have. One of the problems Bolles and I faced early on in our conceptualization of calorie-based flavor preference learning as a hedonic mechanism was to figure out how the rat managed to count calories. We had overwhelming evidence (Mehiel, 1991) that the rat learns to prefer one flavor over another if the flavor is paired with a relatively dense calorie source such as sucrose, starch, or ethanol. Somehow the rat keeps track of the food value of the solutions and uses the flavor as a tag for that postingestive quality of the caloric solution. We liked to talk about the learning in terms of a shift in hedonic response: The rat was learning to like the flavor. However, the identity of the calorie-counting mechanism remained (and still remains) a mystery.

Physiological Mechanisms: The Case for CCK

When I first heard Paul McHugh talk about his work with CCK at a meeting in New York in 1986, it became clear to me that CCK might serve nicely as a calorie counter and could therefore be a stimulus for flavor preferences based on calories. Bolles and I presented data the next day that we saw as evidence against mere exposure effects in flavor–calorie preference learning (Meheil & Bolles, 1986). We had rats drinking twice as much saccharin as Polycose and other rats drinking twice as much Polycose as saccharin; the preference for the Polycose-paired flavor was the same in both groups. McHugh (McHugh & Moran, 1986) talked about the rate of release of CCK at the duodenum, which he claimed was dependent on the caloric density of what was in the stomach. Those results and ours looked like a perfect match. This hormone could be the elusive calorie counter: the way the animal kept track of calories.

Fedorchak and Bolles (1988) subsequently reported that rats do not show CCK's suppression of intake effect when they are tested with a flavor that has not been explicitly paired with caloric intake. Fedorchak's notion was that the rat learns a "nutritive expectancy" during training. This notion of nutritive expectancy grew out of our discussions in which we argued that the nature of the discrimination—the meaning of the preference—was that the rat learns that one flavor means food and the other does not. I thought that the release of CCK became conditioned to the flavor stimulus. In other words, during the normal chain of events, the rat smells, tastes, and then drinks the solution; digestive reflexes occur (e.g., CCK release); and the animal realizes both an energy gain and a psychological shift in preference for the flavor that initiated the chain. Perhaps there is more than one way to think about the effects of that conditioned release of CCK. Perhaps CCK not only acts reflexively at the gut to control stomach emptying but also has a psychological aspect resulting in increased hedonic response (Mehiel, 1991). We conceptualized the rat as if it had a "yummy meter" in its brain and CCK was nudging that meter toward the positive side. Fedorchak's results showed that the flavor had to be explicitly paired with the caloric solution for exogenously administered CCK to suppress intake. I saw those data fitting nicely with the preceding conceptualization. If the flavor caused a conditioned release of CCK, then adding more CCK through injection would result in a higher level of circulating CCK than is found in rats without the conditioned release owing to lack of explicit pairing during conditioning. As a result, one would see more suppression in the explicitly paired group compared to the nonpaired group, which is what Fedorchak found.

For my dissertation, I did a series of experiments looking at the result of antagonizing CCK during conditioning trials and at the effect of artificially creating a "sham CCK release" by injecting it after flavored saccharin drinking. Rats failed to learn a preference for a sucrose-paired flavor over a saccharin-paired flavor when the antagonist proglumide was given following the drinking bout. In addition, rats learned to prefer a flavor paired with saccharin plus CCK injection over a flavor paired with saccharin and a saline injection (Mehiel, 1991). However, these effects have been hard to replicate. In short, CCK is one physiological aspect of learned calorie-based flavor preferences that has been looked at, although the data are equivocal and not very compelling.

Physiological Mechanisms: The Case for Central Opioids

Another issue I looked at as a graduate student is the relationship between calories and endogenous opioid systems. Candice Pert's work (e.g., Pert, Snowman, & Snyder, 1974) identified areas in the brain that have receptors for opiates, and the Wurtmans' work showed that nutrient consumption is at least partly controlled by brain transmitters (J. J. Wurtman, 1985) and that transmitter levels are reciprocally controlled by nutrient consumption (R. J. Wurtman, 1983). Steve Woods's research group was starting to talk about food as a drug (Woods & Strubbe, 1994). In 1994 I focused on how to test behaviorally for opioid responses in the flavor preference paradigm.

Effect of Naloxone on Flavor Preference

Central systems utilizing endogenous opioids as transmitters are believed by some researchers to mediate the psychological experience of reward. For example, naloxone (an opioid antagonist) has been shown to reduce the incentive value of sweetness in humans without affecting levels of hunger (Fantino, Hosotte, & Apelbaum, 1986). By antagonizing the central "reward system" that utilizes brain opioids, naloxone presumably makes food taste less good. It has been found that naloxone has no effect on the latency for mice-killing rats to kill their prey but does greatly increase the latency to eat the mice (Walsh, White, & Albert, 1984). Naloxone reliably shifts preference ratings for sweets such as saccharin and sucrose up the concentration gradient (Cooper, 1983; LeMagnon, Marfaing-Jallat, Miceli, & Devos, 1980; Lynch & Libby, 1983; Siviy & Reid, 1983). "Put plainly, the pleasure or palatability of consumed solid foods or liquids is thought to depend upon endogenous opioid activity" (Cooper & Kirkham,1990, p. 91).

I did several experiments looking at the effect of naloxone on the preference for a flavor that had been paired with calories (Mehiel, 1996). In the first experiment, I tested the idea that naloxone would reduce the expression of a preference for a flavor that had been paired with calories. I conditioned 8 male rats to prefer either cherry or grape flavor by pairing one of the flavors with 10% w/v (weight to volume) dextrose and the other with tap water. Conditioning proceeded in the usual way as described previously. Following four 23-hour exposures to each flavored solution, rats were tested over 2 hours on 2 consecutive days. Prior to one test, rats were injected intraperitoneally with 4 mg/kg naloxone hydrochloride in saline vehicle, 1 ml/kg. Fifteen minutes after the injections, rats were given the usual two-bottle preference test of the two flavors. Prior to the other test, rats were injected with saline vehicle alone, and the same testing procedure followed. Drugs were counterbalanced between rats across test days. The results were that naloxone reduced intake of the CS+ by 55 percent compared to the saline trial. Naloxone had no effect on the CS−.

A second experiment sought evidence that naloxone's effect on preference was not restricted to dextrose-paired flavors. Another group of 8 male rats was conditioned to prefer either cherry or grape flavor by pairings with 5.5% v/v (volume to volume) ethanol. The other flavor was sweetened with 0.25% sodium saccharin. As usual, flavors were counterbalanced across solutions. I invoked a yoking procedure to ensure equal consumption of the conditioning solutions. Each rat's intake of ethanol solution was measured after each odd day of conditioning, and the amount consumed became the amount of saccharin solution offered to that rat on even days. Conditioning lasted 16 days. The testing procedure of Experiment 1 was modified such that each rat was tested four times. Tests were one-bottle tests, either CS+ or CS− and each test was preceded by either 4 mg/kg naloxone hydrochloride intraperitoneally in saline or by saline alone. Tests were 3 hours long. The results of the first experiment essentially were replicated. Naloxone reduced intake of the flavor that had been paired with ethanol but did not reduce intake of the saccharin-paired flavor.

The third experiment looked at the effect of naloxone administration during the conditioning trials. If naloxone reduced intake by reducing palatability, it seemed possible that, during flavor–calorie conditioning trials, no preference for a calorie-paired flavor would develop. I gave rats experience with flavored dextrose and flavored saccharin, but half the rats had naloxone paired with the dextrose and the other half had naloxone paired with the saccharin.

Sixteen adult male rats were assigned to either a naloxone–dextrose (NAL-DEX) condition or a naloxone–saccharin (NAL-SAC) condition by matching of their weights. Grape and cherry Kool-Aid drinks were used as flavor stimuli; the caloric solution was 10% w/v dextrose, and the noncaloric solution was 0.25% w/v saccharin. Naloxone and saline were administered as in the prior experiments. In Phase 1, the rats were trained to drink during a 1-hour period each day for 5 days. In Phase 2, the rats were injected with their respective drug, and 15 minutes later a 1-hour conditioning trial took place. The next day, the rats received the other drug and the other solution. Conditioning proceeded in this manner for 8 days. Each rat in group NAL-DEX had four trials with naloxone injections followed by access to flavored dextrose and four trials with saline injections with access to flavored saccharin. Rats in group NAL-SAC had the same treatments, but the drug–solute relationship was reversed. Following conditioning, all the rats took part in a two-bottle test of cherry- and grape-flavored mixtures of 10% w/v dextrose and 0.25% w/v saccharin.

Naloxone suppressed intake of both flavored saccharin and flavored dextrose in conditioning trials. On the last day of conditioning, mean dextrose solution consumption was 17 ml for rats in group NAL-SAC and 7.9 ml for those in group NAL-DEX. Similarly, consumption of saccharin solutions was suppressed by naloxone. Group NAL-DEX drank 13.2 ml on the last day, whereas group NAL-SAC drank 5.4 ml.

Intakes during the two-bottle test were subjected to analysis of variance, and a significant Group × Flavor interaction was revealed. Rats in group NAL-SAC preferred the dextrose-paired flavor (11 vs. 6.5 ml), whereas rats in group NAL-DEX preferred the saccharin-paired flavor (11.5 vs. 3.5 ml).

It seemed unlikely that the failure of rats to prefer the dextrose-paired flavor in group NAL-DEX was simply an aversion to any solute paired with naloxone. Daily intakes of the naloxone-paired solution increased over conditioning days in both groups. Another explanation might be that the naloxone was interfering with physiological mechanisms (peripheral or central opioid systems) that integrate hedonic responses to flavors. Perhaps during flavor–calorie conditioning, opioid system activity becomes a conditioned response to the flavor CS+. The final experiment in this series was a test of whether or not such activity could be measured indirectly.

Naloxone blocked the expression of preference for a flavor that had been paired with calories over a flavor that had been paired with water. It did so when the calories were in the form of dextrose or when they were from ethanol. When naloxone was given during conditioning trials, the preference learning did not develop.

Opioid System Activity as Conditioned Response

The most exciting of these experiments was the final one, in which I gave the rats the usual flavored calorie versus flavored no-calorie discrimination training and then measured fear in a shock box. I gave the rats a brief taste of either their calorie-paired flavor or their non-calorie-paired flavor and put them in a shock box where they received a small shock every 60 seconds for 8 minutes. Freezing was significantly reduced in the animals that had tasted their calorie-paired flavor.

In this final experiment, I reasoned that because increased levels of endogenous opioids decrease fear and therefore decrease the freezing response to shock (Fanselow, 1991), another way of testing for the contribution of "reward system" activity aroused by flavor–calorie conditioning might be to probe for that activity by using freezing as an index of opioid activity following ingestion of a flavor that had been paired with calories.

Fourteen male rats were conditioned to prefer either orange or grape flavor by pairing one of the flavors with 10% w/v dextrose and the other with 0.25% w/v saccharin. Conditioning proceeded in the manner previously described. Following the conditioning trials, rats were presented with either their calorie-paired flavor or their saccharin-paired flavor for 2 minutes. After the rat had sampled its bottle, it was placed in an operant chamber in which shock was administered. Shocks were delivered at the end of each 60-second period for 8 minutes. The rats were continuously observed and the percentage of time in each minute that the rat was freezing was noted. Observers were blind as to whether the rat had tasted its CS− or CS+ flavor. On the second test day, each rat was given the reverse flavor and was again tested for freezing in the shock box.

The results of the eight freezing observations during each test, the data of interest, were subjected to a repeated measures analysis of variance with dextrose-paired flavor versus saccharin-paired flavor and shock trials as within-rat factors. The rats froze more after tasting their saccharin-paired flavor than after tasting their dextrose-paired flavor, $F(1, 26) = 4.83$, $p < .05$. This finding brought converging evidence to the idea that flavor–calorie preferences may be mediated by endogenous opioid reward system responses.

During flavor–calorie conditioning, the rat learns to like the flavor, and part of the physiology of liking involves activity of endogenous opioid mechanisms; therefore, liking provides analgesia in the shock box. These data appear to provide evidence that learning has an important hedonic component. Long ago, Young (1959) made the point that stimuli have informational value (e.g., nutritive expectancy) as well as affective value (e.g., liking). This idea, though elegant, has turned out to be difficult to provide evidence for.

The Problem With the Two-Bottle Test of Preference

Lately, my own investigations have been focused on the two-bottle test. Typically, in the kind of flavor–calorie experiments described here, one tests the rats for preference learning by giving them a two-bottle test in which they can choose to drink either or both of the flavors that served as stimuli during conditioning. A preference ratio for the flavor that had been paired with calories is computed by forming a ratio of the intake of that flavor to total intake. If a rat drinks only from the bottle containing a calorie-paired flavor, its preference ratio would be 1.0, and if the rat drank equally from both bottles, the ratio would be .50.

I am looking at the possibility that the noncalorie flavor, because it is a Pavlovian CS−, may bring consummatory inhibition to the test. This inhibition may be acting on intake of the calorie-paired flavor (CS+). One can think of the two-bottle test contextually. Perhaps the CS− provides a context in which drinking is not an adaptive response. Of course the CS+ is also present in the test, and it provides a conflicting contextual cue. (It is a wonder the rat drinks at all.) Alternatively, one can think about the problem hedonically. The rat has learned to like the CS+ and has not learned to like the CS−. One predicts that behavior is organized by the hedonic qualities of the stimuli, and to the degree that the CS+ is more hedonically positive than the CS− is hedonically negative, there should be more intake of the CS+. That is of course what does occur; however, it may be profitable to postulate both mechanisms. The presence of the CS+

organizes the rat's behavior so that ingestion results, and the CS− provides some inhibition.

Ed Seiler (1995) and I have begun to examine this idea by mapping conditioned flavor preference learning onto the peak shift procedure. The peak shift phenomenon results when an animal is trained on a CS− and a CS+ and is then given a generalization test across a range of values around the CS+. To the degree that the trained CS− is close in value on some dimension to the CS+, peak response during the CS+ generalization test along that dimension is shifted away from the trained CS− (e.g., see Hanson, 1959, or Honig & Stewart, 1993).

All other things being equal, 0.30% saccharin is about as good as it gets for a rat. Seiler and I examined baseline intakes of various concentrations of saccharin in several groups of naive rats, and as usual, the greatest consumption was at the 0.30% concentration. Subsequently, we trained two new groups of rats to prefer the taste of either 0.24% or 0.16% saccharin over 0.30% saccharin by pairing one of the lower concentrations with Polycose and giving the rats equal exposure to the 0.30% saccharin without any calories in solution. The result of using the different saccharin concentrations as a CS+ and a CS− was that the calories from the Polycose caused the preference to shift away from the 0.30% solution to the weaker concentration. Finally, we gave generalization tests across a range of saccharin concentrations. The rats' peak intake was not at the concentration (either 0.16 or 0.24) that had been the CS+; rather, it was shifted away from the 0.30 CS− level, and the closer to 0.30% the CS+ had been in conditioning, the more they were shifted. In the generalization test, rats preferred concentrations that were even weaker than the CS+. This suggested that the two-bottle test is indeed a candidate for inhibition owing to the presence of the CS− flavor.

Perhaps there is something strange about the two-bottle test. My colleagues and I want to look at relative acceptability, because that is how we conceptualize liking. What could it mean to say that the rat likes the calorie-paired flavor if there is no flavor to compare the liking to? But if the CS− flavor is providing inhibition during the test, then the measure is in some way unclean.

For several years I have been looking at the conditioning mechanisms that control the learning of the flavor preference discrimination and, in particular, looking for typical Pavlovian effects such as CS or US preexposure, retardation, and sensory preconditioning. These phenomena have turned out to be elusive. However, I always used the two-bottle test as a probe for these effects. Lately, with the use of one-bottle tests, like magic, the effects have turned up.

Conclusion

The guiding principle in my work has been and remains the idea that if the rat can learn what it likes, and if it has built-in mechanisms that adjust its liking toward flavors that maximize energy consumption, then it has an elegant learning mechanism that is basically hedonic in the way it is organized. This was the central concept that I learned from Robert Bolles—that behavior is organized hedonically. I keep rediscovering things that Bolles taught me years ago: "The rat is always right. He is doing what he is supposed to. Maybe you just don't understand."

References

Bain, A. (1859). *The emotions and the will.* London: Parker.

Bolles, R. C. (1970). Species-specific defense reactions and avoidance learning. *Psychological Review, 77,* 32–48.

Cooper, S. J. (1983). Effects of opiate agonists and antagonists on fluid intake and saccharin choice in the rat. *Neuropharmacology, 22,* 323–328.

Cooper, S. J., & Kirkham, T. C. (1990). Basic mechanisms of opioids' effects on eating and drinking. In L. D. Reid (Ed.), *Opioids, bulimia, & alcohol abuse and alcoholism* (pp. 91–110). New York: Springer-Verlag.

Fanselow, M. J. (1991). Analgesia as a response to aversive Pavlovian conditional stimuli: Cognitive and emotional mediators. In M. R. Denny (Ed.), *Fear, avoidance, and phobias* (pp. 61–86). Hillsdale, NJ: Erlbaum.

Fantino, M., Hosotte, J., & Apelbaum, M. (1986). An opioid antagonist, naltrexone, reduces preference for sucrose in humans. *American Journal of Physiology, 251,* R91–R96.

Fedorchak, P. M., & Bolles, R. C. (1988). Nutritive expectancies mediate cholecystokinin's suppression-of-intake effect. *Behavioral Neuroscience, 102,* 451–455.

Garcia, J., & Koelling, R. A. (1966). Relation of cue to consequence in avoidance learning. *Psychonomic Science 4,* 123–124.

Gassendi, P. (1993). The life and death of Epicurus. In R. C. Bolles (Ed.), *The study of psychology.* Pacific Grove, CA: Brooks/Cole. (Original work published 1649)

Hanson, H. M. (1959). Effects of discrimination training on stimulus generalization. *Journal of Experimental Psychology, 58,* 321–334.

Honig, W. K., & Stewart, K. E. (1993). Relative numerosity as a dimension of stimulus control: The peak shift. *Animal Learning and Behavior, 21,* 346–354.

LeMagnon, J., Marfaing-Jallat, P., Miceli, D., & Devos, M. (1980). Pain modulating and reward systems: A single brain mechanism? *Pharmacology, Biochemistry, & Behavior, 12,* 729–733.

Locke, J. (1690). *Essay concerning human understanding.*

Lynch, W. C., & Libby, L. (1983). Naloxone suppresses intake of highly preferred saccharin in food deprived and sated rats. *Life Sciences, 33,* 1909–1914.

McHugh, P. R., & Moran, T. H. (1986). The stomach, cholecystokinin, and satiety. *Federation Proceedings, 45,* 1384–1390.

Mehiel, R., & Bolles, R. C. (1986). *Flavor preference learning: Effects of calories and exposure.* Paper presented at the 57th annual meeting of the Eastern Psychological Association, New York.

Mehiel, R. (1991). Hedonic shift conditioning with calories. In R. C. Bolles (Ed.), *The hedonics of taste* (pp. 107–126). Hillsdale, NJ: Erlbaum.

Mehiel, R. (1996). The effects of naloxone on flavor-calorie preference learning indicate involvement of opioid reward systems. *Psychological Record, 46,* 435–450.

Mill, J. S. (1843). *A system of logic.* London: Longman.

Morgan, C. L. (1890). *Animal life and intelligence.*

Pert, C. B., Snowman, A. M., & Snyder, S. H. (1974). Localization of opiate receptor binding in presynaptic membranes of rat brain. *Brain Research, 70,* 184–188.

Reese, W. L. (1980). *Dictionary of philosophy and religion: Eastern and western thought.* Atlantic Highlands, NJ: Humanities Press.

Seiler, E. A. (1995). *Discriminative flavor-calorie conditioning and its relation to the peak shift phenomenon.* Unpublished master's thesis, University of Pennsylvania, Shippensburg.

Siviy, S. M., & Reid, L. D. (1983). Endorphinergic modulation of acceptability of putative reinforcers. *Appetite 4,* 249–257.

Spencer, H. (1855). *Principles of psychology.* London: Longman.

Thorndike, E. L. (1898). Animal intelligence: An experimental study of the associative processes in animals. *Psychological Review Monograph Supplement, 2*(No. 8).

Walsh, M. L., White, L. R., & Albert, D. J. (1984). Dissociation of prey killing and prey eating by naloxone in the rat. *Pharmacology, Biochemistry, & Behavior, 21,* 5–7.

Woods, S. C., & Strubbe, J. H. (1994). The psychobiology of meals. *Psychonomic Bulletin & Review, 1,* 141–155.

Wurtman, J. J. (1985). Neurotransmitter control of carbohydrate consumption. *Annals of the New York Academy of Sciences, 443,* 145–151.

Wurtman, R. J. (1983). Behavioural effects of nutrients. *Lancet, 1*(8334), 1145–1147.

Young, P. T. (1959). The role of affective processes in learning and motivation. *Psychological Review, 66,* 104–125.

Part IV

Defensive Behavior

14

Stimulus, Environmental, and Pharmacological Control of Defensive Behaviors

D. Caroline Blanchard

Robert Bolles's interest in defensive behaviors was, by his own evaluation (Bolles, 1988), a corollary to and by-product of his career-long focus on learning. However, students tend to absorb what they like: During my last two undergraduate years at Hollins College, I took every class or seminar he offered, absorbing a strong conviction that there are "natural," innately organized response patterns, particularly those involving defense, that require little or no specifically relevant experience to occur effectively in normal animals. I recall that Bolles was concerned with the relationship between these natural behavior patterns and learning. Nonetheless, the learning component was always so much less interesting to me that it slipped right on by, leaving me with a belief in the reality of some innate defensive behaviors and a fascination with the roles that these might play in the emotions and emotional psychopathologies of all mammals, including humans.

The other aspect of the "Bollesian" approach to science that I absorbed is a predilection for descriptive work. Bolles was not uninterested in theory, but he was a strong empiricist in an age when detailed and comprehensive descriptions of behavior were not highly valued, much less regarded as necessary. For such enhanced focus on description as has appeared in psychology over the past 30 years, he deserves at least partial credit. Ethological approaches and methodologies, with their clear and strong descriptive focus, clearly predate Bolles's interest in these matters. However, the (belated) acceptance of ethological approaches by experimental, comparative, and physiological psychologists in the United States, beginning in the 1970s and extending to the 1900s and beyond (with quite a way to go), is in considerable part due to the efforts of Bolles and a few others like him. He demonstrated in his own research the value of describing and quantifying behaviors rather than relying on some contrived, machine-mediated, output. For students of Bolles in the early days, when

Preparation of this chapter was supported by National Science Foundation Grant IBN95-11349.

he was often in the laboratory and putting his own highly skilled fingers into everything, it is not optional to watch animals and to describe and classify their reactions. These are essential steps in the progression toward understanding behavior.

My specific belief in the value of studying innate defensive behaviors and my attitude about how to investigate them are what I gained from Bolles. I have no doubt that there was much more and that I am the poorer for not having understood it all. But these were enough, and they have shaped much of my work over a third of a century.

These influences are apparent in this chapter: the focus on defensive behaviors of animals and an approach that involves detailed descriptions of behaviors and behavior patterns. However, considerable divergence from the approach that Bolles used throughout his research is also seen in this chapter. Consideration of how defensive behaviors can provide animal models or analogues of human emotional psychopathologies requires some attention to the "species specificity" of defense. If these behaviors are indeed specific to the rat (and to the laboratory rat at that), then attempts to draw serious parallels to human response tendencies are doomed to recurrent frustration, if not ultimate failure. The question of species specificity can be approached empirically, and attempts to compare defensive behaviors of laboratory and wild rats and of both of these with mice have been a major feature of the work described here. Finally, there is a divergence of which I am not certain that Bolles ever approved. Defensive behaviors have evolved in the context of a range of threat sources and under differing environmental conditions. Even in so impoverished an animal as a laboratory rat, bred for the lack of some specific defenses and raised and maintained in a small cage in near or total isolation, defensive behaviors to the first (noncontact) encounter with an intense threat source such as an approaching predator show sharp differentiations in accord with important features of the environment and of the spatial relationship of the subject and this threat stimulus. This fact suggests the existence of potentially separable defense systems rather than a unified system in which responses are differentiated on the basis of some single stimulus or motivational parameter such as intensity or on the basis of previously reinforced experience. One means of analyzing the differences between biological systems is through pharmacology, and the results of this approach are also described.

Defensive Behaviors and the Stimuli That Elicit Them

Defensive behaviors are activities that occur in response to the host of life-threatening dangers encountered in every natural environment, from predators, from conspecific attack, and from threatening features of the environment (Endler, 1986). Although all three classes of threatening stimuli are undoubtedly factors in the survival of animals in nature, they do not constitute equally convenient stimuli for laboratory research. Little attempt has been made to bring natural environmental threats into the laboratory. Positive environmental hazards (i.e., as opposed to "negative" threat situations involving the absence of necessities such as food or water) include such features as high places, tight places, and poisonous food items, in addition to a few moving dangers such as spreading fire, flood, and earth movements. With the exception of the literature on conditioned responses to poisoned foods and a few studies on developmental aspects of reactivity to the "visual cliff," these dangers are seldom represented in laboratory research.

Moreover, the "hazard" that *is* typically provided in the laboratory, shock, is virtually never encountered in the real world. It could be argued that shock simply represents a class of objects that are painful to touch, such as sharp or very hot things. However, most of these, unlike shock, give consistent visual or thermal evidence of their noxious qualities prior to contact, and involve salient objects for future identification and avoidance. The sudden and unexpected onset of moderate- to high-level pain that characterizes most shock studies is probably quite rare in the real world, and when it does happen, sudden-onset pain is probably more often associated with predator attack than with an environmental feature.

Conspecific attack is the real-world threat most precisely modeled in laboratory situations, in that the model involves the same stimulus as in nature rather than some simulation of it. Nonetheless, laboratory studies of defensive behaviors do not provide a complete counterpart to the natural environment. Even when efforts are made to produce a natural laboratory habitat, typical features of the real world, such as sufficient space to escape to a distant area, are seldom provided. When they are available, they make a difference (Boice & Adams, 1983).

The use of an attacking conspecific as a threat source also involves another problem. In conspecific fighting, there is a strong mutual interdependence of response between attacker and defender (Takahashi & Blanchard, 1982). It is difficult if not impossible for the experimenter to control the attack pattern of the conspecific attacker; efforts to do so are more likely to halt or distort the attack than to fixate its form in a consistent, albeit natural, pattern. The actions of the threat stimulus may vary considerably from attacker to attacker, from second to second within a bout, and most problematically, with changes in the behavior of the attackee. Therefore, conspecific defense is difficult to analyze cleanly, a situation that produces particular problems with the interpretations of studies of the pharmacology of defense (see R. J. Blanchard & Blanchard, 1994, for a discussion of this problem).

In contrast, judicious selection of a predator can enable precise control over the behavior of this animal. The best predator, in terms of experimental control, is probably a graduate student or an advanced undergraduate. These individuals are of a species that frequently kills rats and mice in the real world; they have the requisite speed and stamina to chase and otherwise threaten the subjects; and they are motivated and able to follow a precise script of how they should do this.

The problem immediately arising in this context is that laboratory rats show relatively little defensive reactivity to an approaching human, in part because of the rats' typically extensive experience with people but, more important, because they have been selected and bred over many generations for a failure to do so (only about 16 generations of selection are required; Naumenko et al., 1989). This laboratory–wild rat difference in defensiveness to human approach and handling, one of the earliest documented phenomena of animal psychology (Stone, 1932; Yerkes, 1913), was an important consideration in our use of wild rather than laboratory rats to characterize the full spectrum of antipredator defenses.

Research Choices: The Rationale for Use of Antipredator Defense Models

The defensive behaviors of rats and mice have been investigated in the context of all three of these classes of threat stimuli, albeit with a nonrepresentative threat stimulus, shock, used to model environmental threat. Although environmental threats represent the most varied group of threatening objects or events in nature, because they are typically immobile, they elicit the least elaborate defensive behaviors. Once such a threat has been identified, defense can be successfully accomplished through avoidance. Even for environmental threats that do move, such as floods, the rate of movement is poorly matched to the capabilities of most mammals, being either too rapid for active defensive behaviors to be successful, such as flight, or so slow that these defenses are not challenged. In either case, there is little environmental pressure for development of the rapid and finely tuned defenses that have evolved in response to conspecific and predator threats.

It seems likely that the most elaborate defenses are those made to attacking conspecifics, for the following reasons:

1. Conspecifics have clear targets for attack and, at least in rats (R. J. Blanchard, Blanchard, et al., 1977), body sites on the opponent that they will *not* attack even if these are undefended. These strong preferences make it adaptive for defenders to conceal the target sites for attack even while freely exposing sites that will not be attacked, resulting in specific defensive maneuvers seen only in response to attacking conspecifics (R. J. Blanchard & Blanchard, 1977).
2. Conspecific attackers are close to the size of their attackees, making defensive threat and attack more important components of the defense pattern, because they are effective.
3. Submission signals, either as positive inhibitors of attack or, more passively, in terms of omission of behaviors that incite the attacker (or, in a specific interpretation, as the concealment of targets of attack; Adams, 1979), should be more effective against conspecifics.

Nonetheless, the similarities of antipredator and conspecific defenses are likely to be much greater than the differences. With reference to (1) in the preceding list, predators also show considerable aiming of bites and blows to specific targets on the body of the prey, particularly when the prey is large enough to be difficult to kill (Seidensticker & McDougal, 1993) or large enough to offer a dangerous defense (Ben-David, Pellis, & Pellis, 1991). In addition, rat bites at predators, like those at conspecific attackers, are targeted toward specific body sites (R. J. Blanchard, C. F. Kleinschmidt, C. Fukunaga-Stinson, & D. C. Blanchard, 1980). Regarding (2) in the list, defensive threat or attack appears to act as a deterrent over a surprisingly wide range of discrepancies between prey and predator size (Ben-David et al., 1991). Finally, although positive submission signals that act to reduce attack would not be expected to occur in antipredator defenses (indeed, they may not occur as part of the rat conspecific defense pattern either), it seems likely that one of the functions of freezing is to reduce the probability of predator attack by eliminating movement, an important elicitor of detection or attack in many predators.

Antipredator defense includes most, though perhaps not all, of the defensive behaviors available to rodents. A predator can also serve as a painless and highly controllable threat stimulus. Antipredator defense models thus provide considerable analytic advantages for gathering precise information on defensive behaviors in rodents, their experiential determinants, and the neural and neurochemical systems controlling them.

Defensive Reactions of Wild and Laboratory Rats to Human Approach and Contact: The Fear/Defense Test Battery

The Fear/Defense Test Battery (F/DTB) is a series of tests measuring reactivity of rats, in most cases to the experimenter, in a variety of situations that permit or restrict various activities. Early versions were used in studies of the effects of brain lesions on defensive behaviors (e.g., D. C. Blanchard, Lee, Williams, & Blanchard, 1981), and more recent versions are employed in studies investigating the effects of anxiolytic and potentially anxiolytic drugs on these behaviors (e.g., R. J. Blanchard et al., 1993). In all of these studies, subjects were wild rats. Additional studies compared wild-trapped wild rats, lab-bred wild rats, and lab rats (R. J. Blanchard, Flannelly, & Blanchard, 1986) or "wild-type" and "domesticated" rat strains resulting from selective breeding of wild rats over 35 generations (D. C. Blanchard et al., 1994) for the presence or absence of defensive threat and attack in response to human handling. With the exception of the last study, done in Siberia and involving a nonstandard though generally similar apparatus, the apparatus and procedures for all of these studies have been comparable. Therefore, data are available on control subjects, consisting of predator-exposed but otherwise unmanipulated animals, from over a dozen F/DTB studies performed over a period of nearly 15 years and using subjects from a variety of sources and with different prior experiences.

In the F/DTB, the rat subject is tested in an oval runway several meters long, that permits unlimited forward locomotion. For 11 control groups of wild-trapped wild rats, the percentage avoidance of the experimenter, who walks toward the subject at a rate of 0.5 m/s, ranged from 85 to 100 percent, with a mean of 97.3 percent. The average distance between the experimenter and the subject when the subject turned to move away (avoidance distance is based on trials on which avoidance occurred) ranged from 2.2 to 4.5 m, with a mean of 2.71.

These two measures strongly indicate that wild-trapped wild rats show near-maximum rates of avoidance and that they avoid when the approaching experimenter is several meters distant. The results of a study of naive lab-reared wild rats (R. J. Blanchard et al., 1986) argue strongly against the view that this behavior reflects prior experience: These animals showed 100 percent avoidance and a virtually identical prey–predator avoidance distance of 2.7 m. In the same study, 57 percent of laboratory rats (Long–Evans strain) also showed avoidance, but with an average predator–subject distance of 0.7 m, representing a 75 percent reduction from the distance at which avoidance was elicited in both wild-trapped and lab-reared wild rats.

Following avoidance testing, the oval runway is converted to an inescapable straight alley by closing a door near one end, and the experimenter again slowly approaches the rat, pausing at 5, 4, 3, 2, 1, and 0.5 m from the subject. Freezing during these pauses was extremely high (during 80% or more of the test intervals) when the experimenter was from 5 to 2 m from the subject, declining slightly at 1 m and abruptly at 0.5 m. Defensive threat vocalizations appeared at 1 m and became very likely at 0.5 m. Jump attacks occurred at the 0.5-m distance. Jump attack was the only measure showing reliable differences between wild-trapped and lab-reared wild rats, with the latter making many fewer jump attacks (M = 1.2) than the former (M = 3.9), although still more than the laboratory animals (0). Bites to the experimenter's gloved hand occurred on 100 percent of attempts to pick up the wild-trapped wild rats and on more than 95 percent of pickups of lab-reared wild rats, but bites never occurred in pickups of laboratory rats. A similar level of difference (i.e., near-maximum levels for wild and zero levels for lab rats) was obtained for jump attacks and bites in response to a terminally anesthetized conspecific brought up to the (confined) subject in an additional F/DTB test (R. J. Blanchard et al., 1986).

These comparisons indicate that the defensive behaviors of wild rats are strongly and systematically different from those of laboratory animals and that most points of difference cannot be attributed to differential prior experience. The view that the difference is based on systematic human selection of rats showing less defensive threat and attack as breeding stock during the domestication of laboratory rats is strongly supported by recent findings: Wild rats selected for minimum threat and biting in response to human handling over 35 generations and animals from the same original source that were similarly maintained but selected for continued display of "wild-type" behavior show differences on these F/DTB tests that parallel those found between wild and laboratory rats (D. C. Blanchard et al., 1994). In both sets of comparisons (i.e., between the two lines of wild rats and between wild and lab rats), most defensive behaviors tended to be reduced in the laboratory, or "domesticated-type," animals, but this difference was most profound with reference to defensive attack and biting.

However, one defensive behavior, freezing, may have been increased in laboratory rats. In a study of conspecific encounters (Takahashi & Blanchard, 1982), laboratory rats tended to show more freezing and more defensive upright positioning than wild rats, suggesting that the pattern of wild–lab rat difference involves a shift from more active forms of defense in the wild rats to freezing in laboratory rats. In addition, when laboratory rats were approached by a cat or a shock prod in a circular runway, they showed only about 50 percent levels of flight, with freezing as the dominant reaction on the trials on which flight did not occur (R. J. Blanchard & Blanchard, 1969). This high level of freezing in an *escapable* situation is in contrast to the virtual absence of freezing for wild rats in an escapable runway.

The F/DTB data (summarized in R. J. Blanchard, Blanchard, & Hori, 1989) suggest the following relationships between particular defensive behaviors and the stimuli and situations that elicit them, in familiar situations and in the absence of pain, for wild rats:

1. When approached by a potential predator in an escapable situation, the predominant reaction is flight, which occurs at a relatively consistent (for that type of predator) distance.
2. When approached by a potential predator in an inescapable situation, the predominant reaction is freezing, over a wide range of prey–predator distances. In an escapable situation, immobility with orientation to the predator tends to occur at distances greater than those required to elicit flight.
3. The number of jumps and the average amplitude of jumps in response to abrupt movement or to a sudden sound increase systematically as the prey–predator distance decreases.
4. Freezing declines abruptly at a distance of about 0.5 m, as defensive threat and attack occur. Freezing is, however, near maximal when the predator approaches to between 3 and 1 meter from the subject. In contrast, if the situation involves a clear escape route, flight occurs at about these same predator–prey distances.
5. Defensive threat and attack occur on about 60 percent of trials at the 0.5-m separation (in males more than females), and they are virtually inevitable when actual contact with the predator (or with the head of an anesthetized conspecific) is made.
6. Laboratory rats show sharply reduced flight and defensive threat or attack in response to a human experimenter or to an anesthetized conspecific. Freezing may represent a much stronger and more dominant defensive behavior for laboratory rats in a variety of situations than for wild rats, indicating that the exclusive use of laboratory rats may bias defense analyses toward freezing.

Temporal Patterns of Defensive Behaviors

F/DTB studies analyze relatively immediate reactions to a physically present, approaching predator. A quite different question involves the patterning of defensive behaviors over time following exposure to a predator. To afford the animals maximum choice of response, these patterns have been measured in a seminatural visible burrow system (VBS) habitat with tunnels and burrows and an open area in which the predator (a cat) is presented. Studies (R. J. Blanchard & Blanchard, 1989) of the response to a brief (15 min) presentation of a cat suggest the following sequence of behavior for laboratory rats in a familiar VBS environment:

1. When the cat is presented in the open area of the VBS, rats located in this open area immediately flee to the tunnels.
2. In the tunnels, they freeze consistently for about 30 minutes, with a less consistent but still high level of freezing for several hours thereafter. Freezing invariably involves orientation to the tunnel through which the rat ran in its flight from the cat and through which, presumably, the cat might appear in pursuit.
3. Ultrasonic (18–24 kHz) cries are common during the hour after cat presentation and may serve as "alarm" signals to listening conspecifics (R. J. Blanchard, Blanchard, Agullana, & Weiss, 1991; Brudzynski & Chiu, 1995).
4. As freezing breaks up, the rat approaches the entrance to the open area, showing risk assessment (RA) behaviors such as orientation, "stretch attend," and head out (of the tunnel) and scanning. These constitute the major defenses seen from a period several hours after cat exposure until the animal has essentially returned to normal, perhaps 24 hours later.
5. Latency to reemerge onto the open area where the cat was seen is about 6 hours for dominant males, longer for subordinates.
6. Many nondefensive activities are virtually abolished during this entire sequence, for 24 hours or more.

Although the sequence is initiated by a specific stimulus event, cat presentation, the remainder unfolds without further stimulus change other than that provided by the subjects' own activities. The cat exits the open area quietly when a partition is lifted, at a time when no rats are in visual contact with the open area. My colleagues and I have interpreted this sequence of behaviors as involving a diminution in the perceived intensity of threat over time, in the absence of further threat, mediated largely by feedback from RA activities indicating that the cat is no longer present.

Another Species: Mouse Defensive Behaviors in the VBS and the Mouse Defense Test Battery

The defensive behaviors and patterns described are clearly typical of rats, albeit with some differences between wild and laboratory rats owing to selective breeding, but are they *specific* to rats? This question is important because if each species has its own "species-specific" defensive behaviors, it will be difficult to make generalizations concerning defense from rats to other species, including people. In an effort to determine just how "species-specific" these defensive behaviors are, my colleagues and I recently examined the defenses of Swiss–Webster laboratory mice, first in a mouse-scaled VBS for an overall view of mouse defenses over time (R. J. Blanchard et al., 1995) and second in a Mouse Defense Test Battery (MDTB) for independent elicitation of particular defensive behaviors.

As with rats, cat presentation in the open area of the VBS elicits rapid retreat to the burrows for any mouse on the surface. However, instead of remaining in the depths of the tunnel system, mice return to the tunnel segment nearest the open area, to peer out at the cat and then retreat, about once per minute during the initial 5-minute period of cat presentation. Following these several viewings of the cat, mice retreat down the tunnels and remain there, with a surface reentry latency of over 20 hours. During reemerging sequences, hours after the initial cat presentation, RA again occurs, with head out and scanning.

The initial RA, occurring immediately after cat presentation, is one of two major differences between the mouse and rat defense patterns. The other is a lack of ultrasonic vocalization by mice in this situation (personal observation). These differences are likely related, and both may reflect the more solitary lifestyle of mice: In the absence of an alarm (the vocalizations), each mouse individually must see the threat stimulus. This interpretation is consonant with pilot studies indicating that if mice are held on the surface in a cage and forced to confront the cat, they run deep into the tunnels when released and remain there, without RA ventures to the open area.

The rat–mouse RA timing difference is found also in the MDTB. The MDTB is run in a (mouse-scaled) oval runway, using a hand-held, deeply anesthetized rat "predator," a choice based on the need to be able to control the movements of the predator, as in the F/DTB. It is justified by the status of the rat as a predator of mice (Nikulina, 1991), with hunger enhancing this tendency (Rylov, 1985); by findings (De Catanzaro, 1988) that rat exposure causes disruptions of pregnancy in mice; and by pilot studies in my lab indicating that mice show similar patterns of reactivity to cats and rats, albeit with somewhat reduced intensity of response to the latter.

As with the F/DTB, we now have control (i.e., no drug) data for nearly a dozen MDTB studies (e.g., Griebel, Blanchard, Jung, & Blanchard, 1995). In the escape situation, the mouse turns and runs from the rat when a relatively consistent rat–mouse distance (about 1.1 m) is reached. However, RA occurs even in this situation: The fleeing mouse stops abruptly, often with orientation toward the oncoming rat, and on some occasions with reversal of direction to approach the predator. When the rat is brought close to the mouse in the inescapable alley, the mouse orients to the rat but shows little freezing. Instead, it tends to approach the rat and then withdraw, often to repeat the sequence. When contact with the rat becomes imminent, the mouse shows a defensive threat–attack pattern of upright (boxing) behavior, sonic vocalizations, jump attacks, and bites. With the exception of RA, these behaviors are similar indeed to those of rats in a parallel situation.

These and other findings strongly suggest that, although specific defensive behaviors do not occur in precisely the same form in all species, the term *species-specific* is inaccurate when applied to defensive behaviors generally. Although mice do not show ultrasonic cries in an "alarm" context, a variety of other colonial mammals (e.g., monkeys, Cheney & Seyfarth, 1990; ground squirrels, Owings & Loughry, 1985) and birds (Schmitt, 1991) do. The form of these vocalizations certainly differs among species, but the vocalizations do not appear to be dissimilar for *Rattus norvegicus* and *R. rattus* (see Kaltwasser, 1990, for *R. rattus* calls). In similar fashion, some parameters of particular defenses, such as the timing of RA activities for rats and mice, may differ across species, but the general patterns of RA and many specific RA behaviors appear to be similar. This picture of across-species similarity in function (and often in specific form) of behavior is emerging also for conceptualizations of conspecific juvenile as well as adult attack and defense (Pellis, 1988). This view greatly enhances the value of research on defense because it suggests that an understanding of these behavior patterns and their physiological and pharmacological correlates in experimental animals may be relevant to human defense- or emotion-related behaviors.

Elicitation and Modulation of Defensive Behaviors

The Role of Stimulus Intensity

Defensive behaviors are diverse, yet in certain circumstances each type appears consistently. What mechanisms control this exquisite match between situation and behavior? Stimulus intensity is one traditional mechanism for modulating any behavior, and in the case of defense it assumes additional importance in that the defensive motivation of a "normal" animal or human is viewed as largely dependent on threat stimulus intensity. Fanselow and Lester (1988) used threat intensity, or stimulus imminence, to differentiate among three sets of defensive behaviors: (a) preencounter defenses (represented by compromises in normal activities), (b) postencounter defenses (freezing), and (c) circa-strike defenses (flight, vocalization, biting, and high-activity responses such as to shock). More recently, Fanselow (1994) suggested that this intensity–imminence parameter is the major or possibly sole determinant of the form of defense offered in particular situations.

Threat stimulus intensity dramatically affects important parameters of defense, for natural threat stimuli such as a predator as well as for more easily quantified shock stimulation. Zangrossi and File (1992) reported that exposure to cat odor produces anxiolytic-like responses on the elevated plus-maze for an hour, but not a day, afterward. However, Adamec and Shallow (1993) found a much longer lasting anxiolytic-like plus-maze response after cat exposure, suggesting that a cat is a more potent threat stimulus than is cat odor alone. My group's comparisons of a cat-odor cloth as opposed to a live cat in the VBS (R. J. Blanchard et al., 1989) are fully in accord: The behavior patterns were quite similar, but the animals sequenced through them at a much faster rate when only the cat-odor cloth was presented. These findings suggest that the duration or the speed of sequencing of defensive responses to a threat stimulus may serve as one index of stimulus intensity effects on defensive behavior.

The patterning of defense following cat exposure also suggests a role for intensity: From the time that rats and mice retreat into the burrow system until they return to normal, nondefensive behavior, they sequence through a variety of defenses. These changes in defensive behaviors cannot be based on the activities of the threat stimulus, because the cat not only is invisible to the subjects in the burrow system but also it is gone, having been removed early in the test period while the rats were in the burrows. The 22-kHz vocalizations made by the rats may well influence early defenses in this situation, but these cries cease after an hour or so, and they do not occur in mice at any point in this context. Cat odor may have some modulatory role, but latency to enter the open area where the cat was seen is much shorter when a cat-odor stimulus is placed in the open area *and left in* than when the cat is presented and then removed, counterindicating a crucial role for lingering odors.

Nonetheless, rats do consistently change from a high level of reactivity to fairly normal behavior in the course of 24 hours or so following brief exposure to a cat, and this change involves a specific sequence of defensive behaviors over time. My colleagues and I (D. C. Blanchard, Blanchard, & Rodgers, 1991) suggested that a decline in the intensity of defensiveness is responsible for some of those changes, particularly those that cannot be attributed to alteration of the environment itself, and that risk assessment is the major mechanism for reducing the intensity of defense. The transition from flight (away from the open area and into the burrow) to freezing (in the burrow) does not seem to be a function of reduced intensity. From many informal observations involving the VBS and other studies of arranged rat–cat confrontations (e.g., R. J. Blanchard & Blanchard, 1972), it is known that a rat trapped on the surface with a cat, freezes as its dominant response; this can hardly be attributed to a reduction in threat intensity. However, intensity is hypothesized to modulate the transition from freezing to more active forms of RA, a transition that occurs in a more or less static physical environment for rats deep in the burrow system in the period well after the cat has been removed. Although active RA, including approach and investigation of potential threat stimuli, is incompatible with freezing, freezing animals do show passive RA such as orientation and, later, scanning and sniffing, which provide information on visual and olfactory threat stimuli or the absence of these. If the feedback from such activities suggests that the cat is not present in the burrow, the intensity of defensiveness and the magnitude of freezing both decline. As freezing breaks up, active RA increases and continues as the dominant defense for many hours. Later, as the animal returns to normal, RA also declines. The sequence from freezing to RA to normal behavior appears, therefore, to be based on the rat's (RA-mediated) perception that the intensity or immediacy of threat has declined (D. C. Blanchard et al., 1991). This "inverted U" relationship between threat–defensiveness intensity and RA in rats makes RA an awkward behavior to analyze and interpret. However, this function and its interpretation fit well with data from rat studies on anxiolytic drugs, as I discuss in a subsequent section.

Decreasing predator–subject distance, long viewed as a major determinant of the form of defense (Hediger, 1955, 1968; Ratner, 1967), may also involve an intensity difference. Although freezing increases as the predator approaches, from about 5 meters until the short (1.0 m) distances at which defensive vocalizations and jump attacks are seen, the freezing animal is also preparing for action. Both frequency and magnitude of jumps to a sudden noise or movement increase as contact approaches, and these high-magnitude jumps to the sudden stimulus occur when the predator is at distances at which only freezing would be seen without the sudden stimulus (R. J. Blanchard et al., 1986). A cautionary note, however, is that the jumps seen in this context are not necessarily identical to those made in response to the experimenter as contact approaches. The latter, but not the former, often involve bites, suggesting the commonsensical but important point that biting-type responses seldom occur in the absence of something to be bitten.

The Role of Stimulus and Environmental Support

Although some defense-related phenomena do reflect stimulus intensity, other examples cannot be reasonably interpreted as reflecting an intensity dimension. In the F/DTB, the closing of a door to convert an endless runway into an inescapable straight alley produces a robust behavior change from an average of 97.5 percent flight, in the former, to 100 percent freezing in the latter. This abrupt change in behavior can be attributed to an alteration of threat intensity only if it is assumed (using the Fanselow & Lester, 1988, terminology) that blocking the escape route makes the threat *less* intense or the predator *less* imminent to produce the postcontact defense of freezing rather than the circa-strike defense of flight. As noted previously, trapping a VBS rat on the surface with the cat also produces freezing, whereas flight is virtually instantaneous in this familiar situation when the doors to the burrow are open.

Whereas the foregoing represent particularly salient cases of the role of environmental support stimuli in modulating the form of defensive behaviors, the most elaborate example of the role of stimulus specificity in defensive behavior may be found in the targeting of defensive bites toward specific sites on the body of the attacker (R. J. Blanchard, Blanchard, et al., 1977). This targeting of bites (or other forms of contact) appears to be a general feature of conspecific interactions in mammals (Pellis, 1988; Pellis & Pellis, 1992; Pellis, Pellis, Pierce, & Deswburg, 1992).

There is also evidence of targeting of defensive attack at predators. In fact, studies of the effects of tail shock on bites to specific body parts of a predator (a cat, euthanized because of terminal cancer) have suggested that target stimuli are more important than threat intensity in these bites (R. J. Blanchard et al., 1980). When the terminally anesthetized cat's snout was used as the target stimulus, female rats showed high initial levels of biting, which did not increase with shock. Males showed much lower levels before the shock condition was initiated, and their levels did show an increase when 1.6 mA tail shock was given. When the cat's forepaw was the target, males and females again differed in terms of initial biting levels (moderate vs. very low), but neither showed an increase in biting rates with shock. When the cat's tail was offered, initial rates were low, as were rates during shock, with no indication of an increase during shock. Therefore, not only were initial rates suggestive of a (sex-differentiated) targeting of bites toward the head of the cat, but in five of six (Subject Gender × Target) conditions, there was no evidence of *any* increase in cat biting when shock intensity was increased. In the same study, preshock bites at the snout of an anesthetized male conspecific were low. However, during shock (and in the 2-s period following shock), these increased as a direct function of shock intensity, although at a lower rate for females than for males. Moreover, only males made wounds on the conspecific target, indicating that female bites against male conspecifics are inhibited. In contrast, high rates of biting at a wooden dowel occurred during the 2 second preshock period, as well as the two-second postshock period, and in neither of these, nor to shock itself, was there any indication of an intensity-based enhancement of biting.

These findings suggest a substantial difference in the effects of shock and shock intensity on biting at these three targets, with a clear shock intensity effect only for biting at the snout of an anesthetized conspecific and, in males only, at the snout of a predator. It is striking that the addition of shock and the intensity of the shock added had little effect on bites at the wooden dowel, a fact that is sometimes obscured by procedures in which confined rats are habituated until they show no more bites at a proffered inanimate target before being shocked to "elicit" (disinhibit?) biting. It is also striking that the addition of shock during presentation of the predator's paw or tail produced no increment in biting. Both findings suggest that shock, presented in association with either a moderately threatening (in terms of elicitation of defensive biting prior to shock) predator stimulus (cat's paw) or a (presumably nonthreatening) wooden dowel stimulus, does not necessarily enhance the normal defensive response (biting) seen to predator or conspecific attack.

What these findings do suggest is a considerable amount of specificity in the biting seen in response to these different stimuli. The "inhibited" (i.e., not causing wounds) bites of female rats at a male snout are likely adaptive in reducing the probability that a pained male will show retaliatory attack on the female: Because male rats are much larger than females, this could be a dangerous consequence of female attack on a male. No such inhibition (and a much higher proportion of wounds) was obtained for female bites at the cat's snout, suggesting that the pain-producing potential of bites in the antipredator situation is more likely to reduce than to induce danger from the bitten animal. These data make it clear that shock does not consistently sum with other factors contributing to the ability of a stimulus to elicit defensive behaviors. Moreover, these studies indicate the need for caution in accepting experimenter-designated behaviors (such as dowel biting) as equivalent to other behaviors of similar form but directed at more natural targets (e.g., various sites on the bodies of conspecifics or predators).

Another example of the role of support stimuli in determining defensive behavior can be found in antipredator vocalization. The 22-kHz vocalizations made when a cat is presented to rat groups in a VBS do not occur when rats are exposed alone to a cat (R. J. Blanchard et al., 1991), suggesting that the presence of conspecifics is an important factor in the elicitation of these (alarm?) cries.

As a final example, trimming the mystacial vibrissae of intruders into a rat colony switches their defensive response following conspecific attack from boxing to freezing, with changes of an order of magnitude in each of these behaviors (R. J. Blanchard, Takahashi, et al., 1977). As in the phenomena described previously, stimulus intensity simply cannot account for these changes; they confirm an important role for specific features of the environment and for defensive body structures of the subject itself in the control of the magnitude and form of defensive reactions.

It is notable that the complexity of some of these relationships stands in considerable contrast to the appealing simplicity of findings on (laboratory rat) defensive behaviors to shock in situations that typically do not incorporate variation in the stimulus features that are so important in the control of defensive behaviors. Part of the difference is an emphasis on freezing as the major index of defensiveness, an emphasis that reflects the increased freezing of laboratory rats in contrast to the animals from which they were derived. In particular, this emphasis on freezing has resulted in less attention to some of the subtler aspects of defense, such as ultrasonic vocalization, RA, and the back-defense strategies so important in conspecific attack, which are exquisitely sensitive to features of the environment and the attacker. These defensive behaviors are retained in laboratory rats, and some of them may be observed even in shock situations, albeit in a fashion that makes them less amenable to recognition or interpretation. Finally, having bred the laboratory rat *not* to do certain things (sonic threat vocalization, bite), researchers now induce it to produce these same responses (as well as other, possibly extraneous activities) through the application of shock, a procedure that may provide as much general disinhibition as specific elicitation of particular behaviors. Under these circumstances, it is perhaps no surprise that the important but complex role of modulatory environmental and threat stimulus features has been largely ignored in the psychological literature on defense (see Chapter 15, this volume, for additional consideration of these relationships in the control of freezing and flight).

Differentiation of Defensive Behaviors: Response to Anxiolytic and Panicolytic Drugs

One rationale for attempting to understand the dynamics of specific defensive behaviors is that this understanding may provide insights into the neural and neurochemical systems underlying emotion-related behaviors. Two general hypotheses concerning drug effects on defensive behaviors could be suggested on the basis of conceptualizations of the mechanisms determining and modulating these responses. One is that if intensity alone underlies the sequence of individual defenses, then drugs that increase or decrease defensiveness should produce particular sequences of change, potentially involving all defensive behaviors. The other is that if particular defensive behaviors are differentially modulated by relevant stimulus features, suggesting relatively specific stimulus–response connections, then they may represent essentially different neurobehavioral systems. In this case, a good deal more specificity in drug response would be anticipated.

Studies of the modulation of defensive responses by anxiolytic and panicolytic drugs have largely, but not exclusively, supported the latter interpretation. Briefly (see R. J. Blanchard, Yudko, et al., 1993, for review), in rats classic benzodiazepine (BZP) anxiolytics such as diazepam produce a profile of specific changes in four defense-related behaviors, which can be measured independently in several different tasks: (a) a decrease in proxemic avoidance of threat-related stimuli, (b) an increase in RA measured against a freezing–avoidance baseline, (c) a decrease in RA measured against an RA baseline, and (d) increases in nondefensive behaviors. Partial effects—three of the four changes—were obtained with imipramine and with the 5-HT$_{1A}$ agonist gepirone, both of which have been demonstrated to have some anxiolytic efficacy in clinical tests (e.g., Bernstein, Garfinkel, & Borchardt, 1990), and also with alcohol. The same set of behavioral changes occurred with MK-801, a noncompetitive NMDA antagonist that has not been used clinically. However, no other drug tested with rats (including scopolamine hydrobromide, scopolamine methylbromide, morphine, naloxone, ritanserin, and two 5-HT$_3$ antagonists, ondansetron and MDL 72222) showed any systematic effect on this profile. Moreover, except for a decrease in defensive threat, attack, or both, which declined with most of the anxiolytic drugs as well as with morphine (but increased at intermediate doses of alcohol), no other behaviors gave any suggestion of a systematic change in response to the anxiolytic, as opposed to nonanxiolytic, drugs.

This profile clearly pinpoints RA as the major defensive behavior that changes with anxiolytic drugs. The non-RA measures of the 4-point "anxiolytic profile" are both related to RA: Proximic avoidance is a major factor inhibiting active RA, whereas inhibition of nondefensive behaviors typically accompanies RA. However, there is also an important intensity dimension embedded in this profile, in that animals freezing to high-intensity threat (after cat confrontation) show increased RA when given an anxiolytic drug, suggesting a reduction in defensiveness. Similarly, the administration of anxiolytic drugs to an animal confronted with a less intense threat (cat odor), and showing RA as a baseline behavior, had the effect of reducing this RA. This is precisely the sequence expected from a view that a decline in intensity of defensiveness produces the changes that occur in RA: first an increase and then a decrease as the animal returns to normal after encountering a threat stimulus. However, this change was not equally applicable to all defenses: Behaviors such as freezing and flight showed no systematic response to anxiolytic drugs.

This close association of anxiolytic drugs with RA has also been obtained in more recent mouse studies, with the exception that, because mice show RA even to very intense threat stimuli (i.e., during cat confrontation), only the RA-reducing effects of anxiolytic drugs have been obtained. The classic BZP chlordiazepoxide reduced the RA activities that occur in the fleeing mouse, as did Ro 19-8022, a non-BZP partial agonist at the BZP receptor. The BZP antagonist flumazenil had no effect on this measure, and the BZP inverse agonist Ro 19-4603 increased the same behaviors that had been reduced by the BZP agonists and the partial agonist (Griebel, Blanchard, Jung, & Blanchard, 1995). The atypical BZP alprazolam also reduced RA but only if given on a chronic basis (Griebel, Blanchard, Lee, Masuda, & Blanchard, in press). Other defensive behaviors were not systematically changed, except for defensive threat–attack, which, as in the rat, showed BZP effects similar to those for RA (but was not included in the "anxiolytic profile" because of noncongruent responses to some other anxiolytic drugs). This intriguing profile of BZP-receptor ligand effects for RA is precisely what would be expected from a view that RA behaviors are modulated at the BZP receptor (Griebel, Blanchard, Jung, & Blanchard, 1995), and the pattern of findings from these studies provides strong support for the view that RA responds selectively to anxiolytic drugs, in mice as well as in rats.

However, this same array of BZP-receptor ligands generally failed to alter the clear RA pattern seen in the closed-alley situation, consisting of approaches to the oncoming rat (Griebel, Blanchard, Jung, & Blanchard, 1995). These closed-alley RA behaviors were reduced by 5-HT$_{1A}$ agonists, which in turn generally failed to alter the RA behaviors seen in the escapable situation (Griebel, Blanchard, Jung, Masuda, & Blanchard, 1995). Although the general picture for mice, that both BZP and 5-HT$_{1A}$ agonists tend to reduce RA, is congruent with the earlier rat findings, the two different types of RA behaviors seen in the mouse appear to be rather selectively responsive to the two classes of drugs, both of which are effective against clinical anxiety. This intriguing situation clearly needs further analysis, but it is consistent with studies of rats in indicating a central role for RA in response to anxiolytic drugs, albeit with the possibility that different classes of anxiolytic drugs may have more specific effects within the RA pattern.

Perhaps the most striking finding from these mouse drug studies, relevant to differentiation of defensive behaviors and of the human behavioral pathologies to which they may be related, concerns panicolytic and panicogenic drugs. In an earlier and somewhat different version of the MDTB, the panicogenic drug yohimbine increased flight responses (R. J.

Blanchard, Taukulis, Rodgers, Magee, & Blanchard, 1993). This finding provided support for the suggestion of Deakin and Graeff (1991) that flight may be the core behavioral aspect of panic and encouraged examination of antipanic agents in the MDTB. In this test, three antipanic compounds, alprazolam, imipramine, and fluoxetine, given daily for 2 weeks (i.e., on a chronic basis), reduced flight. However, both imipramine and fluoxetine potentiated flight when this was measured after a single, initial injection (Griebel, Blanchard, Agnes, & Blanchard, 1995), whereas alprazolam had little effect after a single administration (Griebel et al., in press). Notably, classic benzodiazepines (chlordiazepoxide) and a variety of serotonin ligands produced little or no effect on flight responses in the MDTB (Griebel, Blanchard, Jung, & Blanchard, 1995; Griebel, Blanchard, Jung, Masuda, & Blanchard, 1995).

These findings show a particularly striking fit with the clinical effects of the three antipanic compounds. Given on a chronic basis (i.e., after about 2 weeks of treatment), alprazolam, imipramine, and fluoxetine are all effective against panic disorder (e.g., Garakani, Zitrin, & Klein, 1984; Gorman et al., 1987; Schneier et al., 1990). However, the serotonin reuptake inhibitors (imipramine and fluoxetine) tend to exacerbate panic symptoms on initial administration (e.g., Westenberg & Den Boer, 1993).

The drug studies of specific defensive behaviors, like the emerging literature on the neural control of these systems (see chapters in DePaulis & Bandler, 1991, for reviews), indicate a considerable degree of specificity for particular defenses. Although stimulation of particular dorsal and lateral components of the periaqueductal gray matter gives rise to defensive vocalizations and flight (Bandler & Depaulis, 1991), and Fanselow (1991) reported freezing from stimulation of ventral sites, it is interesting that none of these stimulation sites appears to elicit RA behaviors in an important way. This is not unexpected in terms of the clear behavioral and drug response–based separation of RA from these other behaviors and suggests, again, that behavioral analysis should be regarded as a crucial component of attempts to understand neurobehavioral systems.

In an applied context, the most important aspect of these drug effects is that specific defensive behavioral changes, or patterns of behavioral change, can be used to predict the clinical efficacy of drugs against a variety of affective psychopathologies, including generalized anxiety, panic, and potentially depression (McKittrick, Blanchard, Blanchard, McEwen, & Sakai, 1995). More comprehensively, the goal is to understand both behavioral and anatomical–physiological aspects of the defense systems and the stability of these systems across mammals. Such an understanding can only enhance the appreciation of the role of defensive responses and defense-related emotions in both normal and abnormal behavior, including that of people.

This research has wandered rather far from the initial impetus provided by Bob Bolles. At a NATO conference in 1988, he prefaced a talk by declaring, "I have always believed that defensive behaviors are a great nuisance in the study of learning." Like so many other things he said, this wry statement deflected attention from a topic that I believe was quite important to him. The subject of defense would have stopped being such a nuisance to Bolles if he could have conceptualized it in a way that provided some relatively simple and straightforward decision rules amenable to integration into relevant conditioning paradigms.

I remain uncertain whether the approach and the findings described here have produced an advancement toward that goal, or, evidence that it is unlikely to be reached. The delineation of a number of defensive behaviors that are differentially modulated by relevant stimulus and situational features as well as by intensity of threat suggests that these decision rules are not based on any single parameter. Furthermore, these data indicate that some specific defensive behaviors are differentially responsive to drugs that are effective for particular psychopathologies, with intriguing behavioral similarities between these defensive responses and the particular psychopathologies against which those drugs are effective, for example, RA and anxiety (D. C. Blanchard et al., 1991) or flight and panic (Deakin & Graeff, 1991; Griebel, Blanchard, Agnes, & Blanchard, 1995). These parallels suggest important homologies between defense systems across mammals, such that the appearance of either normal or aberrant defense patterns in humans is likely to reflect at least those modulating factors that occur in rodents.

Without discounting an important role for learning in the modulation of defensive behavior, and remaining appreciative of the increasingly sophisticated and successful efforts of those who elect to deal with this complex topic, I am skeptical of the view that conditioning effects per se will ever be capable of providing a reasonably comprehensive explanation of variations either in the defensive behaviors of animals or in emotion-linked psychopathologies. Although defense patterns show important commonalities across species, defensive behaviors represent mechanisms that are strikingly amenable to genetic selection as well as pharmacological manipulation and, moreover, may show important sex differences (e.g., D. C. Blanchard et al., 1991; D. C. Blanchard, Griebel, & Blanchard, 1995; Crepeau & Newman, 1991). This suggests the importance of a focus on defensive behaviors as components of biobehavioral systems that interact with, rather than being determined by, the experiences of the individual. This interaction is the topic of an ongoing collaborative program in my laboratory and a number of others as well, with results (e.g., Albeck et al., in press; D. C. Blanchard, Spencer, et al., 1995; McKittrick et al., 1995) suggesting that the study of chronic defense produces additional complexities on both the physiological and behavioral levels. These results add to my increasingly firm belief that the defense systems are worthy of investigation on their own and not merely as adjuncts to analysis of conditioning processes.

References

Adamec, R. E., & Shallow, T. (1993). Lasting effects on rodent anxiety of a single exposure to a cat. *Physiology and Behavior, 54,* 101–109.

Adams, D. B. (1979). Brain mechanisms for offense, defense, and submission. *Behavioral and Brain Sciences, 2*, 201–241.

Albeck, D. S., McKittrick, C. R., Blanchard, D. C., Blanchard, R. J., Nikulina, J., McEwen, B. S., & Sakai, R. S. (in press). Chronic social stress alters expression of corticotropin-releasing factor and arginine vasopressin mRNA expression in rat brain. *Journal of Neuroscience.*

Bandler, R., & Depaulis, A. (1991). Midbrain periaqueductal gray control of defensive behavior in the cat and the rat. In: A. Depaulis, & R. Bandler (Eds.), *The midbrain periaqueductal grey matter: Functional, anatomical and immunohistochemical organization* (NATO ASI Series A: Vol. 213, pp. 175–198). New York: Plenum Press.

Ben-David, M., Pellis, S. M., and Pellis, V. C. (1991). Feeding habits and predatory behaviour in the marbled polecat (*Vormela peregusna syriaca*): I. Killing methods in relation to prey size and prey behaviour. *Behaviour, 118*, 127–143.

Bernstein, G. A., Garfinkel, B. D., & Borchardt, C. M. (1990). Comparative studies of pharmacotherapy for school refusal. *Journal of American Academy of Child and Adolescent Psychiatry, 29*, 773–781.

Blanchard, D. C., Blanchard, R. J., & Rodgers, R. J. (1991). Risk assessment and animal models of anxiety. In B. Olivier, J. Mos, & J. L. Slangen (Eds.), *Animal models in psychopharmacology* (pp. 117–134). Basel, Switzerland: Birkhauser Verlag.

Blanchard, D. C., Griebel, G., & Blanchard, R. J. (1995). Gender bias in preclinical psychopharmacology: Male models for (predominantly) female disorders. *Journal of Psychopharmacology, 9*, 79–82.

Blanchard, D. C., Lee, E. M. C., Williams, G., & Blanchard, R. J. (1981). Taming of *Rattus norvegicus* by lesions of the mesencephalic central gray. *Physiological Psychology, 9*, 157–163.

Blanchard, D. C., Popova, N. K., Plyusnina, I. Z., Velichko, I. V., Campbell, D., Blanchard, R. J., Nikulina, J., & Nikulina, E. M. (1994). Defensive behaviors of "wild-type" and "domesticated" wild rats in a Fear/Defense Test Battery. *Aggressive Behavior, 20*, 387–398.

Blanchard, D. C., Spencer, R., Weiss, S. M., Blanchard, R. J., McEwen, B. S., & Sakai, R. R. (1995). The visible burrow system as a model of chronic social stress: Behavioral and neuroendocrine correlates. *Psychoendocrinology, 20*, 117–134.

Blanchard, R. J., & Blanchard, D. C. (1969). Passive and active reactions to fear-eliciting stimuli. *Journal of Comparative and Physiological Psychology, 68*, 129–135.

Blanchard, R. J., & Blanchard, D. C. (1972). Effects of hippocampal lesions on the rat's reaction to a cat. *Journal of Comparative and Physiological Psychology, 78*, 77–82.

Blanchard, R. J., & Blanchard, D. C. (1977). Aggressive behavior in the rat. *Behavioral Biology, 21*, 197–224.

Blanchard, R. J., & Blanchard, D. C. (1989). Anti-predator defensive behaviors in a visible burrow system. *Journal of Comparative Psychology, 103*, 70–82.

Blanchard, R. J., & Blanchard, D. C. (1994). Environmental targets and sensorimotor systems in aggression and defense. In S. Cooper & C. A. Hendrie (Eds.), *Ethology and psychopharmacology* (pp. 133–157). New York: Wiley.

Blanchard, R. J., Blanchard, D. C., Agullana, R., and Weiss, S. M. (1991). Twenty-two kHz alarm cries to presentation of a predator, by laboratory rats living in visible burrow systems. *Physiology and Behavior, 50*, 967–972.

Blanchard, R. J., Blanchard, D. C., & Hori, K. (1989). Ethoexperimental approaches to the study of defensive behavior. In R. J. Blanchard, P. F. Brain, D. C. Blanchard, & S. Parmigiani (Eds.), *Ethoexperimental approaches to the study of behavior* (pp. 114–136). Dordrecht, Netherlands: Kluwer Academic.

Blanchard, R. J., Blanchard, D. C., Takahashi, T., & Kelley, M. (1977). Attack and defensive behavior in the albino rat. *Animal Behaviour, 25*, 622–634.

Blanchard, R. J., Flannelly, K. J., & Blanchard, D. C. (1986). Defensive behaviors of laboratory and wild *Rattus norvegicus*. *Journal of Comparative Psychology, 100*, 101–107.

Blanchard, R. J., Kleinschmidt, C. F., Fukunaga-Stinson, C., & Blanchard, D. C. (1980). Defensive attack behavior in male and female rats. *Animal Learning and Behavior, 8*, 177–183.

Blanchard, R. J., Parmigiani, S., Bjornson, C., Masuda, C., Weiss, S. M., & Blanchard, D. C. (1995). Antipredator behavior of Swiss-Webster mice in a visible burrow system. *Aggressive Behavior, 21*, 123–136.

Blanchard, R. J., Takahashi, L. K., Fukunaga, K. K., & Blanchard, D. C. (1977). Functions of the vibrissae in the defensive and aggressive behavior of the rat. *Aggressive Behavior, 3*, 231–240.

Blanchard, R. J., Taukulis, H. K., Rodgers, R. J., Magee, L. K., & Blanchard, D. C. (1993). Yohimbine potentiates active defensive responses to threatening stimuli in Swiss-Webster mice. *Pharmacology, Biochemistry, & Behavior, 44*, 673–681.

Blanchard, R. J., Yudko, E. B., Rodgers, R. J., and Blanchard, D. C. (1993). Defense system psychopharmacology: An ethological approach to the pharmacology of fear and anxiety. *Behavioral Brain Research, 58*, 155–165.

Boice, R., & Adams, N. (1983). Degrees of captivity and aggressive behavior in domestic Norway rats. *Bulletin of the Psychonomic Society, 21*, 149–152.

Bolles, R. C. (1988). *Acquired behaviors: Aversive learning.* Paper presented at the NATO Advanced Study Institute on Ethoexperimental Analysis of Behaviour, Il Ciocco, Italy.

Brudzynski, S. M., & Chiu, E. M. (1995). Behavioural reponses of laboratory rats to playback of 22 kHz ultrasonic calls. *Physiology and Behavior, 57*, 1039–1044.

Cheney, D. L., & Seyfarth, R. M. (1990). *How monkeys see the world.* Chicago: University of Chicago Press.

Crepeau, L. J., & Newman, J. D. (1991). Gender differences in reactivity of adult squirrel monkeys to short-term environmental challenges. Ethopharmacology Conference: Advances in ethopharmacology (Lisek, Czechoslovakia). *Neuroscience and Biobehavioral Reviews, 15*, 469–471.

Deakin, J. F. W., & Graeff, F. G. (1991). 5-HT and mechanisms of defense. *Journal of Psychopharmacology, 5*, 305–315.

De Catanzaro, D. (1988). Effect of predator exposure upon early pregnancy in mice. *Physiology and Behavior, 43*, 691–696.

Depaulis, A., & Bandler, R. (Eds.). (1991). *The midbrain periaqueductal gray matter: Functional, anatomical and immunohistochemical organization* (NATO ASI Series A: Vol. 213). New York: Plenum Press.

Endler, J. A. (1986). Defense against predators. In M. E. Feder & G. V. Lauder, *Predator–prey relationships* (pp. 109–134). Chicago: University of Chicago Press.

Fanselow, M. S. (1991). The midbrain periaqueductal gray as a coordinator of action in response to fear and anxiety. In A. Depaulis & R. Bandler (Eds.), *The midbrain periaqueductal gray matter: Functional, anatomical and immunohistochemical organization* (NATO ASI Series A: Vol. 213, pp. 151–173). New York: Plenum Press.

Fanselow, M. S. (1994). Neural organization of the defensive behavior system responsible for fear. *Psychonomic Bulletin & Review, 1*, 429–438.

Fanselow, M. S., & Lester, L. S. (1988). A functional behavioristic approach to aversively motivated behavior: Predatory imminence as a determinant of the topography of defensive behavior. In R. C. Bolles & M. D. Beecher (Eds.), *Evolution and learning* (pp. 185–211). Hillsdale, NJ: Erlbaum

Garakani, H., Zitrin, C. M., & Klein, D. F. (1984). Treatment of panic disorder with imipramine alone. *American Journal of Psychiatry, 141*, 446–448.

Gorman, J. M., Liebowitz, M. R., Fyer, A. J., Goetz, D., Campeas, R. B., Fyer, M. R., Davies, S. O., & Klein, D. F. (1987). An open trial of fluoxetine in the treatment of panic attacks. *Journal of Clinical Psychopharmacology, 7*, 329–332.

Griebel, G., Blanchard, D. C., Agnes, R., Blanchard, R. J. (1995). Differential modulation of antipredator defensive behavior in Swiss-Webster mice following acute and chronic treatment with imipramine and fluoxetine. *Psychopharmacology, 120*, 57–66.

Griebel, G., Blanchard, D. C., Jung, A., & Blanchard, R. J. (1995). A model of "antipredator" defense in Swiss-Webster mice: Effects of benzodiazepine receptor ligands with different intrinsic activities. *Behavioural Pharmacology, 6*, 732–745.

Griebel, G., Blanchard, D. C., Jung, A., Masuda, C. K., & Blanchard, R. J. (1995) 5-HT$_{1A}$ agonists modulate mouse antipredator defensive behavior differently than the preferential 5-HT$_{2A}$ receptor antagonist pirenperone. *Pharmacology, Biochemistry, and Behavior, 51*, 235–244.

Griebel, G., Blanchard, D. C., Lee, J., Masuda, C. K., & Blanchard, R. J. (in press). Further evidence that the Mouse Defense Test Battery is useful for screening anxiolytic and panicolytic drugs: Effects of acute and chronic treatment with alprazolam. *Neuropharmacology.*

Hediger, H. (1955). *Studies of the psychology and behavior of captive animals in zoos and circuses.* London: Butterworths.

Hediger, H. (1968). *The psychology of animals in zoos and circuses.* New York: Dover.

Kaltwasser, M. T. (1990). Acoustic signaling in the black rat (*R. rattus*). *Journal of Comparative Psychology, 104,* 227–232.

McKittrick, C. R., Blanchard, D. C., Blanchard, R. J., McEwen, B. S., & Sakai, R.R. (1995). Serotonin receptor binding in a colony model of chronic social stress. *Biological Psychiatry, 37,* 383–393.

Naumenko, E. V., Popova, N. K., Nikulina, E. M., Dygalo, N. N., Shishkina, G. T., Borodin, P. M., & Markel, A. L. (1989). Behavior, adrenocortical activity, and brain monoamines in Norway rats selected for reduced aggressiveness towards man. *Pharmacology, Biochemistry, & Behavior, 33,* 85–91.

Nikulina, E. M. (1991). Neural control of predatory aggression in wild and domesticated animals. *Neuroscience and Biobehavioral Reviews, 15,* 545–547.

Owings, D. H., & Loughry, W. J. (1985). Variation in snake-elicited jump-yipping by black-tailed prairie dogs: Ontogeny and snake specificity. *Zeitschrift für Tierpsychologie, 49,* 39–54.

Pellis, S. M. (1988). Agonistic versus amicable targets of attack and defense: Consequences for the origin, function, and descriptive classification of play-fighting. *Aggressive Behavior, 14,* 85–104.

Pellis, S. M., & Pellis, V. C. (1992). Analysis of the targets and tactics of conspecific attack and predatory attack in northern grasshopper mice *Onychomys leucogaster. Aggressive Behavior, 18,* 301–316.

Pellis, S. M., Pellis, V. C., Pierce, J. D., & Dewsbury, D. A. (1992). Disentangling the contribution of the attacker from that of defender in the differences in the intraspecific fighting in two species of voles. *Aggressive Behavior, 18,* 425–435.

Ratner, S. C. (1967). Comparative aspects of hypnosis. In J. E. Gordon (Ed.), *Handbook of clinical and experimental hypnosis* (pp. 550–587). New York: Macmillan.

Rylov, A. I. (1985). Change of predatory intraspecies aggression of male rats under food deprivation. *Zhurnal Vysshei Nervoi Deyatell'nosti, 35,* 875–878.

Schmitt, A. (1991). Adjusting movements in greylag geese during pre-roosting and mass-fleeing. *Bird Behaviour, 9*(1–2), 41–48.

Schneier, F. R., Liebowitz, M. R., Davies, S. O., Fairbanks, J., Hollander, E., Campeas, R., & Klein, D. F. (1990). Fluoxetine in panic disorder. *Journal of Clinical Pharmacology, 10,* 119–121.

Seidensticker, J., & McDougal, C. (1993). Tiger predatory behaviour, ecology and conservation. In N. Dunstone & M. L. Gorman (Eds.), *Mammals as prey* (pp. 105–123). Oxford, England: Clarendon Press.

Stone, C. P. (1932). Wildness and savageness in rats of different strains. In K. S. Lashley (Ed.), *Studies in the dynamics of behavior* (pp. 3–55). Chicago: University of Chicago Press.

Takahashi, L. K., & Blanchard, R. J. (1982). Attack and defense in laboratory and wild Norway and black rats. *Behavioral Processes, 7,* 49–62.

Westenberg, H. G. M., & Den Boer, J. A. (1993). Serotonin and related disorders. In P. M. Vanhoutte, P. R. Saxena, R. Paoletti, N. Brunello, & A. S. Jackson (Eds.), *Serotonin: From cell biology to pharmacology and therapeutics* (pp. 249–254). Boston: Kluwer Academic.

Yerkes, R. M. (1913). The heredity of savageness and wildness in rats. *Journal of Animal Behavior, 3,* 286–296.

Zangrossi, H., & File, S. E. (1992). Behavioral consequences in animal tests of anxiety and exploration of exposure to cat odor. *Brain Research Bulletin, 29,* 381–388.

15

Performance Rules for Problem-Specific Defense Reactions

Ronald A. Sigmundi

This chapter explores the nature of species-specific defense reactions (SSDRs; Bolles, 1970) as theoretical constructs. The purpose is to derive principles of response selection that predict the form and direction of defensive behavior in the rat. The chapter begins with a memory about Bob Bolles and continues with sections on the nature of SSDRs and on the problem-specific response hypothesis. These sections argue, both theoretically and empirically, that SSDRs are responses to innately recognized defensive problems that the rat has faced over the course of evolution. The subsequent section on stages of defense begins a search for the stimulus correlates of these defensive problems by suggesting that SSDRs might reflect antipredator responses organized as antihandling and prehandling defense, each elicited by specific stimulus cues. Prehandling defense is treated again and at length in the section on the freeze–flee decision, leading to the idea that gradients of danger and relative safety enable the rat to recognize innately different types of defensive problems and then to respond accordingly. The chapter next formulates a set of seven performance rules, providing principles of response selection that tie SSDRs to antecedent stimulus conditions. A section on Pavlovian defense discusses the role of Pavlovian conditional and unconditional stimuli (CSs and USs) in the performance rules. The chapter concludes with further comments about Bolles, SSDR theory, and the respondent control of defensive behavior.

Some Memories

It was my good fortune as a graduate student to work with Robert Bolles during the better part of the 1970s. Bolles taught with a light touch, but he was electric in his ability to provide intellectual stimulation. His thinking was deep, yet clever and down-to-earth, and he repeatedly offered fascinating new ways to look at things.

I remember one occasion that seems particularly relevant to the present chapter. Bolles had told his students that he would be away for a couple of days to give a colloquium. The students recognized his destination as a university with strong religious ties. We asked what he was going to talk about, and he replied, "the evolution of behavior." Our alarm was apparent: Was he sure that he wanted to talk about evolution? Would that be a smart thing to do? Did he want to get booed out of the auditorium? His face wrinkled up into his characteristic smile, and he reassured us by saying, "I don't think there'll be a problem. It's just a theory." He later reported that the talk went well.

The point of the story is that his knowledge of the nature of theory was extremely sophisticated. Evidently, by wearing the hat of empirical determinism, he was able to assure members of a potentially hostile audience that evolutionary theory need not threaten their beliefs. Although he did not dwell on metatheory during the 1970s, it must have been one of his earlier interests. This is apparent in his book *Theory of Motivation* (Bolles, 1967, 1975), in which he presents a strong case for empirical determinism as an approach to understanding behavior. The argument is that theoretical constructs are useful in understanding behavior insofar as they help to provide a lawful account of behavior. However, they are just theory; their reality status as causal agents is another issue distinct from their scientific usefulness. That book and that argument have indelibly colored my way of looking at things (see Fanselow & Sigmundi, 1987). The present chapter is no exception. SSDRs and their evolution are viewed here as theoretical constructs, useful only to the extent that they help provide a lawful account of behavior.

The Nature of SSDRs

SSDRs are conceptualized as behavioral adaptations that have evolved through natural selection by defending the animal in dangerous situations. As theoretical constructs, SSDRs need to be described in terms of observable causes and objective response measures. Their linkage to response measures appears to be fairly direct; for example, flight is measured by withdrawal, freezing by immobility, and thigmotaxis by time near environmental structure. Their description in terms of observable causes is more interesting. Three empirically verified properties of respondent defensive behavior are critical to this description. Evidence indicates that defensive behavior (a) is situation-specific, being confined primarily to dangerous settings; (b) exhibits diversity, appearing in a number of different guises such as freezing, flight, and tonic immobility; and (c) is predictable in the sense that response selection is under stimulus control.

That SSDRs are largely specific to dangerous situations is apparent from a number of studies. First, studies show that either innate or Pavlovian danger signals elicit defense reactions (Bouton & Bolles, 1980; Fanselow & Sigmundi, 1986, Experiment 4; Sigmundi, Bouton, & Bolles, 1980). Second, studies also show that Pavlovian danger signals facilitate ongoing aversively motivated behavior and suppress appetitively motivated behavior, whereas safety signals inhibit ongoing aversively motivated behavior. This pattern of results makes sense; as phylogenetic adaptations against danger, SSDRs should be confined to dangerous situations in which their benefits outweigh their costs. The appetitive costs of defense are low in dangerous situations because a rat that engages in appetitive behavior, such as foraging, while in a dangerous situation will have little time to forage before being struck by adversity. The rat might as well spend that precious time engaging in some defensive behavior such as running away. If running away is successful, the rat will live to forage another day, and there will be more total foraging time available to the defensive rat than to the appetitive rat. Under such conditions (i.e., in dangerous situations), natural selection will favor the evolution of SSDRs.

In contrast, if defensive behavior were not confined to dangerous situations, its selective advantage would diminish and SSDRs would not evolve. In safe situations, the probability of injury is too small to favor the use of any defensive behavior that interferes with foraging. The SSDRs would be taking up time better invested in foraging. This is why SSDRs are situation-specific. They have been confined by natural selection to dangerous circumstances.

To achieve this specificity, the rat must be able to distinguish between dangerous and nondangerous situations. There is abundant evidence that the rat can do this. For example, the defense system can be activated by a number of different danger signals, including those that are patently Pavlovian as well as those, such as a cat, stress odor, and dorsal constraint, that may depend on innate recognition mechanisms (Fanselow & Sigmundi, 1987). The rat's recognition of Pavlovian and innate danger signals enables SSDRs to be confined to dangerous situations in which these responses have reduced risk in the rat's evolutionary past.

SSDRs not only are specific to dangerous situations, they also are diverse. The rat is capable of a number of SSDRs, including freezing, fleeing, fighting, threat, thigmotaxis, and tonic immobility. With such diversity, it is not enough to know that a defense reaction will occur in a dangerous situation; it also is important to know which defense reaction will occur. This knowledge is possible only if defense reactions are predictable.

SSDRs are predictable in that they are confined to dangerous situations, but they are also predictable in that the characteristics of the prevailing stimulus situation influence the form of defense. Stimulus characteristics arising from the danger signal and context determine which SSDR will appear in a dangerous situation. For example, in a common fear conditioning chamber, freezing is a highly probable defense reaction in response to either contextual cues or discrete CSs (Sigmundi & Bolles, 1983). By making the chamber long and narrow or by providing escape routes, freezing can be replaced, at least to some extent, by withdrawal-related behaviors (Bolles & Collier, 1976). In addition, a localizable danger signal such as a lightbulb or an approaching shock prod can elicit withdrawal responses and disrupt freezing (Blanchard & Blanchard, 1969b; Karpicke, Christoph, Peterson, & Hearst, 1977, Experiments 4 and 5; Leclerc, 1985; Leclerc & Reberg, 1980). These outcomes indicate that prevailing stimulus characteristics can guide response selection, exerting re-spondent control over the topography of behavior—its form and direction. Therefore, SSDRs appear to be predictable in the sense that they are un-der the topographical control of prevailing stimulus properties as well as the motivational control of danger and safety signals.

The Problem-Specific Response Hypothesis

Given that both the probability and topography of aversively motivated behavior are predictable from the prevailing stimulus array, it makes sense to ask about the basis of this predictability. Why did evolution favor certain stimulus–response correlations and not others? One answer be-gins with the assumption that defensive behavior has functioned to pro-mote fitness in a number of dangerous situations. For example, defensive behavior might help to protect the rat from a number of predatory species. It might help the rat to avoid a predatory encounter or to thwart an attack, once underway. These various situations did not all exert a common se-lection pressure favoring one and the same behavior. If this were the case, there would not be such a diversity of SSDRs. Neither did each situation exert a selection pressure that favored all SSDRs equally. If this were the case, SSDRs would be inherently unpredictable, and there would be no respondent control over their form and direction. Instead, an evolutionary account that is consistent with both the diversity and respondent predict-ability of SSDRs postulates that over the course of its phylogeny, various recurrent defensive problems exerted distinctive selection pressures on the rat's defensive behavior.

Such pressures led to the evolution of a diverse number of SSDRs because different defensive problems required different SSDRs for reso-lution. The distinctive selection pressures also favored the evolution of innate recognition processes that enabled animals to distinguish among the different problems. Innate recognition provided a selective advantage to animals that deployed their defense reactions in appropriate situations. Recognition of these situations evolved to provide the stimulus conditions by which the rat gauges the nature of its plight and directs its responding. Therefore, SSDRs are situation-specific, diverse, and predictable on the basis of antecedent stimulus conditions, because certain stimulus config-urations were phylogenetically valid indicators of recurrent defensive problems and because SSDRs provided adaptive solutions to those prob-lems.

This view has led to the problem-specific response hypothesis. The hypothesis states that SSDRs are not only species-specific and situation-specific but also problem-specific; when the defense system is activated, a problem-specific defense reaction emerges. Its emergence is dictated by stimulus configurations that were correlated in the animal's phylogeny with problem-specific selection pressures. If one wants to predict the to-pography of defensive behavior—its direction and form—one must specify these stimulus configurations.

Analysis of Stages of Defense

The problem-specific response hypothesis suggests that one might start by generating hypotheses about the problem-specific selection pressures that came to bear on the rat over evolutionary time. Because one set of selection pressures was likely provided by the natural predators of the rat, the analysis of predator–prey relationships might prove a useful heuristic for hypotheses about the rat's recognition of defensive problems.

Distance From the Predator

In this vein, Ratner (1967) suggested that the form of defense can be expected to vary with the proximity of the predator. When the predator is far away, one can expect little defensive behavior from the prey. At a closer distance, the rat might engage in antidetection behavior such as freezing or hiding. As the predator draws near, flight might predominate, but when the predator is in contact with the rat, the rat is likely to exhibit violent counterattack and escape behavior, possibly followed by tonic immobility (e.g., Ratner, 1967).

An elaboration of these ideas, including their incorporation into the problem-specific response hypothesis, is possible by considering antipredator defense within the context of optimal foraging theory. Foraging theorists have analyzed predator–prey encounters from the point of view of the predator. They have compartmentalized foraging behavior into a sequence of stages that corresponds to the sequence of problem classes that arise during hunting. The predator must scout for a patch in which to hunt, search the patch for a good prey item, procure the prey item with tactics such as pursuit or ambush, and handle the prey in preparation for consumption. The predator should move through these stages of foraging only when this increases the chance of completing a profitable predatory encounter. The return to an earlier stage of foraging should be governed by the same principle.

To the extent that each stage of foraging requires different capabilities on the part of the predator, each stage might exert distinctive selection pressures on the prey. Each stage might favor distinctive defensive strategies because an effective defense at one stage of foraging might be useless or counterproductive at another. If so, SSDRs might be compartmentalized into a number of distinct stages of defense corresponding to the sequence of problem classes that arise when the prey is being hunted, such as how to avoid detection, procurement, and handling by the predator.

Antidetection, antiprocurement, and antihandling stages of defense have much in common with Ratner's (1967) notion that the proximity of the predator determines the form of defense; however, a classification in terms of stages of defense also leaves open the possibility that additional factors such as the presence of escape routes and places to hide can be important in defining the defensive problem and determining the form of defense.

Antihandling Defense

On the basis of his formulation of defense in terms of distance from the predator, Ratner (1967) indicated that when the predator is in contact with the prey, the prey should exhibit fighting and, in the absence of escape, subsequent tonic immobility. According to the stages of defense analysis, this description characterizes the antihandling stage of defense. Contact by a potential predator should serve as an innate danger signal, activating the defense system and problem-specific defense reactions.

Evidence indicates that this is the case. First, dorsal-tactile stimulation activates struggling in the rat (Brady & Nauta, 1953), sometimes followed by tonic immobility (Ratner, 1967). Second, in the mouse there is evidence that giving a few pinches to the back of the neck activates a naloxone-reversible catatonia (Amir, Brown, Amit, & Ornstein, 1981). Furthermore, Fanselow and Sigmundi (1986) showed that nonhabituated dorsal constraint (being grasped around the back and sides) produces analgesia in the rat. These findings indicate that physical contact with the experimenter is capable of activating both the opioid and SSDR components of the defense system.

On the basis of such data, dorsal-tactile stimulation appears to provide the rat with a defensive cue signifying a phylogenetically recurrent defensive problem. The rat responds with an active defense system that is manifest in opioid release and a defense reaction appropriate to the problem: struggling.

Prehandling Defense

In the stages of defense analysis, one can look at defensive behavior in terms of prehandling as well as antihandling defenses. From this perspective, one might attempt to analyze the rat's behavior in terms of antidetection and antiprocurement tactics. Freezing and flight might have evolved to serve these respective functions.

A long-recognized difficulty with conceptualizing prehandling defense is that, given that the rat has spotted a predator, it is unclear how the rat knows whether the predator has already spotted the rat. If the predator has not, an antidetection strategy such as freezing would be appropriate, but if the predator has already detected the rat, an antiprocurement strategy such as flight might be a better defense. To deploy antidetection and antiprocurement defenses appropriately, the rat must have some indication of whether it has been seen by the predator. What cues might the rat use for such an indication? Such cues would be likely candidates to elicit freezing and flight.

According to Ratner's (1967) hypothesis, the rat responds on the basis of distance from the predator. If the predator is beyond the flight distance, the rat responds as if it is undetected and freezes. If the predator violates the flight distance, the rat responds as if it has been detected and flees. However, other factors are likely involved; for example, flight distance might be expected to vary with the presence versus absence of escape routes.

Blanchard, Fukunaga, and Blanchard (1976) identified the presence versus absence of escape routes as critical to the rat's freeze–flee decision. When confronted with danger and the presence of escape routes, the rat should flee; however, if no escape routes are available, the rat should freeze. It may be that both distance from the predator and presence versus absence of escape routes are stimulus factors that have been phylogenetically correlated with adaptive solutions to antidetection and antiprocurement problems. The stages of defense analysis recognize this possibility. One of the questions left unanswered concerns what makes an escape route. Is it simply the availability of a path away from the predator? This question is examined in a subsequent section on the freeze–flee decision.

Multiplicity of Threats

The analysis in terms of stages of defense emphasizes the multiplicity of biologically important events that can arise at different levels of risk to control defensive behavior. Examples include nociceptive stimuli, constraint, rapid approach by a potential predator, and surprising stimuli. This multiplicity seems critical to an analysis of the Pavlovian basis of defense. The chances are small that a prey animal could withstand repeated nociceptive episodes with a predator, thus precluding the opportunity for many conditioning trials (Bolles, 1970). The availability of important stimuli at earlier stages of predation, when there is less risk, alleviates this problem. If conditioning can occur at lower levels of risk, the opportunity increases for repeated learning trials.

In this regard, the findings of Fanselow and Sigmundi (1986) have indicated that dorsal constraint, implemented by the experimenter grabbing the rat, can function to activate the defense system. Those findings provided evidence that dorsal constraint can trigger the problem-specific defense reaction of struggling. The findings also raise the possibility that dorsal constraint might function as an aversive unconditional stimulus (US) to produce Pavlovian conditioning of the defense system to prehandling stimuli. The prehandling stimuli would then be capable of activating prehandling stages of defense such as antidetection and antiprocurement behaviors.

Fanselow and I addressed this possibility in the following two experiments. Dorsal constraint was paired with a conditional stimulus (CS) composed of contextual cues arising from a semicircular open field apparatus (diameter = 1.2 m). On each of 2 days, individual rats (210-day-old Sprague-Dawley males, $ns = 8$) in the conditioning group were placed in the open field using a handling technique in which they were picked up by the base of the tail. Each rat remained in the open field for 4 minutes and then was removed with the dorsal constraint procedure. Rats in a pseudoconditioning control group received the same treatment except that on Day 1 their placement was into a distinctively different apparatus, a T maze with 13.3-cm-wide alleys, a 30.5-cm-long stem, and arms that spanned 170 cm. Rats in the sensitization control group were placed and removed from the semicircular open field using the tail pickup technique. They did not experience dorsal constraint.

There were no reliable differences in freezing among the groups on Day 1. Group means were 9.6, 3.8, and 5.2 s for the conditioning, pseudoconditioning, and sensitization groups, respectively. However, on Day 2, animals in the conditioning group ($M = 134$ s) froze reliably more than those in either the pseudoconditioning ($M = 82$ s) or sensitization ($M = 61$ s) control groups, $F(2, 21) = 4.26$. The conditioning group froze more than the pooled pseudoconditioning and sensitization groups, $F(1, 21) = 7.89$. The latter two groups did not differ. These results suggest the operation of a Pavlovian conditioning mechanism in the conditioning group whereby the rats associated the trauma of dorsal constraint on Day 1 with the contextual cues arising from the open field. Subsequently, when placed in the open field on Day 2, the open field cues caused the Pavlovian activation of the defense system, which was manifested in the freezing SSDR. These results are consistent with the possibility that dorsal constraint can function as an aversive US in a Pavlovian conditioning paradigm to condition prehandling defensive behaviors to contextual cues. In suggesting that stimuli other than nociception can condition defensive behavior, the results are also consistent with the prediction from the stages of defense analysis that there are a multiplicity of biologically important events that can control defensive behavior at different levels of risk.

The Freeze–Flee Decision

There is another aspect of the results that seems crucial to an understanding of the rat's prehandling defensive strategies. Observations suggested that freezing was confined largely to locations near structure which was provided by the walls of the open field. Because the rats were placed into the center of the open field, they had to move to the walls before freezing there. This suggests that freezing was not the only defense reaction that was occurring. The rats also seemed to have been fleeing in the sense that they displayed thigmotaxic responses (Grossen & Kelley, 1972) by moving toward locations with structure.

A second experiment with Fanselow examined this possibility in more detail by using an observer blind to the treatment condition to monitor not only the time spent freezing but also the location of freezing. In a 2 × 2 random groups design ($ns = 4$), Long-Evans female rats (120 days old) were placed by the tail into either of two open fields (Box A measured 30 × 105 cm; Box B was 51 × 86 cm) for 4 minutes on Day 1 before being removed by dorsal constraint. On Day 2, they were again placed by the tail for 4 minutes into one of the two open fields; one half of the animals were placed into the same open field they had experienced on the previous day, whereas the remaining rats were placed into the second open field.

An analysis of Day 2 freezing indicated that neither the main effect of Day 1 open field nor the main effect of Day 2 open field was significant. However, the interaction was significant: Context-specific freezing was again demonstrated in that rats placed in the same open field on each of the 2 days froze reliably more on Day 2 (M = 72.8 s) than did rats that were shifted to a different open field on Day 2 (M = 25.2 s), $F(1, 12)$ = 5.59. Perhaps more important, nearly 95 percent of all freezing on Day 2 occurred in locations adjacent to the walls and corners of the open field and distant from the experimenter. Because the placement of the rats was into the middle of the open field, near the experimenter's location, ambulation occurred before the freezing response. The rats withdrew from the experimenter and toward structure before freezing.

Such results contrast nicely with work by Suarez and Gallup (1981), who examined the rat's response to the experimenter in an open field test and found that ambulation is not an automatic response to placement in an open field. When their rats were placed in a corner distant from the experimenter, little locomotion occurred.

The present results also bear on work by Grossen and Kelley (1972; Kelley, 1985), who documented in the lab rat that danger increases the rat's thigmotaxic tendencies. When frightened, the rat moves toward environmental structure such as the walls of the test apparatus. The present results extend those findings by demonstrating that freezing follows thigmotaxic movement. Taken together, these findings indicate that the rat ambulates only under certain conditions and freezes only in certain locations. If the rat is not in a suitable location for freezing, ambulation toward that location precedes freezing. However, if the rat is already in a suitable location, freezing occurs there and is not preceded by ambulation.

On the basis of the preceding evidence, the prehandling defense of the rat might conform to a freeze–flee rule such as the following: When in danger, flee to the most suitable accessible location, then freeze (see also Fanselow, Sigmundi, & Williams, 1987).

This performance rule, when used to model prehandling defense, provides a strong heuristic by highlighting three aspects of the freeze–flee decision that are amenable to investigation. The performance rule underscores the importance of understanding the factors that determine (a) what makes a location suitable for freezing, (b) what makes a location accessible, and (c) the sequencing of freezing and flight.

Suitability

What constitutes a suitable location in which to freeze? The preceding evidence from open field tests indicates that freezing occurs distant from the experimenter, next to walls, where no further withdrawal is possible. This evidence is consistent with the view that distance from the predator, absence of escape routes, and presence of structure are all critical in determining a place to freeze. However, there is another study that strikes to the heart of this matter and suggests that a single underlying factor can define the suitability of a location for freezing.

Fanselow and Lester (1988) found in a fear conditioning preparation that the rat confines its freezing to that part of the conditioning chamber that has been associated with Pavlovian safety from shock. In sum, the rat's tendencies to move away from an experimenter toward structure, and to freeze near either structure or Pavlovian safety, suggest that structure signals relative safety. Possibly, structure offers safety in the form of cover and concealment. The implication is that relative safety provides the stimulus configuration that defines for the rat a suitable place to freeze.

Accessibility

Given that the rat is in danger, what defines the accessibility of a suitably safe location? The freeze–flee rule proposes that accessibility is necessary before flight will occur. The question is tantamount to asking what constitutes an escape route for the rat. If one considers this question from a phylogenetic perspective, an escape route would be a path along which the rat could flee to a safer location without increasing the risk that would obtain if the rat froze in place. In this view, an escape route is a path from danger toward relative safety, a path down a gradient of perceived danger.

On this basis, the proposed freeze–flee performance rule can be revised as follows: When in danger, flee to a local minimum of danger—an accessible location of relative safety—then freeze. This rule emphasizes that the pattern of danger confronting the rat determines whether freezing or flight will occur. The pattern of danger has provided the stimulus correlates for effective prehandling defense over the course of phylogeny.

Returning to the conundrum of prehandling defense, consider again how the rat can know whether it has been detected by a predator. First, freezing should be maximally effective in a suitable location for freezing (i.e., a relatively safe place). Second, flight should be maximally effective in a suitable location for flight (i.e., a location with access to relative safety). If freezing and flight are truly antidetection and antiprocurement defenses, respectively, then the rat's location with respect to danger and relative safety should be correlated over phylogeny with whether or not the rat has been detected by a predator. According to this view, in a suitably safe location, the rat should bet that it has not yet been detected and freeze. However, on a gradient of perceived danger—a poor location for freezing—the rat should bet that it has already been spotted by the predator and flee down the gradient to a local minimum of danger before freezing.

The Sequencing of Freezing and Flight

Predictions about the sequencing of freezing and flight follow from the freeze–flee performance rule. Either response might precede the other, depending on whether the rat first encounters a local minimum of danger or a gradient of danger.

There is an implication here for studies of conditioned freezing and aversive-sign tracking. Studies of conditioned freezing indicate that the rat freezes in response to a Pavlovian danger signal (e.g., Blanchard & Blanchard, 1969a; Bouton & Bolles, 1980; Sigmundi & Bolles, 1983; Sigmundi et al., 1980). Studies of aversive sign tracking indicate that the rat flees from Pavlovian danger toward safety (Blanchard & Blanchard, 1969b; Karpicke et al., 1977; Leclerc, 1985; Leclerc & Reberg, 1980; Odling-Smee, 1978). The open field data reported here indicate that both freezing and flight can occur in response to the same danger signal in an aversive-conditioning experiment. If the danger signal appears in a location near the rat, the rat first flees along the gradient of danger determined by distance and then freezes in a part of the apparatus distant from the danger signal. The freeze–flee decision rule predicts, therefore, that freezing will follow flight in studies of either aversive-sign tracking or conditioned freezing when the rat is on a gradient of danger.

Freezing and Flight as Default Responses

At first it might appear that the freeze–flee performance rule suggests that freezing is the preferred response over flight because the rat flees only if it is not in a location suitable for freezing. This view contrasts markedly with the idea that freezing is a passive response that occurs only by default when there are no escape routes. However, it may be a mistake to think of either freezing or flight as a default response. The necessary conditions for flight and for freezing are mutually exclusive. The rat cannot be in two places at once. The rat cannot be located in a local minimum of danger and, at the same time, have access to a safer location. The rat can occupy only one position at a time along a gradient of danger. According to the freeze–flee decision rule, therefore, there are well-defined and mutually exclusive stimulus conditions for both responses, and neither response occurs in lieu of the other.

Both freezing and flight are active defenses. Both are problem-specific defense reactions. It may be more appropriate to refer to freezing as a stationary defense rather than a passive one (cf. Fanselow et al., 1987).

Performance Rules

By performance rules, I mean statements specifying the proximate causes of behavior. In the case of defensive behavior, performance rules should specify the linkages that tie SSDRs to observable antecedent conditions. As theoretical constructs, SSDRs also need linkages to empirical referents on the consequent side. These linkages are fairly direct, tying SSDRs to response measures such as immobility, withdrawal, and struggling. The antecedent linkages are more involved.

The problem-specific response hypothesis maintains that SSDRs are problem-specific defense reactions that arose as adaptations to recurrent defensive problems that have confronted the rat over the course of evolution. The present analysis goes on to suggest the possibility that defensive problems are defined for the rat by the perceived pattern of danger, which in turn is determined by the locations of innate and Pavlovian danger and safety signals. This means that performance rules must specify how the locations of danger and safety signals map onto various SSDRs. Because the following performance rules are concerned with the proximate causes of behavior, I have stripped them of much of the surplus meaning that arose from the phylogenetic analysis:

Rule 1 (the predictability rule): SSDRs are situation-specific, diverse, and predictable. There are a number of different SSDRs, each guided by a distinctive pattern of aversive stimulation.

Rule 2 (the danger rule): Pavlovian and innate danger signals produce gradients of perceived danger. These gradients diminish in strength with distance from the danger signal.

Rule 3 (the safety rule): Pavlovian and innate safety signals inhibit perceived danger, and the gradients of inhibition diminish in strength with distance from the safety signal.

Rule 4 (the response production rule): The amount of perceived danger determines the probability of defense.

Rule 5 (the response selection rule): The rat's location on gradients of perceived danger guides the form of defense.

Rule 6 (the antihandling rule): Contact with a potential predator triggers struggling, possibly followed by tonic immobility.

Rule 7 (the prehandling rule): Rats flee from perceived danger toward relative safety and freeze in locations of relative safety.

Pavlovian Defense

Antecedent stimuli play two roles in regulating defensive behavior. First, their motivational properties trigger response production by activating the defense system. Second, their support properties dictate response selection by creating gradients of danger and relative safety to guide problem-specific defense reactions. This is the case for Pavlovian CSs as well as other stimuli.

Some stimuli have powerful motivational properties but weak support properties, so that response selection must be carried out by other stimuli. An example might be an unlocalized Pavlovian danger signal that can activate the defense system without affecting the pattern of danger in the rat's problem space. In contrast, some stimuli have weak motivational properties but strong support properties, so that activation of the defense system must be carried out by another stimulus. Examples are provided by safety signals; they cannot activate the defense system (although they can deactivate it), but they can modify the pattern of danger in the rat's surroundings. Still other stimuli have powerful motivational and support properties. For example, a localized danger signal can activate the defense system and define the location of maximum danger in the rat's problem space. A second example is provided by predatory handling stimuli that activate the defense system and select antihandling defenses such as struggling and tonic immobility.

Consideration of the role of Pavlovian CSs in response production and selection points to a third way that stimuli can exert respondent control over defensive behavior. Pavlovian USs can condition danger and safety to discrete CSs and contextual cues in the rat's defensive problem space. It is this conditioning that provides Pavlovian CSs with their motivational and response selection properties. The rat's problem space is defined by Pavlovian and innate danger and safety signals, both discrete stimuli and contextual cues. The interrelationships between these CSs, USs, and contextual stimuli determine the pattern of danger confronting the rat. According to the problem-specific response hypothesis, the pattern of danger elicits appropriate defensive behavior by providing antecedent stimulus configurations that have been correlated over phylogeny with recurrent defensive problems.

As a consequence, similarity is the key to response selection in both Pavlovian and non-Pavlovian defense: the similarity of the CS, the US, the context, and their interrelationship to recurrent defensive problems that have confronted the rat over the course of evolution. Pavlovian stimulus substitution theory posits that conditioning causes the CS to become a substitute for the US so that the organism responds to the CS as if it were the US. To the extent that the CS and US share similarities, the CR will look like the UR but be directed at the CS. Although the present formulation views stimulus substitution as a cause for the form of the Pavlovian conditioned response, it is not a substitution of the CS for the US. Instead, the rat's current defensive problem space shares similarities with and becomes a substitute for a prototypical phylogenetic defensive problem. The rat responds to the current situation on that basis.

Conclusion

Robert Bolles had a long-standing interest in the issue of what reinforces avoidance conditioning. His scholarly and empirical work on this topic uncovered the importance of the response requirement for effective avoidance conditioning, and this in turn led to the notion of SSDRs. According to Bolles (1970), rapid avoidance conditioning requires an SSDR as the avoidance response. A particular SSDR will emerge in that role because the avoidance contingency will suppress alternative SSDRs by virtue of either the disrupting or punishing effects of shock.

That viewpoint changed during the 1970s, as Bolles became more and more intrigued with the possibility that the frightened rat engages in little or no learning about response contingencies. Bolles did not think that the frightened rat was that smart, and he did not think that a real-world predator would be forgiving enough to allow the rat to engage in trial-and-error learning. He also had laboratory data indicating that the rapid emergence of freezing as an avoidance response depended on the disruptive rather than the response-contingent punishing effects of shock (Bolles & Riley, 1973). Bolles felt that, instead of response-outcome learning, the rat might rely entirely on respondent behavior to solve its defensive problems. Maybe avoidance conditioning could be explained solely in terms of the respondent control of defense. Bolles was pushing the SSDR envelope.

When focusing solely on a respondent account of behavior, one can no longer use the principle of reinforcement (or punishment) to explain response selection. Things like affordances and behavioral support stimuli must carry the weight. But neither Bolles nor his students understood clearly how such respondent factors would operate. We could not even imagine what a model based on such factors would look like. In the face of such uncertainty, it appears that we tacitly adopted a neutral, atheoretical terminology and began referring to the respondent relationships governing response selection as *performance rules*. If we could at least list the relationships as a set of rules, we might then be able to figure out how to model them with psychological constructs in a more interesting way.

The present chapter was aimed at producing such a set of performance rules with enough detail and enough formality to enable them to support subsequent research on defensive response selection. The rules were initially envisioned as taking the form of an atheoretical catalogue of stimulus–response linkages. Instead, what emerged from the analysis was a catalogue of a different sort with theoretical constructs involving innate recognition and patterns of perceived danger and safety.

References

Amir, S., Brown, Z. W., Amit, Z., & Ornstein, K. (1981). Body-pinches produce long lasting cataleptic-like immobility in mice: Behavioral characterization and effects of naloxone. *Life Sciences, 10,* 1189–1194.

Blanchard, R. J., & Blanchard, D. C. (1969a). Crouching as an index of fear. *Journal of Comparative and Physiological Psychology, 67,* 370–375.

Blanchard, R. J., & Blanchard, D. C. (1969b). Passive and active reactions to fear-eliciting stimuli. *Journal of Comparative and Physiological Psychology, 68,* 129–135.

Blanchard, R. J., Fukunaga, K. K., & Blanchard, D. C. (1976). Environmental control of defensive reactions to a cat. *Bulletin of the Psychonomic Society, 8,* 179–181.

Bolles, R. C. (1967). *Theory of motivation.* New York: Harper & Row.

Bolles, R. C. (1970). Species-specific defense reactions and avoidance learning. *Psychological Review, 71,* 32–48.

Bolles, R. C. (1975). *Theory of motivation* (2nd ed.). New York: Harper & Row.

Bolles, R. C., & Collier, A. C. (1976). The effect of predictive cues on freezing in rats. *Animal Learning & Behavior, 4,* 6–8.

Bolles, R. C., & Riley, A. L. (1973). Freezing as an avoidance response: Another look at the operant-respondent distinction. *Learning and Motivation, 4,* 268–275.

Bouton, M. E., & Bolles, R. C. (1980). Conditioned fear assessed by freezing and by the suppression of three different baselines. *Animal Learning & Behavior, 8,* 429–434.

Brady, J. V., & Nauta, W. J. H. (1953). Subcortical mechanisms in emotional behaviors: Affective changes following septal forebrain lesions in the albino rat. *Journal of Comparative and Physiological Psychology, 46,* 339–346.

Fanselow, M. F., & Lester, L. S. (1988). A functional behavioristic approach to aversively motivated behavior: Predatory imminence as a determinant of the topography of defensive behavior. In R. C. Bolles & M. D. Beecher (Eds.), *Evolution and learning* (pp. 185–211). Hillsdale, NJ: Erlbaum.

Fanselow, M. F., & Sigmundi, R. A. (1986). Species-specific danger signals, endogenous opioid analgesia, and defensive behavior. *Journal of Experimental Psychology: Animal Behavior Processes, 12,* 301–309.

Fanselow, M. F., & Sigmundi, R. A. (1987). Functional behaviorism and aversively motivated behavior: A role for endogenous opioids in the defensive behavior of the rat. *Psychological Record, 37,* 317–334.

Fanselow, M. F., Sigmundi, R. A., & Williams, J. L. (1987). Response selection and the hierarchical organization of species-specific defense reactions: The relationship between freezing, flight, and defensive burying. *Psychological Record, 37,* 381–386.

Grossen, N. E., & Kelley, M. J. (1972). Species specific behavior and acquisition of avoidance behavior in rats. *Journal of Comparative and Physiological Psychology, 81,* 307–310.

Karpicke, J., Christoph, G., Peterson, G., & Hearst, E. (1977). Signal location and positive versus negative conditioned suppression in the rat. *Journal of Experimental Psychology: Animal Behavior Processes, 3,* 105–118.

Kelley, M. J. (1985). Species-typical taxic behavior and event-reinforcer interactions in conditioning. *Learning and Motivation, 16,* 301–314.

Leclerc, R. (1985). Sign-tracking behavior in aversive conditioning: Its acquisition via a Pavlovian mechanism and its suppression by operant contingencies. *Learning and Motivation, 16,* 63–82.

Leclerc, R., & Reberg, D. (1980). Sign-tracking in aversive conditioning. *Learning and Motivation, 11,* 302–317.

Odling-Smee, F. J. (1978). The overshadowing of background stimuli by an informative CS in aversive Pavlovian conditioning with rats. *Animal Learning & Behavior, 6,* 43–51.

Ratner, S. C. (1967). Comparative aspects of hypnosis. In J. E. Gordon (Ed.), *Handbook of clinical and experimental hypnosis* (pp. 550–587). New York: MacMillan.

Sigmundi, R. A., & Bolles, R. C. (1983). CS modality, context conditioning, and conditioned freezing. *Animal Learning & Behavior, 11,* 205–212.

Sigmundi, R. A., Bouton, M. E., & Bolles, R. C. (1980). Conditioned freezing in the rat as a function of shock intensity and CS modality. *Bulletin of the Psychonomic Society, 209,* 254–256.

Suarez, S. D., & Gallup, G. G. (1981). An ethological analysis of open-field behavior in rats and mice. *Learning and Motivation, 12,* 342–363.

16

Species-Specific Defense Reactions: Retrospect and Prospect

Michael S. Fanselow

Robert C. Bolles was a Kuhnian. He believed the greatest leaps in science were caused by the overthrow of prevailing paradigms. According to Kuhn (1962), these leaps were not one-step processes. First, sufficient contrary data had to be collected, enough so that it was generally recognized that the paradigm was wanting. This dissatisfaction with the prevailing view rendered the ground fertile for acceptance of an alternative conceptualization. The alternative had to explain the previous inconsistencies but also be generative, providing a course for new discovery.

The purpose of this chapter is to examine the history and development of and suggest future directions for species-specific defense reaction (SSDR) theory (Bolles, 1970). Because SSDR theory was a reaction to the dominant approach in learning theory at the time, to appreciate it best one must appreciate the previously prevailing paradigms (see Bolles, 1972a, for a complete historical review of avoidance). Before Bolles's SSDR analysis, an instrumental reinforcement view dominated the interpretation of aversively motivated behavior. Avoidance and escape behavior were the major forms of aversively motivated behavior, and they were defined by their reinforcement contingencies. Escape ended some aversive event; avoidance prevented it. A major empirical impetus for this approach was Brogden, Lipman, and Culler's (1938) finding that inevitable conditional stimulus−unconditional stimulus (CS-US) pairings did not foster maximum performance. Rather, response-contingent removal of certain stimuli, such as the CS or US, improved performance.

The major theoretical problem for the reinforcement perspective was postulating what physical event served as reinforcement for avoidance. Living organisms were viewed as unconscious, passively connectionistic machines that could not possibly know the future, so that removal of something not already there could not act to reinforce. The necessary theoretical development came with Miller (1941, 1951) and Mowrer's (1939, 1947) two-factor theories, which pointed to the removal of conditional fear stimuli. The two processes of two-factor theory were the acquisition of fear as a motivator (first factor) and the acquisition of an arbitrary response through fear-reduction reinforcement (second factor). There were other theories proposed during this period that emphasized removal of conditional aversive stimuli (Schoenfeld, 1950) or changes in rate of delivery of the shock (Herrnstein & Hineline, 1966), but they had one essential commonality: They were all reinforcement theories. It was this perspective that SSDR theory revolted against. To Bolles, reinforcement theory was anathema. Something that automatically stamped in a connection between arbitrary bits of stimuli and responses did not square with his views on cognition or his appreciation of the functional nature of behavior.

There are several elements necessary to the development of a Kuhnian analysis: First, one must specify why the prevailing paradigm was so unsatisfactory that it required an alternative. Because Bolles has written extensively on the subject, I establish this point briefly. Second, an alternative paradigm must be described. SSDR theory was not put forth in a single article but developed over a series of articles (Crawford & Masterson, 1982). Because this development has not been completely clear in the literature, I devote considerable space to it. Finally, once the new theory is developed, it must dictate a new paradigm and a particular way of approaching scientific experimentation. This mode of research is what Kuhn called *normal science*. SSDR theory replaced the study of aversive motivation through avoidance learning with an analysis of defensive behavior. I outline some of the major questions raised by such an analysis and some of the progress made on resolving these issues. Finally, I suggest some future directions in the study of mechanisms of defensive behaviors and how an analysis of defensive behavior may provide insight into the complexities of performance in avoidance learning situations.

Reinforcement Theories and Aversively Motivated Behavior

Bolles wrote extensively about the failures of reinforcement theory (see Bolles, 1972b, 1989, for reviews). Here I simply note some of the findings that make this view untenable as far as aversively motivated behavior is concerned.

Reinforcement and Avoidance

Two-factor theory argued that whatever response occurred contiguously with fear reduction would automatically be strengthened. For avoidance responding, this meant that the response had to occur at the same time as a cue that normally preceded shock, and the response had to remove that cue. In other words, there had to be a warning signal and a response contingency, such that the response removed the warning signal. Learning in a prototypical avoidance situation was thought to proceed in the following manner: A rat was placed in a shuttlebox, where it received occasional presentations of a tone followed by shock. Therefore, the rat inevitably received tone–shock pairings. The tone acquired the ability to produce fear, which acted as a nonspecific motivator arousing the animal to action.

This activity would continue until the animal made some response that reduced the fear. The experimenter designed the situation such that some prechosen response could turn off the tone. Two-factor theory took fear reduction caused by warning signal termination, not avoidance of the impending shock, as the major reinforcer. This is because reinforcement theories required a tangible event, such as the removal of something present, for reinforcement. Shock was not there, so its removal was not tangible. In his lectures, Bolles illustrated this point by saying that lots of things did not happen to the rat that made the avoidance response besides not getting shocked. It did not get run over by a yellow Volkswagen either, but that could not be considered a reinforcer.

Owing to heavy indoctrination into the dictates of reinforcement theory in general and two-factor theory in particular, this view may seem plausible to many psychologists. Indeed, years of research that heavily constrained the apparatus used, the responses measured, and the contingencies tested seemed to suggest that the CS-termination contingency accounted for much behavior (e.g., Kamin, 1957; Mowrer & Lamoureaux, 1942). Research that thoroughly manipulated these factors, however, found the inference severely limited (Bolles, Stokes, & Younger, 1966). The backbone of the two-factor theorists' experimentation was the shuttlebox, but even here warning signal termination in isolation had little ability to strengthen behavior. When in combination with the other two potential sources of reinforcement, shock escape and shock avoidance, CS termination had about the same impact as these other two contingencies (Bolles et al., 1966). In the running wheel, Brogden et al.'s apparatus that started aversive learning rolling down the reinforcement road, the situation was even more dire for two-factor theory. Here Bolles et al. (1966) found that the avoidance contingency was the major determinant of behavior, with warning signal termination accounting for little variance. The relative importance of the avoidance and CS-termination contingencies was exactly opposite to that predicted by two-factor theory. Note that by focusing attention on the relative effectiveness of various reinforcement contingencies, the most significant aspect of the Bolles et al. study is missed: The response being examined (wheel running or shuttling) is a more important determinant of performance than any reinforcement contingency, and the impact of a reinforcement contingency depends on what response is examined.

Proponents of two-factor theory have usually held that a demonstration that CS termination contributes to avoidance performance is sufficient support for the theory (see Ayres, in press, for a recent exemplar). For example, Bolles et al. (1966) reported that adding CS termination to the escape contingency in the shuttlebox improved performance from 9 to 31 percent avoidance responses. Manipulating the CS-termination contingency in isolation or collapsing data in a fashion that effectively does so allows one to find a statistically significant effect of the CS-termination contingency (e.g., Kamin, 1957; Mowrer & Lamoreaux, 1942). But two-factor theory cannot explain why, in the Bolles et al. (1966) experiment, adding avoidance to the escape contingency is even more effective than adding the CS-termination contingency: It drives shuttlebox performance from 9 to 37 percent. The theory also does not explain why results change drastically when the running wheel is used; in that case, only the avoidance contingency effectively adds to performance.

One argument that can be made on behalf of two-factor theory is based on its motivational principle rather than its reinforcement principle: Fear energizes elicited behavior, and infrequent responses never get the chance to contact reinforcement (i.e., their operant rate is too low). However, Bolles (1969) examined several behaviors that started at equivalent and relatively high baseline or operant rates such that all responses could make contact with the CS-termination contingency. Even so, a running response readily increased, whereas rearing showed no change over 80 trials. A turning response changed only if it had all three contingencies working for it (CS termination, escape, and avoidance). Even when responses had ample opportunity to contact their consequences, therefore, the results had little to do with the reinforcement contingencies per se; rather, they interacted with the particular response that was being examined. Reinforcement contingencies of any ilk seemed to have little predictive usefulness for avoidance behavior.

Reinforcement in Escape

In contrast to the difficulties in specifying a reinforcement contingency for avoidance, logically identifying the reinforcer for escape is trivial. The termination of the aversive event, usually electric shock in the laboratory arena, should be a potent reinforcer. Rats rapidly come to perform a lever press to escape shock, although they have exceeding difficulty doing the same to avoid a shock (e.g., Dinsmoor & Hughes, 1956). This fact has been taken as an argument against SSDR theory by some writers (e.g., Dinsmoor, 1982; Myers, 1982): If lever pressing does not occur in avoidance situations because it is not an SSDR, then it should not occur in escape situations either. Yet a look under the surface reveals that this robust behavior has little to do with reinforcement. The rat responds to shock with an incredibly short latency (Bolles & McGillis, 1968), so short that it seems likely that the behavior is a prewired reflex. Davis and Burton (1974) carefully measured the rat's contact with the response lever. They found that when shock begins, the rat is reflexively bounced about in the Skinner box. When it bounces against the response lever, the shock ends. The bouncing stops, and the rat is near the lever. The rat begins to freeze on the bar, and shock onset again initiates reflexive activity that terminates the shock. The acquisition of bar-press escape behavior has nothing to do with reinforcement of some arbitrary operant. Perhaps the most conclusive proof of this came from a simple study by Davis (1979) that demonstrated lever-press "escape" in an anesthetized rat. Either reinforcement processes are the same whether or not the central nervous system is shut down or escape behavior is not a reinforced operant.

A Species-Specific Defense Reaction Theory of Avoidance Learning

Bolles (1970) developed an account of avoidance that directly faced the problems of the importance of the response requirement and the inability of reinforcement schedules to alter performance predictably. The solution was simple. Shocks conditioned fear to the apparatus and any predictive cues in the situation. However, this fear differed from the generalized motivator envisioned by two-factor theory. Fear narrowed the response repertoire. The frightened rat did what its species evolved to do when it was afraid; it engaged in species-specific defense reactions. If the experimenter-imposed response requirement was similar to an SSDR, the rat had little trouble. If it was completely incompatible, the rat would never master the situation. Intermediate performance would be achieved when the response requirement matched a low-probability SSDR or only partially matched an SSDR.

According to this approach, rats rapidly learned in what situations they could expect shock, but in such situations they could do only what they were genetically programmed to do. Bolles's view of learning was cognitive; it suggested that the contents of learning were stimulus–stimulus (S-S* where S* was a biologically meaningful event e.g., Bolles, 1972b). Rats learned that certain cues predicted shock and others predicted safety. Bolles was led to this cognitive view, however, for reasons opposite to those that motivated other cognitive learning theorists. Often, it has been observations of the flexibility of behavior that provoked representational interpretations (Bindra, 1976; Tolman, 1932). Tolman's fixed ends–variable means concept is the prototypical example. For Bolles, it was the inflexibility of behavior that led to a cognitive vantage point. Rats in aversively motivated situations could not attach arbitrary responses to the situation. Because response acquisition is the defining characteristic of a stimulus–response (S-R) view, learning could not be of that form. However, rats could rapidly learn what was dangerous and what was safe. Although they quickly learned a representation of the world around them, evolution had programmed in how to deal with that world. The inflexibility of response learning reflected the other side of Bolles's thinking: biological functionalism. In the real world, threats exacted too great a toll to allow slow, trial-and-error learning. Responding could not be arbitrary; it had to be effective immediately on recognition of danger.

By focusing attention on the response requirement and away from reinforcement contingencies, Bolles could account for more of the variance in avoidance experiments. To be sure, there was some residual variability in avoidance behavior, and for SSDR theory to be a complete account of avoidance, this had to be addressed. It was a transition point in SSDR theory when Bolles began emphasizing the study of defense over the study of avoidance. However, he did not make that transition fully in his early writings on SSDR theory, and much effort was spent on trying to account for that residual variance in avoidance behavior (e.g., Bolles, 1970). With hindsight, one could say that the important task was to forget avoidance learning and concentrate on the factors controlling defensive behavior. That was the problem that had to be worked on and that was ignored by the previous reinforcement approach. A comprehensive understanding of defense might even provide insight into the aspects of avoidance that were still elusive (see subsequent discussion). However, Bolles was not yet ready to make the jump completely.

As an explanation of avoidance behavior, therefore, SSDR theory needed to explain why the escape, CS-termination, and avoidance contingencies could control behavior. I argued previously regarding lever-press "escape" behavior that the escape contingency operated because shock elicited reflexive behavior and that reflexive behavior could interact with SSDRs, the required avoidance response, or both. In this respect it is important to note that shock-elicited behavior can differ greatly from the behaviors elicited by stimuli that signal shock (e.g., Fanselow, 1980, 1982).

Bolles argued that in the situations in which CS termination contributed to performance, it did not do so by a fear-reduction mechanism. Instead, the termination of the CS provided feedback for the successful execution of an SSDR (Bolles, 1970, 1971). In the case of flight as an SSDR, execution requires that the animal remove itself from the source of danger. In a runway this is trivial because there is a consistently safe and a consistently dangerous place. In the running wheel, this is more ambiguous because the rat may run away from danger but it never gets anywhere. Finally, in the shuttlebox, the rat runs to a situation paired with shock. On the basis of this interpretation, it would be expected that feedback given when the correct amount of running occurred would assist a flight SSDR to the extent the SSDR needed such assistance.

Bolles and Grossen (1969) demonstrated just this pattern. CS termination or adding a feedback signal (without CS termination) had identical effects, and the effects were graded. Feedback afforded no advantage in the one-way apparatus, a small effect in the wheel, and the greatest effect in the shuttlebox. Bolles argued that this effect could be entirely caused by feedback and have nothing to do with either fear reduction or reinforcement. Rather, feedback could tell the fleeing rat it was "on the right path," providing a "signpost" that directs rather than reinforces behavior (Bolles, 1975, pp. 476–478). Bolles argued that such an informational or directing property of conditional stimuli was an alternative to explanations based on conditioned reinforcement. The stimuli provide a means to an end rather than an end in themselves. According to Bolles (1975), that is why secondary reinforcers hold long chains of behavior together: They indicate to the rat that it is on the correct path (p. 477). Similarly, when the fleeing rat is unsure of where to go, feedback provides a signpost that it is on the correct path. This view bears some resemblance to that of Bolles's mentor, Krechevsky. According to that view, food at the end of a maze did not strengthen response but provided the rat with information that it was using the correct hypothesis to guide its behavior (Krechevsky, 1932).

This is not to say there are no alternative accounts of feedback effects. A feedback cue could be a safety signal that had acquired fear-reducing and hence reinforcing properties. This argument may be inherently unresolvable. For example, Morris (1975) showed that pretraining animals with a shock termination–feedback signal relationship enhanced the beneficial effects of a feedback stimulus on behavior. Is this because the feedback signal had acquired greater fear-reducing properties or because pretraining enhanced its salience? It has also been argued that CS termination is more effective when there is a greater contrast in the level of fear between the CS-on and CS-off conditions (Callen, 1986; McAllister, McAllister, Dieter, & James, 1979). However, this may have more to do with increasing the amount of feedback than with fear reduction. Clearly, a feedback signal may be more effective if it is more salient. Perhaps looking directly at how feedback can direct an SSDR rather than merely change its probability can provide leverage on this issue.

Bolles also demonstrated that the avoidance contingency could make a significant contribution to behavior even in the absence of escape and CS-termination contingencies (Bolles et al., 1966). He addressed this influence in the following way: A multiplicity of SSDRs existed, supposedly arranged in a hierarchy that was initially related to their phylogenetic success. In the avoidance situation, however, if the rat engaged in a particular SSDR but did not successfully avoid shock, that SSDR would be punished. This would reduce the probability of that SSDR occurring and allow one of lower prominence on the hierarchy of SSDRs to emerge. The avoidance contingency would cause the rat to shuffle through its available SSDRs until the one most compatible with the avoidance requirement emerged. The avoidance contingency did not reinforce; rather, punishment reorganized the SSDR hierarchy.

SSDR theory acknowledged that there were several defensive behaviors and that there had to be principles by which the subject of the avoidance experiment came to match its behavior to the requirements of the experiment. This meant that response selection rules had to be formulated, a method that allowed one SSDR from the animal's repertoire of SSDRs to be selected. Bolles's first two SSDR selection rules, feedback stimuli and punishment, were very reinforcement-like, but reinforcement principles, even those of feedback and punishment, were logically incompatible with a fundamental assumption of SSDR theory. Bolles argued that trial-and-error learning was too slow a mechanism to be used by a prey animal to select its responses under predatory pressure. This is just as true of punishment and feedback as it is of fear-reduction reinforcement. The true transition to SSDR theory came when Bolles and Riley (1973) recognized that even SSDRs could not be controlled by their consequences, and a response-strengthening view had to be completely abandoned.

The experiment was simple but critical. Rats were placed on a "Sidman avoidance" schedule, in which they received a shock every 5 seconds unless a freezing response occurred. Freezing delayed subsequent shock by 15 seconds. Almost immediately, rats went to an asymptotic level of freezing. Subsequently, some of these rats were punished for freezing. Punishment immediately suppressed the response, and the denser the shock schedule, the more complete was the suppression. These changes might look like learning through punishment and avoidance to the casual

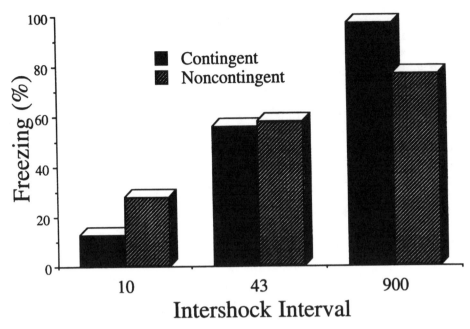

Figure 1. The figure is based on Experiment 2 of Bolles & Riley (1973) and presents the percentage of time rats spent freezing as a function of shock density. For the contingent groups, the 10-second intershock interval (ISI) group was punished as soon as it froze, the 43-second ISI group was punished after it froze for 15 seconds, and the 900-second ISI group could avoid shock by freezing. The ISIs plotted represent the shock densities received by rats with these programmed contingencies.

observer, but this view is an illusion. First, the changes occurred immediately when the schedule was put into effect; there were none of the gradual, incremental changes in behavior that would be expected with response strengthening or weakening. Second, the groups differed extraordinarily in the amount and density (intershock interval) of shock they received. The avoidance group, which froze at a high level, received few shocks at a low density. The rats that showed the lowest levels of freezing—those with the most severe punishment contingencies—received the most shocks at the shortest intershock intervals. More moderate punishment contingencies produced shock frequencies and densities that were intermediate.

Bolles and Riley went on to show that it is the shock density that is the critical determinant of the behavior by examining rats that received noncontingent shock at densities that matched those of the punishment and avoidance groups (see Figure 1). The response contingencies changed behavior not because they directly strengthened behavior but because they indirectly altered the pattern of shock delivery. Why does this occur? First, the behavior elicited by shock is different from the behavior conditioned by shock. Shock elicits a vigorous burst of activity that persists for a brief period beyond shock termination and is completely incompatible with freezing (Fanselow, 1982). Stimuli associated with shock, such as the context the rat is in, can provoke freezing as a conditional response following as little as a single pairing with shock (Fanselow, 1980, 1990). If the rat is given a brief shock, it will be active for a period after shock termination (about 10 s in the Bolles & Riley experiment) and then begin to freeze. If the rat is given no more shock, it will continue to freeze for a prolonged period (until the context–shock association extinguishes). If, instead, the freezing rat is given another shock, freezing will immediately be broken up and replaced with activity. Programming freezing to avoid shock allows the rat to freeze; the subject does so readily and receives little further shock. Freezing remains at a high rate with just enough shock to maintain the context–shock association at a high level. Punishing shock has the opposite effect on behavior. The initial shock causes an activity burst, and as soon as it gives way to freezing, another shock will elicit the next activity burst, and so on. Therefore, shock density, not response contingency, is the critical element (see Figure 1). The effects of avoidance and punishment contingencies are artifacts of their ability to alter the frequency, distribution, and density of shock. Subsequently, I show that the ability of these stimulus factors to determine response form has emerged as a central element in the understanding of defensive behavior.

Of Reinforcement, Rationality, and S-R Mechanisms

For behavior to be controlled by its consequences is pleasing. Laymen find its teleological rationality intuitively satisfying. Mechanists are gratified by their ability to translate this rationality into noncognitive S-R terms. One implication from the Bolles and Riley (1973) experiment is most disquieting, for it suggests that behavior in a fear-provoking situation is inherently irrational.

It has to be recognized that avoidance and punishment provide mirrored descriptions of aversively motivated, response-contingent situations. When a subject avoids by emitting a target response, everything but the target response is punished. Alternatively, punishment of a target response means that all other responses are effective at avoiding. To simplify the argument, imagine dividing all behavior into two exhaustive and mutually exclusive categories, freezing and not freezing (i.e., all behaviors other than freezing). If freezing is punished, the rat should be able to avoid shock by not freezing. This means that if any response is capable of being learned through avoidance, freezing should be suppressed by punishment. However, we have established that this is not the case. Similarly, in a situation in which the rat can avoid shock through freezing, "not freezing" is punished. If not freezing can be suppressed by punishment, the rat should be left with freezing as the only available response. But freezing is not weakened by punishment and is not strengthened by avoidance. This means that in sufficiently fear-provoking situations, behavior in general is not a function of its consequences. Fear falls beyond the purview of both the rationalist and the S-R mechanist.

This argument is not simply an artifact of analyzing responses into two broad categories. Consider the response of running in a situation in which the rat is punished for freezing. If the rat is capable of learning to avoid by running, it should adopt running in that situation, because every time it runs rather than freezes, it avoids shock. However, the Bolles and Riley experiment showed that punishing freezing does not reduce that response and replace it with running. Fanselow and Lester (1988) reached similar conclusions after training freezing in a discriminated avoidance or punishment preparation. They found that the more rats were punished for freezing to a tone, the more they froze to that tone. In 1975, when Bolles wrote, *"We are left with the incredible conclusion, therefore, that no response learning occurs in the avoidance situation"* (p. 364, italics added), he completed the change from the study of reinforcement and avoidance learning to the study of a particular class of behaviors that served a specific biological function: defense. I refer to this general approach, the study of a behavior that solves a particular biological problem or serves a particular adaptive function, as *functional behaviorism*.

The Study of Defense as a Functional Behavior System

Species-specific defense reactions are evolutionary adaptations that arose because they protected members of the species against environmental threats. Each species has its own threats, posing different selection pressures, and evolution has provided sufficient means of defense against those threats to allow reproduction. Unlike paleontologists, psychologists can ignore the species for which this is not so. There may be several threats to one species; for example, the rat may be at risk from both predators and toxins, but the pressures of each may be unique. Finally, even within a single type of threat, there may be species differences (flight may make more sense in a large, fast animal than in a small, slow one). Functional behaviorists cannot approach their topic with the same optimism for sweeping generality as can reinforcement theorists.

It should not be assumed on an a priori basis that there is only one type of solution to a problem. Not all problems are solved by learning; many involve complex prewiring. Functional behaviorists are not without generalities, but these lie with the sorts of questions they strive to answer rather than a set of limited mechanisms they employ as answers. The first step is to specify the biological problem. With Bolles (1970) as instigator, I have chosen the antipredator behavior of the rat. Because this system has both great plasticity (or at least rapid plasticity) and complex prewiring, I have something to say about both characteristics. The next step is to determine what stimuli activate the behavior system. Once the system is activated, the animal's response repertoire becomes limited, but the functional behaviorist must be able to determine which responses belong to the system and which do not. Because the system is composed of multiple responses, another critical question is, What are the mechanisms that select within-system responses? In the present volume, chapters 14 and 15, by Blanchard and Sigmundi, respectively, wrestle with the problem of response selection. The steps outlined here provide a framework for a functional behaviorist's research program.

Activating Stimuli

The stimuli that activate defense illustrate both the complex prewiring and great plasticity referred to previously. Rodents respond to several danger stimuli on the first encounter, and they have clearly evolved complex "feature detectors" capable of extracting exacting environmental information to detect a predator. For example, certain subspecies of deermice respond differentially to predatory and nonpredatory species of snakes (Hirsch & Bolles, 1980), but the critical stimulus dimensions or perceptual apparatus that allows this judgment has yet to be characterized.

The great plasticity of the defensive behavior system lies in the fact that stimuli that predict threat to the external milieu (Garcia & Ervin, 1968) can acquire the ability to conditionally activate the defensive system after only a single experience. The environmental parameters and procedures that foster this Pavlovian learning have been described in detail. Freezing increases with the number and intensity of shock deliveries (Fanselow, 1980, 1982; Fanselow & Bolles, 1979; Fanselow & Tighe, 1988; Young & Fanselow, 1992). It also increases with increasing intertrial intervals (Fanselow, DeCola, & Young, 1993; Fanselow & Tighe, 1988). In that respect, the behavior appears to be like any Pavlovian conditional response. It is an adaptively specialized form of Pavlovian conditioning in that, like conditional taste aversion, it shows significant acquisition with only a single trial, and asymptote is reached after very few CS-US pairings (Fanselow, 1981, 1986, 1990; Young & Fanselow, 1992). There is some degree of stimulus specificity as well. For example, tone CSs show conditional freezing more readily than light CSs (Ayres, Axelrod, Merker, Muchnik, & Vigorito, 1985; Helmstetter & Fanselow, 1989; Kim, Rivers, Bevins, & Ayres, 1996; Lester & Fanselow, 1992; Sigmundi & Bolles, 1983; Sigmundi, Bouton, & Bolles, 1980).

Perhaps even more impressive is the progress being made on characterizing and localizing the synaptic mechanisms of this plasticity (for a review, see Maren & Fanselow, 1996). Information about conditional and unconditional stimuli converges on the amygdala and results in a long-term potentiation mediated by the neurotransmitter glutamate in the circuits that mediate freezing (Clugnet & LeDoux, 1990; Maren & Fanselow, 1995; Quirk, Repa, & LeDoux, 1995; Romanski, Clugnet, Bordi, & LeDoux, 1993). Blocking the NMDA subtype of glutamate receptors in the amygdala during conditioning blocks the acquisition of SSDRs to environmental stimuli paired with noxious events (Fanselow & Kim, 1994; Miserendino, Sananes, Melia, & Davis, 1990). By focusing on a specific SSDR, freezing, researchers have been able to determine the different neural sites necessary for plasticity to discrete and contextual CSs (Kim & Fanselow, 1992; Phillips & LeDoux, 1992). By combining this technique with a transgenic mouse approach, considerable progress is underway in discovering the subcellular mechanisms of this plasticity (Bourtchuladze et al., 1994; Mayford, Abel, & Kandel, 1995; Tonegawa et al., 1995).

Species-Specific Defense Reactions and Response Selection

Traditionally, learning theorists have used reinforcement concepts to explain response selection. I have argued that SSDR theory has pushed researchers away from reinforcement and toward other mechanisms of response selection. Subsequently, there has been at least one attempt to incorporate a reinforcement principle into an SSDR analysis. Masterson and Crawford (1982) argued that activation of the animal's defensive system not only limits the animal's response repertoire but also provides sensory templates that make certain stimuli reinforcing. This approach adds a reinforcement rule to SSDR theory's response limitation rule. The necessity of such a reinforcement principle is not readily apparent. If the response repertoire of the subject is limited, why do those responses need reinforcement? It seems that this reinforcement principle does not explain anything that is not already explained by the response limitation principle. What is still needed is a rule for determining which SSDRs are selected from the set of responses.

In the preceding discussion of the Bolles and Riley (1973) experiment, it was argued that shock density is a critical determinant of behavior. Another major determinant of defensive behavior is the distance between threat and subject (Fanselow & Lester, 1988; Ratner, 1967; Rovee, Kaufman, & Collier, 1977). Fanselow and Lester (1988) suggested that both factors could be related to a single continuous dimension they labeled *predatory imminence*, which in terms of its antecedent conditions resembles the intuitive concept of fear.

Because the two-factor theorist also relied on a fear construct, it may be illustrative to highlight the similarities and differences between these notions of fear. Both assumed that fear is produced as a Pavlovian conditional reaction, but conditioning currently is more formally defined and has a more "cognitive" or representational flavor (see chapters 17 and 19, this volume). Two-factor theory virtually ignored the ability of innate stimuli to produce fear. The predatory imminence construct draws attention to the ability of innate danger stimuli to produce fear and the fact that their physical distance is inversely related to fear. An even more striking difference between the two conceptualizations concerns how fear translates into performance. The two-factor theorist's version of fear was as a nonspecific motivator; its performance-generating properties were a generalized motivator like hunger (e.g., Hull, 1943). The current approach views fear as a limiter and selector of responses. It determines both the amount and the form of defense.

As fear increases, defensive responses increase and other types of behavior are suppressed. When fear reaches certain levels, behavior changes in form, and this second form of defense increases until another shift in defensive strategy is obtained. This shifting in form of defense is not unique in animal behavior. For example, it characterizes the locomotion of horses. To achieve linear increases in speed, horses start by walking, and the rate of this response increases gradually until the horse shifts to a trotting response. Trotting gradually increases until the horse breaks into a gallop. Therefore, linear increases in speed are achieved by changes within a topography, followed by shifts in topography.

By analogy, fear may increase linearly because of the spatial or temporal proximity of threat (i.e., predatory imminence). I have termed the form of defense applied to low levels of threat *preencounter responses*; they occur before the subject has detected a particular threat in a situation that is associated with a small increase in danger. This is likely to occur when the rat is moving between locations, such as when leaving a nesting area for a foraging ground. The rat adjusts its meal patterns as a function of threat, taking less frequent meals that more effectively exploit patches of food that are encountered (Fanselow, Lester, & Helmstetter, 1988). This strategy serves to protect total caloric intake (see chapter 4, this volume) while reducing time at risk in the foraging situation. Rats also move through such environments in a cautious manner, characterized by stretched approach postures that may have an information-gathering function (see chapter 14, this volume; Pinel & Mana, 1989; Pinel, Mumby, Dastur, & Pinel, 1994). Information gathering can serve to change the level of perceived risk and predatory imminence allowing for changes in defensive topography. Also, these cautious movements may result in refusal to enter a particular location or retreat from a particular environment, a response that can be said to represent a form of flight.

If an actual threat is detected (e.g., a cat or a CS that had been associated with shock is identified), behavioral topography switches to *postencounter defense*, which is dominated by freezing. Although the most striking feature of freezing is its profound suppression of movement, it would be a mistake to think of it as a unidimensional behavior. Freezing is influenced by features of the environment. The location of freezing is predictable: It occurs next to objects (thigmotaxis, e.g., Grossen & Kelley, 1972), under shelters (chapter 15, this volume), and near safety signals (Fanselow & Lester, 1988). If freezing has preferred locations, the rat must somehow get to those locations. This movement to a location to freeze could be described as another form of flight (see Sigmundi's analysis of the freeze–flee decision rule in chapter 15, this volume).

The final stage of defense comes at the time surrounding predator–prey contact, which I have termed *circa-strike behavior*. At this point, freezing is disrupted and replaced by more violent forms of defense such as jumps and biting acts (Blanchard, Blanchard, & Hori, 1989). The behavior is also characterized by loud, broad-spectrum vocalizations. This behavior appears designed to give the predator pause and the prey a chance to escape its clutches, which would result in a decrease in predatory imminence and a change in defensive behavioral topography. If the rat escapes, predatory imminence would decrease a bit, and the postencounter defensive pattern would return. If it fails to escape, it will make no future contributions to the gene pool.

Future Directions for SSDR Theory

Understanding Flight

Bolles and others looked at freezing and flight as discrete alternative responses. Flight is more complex than that. At each stage of defense, there is a response; each might be labeled as flight but is really an integrated component of the defensive strategy occurring at that time. Perhaps the term *flight* is too broad and should be replaced by a detailed description of the locomotor behavior and the factors that control it in each stage of defense. A reanalysis of flight is one area within SSDR theory that needs future development. Here I provide a footing for such reanalysis by suggesting that flight has different forms that are specific to the stage of defense. An important feature is that flight is viewed as a facilitator for, not a competitor with, the other behaviors that occur at a particular level of defense.

During preencounter defense, the animal may withdraw to the nest area while cautiously foraging or exploring an environment. This behavior can be taken as a form of flight; note that it occurs when the level of predatory imminence is quite low, lower than that sufficient for freezing. For example, foraging rats may carry food to a location with cover and consume it there (Whishaw, 1993).

However, this sort of locomotion should not be confused with that seen at higher levels of predatory imminence. During postencounter defense, rats move to an optimal location to freeze. Here, the movement is a component of the freezing module. The rat usually ends up freezing in corners, especially dark ones, under cover, and near safety signals (see chapters 14 and 15, this volume; Fanselow & Lester, 1988). It is necessary to be able to detail formally this aspect of postencounter defense; a future direction of SSDR research is to specify more precisely when the rat will move to a location to freeze. Heretofore, there has been too much concentration on the sheer level of freezing. When a rat is placed in a box it previously received shock in, it generally does not freeze immediately; often, freezing increases over the first minute or so (e.g., Fanselow, 1982). This recruitment time is largely unaccounted for, but some portion of it may reflect the rat's localizing and moving to the safest place to freeze. This recruitment period is relatively long; it cannot take the rat a full minute or two to move to the back corner of a small conditioning chamber. Perhaps the rat accomplishes this movement in several steps, each one to a local minimum of safety (e.g., see chapter 15, this volume). At present, this movement is not adequately detailed.

These two forms of locomotion are both retreats toward a particular location: a safer place to eat or a better place to freeze. The locomotion that occurs during circa-strike defense is locomotion away from something—the threat that is contacting the prey at that instant. In that sense, it is directed in a different way and again should be thought of as distinct from the other two forms of defensive locomotion. This violent escape behavior is characterized by vocalizations, jumps, and even biting at the predator (Blanchard et al., 1989). The locomotion provides part of a coordinated defense against a proximal threat and has been described in considerable detail by Blanchard, Flanelly, and Blanchard (1986).

Perceptual Mechanisms

Much progress has been made in identifying the neural mechanisms that subserve the defensive behavior system, but there are some fundamental questions that remain. One has to do with the perceptual apparatus that allows prey species to recognize their predators innately. What are the critical features and how are they extracted? What brain areas make the judgment that a particular animal is a predator? Once the assessment is made, the prey must make a judgment about the threat of that predator. How far away is it? Is it approaching? Is it on an intercept or a tangential course? All these factors influence defensive behavior (Walther, 1969). The animal must have the neural apparatus to respond to the level of predatory imminence. Presently, it is thought that the amygdala is the structure that can learn about new danger stimuli and that receives information about innate danger. (For recent reviews of the involvement of the amygdala in learned fear, see Davis, Rainnie, & Cassell, 1994; LeDoux, 1993; Maren & Fanselow, 1996.) The amygdala is also critical for reactions to innate dangers. Rats with amygdalar lesions do not react to cats (Blanchard & Takahashi, 1988; Fox & Sorenson, 1994), and a human with selective damage to the amygdala did not react to human faces that were expressing fear (Adolphs, Tranel, Damasio, & Damasio, 1994).

Once the level of predatory imminence has been assessed, the prey engages and coordinates the set of responses appropriate for that level of imminence. I have begun to analyze this capacity of the animal by determining midbrain contributions to defense (e.g., Fanselow, 1991). Information from the amygdala seems to activate the behavioral components of postencounter defenses (e.g., freezing) through projections to the ventral portions of the periaqueductal gray. The autonomic components seem to arise from projections from the amygdala to the hypothalamus (LeDoux, Iwata, Cicchetti, & Reis, 1988). Circa-strike reactions are mediated by more dorsal portions of the periaqueductal gray that are activated directly by nociceptive input and by other stimuli associated with contact, perhaps mediated through the superior colliculus (Fanselow, 1991, 1994). The superior colliculus can provide sufficient localization of the threat to allow circa-strike (escape locomotion, jump–bite attacks) to be appropriately directed (Dean, Redgrave, & Westby, 1989; Redgrave & Dean, 1991). The individual behavioral and autonomic components of circa-strike behavior are organized into longitudinal columns within the dorsolateral periaqueductal gray (Depaulis, Keay, & Bandler, 1992). Switching between circa-strike and postencounter modes of defense may be accomplished by an inhibitory connection between the dorsolateral and ventral periaqueductal gray or amygdala (Fanselow, DeCola, De Oca, & Landeira-Fernandez, 1995).

The anatomical location of preencounter defense is still unknown. Additionally, further clarification is needed on how the sensorimotor coordination of the different components of a particular mode of defense is achieved.

A Final Word About Avoidance Behavior

In moving to an analysis of defensive behavior, I have left the original problem that Bolles faced, behavior in the avoidance training situation, far behind. I believe that this change in orientation facilitated the recent remarkable progress in the understanding of aversively motivated behavior. The avoidance learning experiments of the past were an inefficient way to study defensive behavior. Until there is a better understanding of defense, one cannot hope to have a complete understanding of an animal's behavior in such situations. Even so, the analysis of defensive behavior so far may give us some pointers.

First, the avoidance contingency is successful because it influences shock density. The rat is placed on different points of the predatory imminence continuum so that different sets of behavior are available to it. For example, Helmstetter and Fanselow (1993) found that rats that received very low rates of shock when they were foraging and earning food adjusted their meal patterns in a way that reduced the amount of shock. This of course kept shock density low, and the rats stayed in the preencounter mode with its altered meal patterns. When these researchers increased shock frequency to a higher rate, meal pattern alterations were abandoned and feeding was generally suppressed. This occurred as the rat entered the postencounter mode characterized by freezing. The point here is that, as found in the Bolles and Riley (1973) experiment, when a particular SSDR results in avoidance of shock, shock density changes, and density is an automatic determinant of response topography. Altering context fear or probing a Pavlovian CS onto an avoidance response baseline may also be expected to change a rat's perception of predatory imminence and therefore cause a shift in the magnitude or form of behavior (e.g., McAllister et al., 1979; Rescorla & LoLordo, 1965).

In most avoidance situations, the level of shock received, even by the well-trained rat, is not zero. It appears that presentation of a single threat causes the rat to backward cycle through the stages of predatory imminence. For example, Blanchard et al. (1989) showed that following a single encounter with a cat, a rat shows escape locomotion (circa-strike), followed by prolonged periods of freezing in a burrow (postencounter). Then the rat begins to leave the burrow with stretched approach postures (preencounter defense). A single shock has a similar effect, causing an initial activity burst that is followed by freezing (Fanselow, 1982). A single readministration of shock in an avoidance situation can break up an ongoing behavior pattern and cause the rat to cycle through its defensive repertoire. Such features have yet to be explored in avoidance situations but may make a strong contribution.

I have pointed out that rats choose locations within which to freeze. A local area of minimum danger may act as an attractor for freezing. Features such as feedback signals, conditional stimuli, and the construction of the environment may provide support for the rat to move to locations in an avoidance or escape situation. The simplest and most obvious example is the rat's freezing on a lever in the lever-press escape task. Similar features may operate in a shuttle avoidance situation as well. The termination of a danger signal or the onset of a safety signal may tell the rat it has reached a local area of minimum danger, and it will stay there and begin to freeze. Perhaps that is why pretraining a feedback signal as a safety signal enhances its efficacy (Morris, 1975). When the warning signal turns on, the sudden heightening of fear may push the rat briefly into the circa-strike mode, eliciting escape locomotion that results in a shuttle response. In trying to describe how various response contingencies interact to produce the totality of behavior in an avoidance experiment, Bolles (1975) said, "The general rule seems to be that there is no general rule" (p. 336). Perhaps by focusing on how the environment controls defensive behavior, researchers may find those elusive generalities.

References

Adolphs, R., Tranel, D., Damasio, H., & Damasio, A. (1994). Impaired recognition of emotion in facial expressions following bilateral damage to the human amygdala. *Nature, 372,* 669–672.

Ayres, J. J. B. (in press). Fear conditioning and avoidance. In W. O'Donohue (Ed.), *Learning and behavior therapy.* Boston: Allyn & Bacon.

Ayres, J. J. B., Axelrod, H., Merker, E., Muchnik, F., & Vigorito, M. (1985). Concurrent observations of barpress suppression and freezing: Effects of CS modality and on-line vs. off-line training upon posttrial behavior. *Animal Learning & Behavior, 13,* 44–50.

Bindra, D. (1976). *A theory of intelligent behavior.* New York: Wiley.

Blanchard, D. C., & Takahashi, S. N. (1988). No change in intermale aggression after amygdala lesions which reduce freezing. *Physiology & Behavior, 42,* 613–616.

Blanchard, R. J., Blanchard, D. C., & Hori, K. (1989). An ethoexperimental approach to the study of defense. In R. J. Blanchard, P. F. Brain, D. C. Blanchard, & S. Parmigiani (Eds.), *Ethoexperimental approaches to the study of behavior* (pp. 114–136). NATO ASI Series D, Vol. 48. Boston: Kluver Academic.

Blanchard, R. J., Flannelly, K. J., & Blanchard, D. C. (1986). Defensive behaviors of laboratory and wild *Rattus norvegicus. Journal of Comparative Psychology, 100,* 101–107.

Bolles, R. C. (1969). Avoidance and escape learning: Simultaneous acquisition of different responses. *Journal of Comparative and Physiological Psychology, 68,* 355–358.

Bolles, R. C. (1970). Species-specific defense reactions and avoidance learning. *Psychological Review, 77,* 32–48.

Bolles, R. C. (1971). Species-specific defense reactions. In F. R. Brush (Ed.), *Aversive conditioning and learning.* New York: Academic Press.

Bolles, R. C. (1972a). The avoidance learning problem. In G. H. Bower (Ed.), *The psychology of learning and motivation, 6.* New York: Academic Press.

Bolles, R. C. (1972b). Reinforcement, expectancy, and learning. *Psychological Review, 79,* 394–409.

Bolles, R. C. (1975). *Theory of motivation* (2nd ed.). New York: Harper & Row.

Bolles, R. C. (1989). Acquired behaviors: Aversive learning. In R. J. Blanchard, P. F. Brain, D. C. Blanchard, & S. Parmigiani (Eds.), *Ethoexperimental approaches to the study of behavior* (pp. 167–179). NATO ASI Series D, Vol. 48. Boston: Kluver Academic.

Bolles, R. C., & Grossen, N. E. (1969). Effects of an informational stimulus on the acquisition of avoidance behavior in rats. *Journal of Comparative and Physiological Psychology, 68,* 90–99.

Bolles, R. C., & McGillis, D. B. (1968). The non-operant nature of the bar press escape response. *Psychonomic Science, 11,* 261–262.

Bolles, R. C., & Riley, A. L. (1973). Freezing as an avoidance response: Another look at the operant-respondent distinction. *Learning and Motivation, 4,* 268–275.

Bolles, R. C., Stokes, L. W., & Younger, M. S. (1966). Does CS termination reinforce avoidance behavior? *Journal of Comparative and Physiological Psychology, 62,* 201–207.

Bourtchuladze, R., Frenguelli, B., Blendy, J., Cioffi, D., Schutz, G., & Silva, A. J. (1994). Deficient long-term memory in mice with a targeted mutation of the cAMP-responsive element-binding protein. *Cell, 79,* 59–68.

Brogden, W. J., Lipman, E. A., & Culler, E. (1938). The role of incentive in conditioning and learning. *American Journal of Psychology, 51,* 109–117.

Callen, E. J. (1986). Fear of the CS and of the context in two-way avoidance learning: Between- and within-subjects manipulations. *Animal Learning & Behavior, 14,* 89–89.

Clugnet, M. C., & LeDoux, J. E. (1990). Synaptic plasticity in fear conditioning circuits: Induction of LTP in the lateral nucleus of the amygdala by stimulation of the medial geniculate body. *Journal of Neuroscience, 10,* 2818–2824.

Crawford, M., & Masterson, F. A. (1982). Species-specific defense reactions and avoidance learning: An evaluative review. *Pavlovian Journal of Biological Science, 17,* 204–214.

Davis, H. (1979). Leverpress escape behavior in a clinically unconscious rat. *Physiology & Behavior, 22,,* 599–600.

Davis, H., & Burton, J. (1974). The measurement of response force during a leverpress shock escape procedure in rats. *Journal of the Experimental Analysis of Behavior, 22,* 433–440.

Davis, M., Rainnie, D., & Cassell, M. (1994). Neurotransmission in the rat amygdala related to fear and anxiety. *Trends in Neurosciences, 17,* 208–214.

Dean, P., Redgrave, P., & Westby, G. W. M. (1989). Event or emergency? Two response systems in the mammalian superior colliculus. *Trends in Neuroscience, 12,* 137–147.

Depaulis, A., Keay, K. A., & Bandler, R. (1992). Longitudinal neuronal organization of defensive reactions in the midbrain periaqueductal gray region of the rat. *Experimental Brain Research, 90,* 307–318.

Dinsmoor, J. A. (1982). Is this defense needed? *Behavioral and Brain Sciences, 5,* 679.

Dinsmoor, J. A., & Hughes, L. H. (1956). Training rats to press a bar to turn off shock. *Journal of Comparative and Physiological Psychology, 49,* 235–238.

Fanselow, M. S. (1980). Conditional and unconditional components of post-shock freezing. *Pavlovian Journal of Biological Sciences, 15,* 177–182.

Fanselow, M. S. (1981). Naloxone and Pavlovian fear conditioning. *Learning & Motivation, 12,* 398–419.

Fanselow, M. S. (1982). The post-shock activity burst. *Animal Learning & Behavior, 190,* 448–454.

Fanselow, M. S. (1986). Associative vs. topographical accounts of the immediate shock freezing deficit in rats: Implications for the response selection rules governing species-specific defensive reactions. *Learning and Motivation, 17,* 16–39.

Fanselow, M. S. (1990). Factors governing one trial contextual conditioning. *Animal Learning & Behavior, 18,* 264–270.

Fanselow, M. S. (1991). The midbrain periaqueductal gray as a coordinator of action in response to fear and anxiety. In A. Depaulis & R. Bandler (Eds.), *The midbrain periaqueductal gray matter: Functional, anatomical and immunohistochemical organization* (pp. 151–173). NATO ASI Series. New York: Plenum Press.

Fanselow, M. S. (1994). Neural organization of the defensive behavior system responsible for fear. *Psychonomic Bulletin and Review, 1,* 429–438.

Fanselow, M. S., & Bolles, R. C. (1979). Naloxone and shock elicited freezing in the rat. *Journal of Comparative and Physiological Psychology, 93,* 736–744.

Fanselow, M. S., DeCola, J. P., De Oca, B., & Landeira-Fernandez, J. (1995). Ventral and dorsolateral regions of the midbrain periaqueductal gray control different stages of defensive behavior: Dorsolateral PAG lesions enhance the defensive freezing produced by massed and immediate shock. *Aggressive Behavior, 21,* 63–77.

Fanselow, M. S., DeCola, J. P., & Young, S. L. (1993). Mechanisms responsible for reduced contextual conditioning with massed unsignaled unconditional stimuli. *Journal of Experimental Psychology: Animal Behavior Processes, 19,* 121–137.

Fanselow, M. S., & Kim, J. J. (1994). Acquisition of contextual Pavlovian fear conditioning is blocked by application of an NMDA receptor antagonist D,L-2-amino-5-phosphono-valeric acid to the basolateral amygdala. *Behavioral Neuroscience, 108,* 210–212.

Fanselow, M. S., & Lester, L. S. (1988). A functional behavioristic approach to aversively motivated behavior: Predatory imminence as a determinant of the topography of defensive behavior. In R. C. Bolles & M. D. Beecher (Eds.), *Evolution and learning* (pp. 185–212). Hillsdale, NJ: Erlbaum.

Fanselow, M. S., Lester, L. S., & Helmstetter, F. J. (1988). Changes in feeding and foraging patterns as an antipredator defensive strategy: A laboratory simulation using aversive stimulation in a closed economy. *Journal of the Experimental Analysis of Behavior, 50,* 361–374.

Fanselow, M. S., & Tighe, T. J. (1988). Contextual conditioning with massed versus distributed unconditional stimuli in the absence of explicit conditional stimuli. *Journal of Experimental Psychology: Animal Behavior Processes, 14,* 187–199.

Fox, R. J., & Sorenson, C. A. (1994). Bilateral lesions of the amygdala attenuate analgesia induced by diverse environmental challenges. *Brain Research, 648,* 215–221.

Garcia, J., & Ervin, F. R. (1968). Gustatory-visceral and telereceptor-cutaneous conditioning-adaptation in internal and external milieus. *Communications in Behavioral Biology, 1,* 389–415.

Grossen, N. E., & Kelley, M. J. (1972). Species-specific behavior and acquisition of avoidance in rats. *Journal of Comparative and Physiological Psychology, 81,* 307–310.

Helmstetter, F. J., & Fanselow, M. S. (1989). Differential second-order aversive conditioning using contextual stimuli. *Animal Learning & Behavior, 17,* 205–212.

Helmstetter, F. J., & Fanselow, M. S. (1993). Aversively motivated changes in meal patterns of rats in a closed economy: The effects of shock density. *Animal Learning & Behavior, 21,* 168–175.

Herrnstein, R. J., & Hineline, P. N. (1966). Negative reinforcement as shock frequency reduction. *Journal of the Experimental Analysis of Behavior, 9,* 421–430.

Hirsch, S. M., & Bolles, R. C. (1980). On the ability of prey to recognize predators. *Zeitschrift für Tierpsychologie, 54,* 71–84.

Hull, C. L. (1943). *Principles of behavior.* New York: Appleton.

Kamin, L. J. (1957). The effects of termination of the CS and avoidance of the US on avoidance learning: An extension. *Canadian Journal of Psychology, 11,* 48–56.

Kim, J. J., & Fanselow, M. S. (1992). Modality-specific retrograde amnesia of fear. *Science, 256,* 675–677.

Kim, S. D., Rivers, S., Bevins, R. A., & Ayres, J. J. B. (1996). Conditioned stimulus determinants of conditioned response form in Pavlovian fear conditioning. *Journal of Experimental Psychology: Animal Behavior Processes, 22,* 87–104.

Krechevsky, I. (1932). Hypotheses in rats. *Psychological Review, 39,* 516–532.

Kuhn, T. S. (1962). *The structure of scientific revolutions.* Chicago: University of Chicago Press.

LeDoux, J. E. (1993). Emotional memory systems in the brain. *Behavioural Brain Research, 58*(1–2), 69–79.

LeDoux, J. E., Iwata, J., Cicchetti, P., & Reis, D. J. (1988). Different projections of the central amygdaloid nucleus mediate autonomic and behavioral correlates of conditioned fear. *Journal of Neuroscience, 8,* 2517–2529.

Lester, L. S., & Fanselow, M. S. (1992). Nocturnality as a defensive behavior in the rat: An analysis in terms of selective association between light and aversive stimulation. *Psychological Record, 42,* 221–253.

Maren, S., & Fanselow, M. S. (1995). Synaptic plasticity in the basolateral amygdala induced by hippocampal formation *in vivo. Journal of Neuroscience, 15,* 7548–7564.

Maren, S., & Fanselow, M. S. (1996). The amygdala and fear conditioning: Has the nut been cracked? *Neuron, 16,* 237–240.

Masterson, F. A., & Crawford, M. (1982). The defense motivation system: A theory of avoidance behavior. *Behavioral & Brain Sciences, 5,* 661–696.

Mayford, M., Abel, T., & Kandel, E. R. (1995). Transgenic approaches to cognition. *Current Opinion in Neurobiology, 5,* 141–148.

McAllister, W. R., McAllister, D. E., Dieter, S. E., & James, J. H. (1979). Preexposure to situational cues produces a direct relationship between two-way avoidance learning and shock intensity. *Animal Learning & Behavior, 7,* 165–173.

Miller, N. E. (1941). An experimental investigation of acquired drives. *Psychological Bulletin, 38,* 534–535.

Miller, N. E. (1951). Learnable drives and rewards. In S. S. Stevens (Ed.), *Handbook of experimental psychology* (pp. 435–472). New York: Wiley.

Miserendino, M. J. D., Sananes, C. B., Melia K. R., & Davis, M. (1990). Blocking of acquisition but not expression of conditioned fear-potentiated startle by NMDA antagonists in the amygdala. *Nature, 345,* 716–718.

Morris, R. G. (1975). Preconditioning of reinforcing properties to an exteroceptive feedback stimulus. *Learning & Motivation, 6,* 289–298.

Mowrer, O. H. (1939). A stimulus-response analysis of anxiety and its role as a reinforcing agent. *Psychological Review, 46,* 553–564.

Mowrer, O. H. (1947). On the dual nature of learning: A reinterpretation of "conditioning" and "problem solving." *Harvard Educational Review, 17,* 102–148.

Mowrer, O. H., & Lamoureaux, R. R. (1942). Avoidance conditioning and signal duration: A study of secondary motivation and reward. *Psychological Monographs, 54*(5, Whole No. 247).

Myers, A. K. (1982). Reinforcement of avoidance behavior. *Behavioral & Brain Sciences, 5,* 681–682.

Phillips, R. G., & LeDoux, J. E. (1992). Differential contribution of amygdala and hippocampus to cued and contextual fear conditioning. *Behavioral Neuroscience, 106,* 274–285.

Pinel, J. P. J., & Mana, M. J. (1989). Adaptive interactions of rats with dangerous inanimate objects: Support for a cognitive theory of defensive behavior. In R. J. Blanchard, P. F. Brain, D. C. Blanchard, & S. Parmigiani (Eds.), *Ethoexperimental approaches to the study of behavior* (pp. 137–150). NATO ASI Series D, Vol. 48. Boston: Kluver Academic.

Pinel, J. P. J., Mumby, D. G., Dastur, F. N., & Pinel, J. G. (1994). Rat (*Rattus norvegicus*) defensive behavior in total darkness: Risk-assessment function of defensive burying. *Journal of Comparative Psychology, 108,* 140–147.

Quirk, G. J., Repa, J. C., & LeDoux, J. E. (1995). Fear conditioning enhances short-latency auditory responses of the lateral amygdala neurons: Parallel recordings in the freely moving rat. *Neuron, 15,* 1029–1039.

Ratner, S. C. (1967). Comparative aspects of hypnosis. In J. E. Gordon (Ed.), *Handbook of clinical and experimental hypnosis* (pp. 550–587). New York: Macmillan.

Redgrave, P., & Dean, P. (1991). Does the PAG learn about emergencies from the superior colliculus? In A. Depaulis & R. Bandler (Eds.), *The midbrain periaqueductal gray matter: Functional, anatomical and immunohistochemical organization* (pp. 199–209). NATO ASI Series. New York: Plenum Press.

Rescorla, R. A., & LoLordo, V. M. (1965). Inhibition of avoidance behavior. *Journal of Comparative and Physiological Psychology, 59,* 406–412.

Romanski, L. M., Clugnet, M. C., Bordi, F., & LeDoux, J. E. (1993). Somatosensory and auditory convergence in the lateral nucleus of the amygdala. *Behavioral Neuroscience, 107,* 444–450.

Rovee, C. K., Kaufman, L. W., & Collier, G. H. (1977). Components of predation defense behavior in chickens: Evidence for endogenous rhythmicity. *Physiology & Behavior, 19,* 663–671.

Schoenfeld, W. N. (1950). An experimental approach to anxiety, escape, and avoidance behavior. In P. H. Hoch & J. Zubin (Eds.), *Anxiety* (pp. 70–99). New York: Grune & Stratton.

Sigmundi, R. A., & Bolles, R. C. (1983). CS modality, context conditioning, and conditioned freezing. *Animal Learning and Behavior, 11,* 205–212.

Sigmundi, R. A., Bouton, M. E., & Bolles, R. C. (1980). Conditioned freezing in the rat as a function of shock intensity and CS modality. *Bulletin of the Psychonomic Society, 15,* 254–256.

Tolman, E. C. (1932). *Purposive behavior in animals and men.* New York: Appleton.

Tonegawa, S., Li, Y., Erzurumlu, R. S., Jhaveri, S., Chen, C., Goda, Y., Paylor, R., Silva, A. J., Kim, J. J., Wehner, J. M., Stevens, C. F., & Abeliovich, A. (1995). The gene knockout technology for the analysis of learning and memory, and neural development. *Progress in Brain Research, 105,* 3–14.

Walther, F. R. (1969). Flight behaviour and avoidance of predators in Thompson's gazelle. *Behaviour, 34,* 184–221.

Whishaw, I. Q. (1993). Activation, travel distance, and environmental change influence food carrying in rats with hippocampal, medial thalamic and septal lesions: Implications for studies on hoarding and theories of hippocampal function. *Hippocampus, 3,* 373–385.

Young, S. L., & Fanselow, M. S. (1992). Associative regulation of Pavlovian fear conditioning: US intensity, incentive shifts and latent inhibition. *Journal of Experimental Psychology: Animal Behavior Processes, 18,* 400–413.

Part V

Cognition in Animal Learning

17

Bolles's Psychological Syllogism

Anthony Dickinson

Twenty-five years ago, Robert Bolles (1972) published an article in the *Psychological Review* that has provided an enduring theoretical framework for my research. At that time I had just completed my doctoral thesis on the behavioral effects of septal lesions, an enterprise undertaken in the hope that the "functioning of brain-injured organisms is . . . likely to reveal the 'natural fracture lines' of behavior" (Thomas, Hostetter, & Barker, 1968, p. 264). The attractiveness of such an uncertain research strategy has to be seen within the context of the theoretical vacuum of the preceding decade or so, a vacuum induced by the apparently insoluble dispute between the cognitive (e.g., Tolman, 1932, 1949a, 1949b) and stimulus–response (S-R)/reinforcement neobehaviorists (e.g., Guthrie, 1935; Hull, 1943, 1952).

In the early 1950s, the view emerged that the dispute was, to use Kendler's (1952) phrase, "a theoretical blind alley," a pseudoproblem that could never be resolved by the rat's ability to recognize and avoid dead ends in a maze or, for that matter, by any other form of empirical evidence. Kendler's radical operationalism did not pass unchallenged, however. For example, in one of the great satires of psychology, "The Circumnavigation of Cognition," Ritchie (1953) mounted a staunch defense of the reality and causal efficacy of psychological processes by demonstrating the absurdity of operational behaviorism. Such behaviorism, he argued, is akin to claiming that the concept of a spherical world should be replaced by an operational description of a circumnavigation. Ritchie's conceptual analysis failed to navigate behavioral psychology back to the harbor of enlightenment, however, and the subject descended into an atheoretical dark age for the next 2 decades. Unfortunately, my formative student years were passed toward the fagend of this period, and I knew no better than to take up the hit-and-miss research strategy advocated by Thomas et al. (1968) in the hope that the septum was a fracture point for psychology.

I thank my past students and colleagues, especially Chris Adams, David Nicholas, Gerry Dawson, and Andy Watt, for their contributions to this research, and I thank Fred Westbrook and Jacques Mirenowicz for their comments on an earlier draft of the chapter. A special acknowledgment is due to Bernard Balleine, who not only conducted but also inspired most of the research on incentive learning. Finally, I thank the Biotechnology and Biological Sciences Research Council and the European Commission for their continued support of this research.

My thesis served only to confound this hope. Discerning any psychological structure in my research was an exercise in post hoc and special pleading (Dickinson, 1974), and I came to the conclusion that understanding of the brain processes controlling behavior is predicated on psychological theory rather than vice versa. It was clear, however, that an adequate psychological theory of acquired behavior was sadly lacking, for at that time even such fundamental questions as what is learned in the basic conditioning procedures were unanswered. Clearly, the most pressing need was for purely psychological research, and it was in this context that Bolles's (1972) theory along with other cognitive accounts (e.g., Estes, 1969; Irwin, 1971), had such an impact in reestablishing the primacy of psychological theory in the research agenda.

Bolles's thesis is simple: Exposure to stimulus-outcome (S-S*) and response-outcome (R-S*) contingencies leads to the acquisition of S-S* and R-S* expectancies, respectively, that represent these relations. The two expectancies are "synthesized" or combined in a "psychological syllogism" so that in the presence of the cue S, the animal is likely to perform response R. More specifically, "the probability of a response increases with (a) the strength of the S-S* expectancy, (b) the strength of the R-S* expectancy, and (c) the value of S*" (Bolles, 1972, p. 404), although each of these strengths is manifested in behavior only by interaction with the other terms of the psychological syllogism. The value of S* is determined not only by the nature of S* itself but also by the animal's current motivational state. Not surprisingly, therefore, a food S* is assumed to have a higher positive value when the animal is hungry than when it is sated. Finally, an aversive S* has negative value that inhibits R in the presence of S through the appropriate expectancies.

Although Bolles's (1972) theory offered a succinct, cognitive account of acquired behavior, its impact was somewhat undercut by the absence of any compelling empirical evidence for the independent contributions of S-S* and R-S* expectancies. The classic latent learning studies (MacCorquodale & Meehl, 1954; Thistlethwaite, 1951) had uniformly employed behavioral tasks involving spatial locomotion in which the roles of the S-S* and R-S* contingencies are inevitably confounded. Evidence for S-S* expectancies was not long in coming, however. Three years later, Holland and Rescorla (1975) demonstrated that postconditioning devaluation of S* reduced subsequent performance following Pavlovian training. Initially, an appetitive response was conditioned to a stimulus S that signaled the delivery of a food S* to their rats. The value of the food S* was then reduced by associating its consumption with the induction of gastric malaise. It is important that this aversion conditioning occurred in the absence of the signal S, so that any change in the animals' responses to S could not reflect a direct association between S and the malaise. Finally, to assess whether the devaluation of S* had an effect on these responses to S, the signal was presented by itself in an extinction test.

On the reasonable assumption that the aversion conditioning reduces the positive value of S*, expectancy theory anticipates that such a devaluation treatment should attenuate performance on test. By contrast, if the food S* simply serves to reinforce an S-R connection during Pavlovian conditioning, any subsequent change in the properties of S* would not affect the test performance. The results of the study clearly favored a role for expectancies in that the animals for whom the food S* had been devalued responded less frequently on test than control subjects that did not receive the aversion conditioning.

Bolles's theory assumes that the conditioning and devaluation effect observed by Holland and Rescorla (1975) were mediated by the interaction of an S-S* expectancy representing the Pavlovian contingency in force during training with a previously learned or innate R-S* expectancy (the law of prior expectancies). At that time, however, there was no independent evidence for R-S* expectancies comparable to that offered by Holland Rescorla (1975) for S-S* expectancies, and the attempt to provide such evidence was the starting point for my own research program.

In this chapter I describe the development of this program within the framework provided by Bolles's syllogism. I begin by discussing the evidence for R-S* expectancies from studies of the S* devaluation in instrumental conditioning, before turning to the issue of the interaction of S-S* and R-S* expectancies. In certain cases, revaluing an S* depends upon incentive learning, which I then describe, leading into a discussion of the psychological processes and brain structures involved in determining S* value. The final section of the chapter considers the scope of the syllogism's account of instrumental behavior and the internal consistency of the theory.

R-S* Expectancies

The initial attempts to demonstrate an S* devaluation effect in instrumental procedures met with little success. In an instrumental analogue of the Holland and Rescorla (1975) study conducted in my laboratory, Adams (1980) trained hungry rats to press a lever for a good S* before devaluing this S* by associating its consumption with toxicosis induced by injections of lithium chloride (LiCl). Even though this aversion treatment both suppressed consumption of the food S* and abolished its reinforcing properties, Adams could detect no effect of this devaluation on lever pressing in a subsequent extinction test. He was not alone in failing to demonstrate a role for an R-S* expectancy in free-operant performance; both Morrison and Collyer (1974) and Holman (1975) had previously reported failures to detect any impact of S* devaluation by aversion conditioning.

A notable feature of these three studies is that they all trained the instrumental response on an interval schedule. In retrospect, this was the least appropriate schedule to employ if, as Bolles (1972) maintained, the strength of the R-S* expectancy represents the strength of the instrumental contingency. At moderate and high rates of responding, the instrumental contingency arranged by an interval schedule is weak in the sense that the S* or reinforcement rate is relatively independent of the response rate. For example, if an interval schedule makes a reinforcer available on average once every minute, the overall reinforcement rate is little affected by whether the animal performs at a rate of 10 or 20 responses per minute. This relative independence contrasts with the contingency in force on a ratio schedule, under which there is a constant relation between response and S* rates. The fact that animals consistently respond faster on ratio than on matched interval schedules shows that they are sensitive to this difference in contingency (e.g., Dawson & Dickinson, 1990).

Given this analysis, clearly the next step was to investigate the effect of S* devaluation following ratio training. In fact, the magnitude of the devaluation effect was evaluated following training on ratio and interval schedules matched for either the probability of S* (given a response) or the rate of S* (Dickinson, Nicholas, & Adams, 1983). The results were unequivocal. Although this study replicated the absence of any detectable effect of devaluation following interval training, the rats trained on the ratio schedule pressed less during the extinction test when an aversion had been conditioned to the food S*. The dissociation between interval and ratio performance was also observed following S* devaluation through specific satiety. As well as failing to find a devaluation effect with aversion conditioning, Holman (1975) also reported that when hungry rats were trained to lever press for a saccharin solution on an interval schedule, prefeeding the animals with saccharin just prior to an extinction test had no detectable effect on instrumental performance. I replicated Holman's finding following interval training but also observed a significant devaluation effect induced by saccharin prefeeding when lever pressing was trained on a ratio schedule (Dickinson, 1987).

These studies suggest that instrumental performance established and maintained by a reasonably strong R-S* contingency, such as that engendered by a ratio schedule, is mediated by a corresponding expectancy. Before drawing this conclusion, however, one should note a possible confounding factor. Bolles's theory assumes that arranging an R-S* contingency inevitably brings about an S-S* relation. Indeed, this stimulus relation is necessary for the acquisition of the S-S* expectancy required to complete the psychological syllogism. In the type of nondifferential conditioning procedures employed in the original instrumental devaluation studies, it is the contextual cues of the conditioning environment that play the role of the stimulus S. Thus, the S-S* expectancy engendered by instrumental training simply reflects that the animals come to expect S* in the training environment. The presence of this S-S* relation means, however, that the devaluation effects observed in these studies may have been mediated by the S-S* rather than the R-S* contingency and hence these effects cannot be taken as unequivocal evidence for R-S*.

To determine the role of the R-S* contingency, Adams and I (Adams & Dickinson, 1981) trained hungry rats to lever press on a conjoint schedule using two different food S*s. The aim of this schedule is to establish a common relation between the contextual cues S and the two S*s but differing contingencies between lever pressing and each of the S*s. Under this schedule there is a positive, R-S* contingency between lever pressing and one of the S*s but a negative, R—no S* contingency between the other

S* and the response. These contingencies are implemented by arranging that lever pressing delivers the positive S* (S*+) on a ratio schedule. By contrast, lever presses postpone the delivery of a scheduled negative S* (S*−). The important feature of this conjoint schedule is that it ensures that S*+ and S*− occur equally frequently within the training context and so should establish equally strong positive S-S*+ and S-S*− expectancies. To the extent that any devaluation effect is mediated by the S-S* contingency alone, devaluing either S*+ or S*− should have a comparable impact on test performance.

Devaluing S*+ and S*−, on the other hand, should have contrasting effects on performance if the effect of S* value is also mediated by the instrumental contingencies. Whereas devaluing S*+ should attenuate lever pressing on test, there is no reason to expect a comparable effect from devaluing S*−, which is presented in a negative relation with lever pressing. Indeed, there are grounds for supposing that devaluing an S*− might augment performance if it becomes aversive as a result of this treatment. In his discussion of avoidance performance, Bolles (1972, pp. 406–407) argued that when S* is aversive, an S-S* expectancy has to interact with an R−no S* expectancy engendered by a negative contingency if the animal is to perform the target response. To the extent that the animals learn about the negative relation between lever pressing and S*−, devaluing S*− should augment performance of this response.

In summary, if the effect of devaluation is mediated solely by S-S* expectancies, devaluing either S*+ or S*− should have a comparable effect on test performance. On the other hand, devaluing S*+ should depress performance and devaluing S*− elevate it if R-S* and R−no S* expectancies control instrumental action. The results of the Adams and Dickinson (1981) study clearly favored a role for instrumental expectancies in that the animals pressed the lever less on test following aversion conditioning with S*+ rather than with S*−.

The contribution of the R-S* contingency was confirmed in an elegant study by Colwill and Rescorla (1985) using a choice procedure. They trained hungry rats to perform two responses, lever pressing and chain pulling, to receive different food S*s. They then conditioned an aversion to one of the S*s, but not to the other, before giving the animal a choice between the two responses in extinction. In this test, the performance of the response associated with the devalued S* during training was reduced relative to the other action. Again, this procedure equates the relation between the contextual cues S and the two S*s so that any difference must have been mediated by the instrumental R-S* contingency and, by implication, by the corresponding expectancy.

S-S* Expectancies

Although in retrospect the relative sensitivities of interval and ratio performance to S* devaluation make sense in terms of the strength of the instrumental contingencies arranged by the two schedules, the initial expectation that interval performance should be sensitive to outcome devaluation was based on a classic irrelevant incentive effect reported by Krieckhaus and Wolf (1968). In this study, the value of S* was manipulated by shifting between motivational states. Initially, thirsty rats were trained to lever press on an interval schedule for one of three S*s: a sodium solution, water, or a solution of a nonsodium salt. The animals were then tested in extinction following the induction of a sodium appetite. Significantly, test performance was higher when the training S* was saline rather than a nonsodium outcome, a difference that did not emerge when testing occurred either under thirst or in the absence of any explicit deprivation or appetite induction (Dickinson & Nicholas, 1983a).

One interpretation of this finding is that animals learn about the various properties of an S*, such as the sodium content, during instrumental training whether or not they are relevant to the current motivational state. The induction of the sodium appetite then reduces the value of S*s with properties irrelevant to this test state while maintaining that of the saline, a difference that is then reflected in the test performance. In the present context, the important feature of the study by Krieckhaus and Wolf (1968) is the substantial revaluation effect observed even though the animals were trained on an interval schedule, a finding that stands in marked contrast to the failure to detect devaluation effects following aversion conditioning under similar training conditions.

One explanation of this discrepancy is that the irrelevant incentive effect induces a larger shift in S* value than does aversion conditioning, with the result that the change in value can be detected even though it is mediated through the relatively weak R-S* expectancy engendered by interval training. If this is so, an even larger revaluation effect should be observed following ratio training, a prediction that was not substantiated in a direct comparison of the magnitude of this irrelevant incentive effect following training on matched ratio and interval schedules. Whether the rats were trained on the ratio or interval contingency, those trained with a sodium S* pressed more on test under a sodium appetite than those trained with a potassium S* (Dickinson & Nicholas, 1983b).

The fact that the irrelevant incentive effect is not sensitive to the difference between ratio and interval contingencies led me to wonder whether this form of S* revaluation is mediated by the R-S* contingency. The alternative, of course, is that the effects of changing the relative values of the saline and nonsodium S*s act through an S-S* relation rather than the instrumental R-S* association. I have already noted that in a free-operant procedure, such as that employed in the irrelevant incentive studies, the contextual cues play the role of S. Therefore, the next step in the analysis was to determine whether or not R-S* expectancies make any contribution to the irrelevant incentive effect.

The initial study addressing this issue employed the conjoint training schedule used by Adams and Dickinson (1981) to demonstrate the role of the R-S* relation in the case of S* devaluation by aversion conditioning. It may be recalled that this schedule arranges equivalent associations between the contextual Ss and two S*s but different relations between each

S* and the instrumental response. Thirsty rats were trained to lever press with two S*s, a saline and a nonsodium outcome, either a potassium solution or plain water. For some animals, the saline acted as S*+ by being presented in a positive R-S* contingency, and the other outcome acted as S*− in a negative contingency. This contingency–S* assignment was reversed for the remaining animals. If the revaluation of these S*s produced by the induction of a sodium appetite is mediated by the R-S* contingency and therefore by the corresponding expectancy, one would expect animals trained with the saline as S*+ should press more on test than those trained with this solution as S*−. In fact, no such difference was detected (Dickinson & Nicholas, 1983a), and subsequent assessments of the role of the R-S* using the choice procedure developed by Colwill and Rescorla (1985) yielded the same conclusion (Dickinson, 1986), namely, that the irrelevant incentive effect induced by a sodium appetite is not mediated by the R-S* contingency.

This conclusion is not restricted to motivational revaluation based on a sodium appetite. Dickinson and Dawson (1987b) used a shift from hunger to thirst to change the relative values of a sucrose solution and food pellets. Initially, hungry rats were trained to press a lever for either a sucrose solution or food pellets before their performance was tested in extinction. When the motivational state was shifted from hunger to thirst, a state in which the sucrose solution has a higher value than the food pellets, those trained with the sucrose pressed the most in an extinction test. This was not due to the fact that the sucrose has a higher S* value irrespective of the animals' motivational state because no difference was observed when the animals were tested hungry. Like the irrelevant incentive effect based on a sodium appetite, the revaluation induced by the hunger-to-thirst transition does not appear to be mediated by the R-S* contingency. In one experiment (Dickinson & Dawson, 1987b, Experiment 3), hungry rats were trained to lever press and chain pull for the sucrose solution and food pellets on a concurrent schedule to equate the S-S* contingencies for the two outcomes while arranging different R-S* relations. When these animals were subsequently given a choice between the two actions while thirsty, they showed no reliable preference for the one trained with the sucrose solution.

Taken together, these results suggest that R-S* expectancies often play a minimal role in mediating the effects of S* revaluation brought about by simple transitions between motivational states, at least with the instrumental training procedures employed in my laboratory (but see Dickinson & Balleine, 1990). Given this conclusion, the implication is that the standard irrelevant incentive effect is mediated primarily by the S-S* expectancy that inevitably arises from instrumental training. Although there is now considerable evidence from my laboratory that this is so (see Dickinson & Balleine, 1990; Dickinson & Dawson, 1987a), perhaps the most informative demonstration comes from a recent experiment concluded in my laboratory by Balleine (1994) using a Pavlovian-instrumental transfer design. The standard procedure for demonstrating the influence of an S-S* relation on instrumental performance is to train the Pavlovian association independently before presenting S while the animals are performing the instrumental response. Thus, in Balleine's study hungry rats experienced an S-S* contingency in the first stage. S* was the sucrose solution for half of the animals and the food pellets for the remainder. The motivational state of the animals was then shifted to thirst, and the animals were taught to press a lever for a water S*. Finally, when lever pressing was tested in the presence of S, Balleine observed an irrelevant incentive effect in that the stimulus associated with the sucrose elevated lever pressing, whereas that associated with the food pellets depressed it. The latter finding is of particular interest because it suggests that dry food, such as the standard reward pellets used, may have a negative S* value when the animals are thirsty.

In summary, these studies of the irrelevant incentive effect demonstrate, in accord with the psychological syllogism, a role for S-S* expectancies in the control of instrumental performance. What remains more problematic for Bolles's theory, however, is the failure to detect any contribution from R-S* expectancies through putative changes in the relative values of S*s brought about by shifts in motivational state.

Incentive Learning

To recap, the psychological syllogism assumes that performance results from the interaction of two representations, the S-S* and R-S* expectancies, with the value of S*. Although Bolles did not specify the nature of this interaction in detail, he suggested that it might be multiplicative in line with the classical formulation of the interaction between learning and motivational processes in neobehaviorist theory (e.g., Hull, 1943, 1952). Within the present context, the implication of this claim is that the ability to detect, for example, an R-S* expectancy by changing the value of S* may well depend on the magnitude of this change.

This point can be illustrated by reconsidering the study by Dickinson and Dawson (1987b, Experiment 3) that has already been discussed. Hungry rats were trained concurrently to perform one action, either lever pressing or chain pulling, for the sucrose solution and the other for the food pellets on interval schedules. These animals were then tested in extinction while thirsty. The rationale of this study was that the shift to thirst would enhance the value of the sucrose relative to the pellets and thus reveal that the respective responses were mediated by R–sucrose and R–pellet expectancies by changing their relative performance appropriately. We expected the thirsty animals to perform the response trained with the sucrose solution more than the one trained with the food pellets during the extinction test. Our failure to observe such a difference, however, may have been due to the fact that the concurrent schedule did not establish sufficiently strong R–sucrose and R–pellet expectancies to allow a reliable difference in performance to be detected with the change in the relative values of the pellets and sucrose solution brought about by the shift from hunger to thirst.

If performance is determined by the product of the strength of the R-S* expectancy and the value of S*, the ability to detect the R–sucrose and R–pellet expectancies depends on the magnitude of the change in the S* values produced by a revaluation procedure. S* revaluation by aversion conditioning produces large enough changes in the relative values of the S*s to allow the R-S* expectancies established by concurrent training to be detected (e.g., Colwill & Rescorla, 1985). By contrast, the relative revaluation of the food pellets and sucrose solution produced by the motivational shift may not be sufficient to support a reliable difference in performance mediated by the R–sucrose and R–pellet expectancies.

This analysis led me to consider whether the change in the relative values of the sucrose solution and food pellets brought about by a shift from hunger to thirst could be enhanced. In his classic articles on the interaction of motivational and cognitive processes, Tolman (1949a, 1949b) argued that a simple shift in motivational state does not necessarily produce a substantial change in the incentive value. Rather, he claimed that the ability of a motivational state to determine the value of a relevant "goal-object" depends on the acquisition of a "cathexis" for that S*. Moreover, the cathexis is acquired through consummatory contact with the S*:

> It would seem that animals or human beings acquire positive cathexes for new foods, drinks, sex-objects, etc., by trying out the corresponding consummatory responses upon such objects and finding that they work—that, in short, the consummatory reactions to these new objects do reduce the corresponding drives. (Tolman, 1949a, p. 146)

Although there was little or no evidence for Tolman's cathexis process, Dawson and I decided to investigate whether we could enhance the change in the incentive value brought about by a shift in motivational state by allowing the animals consummatory contact with the S*s in the shifted state. We have reported on a number of irrelevant incentive studies employing the cathexis process, or what we refer to as *incentive learning* (Dickinson & Dawson, 1988, 1989), but I shall illustrate the general result with an unpublished experiment (Dickinson & Watt, 1992).

The design of this experiment is illustrated in Table 1.[1] During the initial, incentive training stage, the motivational state of the animals was alternated daily between hunger and thirst by the appropriate schedule of food and water deprivation in the home cages. The purpose of this stage was to allow the animals in Group Thirst, but not those in Group Hunger, to learn about the relative values of the food pellets and the sucrose solution when thirsty or, in Tolman's words, to acquire the appropriate cathexes for these S*s under thirst. On days when they were thirsty, the rats in Group Thirst were placed in the operant chambers, where they received noncontingent presentations of the food pellets and sucrose solution with the levers and chains withdrawn. Group Hunger received the

---

[1]The procedure employed in this study was identical to that of Experiment 1a reported by Dickinson and Dawson (1989) except that during the test session the animals had access to both the chain and the lever.

Table 1. Incentive and Instrumental Training for Thirst and Hunger

Group	Incentive Training Thirst	Hunger	Instrumental Training Hunger	Test Thirst
Thirst	Suc, Pel	———	R1 → Suc, R2 → Pel	R1 → 0, R2 → 0
Hunger	———	Suc, Pel		

Note: R1 and R2; lever press and chain pull; Suc: sucrose solution; Pel: food pellets; 0: no outcome

same treatment except that these rats were exposed to the outcome on days when they were hungry. This incentive training was intended to give Group Thirst, but not Group Hunger, the opportunity to learn that the sucrose solution has a higher value than the food pellets under conditions of thirst. The hope was that this training would enhance the change in the relative values of the two S*s for Group Thirst produced by the subsequent shift from instrumental training under hunger to testing under thirst. To investigate whether this was so, each animal was then trained, while hungry, to press a lever and pull a chain on a concurrent schedule for the sucrose solution and pellets, with the action–outcome assignment counterbalanced within each group. Finally, all animals were transferred to a water-deprivation schedule, and the performance of the two actions was assessed in extinction.

If the performance of the two responses is mediated by the appropriate R-S* expectancies, then the action trained with the sucrose outcome should be performed more frequently than the one trained with the pellet outcome, on the assumption, of course, that the sucrose has a higher value than the pellets when the animals are thirsty. I have already noted, however, the failure to detect this difference previously, a result confirmed in the present study. The right-hand panel of Figure 1 shows that the animals in Group Hunger performed both actions with equal frequency during the test. By contrast, when the animals were allowed to learn about the relative values of the two outcomes while thirsty prior to instrumental training, the test performance revealed that the R-S* expectancies controlled instrumental performance. The left-hand panel of Figure 1 shows that the animals in Group Thirst performed the action trained with the sucrose outcome more than the one trained with the pellets.[2] Moreover, other studies have shown that this incentive training is effective when given not only prior to instrumental training but also between the end of instrumental training and testing (Dickinson & Dawson, 1988, 1989).

Devaluing an S* by a downshift in motivation in combination with incentive learning has now been used in a variety studies to demonstrate a role for R-S* expectancies in the control of instrumental performance

---

[2]There was a significant effect of outcome type (sucrose solution vs. food pellets) when the animals had received incentive pretraining while thirsty, $F(1, 5) = 9.35$, $p < .05$, but not when they had received pretraining while hungry, $F(1, 6) = 1.36$, $p > .25$.

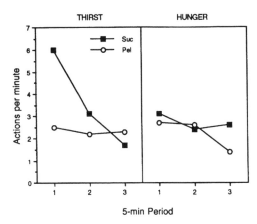

Figure 1. Mean rate of lever pressing and chain pulling during an extinction test conducted while the animals were thirsty. Performance is shown separately for the actions trained with either the food pellets (Pel) or the sucrose solution (Suc). The left- and right-hand panels display the performance of the animals which received incentive training while they were either thirsty or hungry, respectively (see Table 1).

(e.g., Balleine, 1992; Lopez, Balleine, & Dickinson, 1992). A good illustration of the generality of the effect comes from a study of the control of instrumental performance by a downshift in the level of hunger (Balleine & Dickinson, 1994, Experiment 2). In this experiment, rats were trained to press a lever and pull a chain for food pellets and a maltodextrin solution while in a state of hunger induced by food deprivation. During a subsequent reexposure stage, which in this case took place in separate feeding cages rather the operant chambers, the animals were reexposed to one of the outcomes while hungry but to the other outcome while in the nondeprived state. Such reexposure allows the animals to learn about the relatively low value of food in the nondeprived state but only for one of the training outcomes, namely, the one reexposed when the animals are not hungry. As a consequence, the animals should assign a lower value to this outcome on test and therefore perform the associated action less frequently. As the left-hand panel of Figure 2 shows, the effect of incentive learning was evident when the animals were tested in the undeprived state. The action trained with the outcome reexposed in the nondeprived state was performed less frequently than the action whose outcome was reexposed under deprivation.

In the present context, the importance of these and other demonstrations of incentive learning (see Dickinson & Balleine, 1994, 1995, for reviews) is that they confirm the role of R-S* expectancies in the control of performance. Unless an animal knows which action causes which outcome, there is no basis on which the modulation of S* value by incentive learning could selectively control the appropriate instrumental action. Therefore, these studies demonstrate that R-S* expectancies contribute to the process by which primary motivational states, such as hunger and thirst, control instrumental action.

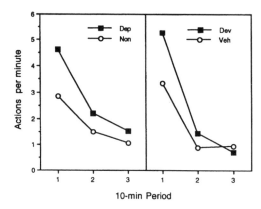

Figure 2. Mean rate of lever pressing and chain pulling during an extinction test conducted while the animals were not food deprived. In the left-hand panel performance is shown separately for the actions trained with outcomes reexposed while the animals were either food deprived (Dep) or non-deprived (Non). In the right-hand panel performance is shown separately for the actions trained with outcomes reexposed following an injection of either devazepide (Dev) or vehicle (Veh). These animals were not food deprived during the reexposure.

S* Value

Having established the contribution of S-S* and R-S* expectancies to performance, I consider the final term of the syllogism, S* value. The analysis so far has assumed that the effective procedures for manipulating S* value are known. Indeed, because of the interactive nature of the syllogism, manipulations of S* value have been used to detect the operation of S-S* and R-S* expectancies, and the very success of these manipulations validates them as factors controlling S* value. As I have shown, the opportunity for incentive learning is an important determinant of S* value, an observation that raises the question of what is learned about S* during incentive training.

From a functional perspective, the value of S* should be determined by its impact on the biological state of the animal so that in the case of hunger, for example, S* value reflects the effect of the outcome on the animal's nutritional state. Incentive learning should, therefore, involve learning that the S* is associated with certain feedback consequences. This is surely what Tolman meant when he referred to finding out that consummatory responses on goal objects "work." In fact, the clearest evidence that the feedback induced by consummatory contact may play a role in determining incentive value comes not from procedures in which the animal finds that such responses "work" but from those in which they do not work.

An obvious interpretation of the devaluation produced by aversion conditioning is that an animal learns about the association between S* and toxicosis, and it is this knowledge that produces the devaluation. Although there is good evidence that such predictive learning can mediate S* devaluation under certain circumstances (Balleine & Dickinson, 1992;

Rescorla, 1992), Garcia (1989) offered a somewhat different account of flavor-aversion conditioning. Rather than reflecting knowledge of the predictive relation between the flavor and illness acquired during conditioning, Garcia argued that the aversion is due to the fact that contact with the flavored S* now induces noxious rather than appetitive feedback and that it is this change in the feedback consequences that suppresses intake. Balleine and I considered whether outcome devaluation by aversion conditioning may depend, at least in part, on experiencing the changed feedback consequences produced by contact with the S*.

To investigate this idea, we (Balleine & Dickinson, 1991) trained thirsty animals to lever press and chain pull for a saline and sucrose solution in a single session. An aversion was then conditioned to both S*s by inducing gastric malaise immediately after this session through an injection of LiCl. To determine whether experience with feedback consequences makes a contribution to any devaluation effect resulting from this aversion conditioning, all animals were then given a brief reexposure to one of the S*s, either the saline or the sucrose solution, in separate drinking cages. Finally, the animals were returned to the operant chambers, where they could choose between the two actions in extinction. A reliable incentive learning effect was observed in that, during this test, the action trained with the reexposed S* was performed less frequently than the other action, trained with the nonreexposed S*.

Balleine and I interpreted this incentive learning effect as evidence that contacting the S* during reexposure induces conditioned nausea (Meachum & Bernstein, 1990) and that it is the experience of the S* in association with this feedback consequence that leads to the devaluation of S*. An obvious prediction from this account is that the devaluation produced at reexposure should be attenuated by blocking the conditioned malaise. My group recently did this by using the antiemetic ondansetron (Balleine, Garner, & Dickinson, 1995), which is a potent and selective antagonist of the 5-HT3 receptors. As in the previous study, thirsty animals were trained to lever press and chain pull for the saline and sucrose solution in a single session, which was followed by a LiCl injection. In this study, however, both S*s were reexposed, the only difference being that one was reexposed following an injection of ondansetron and the other following an injection of saline. This antiemetic should block any noxious feedback and, as a consequence, an S* experienced under ondansetron should suffer less devaluation. This expectation was fulfilled; on test the animals performed the action trained with the S* reexposed under ondansetron more than the one trained with the S* reexposed under saline.

The finding that incentive learning depends on the feedback consequences elicited by contact with S* during reexposure in turn raises the issue of how this feedback determines incentive value. Again, the obvious answer is that the animal simply learns an association, in this case between S* and the feedback. An alternative, however, is that the feedback modulates the animal's affective or hedonic reactions to the S* itself. Not only does flavor-aversion conditioning reinforced by LiCl endow the flavor with the capacity to elicit response patterns characteristic of gastric malaise, but also it changes the pattern of responses to the flavored food or fluid. Grill and Berridge (1985) noted that the fixed-action patterns elicited by contact with a food or fluid appear to index an animal's affective and hedonic evaluation of the commodity. An attractive commodity (e.g., sugar solution) elicits positive, ingestive responses, such as paw licking and tongue protrusions in the rat, whereas distasteful commodities (e.g., quinine solution) elicit aversive reactions, such as gaping and head shaking. The relevance of this observation is that aversion conditioning shifts the responses elicited by a commodity that is initially attractive from the ingestive to the aversive pattern (Berridge, Grill, & Norgren, 1981; Pelchat, Grill, Rozin, & Jacobs, 1983). Rather than learning about the feedback consequences of S*, it is possible that in the case of a flavor aversion the feedback changes the animal's hedonic reactions to the S* itself and that the assignment of S* value is based directly on this new affective evaluation.

The argument is that incentive value is grounded on the affective and hedonic reactions elicited by S* and that the feedback simply acts to modulate these reactions. A test of this idea requires a treatment that alters an animal's hedonic responses to the S* without altering the feedback consequences. In the case of attractive foods, the administration of a benzodiazepine (BZP) appears to be an ideal method. Berridge and Treit (1986) reported that positive ingestive reactions elicited by foods are enhanced by the administration of a BZP, indicating that these drugs augment the hedonic response to attractive foods. If this is so, a prediction of the hedonic theory is that the incentive value of a food S* is enhanced by experiencing the food under the influence of a BZP.

To test this prediction, trained undeprived rats were trained to lever press and chain pull for food pellets and maltodextrin solution before administering incentive training to alter the relative S* values of the two outcomes (Balleine, Ball, & Dickinson, 1994). One outcome was reexposed following an injection of the BZP drug midazolam, whereas the animals experienced the other S* following control injections of the water vehicle used for delivering the drug. If animals assign S* value on the basis of their hedonic reactions to the outcome, a higher value should be assigned to an S* experienced under midazolam than to the one reexposed under the vehicle. To test whether this is so, the animals were returned to the operant chambers, where they were given a choice between the two actions in extinction. This test was given following an injection of midazolam to reinstate the conditions under which the animals experienced the augmented outcome during reexposure.

The prediction of the hedonic theory was confirmed; the rats performed the action trained with the outcome that was reexposed under the drug more frequently than the alternative action that was reexposed following a water injection. It is not clear how this drug-based incentive learning effect can be explained in terms of learning about the feedback consequences of the food outcome because the animals were not in a nutritional deficit at the time of reexposure. Rather, it appears that the midazolam enhanced the animals' hedonic response to the food outcome, as a result of which they assigned a higher S* value to this outcome.

One of the enduring mysteries of psychology is why motivationally significant events do not act solely as goals of action but also generate affective or hedonic experiences, such as pleasure and elation (and, of course, pain and distress in the case of noxious events). One explanation is that such experiences provide the animal with a psychological marker of the biological significance of an outcome on which it can ground the assignment of S* value. According to this account, motivational states such as hunger act by modulating the animal's affective reactions to S* and, by this process, determine its incentive value. Berridge's (1991) observation that the ingestive reactions elicited by a mixed sugar–quinine solution are modulated by the degree of food deprivation provides direct support for this hedonic theory of motivation.

In an attempt to understand the mechanism by which hunger controls the assignment of S* value during incentive learning Balleine and I have focused on the role of the gut peptide cholecystokinin (CCK), which it has been claimed (Smith & Gibbs, 1992) mediates short-term satiety. On the basis of this claim, we speculated that experiencing a food outcome in the presence of CCK may be the factor causing the assignment of a low S* value. We employed two experimental strategies to assess this idea, the first of which involved attempting to block the action of endogenous CCK. As I have already noted, we demonstrated a role of incentive learning in the motivational control of instrumental action by a reduction in food deprivation (Balleine & Dickinson, 1994, Experiment 2). To recap, hungry rats were trained to lever press and chain pull for food pellets and maltodextrin solution before performance was tested in extinction when the animals were not food-deprived. Prior to this test, however, the animals had experienced one of the outcomes, but not the other, in the undeprived state, an experience that we assumed would lead the animals to assign a low S* value to the first outcome. As the left-hand panel of Figure 2 illustrates, the effect of incentive learning was manifested in the extinction test by a reduction in the performance of the action associated with the outcome reexposed in the nondeprived state.

Given this basic devaluation effect, Balleine and I were interested in determining whether the crucial feature of the incentive learning experience was that the target outcome was exposed in the presence of high endogenous levels of CCK owing to the nondeprived state of the animals at the time. To assess this idea, we repeated the training and reexposure regimen except for the fact that the animals had experience with both outcomes in the nondeprived state during the reexposure between training and testing (Balleine & Dickinson, 1994, Experiment 4). Prior to the reexposure to one of the outcomes, however, the animals were injected with the selective CCK-A antagonist devazepide. If the assignment of S* value to a food outcome is determined by the effective CCK level, the impact of endogenous CCK during reexposure would be counteracted by the devazepide, with the consequence that the outcome exposed under the drug would retain a high S* value. In confirmation of this prediction, the right-hand panel of Figure 2 shows that when the animals were tested in the nondeprived state, they showed a preference for the action trained with the outcome reexposed under the antagonist. A comparison of the two panels of Figure 2 illustrates that outcome reexposure following food deprivation and following administration of devazepide has a comparable effect on maintaining S* value.

The second strategy for investigating the role of CCK in the control of S* value sought to block an upshift in value by the administration of an exogenous version of the peptide. Except for the S* revaluation brought about by the BZP drug, the cases considered so far have all been examples of devaluation. However, Balleine (1992) demonstrated that an upshift in the degree of food deprivation, when combined with the appropriate incentive training, can enhance the value of a food S*. Once again, he trained rats on the standard concurrent schedule with two actions and two food S*s, but in this case the animals were undeprived during training. These animals were subsequently tested in extinction following a period of food deprivation. During this test, they showed preference for the action trained with an S* that they had previously experienced in the deprived state during an incentive learning phase. Our interpretation of this result is that during this incentive training the animals experienced the food outcome as hedonically positive because of the low level of endogenous CCK in the undeprived state, and consequently they had assigned a high S* value to it, a value that was then manifested in the subsequent instrumental test. If this is so, it should be possible to prevent this elevation of S* value by artificially enhancing the CCK level during incentive learning.

To test this prediction nondeprived rats were trained to press a lever and pull a chain for food pellets and a maltodextrin solution (Balleine, Davies, & Dickinson, 1995). The animals then received reexposure to both outcomes while deprived, a treatment that was expected to elevate their S* values. Prior to reexposure to one of the outcomes, however, the animals were injected with exogenous CCK in the expectation that this treatment would block the enhancement of S* value for this outcome. This prediction was confirmed; on test the animals showed a preference away from the action trained with the outcome reexposed under CCK.

In summary, studies of incentive learning suggest that primary motivational states do not necessarily modulate S* value automatically but that animals can learn about the value of an S* in a particular state. In addition to its role in hunger and aversion, incentive learning contributes to the control of instrumental action by thermal states (Hendersen & Graham, 1979), thirst (Lopez et al., 1972), and possibly sexual arousal (Everitt & Stacey, 1987).

Brain Mechanisms Revisited

In general, the research undertaken over the past 25 years confirms the importance of the structures and processes of the psychological syllogism.

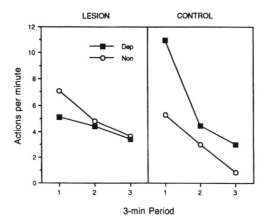

Figure 3. Mean rates of lever pressing and chain pulling during an extinction test conducted while the animals were not food deprived. The left-hand panel displays the performance of animals with lesions of the gustatory cortex, whereas the performance of the control animals is shown in the right-hand panel. Performance is shown separately for actions trained with outcomes reexposed while the animals were either food deprived (Dep) or non-deprived (Non).

Both S-S* and R-S* expectancies have a role in the control of instrumental action, and the analysis of the processes determining the assignment of S* value had advanced. Indeed, the progress has warranted a return to the research issue on which I initially embarked. Whereas in the theoretical vacuum of the 1960s I had hoped that the pattern of behavioral dysfunction produced by neural interventions would reveal the psychological structures and processes of instrumental action, I now have sufficient confidence in the present psychological understanding to reverse the research strategy and ask how the brain implements these processes and structures.

Balleine and I chose to reengage in this enterprise by investigating the neural structures encoding S*s. Our research on incentive learning indicates that in the case of food S*s this process involves learning about the relation between the sensory properties of the S*, such as its taste, and the hedonic reactions that it elicits. This conclusion immediately led us to consider a role for the insular cortex in incentive learning, because this structure has been implicated in gustatory learning (Braun, 1990; Braun, Lasiter, & Kiefer, 1982). Consequently, we investigated the effect of bilateral excitotoxic lesions of the gustatory cortex on devaluation of S* by incentive learning. In general terms, the experiment employed our standard procedure. Food-deprived rats were trained to lever press and chain pull for two S*s, food pellets and the maltodextrin solution, before receiving the incentive training. During this phase, they were exposed to one of the outcomes when undeprived so that they had the opportunity to learn about the relative low value of the S* in this state. The animals also received exposure to the other S*, but in this case when they were food-deprived.

Figure 3 illustrates the effect of this reexposure when the animals were subsequently given a choice between the two actions in an extinction test during which they were undeprived. The unoperated control animals exhibited the standard incentive learning effect in that they performed the action trained with the S* reexposed in the nondeprived state less than the other action (compare the right-hand panel of Figure 3 with the left-hand panel of Figure 2[3]). The reexposure allowed the animals to learn about the relative low value of the S* in the undeprived state, so that when they were once again placed in this state, their performance was controlled by this low value. The important finding, however, was the absence of any evidence for an incentive learning effect in the lesioned animals. Although they learned to lever press and chain pull as readily as the normal rats, the left-hand panel of Figure 3 shows that the incentive training had no effect on their performance in the extinction test.

It is unlikely that the lesion disrupted either taste sensitivity or the capacity of the taste of the S*s to elicit positive hedonic responses. It has long been known that cortical lesions affect neither the ingestive responses, which are indicative of hedonic evaluation in the rat (Grill & Berridge, 1985), nor the sensitivity of such responses to variations in the gustatory properties of the test food or fluid. Therefore, our favored interpretation is that rats normally encode food S*s in the expectancies of the syllogism and in the representation of incentive value in terms of their gustatory properties and that this encoding is mediated by the gustatory cortex. In the absence of a functional cortical representation of the S*, the process of the psychological syllogism cannot be engaged to control instrumental behavior. Whatever the merits of this particular interpretation, however, this study illustrates how questions about neural function can be guided by psychological theory.

Beyond the Psychological Syllogism

Although the psychological syllogism captures important aspects of the cognitive structures and processes controlling instrumental action, I have two main reservations about the theory. The first concerns whether or not the syllogism provides an exhaustive account of instrumental behavior and the second relates to the internal consistency of the theory. I shall consider each of these issues in turn.

There are a number of reasons for believing that instrumental behavior can be controlled by processes that lie outside the scope of the syllogism. For example, if dysfunction of the gustatory cortex prevents encoding of the food S* within R-S* and S-S* expectancies, and the assignment of S* value, what is the process underlying acquisition and maintenance

---

[3]The absolute levels of performance in the two figures should not be compared directly owing to differences in the training schedules in the two studies. The test performance displayed in Figure 2 is for actions trained on concurrent variable interval schedules, whereas the two actions were trained in separate sessions on ratio schedules in the lesion study.

of performance in the dysfunctional animals? One possibility is a simple S-R habit mechanism of the type envisaged by traditional reinforcement theory. Indeed, Bolles (1972, pp. 405–406) explicitly considered the possibility that the "automatic" habits produced by extended training might be mediated by an S-R mechanism. In accord with this claim, such training can render instrumental performance impervious to S* devaluation by both aversion conditioning (Adams, 1982) and motivational shifts coupled with incentive learning (Dickinson, Balleine, Watt, Gonzalez, & Boakes, 1995), suggesting that after extended training, behavior is no longer controlled by the expectancies of the syllogism. On the basis of this behavioral autonomy, I suggested a dual-process theory of instrumental behavior in which performance is jointly controlled by an S-R association and an R-S* expectancy with relative contributions of these two structures varying with the amount and schedule of training (Dickinson, 1985, 1989; Dickinson et al., 1995).

My second concern is more of a challenge to the theory and addresses the central tenet of the syllogism. By denoting the interaction between the S-S* and R-S* expectancies as syllogistic in the causation of behavior, Bolles implied that this interaction is rational in character. In this respect, there is no problem with the interaction between the R-S* expectancy and the S* value. If S* currently has a positive value and an animal also has R-S* expectancy (i.e., it believes that performing R causes access to S*), it is entirely rational to perform response R. Indeed, this is the standard process of practical inference. What is more problematic, however, is whether an S-S* expectancy can also play a rational role in the production of response R.

The case of avoidance behavior is uncontentious. As I have already described, Bolles argued that when S* is aversive and thus has a negative value, avoidance behavior is generated by the interaction of S-S* and R−no S* expectancies. This interaction is, of course, entirely rational; in the presence of a stimulus that predicts an aversive S*, it is a rational course of action to perform a response that causes the omission of S*. What is less clear, however, is whether an S-S* expectancy has any implication for the performance of an action based on an R-S* expectancy when S* has a positive value. In fact, there are grounds for arguing that an S-S* expectancy should reduce rather than facilitate performance. If an animal expects a valued S* to occur in the presence of cue S, the performance of an action that it also believes will cause that same S* is redundant in the context of S. By analogy with the avoidance syllogism, the stimulus premise that rationalizes the performance of a response R for a positively valued S* within a syllogism with an R-S* expectancy is an expectancy with S−no S* content.

Bolles maintained that the syllogism took S-S* and R-S* expectancies as premises because he wanted to encompass Pavlovian conditioning within its scope. As I have already noted when discussing the Holland and Rescorla (1975) devaluation study, Bolles assumed that Pavlovian conditioning reflects the interaction of an S-S* expectancy acquired during this conditioning with a previously learned or innate R-S* expectancy. There are good reasons, however, to doubt this explanation of Pavlovian conditioning. In this respect, the most appropriate paradigm in which to investigate the syllogistic theory is a Pavlovian–instrumental transfer procedure in which the nature of the S-S* and R-S* expectancies can be manipulated independently. The central tenet of the theory is that the two expectancies interact by virtue of the fact that they represent a common S*, because it is this feature of the interaction that warrants its characterization as syllogistic. Therefore, a Pavlovian stimulus established under an S-S* contingency should potentiate an instrumental response established by an R-S* contingency in a transfer test to the extent that stimulus and response are trained with a common S*. Although there are examples that accord with this prediction (e.g., Colwill & Rescorla, 1988; Trapold, 1970), there are also cases in which the greatest transfer is seen when the Pavlovian and instrumental training involve different S*s.

Dawson and I (Dickinson & Dawson, 1987a) demonstrated greater Pavlovian instrumental transfer across different S*s using an irrelevant procedure. Hungry rats were exposed to Pavlovian pairings of one stimulus, S_{pel}, with food pellets and another, S_{suc}, with a sucrose solution. At the same time, an R–pellet expectancy was established by training the animals to lever press for the food pellets. On test, the animals were exposed, for the first time, to the lever in the presence of the two Pavlovian stimuli in extinction.

If the interaction between S-S* and R-S* expectancies is mediated by a common S*, as the psychological syllogism claims, then S_{pel} should facilitate lever pressing more than S_{suc} because a pellet S* was used as the instrumental outcome. Although this was the effect observed when the animals were tested hungry, exactly the opposite outcome occurred under thirst. When the animals were thirsty on test, they pressed more in the presence of S_{suc} than S_{pel}, a result clearly at variance with the syllogism. Dickinson and Balleine (1990) also reported greater transfer across- than within-S* type following a shift from training under thirst to testing under hunger. In these cases, the S-S* expectancy does not appear to interact with the R-S* expectancy through a syllogistic process to determine performance; rather, the stimulus appears to exert a general motivating effect on behavior. The stimulus S_{suc} exerted greater facilitation on behavior than S_{pel} simply because its associated S* was relevant to the test state of thirst.

In conclusion, there are both empirical and theoretical grounds, therefore, for challenging the claim that S-S* and R-S* expectancies interact to control behavior through syllogistic processes. I have already appealed to a noncognitive mechanism in the form of S-R habits to explain instances of resistance to S* revaluation, and I suggest that the facilitatory effect of an S-S* expectancy can also involve a noncognitive process, although in this case one of general motivation or activation (Rescorla & Solomon, 1967).

Whether or not the psychological syllogism survives further empirical examination, it remains a significant theoretical statement of its time. It marked the end of a period during which the study of learning suffered a theoretical vacuum and reinstated the role of cognition in theories of conditioning. It is for this reason that I have always found Robert Bolles's contribution to be both an inspirational and a guiding influence on my own research.

References

Adams, C. D. (1980). Post-conditioning devaluation of an instrumental reinforcer has no effect on extinction performance. *Quarterly Journal of Experimental Psychology, 32,* 447–458.

Adams, C. D. (1982). Variations in the sensitivity of instrumental responding to reinforcer devaluation. *Quarterly Journal of Experimental Psychology, 34B,* 77–98.

Adams, C. D., & Dickinson, A. (1981). Instrumental responding following reinforcer devaluation. *Quarterly Journal of Experimental Psychology, 33B,* 109–122.

Balleine, B. (1992). Instrumental performance following a shift in primary motivation depends upon incentive learning. *Journal of Experimental Psychology: Animal Behavior Processes, 18,* 236–250.

Balleine, B. (1994). Asymmetrical interactions between thirst and hunger in Pavlovian-instrumental transfer. *Quarterly Journal of Experimental Psychology, 47B,* 211–231.

Balleine, B., Ball, J., & Dickinson, A. (1994). Benzodiazepine-induced outcome revaluation and the motivational control of instrumental action in rats. *Behavioral Neuroscience, 108,* 573–589.

Balleine, B., Davies, A., & Dickinson, A. (1995). Cholecystokinin attenuates incentive learning in rats. *Behavioral Neuroscience, 109,* 312–319.

Balleine, B., & Dickinson, A. (1991). Instrumental performance following reinforcer devaluation depends upon incentive learning. *Quarterly Journal of Experimental Psychology, 43B,* 279–296.

Balleine, B., & Dickinson, A. (1992). Signalling and incentive processes in instrumental reinforcer devaluation. *Quarterly Journal of Experimental Psychology, 45B,* 285–301.

Balleine, B., & Dickinson, A. (1994). Role of cholecystokinin in the motivational control of instrumental action in rats. *Behavioral Neuroscience, 108,* 590–605.

Balleine, B., Garner, C., & Dickinson, A. (1995). Instrumental outcome devaluation is attentuated by the anti-emetic ondansetron. *Quarterly Journal of Experimental Psychology, 48B,* 235–251.

Berridge, K. C. (1991). Modulation of taste affect by hunger, caloric satiety, and sensory-specific satiety in the rat. *Appetite, 16,* 103–120.

Berridge, K. C., Grill, H. J., & Norgren, R. (1981). Relation of consummatory responses and preabsorptive insulin release to palatability and learned taste aversions. *Journal of Comparative and Physiological Psychology, 95,* 363–382.

Berridge, K. C., & Treit, D. (1986). Chlordiazepoxide directly enhances positive ingestive reactions. *Pharmacology, Biochemistry, & Behavior, 24,* 217–221.

Bolles, R. C. (1972). Reinforcement, expectancy, and learning. *Psychological Review, 95,* 394–409.

Braun, J. J. (1990). Gustatory cortex: Definition and function. In B. Kolb & R. Tees (Eds.), *The cerebral cortex of the rat* (pp. 407–430). Cambridge, MA: MIT Press.

Braun, J. J., Lasiter, P. S., & Kiefer, S. W. (1982). The gustatory neocortex of the rat. *Physiological Psychology, 10,* 13–45.

Colwill, R. C., & Rescorla, R. A. (1985). Postconditioning devaluation of a reinforcer affects instrumental responding. *Journal of Experimental Psychology: Animal Behavior Processes, 11,* 120–132.

Colwill, R. M., & Rescorla, R. A. (1988). Associations between the discriminative stimulus and the reinforcer in instrumental learning. *Journal of Experimental Psychology: Animal Behavior Processes, 14,* 155–164.

Dawson, G. R., & Dickinson, A. (1990). Performance on ratio and interval schedules with matched reinforcement rates. *Quarterly Journal of Experimental Psychology, 42B,* 225–239.

Dickinson, A. (1974). Response suppression and facilitation by aversive stimuli following septal lesions in rats: A review and model. *Physiological Psychology, 2,* 444–456.

Dickinson, A. (1985). Actions and habits: The development of behavioural autonomy. *Philosophical Transactions of the Royal Society (London), B308,* 67–78.

Dickinson, A. (1986). Re-examination of the role of the instrumental contingency in the sodium-appetite irrelevant incentive effect. *Quarterly Journal of Experimental Psychology, 38B,* 161–172.

Dickinson, A. (1987). Instrumental performance following saccharin pre-feeding. *Behavioural Processes, 14,* 147–154.

Dickinson, A. (1989). Expectancy theory in animal conditioning. In S. B. Klein & R. R. Mowrer (Eds.), *Contemporary learning theories: Pavlovian conditioning and the status of traditional learning theories* (pp. 279–308). Hillsdale, NJ: Erlbaum.

Dickinson, A., & Balleine, B. (1990). Motivational control of instrumental performance following a shift from thirst to hunger. *Quarterly Journal of Experimental Psychology, 42B,* 413–431.

Dickinson, A., & Balleine, B. (1994). Motivational control of goal-directed action. *Animal Learning & Behavior, 22,* 1–18.

Dickinson, A., & Balleine, B. (1995). Motivational control of instrumental action. *Current Directions in Psychological Science, 4,* 162–167.

Dickinson, A., Balleine, B., Watt, A., Gonzalez, F., & Boakes, R. A. (1995). Motivational control after extended instrumental training. *Animal Learning & Behavior, 23,* 197–206.

Dickinson, A., & Dawson, G. R. (1987a). Pavlovian processes in the motivational control of instrumental performance. *Quarterly Journal of Experimental Psychology, 39B,* 201–213.

Dickinson, A., & Dawson, G. R. (1987b). The role of the instrumental contingency in the motivational control of performance. *Quarterly Journal of Experimental Psychology, 39B,* 77–93.

Dickinson, A., & Dawson, G. R. (1988). Motivational control of instrumental performance: the role of prior experience of the reinforcer. *Quarterly Journal of Experimental Psychology, 40B,* 113–134.

Dickinson, A., & Dawson, G. R. (1989). Incentive learning and the motivational control of instrumental performance. *Quarterly Journal of Experimental Psychology, 41B,* 99–112.

Dickinson, A., & Nicholas, D. J. (1983a). Irrelevant incentive learning during instrumental conditioning: The role of drive-reinforcer and response-reinforcer relationships. *Quarterly Journal of Experimental Psychology, 35B,* 249–263.

Dickinson, A., & Nicholas, D. J. (1983b). Irrelevant incentive learning during training on ratio and interval schedules. *Quarterly Journal of Experimental Psychology, 35B,* 235–247.

Dickinson, A., Nicholas, D. J., & Adams, C. D. (1983). The effect of the instrumental training contingency on susceptibility to reinforcer devaluation. *Quarterly Journal of Experimental Psychology, 35B,* 35–51.

Dickinson, A., & Watt, A. (1992). *Incentive learning and the transfer of instrumental performance from hunger to thirst.* Unpublished manuscript.

Estes, W. K. (1969). Reinforcement in human learning. In. J. T. Tapp (Ed.), *Reinforcement and behavior.* New York: Academic Press.

Everitt, B. J., & Stacey, P. (1987). Studies of instrumental behavior with sexual reinforcement in male rats (*Rattus norvegicus*): II. Effects of preoptic area lesions, castration, and testosterone. *Journal of Comparative Psychology, 101,* 407–419.

Garcia, J. (1989). Food for Tolman: Cognition and cathexis in concert. In T. Archer & L.-G. Nilsson (Eds.), *Aversion, avoidance and anxiety* (pp. 45–85). Hillsdale, NJ: Erlbaum.

Grill, H. J., & Berridge, K. C. (1985). Taste reactivity as a measure of the neural control of palatability. In J. M. Sprague & A. N. Epstein (Eds.), *Progress in psychobiology and physiological psychology,* (Vol. 11, pp. 1–61). San Diego, CA: Academic Press.

Guthrie, E. R. (1935). *The psychology of learning.* New York: Harper.

Hendersen, R. W., & Graham, J. (1979). Avoidance of heat by rats: Effects of thermal context on the rapidity of extinction. *Learning and Motivation, 10,* 351–363.

Holland, P. C., & Rescorla, R. A. (1975). The effect of two ways of devaluing the unconditioned stimulus after first- and second-order appetitive conditioning. *Journal of Experimental Psychology: Animal Behavior Process, 1*, 355–363.

Holman, E. W. (1975). Some conditions for the dissociation of consummatory and instrumental behavior in rats. *Learning and Motivation, 6*, 358–366.

Hull, C. L. (1943). *Principles of behavior*. New York: Appleton-Century-Crofts.

Hull, C. L. (1952). *A behavior system*. New Haven, CT: Yale University Press.

Irwin, F. W. (1971). *Intentional behavior and motivation: A cognitive theory*. Philadelphia: Lippincott.

Kendler, H. H. (1952). "What is learned?"—a theoretical blind alley. *Psychological Review, 59*, 269–277.

Krieckhaus, E. E., & Wolf, G. (1968). Acquisition of sodium by rats: Interaction of innate mechanisms and latent learning. *Journal of Comparative and Physiological Psychology, 65*, 197–201.

Lopez, M., Balleine, B., & Dickinson, A. (1992). Incentive learning and the motivational control of instrumental performance by thirst. *Animal Learning and Behavior, 20*, 322–328.

MacCorquodale, K., & Meehle, P. E. (1954). Edward C. Tolman. In W. K. Estes, S. Koch, K. MacCorquodale, P. E. Meehl, C. G. Mueller, Jr., W. N. Schoenfeld, & W. S. Verplanck (Eds.), *Modern learning theory* (pp. 177–266). New York: Appleton-Century-Crofts.

Meachum, C. L., & Bernstein, I. L. (1990). Conditioned responses to a taste conditioned stimulus paired with lithium chloride administration. *Behavioral Neuroscience, 104*, 711–715.

Morrison, G. R., & Collyer, R. (1974). Taste-mediated conditioned aversion to an exteroceptive stimulus following LiCl poisoning. *Journal of Comparative and Physiological Psychology, 80*, 51–55.

Pelchat, M. L., Grill, H. J., Rozin, P., & Jacobs, J. (1983). Quality of acquired responses to taste by *Rattus norvegicus* depends upon type of associated discomfort. *Journal of Comparative and Physiological Psychology, 97*, 140–153.

Rescorla, R. A. (1992). Depression of an instrumental response by a single devaluation of its outcome. *Quarterly Journal of Experimental Psychology, 44B*, 123–136.

Rescorla, R. A., & Solomon, R. L. (1967). Two-process learning theory: Relationship between Pavlovian conditioning and instrumental learning. *Psychological Review, 74*, 151–182.

Ritchie, B. F. (1953). The circumnavigation of cognition. *Psychological Review, 60*, 216–221.

Smith, G. P., & Gibbs, J. (1992). The development and proof of the CCK hypothesis of satiety. In C. T. Dourish, S. J. Cooper, S. D. Iversen, & L. L. Iversen (Eds.), *Multiple cholecystokinin receptors in the CNS* (pp. 166–182). London: Oxford University Press.

Thistlethwaite, D. (1951). A critical review of latent learning and related experiments. *Psychological Review, 48*, 97–129.

Thomas, G. J., Hostetter, G., & Barker, D. J. (1968). Behavioral functions of the limbic system. In E. Stellar & J. M. Sprague (Eds.), *Progress in physiological psychology* (Vol. 2, pp. 229–311). New York: Academic Press.

Tolman, E. C. (1932). *Purposive behavior in animals and man*. New York: Century.

Tolman, E. C. (1949a). The nature and function of wants. *Psychological Review, 56*, 357–369.

Tolman, E. C. (1949b). There is more than one kind of learning. *Psychological Review, 56*, 144–155.

Trapold, M. A. (1970). Are expectancies based upon different positive reinforcing events discriminably different? *Learning and Motivation, 1*, 129–140.

18

The Neurobiology of Memory for Aversive Emotional Events

Larry Cahill, Benno Roozendaal,
and James L. McGaugh

Understanding brain mechanisms of information storage is a central goal of neuroscience. Discoveries of recent years have substantially altered many conceptions of how the brain learns and remembers. Perhaps most notably, the idea that "memory" exists and can be studied as a single, homogeneous entity has been almost completely abandoned. There appear to be many types of memory subserved by interactions among many different brain regions (Squire, Knowlton, & Musen, 1993). Direct study of brain memory systems has even begun to resolve long-standing issues that dominated purely psychological investigations of memory (Packard & McGaugh, 1996).

This chapter reviews evidence for another view of memory storage processes derived from neurophysiological investigations: In addition to systems serving as sites of stored information, there are *neuromodulatory systems* (Gold & McGaugh, 1975) that function to modulate the storage of information. It is an idea that likely would have appealed to Robert Bolles, who emphasized the need for functional significance in theories of learning (Bolles, 1970). At present, the evidence indicates that there are two primary, interacting components critical to neuromodulation of memory: peripheral stress hormones released during emotionally stressful learning situations (especially adrenal hormones) and influences mediated by the amygdaloid complex (AC).

We focus here on the role of these components in memory for aversive learning situations for two main reasons. First, much of the evidence for the existence of neuromodulatory systems comes from experiments using aversive training paradigms. Second, it is known that stress hormones are more consistently released, and generally released to a greater degree, during aversive training than during appetitive learning situations (Coover, Hart, & Frey, 1986; Gold, 1989). Although we do not discuss the issue here, it seems likely that memory-modulatory processes are active

The research reported in this chapter was supported by R. W. and L. Gerard Family Trust Fellowship (BR) and USPHS Research Grant MH12526 from the National Institute of Mental Health and National Institute on Drug Abuse (JLM).

during appetitive learning situations of sufficient emotional intensity to elicit hormonal responses. The focus of inquiry is not on the reactions induced by aversive stimulation (Bolles, 1970) but on the influences of the stimulation on systems involved in modulating the storage of information.

The evidence reviewed here indicates that memory storage for emotional events is modulated (i.e., enhanced or impaired) by interactions between central and peripheral nervous system processes. Accordingly, we suggest that it is no longer sufficient to speak of "brain" memory storage mechanisms without speaking of peripheral modulatory influences, at least for emotionally arousing learning situations. This chapter summarizes some of the evidence on which this view rests.

Peripheral Stress Hormones and Memory

The earliest experiments to suggest that adrenal hormones affect learning processes used pretraining manipulations of pituitary-adrenal hormones (injections or adrenalectomy). For example, Mirsky, Miller, and Stein (1953) studied the effects of pretraining injections of adrenocorticotropic hormone (ACTH) on learned behavioral responses to stressful situations in monkeys and found that the injections profoundly altered extinction behavior. Subsequently, de Wied (1966) found effects of injection of ACTH and related peptides on extinction of avoidance behavior in rats. However, the discovery that drugs given *after* a training experience can act in a retrograde fashion to affect memory (Breen & McGaugh, 1961; McGaugh, 1966; McGaugh & Herz, 1972) raised the possibility that stress hormones released after an acute stressful event may affect memory for that event (Gold & McGaugh, 1975). The first person to recognize this possibility apparently was Ralph Gerard (1961), who noted evidence that memory is susceptible to posttraining drug influences and suggested that the release of epinephrine after a "vivid emotional experience" could "hasten the fixation process" of memory for the experience (p. 29–30).

Adrenomedullary Hormones

Gold and van Buskirk (1976) were the first to demonstrate the validity of Gerard's prediction. They found that posttraining injections of the adrenergic stress hormone epinephrine could affect memory storage in rats trained in a one-trial aversive-learning paradigm. Injections of epinephrine administered immediately after the learning trial resulted in improved memory when the rats were tested 1 day later. In what has become a familiar pattern, the dose response curve obtained was an inverted-U: Optimal enhancing effects on memory were seen at midrange doses, whereas higher or lower doses were less effective. Furthermore, the effects occurred only when the hormone was given soon after the training experience, indicating that the hormone acted on memory storage mechanisms.

Posttraining effects of peripherally injected catecholamines on memory in animal experiments have been subsequently reported many times in many learning situations (McGaugh, 1989). However, only a few experiments have investigated the effects of catecholamines on memory in humans. For example, Christianson, Nillson, Mjorndal, Perris, and Tjellden (1986) found no effect of epinephrine injections on short-term (12 min) memory in normal humans. However, the animal literature indicates that epinephrine affects long-term memory and makes few if any predictions about its potential effects on short-term memory. Indeed, a recent report (Costa-Miserachs, Portell-Cortes, Aldavert-Vera, Torras-Garcia, & Morgado-Bernal, 1994) suggests that, under certain circumstances, effects of epinephrine on memory may not become evident until many days after a training experience.

Recently, we studied the role of catecholamines in the memory of humans (Cahill, Prins, Weber, & McGaugh, 1994). Specifically, we compared the effect of blockade of beta-adrenergic receptors (at which both epinephrine and norepinephrine act) on memory for emotionally neutral and emotionally charged events. Participants took either a placebo or the beta-adrenergic blocking drug propranolol (40 mg) 1 hour prior to viewing either an emotionally neutral story or a closely matched but more emotionally arousing story. Both stories described a young boy walking with his mother to visit his father at work. In the emotionally arousing story, the boy is critically injured in an automobile accident, whereas in the neutral story the boy watches a disaster drill. Retention of the stories was tested in a surprise memory test 1 week later. As expected, participants given placebo showed enhanced retention of the emotional story compared to those who viewed the neutral story. Propranolol administration had no effect on memory for the neutral story, but it impaired memory for the arousing story (see Figure 1). The results are consistent with other recent evidence indicating that chronic beta-blocker treatment in elderly persons impairs the enhancing effect of physical activity on memory (Nielson & Jensen, 1994). Taken together, these studies strongly support the view derived from animal studies that enhanced memory associated with arousal in humans involves the activation of beta-adrenergic receptors, although these receptors are not required for regulating memory storage in nonarousing conditions.

There are several indications that beta-adrenergic receptors outside the central nervous system are critical to the effects of emotion on memory. Most fundamental is the fact that the principal catecholamine hormones released during stress (epinephrine and norepinephrine) do not easily pass the blood–brain barrier (Wiener, 1985). Furthermore, peripheral injections of sotalol, a beta-adrenergic blocker that does not cross the blood–brain barrier, block the effect of epinephrine on memory (Introini-Collison, Saghafi, Novack, & McGaugh, 1992). Also, the effects of numerous drugs and hormones injected peripherally are blocked by vagotomy (Flood & Morley, 1988; Williams & Jensen, 1991). Given this evidence, it seems likely that the impairing effect of propranolol on emotionally influenced memory observed by Cahill et al. (1994) was due, at least in part, to its

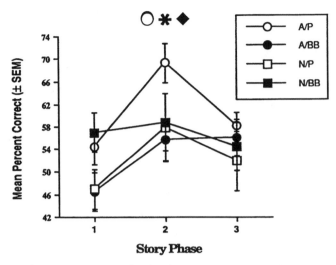

Figure 1. Performance on a multiple-choice memory test for participants taking either a placebo or propranolol 1 hour before viewing either an emotional or a neutral story. The emotional story elements were introduced into the middle phase of the emotional story (Phase 2). Enhanced memory for these elements was seen only in the placebo group: Memory in the arousal story–placebo group for Story Phase 2 was significantly better than for either Phase 1 (O, $p < .01$) or Phase 3 ($\star$, $p < .05$). No other group showed any significant differences in retention between any story phases. Propranolol blocked the enhancing effect of emotion on memory ($\blacklozenge$, $p < .02$) compared to the arousal/beta-blocker (A/BB) group score for Story Phase 2. Memory was tested 1 week after story viewing. A/P = arousal story–placebo; A/BB = arousal story–beta-blocker; N/P = neutral story–placebo; N/BB = neutral story–beta-blocker. From "β-Adrenergic Activation and Memory for Emotional Events," by L. Cahill, B. Prins, M. Weber, & J. L. McGaugh, 1994, *Nature, 371,* p. 703. Reprinted with permission.

actions at peripheral beta-adrenergic receptors. This important issue deserves additional study in humans.

Adrenocortical Hormones

In addition to the role of adrenomedullary hormones, there is considerable evidence that hormones of the adrenal cortex are also involved in memory storage in animals and humans (for reviews see Bohus, 1994; de Kloet, 1991; McEwen & Sapolsky, 1995). For example, short-term adrenalectomy impairs spatial memory of rats in a water maze (Oitzl, Sutanto, & de Kloet, 1990; Roozendaal, Portillo-Marquez, & McGaugh, 1995). Systemic posttraining administration of dexamethasone, a synthetic glucocorticoid, restored memory of ADX rats, whereas similar doses of corticosterone had no effect (Roozendaal, Portillo-Marquez, & McGaugh, 1995).

The differential effect of the two glucocorticoids can be explained by the existence of two receptor types for corticosterone in the brain: mineralocorticoid receptors (MR or Type I) and glucocorticoid receptors (GR or Type II; McEwen, Weiss, & Schwartz, 1966; de Kloet, 1991). These two receptor types differ in their affinity for corticosterone and synthetic ligands. MRs have the highest affinity for the natural steroid corticosterone, whereas GRs have a high affinity for synthetic ligands such as dexamethasone and RU 28362 but a 10-fold lower affinity for corticosterone than do MRs (Reul & de Kloet, 1985; Reul, de Kloet, van Sluys, Rijnberk, & Rothuizen, 1990; Sutanto & de Kloet, 1987). Because of the differential binding affinity for the two receptor types, basal levels of circulating corticosterone primarily bind to MRs, whereas GRs become occupied during stress and at the circadian peak. The finding that dexamethasone restores spatial memory strongly implicates activation of GRs in memory storage.

An involvement of GRs in memory storage is further supported by the finding that administration of the selective GR antagonist RU 38486 to adrenally intact rats impairs memory for a spatial water maze task, whereas MR blockade with the selective antagonist RU 28318 does not (although it does alter search–escape strategies and the reactivity to spatial novelty (Oitzl & de Kloet, 1992; Roozendaal, Portillo-Marquez, & McGaugh, 1995).

In the inhibitory avoidance task, dual effects of glucocorticoids on memory have been found, depending on the dose used: Low doses of corticosterone enhance, whereas very high doses impair, inhibitory avoidance retention (Cottrell & Nakajima, 1977; Kovacs, Telegdy, & Lissak, 1977). In a recent study, we showed that the GR agonists dexamethasone and RU 28362 enhance memory for inhibitory avoidance training, indicating that GRs are also involved in this type of memory (Roozendaal & McGaugh, 1996). In chicks, corticosterone enhanced memory in a passive avoidance paradigm, and this effect was antagonized in animals pretreated with a GR, but not an MR, antagonist (Sandi & Rose, 1994). In contrast to the involvement of glucocorticoids in memory storage in the inhibitory avoidance paradigm, glucocorticoids seem not to affect active shock avoidance learning (Bohus & Lissak, 1968).

In contrast to the effects of acute administration, chronic or repeated exposure to glucocorticoids generally impairs cognitive function in both animals (Luine, Villegas, Martinez, & McEwen, 1994) and humans (Newcomer, Craft, Hershey, Askins, & Bardgett, 1994). Similar disruptive effects of glucocorticoids on cognition have been found in human patients suffering from sustained hypercortisolism and Cushing's syndrome (Starkman, Gebarski, Berent, & Schteingart, 1992).

Interactions Between Adrenomedullary and Adrenocortical Hormones

The evidence reviewed indicates that both adrenomedullary and adrenocortical hormones can modulate memory storage. Additional findings suggest that these two stress hormone systems interact in their effects on memory storage.

Borrell and colleagues (Borrell, de Kloet, Versteeg, & Bohus, 1983; Borrell, de Kloet, & Bohus, 1984) reported that short-term adrenalectomy

(ADX) produced an impairment of memory for inhibitory avoidance training. Adrenomedullectomy (ADMX) produced a similar memory impairment, indicating that the memory impairing effect is caused primarily by the absence of adrenomedullary hormones. This conclusion is supported by evidence that administration of epinephrine or norepinephrine to ADX or ADMX rats attenuated the memory impairment (Borell et al., 1983, 1984). However, the effectiveness of epinephrine in ADMX rats for modulating memory storage was dramatically decreased compared to the effect in ADX rats. ADMX rats required a dose of epinephrine about 1,000 times higher than ADX rats to attenuate the memory impairment. These findings suggest that circulating glucocorticoids influence the memory restoring effect of epinephrine.

Administration of low doses of corticosterone to ADX rats also decreases the sensitivity to epinephrine. In contrast, administration of dexamethasone, a synthetic GR agonist, does not affect epinephrine sensitivity, indicating that the glucocorticoid–adrenergic interaction in ADX rats is probably mediated through MRs and not GRs.

Evidence for a learning-related interaction between adrenomedullary and adrenocortical hormones in adrenally intact rats comes from a recent experiment from our laboratory (Roozendaal, Carmi, & McGaugh, 1996). We examined glucocorticoid–adrenergic interactions on memory storage in rats injected with metyrapone, an 11-beta-hydroxylase inhibitor, the rate-limiting enzyme in the synthesis of corticosterone (Strashimirov & Bohus, 1966). Metyrapone treatment does not completely block the release of corticosteroids, but it greatly reduces the elevation of corticosterone following emotionally arousing events like inhibitory avoidance training. Basal levels of corticosterone are not appreciably affected (Freo, Holloway, Kalogeras, Rapoport, & Soncrant, 1992). Rats were injected with metyrapone (50 mg/kg) or vehicle 90 minutes before training in an inhibitory avoidance apparatus and with epinephrine (0.1 mg/kg), amphetamine (1.0 mg/kg), or 4-OH amphetamine (2.0 mg/kg, a peripherally acting derivative of amphetamine) immediately after training. Both amphetamine drugs are known to enhance memory, at least in part, by stimulating the release of epinephrine from the adrenal medulla (Martinez et al., 1980; Wiener, 1985). All three adrenergic drugs enhanced retention of the training experience, tested 48 hours later (Figure 2). Metyrapone administration alone did not affect memory, but it completely blocked the memory enhancing effects of the posttraining adrenergic drug treatments. These results indicate that stress-induced increases in plasma levels of glucocorticoids are required to induce the memory enhancing effects of epinephrine and amphetamine.

This conclusion differs from that of Borrell and colleagues (1983, 1984), whose primary conclusion was that glucocorticoids decrease the effectiveness of epinephrine. However, it should be noted that in ADX rats (used in their experiments), both MR and GR are deprived of glucocorticoids, whereas metyrapone treatment primarily affects binding of corticosterone to GRs. It is possible that both of the corticosteroid receptor types influence adrenergic effects on memory storage, albeit in different

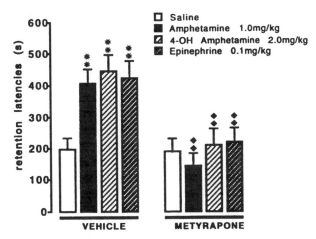

Figure 2. Effects of corticosteroid synthesis blockade with metyrapone (50 mg/kg) on the enhancement of memory produced by posttraining injections of amphetamine (1.0 mg/kg), 4-OH amphetamine (2.0 mg/kg), or epinephrine (0.1 mg/kg) in an inhibitory avoidance task. Metyrapone pretreatment completely blocked the memory enhancement produced by each of these drugs ($n = 9-20$ animals per group). ★★ $p < .01$ compared to the corresponding saline group; ♦ ♦ $p < .01$ compared to the corresponding vehicle pretreatment group. Error bars represent *SEM*. From "Adrenocortical Suppression Blocks the Memory-Enhancing Effects of Amphetamine and Epinephrine," by B. Roozendaal, O. Carmi, & J. L. McGaugh (1996), *Proceedings of the National Academy of Science, 93,* 1431. Reprinted with permission.

ways. In any case, the available evidence supports the general conclusion that adrenergic and glucocorticoid stress hormone systems are intimately coupled during processes of memory storage.

Involvement of the Amygdaloid Complex

A large body of evidence implicates the AC in learning during emotionally negative learning situations (e.g., Cahill & McGaugh, 1991; Davis, 1992; Fanselow & Kim, 1994; Gallagher, Kapp, & Pascoe, 1982; Goddard 1964; Helmstetter & Bellgowan, 1994; LeDoux, 1995). Substantial evidence also suggests that the AC is critical to the memory-modulating effects of stress hormones, which are known to be released during aversive-learning situations (recently reviewed in McGaugh et al., 1995). In general, the evidence suggests that the degree to which the AC is involved in a learning situation is related to the degree to which the learning conditions induce stress hormone release (Cahill & McGaugh, 1990).

The general conclusion that the AC is involved in learning especially during emotionally arousing situations receives considerable support from recent studies involving humans. Perhaps most informative are results obtained from patients with Urbach–Wiethe disease, a rare genetic disorder that sometimes causes a selective, bilateral AC lesion (Hofer, 1973).

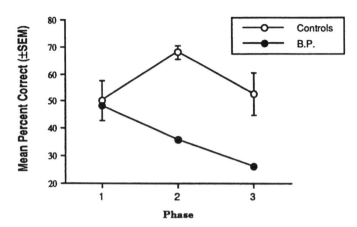

Figure 3. Retention of a short story by controls ($n = 6$) and patient B.P., who has a selective, bilateral AC lesion. The results show performance on a multiple-choice test given 1 week after story viewing. Controls show the expected increase in memory for the phase of the story in which the emotional elements were introduced (Phase 2). In contrast, B.P. showed no evidence of enhanced memory for the emotional story elements. From "The amygdala and emotional memory," by L. Cahill, R. Babinsky, H. Markowitsch, & J. L. McGaugh, 1995, *Nature, 377,* p. 295. Reprinted with permission.

Investigations of the conscious recall in such patients have suggested that they suffer from a selective memory deficit for emotional material (Babinsky et al., 1993; Markowitsch et al., 1994).

Recently, we confirmed this view using the same experimental paradigm used previously to examine beta-adrenergic involvement in emotional memory (Cahill et al., 1994). In this study (Cahill, Babinsky, Markowitsch, & McGaugh, 1995), a patient with Urbach–Wiethe disease (B.P.) with selective, bilateral AC damage and control participants viewed a slightly modified version of the emotionally arousing story described earlier. All received a surprise memory test 1 week later. Consistent with our earlier findings (Cahill et al., 1994), control participants recalled the story phase in which the emotional story elements were introduced (Phase 2) better than the relatively nonemotional initial story phase (Phase 1; see Figure 3). In sharp contrast, B.P. displayed no evidence of enhanced Phase 2 memory despite normal Phase 1 memory. It is interesting that B.P. rated the emotionality of the story slightly higher than the average for the controls. Thus, B.P. failed to show enhanced memory associated with emotion in this paradigm despite having a normal self-described emotional reaction to the story. These findings suggest that the AC is critical to processes that translate emotional arousal into enhanced long-term conscious recall.

Finally, specific neurochemical interactions within the AC appear critical to its role in learning during aversive situations (reviewed in McGaugh et al., 1995). Most relevant to the present discussion, direct beta-adrenergic manipulation of the AC profoundly affects memory. For example, researchers from several laboratories have reported that posttraining intra-AC injections of adrenergic agents modulate memory. In general, injections of appropriate doses of beta-adrenergic agonists enhance, and of antagonists impair, memory (Gallagher, Kapp, Pascoe, & Rapp, 1981; Liang, Juler, & McGaugh, 1986; Liang, McGaugh, & Yao, 1990). Some experiments suggest that alpha-adrenergic receptors in the amygdala do not participate in learning (McGaugh, Introini-Collison, & Nagahara, 1988). Finally, recent evidence indicates that adrenergic influences themselves may affect memory by acting on "downstream" cholinergic mechanisms within the AC (Introini-Collison, Dalmaz, & McGaugh, 1996).

Involvement of Individual Amygdalar Nuclei in Memory Modulation

So far, the involvement of the AC in the modulation of memory by peripheral hormones has been discussed with reference to the AC as a whole. However, considerable evidence indicates that the individual AC nuclei subserve different roles in learning (Sarter & Markowitsch, 1985). For example, recent studies suggest that AC nuclei are differentially involved in modulating hormonal and neuromodulatory influences on memory for inhibitory avoidance training. Selective lesions of the basolateral nucleus (BLA), but not other AC nuclei, block the memory impairing effect of diazepam in this paradigm (Tomaz, Dickinson-Anson, & McGaugh, 1992). Moreover, injections of diazepam into the BLA, but not the central nucleus (CEA), induce amnesia for inhibitory avoidance training (de Souza-Silva & Tomaz, 1995). Inactivation of the BLA (with lidocaine) after training induces retrograde amnesia, whereas an inactivation of the CEA does not (Parent & McGaugh, 1994). Considered together with our finding concerning the patient with an amygdalar lesion described earlier (Cahill et al., 1995), whose lesion is primarily in the BLA, these findings suggest that the BLA might be the primary amygdalar area involved in mediating modulatory effects of stress hormones on memory for aversive experiences.

A recent study examined this implication for memory enhancement by glucocorticoids (Roozendaal & McGaugh, 1996). Rats with lesions of either the BLA or CEA or sham lesions were trained in an inhibitory avoidance task. Systemic injections of either vehicle, corticosterone (0.3 mg/kg) or the more selective GR agonist dexamethasone (0.3 mg/kg), were administered immediately after training. Retention in animals with lesions of the CEA was impaired, but retention in animals with BLA lesions was unimpaired. The finding that lesions of the BLA alone did not affect retention is consistent with previous reports (Tomaz et al., 1992) and indicates that an intact BLA is not required for acquisition or expression in this task. The retention impairment of animals with CEA lesions is consistent with the observation that the CEA is involved in fear conditioning (LeDoux, 1995; Roozendaal, Koolhaas, & Bohus, 1993). As shown in Figure 4, dexamethasone enhanced retention in sham-operated controls as well as in animals with lesions of the CEA, but it did not enhance retention of

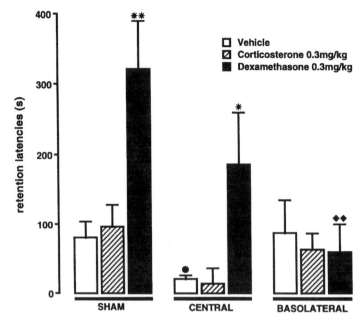

Figure 4. Effect of basolateral or central AC lesions on memory enhancement by dexamethasone in an inhibitory avoidance task. Rats with lesions in either the central or basolateral nuclei or with sham lesions were treated with either saline, corticosterone, or dexamethasone immediately following training. Retention was tested 48 hours later. Central, but not basolateral, lesions impaired retention; however, basolateral, but not central, lesions blocked the retention enhancement produced by dexamethasone ($n = 8–13$ animals per group). ⋆ $p < .05$, ⋆⋆ $p < .01$ compared to the corresponding vehicle group; • $p < .05$ compared to the vehicle–sham group; ◆ ◆ $p < .01$ compared to the sham lesion–dexamethasone group. Error bars represent *SEM*. From "Amygdaloid Nuclei Lesions Differentially Affect Glucocorticoid-Induced Memory Enhancement in an Inhibitory Avoidance Task," by B. Roozendaal & J. L. McGaugh, 1996, *Neurobiology of Learning and Memory, 65,* p. 4. Reprinted with permission.

animals with BLA lesions. Posttraining corticosterone did not affect retention. These findings indicate that the BLA is selectively involved in the modulation of memory formation by glucocorticoids.

Selective lesions of the BLA, and not the CEA, not only disrupt memory-modulatory effects in an inhibitory avoidance task but also block the effects of glucocorticoid manipulations on memory for spatial learning in a water maze (Roozendaal et al., 1995). Removal of the adrenal glands 4–5 days prior to training impaired memory for this task, and immediate posttraining systemic injections of dexamethasone (0.3 mg/kg), but not corticosterone (0.3 mg/kg), attenuated this ADX-induced memory impairment in rats with an intact amygdala. Lesions of the BLA blocked the effects of ADX and glucocorticoids on retention. In contrast, lesions of the CEA itself impaired acquisition and retention performance but did not block the glucocorticoid-induced modulation of memory.

Evidence for Amygdala–Hippocampus Interactions in Learning

There are at least two different views of the role of the AC in learning. Some researchers suggest that the AC functions as a critical link in a learning circuit (e.g., Davis, 1992; LeDoux, 1995). Alternatively, investigations in our laboratory have suggested that the AC functions to modulate memory processes in other brain structures during emotionally arousing situations (discussed recently by Packard, Williams, Cahill, & McGaugh, 1995). Identification of the brain site or sites at which the AC may modulate memory processes remains an important step in the understanding of the role of this structure in memory.

Considerable evidence suggests that the AC may modulate memory processing in the hippocampus. Anatomical evidence is consistent with the possibility that the AC can influence hippocampus-based memory (Krettek & Price, 1977). Furthermore, we have observed c-Fos expression in the dorsal hippocampus following injections of NMDA into the AC (Cahill, 1993; Packard et al., 1995), providing evidence of a functional connection between the AC and the hippocampus. We have also recently shown that AC stimulation modulates hippocampus-dependent spatial learning (Packard, Cahill, & McGaugh, 1994). Finally, as noted previously, BLA lesions block the memory modulatory effects of drugs on spatial memory.

Electrophysiological experiments also suggest that the AC modulates hippocampal function. Thomas, Assaf, and Iverson (1984) showed that AC stimulation modulates neurotransmission from the entorhinal cortex to the dentate gyrus. More recent evidence indicates that lesions of the BLA attenuate the induction of long-term potentiation (LTP) in the dentate gyrus in vivo (Ikegaya, Saito, & Abe, 1994, 1995). Tetanic stimulation of the medial perforant path evoked LTP in the dentate gyrus granule cell synapses. However, lesions of the BLA or temporary BLA inactivation with tetracaine significantly attenuated the magnitude of the LTP. The finding that BLA, but not CEA, lesions modulate hippocampal LTP (Ikegaya et al., 1994) parallels the finding (discussed previously) that BLA, but not CEA, lesions block memory modulation by peripherally administered drugs. Therefore, behavioral, electrophysiological, and pharmacological studies imply that influences from the BLA are required for normal memory processing by the hippocampus.

A recent study (Roozendaal & McGaugh, 1997) examined this implication by investigating whether the memory impairing effect of direct, intrahippocampal infusions of a specific GR antagonist (RU 38486) is attenuated by AC lesions. Rats with lesions of the BLA or CEA or with sham lesions received RU 38486 (3 or 10 ng) or vehicle directly into the dorsal hippocampus shortly before training in a spatial version of the water maze. Rats received five to seven training trials, and retention was tested 48 hours later. The results are shown in Figure 5. The AC nuclei lesions had no effect by themselves on retention. Intrahippocampal infusion of RU 38486 (which did not affect acquisition) impaired retention performance

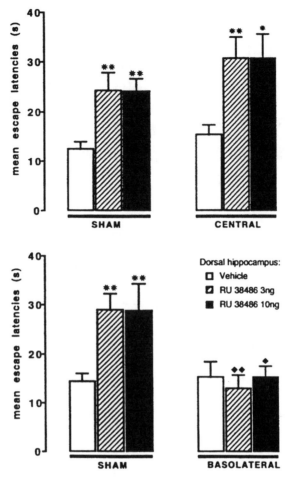

Figure 5. Forty-eight-hour retention test performance in a spatial water maze task. Rats with lesions of the central or basolateral AC nucleus or with sham lesions received intrahippocampal infusions of the specific GR antagonist RU 38486 shortly before training. Intrahippocampal RU 38486 infusion impaired retention (rats required more time to find the hidden platform). Lesions of the basolateral AC completely blocked this effect. $\star$ $p < .05$, $\star\star$ $p < .01$ compared to the corresponding vehicle group; $\blacklozenge$ $p < .05$, $\blacklozenge\blacklozenge$ $p < .01$ compared to the sham lesion–RU 38486 injected group. From "Basolateral Amygdala Lesions Block Glucocorticoid-Induced Modulation of Memory for Spatial Learning," by B. Roozendaal & J. L. McGaugh, 1997, *European Journal of Neuroscience, 9,* p. 80. Reprinted with permission.

of animals with sham and CEA lesions. However, this memory impairment was completely blocked by lesions of the BLA. These data support the view that output from the BLA is required for the modulation of memory processes occurring in other brain structures, including the hippocampus. It is also possible that amygdalofugal influences interact with influences to the amygdala from the hippocampus to modulate memory (Maren & Fanselow, 1995).

Conclusion

Despite the complexity to be expected in neurobiological mechanisms of memory modulation for aversive events, a fairly consistent picture of their nature is emerging. Aversive-learning situations activate both adrenocortical and adrenomedullary stress hormone systems. These in turn interact to affect memory (especially memory storage) for the aversive events. The brain region most clearly implicated in these mnemonic effects to date is the AC. The AC in turn likely affects memory through its influences on other brain structures, especially the hippocampus. We argued that findings from many different experimental approaches, involving both experimental animals and humans, now converge to support this view.

References

Babinsky, R., Calabrese, P., Durwen, H. F., Markowitsch, H. J., Brechtelsbauer, D., Heuser, L., & Gehlen, W. (1993). The possible contribution of the amygdala to memory. *Behavioural Neurology, 6,* 167–170.

Bohus, B. (1994). Humoral modulation of learning and memory processes: Physiological significance of brain and peripheral mechanisms. In J. Delacour (Ed.), *The memory systems of the brain* (pp. 337–364). Singapore: World Scientific.

Bohus, B., & Lissak, K. (1968). Adrenocortical hormones and avoidance behavior in rats. *International Journal of Neuropharmacology, 7,* 301–306.

Bolles, R. C. (1970). Species-specific defense reactions and avoidance learning. *Psychological Review, 77,* 32–48.

Borrell, J., de Kloet, E. R., & Bohus, B. (1984). Corticosterone decreases the efficacy of adrenaline to affect passive avoidance retention of adrenalectomized rats. *Life Sciences, 34,* 99–107.

Borrell, J., de Kloet, E. R., Versteeg, D. H. G., & Bohus, B. (1983). Inhibitory avoidance deficit following short term adrenalectomy in the rat: The role of adrenal catecholamines. *Behavioral and Neural Biology, 39,* 241–258.

Breen, R. A., & McGaugh, J. L. (1961). Facilitation of maze learning with posttrial injections of picrotoxin. *Journal of Comparative and Physiological Psychology, 54,* 498–501.

Cahill, L. (1993). [Fos expression in hippocampus and related structures following amygdala stimulation.] Unpublished raw data.

Cahill, L., Babinsky, R., Markowitsch, H., & McGaugh, J. L. (1995). The amygdala and emotional memory. *Nature, 377,* 295–296.

Cahill, L., & McGaugh, J. L. (1990). Amygdaloid complex lesions differentially affect retention of tasks using appetitive and aversive reinforcement. *Behavioral Neuroscience, 104,* 532–543.

Cahill, L., & McGaugh, J. L. (1991). NMDA-induced lesions of the amygdaloid complex block the retention enhancing effect of post-training epinephrine. *Psychobiology, 19,* 206–210.

Cahill, L., Prins, B., Weber, M., & McGaugh, J. L. (1994). β-Adrenergic activation and memory for emotional events. *Nature, 371,* 702–704.

Christianson, S. A., Nillson, L. G., Mjorndal, T., Perris, C., & Tjellden, G. (1986). Psychological versus physiological determinants of emotional arousal and its relationship to laboratory induced amnesia. *Scandinavian Journal of Psychology, 27,* 300–310.

Coover, G. D., Hart, R. P., & Frey, M. J. (1986). Corticosterone, free fatty acid and glucose responses of rats to footshock, fear, novel stimuli, and instrumental reinforcement. *Psychoneuroendocrinology, 11,* 373–388.

Costa-Miserachs, D., Portell-Cortes, I., Aldavert-Vera, L., Torras-Garcia, M., & Morgado-Bernal, I. (1994). Long-term memory facilitation in rats by posttraining epinephrine. *Behavioral Neuroscience, 108,* 469–474.

Cottrell, G. A., & Nakajima, S. (1977). Effects of corticosteroids in the hippocampus on passive avoidance behavior in the rat. *Pharmacology, Biochemistry, and Behavior, 7,* 277–280.

Davis, M. (1992). The role of the amygdala in fear and anxiety. *Annual Review of Neuroscience, 15,* 353–375.

de Kloet, E. (1991). Brain corticosteroid receptor balance and homeostatic control. *Frontiers in Neuroendocrinology, 12,* 95–164.

de Souza-Silva, M. A., & Tomaz, C. (1995). Amnesia after diazepam infusion into basolateral but not central amygdala of *Rattus norvegicus. Neuropsychobiology, 32,* 31–36.

de Wied, D. (1966). Inhibitory effect of ACTH and related peptides on extinction of conditioned avoidance behavior in rats. *Proceedings of the Society for Experimental Biology (New York), 122,* 28–32.

Fanselow, M. S., & Kim, J. J. (1994). Acquisition of contextual Pavlovian fear conditioning is blocked by the application of an NMDA receptor antagonist, D,L-2-amino-5-phosphonovaleric acid to the basolateral amygdala. *Behavioral Neuroscience, 108,* 210–212.

Flood, J. F., & Morley, J. E. (1988). Effects of bombesin and gastric releasing peptide on memory processing. *Brain Research, 460,* 314–322.

Freo, U., Holloway, H. W., Kalogeras, K., Rapoport, S. E., & Soncrant, T. T. (1992). Adrenalectomy or metyrapone-pretreatment abolishes cerebral metabolic responses to the serotonin agonist 1-(2,5-dimethoxy-4-iodophenyl)-2-aminopropane (DOI) in the hippocampus. *Brain Research, 586,* 256–264.

Gallagher M., Kapp, B. S., & Pascoe, J. P. (1982). Enkephalin analogue effects in the amygdala central nucleus on conditioned heart rate. *Pharmacology, Biochemistry, and Behavior, 17,* 217–222.

Gallagher, M., Kapp, B. S., Pascoe, J. P., & Rapp, P. R. (1981). A neuropharmacology of amygdala systems which contribute to learning and memory. In Y. Ben-Ari (Ed.), *The amygdaloid complex.* Amsterdam: Elsevier.

Gerard, R. W. (1961). The fixation of experience. In J. F. Delafresnaye (Ed.), *Brain mechanisms and learning* (pp. 21–35). Springfield, IL: Charles C Thomas.

Goddard, G. (1964). Amygdaloid stimulation and learning in the rat. *Journal of Comparative and Physiological Psychology, 58,* 23–30.

Gold, P. E. (1989). Neurobiological features common to memory modulation by many treatments. *Animal Learning & Behavior, 17,* 94–100.

Gold, P. E., & McGaugh, J. L. (1975). A single-trace, two-process view of memory storage processes. In D. Deutsch & J. A. Deutsch (Eds.), *Short-term memory* (pp. 355–378). New York: Academic Press.

Gold, P., & van Buskirk, R. (1976). Enhancement and impairment of memory processes with posttrial injections of adrenocorticotropic hormone. *Behavioral Biology, 16,* 387–400.

Helmstetter, F. J., & Bellgowan, P. S. (1994). Effects of muscimol applied to the basolateral amygdala on acquisition and expression of contextual fear conditioning in rats. *Behavioral Neuroscience, 108,* 1005–1009.

Hofer, P. A. (1973). Urbach-Wiethe disease: A review. *Acta Dermato-Venereologica, 53*(Suppl. 71), 5–31.

Ikegaya, Y., Saito, H., & Abe, K. (1994). Attenuated hippocampal long-term potentiation in basolateral amygdala-lesioned rats. *Brain Research, 656,* 157–174.

Ikegaya, Y., Saito, H., & Abe, K. (1995). Requirement of basolateral amygdala neuron activity for the induction of long-term potentiation in the dentate gyrus in vivo. *Brain Research, 671,* 351–354.

Introini-Collison, I., Dalmaz, C., & McGaugh, J. L. (1996). Amygdala β-noradrenergic influences on memory storage involved cholinergic activation. *Neurobiology of Learning and Memory, 65,* 57–64.

Introini-Collison, I., Saghafi, D., Novack, G., & McGaugh, J. (1992). Memory-enhancing effects of posttraining dipivefrin and epinephrine: Involvement of peripheral and central adrenergic receptors. *Brain Research, 572,* 81–86.

Kovacs, G. L., Telegdy, G., & Lissak, K. (1977). Dose-dependent action of corticosteroids of brain serotonin content and passive avoidance behavior. *Hormones and Behavior, 8,* 155–165.

Kretteck, J. E., & Price, J. L. (1977). Projections from the amygdaloid complex and adjacent olfactory structures to the entorhinal cortex and to the subiculum in the rat and cat. *Journal of Comparative Neurology, 172,* 723–752.

LeDoux, J. E. (1995). Emotion: Clues from the brain. *Annual Review of Psychology, 46,* 209–235.

Liang, K. C., Juler, R., & McGaugh, J. L. (1986). Modulating effects of posttraining epinephrine on memory: Involvement of the amygdala noradrenergic system. *Brain Research, 368,* 125–133.

Liang, K. C., McGaugh, J. L., & Yao, H. (1990). Involvement of amygdala pathways in the influence of posttraining amygdala norepinephrine and peripheral epinephrine on memory storage. *Brain Research, 508,* 225–233.

Luine, V., Villegas, M., Martinez, C., & McEwen, B. S. (1994). Repeated stress causes reversible impairments of spatial memory performance. *Brain Research, 639,* 167–170.

Maren, S., & Fanselow, M. S. (1995). Synaptic plasticity in the basolateral amygdala induced by hippocampal formation stimulation *in vivo. Journal of Neuroscience, 15,* 7548–7564.

Markowitsch, H. J., Calabrese, P., Wuerker, M., Durwen, H. F., Kessler, J., Babinsky, R., Brechtelsbauer, D., Heuser, L., & Gehlen, W. (1994). The amygdala's contribution to memory: A study on two patients with Urbach-Wiethe disease. *NeuroReport, 5,* 1349–1352.

Martinez, J. L., Jensen, R. A., Messing, R. B., Vasquez, B. J., Soumireu-Mourat, B., Geddes, D., Liang, K. C., & McGaugh, J. L. (1980). Central and peripheral actions of amphetamine on memory storage. *Brain Research, 182,* 157–166.

McEwen, B. S., & Sapolsky, R. M. (1995). Stress and cognitive function. *Current Opinion in Neurobiology, 5,* 205–216.

McEwen, B. S., Weiss, J. M., & Schwartz, L. S. (1966). Selective retention of corticosterone by limbic structures in the rat brain. *Nature, 220,* 911–912.

McGaugh, J. L. (1966). Time-dependent processes in memory storage. *Science, 153,* 1351–1358.

McGaugh, J. L. (1989). Involvement of hormonal and neuromodulatory systems in the regulation of memory storage. *Annual Review of Neuroscience, 12,* 255–287.

McGaugh, J. L., Cahill, L., Parent, M. B., Mesches, M. H., Coleman-Mesches, K., & Salinas, J. (1995). Involvement of the amygdala in the regulation of memory storage. In J. L. McGaugh, F. Bermudez-Rattoni, & R. A. Prado-Alcala (Eds.), *Plasticity in the central nervous system.* Hillsdale, NJ: Erlbaum.

McGaugh, J. L., & Herz, M. J. (1972). *Memory consolidation.* San Francisco: Albion.

McGaugh, J. L., Introini-Collison, I. B., & Nagahara, A. (1988). Memory-enhancing effects of post-training naloxone: Involvement of β-adrenergic influences in the amygdaloid complex. *Brain Research, 446,* 37–49.

Mirsky, I., Miller, R., & Stein, M. (1953). Relation of adrenocortical activity and adaptive behavior. *Psychosomatic Medicine, 15,* 574–584.

Newcomer, J. S., Craft, S., Hershey, T., Askins, K., & Bardgett, M. E. (1994). Glucocorticoid-induced impairment in declarative memory performance in adult humans. *Journal of Neuroscience, 14,* 2047–2053.

Nielson, K. A., & Jensen, R. A. (1994). Beta-adrenergic receptor antagonist antihypertensive medications impair arousal-induced modulation of working memory in elderly humans. *Behavioral and Neural Biology, 62,* 190–200.

Oitzl, M. S., & de Kloet, E. R. (1992). Selective corticosteroid antagonists modulate specific aspects of spatial orientation learning. *Behavioral Neuroscience, 108,* 62–71.

Oitzl, M. S., Sutanto, W., & de Kloet, E. R. (1990). Mineralo- and glucocorticoid receptor function in a spatial orientation task. *Journal of Steroid Biochemistry, 26,* 72S.

Packard, M. G., Cahill, L., & McGaugh, J. L. (1994). Amygdala modulation of hippocampal-dependent and caudate nucleus-dependent memory processes. *Proceedings of the National Academy of Science, 91,* 8477–8481.

Packard, M. G., & McGaugh, J. L. (1996). Inactivation of hippocampus or caudate nucleus with lidocaine differentially affects expression of place and response learning. *Neurobiology of Learning and Memory, 65,* 65–72.

Packard, M., Williams, C. L., Cahill, L., & McGaugh, J. L. (1995). The anatomy of a memory modulatory system: From periphery to brain. In N. E. Spear, L. P. Spear, & M. L. Woodruff (Eds.), *Neurobehavioral plasticity* (pp. 149–185). Hillsdale, NJ: Erlbaum.

Parent, M. B., & McGaugh, J. L. (1994). Posttraining infusion of lidocaine into the amygdala basolateral complex impairs retention of inhibitory avoidance training. *Brain Research, 661,* 97–103.

Reul, J. M. H. M., & de Kloet, E. R. (1985). Two receptor systems for corticosterone in rat brain: Microdistribution and differential occupation. *Endocrinology, 117,* 2505–2512.

Reul, J. M. H. M., de Kloet, E. R., van Sluys, F. J., Rijnberk, A., & Rothuizen, J. (1990). Binding characteristics of mineralocorticoid and glucocorticoid receptors in dog brain and pituitary. *Endocrinology, 127,* 907–915.

Roozendaal, B., Carmi, O., & McGaugh, J. L. (1996). Adrenocortical suppression blocks the memory-enhancing effects of amphetamine and epinephrine. *Proceedings of the National Academy of Science, 93,* 1429–1433.

Roozendaal, B., Koolhaas, J. M., & Bohus, B. (1993). The central amygdala is involved in conditioning but not in retention of active and passive shock avoidance in male rats. *Behavioral and Neural Biology, 59,* 143–149.

Roozendaal, B., & McGaugh, J. L. (1996). Amygdaloid nuclei lesions differentially affect glucocorticoid-induced memory enhancement in an inhibitory avoidance task. *Neurobiology of Learning and Memory, 65,* 1–8.

Roozendaal, B., & McGaugh, J. L. (1997). Basolatera amygdala lesions block the memory-enhancing effect of glucocorticoid administration in the dorsal hippocampus of rats. *European Journal of Neuroscience, 9,* 76–83.

Roozendaal, B., Portillo-Marquez, G., & McGaugh, J. L. (1995). Basolateral amygdala lesions block glucocorticoid-induced modulation of memory for spatial learning. *Behavioral Neuroscience, 110,* 1074–1083.

Sandi, C., & Rose, S. P. R. (1994). Corticosterone enhances long-term potentiation in one day-old chicks trained in a weak passive avoidance learning paradigm. *Brain Research, 647,* 106–112.

Sarter, M., & Markowitsch, H. (1985). Involvement of the amygdala in learning and memory: A critical review with emphasis on anatomical relations. *Behavioral Neuroscience, 99,* 342–380.

Squire, L. R., Knowlton, B., & Musen, G. (1993). The structure and organization of memory. *Annual Review of Psychology, 44,* 453–495.

Starkman, M., Gebarski, S., Berent, S., & Schteingart, D. (1992). Hippocampal formation volume, memory dysfunction, and cortisol levels in patients with Cushing's syndrome. *Biological Psychiatry, 32,* 756–765.

Strashimirov, D., & Bohus, B. (1966). Effect of 2-methyl-1,2-bis-(3-pyridyl)-1-propanone (SU-4885) on adrenocortical secretion in normal and hypophysectomized rats. *Steroids, 7,* 171–180.

Sutanto, W., & de Kloet, E. R. (1987). Species-specificity of corticosteroid receptors in hamster and rat brains. *Endocrinology, 121,* 1405–1411.

Thomas, S. R., Assaf, S. Y., & Iverson, S. D. (1984). Amygdaloid complex modulates neurotransmission from the entorhinal cortex to the dentate gyrus of the rat. *Brain Research, 307,* 363–365.

Tomaz, C., Dickinson-Anson, H., & McGaugh, J. L. (1992). Basolateral amygdala lesions block the diazepam-induced anterograde amnesia in an inhibitory avoidance task. *Proceedings of the National Academy of Science, 89,* 3615–3619.

Wiener, N. (1985). Norepinephrine, epinephrine, and the sympathetic amines. In A. G. Goodman, L. S. Goodman, T. W. Rall, & F. Murad (Eds.), *The pharmacological basis of therapeutics* (7th ed.). New York: Macmillan.

Williams, C., & Jensen, R. A. (1991). Vagal afferents: A possible mechanism for the modulation of peripherally acting agents. In R. C. A. Frederickson, J. L. McGaugh, & D. L. Felten (Eds.), *Peripheral signaling of the brain in neural-immune and cognitive function* (pp. 467–472). New York: Hogrefe & Huber.

19

Signals for Whether Versus When an Event Will Occur

Mark E. Bouton

Robert Bolles was an early student of what is now called "animal cognition." He was interested in what animals actually learn about; that is, the
content of their learning. During the 1970s, he was fond of arguing that
different stimuli in the animal's environment have different functional
roles and that they might also provide different kinds of information. In
this chapter, I present the history of one idea from the 1970s, a distinction
Bolles made between cues that signal *whether* an event will occur versus
those that signal *when* it will occur. The idea had a brief direct effect on
research in Bolles's own laboratory, and an enduring indirect effect on my
own. In my view, the "whether-when" distinction anticipated current research on the role of context, occasion setting, and timing processes in
animal learning, and it still provides a framework for understanding how
they interrelate. This chapter presents the original distinction, and then
focuses on how *whether* signals might actually operate.

The Whether-Versus-When Distinction

When I first arrived at the University of Washington to do graduate work
with Bolles in 1975, most of the research activity in his laboratory was
connected in some way with two articles he had recently written. The first
was the famous article on species-specific defense reactions (SSDRs;
Bolles, 1970), which was the inspiration for a large number of studies of
defensive behavior. The second was "Reinforcement, Expectancy, and
Learning" (Bolles, 1972). In the latter article, Bolles had pointed out that
reinforcement does not always work; that in any situation the animal has
a chance to learn about its behavior and about stimuli in the environment;
and that as far as he was concerned, animals usually learn relatively little
about their behavior and relatively more about the environment. This

Preparation of this chapter was supported by Grant IBN 92-09454 from the National
Science Foundation. I thank Juan M. Rosas and Robert A. Boakes for their comments and
James Byron Nelson for his contribution to the work on inhibition and occasion setting
described here.

statement reflects the direction that SSDR theory took (see chapter 16, this volume). For years afterward, Bolles wrote that animals do not need to learn much about their behavior (e.g., Bolles, 1978, 1984). In the 1972 article, stimulus learning was called the "primary law of learning." Bolles and I shared an interest in the primary law: how animals use and acquire information from the environment.

I joined Bob and Alexis Collier, a more senior graduate student, in a number of discussions of stimulus learning. It was here that I first encountered the distinction between whether and when. The idea was that even in a simple classical conditioning experiment, cues might signal several different things. They might predict *whether* an event, like the food or shock unconditioned stimulus (US), would occur. And they might also predict *when* it was going to happen. Any conditioned stimulus (CS) could have either of these signaling functions, which are confounded in most conditioning experiments. The challenge was to find a way to separate them.

The whether-versus-when distinction had a brief but brilliant history in the Bolles lab. It first came to Seattle with John J. B. Ayres, who spent a sabbatical leave there in 1973–1974. Collier and R. G. M. Morris, who visited the lab in the summer of 1975, had conducted an experiment attempting to separate the *whether* and *when* functions that was presented at the Eastern Psychological Association meeting the next spring (Collier, Morris, & Bolles, 1976). In that experiment, a *whether* signal, a variable-duration (25–165 s) cue whose offset coincided with shock 100 percent of the time, appeared to control more conditioned fear than an embedded *when* signal, a shorter (20 s) fixed-duration cue whose offset coincided with shock only 25 percent of the time. The result was interesting but also consistent with other models that did not invoke a distinction between *whether* and *when* (e.g., Rescorla & Wagner, 1972). To my knowledge, the experiment was never followed up.

By the time I first heard about the whether-versus-when distinction, it had taken on what seemed to be a purely Bollesian character. It was not a fact or even a theory but a cute idea that lacked only a little evidence to help shore it up. We briefly focused on the *when* function, the temporal aspects of conditioning. I ran one or two unpublishable experiments on inhibition of delay. We also examined trace conditioning (Bolles, Collier, Bouton, & Marlin, 1978). Collier's dissertation (Collier, 1977) examined whether rats preferred shocks that were signaled by cues that provided temporal information. Since those early days, researchers in the field have become quite interested in the timing processes in conditioning (e.g., Desmond & Moore, 1988; Gallistel, 1990; Gibbon & Balsam, 1981; Kehoe, Horne, Macrae, & Horne, 1993; Miller & Barnet, 1993). Although there is still much to learn about the subject, it is now much less controversial to say that a CS can signal *when*. Indeed, now that timing is generating so much interest, it is worth noting that the Bollesian distinction emphasizes two processes: Stimuli do not only signal *when*; they can also signal *whether*. Neither function subsumes the other. It is just as important to appreciate the mechanisms of *whether* signaling as those of signaling *when*.

The Contextual Control of Extinction

The whether–when distinction more or less disappeared from consciousness in the Bolles lab by early 1976. I do not remember talking to Bolles much about it in the many conversations we had after that time. I was soon running experiments of a completely different type. Using rat subjects, I conditioned fear of a tone by pairing the tone with shock in one box, Context A, and then extinguished the fear in another box, Context B, by presenting the tone there repeatedly without shock. Once extinction was complete, I tested the tone back in the first context or possibly in a third context. The designs were intended to establish whether extinction was specific to its context. I have run a large number of experiments like this since then, but in those early days, there was little evidence that a context could control conditioned fear. I found, of course, that it could do so in a big way. When the tone was returned to the original conditioning context, it evoked strong fear again after extinction (Bouton & Bolles, 1979a). I now call this effect the *renewal effect* (for reviews, see Bouton, 1991, 1993).

For me, the early renewal experiments were a test of the Rescorla–Wagner model (e.g., Rescorla & Wagner, 1972). That model, which was relatively new at the time, provided a rigorous, interesting account of stimulus learning. It often explained phenomena by invoking the hypothetical conditioning of contextual cues. The renewal results confirmed that contexts can be important, although some of the data were inconsistent with the specifics of the model. I also thought the experiments told something fundamental about extinction. However, it recently struck me that the renewal design, as well as my long history of subsequent research on the context problem, might also shed some light on the whether-versus-when distinction. In fact, although I do not think it is likely, I cannot reject the possibility that Bolles understood the early experiments on contextual control in this way: The renewal design begins to separate the *whether* and *when* functions.

The idea is illustrated in Figure 1, a sketch of a hypothetical situation in which a tone is paired with shock in Context A and then presented without shock in Context B. The figure gives a sense of the timing of events, although time is not to scale. In a typical fear conditioning experiment in my laboratory, the rat is in the context for about 90 minutes, whereas each of the CSs lasts 60 seconds. As the figure illustrates, the tone is a relatively accurate predictor of when the next shock will occur. In contrast, the context provides only gross temporal information; it is much less precise. On the other hand, over the entire experiment, the context is a better predictor of whether the tone–shock relation is in force. Because the tone is paired with shock only some of the time, it is not a very good *whether* cue. The context and the tone may naturally convey

Contextual Control

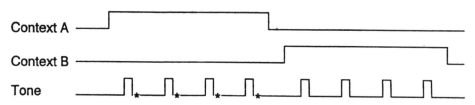

Figure 1. Temporal characteristics of an experiment on contextual control. Time moves from left to right.

different types of information: The context signals *whether*, and the CS signals *when*.

Occasion Setting

Figure 2 illustrates another kind of experiment I became involved with in the 1980s and 1990s. It illustrates procedures that produce *occasion setting*, a type of behavioral control that has attracted considerable attention recently (see Holland, 1992; Swartzentruber, 1995, for reviews). The figure illustrates two types of discriminations. In both, there is a *target* CS, such as a tone, that is sometimes paired with a US, and there is a *feature* CS, such as a light, that marks trials on which the target is paired or not paired with the US. In the feature-positive paradigm, the feature marks the positive trials; in the feature-negative paradigm, the feature marks the negative trials. It is not surprising that the subject learns to respond

Occasion Setting

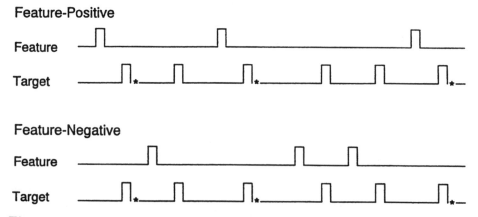

Figure 2. Temporal characteristics of experiments on occasion setting. *Top.* A feature-positive discrimination producing positive occasion setting. *Bottom.* A feature-negative discrimination producing negative occasion setting.

appropriately. However, what the subject learns can depend on when the feature is presented in time (e.g., Holland, 1983, 1984). If the feature is presented simultaneously with the target, it becomes a simple excitor (in the positive discrimination) or a simple inhibitor (in the negative discrimination), as predicted by models of compound conditioning (e.g., Rescorla & Wagner, 1972). However, if the feature and target are presented serially so that the feature occurs sometime before the target comes on (as shown in Figure 2), the animal learns that the feature "sets the occasion" for the meaning of the target. Characterizing this process and distinguishing it from other conditioning processes is an important issue for current conditioning theory (see Holland, 1992; Rescorla, 1985; Wagner & Brandon, 1989; Wilson & Pearce, 1990, for various views). To put it casually for now, the occasion-setting feature seems to signal something like "the tone will be reinforced" or "the tone will not be reinforced" instead of signaling the US or no US more directly.

The point is that when the feature is remote in time, it is not as precise as the target is at signaling when the US will happen. On the other hand, it is more accurate than the target about whether the US will occur. Holland (e.g., 1992, Figure 9) showed that, at least to a first approximation, there is a trade-off between these functions. For example, when the positive feature is presented close in time to the US, the feature elicits a conditioned response that anticipates delivery of the US. However, when the feature is presented more remotely in time, it elicits less anticipatory responding. Now the animal responds primarily to the target, so that the response occurs close in time to the upcoming US. However, responses to the target occur only on the trials that are marked by the feature. The target provides the *when* information, whereas the occasion-setting feature signals *whether* the US will occur.

I did not know it in 1975, but the whether-versus-when distinction anticipated two important issues (besides timing) in conditioning theory: contextual control and occasion setting. In what follows, I will ask what the research I have done since leaving Bolles's laboratory might tell us about the mechanisms of *whether* signaling.

Relevant Aspects of Contextual Control

The Renewal Effect

Figure 3 shows the results of two experiments I ran with my own graduate students after I moved to the University of Vermont and built a laboratory that was specifically designed to run experiments on contextual control. The experiments in Figure 3 illustrate the renewal effect. The upper panel shows results of a fear conditioning experiment (Bouton & King, 1983, Experiment 1) that expanded on the experiments I had conducted with Bolles. The lower panel shows results of an appetitive conditioning experiment in which the tone was paired with food pellets instead of shock

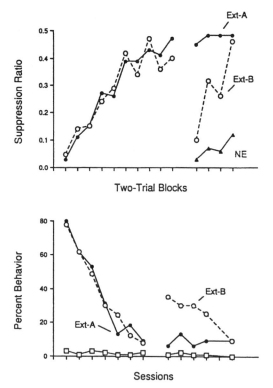

Figure 3. The renewal effect in fear conditioning (top) and appetitive conditioning (bottom). In both experiments, extinction (shown at left) was conducted either
in the context in which conditioning had occurred (Ext-A) or in a different context
(Ext-B). Testing for all groups (shown at right) was conducted in Context A, the
original conditioning context. *Top.* Y axis is the standard suppression ratio, in
which the number of operant responses made in the conditioned stimulus (CS) is
divided by that quantity summed with the number of responses made during an
equally long period immediately before the CS. Ratios of 0 indicate total suppression and maximal fear; ratios of 0.5 indicate no fear. NE = no extinction. From
"Contextual Control of the Extinction of Conditioned Fear: Tests for the Associative Value of the Context," by M. E. Bouton and D. A. King, 1983, *Journal of
Experimental Psychology: Animal Behavior Processes, 9,* p. 252. Adapted with permission of the American Psychological Association. *Bottom.* Y axis shows the percentage behavior judged to be "head jerking," an appetitive response shown by
rats to auditory CSs. Squares describe a conditioning control group that received
unpaired presentation of tone and food. From "Context Effects on Conditioning,
Extinction, and Reinstatement in an Appetitive Conditioning Preparation," by M.
E. Bouton and C. A. Peck, 1989, *Animal Learning & Behavior, 17,* p. 190. Adapted
with permission of the Psychonomic Society.

(Bouton & Peck, 1989, Experiment 1). In the first phase of both experiments, which is not shown, conditioning trials (tone-shock or tone-food)
were given in Context A. The contexts were provided by counterbalanced
sets of conditioning boxes that differed in several ways: their location in
the lab, their visual and olfactory properties, and the style of their floors.

In the extinction phases shown at left, the tone was presented alone either in Context A, where conditioning had occurred, or in Context B. As the extinction data show, the change of context after conditioning had no effect on the course of extinction; performance was the same in either Context A or Context B. A context switch after conditioning typically has little effect on performance resulting from either fear conditioning or appetitive conditioning.

In contrast, a context switch effect emerged in the final test shown at the right in Figure 3. At this point, all the rats were returned to the original conditioning context (Context A) and were presented with the tone alone. There was a clear renewal effect. In either fear conditioning or appetitive conditioning, extinguished responding was renewed when Group Ext-B was returned to the conditioning context. Extinction effects are not permanent, therefore; performance evoked by an extinguished CS is controlled by the context in which it occurs.

Reinstatement

The experiments shown in Figure 3, like other renewal experiments, suggest that the context has an especially potent effect on performance after extinction. A similar point was made in a converging set of experiments that investigated *reinstatement* (e.g., Rescorla & Heth, 1975). If the animal is exposed to the US after extinction, the US presentations can reinstate performance to the tone. However, as Bolles and I originally discovered (Bouton & Bolles, 1979b), this effect depends almost completely on the context. For example, US presentations in an irrelevant context have little impact on performance (Bouton, 1984; Bouton & Bolles, 1979b; Bouton & King, 1983, 1986; Bouton & Peck, 1989). To produce reinstatement, the US must be re-presented in the context in which testing is to occur. The US presentations condition the background, and when the tone is tested in an excitatory background, it elicits responding again, perhaps because contextual conditioning sets the occasion for conditioning (Bouton, Rosengard, Achenbach, Peck, & Brooks, 1993). The strength of reinstatement can be predicted from the strength of contextual conditioning when it is measured ahead of time (Bouton, 1984; Bouton & King, 1983), but most important, the performance-augmenting effect of context conditioning is peculiar to an extinguished CS. If a CS that has never undergone extinction is tested in the presence of the same contextual conditioning, CS performance is not affected (Bouton, 1984; Bouton & King, 1986; Bouton et al., 1993). This is once again true in either fear or appetitive conditioning, and it is also true when conditioned and conditioned-then-extinguished CSs are carefully equated for the amount of responding they evoke prior to the test (Bouton, 1984). These findings converge on the results shown in Figure 3 in suggesting that an extinguished CS is more sensitive to context than are CSs that have never been extinguished.

Variations and Mechanisms

On the other hand, it is worth noting that the renewal effect also occurs in other conditioning paradigms besides extinction. The phenomenon has now been demonstrated in nearly every paradigm in which the CS is given a second meaning in a second phase (Bouton, 1993). For example, my colleagues and I have shown renewal in counterconditioning (Peck & Bouton, 1990), discrimination reversal learning (Bouton & Brooks, 1993; see also Spear et al., 1980; Thomas, McKelvie, Ranney, & Moye, 1981), latent inhibition (Bouton & Bolles, 1979a; Bouton & Swartzentruber, 1989), and reacquisition after extinction (Bouton & Swartzentruber, 1989). The effect has also been observed in verbal learning experiments in which humans learn a list of words in one context, a second list in another, and are then returned to the original context and tested for recall (Greenspoon & Ranyard, 1957). (It is interesting that the paradigms that support renewal often also support spontaneous recovery: When time is allowed to pass after Phase 2, Phase 1 performance may recover over time; see Bouton, 1993, for a review.) Because of the parallels between extinction and the other paradigms, I believe extinction represents a general retroactive interference process (Bouton, 1993). Contextual cues turn out to be important in every paradigm in which incompatible information is learned in successive phases of the experiment.

There are several issues worth mentioning about renewal in extinction. First, it occurs with many kinds of contextual stimuli. For example, it happens with the interoceptive contexts provided by drugs: If rats receive fear extinction in the "context" provided by a benzodiazepine tranquilizer such as chlordiazepoxide or diazepam, fear is renewed when the animal is removed from that context and tested in the original, sober state (Bouton, Kenney, & Rosengard, 1990). The same effect has been shown with alcohol (Cunningham, 1979). In avoidance procedures, renewal has also been produced by contexts provided by correlates of stress or emotion. If adrenocorticotropic hormone (ACTH) is secreted as it normally is during avoidance training and the avoidance response is then extinguished, an injection of ACTH after extinction can cause avoidance performance to be renewed (e.g., Ahlers & Richardson, 1985; Richardson, Riccio, & Devine, 1984). These sorts of findings encourage the view that the experiments on apparatus contexts generalize to a variety of contextual cues.

Second, it is known that renewal happens in a number of different contextual arrangements. The results shown in Figure 3 occurred when conditioning, extinction, and testing were conducted in Contexts A, B, and A, respectively; however, renewed performance has also been seen when the phases occur in Contexts A, B, and C (e.g., Bouton & Brooks, 1993). Most recently, a colleague and I showed the effect when conditioning and extinction both occur in Context A and testing occurs in a second context, Context B (Bouton & Ricker, 1994). Therefore, renewal does not depend on returning the CS to the original conditioning context; a switch out of the extinction context can be enough. The results further reinforce the view that extinction performance is more context-dependent than is conditioning performance. To produce a renewal of conditioning performance in the AAB design, conditioning must generalize across contexts more than extinction does. This is also true in the ABC design.

Finally, the contexts do not have the properties ordinarily expected of excitatory or inhibitory CSs. In our early experiments (Bouton & Bolles, 1979a) Bolles was quickly convinced that the context had a special role. I liked the idea but wanted to approach it carefully. There was the Rescorla–Wagner model (Rescorla & Wagner, 1972) to deal with, as well as the whole history of associative learning. During conditioning, Context A could clearly become a conditioned excitor; it was associated with the US. During extinction, Context B could become a conditioned inhibitor; it was associated with nonreinforcement of an excitor, exactly the condition the model specifies as the one producing conditioned inhibition. My students and I ran the relevant tests for these properties (Bouton & King, 1983; Bouton & Swartzentruber, 1986), and Bolles's intuition appears to have been right: Context A does not have the properties one would expect of an excitor, and Context B does not have the properties of a conditioned inhibitor. By the mid-1980s, it was becoming clear that our contexts had properties that paralleled the ones that were beginning to emerge for occasion setters (Holland, 1983, 1985; Rescorla, 1985). Contexts control performance to the CS, but they are not merely associated with the US or the absence of the US (Bouton & Swartzentruber, 1986). They signal something like *whether* the tone–shock or tone–food relation is in force.

A Model of Context in Extinction

My colleagues and I recently suggested a simple model of extinction that summarizes much of the data (Bouton, 1994b; Bouton & Nelson, 1994; Bouton & Ricker, 1994). The model (see Figure 4) describes a hypothetical

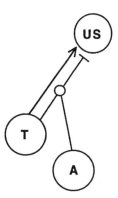

Figure 4.   Hypothetical memory structure for extinction. T = tone CS; US = unconditioned stimulus; A = context. From "Context-Specificity of Target Versus Feature Inhibition in a Feature Negative Discrimination," by M. E. Bouton and J. B. Nelson, 1994, *Journal of Experimental Psychology: Animal Behavior Processes, 20,* p. 62. Reprinted with permission of the American Psychological Association.

memory structure that results from extinction. Like many memory models, it supposes that memory consists of nodes or units that represent items in the world and the associations or connections between them that are learned (e.g., McClelland & Rumelhart, 1985; see also Anderson & Bjork, 1994). Connections can be either excitatory (arrow) or inhibitory (blocked line). The model assumes that during conditioning, the tone is associated with the US. As a consequence, when the tone is presented again, the corresponding memory node is activated, and through the connection, it activates the US node, thus generating performance (Rescorla, 1973, 1974). During extinction, this association remains intact; a new inhibitory tone–shock association is learned. After extinction, the CS therefore has two associations with the US. Its meaning is "ambiguous" (Bouton, 1984, 1994b; Bouton & Bolles, 1985), and like other ambiguous stimuli (such as ambiguous words), the performance it evokes depends on the current context.

The model gives the context a specific role. It proposes that, unlike the tone itself, the context (Stimulus A in the figure) does not work through a direct association with the US. This idea is consistent with the results mentioned previously suggesting that the context is not merely a simple excitor or inhibitor. Instead, the context excites an intermediate node that functions as an AND gate. The AND gate requires input from both the context and the CS to activate the next link, the inhibitory link that suppresses the US. Once this final link is activated, the US node's activation is suppressed, canceling the effect of the original excitatory link. However, this part of the mechanism requires input from both the CS and the context. Outside of the extinction context, the inhibitory link is not activated, and the renewal effect is observed. In effect, renewal occurs because the inhibitory link is not retrieved outside the extinction context.

The major impact of the context in extinction, therefore, is on the inhibitory association of the CS. This idea is consistent with my group's research suggesting that extinction is context-dependent whereas conditioning is much less so (e.g., see Figure 3). According to the model, the influence of the context on behavior is primarily inhibitory; responding is on unless the context switches it off. Later, I develop the idea that *whether* signals often operate this way, by switching the target CS's second-learned, inhibitory association.

To expand the extinction model just a little, we explicitly assumed that "context" is provided by many different types of background cues (see also Spear, 1978). I mentioned previously that drug states and correlates of emotion may provide contexts; so may the memory of recent events and even the associative status of the background (see Bouton & Nelson, in press). I have also suggested that internal and external cues that may change with the passage of time may provide a succession of contexts (Bouton, 1988, 1993). A retention interval may change the context, therefore. Once this possibility is acknowledged, the model provides an account of spontaneous recovery, one of the best-known but least-understood effects in conditioning theory. (It is somewhat surprising to realize that no contemporary conditioning model anticipates it or explains it.) The context model suggests that the passage of time after extinction merely moves the subject to a new temporal context. The inhibitory association is not activated. Spontaneous recovery is the renewal effect that occurs when the CS is tested outside the temporal extinction context.

The model suggests that both spontaneous recovery and renewal occur because the animal fails to retrieve inhibition. Consistent with this hypothesis, spontaneous recovery and renewal are both attenuated if the animal is reminded of extinction with a retrieval cue just before the test (Brooks & Bouton, 1993, 1994). These results suggest that the two effects result from the same mechanism, a failure to retrieve extinction, as the model predicts.

The extinction model embodies the idea that extinction is essentially a retrieval problem. Memories of conditioning and extinction are both available after extinction. Performance depends on which is retrieved. The context, a Bollesian *whether* signal, serves mostly to switch or activate an inhibitory link that is learned in extinction.

Inhibition Switching in Occasion Setting

The Feature-Negative Discrimination

The idea that the context modulates inhibition in extinction might have general implications for the understanding of inhibition. There are other well-known ways to produce inhibition in learning experiments. Perhaps the context is important in many of them.

On the basis of this idea, Byron Nelson and I investigated the role of context in feature-negative (FN) discrimination (Bouton & Nelson, 1994; Nelson & Bouton, 1996). In this paradigm, a target CS is reinforced when presented on its own but nonreinforced when presented in compound with a feature CS (i.e., T+, LT−). Provided the compound is simultaneous, the feature (L) becomes a classic conditioned inhibitor, passing the well-known tests of inhibition (Rescorla, 1969; Williams, Overmier, & LoLordo, 1992): It is difficult to convert into an excitor when it is paired with the US (it passes the retardation test), and it suppresses performance to another excitor when the two stimuli are presented together (it produces inhibitory summation in the summation test). The feature-negative procedure is often thought to be one of the most fundamental means of producing inhibition, because it is embedded in many other inhibitory conditioning procedures (e.g., Wagner & Rescorla, 1972). Of course, Nelson and I also knew that the FN procedure—especially in the serial form illustrated in Figure 2—could also generate negative occasion setting.

The conventional way to view what is learned in the FN discrimination is sketched in Panel A of Figure 5 (e.g., Rescorla & Holland, 1977; Rescorla & Wagner, 1972). On trials in which the tone target is reinforced, an excitatory association with the US develops, and on trials when the light–tone compound is nonreinforced, the light feature acquires inhibi-

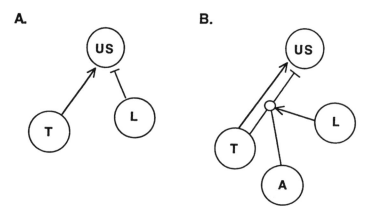

Figure 5. Hypothetical memory structures resulting from feature-negative discrimination training. *Panel A.* Conventional description of inhibition acquired in the feature-negative discrimination. *Panel B.* Inhibition switching by a negative occasion setter (L). Note that L now activates the context-specific inhibitory link learned when the tone is nonreinforced (i.e., undergoes extinction; see Figure 4). T = tone target CS; L = inhibitory feature CS; US = unconditioned stimulus; A = context. Panel B from "Context-Specificity of Target Versus Feature Inhibition in a Feature Negative Discrimination," by M. E. Bouton and J. B. Nelson, 1994, *Journal of Experimental Psychology: Animal Behavior Processes, 20,* p. 62. Reprinted with permission of the American Psychological Association.

tion. The feature is a pure inhibitor; it has only the inhibitory association with the US. The inhibitory association can be conceptualized in two ways. In the Rescorla–Wagner model or in connectionist models that also use the so-called delta rule (e.g., McClelland & Rumelhart, 1985; see Sutton & Barto, 1981), it has a negative value. The tone's excitatory association, in contrast, has a positive one. When the tone is presented alone, it excites the US representation; when it is presented with the light, the light's negative value subtracts from it (Rescorla & Wagner, 1972) and no performance is observed. Alternatively, the inhibitory association may raise the threshold beyond which the US node must be activated to excite the response (e.g., Rescorla, 1979, 1985). The latter description has not been spelled out in much mechanistic detail, but by either means, the light suppresses performance to the tone and thus passes the summation test. It also passes the retardation test, because when the light and US are paired, the negative association must be converted into a positive one (Rescorla & Wagner, 1972), or threshold raising might make the US less effective when it is paired with the light.

The experiments Nelson and I ran seem to have uncovered a second mechanism of inhibition, which is illustrated in Panel B. The new mechanism builds directly on a previous account of extinction (see Figure 4); we discovered a new role for the inhibition switching mechanism presented there. Panel B recognizes that the target CS, like an extinguished CS, is associated with both reinforcement and nonreinforcement during training; consequently, it may acquire the same excitatory and inhibitory associations as an extinguished CS. Also as before, the target's inhibitory association may be "gated" by the context. The new idea is that the feature may inhibit behavior by activating the target's *own* inhibitory association with the US. In the model, it provides an additional input to the familiar AND gate. In the mechanism shown, if target performance is to be suppressed, the AND gate must now receive inputs from the target, the feature, and the context. The new mechanism of inhibition is essentially the same as the one uncovered in extinction. The evidence suggests that either the Panel A or the Panel B mechanism (or both) may be learned in a given FN discrimination, but Panel B describes negative occasion setting. *Whether* signals—provided by either contexts or discrete negative occasion setters—appear to work by modulating the target's own inhibitory association with the US.

Context Effects in Negative Occasion Setting

Nelson and I arrived at this conclusion after running two types of experiments, the designs of which are illustrated in Table 1. In the first type, we asked what happens to inhibition to the feature when the context is switched after FN training. In one experiment (Bouton & Nelson, 1994, Experiment 2), we intermixed an equal number of sessions in two contexts during a training phase. In Context A, the rats received a T+/LT− discrimination; a tone was paired with food when it was presented alone but

Table 1. Designs for Experiments on Effects Context on Inhibition and Negative Occasion Setting

Training		Testing
Context specificity of the feature		
A: T+, LT−		A: T, LT
B: T+, KT−	and/or	B: T, LT
Context specificity of the target		
A: L+, TL−		A: L, TL
B: K+, TK−	and/or	B: L, TL

Note. The rats received intermixed training with both session types shown. The first design tests the context specificity of inhibition to the feature, and the second design tests context specificity of the target. In the illustrations, the focal stimulus is always L. A and B are contexts; T, L, and K are tone, light-off, and keylight CSs, respectively. + = reinforced; − = nonreinforced. The designs are from "Context-Specificity of Target Versus Feature Inhibition in a Feature Negative Discrimination," by M. E. Bouton and J. B. Nelson, 1994, *Journal of Experimental Psychology: Animal Behavior Processes, 20,* 51–65; "The Effects of a Context Switch Following Serial and Simultaneous Feature-Negative Discriminations," by J. B. Nelson and M. E. Bouton, 1996, *Learning and Motivation, 28,* 56–84.

was presented without food when it was combined with a light.[1] (The compound was simultaneous.) In Context B, the rats received a similar treatment, except now a "keylight" CS (onset of a small light mounted in the wall) served as the feature. That is, the rats received T+/KT− in Context B. The two types of sessions made Contexts A and B equally familiar and equally associated with reinforcement, nonreinforcement, and the tone. In the crucial test, we focused on inhibition to the light. Different groups were tested with the LT compound in either Context A or Context B. Notice that the tone had been "inhibited" in both contexts before the test; however, the light was new to Context B. If inhibition to the feature is context-specific, there should be more responding in the LT compound—less inhibition to the feature—in Context B.

This hypothesis was quickly disconfirmed. The context switch caused no disruption of the light's ability to turn off responding to the tone. Figure 6 shows the results of a more recent version of the same experiment (Nelson & Bouton, 1997, Experiment 2) in which we used a within-subject test procedure that was potentially more powerful. We tested each rat in both A and B in a counterbalanced sequence. And more interestingly, we also examined the effect of the context switch after different groups had received either simultaneous FN training (as before) or serial FN training (in which L came on and then went off at the instant T came on). Inhibition to the feature trained with either procedure transferred perfectly to the new context. Inhibition to the feature was not reduced by a context change.

When the feature was switched to the new context, it was tested in compound with a target that had already been inhibited there. In the Panel B mechanism, all the inputs to the AND gate were ready to go. However, Panel B has another, more interesting, implication. If the *target* is switched to a new context, it is more difficult to activate its inhibitory association: The context switch removes the crucial input to the AND gate from the original context. According to Panel B, *responding to the target should be more difficult to inhibit when it is tested in a new context.*

That is exactly what our experiments showed (Bouton & Nelson, 1994, Experiments 3 and 4). In one of them (Experiment 3; see Table 1), rats again received intermixed training in Context A and Context B. In Context A, they received L+/TL− training (the light was now a target rather than a feature). In Context B, they received K+/TK−. As in the previous design, the procedure equated the two contexts on their familiarity and on their associations with reinforcement, nonreinforcement, and the tone. In this case, however, the feature was common across the contexts and the *targets* were unique. In the final test, different groups were tested with TL in Context A or Context B. In Context A, TL was the feature−target combination that had been trained all along, but in Context B, although the

---

[1]The "light" (L) in these experiments was an offset of the houselights that caused complete darkness. We often focus on this CS or on a pure 3000-Hz tone, because the rat perceives these cues as the same stimulus when they are presented in different contexts (e.g., there is no generalization decrement after a context switch). Therefore, any effect of a context switch cannot be the result of the CS "looking" or "sounding" different.

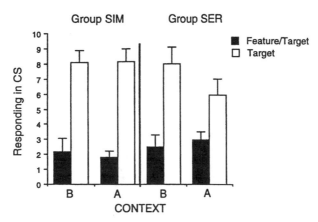

Figure 6. Effects of a context switch on inhibition conditioned to a *feature* after feature-negative training. Group Sim received a simultaneous feature-negative discrimination; Group Ser received a serial one. Context A was the context in which the discrimination was trained; the feature had never been presented before in Context B. See text and top of Table 1 for further explanation. From "The Effects of a Context Switch Following Serial and Simultaneous Feature-Negative Discriminations," by J. B. Nelson and M. E. Bouton, *Learning and Motivation*, 1996, 28, 56–84. Adapted with permission of Academic Press, Inc.

feature had been trained there, the target had not. The design examined the effect of switching the target, not the feature, to a new context.

The results were once again clear. The context switch made responding to the target more difficult to inhibit in Context B. Figure 7 shows the results of a recent version of the experiment (Nelson & Bouton, 1996, Experiment 1), which again used a within-subject test procedure and also examined both simultaneously and serially trained groups.[2] Recall that the serial procedure is the one that produces negative occasion setting. In the simultaneous group (left), the feature inhibited the target in Context A, where the discrimination was originally trained. However, the target was not as readily inhibited in Context B, where it had not been presented before. This was the only effect of switching the target to the new context; as usual, there was no loss of excitation itself when the target was tested alone in Context B. The context switch specifically made responding to the target more difficult to inhibit.

The serially trained group (at right) showed the same result, except the effect was even more pronounced. Here again, the feature inhibited responding in Context A, where the discrimination had been trained, but the target was much more difficult to inhibit when it was switched to Context B. In fact, in the serial group, the feature produced no detectable inhibition of responding to the target tested in the new context. The target's "inhibitability" was completely lost. The results are consistent with

---

[2]The identities of the CSs were also different from the preceding descriptions. In this experiment, the rats received T+/LT− in Context A and N+/LN− in Context B before tests of T and LT in A and B. N was an intermittent white noise.

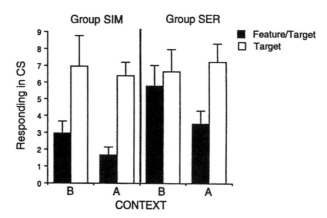

Figure 7. Effects of a context switch on inhibition conditioned to the *target* after feature-negative training. Group Sim received a simultaneous feature-negative discrimination; Group Ser received a serial one. Context A was the context in which the discrimination was trained; the target had never been presented before in Context B. See text and bottom of Table 1 for further explanation. From "The Effects of a Context Switch Following Serial and Simultaneous Feature-Negative Discriminations," by J. B. Nelson and M. E. Bouton, *Learning and Motivation*, 1996, 28, 56–84. Adapted with permission of Academic Press, Inc.

the idea that the serial procedure encourages the inhibition mechanism shown in Panel B. The feature worked exclusively by activating the target's context-specific inhibitory association. When the context input was removed, the inhibition was completely lost. The simultaneous procedure, in contrast, produced a mixture of the Panel B and Panel A mechanisms. The Panel B mechanism was the part that was lost with the context switch, but the Panel A mechanism remained, and regardless of the context, the feature could suppress the US representation directly. No other extant account of inhibition or occasion setting predicts or explains the pattern of results (see Bouton & Nelson, 1994; Nelson & Bouton, 1996).

Hallmarks of Negative Occasion Setting

The model, which builds directly on my group's account of extinction, also accounts for other classic hallmarks of negative occasion setters. I mentioned earlier that a traditional inhibitor is slow to be converted into an excitor when it is paired with a US (the retardation test). One of the properties of a negative occasion setter, however, is that it is not retarded in its conversion into an excitor (e.g., Holland, 1984). The models in Figure 5 account for the difference. As described previously, the traditional Panel A mechanism allows retardation because the inhibitor–US pairings must overcome the inhibitor's negative association with the US. However, in the Panel B mechanism, the feature has no direct inhibitory association with the US; its "inhibition" is not manifested unless the target is also present. Therefore, when it is paired with the US on its own, there is no basis for retardation. Consistent with this account and with earlier experiments on negative occasion setting, the serial feature trained in the experiment shown in Figure 7 (Nelson & Bouton, 1996, Experiment 1) became an excitor more quickly than the simultaneous feature when the two stimuli were paired with the US (Figure 8).

A second hallmark of occasion setting also follows. After a traditional inhibitor is converted into an excitor, its ability to inhibit responding to the target is abolished (Holland, 1984), although perhaps not irrevocably (Rescorla, 1985). This result follows from the traditional view (Panel A), because the stimulus has been converted from negative to positive (the Rescorla–Wagner model assumes independence-of-path). Even if the original inhibitory association remained after excitatory conditioning (e.g., Bouton, 1993), converting the stimulus to a net excitor would cause net excitation, and thus excitatory summation, in the compound. In contrast, a negative occasion setter still inhibits responding to the target after it has been converted into an excitor (Holland, 1984). This paradoxical result is consistent with the Panel B model. Excitatory conditioning of the feature on its own would add an excitatory link between the feature and the US, but it would not change the target's associations or the feature's interaction with them. Therefore, although the new excitatory link would attenuate the feature's ability to "inhibit," the feature should still be able to activate the target's inhibitory association and produce some inhibition of responding to the target. This pattern was observed in one of my group's recent experiments (Nelson & Bouton, 1996, Experiment 2; see also Pearce & Wilson, 1991).

The Panel B model also begins to address a third hallmark of negative occasion setting. A traditional inhibitor's ability to suppress responding to its target can "transfer" and suppress responding to another target. For example, if animals receive intermixed T+, LT−, and N+ trials, the light will ultimately suppress responding to N as well as T (e.g., Rescorla &

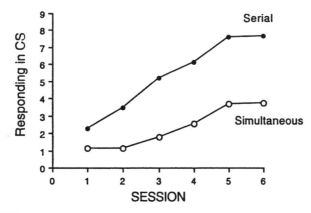

Figure 8. Effects of reinforcing the feature after serial and simultaneous feature-negative discrimination training. From "The Effects of a Context Switch Following Serial and Simultaneous Feature-Negative Discriminations," by J. B. Nelson and M. E. Bouton, *Learning and Motivation*, 1996, 28, 56–84. Adapted with permission of Academic Press, Inc.

Holland, 1977). The Panel A mechanism is consistent with this result (not surprisingly, because it is partly based on it); the feature suppresses the US node regardless of the excitor that excites it. However, a negative occasion setter's ability to transfer is more restricted. In the type of experiment just described, if L were a negative occasion setter (owing to serial training), it would suppress responding to T but not N (e.g., Holland & Lamarre, 1984). This result is consistent with the Panel B mechanism: No direct suppression of the US representation is possible, and N has no inhibitory association with the US that the feature could activate or modulate.

Later research established that the effects of occasion setters transfer better if the transfer target has been in an occasion-setting relationship itself (e.g., Lamarre & Holland, 1987; Rescorla, 1985) or if the transfer target is under the influence of extinction (e.g., Swartzentruber & Rescorla, 1994; but see Holland, e.g., 1986). These results are consistent with the spirit of the Panel B model, because in either case the transfer target's training would give it an inhibitory association that the occasion setter can modulate. The Panel B model is not specific about how transfer would occur (but see Bouton & Nelson, 1994). The model nonetheless provides an insight into why the transfer target's conditioning history is important: Nonreinforcement generates an inhibitory target–US relation, which the feature is in the business of modulating. The transfer issue remains one of the most complex of the many questions that surround occasion setting.

It is interesting to see how easily our experiments on inhibition and negative occasion setting can be linked to the original renewal experiments I ran in Bolles's lab. Bolles gave his students a respect for programmatic research, and he was instrumental in helping me launch a research program of my own. Now that program seems to reach even further back, to the old whether–when distinction. *Whether* signals (i.e., contexts or occasion setters) seem to work by switching inhibition. In this scheme, target excitation may function as a timing process that brings behavior into temporal alignment with biologically significant events in the world. (A more specific timing mechanism could be added.) *Whether* signaling comes into play in extinction and negative occasion setting; here, the target continues to signal *when* unless a *whether* signal turns it off, apparently by activating an inhibition process that is carried by the target itself.

Discussion

I have not said anything about the other side of the occasion-setting coin, namely, the *positive* occasion setting that can arise in serial feature-positive discriminations (see Figure 2). To comment in any detail would be to go beyond what we have been able to produce so far in the laboratory. However, a case can already be made for the idea that positive occasion setters also switch inhibition. Instead of activating target inhibition, however, a positive occasion setter probably inhibits it ("Inhibition of inhibition," Bolles would have said. "Marvelous!"). Swartzentruber and Rescorla

(1994) found that serially trained positive and negative features both modulated performance to a target CS that was undergoing extinction. The
positive feature enhanced responding to the CS, whereas the negative one
suppressed it. More important, neither feature affected responding to a
target CS that was undergoing conditioning instead of extinction. The idea
is that the extinguishing target would be acquiring an inhibitory link,
whereas the conditioning target would not.[3] The actions of both features
apparently required the presence of that inhibition; the positive and negative features respectively inhibited and excited it. These ideas bear some
resemblance to those of Rescorla (e.g., 1985); however, unlike Rescorla, I
accept two inhibitory processes (Figure 5) rather than one, and I also anticipate a role for the context.[4]

I must further clarify the type of inhibition that *whether* signals
switch or modulate. As Figure 6 illustrates, contextual *whether* signals did
not switch conditioned inhibition per se; inhibition conditioned to the feature was not affected by a change of context. Instead, what contexts (and
perhaps other types of *whether* signals) actually modulate is the *second
thing that is learned about the target CS*. The inhibition learned in extinction is clearly such a second thing. The same is true of target inhibition
in the FN design, because by most accounts excitation must be learned
before inhibition can follow. It is worth mentioning that the target was
first paired with the US alone before Nelson and I began FN training in
our FN experiments. Furthermore, second-learned associations do seem
to be context-specific regardless of their inhibitory or excitatory status.
For example, in an unpublished dissertation experiment, Nelson (1995)
found that responding to a conditioned excitor was reduced with a context
switch if the excitor had first been trained as a conditioned inhibitor (i.e.,
a feature in an FN discrimination). As usual, without the initial inhibitory
training, responding to the excitor was not lost. Swartzentruber and Bouton (1992), as well as de Brugada, Garcia-Hoz, Bonardi, and Hall (1995),
reported compatible results with excitors that were initially put through
a latent inhibition treatment. Nelson is currently asking whether an inhibitory feature first trained as an excitor analogously loses its inhibition
with a context switch. The point is, regardless of whether it is conditioned
inhibition or excitation, the first thing learned about a CS is not specific
to the context, whereas the second thing learned about it is. The inhibitory
process modulated by the *whether* signal is not conditioned inhibition. It

---

[3]The target stimuli were trained in a discrimination reversal in which X+/Y− training
preceded the current extinction and conditioning (X−/Y+). It is possible, but not likely, that
Y acquired an inhibitory association in Phase 1. Inhibition was not tested to Y, but other
experiments in the same laboratory using the same general methods commonly have found
no inhibition to Y after X+/Y− and often use the treatment as an inhibitory conditioning
control (e.g., Rescorla, 1985).

[4]Holland (e.g., 1985) originally offered yet another view. He proposed that the target
acquires a simple excitatory association and that positive occasion setters excite it and
negative occasion setters inhibit it. This view does not acknowledge a role for context or the
importance of the target's training history. (The latter, but not the former, was later addressed by assuming that occasion-set targets become stored in a "conditional memory system"; e.g., Holland, 1992.)

is more like *retroactive* inhibition: the suppression of first-learned information by something learned subsequently.

It is interesting to wonder why the second thing learned about a stimulus is more context-specific than the first. At present, I can only offer speculations. The context provides little information until the CS has two meanings to disambiguate. During initial learning, the animal may learn that the CS is the best signal of the US. As Phase 2 begins and the predicted US does not happen, any change of context has predictive usefulness, and the animal may begin to pay more attention to the context (cf. Darby & Pearce, 1995). There are also functional reasons why learning and memory might be organized in this way (Bouton, 1994a). A conditioning trial provides an opportunity to sample from and make inferences about the rest of the world (e.g., Staddon, 1988). If a tone is paired with shock, conditioning allows the inference that other presentations of the tone will also be paired with shock. However, if the world is composed of two types of trials (e.g., tone–shock and tone–no shock trials), the animal is statistically more likely to encounter the more common type first. An early encounter with one type of trial would, on average, reflect its dominance in the population. Subsequent samples of another type of trial would likely be exceptions to the rule. In this sense, treating the second type of trial as less probable in a new context is an adaptation to a statistical feature of sampling items from real populations. Evolution may have designed memory to treat second-learned information as an exception to the rule. It may pay to forget extinction or other second associations with changes of physical or temporal context (see Bouton, 1994a, for other reasons).[5]

These comments seem quite removed from the Bollesian whether-versus-when distinction. What, in the last analysis, can be said about that idea? It should be acknowledged that *whether* signals are probably also equipped to convey some *when* information; the whether–when distinction cannot be hard and fast. The temporal regularities of most occasion-setting procedures could give occasion setters *when*-signaling capabilities. Even a 90-minute exposure to a context provides gross temporal information about the US, especially if viewed from the perspective of the animal's 24-hour day. However, this does not mean that occasion setting and contextual control can be reduced to the laws that govern the actions of simpler *when* signals. As I have indicated, the evidence suggests that occasion setters and contexts are different from such simple eliciting CSs; their ability to control responding to an embedded cue seems independent of the response they control directly themselves (e.g., Holland, 1985, 1992; Nelson & Bouton, 1996). Any theory of conditioning, including ones that might emphasize timing and *when* signaling, needs to recognize a difference between ordinary eliciting CSs and the *whether* signals that control responding to them.

---

[5]The exception to the second-association rule is latent inhibition, which appears to be context-specific (see Bouton, 1993; Hall, 1991) even though it is the first thing learned about the CS.

Still, it is instructive to note that even features that can provide fairly precise temporal information can become *whether* signals (occasion setters) under some circumstances. Specifically, when a positive feature occurs simultaneously with the target, it can become an occasion setter, provided it is relatively weak and nonsalient (Holland, 1989). This finding suggests that contexts may be similar to occasion setters, not because they are imprecise temporal cues but because they are a relatively nonsalient part of the background. One explanation of the Holland (1989) result is that a weak simultaneous feature (or the trace of a serial feature) is not very effective at overshadowing the target. The target therefore acquires strong excitation, which in turn allows it to acquire more inhibition when it is nonreinforced (Rescorla, 1988). The development of occasion setting may depend, therefore, on conditions that encourage strong target inhibition (e.g., Holland, 1992; Rescorla, 1988). Perhaps this is the factor that most directly drives acquisition of what I am calling the *whether* function.

Conclusion

The understanding of contextual control and occasion setting is still far from complete. The focus is also a long way from the original whether-versus-when distinction, although that is not a bad thing—the distinction is now over 20 years old. The approach I have taken is more mechanistic and associationistic than Bolles might have liked. In the long run, I have been attracted to connectionistic "bubble models" because they add precision to the discussion, revealing hidden assumptions and making new predictions. This chapter illustrates their value in this sense. Bolles taught me that good theories are good precisely because they generate testable hypotheses. On this level, perhaps the most essential level, the bubble models succeed. I believe Bolles ultimately would have agreed.

Bolles also would have agreed with another thing: He was right about the main issue in 1975. The whether-versus-when distinction merely represents the larger insight he had about stimulus learning, that conditioning involves multiple kinds of information. In current terms, *when* signals are cues that control behavior by entering into direct associations with significant events. *Whether* signals are the superordinate cues that control these eliciting cues, perhaps by switching or retrieving their inhibition. Some version of the original whether–when distinction may well be essential for a complete understanding of stimulus learning.

References

Ahlers, S. T., & Richardson, R. (1985). Administration of dexamethasone prior to training blocks ACTH-induced recovery of an extinguished avoidance response. *Behavioral Neuroscience, 99,* 760–764.

Anderson, M. C., & Bjork, R. A. (1994). Mechanisms of inhibition in long-term memory: A new taxonomy. In D. Dagenbach & T. H. Carr (Eds.), *Inhibitory processes in attention, memory, and language.* San Diego, CA: Academic Press.

Bolles, R. C. (1970). Species-specific defense reactions and avoidance behavior. *Psychological Review, 77,* 32–48.

Bolles, R. C. (1972). Reinforcement, expectancy, and learning. *Psychological Review, 79,* 394–409.

Bolles, R. C. (1978). The role of stimulus learning in defensive behavior. In S. H. Hulse, H. Fowler, & W. K. Honig (Eds.), *Cognitive processes in animal behavior* (pp. 89–108). Hillsdale, NJ: Erlbaum.

Bolles, R. C. (1984). Species-typical response predispositions. In P. Marler & H. S. Terrace (Eds.), *The biology of learning* (pp. 435–446). Berlin: Springer-Verlag.

Bolles, R. C., Collier, A. C., Bouton, M. E., & Marlin, N. A. (1978). Some tricks for ameliorating the trace-conditioning deficit. *Bulletin of the Psychonomic Society, 11,* 403–406.

Bouton, M. E. (1984). Differential control by context in the inflation and reinstatement paradigms. *Journal of Experimental Psychology: Animal Behavior Processes, 10,* 56–74.

Bouton, M. E. (1988). Context and ambiguity in the extinction of emotional learning: Implications for exposure therapy. *Behavior Research and Therapy, 26,* 137–149.

Bouton, M. E. (1991). Context and retrieval in extinction and in other examples of interference in simple associative learning. In L. W. Dachowski & C. F. Flaherty (Eds.), *Current topics in animal learning: Brain, emotion, and cognition* (pp. 25–53). Hillsdale, NJ: Erlbaum.

Bouton, M. E. (1993). Context, time, and memory retrieval in the interference paradigms of Pavlovian learning. *Psychological Bulletin, 114,* 80–99.

Bouton, M. E. (1994a). Conditioning, remembering, and forgetting. *Journal of Experimental Psychology: Animal Behavior Processes, 20,* 219–231.

Bouton, M. E. (1994b). Context, ambiguity, and classical conditioning. *Current Directions in Psychological Science, 3,* 49–53.

Bouton, M. E., & Bolles, R. C. (1979a). Contextual control of the extinction of conditioned fear. *Learning and Motivation, 10,* 445–466.

Bouton, M. E., & Bolles, R. C. (1979b). Role of conditioned contextual stimuli in reinstatement of extinguished fear. *Journal of Experimental Psychology: Animal Behavior Processes, 5,* 368–378.

Bouton, M. E., & Bolles, R. C. (1985). Contexts, event-memories, and extinction. In P. D. Balsam & A. Tomie (Eds.), *Context and learning* (pp. 133–166). Hillsdale, NJ: Erlbaum.

Bouton, M. E., & Brooks, D. C. (1993). Time and context effects on performance in a Pavlovian discrimination reversal. *Journal of Experimental Psychology: Animal Behavior Processes, 19,* 165–179.

Bouton, M. E., & Brooks, D. C. (1993). Time and context effects on performance in a Pavlovian discrimination reversal. *Journal of Experimental Psychology: Animal Behavior Processes, 19,* 165–179.

Bouton, M. E., Kenney, F. A., & Rosengard, C. (1990). State-dependent fear extinction with two benzodiazepine tranquilizers. *Behavioral Neuroscience, 104,* 44–55.

Bouton, M. E., & King, D. A. (1983). Contextual control of the extinction of conditioned fear: Tests for the associative value of the context. *Journal of Experimental Psychology: Animal Behavior Processes, 9,* 248–265.

Bouton, M. E., & King, D. A. (1986). Effect of context on performance to conditioned stimuli with mixed histories of reinforcement and nonreinforcement. *Journal of Experimental Psychology: Animal Behavior Processes, 12,* 4–15.

Bouton, M. E., & Nelson, J. B. (1994). Context-specificity of target versus feature inhibition in a feature negative discrimination. *Journal of Experimental Psychology: Animal Behavior Processes, 20,* 51–65.

Bouton, M. E., & Nelson, J. B. (in press). The role of context in classical conditioning: Some implications for cognitive behavior therapy. In W. O'Donohue (Ed.), *Learning and behavior therapy.* Needham Heights, MA: Allyn & Bacon.

Bouton, M. E., & Peck, C. A. (1989). Context effects on conditioning, extinction, and reinstatement in an appetitive conditioning preparation. *Animal Learning & Behavior, 17,* 188–198.

Bouton, M. E., & Ricker, S. T. (1994). Renewal of extinguished responding in a second context. *Animal Learning & Behavior, 22,* 317–324.

Bouton, M. E., Rosengard, C., Achenbach, G. G., Peck, C. A., & Brooks, D. C. (1993). Effects of contextual conditioning and unconditional stimulus presentation on performance in appetitive conditioning. *Quarterly Journal of Experimental Psychology, 46B*, 63–95.

Bouton, M. E., & Swartzentruber, D. (1986). Analysis of the associative and occasion-setting properties of contexts participating in a Pavlovian discrimination. *Journal of Experimental Psychology: Animal Behavior Processes, 12*, 333–350.

Bouton, M. E., & Swartzentruber, D. (1989). Slow reacquisition following extinction: Context, encoding, and retrieval mechanisms. *Journal of Experimental Psychology: Animal Behavior Processes, 15*, 43–53.

Brooks, D. C., & Bouton, M. E. (1993). A retrieval cue for extinction attenuates spontaneous recovery. *Journal of Experimental Psychology: Animal Behavior Processes, 19*, 77–89.

Brooks, D. C., & Bouton, M. E. (1994). A retrieval cue for extinction attenuates response recovery (renewal) caused by a return to the conditioning context. *Journal of Experimental Psychology: Animal Behavior Processes, 20*, 366–379.

Collier, A. C. (1977). Preference for shock signals as a function of the temporal accuracy of the signals. *Learning and Motivation, 8*, 159–170.

Collier, A. C., Morris, R. G. M., & Bolles, R. C. (1976). *The overshadowing of a cue predicting when shock will occur by a cue predicting whether it will occur.* Paper presented at the meeting of the Eastern Psychological Association, New York.

Cunningham, C. L. (1979). Alcohol as a cue for extinction: State dependency produced by conditioned inhibition. *Animal Learning & Behavior, 7*, 45–52.

Darby, R. J., & Pearce, J. M. (1995). Effects of context on responding during a compound stimulus. *Journal of Experimental Psychology: Animal Behavior Processes, 21*, 143–154.

de Brugada, I., Garcia-Hoz, V., Bonardi, C., & Hall, G. (1995). Role of stimulus ambiguity in conditional learning. *Journal of Experimental Psychology: Animal Behavior Processes, 21*, 275–284.

Desmond, J. E., & Moore, J. W. (1988). Adaptive timing in neural networks: The conditioned response. *Biological Cybernetics, 58*, 405–415.

Gallistel, C. R. (1990). *The organization of learning.* Cambridge, MA: MIT Press.

Gibbon, J., & Balsam, P. (1981). Spreading association in time. In C. M. Locurto, H. S. Terrace, & J. Gibbon (Eds.), *Autoshaping and conditioning theory* (pp. 219–253). New York: Academic Press.

Greenspoon, J., & Ranyard, R. (1957). Stimulus conditions and retroactive inhibition. *Journal of Experimental Psychology, 53*, 55–59.

Holland, P. C. (1983). Occasion setting in Pavlovian feature positive discriminations. In M. L. Commons, R. J. Herrnstein, & A. R. Wagner (Eds.), *Quantitative analyses of behavior: Discrimination processes* (Vol. 4, pp. 183–206). New York: Ballinger.

Holland, P. C. (1984). Differential effects of reinforcement of an inhibitory feature after serial and simultaneous feature negative discrimination training. *Journal of Experimental Psychology: Animal Behavior Processes, 10*, 461–475.

Holland, P. C. (1985). The nature of conditioned inhibition in serial and simultaneous feature negative discriminations. In R. R. Miller & N. E. Spear (Eds.), *Information processing in animals: Conditioned inhibition* (pp. 267–297). Hillsdale, NJ: Erlbaum.

Holland, P. C. (1986). Temporal determinants of occasion setting in feature-positive discriminations. *Animal Learning & Behavior, 17*, 269–279.

Holland, P. C. (1989). Occasion setting with simultaneous compounds in rats. *Journal of Experimental Psychology: Animal Behavior Processes, 15*, 183–193.

Holland, P. C. (1992). Occasion setting in Pavlovian conditioning. In G. Bower (Ed.), *The psychology of learning and motivation* (Vol. 28, pp. 69–125). Orlando, FL: Academic Press.

Holland, P. C., & Lamarre, J. (1984). Transfer of inhibition after serial and simultaneous feature negative discrimination training. *Learning and Motivation, 15*, 219–243.

Kehoe, E. J., Horne, P. S., Macrae, M., & Horne, A. J. (1993). Real-time processing of serial stimuli in classical conditioning of the rabbit's nictitating membrane response. *Journal of Experimental Psychology: Animal Behavior Processes, 19*, 265–283.

Lamarre, J., & Holland, P. C. (1987). Transfer of inhibition after serial feature negative discrimination training. *Learning and Motivation, 18*, 319–342.

McClelland, J. L., & Rumelhart, D. E. (1985). Distributed memory and the representation of general and specific information. *Journal of Experimental Psychology: General, 114,* 159–188.

Miller, R. R., & Barnet, R. C. (1993). The role of time in elementary associations. *Current Directions in Psychological Science, 2,* 106–111.

Nelson, J. B. (1995). [Prior inhibition training makes an excitor context-specific] Unpublished raw data, University of Vermont.

Nelson, J. B., & Bouton, M. E. (1996). The effects of a context switch following serial and simultaneous feature-negative discriminations. *Learning and Motivation, 28,* 56–84.

Pearce, J. M., & Wilson, P. N. (1991). Failure of excitatory conditioning to extinguish the influence of a conditioned inhibitor. *Journal of Experimental Psychology: Animal Behavior Processes, 17,* 519–529.

Peck, C. A., & Bouton, M. E. (1990). Context and performance in aversive-to-appetitive and appetitive-to-aversive transfer. *Learning and Motivation, 21,* 1–31.

Rescorla, R. A. (1969). Pavlovian conditioned inhibition. *Psychological Bulletin, 72,* 77–94.

Rescorla, R. A. (1973). Effect of US habituation following conditioning. *Journal of Comparative and Physiological Psychology, 82,* 137–143.

Rescorla, R. A. (1974). Effect of inflation of the unconditioned stimulus value following conditioning. *Journal of Comparative and Physiological Psychology, 86,* 101–106.

Rescorla, R. A. (1979). Conditioned inhibition and extinction. In A. Dickinson & R. A. Boakes (Eds.), *Mechanisms of learning and motivation: A memorial volume to Jerzy Konorski* (pp. 83–110). Hillsdale, NJ: Erlbaum.

Rescorla, R. A. (1985). Conditioned inhibition and facilitation. In R. R. Miller & N. E. Spear (Eds.), *Information processing in animals: Conditioned inhibition* (pp. 199–326). Hillsdale, NJ: Erlbaum.

Rescorla, R. A. (1988). Facilitation based on inhibition. *Animal Learning & Behavior, 16,* 169–176.

Rescorla, R. A., & Heth, C. D. (1975). Reinstatement of fear to an extinguished conditioned stimulus. *Journal of Experimental Psychology: Animal Behavior Processes, 1,* 88–96.

Rescorla, R. A., & Holland, P. C. (1977). Associations in Pavlovian conditioned inhibition. *Learning and Motivation, 8,* 429–447.

Rescorla, R. A., & Wagner, A. R. (1972). A theory of Pavlovian conditioning: Variations in the effectiveness of reinforcement and nonreinforcement. In A. H. Black & W. F. Prokasy (Eds.), *Classical conditioning: II. Current research and theory* (pp. 64–99). New York: Appleton-Century-Crofts.

Richardson, R., Riccio, D. C., & Devine, L. (1984). ACTH-induced recovery of extinguished avoidance responding. *Physiological Psychology, 12,* 184–192.

Spear, N. E. (1978). *The processing of memories: Forgetting and retention.* Hillsdale, NJ: Erlbaum.

Spear, N. E., Smith, G. J., Bryan, R., Gordon, W., Timmons, R., & Chiszar, D. (1980). Contextual influences on the interaction between conflicting memories in the rat. *Animal Learning & Behavior, 8,* 273–281.

Staddon, J. E. R. (1988). Learning as inference. In R. C. Bolles & M. D. Beecher (Eds.), *Evolution and learning* (pp. 59–78). Hillsdale, NJ: Erlbaum.

Sutton, R. S., & Barto, A. G. (1981). Toward a modern theory of adaptive networks: Expectation and prediction. *Psychological Review, 88,* 135–170.

Swartzentruber, D. (1995). Modulatory mechanisms in Pavlovian conditioning. *Animal Learning & Behavior, 23,* 123–143.

Swartzentruber, D., & Bouton, M. E. (1992). Context sensitivity of conditioned suppression following preexposure to the conditioned stimulus. *Animal Learning & Behavior, 20,* 97–103.

Swartzentruber, D., & Rescorla, R. A. (1994). Modulation of trained and extinguished stimuli by facilitators and inhibitors. *Animal Learning & Behavior, 22,* 309–316.

Thomas, D. R., McKelvie, A. R., Ranney, M., & Moye, T. B. (1981). Interference in pigeons' long-term memory viewed as a retrieval problem. *Animal Learning & Behavior, 9,* 581–586.

Wagner, A. R., & Brandon, S. E. (1989). Evolution of a structured connectionist model of Pavlovian conditioning: AESOP. In S. B. Klein & R. R. Mowrer (Eds.), *Contemporary learning theories: Pavlovian conditioning and the status of traditional learning theory* (pp. 149–190). Hillsdale, NJ: Erlbaum.

Wagner, A. R., & Rescorla, R. A. (1972). Inhibition in Pavlovian conditioning: Application of a theory. In R. A. Boakes & M. S. Halliday (Eds.), *Inhibition and learning* (pp. 301–336). London: Academic Press.

Williams, D. A., Overmier, J., & LoLordo, V. M. (1992). A reevaluation of Rescorla's early dictums about Pavlovian conditioned inhibition. *Psychological Bulletin, 111,* 275–290.

Wilson, P. N., & Pearce, J. M. (1990). Selective transfer of responding in conditional discriminations. *Quarterly Journal of Experimental Psychology, 42B,* 41–58.

Appendix _____

The Publications of Robert C. Bolles

1954

Bolles, R. C., & Petrinovich, L. (1954). A technique for obtaining rapid drive discrimination in the rat. *Journal of Comparative and Physiological Psychology, 47,* 378–380.
Petrinovich, L., & Bolles, R. C. (1954). Deprivation states and behavioral attributes. *Journal of Comparative and Physiological Psychology, 47,* 450–453.

1956

Bolles, R. C., & Bailey, D. E. (1956). The importance of object recognition in size constancy. *Journal of Experimental Psychology, 55,* 222–225.
Bolles, R. C., & Petrinovich, L. (1956). Body weight changes and behavioral attributes. *Journal of Comparative and Physiological Psychology, 49,* 177–180.

1957

Petrinovich, L., & Bolles, R. C. (1957). Delayed alternation: Evidence for symbolic processes in the rat. *Journal of Comparative and Physiological Psychology, 50,* 363–365.

1958

Bolles, R. C. (1958). Occam's razor and the science of behavior. *Psychological Reports, 3,* 321–324.
Bolles, R. C. (1958). A replication and further analysis of a study on position reversal learning in hungry and thirsty rates. *Journal of Comparative and Physiological Psychology, 51,* 349.
Bolles, R. C. (1958). The usefulness of the drive concept. *Nebraska Symposium on Motivation.* Lincoln: University of Nebraska Press.
Bolles, R. C., & Messick, S. (1958). Statistical utility in experimental inference. *Psychological Reports, 4,* 223–227.
Bolles, R. C., & Messick, S. (1958). Statistical utility and components of variance. *Psychological Reports, 4,* 714.

1959

Bolles, R. C. (1959). The effect of altering the middle of the list during serial learning. *American Journal of Psychology, 72,* 577–580.
Bolles, R. C. (1959). Group and individual performance as a function of intensity and kind of deprivation. *Journal of Comparative and Physiological Psychology, 52,* 579–585.

Bolles, R. C., & Ballou, N. E. (1959). Calculated activities and abundances of U^{235} fission products. *Nuclear Science and Engineering, 5,* 156–185.

Bolles, R. C., Hulicka, I. M., & Hanly, B. (1959). Colour judgment as a function of stimulus conditions and memory colour. *Canadian Journal of Psychology, 13,* 175–185.

Gagne, R. M., & Bolles, R. C. (1959). A review of factors in learning efficiency. In E. Galanter (Ed.) *Teaching machines.* New York: Wiley.

1960

Bolles, R. C. (1960). Grooming behavior in the rat. *Journal of Comparative and Physiological Psychology, 53,* 306–310.

Bolles, R. C., & Morlock, H. (1960). Some asymmetrical drive summation phenomena. *Psychological Reports, 7,* 373–378.

1961

Bolles, R. C. (1961). Generalization of deprivation-produced stimuli. *Psychological Reports, 9,* 623–626.

Bolles, R. C. (1961). The interaction of hunger and thirst in the rat. *Journal of Comparative and Physiological Psychology, 54,* 580–584.

Bolles, R. C. (1961). Is the "click" a token reward? *Psychological Record, 11,* 163–168.

Bolles, R. C. (1961). Percentage timing reinforcement schedules. *Psychological Record, 11,* 349–354.

de Lorge, J., & Bolles, R. C. (1961). Effects of food deprivation on exploratory behavior in a novel situation. *Psychological Reports, 9,* 599–606.

1962

Bolles, R. C. (1962). The difference between statistial hypotheses and scientific hypotheses. *Psychological Reports, 11,* 639–645.

Bolles, R. C. (1962). A psychophysical study of hunger in the rat. *Journal of Experimental Psychology, 63,* 387–390.

Bolles, R. C. (1962). The readiness to eat and drink: The effect of deprivation conditions. *Journal of Comparative and Physiological Psychology, 55,* 230–234.

Bolles, R. C., & de Lorge, J. (1962). Effect of hunger on exploration in a familiar locale. *Psychological Reports, 10,* 54.

Bolles, R. C., & de Lorge, J. (1962). Exploration in a Dashiell maze as a function of prior deprivation, current deprivation, and sex. *Canadian Journal of Psychology, 16,* 221–227.

Bolles, R. C., & de Lorge, J. (1962). The rat's adjustment to a-diurnal feeding cycles. *Journal of Comparative and Physiological Psychology, 55,* 760–762.

1963

Bolles, R. C. (1963). Effect of food deprivation upon the rat's behavior in its home cage. *Journal of Comparative and Physiological Psychology, 56,* 456–460.

Bolles, R. C. (1963). A failure to find evidence of the estrus cycle in the rat's activity level. *Psychological Reports, 12,* 530.

Bolles, R. C. (1963). Psychological determinism and the problem of morality. *Journal for the Scientific Study of Religion, 2,* 182–189.

Bolles, R. C. (1963). The statistician's role. *Psychological Reports, 12,* 782.

Duda, J. J., & Bolles, R. C. (1963). Effects of prior deprivation, current deprivation, and weight loss on the activity of the hungry rat. *Journal of Comparative and Physiological Psychology, 56,* 569–571.

1964

Bolles, R. C., & Popp, R. J. (1964). Parameters affecting the acquisition of Sidman avoidance. *Journal of the Experimental Analysis of Behavior, 7,* 315–321.

Bolles, R. C., & Seelbach, S. E. (1964). Punishing and reinforcing effects of noise onset and termination for different responses. *Journal of Comparative and Physiological Psychology, 58,* 127–131.

Bolles, R. C., & Stojkiewicz, L. W. (1964). A simple fast pulse former. *Journal of the Experimental Analysis of Behavior, 7,* 308.

Bolles, R. C., Sulzbacher, S. I., & Arant, H. (1964). Innateness of the adrenalectomized rat's acceptance of salt. *Psychonomic Science, 1,* 21–22.

Bolles, R. C., & Woods, P. J. (1964). The ontogeny of behavior in the albino rat. *Animal Behaviour, 12,* 427–441.

Chapman, J. A., & Bolles, R. C. (1964). Effect of UCS duration on classical avoidance learning of the bar-press response. *Psychological Reports, 14,* 559–563.

1965

Bolles, R. C. (1965). Consummatory behavior in rats maintained a-periodically. *Journal of Comparative and Physiological Psychology, 60,* 239–243.

Bolles, R. C. (1965). Effects of deprivation conditions upon the rat's home cage behavior. *Journal of Comparative and Physiological Psychology, 60,* 244–248.

Bolles, R. C. (1965). Readiness to eat: Effects of age, sex, and weight loss. *Journal of Comparative and Physiological Psychology, 60,* 88–92.

Bolles, R. C., & Rapp, H. M. (1965). Readiness to eat and drink: Effect of stimulus conditions. *Journal of Comparative and Physiological Psychology, 60,* 93–97.

Bolles, R. C., & Stokes, L. W. (1965). Rat's anticipation of diurnal and a-diurnal feeding. *Journal of Comparative and Physiological Psychology, 60,* 290–294.

Bolles, R. C., & Warren, J. A. (1965). The acquisition of bar press avoidance as a function of shock intensity. *Psychonomic Science, 3,* 297–298.

Bolles, R. C., & Warren, J. A. (1965). Effects of delayed UCS termination on classical avoidance learning of the bar-press response. *Psychological Reports, 17,* 689–690.

Weinstock, R., White, R. T., & Bolles, R. C. (1965). Incentive value of saccharin as a function of concentration and deprivation conditions. *Psychonomic Science, 3,* 103–104.

Woods, P. J., & Bolles, R. C. (1965). Effects of current hunger and prior eating habits on exploratory behavior. *Journal of Comparative and Physiological Psychology, 59,* 141–143.

1966

Bolles, R. C. (1966). Criminal law and experimental psychology. In R. Slovenko (Ed.), *Crime, law and corrections.* Springfield, IL.: Charles C Thomas.

Bolles, R. C. (1966). Shock density and effective shock intensity: A comparison of different shock scramblers. *Journal of the Experimental Analysis of Behavior, 9,* 553–556.

Bolles, R. C., & Ogilvie, R. D. (1966). Effects of a-diurnal lighting and feeding on the rat's diurnal activity cycle. *Journal of Comparative and Physiological Psychology, 62,* 141–143.

Bolles, R. C., Stokes, L. W., & Younger, M. S. (1966). Does CS termination reinforce avoidance behavior? *Journal of Comparative and Physiological Psychology, 62,* 201–207.

Bolles, R. C., & Warren, J. A. (1966). Effects of delay on the punishing and reinforcing effects of noise onset and termination. *Journal of Comparative and Physiological Psychology, 61,* 475–477.

Bolles, R. C., Warren, J. A., & Ostrov, N. (1966). The role of the CS-US interval in bar press avoidance learning. *Psychonomic Science, 6,* 113–114.

1967

Bolles, R. C. (1967). The syntax of the mind. *Psychological Reports, 21,* 493–498.

Bolles, R. C. (1967). *Theory of motivation.* New York: Harper.

Bolles, R. C., & Tuttle, A. V. (1967). A failure to reinforce instrumental behavior by terminating a stimulus that had been paired with shock. *Psychonomic Science, 9,* 255–256.

Bolles, R. C., & Younger, M. S. (1967). The effect of hunger on the threshold of behavioral arousal. *Psychonomic Science, 7,* 243–244.

Warren, J. A., & Bolles, R. C. (1967). A reevaluation of a simple contiguity interpretation of avoidance learning. *Journal of Comparative and Physiological Psychology, 64,* 179–182.

1968

Bolles, R. C. (1968). Anticipatory general activity in thirsty rats. *Journal of Comparative and Physiological Psychology, 65,* 511–513.

Bolles, R. C. (1968). Autonomic indices of fear: The collapse of an idea. *Psychological Reports, 23,* 1249–1250.

Bolles, R. C., Duncan, P. M., Grossen, N. E., & Matter, C. F. (1968). Relationship between activity level and body temperature in the rat. *Psychological Reports, 23,* 991–994.

Bolles, R. C., & McGillis, D. B. (1968). The non-operant nature of the bar-press escape response. *Psychonomic Science, 11,* 261–262.

Bolles, R. C., Rapp, H. M., & White, G. C. (1968). Failure of sexual activity to reinforce female rats. *Journal of Comparative and Physiological Psychology, 65,* 311–313.

Collier, G. H., & Bolles, R. C. (1968). Hunger, thirst, and their interaction as determinants of sucrose consumption. *Journal of Comparative and Physiological Psychology, 66,* 633–641.

Collier, G., & Bolles, R. C. (1968). Some determinants of intake of sucrose solutions. *Journal of Comparative and Physiological Psychology, 65,* 379–383.

Grossen, N. E., & Bolles, R. C. (1968). Effects of a classical conditioned 'fear signal' and 'safety signal' on nondiscriminated avoidance behavior. *Psychonomic Science, 11,* 321–322.

1969

Bolles, R. C. (1969). Avoidance and escape learning: Simultaneous acquisition of different responses. *Journal of Comparative and Physiological Psychology, 68,* 355–358.

Bolles, R. C. (1969). The role of eye movements in the Muller-Lyer illusion. *Perception & Psychophysics, 6,* 175–176.

Bolles, R. C., & Duncan, P. M. (1969). Daily course of activity and subcutaneous body temperature in hungry and thirsty rats. *Physiology & Behavior, 4,* 87–89.

Bolles, R. C., & Grossen, N. E. (1969). Effects of an informational stimulus on the acquisition of avoidance behavior in rats. *Journal of Comparative and Physiological Psychology, 68,* 90–99.

Bolles, R. C., Grossen, N. E., & Hargrave, G. E. (1969). The effects of an escape contingency upon running wheel and one-way avoidance learning. *Psychonomic Science, 16,* 33–34.

Bolles, R. C., & Sanders, G. H. (1969). What does the ultrasonic activity recording device measure? *Behavior Research Methods and Instrumentation, 1,* 180–182.

Grossen, N. E., Kostansek, D. J., & Bolles, R. C. (1969). Effects of appetitive discriminative stimuli on avoidance behavior. *Journal of Experimental Psychology, 81,* 340–343.

1970

Bolles, R. C. (1970). The cue value of illumination change in anticipatory general activity. *Learning and Motivation, 1,* 177–185.

Bolles, R. C. (1970). Interactions with motivation. In M. H. Marx (Ed.), *Learning: Interactions.* New York: Macmillan.

Bolles, R. C. (1970). Species-specific defense reactions and avoidance learning. *Psychological Review, 77,* 32–48.

Bolles, R. C. (1970). What reinforces avoidance behavior? In J. M. Foley, R. A. Lockhart, & D. M. Messick (Eds.), *Contemporary readings in psychology.* New York: Harper.

Bolles, R. C., & Grossen, N. E. (1970). Function of the CS in shuttle-box avoidance learning by rats. *Journal of Comparative and Physiological Psychology, 70,* 165–169.

Bolles, R. C., & Grossen, N. E. (1970). The noncontingent manipulation of incentive motivation. In J. M. Reyneirse (Ed.), *Current issues in animal learning.* Lincoln: University of Nebraska Press.

Bolles, R. C., Grossen, N. E., Hargrave, G. E., & Duncan, P. M. (1970). Effects of conditioned appetitive stimuli on the acquisition and extinction of a runway response. *Journal of Experimental Psychology, 85,* 138–140.

Bolles, R. C., Hargrave, G. E., & Grossen, N. E. (1970). Avoidance learning as a function of CS quality and CS termination on escape trials. *Psychological Reports, 26,* 27–32.

1971

Bolles, R. C. (1971). Aversive control. A review of B. A. Campbell and R. M. Church's *Punishment and aversive behavior. Journal of the Experimental Analysis of Behavior, 16,* 283–288.

Bolles, R. C. (1971). Bekraftigung. In E. S. Esynck (Ed.), *Lexicon der Psychologie.* Freiburg, Germany: Verlag.

Bolles, R. C. (1971). Species-specific defense reactions. In F. R. Brush (Ed.), *Aversive conditioning and learning.* New York: Academic.

Bolles, R. C., Moot, S. A., & Grossen, N. E. (1971). The extinction of shuttlebox avoidance. *Learning and Motivation, 2,* 324–333.

Hargrave, G. E., & Bolles, R. C. (1971). Rat's aversion to flavors following induced illness. *Psychonomic Science, 23,* 91–92.

1972

Bolles, R. C. (1972). The avoidance learning problem. In G. Bower (Ed.), *Learning and motivation* (Vol 6). New York: Academic Press.

Bolles, R. C. (1972). Reinforcement, expectancy, and learning. *Psychological Review, 79*, 394–409.

Bolles, R. C., & Moot, S. A. (1972). Derived motives. *Annual Review of Psychology*, pp. 51–72.

1973

Bolles, R. C. (1973). The comparative psychology of learning: The selective association principle and some problems with "general" laws of learning. In G. Bermant (Ed.), *Perspectives on animal behavior*. Glenview, IL: Scott Foresman.

Bolles, R. C. (1973). *Teoria de la motivacion*. Spanish edition of *Theory of motivation*. (There are also Japanese and International editions, not listed here.)

Bolles, R. C., & Moot, S. A. (1973). The rat's anticipation of two meals a day. *Journal of Comparative and Physiological Psychology, 83*, 510–514.

Bolles, R. C., & Riley, A. L. (1973). Freezing as an avoidance response: Another look at the operant-respondent distinction. *Learning and Motivation, 4*, 268–275.

Bolles, R. C., Riley, A. L., & Laskowski, B. (1973). A further demonstration of the learned safety effect in food-aversion learning. *Bulletin of the Psychonomic Society, 1*, 190–192.

Weisinger, R. S., Parker, L. F., & Bolles, R. C. (1973). Effects of amount of reward on acquisition of a black–white discrimination. *Bulletin of the Psychonomic Society, 2*, 27–28.

1974

Bolles, R. C. (1974). Cognition and motivation: Some historical trends. In B. Weiner (Ed.), *Cognitive views of human motivation*. New York: Academic Press.

Bolles, R. C. (1974). Review of R. A. Hinde & J. Stevenson-Hinde's *Constraints on learning*. *American Journal of Psychology, 87*, 298–302.

Bolles, R. C., Riley, A. L., Cantor, M. B., & Duncan, P. M. (1974). The rat's failure to anticipate regularly scheduled daily shock. *Behavioral Biology, 11*, 365–372.

Moot, S. A., Nelson, K., & Bolles, R. C. (1974). Avoidance learning in a black and white shuttlebox. *Bulletin of the Psychonomic Society, 4*, 501–502.

Moot, S. A., Overby, L. P., & Bolles, R. C. (1974). Discrimination learning with an avoidance procedure. *Bulletin of the Psychonomic Society, 3*, 129–130.

1975

Bolles, R. C. (1975). Learning, motivation, and cognition. In W. K. Estes (Ed.), *Handbook of learning and cognitive processes*. Hillsdale, NJ: Erlbaum.

Bolles, R. C. (1975). *Learning theory*. New York: Holt.

Bolles, R. C. (1975). *Theory of motivation* (2nd ed.). New York: Harper.

Bolles, R. C., & Nelson, K. (1975). The role of intertrial interval in the learning of two simple avoidance tasks. *Animal Learning & Behavior, 3*, 157–160.

Bolles, R. C., Uhl, C. N., Wolfe, M., & Chase, P. B. (1975). Stimulus learning versus response learning in a discriminated punishment situation. *Learning and Motivation, 6*, 439–447.

1976

Bolles, R. C. (1976). Some relationships between learning and memory. In D. L. Medin, W. A. Roberts, & R. T. Davis (Eds.), *Processes of animal memory*. Hillsdale, N.J.: Erlbaum.

Bolles, R. C., & Collier, A. C. (1976). The effect of predictive cues on freezing in rats. *Animal Learning & Behavior, 4*, 6–8.

Bolles, R. C., Moot, S. A., & Nelson, K. (1976). Note on the invariance of response latency in shuttlebox avoidance behavior. *Learning and Motivation, 7*, 108–116.

1977

Bolles, R. C. (1978). The more things change . . . *Behavioral and Brain Sciences, 1*, 53–54.

Bolles, R. C. (1978). The role of stimulus learning in defensive behavior. In S. H. Hulse, H. Fowler, & W. K. Honig (Eds.), *Cognitive processes in animal behavior*. Hillsdale, N.J.: Erlbaum.

Bolles, R. C. (1978). Whatever happened to motivation? *Educational Psychologist, 13*, 1–13.

Bolles, R. C., Collier, A. C., Bouton, M. E., & Marlin, N. A. (1978). Some tricks for ameliorating the trace-conditioning deficit. *Bulletin of the Psychonomic Society, 11*, 403–406.

Bolles, R. C., & Treichler, F. R. (1977). Deprivation, weight loss and intake in the rat as a function of age: Evidence for an obligatory growth factor. *Biobehavioral Reviews, 1*, 207–212.

1979

Bolles, R. C. (1979). The functional significance of behavior. *Behavioral and Brain Sciences, 1*, 29–30.

Bolles, R. C. (1979). *Learning theory* (2nd ed.). New York: Holt.

Bolles, R. C. (1979). The nonextinction of fear: Operation bootstrap. *Behavioral and Brain Sciences, 1*, 167–168.

Bolles, R. C. (1979). Scholar's progress: Review of B. F. Skinner's *Particulars of my life* and *The shaping of a behaviorist*. *Science, 204*, 1073–1074.

Bolles, R. C. (1979). Toy rats and real rats. *Behavioral and Brain Sciences, 1*, 103.

Bouton, M. E., & Bolles, R. C. (1979). Contextual control of the extinction of conditioned fear. *Learning and Motivation, 10*, 445–466.

Bouton, M. E., & Bolles, R. C. (1979). Role of conditioned contextual stimuli in reinstatement of extinguished fear. *Journal of Experimental Psychology: Animal Behavior Processes, 5*, 368–378.

Fanselow, M. S., & Bolles, R. C. (1979). Naloxone and shock-elicited freezing in the rat. *Journal of Comparative and Physiological Psychology, 93*, 736–744.

Fanselow, M. S., & Bolles, R. C. (1979). Triggering of the endorphin analgesia reaction by a cue previously associated with shock: Reversal by naloxone. *Bulletin of the Psychonomic Society, 14*, 88–90.

1980

Bolles, R. C. (1980). Ethological learning theory. In G. M. Gazda & R. J. Corsini (Eds.), *Theories of learning*. Itasca, IL: Peacock.

Bolles, R. C. (1980). Historical note on the term "appetite." *Appetite, 1*, 1–4.

Bolles, R. C. (1980). Review of J. Alcock's *Animal behavior. Quarterly Review of Biology, 55,* 94.

Bolles, R. C. (1980). Some functionalistic thoughts about regulation. In F. M. Toates & T. R. Halliday (Eds.), *Analysis of motivational processes.* London: Academic Press.

Bolles, R. C. (1980). Stress-induced overeating? A response to Robbins and Frey. *Appetite, 1,* 229–230.

Bolles, R. C. (1980). Wundt and after: Review of E. Hearst's *The first century of experimental psychology. Science, 208,* 715–716.

Bolles, R. C., & Fanselow, M. S. (1980). A perceptual-defensive-recuperative model of fear and pain. *Behavioral and Brain Sciences, 3,* 291–323.

Bolles, R. C., Holtz, R., Dunn, T., & Hill, W. (1980). Comparisons of stimulus learning and response learning in a punishment situation. *Learning and Motivation, 11,* 78–96.

Bouton, M. E., & Bolles, R. C. (1980). Conditioned fear assessed by freezing and by the suppression of three different baselines. *Animal Learning & Behavior, 8,* 429–434.

Collier, A. C., & Bolles, R. C. (1980). The ontogenesis of defensive reactions to shock in preweanling rats. *Developmental Psychobiology, 13,* 141–150.

Fanselow, M. S., Sigmundi, R. A., & Bolles, R. C. (1980). Naloxone pretreatment enhances shock-elicited aggression. *Physiological Psychology, 8,* 369–371.

Hirsch, S. M., & Bolles, R. C. (1980). On the ability of prey to recognize predators. *Zeitschrift für Tierpsycholiogie, 54,* 71–84.

Sigmundi, R. A., Bouton, M. E., & Bolles, R. C. (1980). Conditioned freezing in the rat as a function of shock intensity and CS modality. *Bulletin of the Psychonomic Society, 15,* 254–256.

1981

Bolles, R. C. (1981). Emotion. In D. McFarland (Ed.), *The Oxford companion to animal behaviour.* Oxford, England: Oxford University Press.

Bolles, R. C. (1981). On a clear day you can see behavior. *Behavioral and Brain Sciences, 4,* 619–620.

Bolles, R. C. (1981). A parallel to dominance competition. *Behavioral and Brain Sciences, 4,* 433–434.

Bolles, R. C. (1981). Trouble in reinforcementland. *Behavioral and Brain Sciences, 4,* 390.

Bolles, R. C., Hayward, L., & Crandall, C. (1981). Conditioned taste preferences based on caloric density. *Journal of Experimental Psychology: Animal Behavior Processes, 7,* 59–69.

Kaufman, M. A., & Bolles, R. C. (1981). A nonassociative aspect of overshadowing. *Bulletin of the Psychonomic Society, 18,* 318–320.

1982

Bolles, R. C. (1982). Motivation and reinforcement? *Behavioral and Brain Sciences, 5,* 667–668.

Bolles, R. C., & Fanselow, M. S. (1982). Endorphins and behavior. *Annual Review of Psychology,* 87–101.

Bolles, R. C., & Fanselow, M. S. (1982). Is there one motivational system or two? *Behavioral and Brain Sciences, 5,* 606–608.

Fanselow, M. S., & Bolles, R. C. (1982). Independence and competition in aversive motivation. *Behavioral and Brain Sciences, 5,* 320–321.

1983

Bolles, R. C. (1983). The explanation of behavior. *Psychological Record, 33,* 31–48.

Bolles, R. C. (1983). A mixed model of taste preferences in the rat. In R. L. Mellgren (Ed.), *Cognition and animal behavior.* Norman, OK: University of Oklahoma Press.

Sigmundi, R. A., & Bolles, R. C. (1983). CS modality, context conditioning, and conditioned freezing. *Animal Learning & Behavior, 11,* 205–212.

1984

Bolles, R. C. (1984). Species-typical response predispositions. In P. Marler & H. S. Terrace (Eds.), *The biology of learning.* Berlin: Springer-Verlag.

Bolles, R. C. (1984). On the status of causal modes. *Behavioral and Brain Sciences, 7,* 482–483.

Mehiel, R., & Bolles, R. C. (1984). Learned flavor preferences based on caloric outcome. *Animal Learning & Behavior, 12,* 421–427.

1985

Bolles, R. C. (1985). Associative processes in the formation of conditioned food aversions: An emerging functionalism? In N. S. Braveman & P. Bronstein (Eds.), *Experimental assessment and clinical applications of conditioned taste aversions. Annals of the New York Academy of Science, 443,* 1–24.

Bolles, R. C. (1985). A cognitive, nonassociative view of inhibition. In R. R. Miller & N. E. Spear (Eds.), *Information processing in animals: Conditioned inhibition.* Hillsdale, NJ: Erlbaum.

Bolles, R. C. (1985). Making behavior interesting: Review of J. E. R. Staddon's *Adaptive behavior and learning. Contemporary Psychology, 30,* 437–438.

Bolles, R. C. (1985). Short term memory and attention. In L. Nilsson & T. Archer (Eds.), *Perspectives on learning and memory.* Hillsdale, NJ: Erlbaum.

Bolles, R. C. (1985). The slaying of Goliath: What happened to reinforcement theory. In T. D. Johnston & A. R. Peitrewicz (Eds.), *The ethological study of learning.* Hillsdale, NJ: Erlbaum.

Bouton, M. E., & Bolles, R. C. (1985). Contexts, event-memories, and extinction. In P. D. Balsam & A. Tomie (Eds.), *Context and learning.* Hillsdale, NJ: Erlbaum.

1986

Fedorchak, P. M., & Bolles, R. C. (1986). Differential outcome effect using a biologically neutral outcome difference. *Journal of Experimental Psychology: Animal Behavior Processes, 12,* 125–130.

1987

Fedorchak, P. M., & Bolles, R. C. (1987). Hunger enhances the expression of calorie- but not taste-mediated conditioned flavor preferences. *Journal of Experimental Psychology: Animal Behavior Processes, 13,* 73–79.

1988

Bolles, R. C. (1988). Nativism, naturalism, and niches. In R. C. Bolles & M. D. Beecher (Eds.), *Evolution and learning.* Hillsdale, NY: Erlbaum.

Bolles, R. C. (1988). Why you should avoid statistics. *Biological Psychiatry, 23,* 79–85.

Bolles, R. C., & Beecher, M. D. (Eds.). (1988). *Evolution and learning.* Hillsdale, NJ: Erlbaum.

Bolles, R. C., & Mehiel, R. (1988). Away with rat chow! *Appetite, 11,* 40–41.

Fedorchak, P. M., & Bolles, R. C. (1988). Nutritive expectancies mediate cholecystokinin's suppression of intake effect. *Behavioral Neuroscience, 102,* 451–455.

Mehiel, R., & Bolles, R. C. (1988). Hedonic shift learning based on calories. *Bulletin of the Psychonomic Society, 26,* 459–462.

Mehiel, R., & Bolles, R. C. (1988). Learned flavor preferences based on calories are independent of initial hedonic value. *Animal Learning & Behavior, 16,* 383–387.

1989

Bolles, R. C. (1989). Acquired behaviors: Aversive learning. In R. J. Blanchard, P. F. Brain, D. C. Blanchard, & S. Parmigiani (Eds.), *Ethoexperimental approaches to the study of behavior.* Dordrecht, Netherlands: Kluwer.

Bolles, R. C. (1989). The monkey see, monkey do phenomenon. Review of T. R. Zentall & B. G. Galef's *Social learning. Contemporary Psychology, 34,* 833–834.

1990

Bolles, R. C. (1990). Where did everybody go? *Psychological Science, 1,* 107–113.

Bolles, R. C. (1990). A functionalistic approach to feeding. In E. D. Capaldi & T. Powley (Eds.), *Taste, experience, and feeding* (pp. 3–13). Washington, DC: American Psychological Association.

1991

Bolles, R. C. (Ed.), (1991). *The hedonics of taste.* Hillsdale, NJ: Erlbaum.

Bolles, R. C. (1991). Hedonism. In. R. C. Bolles (Ed.), *The hedonics of taste.* Hillsdale, NJ: Erlbaum.

1992

Bolles, R. C. (1992). Miller's acquired drive study. *Journal of Experimental Psychology: General, 121,* 10.

1993

Bolles, R. C. (1993). *The story of psychology.* Pacific Grove, CA: Brooks/Cole.

1994

Bolles, R. C. (1994). The response problem. *Behavioral and Brain Sciences, 17,* 135–136.

1995

Dewsbury, D. A., & Bolles, R. C. (1995). The founding of the Psychonomic Society. *Psychonomic Bulletin and Review, 2,* 216–233.

1996

Ramsay, D. S., Seeley, R. J., Bolles, R. C., & Woods, S. C. (1996). Ingestive homeostasis: The primacy of learning. In. E. D. Capaldi (Ed.), *Why we eat what we eat: The psychology of eating* (pp. 11–27). Washington, DC: American Psychological Association.

Author Index

Numbers in italics refer to listings in the reference sections.

Subject Index

About the Editors

Mark E. Bouton and **Michael S. Fanselow** received their graduate training from Robert C. Bolles in the late 1970s. Both received PhDs in biobehavioral psychology from the University of Washington in 1980.

Dr. Bouton took a position at the University of Vermont, on the "west coast of New England," where he is now Professor of Psychology. His research focuses on the role of context in the learning and memory processes involved in classical conditioning. This work has received continuous support from the National Science Foundation since 1981. Dr. Bouton has received Fulbright and James McKeen Cattell Sabbatical Awards, and he is currently the Editor of the *Journal of Experimental Psychology: Animal Behavior Processes*. He enjoys skiing and huddling by a woodstove during the scenic but frosty Vermont winters.

Dr. Fanselow held positions at Rensselaer Polytechnic Institute and Dartmouth College and is now Professor of Psychology at the University of California, Los Angeles. His research is on the neural basis of learned fear and fear-motivated defensive behavior. This work has been supported by the National Science Foundation and National Institute of Mental Health. Dr. Fanselow has received the Troland Award from the National Academy of Sciences, the Distinguished Early Career Award, and the D. O. Hebb Young Scientist award from the American Psychological Association. He enjoys hiking and sipping California wine on warm Los Angeles winter evenings.